Managerial Economics

Economic Tools for
Today's Decision Makers

FOURTH EDITION

Paul G. Keat

*Thunderbird, The American Graduate School
of International Management*

Philip K. Y. Young

*Thunderbird, The American Graduate School
of International Management*

Prentice
Hall

Upper Saddle River, New Jersey 07458

To my wife, Sheilah, and my children, Diana and Andrew — P.G.K.
To my wife, Ilse, and my children, Christopher and Adriana — P.K.Y.Y.

Library of Congress Cataloging-in-Publication Data

Keat, Paul G.
    Managerial economics: economic tools for today's decision makers/
Paul G. Keat, Philip K.Y. Young—4th ed.
        p. cm.
    Includes index.
    ISBN 0-13-035335-3 (cloth)
        1. Managerial economics. I. Young, Philip K. Y. II. Title.

HD30.22 .K39 2003
338.5'024'658—dc21

2002075499

AVP/Executive Editor: Rod Banister
Editor-in-Chief: PJ Boardman
Managing Editor (Editorial): Gladys Soto
Assistant Editor: Marie McHale
Editorial Assistant: Lisa Amato
Media Project Manager: Victoria Anderson
Executive Marketing Manager: Kathleen Mclellan
Marketing Assistant: Christopher Bath
Managing Editor (Production): John Roberts
Production Editor: Maureen Wilson
Permissions Coordinator: Suzanne Grappi

Associate Director, Manufacturing:
    Vincent Scelta
Production Manager: Arnold Vila
Manufacturing Buyer: Michelle Klein
Cover Design: Kiwi Design
**Full-Service Project Management
    and Composition:** Compset Inc.
Project Manager: Janet Domingo
Printer/Binder: Courier-Westford

Credits and acknowledgments borrowed from other sources and reproduced, with permission, in this textbook appear on appropriate page within text.

Pearson Education LTD.
Pearson Education Australia PTY, Limited
Pearson Education Singapore, Pte. Ltd.
Pearson Education North Asia Ltd.
Pearson Education, Canada, Ltd.
Pearson Educación de Mexico, S.A. de C.V.
Pearson Education–Japan
Pearson Education Malaysia, Pte. Ltd.

10 9 8 7 6 5 4 3 2 1
ISBN 0-13-035335-3

BRIEF CONTENTS

CONTENTS

Contents

PREFACE

One day after class, a student in one of our courses commented on the managerial economics text then being used: "This book is very dry. What it needs is a plot!" To a large extent, the idea for this text stemmed from this remark. This is a text that we believe will excite readers about managerial economics as well as inform them about this vital part of management education. Each chapter begins with a "Situation," in which managers in a fictional company, Global Foods, Inc., must make certain key decisions about their products in the beverage industry. After the relevant economic concepts or tools of analysis are presented, each chapter ends with a "Solution," a suggested way in which these concepts or tools can be used to help managers make the best decision.

The heart of managerial economics is the microeconomic theory of the firm. Much of this theory was formalized in a textbook written over 100 years ago by Professor Alfred Marshall of Cambridge University. Indeed, if readers were to refer to his *Principles of Economics* (1890), they would find many of the diagrams and equations presented in this text as well as in all other texts in managerial economics. To be sure, the world has changed greatly since Marshall's ideas were developed. Market structures other than the "perfectly competitive model" are now much more important. Technology moves at such a rapid pace that the rate of obsolescence of products is now often measured in months rather than years. Competition among firms is frequently conducted on a global scale rather than a local or national one. Multinational firms invest, manufacture, and sell around the world. In so doing, they sometimes buy out their global competitors or form alliances or joint ventures with them. In recent years, the Internet and e-commerce have become critical elements of most businesses.

Yet through all of these changes, basic microeconomic principles such as supply and demand, elasticity, short-run and long-run shifts in resource allocation, diminishing returns, economies of scale, and pricing according to marginal revenue and marginal cost continue to be important tools of analysis for managerial decision makers. In fact, the overall objective of this text is to demonstrate to our readers that the application of microeconomic theory has stood the test of time and continues to be relevant to many facets of modern business decision making.

One of the key reasons for managers to learn in studying economic analysis is the importance of understanding shifts in market demand and supply. In the first edition (1992), we cited Sun Microsystems as a good example of a company that was able to succeed in a market known for its rapidly changing supply and demand. At the time, we pointed out Sun's leadership in production and marketing of workstations as evidence of this. In our second edition (1996), we observed how Campbell Soup and Grand Met, two leading global food manufacturers, were trying to take advantage of the growing demand for salsa and Mexican foods by buying food companies that produced these products. In the third edition, we noted that two dominant industry leaders, Levi's and Kellogg's, were being seriously challenged in their respective markets because of their inability to keep up with changing tastes, preferences, and life-styles (i.e., demand shifts) as well as pricing and product pressures from competitors (i.e., supply shifts.).

For this edition, we can point out an entire industry that has been roiled by the changing forces of supply and demand: the recording industry. Based on units shipped, music sales in the United States declined almost 10 percent in 2001. This decrease is apparently more of a structural trend than a result of that year's recession. In 2000, sales declined about 7 percent. The specific culprit in the falling demand for CDs seems to be the growing force of substitutes for music CDs such as video games, pay-per-view and DVD players, and the high-speed Internet. The last mentioned factor is the ultimate threat, enabling consumers to download selected music free of charge. To make matters worse, there are serious "supply-side" problems relating to the musical artists who are the "inputs" in the production process. A number of well-known stars (and their lawyers) are beginning to express publicly their distrust of the record companies' accounting for revenues and their commissions from sales as well as certain terms and conditions of recording contracts. In particular, some of the stars are demanding seven-year contracts rather than contracts based on a predetermined number of record albums. All of this clearly represents the "changing economics of the recording industry."[1]

Our text presents numerous examples of firms such as those cited above that are facing changing market conditions. We point out a few here simply to give readers some introductory examples of just how relevant and fresh economic analysis can be. We are well aware of the reputation that economics courses have among some business students of being "too theoretical and not practical enough for the real world." In our opinion, nothing could be further from the truth. We know that the instructors in managerial economics will agree with us on this matter. We hope that this text will serve as a solid supplement to their classroom efforts to demonstrate to their students the importance and utility of economic theory for business decision making.

This text is designed for upper-level undergraduate courses and first-year MBA courses in managerial economics and applied economics. Very often, we have found that MBA students enter the managerial economics course with varying degrees of preparation for the subject. The first two chapters are a general introduction to economics and economic reasoning, and chapter 3 reviews the basic elements of supply and demand theory. The appendix to chapter 2 reviews the mathematics that can be used to help explain the material in selected chapters. We have purposely limited the use of calculus in this text. Thus, this appendix is intended primarily for those instructors and students who desire the economy of expression gained by using calculus and who want a general review of this mathematical technique. In addition, we have included brief mathematical appendices at the end of as well as within selected chapters.

---

[1]This information is based on Bernard Weinraub, "For the Industry, Less to Celebrate at the Grammys," *New York Times*, February 25, 2002.

In addition to discussing the applications of economic theory to the firm, our text (as is the custom with all texts in managerial economics) includes chapters on various tools of analysis that are helpful to business decision makers but that are not part of the core of traditional microeconomic theory. They are demand, production and cost estimation using regression analysis, forecasting, linear programming, capital budgeting, and risk analysis. Another subject, the role of government, can often be found in microeconomics texts under the heading of "market externalities." We are able to treat all of these subjects only in an introductory fashion. However, we hope that we have provided enough discussion and explanation on these topics to give readers a solid understanding of how they can be used in managerial decision making.

IMPROVEMENTS IN THE FOURTH EDITION

In this fourth edition, we have sought to improve on the previous editions by incorporating what we continue to learn from using the book in our classes. In addition, we received a number of useful comments from the faculty selected by Prentice Hall to review this edition's draft. One way in which we have tried to keep the material fresh and current is to incorporate many recent business examples from the popular press. At the same time, we have kept some of the examples that have appeared in our previous three editions. In our view, the passing of time has not diminished their powerful teaching points.

Our examples and applications are presented as integral parts of the general narrative. We have deliberately chosen not to use "boxed or shaded" sections of stories scattered all throughout the book. Our reviewers have told us that practice tends to be distracting for the reader. At the end of almost each chapter, we do have a specific "International Application" that demonstrates one or more of the chapter's key teaching points in a global context. We introduced this feature in the third edition and reviewers and students have told us that they found it to be quite helpful. As we initiated in the first edition, we also have our ongoing case of "Global Foods," the hypothetical food and beverage company that faces problems and challenges relating to the topics presented in each chapter. We recognize that with the ease of accessing library data bases and information on the Internet, any new example that we cite, no matter how recent, can be easily supplanted by more current information. Our hope is that our discussion in the text will motivate readers to update these examples or to find their own appropriate examples of the theoretical concepts presented in the text.

The following major changes and additions have been made in this fourth edition.

- An entirely new chapter on the "new economy" has been added (see chapter 12). Despite the recent collapse of the dot-coms, the Internet and all of its applications have definitely changed the nature of the way firms do business. Moreover, well-known dot-coms such as Amazon and Yahoo! are still in business (at least at the time this preface is being written), and companies such as e-Bay are in fact quite profitable. In this chapter, we provide a basic introduction to business activities involving the Internet such as B2C and B2B. More important, we link these activities to the fundamentals of managerial economics.

- Chapter 10 (Pricing and Output Decisions: Monopolistic Competition and Oligopoly) has been greatly expanded and rewritten. Given the increasing consolidation in many industries over the past decade, business behavior and managerial decision making in oligopoly markets have become more relevant and important than ever before. We also provide much more on game theory.
- Well over half of the "International Applications" are new and different from those provided in the previous edition. The global business scene is interesting and rapidly changing. We want our readers to be as excited about doing business outside the United States as they might be about doing business in the home market. In fact, as future managers, they may have no choice in the matter. Therefore, the international dimension of business is the one area that we want to be as current as possible in the use of our examples.
- An appendix on Asymmetric Information has been added (see Appendix B at end of the text). This topic has become increasingly important in recent years. In 2001, the developers of this theory received the Nobel Prize in Economics for their path-breaking work on the subject. This has no doubt added further interest in the field.
- According to several reviewers, one of the most useful and unique aspects of our text is the final chapter in which we try to incorporate as many of the concepts introduced throughout the text into the analysis of one real case: the situation facing selected firms in the semiconductor industry. In this fourth edition, we use the most current analysis by Standard & Poor's of the semiconductor industry available to us at the time the edition was being written. We also update the activities of the actual company that we used in the third edition, Standard Microsystems Corporation, and talk about several other companies in the industry as well.
- In the first and second editions, the major strategic move made by our hypothetical "Global Foods Corporation" was its entry into the soft drink market. In the third edition, the company decided to expand into bottled water. We decided to keep the strategic focus and almost all of the "Situations" and "Solutions" essentially unchanged in this fourth edition. However, in chapter 7 (The Theory and Estimation of Production) we decided to use a new situation and solution as a way of bringing attention to an important management tool called "supply chain management."
- We have also updated many of the examples and some of the sections that we presented in the previous editions. For example, the section on linear programming has been expanded considerably. In chapter 15 (Government and Industry: Challenges and Opportunities for Today's Managers), we have added information about the deregulation of electric utilities and more material on mergers and acquisitions.
- *Special note to instructors:* Several reviewers recommended that we try to link the situations and solutions more closely to the material in each chapter. We believe that this is one of the more intangible and subjective elements of teaching that would be best done in the classroom environment. Therefore, we have provided in the Instructor's Manual some guidelines on how instructors can make better

use of these situations and solutions for classroom discussions in order to underscore the key teaching points of each chapter.

ANCILLARY MATERIALS

The Companion Website (http://ww.prenhall.com/keat) has been designed specifically to accompany this text. It includes the following features:

Online study guide: Prepared by Professor David Eaton of Murray State University, these Online quizzes offer students another opportunity to sharpen their problem-solving skills and to assess their understanding of the text material. It has been completely revised for this edition. It includes an all-new set of short-answer, analytical questions that require students to further analyze the concepts covered in each chapter. The Online Study Guide grades each question submitted by the student, provides immediate and detailed feedback for correct and incorrect answers, and allows students to e-mail results to up to four e-mail addresses.

Excel® Spreadsheets: More than two dozen spreadsheet templates accompany the text and are intended to help students solve many of the questions raised in text discussions. An index of the applications is printed on the inside of the front cover of this book. This student aid can be downloaded from the Companion Website.

PowerPoint Presentation: This lecture presentation tool, prepared by Professors Benjamin F. Blair and Jon Rezek of Mississippi State University, can be downloaded by instructors. It offers outlines and summaries of important text material, tables and graphs, and additional examples. The package will allow instructors to make full-color, professional-looking presentations while providing the ability to create custom handouts for students.

Instructor's Manual and Test Bank: This manual provides answers to all of the questions and problems found in the text, as well as a group of multiple-choice and short-answer questions. Instructors can download the manual.

ACKNOWLEDGMENTS

We wish to thank our colleagues at Thunderbird, The American Graduate School of International Management, and former colleagues at IBM and Pace University for their assistance and encouragement in our work on this and the previous three editions of this text. We are particularly grateful to Dr. Jack Yurkiewicz, professor of management science at Pace University, and Sylvia Von Bostel, of Booz-Allen & Hamilton, for their contributions to the third and fourth editions. Further, we wish to acknowledge the contributions of Dr. Shannon B. Mudd to this edition. We also wish to thank Robin Cole for helping us to write the case used in Chapter 7. This case is based on her actual experience in the soft drink industry.

We also thank Professor David Eaton of Murray State University for writing the Online Study Guide, and Professors Benjamin F. Blair and Jon Rezek of Mississippi State University for preparing the PowerPoint Presentations.

Our appreciation also goes to the reviewers of all four editions of this text: Michael J. Applegate, Oklahoma State University; Robert Britt, West Virginia University; Peter Brust, University of Tampa; Charles Callahan, III, State University of New York, College at Brockport; John Conant, Indiana State University; Lewis Freiberg, Northeastern Illinois University; Edward H. Heinze, Valparaiso University; George Hoffer, Virginia Commonwealth University; Al Holtmann, University of Miami; Richard A. Jenner, San Francisco State University; Douglas Lamdin, University of Maryland, Baltimore County; Dale Lehman, Fort Lewis College; Jerry Manahan, Midwestern State University; Cynthia McCarty, Jacksonville State University; Yale L. Meltzer, College of Staten Island; L. W. (Bill) Murray, University of San Francisco; Jan Palmer, Ohio University–Athens; Leila J. Pratt, The University of Tennessee at Chattanooga; L. B. Pulley, University of Virginia; Mathew Roelofs, Western Washington University; Roy Savoian, Lynchburg College; Frederica Shockley, California State University–Chico; Ken Slaysman, York College of PA; William Doyle Smith, University of Texas at El Paso; Robert Stuart, Rutgers University; James Tallant, Cape Fear Community College; Mo-Yin Tam, University of Illinois at Chicago; Yien-I Tu, University of Arkansas; Daryl N. Winn, University of Colorado; Richard Winkelman, Arizona State University; Richard Zuber, University of North Carolina at Charlotte; Habib Zuberi, Central Michigan University.

In closing, we would like to express our appreciation to the helpful, encouraging, and patient team at Prentice Hall, including Rod Banister, executive editor; Gladys Soto, managing editor; Maureen Wilson, production editor; Marie McHale, assistant editor; Lisa Amato, editorial assistant; Victoria Anderson, media project manager and Suzanne Grappi, permissions coordinator.

ABOUT THE AUTHORS

Paul G. Keat has been a member of the Global Business Faculty at Thunderbird, The American Graduate School of International Management, for the past fifteen years. At present he is an Associate Professor Emeritus and Director of Research, CIBER Trade Assistance Service. Prior to his coming to Thunderbird he was for many years associated with the International Business Machines Corporation in professional and managerial capacities.

His education includes a B.B.A. in accounting from the Baruch School of the City University of New York, an M.A. from Washington University, and a Ph.D. in economics from the University of Chicago.

Dr. Keat began his IBM career in the department of economic research and then moved into the long-range planning area. Later, as a member of the finance function, he spent several years at IBM's European headquarters in Paris, as manager in the financial planning area, and then as the financial manager for the company's European software business. After his return to the United States, Dr. Keat served as manager in the pricing area of one of the company's manufacturing groups. Before leaving IBM in 1987 he was associated with the company's International Finance, Planning and Administration School (IFPA), where he taught managerial economics, lectured on finance in a number of company-related courses, and managed academic courses. He also taught at IBM's IFPA school at La Hulpe, Belgium.

Dr. Keat has taught at several U.S. universities, including Washington University, CUNY, and Iona College. He was an adjunct professor of finance at the Lubin Graduate School of Business at Pace University, and he also taught in Pace's Executive MBA program.

Philip K.Y. Young is Clinical Professor of Management at Thunderbird, The American Graduate School of International Management. In this capacity, he conducts executive education programs for Thunderbird corporate clients throughout the world. Prior to this, he was Professor of Economics at the Lubin School of Business at Pace University. Dr. Young has over 20 years of experience developing and teaching in executive development programs. He served as the first visiting professor at the International Finance, Planning and Administration School of the IBM Corporation, where he developed and taught courses for IBM in both the United States and LaHulpe, Belgium.

Among the companies that currently utilize his teaching services are IBM, Verizon, British Telecom, SBC, ST Microelectronics, MasterCard International, Booz-Allen & Hamilton, and Dow Chemical. He teaches in executive programs for these and other companies in the United States, Latin America, Western and Central Europe, and Asia.

He has a B.A. from the University of Hawaii, a master's in international affairs from Columbia University, and a Ph.D. in economics from New York University.

Chapter 1

Introduction

The Situation

 The last of the color slides was barely off the screen when Bob Burns, the CEO of Global Foods, Inc., turned to his board of directors to raise the question that he had been waiting all week to ask. "Well, ladies and gentlemen, are you with me in this new venture? Is it a 'go'? Shall we get into the soft drink business?"

"It's not that easy, Bob. We need some time to think it over. You're asking us to endorse a very major *decision*, one that will have a long-term impact on the direction of the company."

"I appreciate your wish to deliberate further, Dr. Breakstone," Bob responded, "but I would like to reach a decision today. As the president of a major university, you have been especially valuable in advising this company in matters relating to social and governmental policies. But we must diversify our business very soon in order to maintain the steady growth in profits that we have achieved in recent years. As my presentation showed, the manufacturing and marketing of our own brand of soft drink is one of the best ways to do this. It represents a significant diversification, yet it is very closely related to our core business: food.

"The *economics* of the soft drink market tell us that we would be foolish to pass up the kind of *investment return* that the market offers to those newcomers willing to take the *risk*. The food business is generally a mature one. On the other hand, our *forecast* indicates that there is still a lot of room for growth in the soft drink market. To be sure, there is a tremendous amount of *competition* from the 'red team' and the 'blue team.' But we already have expertise in the food business, and it should carry over into the beverage market."

(Continued)

"That's just it, Bob," interjected another board member. "Are we prepared to take this risk? You yourself acknowledged that the *market power* wielded by the two dominant companies in this business is not to be taken lightly. Others have tried to take market share from them and have failed miserably. Moreover, the projections that you have shown for a growing soft drink market are based on the *assumption* that the growth rate will remain the same as it has been in the past ten years or so. As we all know, the soft drink market has been growing, but it has also been very fickle. Only recently, Americans were on a health kick, and fruit juices and bottled waters along with health foods were in fashion. Now it seems that soft drinks are back in style again. Who knows what people will want in the future? Maybe we'll all go back to drinking five cups of coffee a day. And what about all the money that we're going to have to spend up front to *differentiate* our product? As you well know, in the processed-food business, establishing brand recognition—not to mention brand loyalty—can be extremely difficult and costly."

"Well, ladies and gentlemen, all your concerns are certainly legitimate ones, and believe me, I have given much thought to these drawbacks. This is one of the biggest decisions that I will have made since becoming CEO. My staff has spent hundreds of hours analyzing all available data to arrive at a judgment. Our findings indicate a strong probability of earning an above-average return on an investment in the soft drink business, a return commensurate with the kind of risk we know exists in that market. But if we could make all our decisions with 100 percent certainty simply by feeding numbers into a computer, we'd all be out of a job. To be sure, details on production, cost, pricing, distribution, advertising, financing, and organizational structure remain to be ironed out. However, if we wait until all these details are worked out, we may be missing a window of opportunity that might not appear again in this market for a long time. I say that we should go ahead with this project as soon as possible. And unanimity among the board members will give me greater confidence in this endeavor."

INTRODUCTION: ECONOMICS AND MANAGERIAL DECISION MAKING

Managerial Economics is one of the most important and useful courses in your curriculum of studies. It will provide you with a foundation for studying other courses in finance, marketing, operations research, and managerial accounting. It will also provide you with a theoretical framework for tying together courses in the entire curriculum so that you can have a cross-functional view of your studies.

Economics is "the study of the behavior of human beings in producing, distributing and consuming material goods and services in a world of scarce resources."[1]

---

[1]Campbell McConnell, *Economics*, New York: McGraw-Hill, 1993, p. 1.

Management is the discipline of organizing and allocating a firm's scarce resources to achieve its desired objectives.[2] These two definitions clearly point to the relationship between economics and managerial decision making. In fact, we can combine these two terms and define **managerial economics** as the use of economic analysis to make business decisions involving the best use of an organization's scarce resources.

Joel Dean, the author of the first managerial economics textbook, defines managerial economics as "the use of economic analysis in the formulation of business policies." He also notes a "big gap between the problems of logic that intrigue economic theorists and the problems of policy that plague practical management [which] needs to be bridged in order to give executives access to the practical contributions that economic thinking can make to top-management policies."[3]

William Baumol, a highly respected economist and industry consultant, stated that an economist can use his ability to build theoretical models and apply them to any business problem, no matter how complex, break it down into essential components, and describe the relationship among the components, thereby facilitating a systematic search for an optimal solution. In his extensive experience as a consultant to both industry and government, he found that every problem that he worked on was helped in some way by "the method of reasoning involved in the derivation of some economic theorem."[4]

William H. Meckling, the former dean of the Graduate School of Management at the University of Rochester, expressed a similar sentiment in an interview conducted by *The Wall Street Journal*. In his view, "economics is a discipline that can help students solve the sort of problems they meet within the firm." Recalling his experience as the director of naval warfare analysis at the Center for Naval Analysis and as an economic analyst at the Rand Corporation, one of the nation's most prominent think tanks, Meckling stated that these institutions are "dominated by physical scientist types, really brilliant people." But he went on to say that "the economists knew how to structure the problems . . . the rest of the people knew a lot about technical things but they had never thought about how you structure big issues."[5]

As it has evolved in undergraduate and graduate programs over the past half century, managerial economics is essentially a course in applied microeconomics that includes selected quantitative techniques common to other disciplines such as linear programming (management science), regression analysis (statistics, econometrics, and management science), capital budgeting (finance), and cost analysis (managerial and cost accounting). Looked at from our perspective as economists, we see that in fact many disciplines in business studies have drawn from the core of microeconomics for concepts and theoretical support. For example, the economic analysis of demand and price elasticity can be found in most marketing texts. The division of markets into four types—perfect competition, pure monopoly, monopolistic competition, and oligopoly—is generally the basis for the analy-

---

[2]For books supporting this definition, see Peter Drucker, *Management,* New York: Harper & Row, 1973.
[3]Joel Dean, *Managerial Economics,* Englewood Cliffs, NJ: Prentice-Hall, 1951, p. vii.
[4]William Baumol, "What Can Economic Theory Contribute to Managerial Economics?" *American Economic Review,* 51, 2 (May 1961), p. 114.
[5]"Economics Has Much to Teach the Businessman," *The Wall Street Journal,* May 3, 1983.

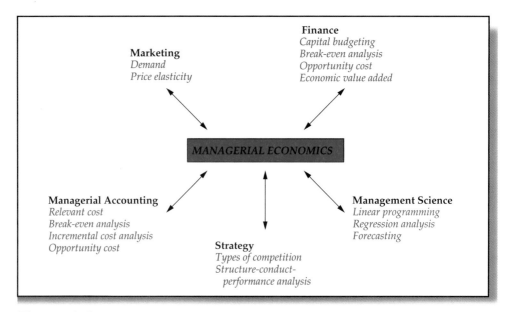

Figure 1.1
Managerial Economics and Other Business Disciplines

sis of the competitive environment presented in books on corporate strategy and marketing strategy.[6]

There are a number of other examples to be found. The economic concept of opportunity cost serves as the foundation for the analysis of relevant cost in managerial accounting and for the use of the "hurdle rate"[7] in finance. As you will see in the next chapter, opportunity cost also plays an important part in understanding how firms create "economic value" for their shareholders. Finally, in recent years, certain authors have linked their managerial economics texts thematically with strategy and human resources.[8] Figure 1.1 illustrates our view that managerial economics is closely linked with many other disciplines in a business curriculum.

Our approach in this text is to show that linkages of economics with other business functions, while maintaining a focus on the heart of managerial economics: the microeconomic theory of the behavior of consumers and firms in competitive markets. When clearly understood and exemplified in actual business examples, this theory provides managers with a basic framework for making key business decisions about the allocation of their firm's scarce resources. In making these decisions managers must deal essentially with the questions below listed in abridged form:

[6]Professor Michael Porter, whose books on strategy have greatly influenced this field of study, is himself a Ph.D. in economics.
[7]Essentially, this is a company's cost of funds expressed as a percentage (e.g., 15%). Any project funded by the company should have a rate of return that is greater than this level.
[8]See for example, David Besanko et al., *Economics of Strategy*, New York: John Wiley & Cons, 2000, and James A. Brickley et al., *Managerial Economics and Organizational Architecture*, New York, Irwin, McGraw-Hill, 1997.

1. What are the economic conditions in a particular market in which we are or could be competing? In particular:
   a. Market structure?
   b. Supply and demand conditions?
   c. Technology?
   d. Government regulations?
   e. International dimensions?
   f. Future conditions?
   g. Macroeconomic factors?
2. Should our firm be in this business?
3. If so, what price and output levels should we set in order to maximize our economic profit or minimize our losses in the short run?
4. How can we organize and invest in our resources (land, labor, capital, managerial skills) in such a way that we maintain a competitive advantage over other firms in this market?
   a. Cost leader?
   b. Product differentiation?
   c. Focus on market niche?
   d. Outsourcing, alliances, mergers, acquisitions?
   e. International dimension—regional or country focus or expansion?
5. What are the risks involved?

Perhaps the most fundamental management question is #2, which concerns whether or not a firm should be in the business in which they are operating. This is the very question addressed by Bob Burns and the rest of the board of directors of Global Foods in this chapter's "Situation."

Note that question #5 has to do with a firm's risk. Uncertainty pervades our everyday lives, especially when we are considering what may happen in the future—near or far. And uncertainty, or risk, is always present in the operations of a business. Of course, there are some things that are fairly certain. A company that buys steel can get a price quote and be certain what it will pay for a ton. A company with temporary excess cash to invest for a short period of time can ascertain the interest rate it will earn. An investor purchasing a U.S. Treasury bill is virtually certain that she will be repaid in full at maturity.

However, when it comes to future impacts, very few things are certain. We can define risk or uncertainty (we will explain the difference between these two terms in chapter 14) as a chance or possibility that actual future outcomes will differ from those expected today. Actually we are usually only concerned with unfavorable results. Thus we can say that risk is the possibility that the outcomes of an action will turn out to be worse than expected. Typical of the types of risk that businesses face would include:

- Changes in demand and supply conditions
- Technological changes and the effect of competition
- Changes in interest rates and inflation rates
- Exchange rate changes for companies engaged in international trade
- Political risk for companies with foreign operations

You may not literally see the term *risk* in many of the chapters of this book. In some of the chapters we implicitly assume that we know the level of demand, the product price, production cost, and the economic profit resulting from operations. However, we really know that risk is present in most situations. Therefore, we have devoted a complete chapter to the subject of risk and uncertainty. In chapter 14 we show how business can attempt to quantify risk and how decisions are made under these conditions. But this is not all. Chapters 5 (demand estimation) and 6 (forecasting) deal with estimating the effects of changes in the variables that determine demand for products and with predicting future results based on past experience if we have sufficient historical data or estimating what may happen in the future even if we have no past data. Furthermore, in chapter 16, we discuss the risks faced by the semiconductor industry and specifically those encountered by the Standard Microsystems Corporation. As you will see when you study this chapter, public companies like SMSC actually must specify the risks they face when they prepare their annual report to the Security and Exchange Commission, the so-called 10K report. The more familiar you become with the risk sections of these reports, the more you will realize that managers cannot avoid risk and they must confront and deal with it every day. It is our firm belief that mastering the principles offered in this text will help you as managers to rationally assess and deal with the various types of business risks that firms must address all the time in the operations of their business.

THE ECONOMICS OF A BUSINESS

Another way to appreciate the study of managerial economics in a business curriculum is to consider how the material covered in this text relates to what we call the **economics of a business.** By this we mean "the key factors that affect the ability of a firm to earn an acceptable rate of return on its owners' investment." (See chapter 2 for a discussion of financial goals of a firm such as return on investment, profit maximization, and economic value added.) The most important of these factors are competition, technology, and customers.

The impact of changing economics on well-established companies can be better understood and appreciated within the framework of a 'four-stage model' of change. This model is shown in Figure 1.2.

Stage I can be called "the good old days" for companies such as IBM, Kodak, Sears, and any number of other solid, blue-chip companies whose dominance of the market allowed them to achieve high profit margins by simply marking up their costs to provide them with a suitable level of profit. Then changes in technology, competition, and customers put pressures on their profit margins as well as market share and forced them into Stage II, where they sought refuge through cost cutting, downsizing, restructuring, and reengineering. In the United States, this began to occur in the 1980s and continued on to the early 1990s, when consultants such as Michael Hammer touted the benefits of "reengineering" as a means of dealing with these changes.[9]

---

[9]Michael Hammer and James Champy, *Reengineering the Corporation*, New York: Harper Collins, 1993.

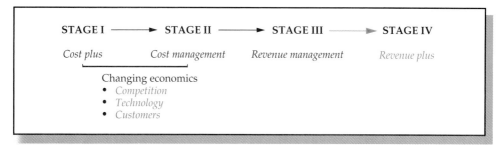

Figure 1.2
Four Stages of Change

From the mid 1990s on, companies sought to enter Stage III when they realized that the continual focus on cost had its limits insofar as its ability to increase profits. After all, there is only so much money that a company can save by reducing its workforce or by becoming more efficient. Therefore, in Stage III "top-line growth" became the major focus.[10] Although companies may have reaffirmed their ability to grow their top line, Wall Street analysts questioned their ability to grow in a *profitable* manner. Thus Stage IV becomes a necessary part of a company's full recovery from the impact of changing economics.[11]

Avon is a good example of a well-established company that has gone through the first three stages and is seeking a firm footing in Stage IV. Stage I for Avon lasted until the latter part of the 1970s. As more and more women began to enter the workforce on a full-time basis, the effectiveness of Avon's vaunted sales force (the "Avon ladies") began to decline. In the 1980s, Avon chose to deal with this change by diversifying rather than taking the full brunt of cost cutting implied in Stage II. In the late 1980s, they were actually faced with the threat of a hostile takeover by Amway. By the early 1990s, Avon divested itself of its acquisitions and started its way through Stage II by consolidating its manufacturing facilities and call centers worldwide. In 1997, just about the time we were beginning work on the third edition of this text, Avon embarked on a substantial reengineering program that aimed to save it hundreds of millions of dollars. Because Avon had to make up for lost time due to its excursions into diversification, its entry into Stage III overlapped that of Stage II. The mid-1990s marked the beginning of Stage III, when Avon expanded aggressively into emerging markets such as China, India, Central Europe, and Russia. It also continued to grow in Latin America, a region of the world in which it had already developed a considerable amount of business. In their U.S. and Western European markets, Avon is spending more on marketing to improve and modernize the image of Avon products. For example, it recently opened "Avon Centre" in the fashionable Trump Tower building on Fifth Avenue in New York City.

In 1999, Avon appointed its first woman CEO, Andrea Jung, to lead the company into Stage IV. By early 2002, both stock analysts and the media seemed to agree that she

---

[10]See for example Robert G. Cross, *Revenue Management*, New York: Broadway Books, 1997.
[11]For a more recent book on "profitable growth," see Ram Charan and Noel M. Tichy, *Every Business Is a Growth Business*, New York: Random House, 1998.

and her team had done a solid job in improving both its growth and its profitability. Key moves included the development of retail channels of distribution, simplifying its line of products and focusing on some of its best selling products. In addition it launched a new line of cosmetics sold through the J.C. Penney stores and has also started to develop products for younger shoppers. Mindful of the opportunities as well as threats of online shopping, Avon is trying to straddle its traditional direct sales channel and the "new economy" by encouraging its representatives to set up their own web sites.[12]

There are numerous other examples of well-established corporations that were forced by changes in customers, competition, or technology to go from Stage I to Stage II and have had to change their strategies in order to move on to Stages III and IV. In our previous edition, we cited Kodak, IBM, and Sears as three of the more well-known stories. IBM, under the leadership of CEO Lou Gerstner, has recovered largely because of its expansion into computer services and consulting. Kodak is still trying to prove that it has a viable strategy to develop a growing and profitable business in the digital era. Sears repositioned itself as a women's clothing store (e.g., "Come see the softer side of Sears") but is still facing tough competition from all sides, from retail giant Wal-Mart to the specialty chains such as Old Navy.[13]

The four stages of change model provides more than just a framework to judge current business events. The model also underscores the importance of various topics covered in this text. For example, in Stage I when the company dominates the market, the monopoly model whereby firms are free to price their products using the "MR = MC rule" (you will learn about this in chapter 9) would be particularly useful. In Stage II, when the company must engage in cost cutting in response to changing competition, customers, and technology, the material in chapters 7 and 8 on cost and production and in chapter 9's section on highly competitive markets become vital to understand. In Stage III, when the company tries to grow its way out of its decline, chapters 4, 5, and 6 provide critical information. These chapters cover the qualitative and quantitative analysis of demand, the keys to growing revenue. Finally in Stage IV, when the company strives for profitable growth, just about all the material in this text can prove helpful.

A BRIEF REVIEW OF IMPORTANT ECONOMIC TERMS AND CONCEPTS

For purposes of study and teaching, economics is divided into two broad categories: microeconomics and macroeconomics. The former concerns the study of individual consumers and producers in specific markets, and the latter deals with the aggregate

---

[12]"A Makeover Has Avon Looking Good," *BusinessWeek,* January 22, 2002. Also see a cover story on Ms. Jung in *BusinessWeek,* September 18, 2000.

[13]These three companies are always in the news. See, for example, the cover story on the newly appointed IBM CEO in *BusinessWeek,* February 11, 2002 and "Film vs. Digital: Can Kodak Build a Bridge," *BusinessWeekOnline,* August 2, 1999, and "Kodak is the Picture of Digital Success (But can the fast-selling EasyShare alter its profit picture?)," *BusinessWeekOnline,* January 14, 2002. A complete listing of Sears' business moves can be found by at www.yahoo.marketguide.com. Among the more important of Sears' recent activities relating to managerial economics are launching a B2B retail exchange with various partners, developing a strategic alliance with Compaq, closing outmoded or outdated stores, and opening 15 new full-line stores and remodeling 50 stores in 2002.

economy. Topics in microeconomics include supply and demand in individual markets, the pricing of specific outputs and inputs (also called factors of production, or resources), production and cost structures for individual goods and services, and the distribution of income and output in the population. Topics in macroeconomics include analysis of the gross domestic product (also referred to as "national income analysis"), unemployment, inflation, fiscal and monetary policy, and the trade and financial relationships among nations.

Microeconomics is the category that is most utilized in managerial economics. However, certain aspects of macroeconomics must also be included because decisions by managers of firms are influenced by their views of the current and future conditions of the macroeconomy. For example, we can well imagine that the management of a company producing capital equipment (e.g., computers, machine tools, trucks, or robotic instruments) would indeed be remiss if they did not factor into their sales forecast some consideration of the macroeconomic outlook. For these and other companies whose businesses are particularly sensitive to the business cycle, a recession would have a very unfavorable effect on their sales, whereas a robust period of economic expansion would be beneficial. But for the most part, managerial economics is based on the variables, models, and concepts that embody microeconomic theory.

As defined in the previous section, economics is the study of how choices are made regarding the use of scarce resources in the production, consumption, and distribution of goods and services. The key term is *scarce resources*. **Scarcity** can be defined as a condition in which resources are not available to satisfy all the needs and wants of a specified group of people. Although scarcity refers to the supply of a **resource,** it makes sense only in relation to the demand for the resource. For example, there is only one Mona Lisa. Therefore, we can safely say that the supply of this particular work of art by da Vinci is limited. Nevertheless, if for some strange reason no one wanted this magnificent work of art, then in purely economic terms it would not be considered scarce. Let us take a less extreme and certainly more mundane example: broken glass on the streets of New York City. Here we have a case of a "resource" that is not scarce not only because there is a lot of broken glass to be found, but also because nobody wants it! Now suppose there were a new art movement inspired by the use of materials retrieved from the streets of urban areas, with broken glass from the streets of New York being particularly desirable. The once-plentiful resource would fast become a "scarce" commodity.

The relative nature of scarcity is represented in Figure 1.3. As can be seen in the figure, the supply of resources is used to meet the demand for these resources by the population. Because the population's needs and wants exceed the ability of the resources to satisfy all the demands, scarcity exists.

In an introductory economics course, the concept of scarcity is usually discussed in relation to an entire country and its people. For example, you will probably recall from your first course in economics the classic example of "guns" (representing a country's devotion of resources to national defense) versus "butter" (representing the use of resources for peacetime goods and services). To be sure, scarcity is a condition individual consumers and producers must also deal with. This text is primarily concerned with the way in which managers of the producing organizations contend

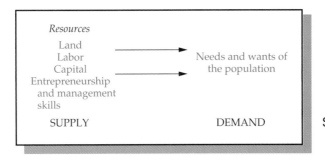

Figure 1.3
Supply, Demand, and Scarcity

with scarcity. But before discussing this particular aspect of the problem, let us review the condition of scarcity from the perspective of an entire country.

The intent of the "guns versus butter" example is to illustrate that scarcity forces a country to choose the amounts of resources that it wishes to allocate between defense and peacetime goods and services. In so doing, its people must reckon with the **opportunity cost** of their decision. This type of cost can be defined as the amount or subjective value that must be sacrificed in choosing one activity over the next best alternative. In the "guns versus butter" example, one activity involves the production of war goods and services, and the other pertains to peacetime good and services. Because of the scarcity of resources, the more that the country allocates to guns, the less it will have to produce butter, and vice versa. The opportunity cost of additional units of guns are the units of butter that the country must forgo in the resource allocation process. The opposite would apply as resources are allocated more for the production of butter than for guns.

In the presence of a limited supply relative to demand, countries must decide how to allocate their scarce resources. This decision is central to the study of economics. In fact, economics has been defined as "the science which studies human behavior as a relationship between ends and scarce means which have alternative uses."[14] Essentially, the allocation decision can be viewed as comprising three separate choices:

1. *What* goods and services should be produced and in what quantities?
2. *How* should these goods and services be produced?
3. *For whom* should these goods and services be produced?

These are the well-known *what, how,* and *for whom* questions found in the introductory chapter of all economic principles textbooks.

The first question incorporates the "guns versus butter" decision. Should a country with scarce resources produce guns? Should it produce butter? If so, how much butter and how many guns? The same applies to the countless other goods and services or product groups that a country is capable of producing.

The second question involves the allocation of a country's resources in the production of a particular good or service. Suppose a country decides to produce a cer-

---

[14]Lionel Robbins, *An Essay on the Nature and Significance of Economic Science,* 2nd ed., London: Macmillan and Co., Ltd., 1935, p. 16.

tain amount of butter. What amounts of land, labor, capital, and entrepreneurial efforts should it devote to this end? Should it use more workers than machinery (a labor-intensive process) or vice versa (a capital-intensive process)? The important point to remember about this question is that it is an economic and not a technical one. It is not asking which formula or recipe should be used to make butter; it is asking what combination of the factors of production should be used in producing a given amount of the product.

The meaning of the third question should be readily apparent. It is a decision that must be made about the distribution of a country's output of goods and services among the members of its population.

All countries must deal with these three basic questions because all have scarce resources. Scarcity is a more serious problem in some countries than in others, but all have needs and wants that cannot be completely met by their existing resources. Precisely how these countries go about making allocation decisions is the question to which we now turn.

There are essentially three ways a country can answer the questions of what, how, and for whom. These ways, referred to as *processes,* are as follows:

1. **Market process:** The use of supply, demand, and material incentives to answer the questions of what, how, and for whom.
2. **Command process:** The use of the government or some central authority to answer the three basic questions. (This process is sometimes referred to as the *political process.*)
3. **Traditional process:** The use of customs and traditions to answer the three basic questions.

Countries generally employ a combination of these three processes to allocate their scarce resources. The market process is predominant in the United States, although the command process plays an important role. Hence, the United States is said to have a mixed economy. Based on the levels of spending by the federal, state, and local governments, we can state that approximately one-fifth of the goods and services produced in the United States are influenced by the command process. The command process does not necessarily mean that a government literally orders the production of certain amounts of guns, butter, or other goods or services; rather, a government may use the material incentives of the market process to allocate resources in certain ways, a process often referred to as *indirect command.* For example, the government offers defense contractors the opportunity to earn a profit by producing military goods and services. In addition, the government can control the allocation of resources in a more direct way through various laws governing the actions of both consumers and producers. For example, the government controls manufacturing and distribution through such agencies as the Food and Drug Administration. It attempts to control consumer use of certain foods and drugs through various laws and regulations. A simple but important example of this pertains to the tobacco industry. Over the past several decades, the U.S. government has made determined efforts to convince people to stop smoking. These efforts range from warnings on cigarette packages to the banning of smoking on airline flights. Prohibition during the 1920s offers another example of the government's efforts to stop the consumption of certain goods or services.

In addition to using rules and regulations and its fiscal power, the government can also influence the allocation of scarce resources through subsidies, tariffs, and quotas. Further discussion of these aspects of the command process in the U.S. economy is found in other sections of this chapter and throughout the rest of the text. In fact, chapter 15 is devoted to a discussion of the role of government in the market economy.

The traditional process is also at work in the U.S. economy, but this process can be better understood by considering its impact on different countries throughout the world, particularly those whose economies are still developing. Examples of the traditional process are found in the eating habits, and in the patterns of work and social interaction in such countries. Two examples of how the traditional process influences the allocation of scarce resources are religious restrictions on certain foods, such as beef and pork, and hiring practices based primarily on familial relationships. A branch of anthropology called economic anthropology is particularly concerned with the impact of customs and traditions on the economic questions of what, how, and for whom. In the business curriculum, students will find this subject of particular importance in courses on international business.

Because of the predominance of the market process in the U.S. economy, our discussion of the allocation of scarce resources is based on the assumption that managers operate primarily through the mechanisms of supply, demand, and material incentive (i.e., the profit motive). Their decisions about what goods to produce, how they should be produced, and for whom they should be produced are essentially market oriented. That is, firms choose to produce certain goods and services because, given the demand for these products and the cost of using scarce resources, they can earn sufficient profit to justify their particular use of these resources. Moreover, they combine their scarce resources to produce maximum output in the least costly way. Finally, they supply these goods and services to those segments of the population expected to provide the most material reward for their efforts.

Table 1.1 compares the three basic questions from the standpoint of a country and from the standpoint of a company, where they form the basis of the **economic decisions for the firm.** From the firm's point of view, question 1 is the product decision. At some particular time, a firm may decide to provide new or different goods or services or to stop providing a particular good or service. For example, Gateway

Table 1.1
The Three Basic Economic Questions

FROM THE STANDPOINT OF A COUNTRY	FROM THE STANDPOINT OF A COMPANY
1. What goods and services should be produced?	1. The product decision
2. How should these goods and services be produced?	2. The hiring, staffing, procurement, and capital-budgeting decisions
3. For whom should these goods and services be produced?	3. The market segmentation decision

2000, the seller of personal computers through direct mail, decided in 1997 to expand its range of product offerings to include servers as well as PCs. Also in that year, Mercedes began selling its version of a sports utility vehicle to compete in the high end of this market. As an example of new services, consider the wireless companies' offering of digital services (as opposed to the older analog services), typical of the many product introductions taking place in the information technology and communications industry. And as you will see in the next chapter, Global Foods decides to sell bottled water in addition to carbonated soft drinks. Bottled water actually represents the fastest growing segment of the nonalcoholic beverage market, and certainly our fictional company does not want to get left behind.

Question 2 is a basic part of a manager's responsibility. It involves personnel practices such as hiring and firing as well as questions concerning the purchase of items ranging from raw materials to capital equipment. For example, the decision to automate certain clerical activities using a network of personal computers results in a more capital-intensive mode of production. The resolution to use more supplementary, part-time workers in place of full-time workers is another example of a management decision concerning how goods and services should be produced. A third example involves the selection of materials in the production of a certain item (e.g., the combination of steel, aluminum, and plastic used in an automobile).

The firm's decision concerning question 3 is not completely analogous to that of a country. Actually, a firm's decision regarding *market segmentation* (a term used in the marketing field) is closely related to question 1 for a country. In deciding what segment of the market to focus on, the firm is not literally deciding who gets the good or service. For example, suppose a firm decides to target a certain demographic segment by selling only a "high-end" or premium version of a product. However, the way in which a company markets the product (which includes its pricing and distribution policies) makes certain segments of the market more likely to purchase the product.

Perhaps one of the best ways to link the economic problem of making choices under conditions of scarcity with the tasks of a manager is to consider the view put forth by Professor Robert Anthony that a manager is essentially a person who is responsible for the allocation of a firm's scarce resources.[15]

It is interesting to note that "managers" or "management skills" was not delineated as a separate factor of production by early economic theorists. The four traditional categories of resources are land, labor, capital, and entrepreneurship. The last category can be treated as broad enough to include management, but the two classifications do involve different characteristics or skills.

The term *entrepreneurship* is generally associated with the ownership of the means of production. But in addition, it implies willingness to take certain risks in the pursuit of goals (e.g., starting a new business, producing a new product, or providing a different kind of service). Management, on the other hand, involves the abil-

---

[15]Actually, Anthony divided the planning and control process in a firm into three activities: strategic planning (i.e., setting the firm's overall objectives), management control (i.e., making sure that scarce resources are obtained and used effectively and efficiently in the firm's accomplishment of its objectives), and operational control (i.e., making sure that specific tasks are carried out effectively and efficiently). These ideas were first put forth in R. N. Anthony, *Planning and Control Systems: A Framework for Analysis,* Boston: Harvard Business School, Division of Research, 1965.

ity to organize and administer various tasks in pursuit of certain objectives. An important part of a manager's job is to monitor and guide people in an organization. In the words of Peter Drucker, who has been called "the founding father of the science of management,"

> It is "management" that determines what is needed and what has to be achieved [in an organization]. . . . Management is work. Indeed, it is the specific work of a modern society, the work that distinguishes our society from all earlier ones. . . . As work, management has its own skills, its own tools, its own techniques.[16]

Part of being a good manager involves taking risks, so experts have advised managers to become more "entrepreneurial." By the same token, entrepreneurs may require professional management expertise to run their venture more effectively. Michael Dell, founder of Dell Computer Corporation, is perhaps one of the best examples of an entrepreneur who required professional management at some point in the development of his company. Back in the mid 1990s, Dell's rapid growth created serious process and control problems. To his credit, Michael Dell brought in seasoned executives from large corporations to help the company deal with these problems.

By 2000, Dell had established itself as the clear-cut leader in the highly competitive personal computer market. In the United States that year, its 9.4 million units sold was 19.1 percent of the market. This was followed by Compaq with 7.6 million units or a 15.4 percent market share. The numbers for Hewlett-Packard, Gateway, and IBM were 5.6 million and 11.4 percent, 4.2 million and 8.6 percent, and 2.6 million and 5.4 percent, respectively.[17] Despite a difficult year in 2001, Dell still managed to increase its sales faster than its closest competitors. The success of Dell's company today indicates the importance of professional management in rapidly growing start-ups.

Some economists cite management skills as a separate factor of production. Others include them in the general category of entrepreneurship. Still others combine entrepreneurship and management skills into one category, as we have done. An interesting treatment of the subject was given by Alfred Marshall, whose work in economic theory about 100 years ago still provides much of the foundation for modern microeconomics. Marshall used the building trade to illustrate certain differences between managerial and entrepreneurial skills and activities. According to Marshall, individuals may well be able to manage the construction of their own homes even though they are less efficient than a professional contractor would be. However, it is another matter when housing construction is carried out on a large scale.

> When this [housing construction] is done on a large scale, as for instance in opening a new suburb, the stakes at issue are so large as to offer an attractive field to powerful capitalists with a very high order of general business ability, but perhaps with not much technical knowledge of the building trade. They rely on their own judgment for the decision as to what are

---

[16]Drucker, *Management*, p. xi.
[17]Market Share Reporter, 2002.

likely to be the coming relations of demand and supply for different kinds of houses; but they entrust to others the *management of details* [emphasis added]. They employ architects and surveyors to make plans in accordance with their general directions, and then enter into contracts with professional builders for carrying them out. But they themselves *undertake the chief risks of the business* [emphasis added], and control its general direction.[18]

You may be somewhat surprised at the freshness of observations made a century ago. You may also feel that Marshall was referring simply to management tasks and responsibilities at different levels. Putting Marshall's ideas in terms of today's large corporation, what he refers to as "the decision as to what are likely to be the coming relations of demand and supply" most likely involves strategic decisions made by upper management. What he terms "the management of details" is usually carried out by lower levels of management (e.g., by first-line supervisors).

Regardless of how the classification is handled, it is important to be aware of the distinction between the two factors. Obviously, the content of this text is devoted to developing management skills. Nonetheless, a mastery of the economic principles presented in this book could well lead to a sharpening of one's entrepreneurial skills by helping to assess the market conditions and risks involved in a particular venture.

THE CASE OF GLOBAL FOODS, INC.: SITUATIONS AND SOLUTIONS

Prior sections of this chapter cited various reasons why an understanding of economics is important to managerial decision making. An effective way of demonstrating this importance is to cite real-world examples gleaned from the popular press and distilled from the findings of research studies on the use of economics in managerial decision making. All other texts in managerial economics do this, and this book is no exception. But in addition, we hope to show how economic terms and concepts can be applied to managerial decision making through the use of a series of hypothetical situations such as the one presented at the beginning of this chapter. In fact, each chapter will begin with a *situation* requiring some sort of decision or action relating directly to the subject matter of the chapter. For example, in this chapter, a decision must be made about whether to enter the soft drink market. This is a fundamental business decision involving the allocation of a firm's scarce resources, a major theme of this chapter.

At the end of each chapter, a *solution* for the situation will be presented based on the knowledge gained from reading the chapter. We use the term *solution* rather loosely because it may not involve a specific answer, as one might expect in the solution to a mathematical problem. In our view, the ambiguity of a solution is very much in keeping with conditions in the real world. Very often in an actual business

---

[18]Alfred Marshall, *Principles of Economics*, 8th ed., Philadelphia: Porcupine Press, 1920, reprinted 1982, pp. 245–46. (First edition published in 1890.)

problem, there is no unique formula that one can use to compute the answer.[19] Either the formula does not exist or is not entirely applicable to the problem, or the problem itself is not amenable to a straightforward quantitative solution technique. And even when a specific numerical solution is achieved—as is the case in chapter 13 on capital budgeting—there may be other considerations of a qualitative nature that temper the acceptability of the solution. Therefore, the solutions offered at the end of the chapters are only suggested outcomes of the situations. (You may wish to consider alternative ways for the managers depicted in the situations to deal with their tasks or problems.)

The situations used throughout the book are based on one industry and one firm in that industry. As you have already learned, we will be using the soft drink industry. Moreover, we will be following the trials and tribulations of the managers of Global Foods, Inc., and, in certain cases, the managers of firms that do business with Global. This will help to tie together the disparate aspects of economic analysis. Also, we felt that a focus on one firm in one industry will create added interest in the events depicted in the situations, further motivating mastery of each chapter's material.

A number of industries were initially considered. We chose the soft drink industry based on the following criteria:

1. The industry should be one that all readers can relate to as consumers.
2. The goods or services sold in the industry should be essentially nontechnical, and the means of production should be relatively easy for the layperson to understand.
3. The competitive environment should be very intense.
4. Information about the industry should be readily available (e.g., from trade journals and research monographs), and news about current activities in this industry should be frequently reported in the popular media.

The soft drink industry closely meets all of these criteria. Just about everyone consumes this product, and the product itself is rather simple: carbonated water, sweeteners, and various flavorings. The packaging is also uncomplicated. Soft drinks are sold today in 12-ounce aluminum cans, in 1- and 2-liter plastic bottles, and in glass bottles. The making of the syrup and the bottling of the beverage involve various manufacturing processes that are relatively easy to understand. The two most important trade publications in the soft drink industry are *Beverage World* and *Beverage Digest*. We found them to be excellent sources of background information on the industry. Moreover, the major soft drink companies are constantly reported on in major periodicals. Recent articles from these sources will be cited throughout the text.

---

[19]For example, an article in *Investor's Business Daily,* February 7, 2002, points out that analysts are starting to seriously question the wisdom of Pepsi's acquisition of Quaker Oats, which was done primarily to gain ownership of that company's leading brand, Gatorade. Last year, Gatorade exhibited only a 6 percent growth. Previously, the brand had consistently achieved annual double digit growth. It would be ironic if Pepsi falters with this brand, because Quaker Oat's failure to generate a decent return on its acquisition of Snapple caused it to lose hundreds of millions of dollars. In fact, this failure eventually weakened the company to the point where it was ripe for acquisition by Pepsi. Thus we see in the real world that the acquisition of a leading brand may not be the solution for a firm's slumping growth.

The situations used in each chapter, along with the characters portrayed at Global, are entirely fictitious. However, the features of each situation closely resemble actual business problems or circumstances that managers must often address. The verity of the issues involved in each situation is based on the authors' experiences in private industry as well as on extensive interviews with managers from various companies in the soft drink business. The following section gives a summary of the situations and solutions presented in the chapters. The main decisions to be made by the characters portrayed in the situations are included under the heading "Key Question."

Summary of the Situations and Solutions

1 Introduction

Situation: Bob Burns, CEO of Global Foods, Inc., asks the board of directors to approve a decision to enter the soft drink business.
Key Question: "Should we enter the soft drink business?"
Solution: The Board approves the decision, and Global Foods enters the soft drink business.

2 The Firm and Its Goals

Situation: In an effort to increase the company's revenues, Bob Burns considers entry into the bottled water market, the fastest-growing segment of the nonalcoholic beverage industry.
Key Question: "How can we improve the value of our company when the Wall Street analysts are judging us primarily on our ability to grow our revenue and profit?"
Solution: Bob decides to take Global Foods into the bottled water business.

3 Supply and Demand

Situation: Ross Harris, senior purchasing agent for Global Foods, and Kathy Martinez, staff associate for a major producer of high-fructose corn syrup (HFCS), must prepare studies for their respective companies as a prelude to a major contract negotiation between the suppliers and users of HFCS.
Key Question: "What is the best time period within which to lock in the price of HFCS?"
Solution: The suppliers and users of HFCS agree to a compromise in which the price of HFCS is to be established every 3 months instead of every 12 months.

4 Demand Elasticity

Situation: Henry Caulfield, the proprietor of a "Gas 'n Go" convenience store, must evaluate the desirability of various pricing schedules for soft drinks set by the major beverage companies.

Key Question: "For what price should I sell this new soft drink?"
Solution: He decides that the relative inelasticity of the products in question makes it difficult to increase sales by lowering the price.

5 Demand Estimation

Situation: Jennifer Harrah, senior research associate of a market research firm, is assigned the task of producing a statistical model that will help to explain the determinants of soft drink consumption. Her firm's client is Global Foods, Inc.
Key Question: "What are the key determinants of demand for soft drinks, and what are their quantitative impacts on sales?"
Solution: Jennifer estimates the quantitative impacts of a selected number of factors on soft drink sales with the use of multiple regression analysis.

6 Forecasting

Situation: Frank Robinson, newly appointed head of Global's forecasting department, is asked to estimate the next year's sales of Citronade, the company's lemon-lime soda.
Key Question: "What will next year's sales for Citronade be?"
Solution: Frank uses a trend analysis, adjusted seasonally as well as cyclically, to forecast the coming year's sales.

7 The Theory and Estimation of Production

Situation: Christopher Lim, production manager, is concerned about the best way to bottle the water that the company now intends to sell. To differentiate Global Foods' product in a highly competitive market, the marketing people want to use glass bottles. In Chris's view, this may help in the marketing of the product, but may well increase production costs significantly.
Key Question: "Should we package the water in glass bottles?"
Solution: Chris recommends that plastic bottles should be used to package both the carbonated soft drink and the bottled water products.

8 The Theory and Estimation of Cost

Situation: Shayna Bottling Company, an independent bottler of Global Foods soft drinks, is looking for new ways to increase the profitability of its soda production. Adam Michaels, the Plant Manager, receives a marketing flyer from a new potential supplier in the next state, Lawrence Aluminum Products.
Key Question: Should the company stay with its current main supplier in the next town, Kayla Containers, Inc., or switch to this new supplier?
Solution: Shayna Soda Co. decides to stay with Kayla Containers, Inc., after considering all of the other factors involved in the switch. Raw material costs were lower with Lawrence Aluminum, but other associated costs resulted in a net increase.

9   Pricing and Output Decisions: Perfect Competition and Monopoly

Situation: Frank Robinson is appointed product manager of the new bottled water product. One of his first tasks is to recommend a price for the product.
Key Question: "What price should we charge for our new product?"
Solution: After analyzing the demand elasticity and short-run cost structure of the product, Frank recommends a price based on the MR = MC rule.

9   Appendix B   Break-Even Analysis (Volume-Cost-Profit)

Situation: Suzanne Prescott, a senior analyst for the bottled water division, is asked to prepare a profit plan for the coming year.
Key Question: "What is the profit outlook for the coming year for our bottled water product, Waterpure?"
Solution: She uses break-even analysis to forecast the coming year's profit for this product. She also uses sensitivity analysis to provide best-case and worst-case scenarios.

10   Pricing and Output Decisions: Monopolistic Competition and Oligopoly

Situation: The Management Committee of Global Foods asks Frank to reconsider his pricing recommendation because his analysis did not take into account certain competitive and market issues.
Key Question: "What is the best price for a product, given its demand, cost, and competition?"
Solution: After much debate, the management committee, with Frank's additional help, decides to set the price of its product slightly lower than the premium-priced competitors but slightly higher than the "value brands."

11   Special Pricing Practices

Situation: Rebecca James must decide what price bid she should submit to a large airport caterer that wishes to award a contract to a single supplier.
Key Question: "How should the bid price be set to give Global Foods a good shot at obtaining the large caterer's contract?"
Solution: Since demand elasticities differ in different markets, the price offered in this price-sensitive market will have to be sufficiently low to give Global a good chance of winning the contract.

12   Economic Decision-Making in the Twenty-First Century: The Old Economics of the New Economy

Situation: Global Foods is concerned about a rival start-up called "Kwench" that operates as a virtual supplier of a "new age" beverage. Nicole Goodman, vice president of marketing works with a consultant to develop a competitive response.

Key Question: Should the company start its own B2B exchange in order to move quickly to counteract Kwench's entry into the marketplace or should it just try to acquire the upstart?

Solution: Global Foods decides to initiate a joint venture with Kwench. Kwench provides the brand recognition and Global Foods provides the distribution channel.

13 Capital Budgeting

Situation: George Kline, the manager of Global's capital planning department, is considering two new project proposals. One involves the expansion of company activities into a new geographical region, and the other involves the purchase of a new depalletizing machine to replace the one currently in use.

Key Questions: "Should we expand into a new geographical area? Should we replace one of our depalletizers?"

Solution: Using capital budgeting techniques involving the calculation of net present value and internal rates of return, George recommends that the firm accept the first project proposal and reject the second one.

14 Risk and Uncertainty

Situation: George is asked by the firm's treasurer to consider the risk involved in going ahead with the project to expand into a new geographical area.

Key Question: "What is the extent of our risk in expanding our geographic area?"

Solution: After considering various acceptable ways to adjust a capital project for risk, George decides to rely primarily on sensitivity analysis. In addition to his original findings, George presents the treasurer with an optimistic and a pessimistic set of results.

15 The Role of Government in the Market Economy

Situation: Bill Adams, the chief information officer (CIO) of Global Foods, Inc., is told by CEO Bob Burns that Global Foods must outsource its telecommunications network. Although Bill does not agree, he tries to make the best of it by trying to find the best company to handle Global Foods' telecommunications requirements.

Key Question: "Which telecommunications company is best equipped to handle Global Foods' voice and data communications requirements?"

Solution: No specific solution is offered, but the main point of this situation is that increasing deregulation in industries such as telecommunication has given companies such as Global Foods many more options in running their business operations.

16 Managerial Economics in Action: Competing in the Semiconductor Industry

This chapter focuses on the semiconductor industry. Because of this industry's intensity of competition, sensitivity to the business cycle, and fast-moving changes in technology, it makes a dramatic real-world setting in which to examine how the concepts and tools of analysis presented in this text can be helpful to managers. All the material in this chapter is factual. Therefore, no situation or solution for a fictional company such as Global Foods will be needed.

INTERNATIONAL APPLICATION: REINVENTING THE CORPORATION

 This chapter talked about what happens to a company when it is buffeted by changing "economics" (e.g., changing customers, competition, and technology). In order to adjust to these changes, managers often must decide to make major shifts in the focus of their business and to reallocate the firm's scarce resources to support these shifts. Sometimes the change in focus is so great that the company exits completely from its core business and enters into completely different businesses. Such has been the case for two companies; one should be well-known at least in name, and the other may be unknown to most readers.[20] The companies are Western Union and VNU.

One of the authors recalls a movie that he saw when rather young about the Pony Express. What made a big impression on him was that no matter how fast the ponies or how skilled the riders, they could not outrun the telegraph. Have you ever wondered what happened to Western Union Telegraph, at one time one of the most powerful companies in the United States?[21] It is undoubtedly a prime example of a company that has been subjected to immense changes in customers, competition, and technology since the days of the Pony Express. Through all these changes, it has managed to survive and is now doing well as a subsidiary of First Data Corporation, the world's largest third-party processor of credit card transactions.[22]

Many aspects of the Western Union case are fascinating and relevant to managerial economics. The two that we would like to point out are (1) its shift in focus from telegraph communications to a financial services company, and (2) the expansion from its beginnings in a regional section of the United States to its position today as a global organization with over 100,000 agent locations around the world. The details of this shift in focus and its global expansion are well beyond the scope of this text. But here are a few highlights:

1851 Western Union's predecessor company, the New York and Mississippi Valley Printing Telegraph Company, is formed by a group of businessmen in Rochester, NY.

1856 The New York and Mississippi Valley Printing Telegraph Company changes its name to Western Union Telegraph Company, signifying the acquisition of various competing firms.

1861 Completes the first transcontinental telegraph line, providing fast communications during the Civil War.

---

[20]A few readers may have been beneficiaries of Western Union's money transfer services.
[21]In 1884, it was selected as one of the original 11 stocks tracked by the first Dow Jones Index.
[22]Go to www.westernunion.com and www.firstdata.com for more details on both Western Union and First Data Corporation.

1871 Introduces Western Union Money Transfer (registered trademark) service, which soon becomes the company's primary business.

1914 Introduces the first consumer charge card.

1933 Introduces singing telegrams.

1970 Offers next-day delivery via postal service.

1974 Launches Westar I, the first domestic communications satellite.

1989 Launches Quick Collect (registered trademark), a service that provides creditors with a fast and secure method for collecting delinquent accounts via flat-rate money transfers. Also, Rapid Money Transfer service becomes available outside North America.

1992 Initiates Western Union money order service.

1993 Introduces *Dinero en Minutos* (registered trademark), making funds sent from the U.S. to Mexico available in minutes.

1994–95 Becomes part of First Data Corporation.

2000 Launches Westernunion.com as a means of transferring funds over the Internet.

2001 Celebrates 150th anniversary, has a network of over 100,000 agent locations around the world.[23]

The other company that impressed us with its ability to refocus its product lines as well as the geography of its operations is VNU. Western Union began as a regional American company in communications that eventually became a global leader in money-transfer services. VNU is a Dutch company that began in publishing and is now a global leader in marketing and media information. Much of its revenue in fact comes from its businesses in the United States. Perhaps the best way to appreciate this transformation is to read what the company says about itself.

Since 1964, VNU has expanded from a Dutch publishing firm into a major international Media and Information Company, with leading market positions and brands in Marketing Information, Media Measurement, Business Information and Directories. With 180 trade magazines, 125 trade shows, 115 directories and "yellow pages," over 250 Internet sites and thousands of market data reports, we provide millions of people around the world with business and professional intelligence.[24]

VNU used both acquisitions and divestment in order to implement its strategy of becoming an international media and information company. Recent moves include the acquisition of World Directories in 1999, Nielsen Media Research in 1999, and ACNielsen in 2001.[25] It also sold its consumer information and educational publishing divisions in 2001. We can imagine that the sale of these groups must have been a difficult decision because they were the foundations of the original VNU.[26]

---

[23]These were taken, some almost verbatim, from the Western Union web site. Only certain highlights were selected for this section. For a full listing, please click on to "History" from the home page.

[24]From the company brochure. Full details about VNU, its history and its strategy can be found at www.vnu.com. In the authors' opinion, it contains one of the clearest explanations of a company strategy that we have found on any corporate web site.

[25]ACNielsen's business of collecting and analyzing information in various consumer markets is noted in Chapter 5.

[26]The divestiture of a business that a company starts out with must be difficult, simply for "emotional reasons." Imagine what IBM went through in abandoning the typewriter business or the difficult time Sears must have had in getting rid of its catalog.

The Solution

After about an hour of heated debate, Bob had a suggestion to make to the board. "Look, we've been discussing this to such an extent that perhaps the key arguments I made in my presentation have gotten lost or confused. Let me summarize the seven key reasons why we want to enter the soft drink business, and then let's vote on this matter.

"1. *Outlook for the industry:* Prospects for growth in the industry continue to be strong. Therefore, we can expect the demand for our products to be a part of this positive industry trend.

"2. *Market size and structure:* Although the industry is dominated by Coca-Cola and Pepsi-Cola, we believe there is still room for the entry of niche marketers. A number of regional and specialty companies have emerged over the past few years, particularly those offering sparkling fruit juices. We believe we can be as successful, if not more successful, than these new entrants.

"3. *Manufacturing, packaging, and distribution:* Our experience in the manufacturing of food products will give us a significant head start when we enter the soft drink business. Moreover, we do not plan to build bottling facilities from scratch. Instead, we look to purchase and consolidate existing bottling plants currently owned and operated by independent firms or by multiple franchise operations. We are also encouraged by the number of new cost-reducing technologies that have been introduced and the fact that the cost of the artificial sweetener aspartame should decline now that Monsanto's patent has expired.

"4. *Transportation and distribution:* We already have a well-managed fleet of vehicles that deliver our food products. We also have important influence and contacts in the retail food business. These will be essential in establishing a presence on the shelves of supermarkets and convenience stores throughout the country.

"5. *Pricing, advertising, and promotion:* As the 'new kid on the block,' we recognize that we will have to enter the market as a price follower. However, in time, as our products are developed and marketed, we should be able to establish some independence either to raise or lower our prices in comparison with the rest of the industry. As far as advertising and promotion are concerned, we have an excellent advertising agency that has served us well with our current product line. However, we shall be flexible enough to consider other agencies if the need arises. Moreover, our experience with various promotional programs (e.g., discount coupons through direct mail and magazine inserts) should be transferable to the soft drink industry. Most important, all advertising and promotional efforts should be greatly aided by the fact that our company name—Global Foods—enjoys a high degree of consumer recognition (along with the specific brand names of our products).

(Continued)

"6. *New products:* As you have seen in the detailed report, we have exciting plans for several new products as well as a full line of naturally and artificially sweetened carbonated drinks. Through an independent market research company, we have tested consumer preferences for our new offerings. The results have been most satisfactory.

"7. *Financial considerations:* As stated at the very beginning of this presentation, our main goal is to create value for our shareholders. We must continue to grow in a profitable manner if we are to continue satisfying the financial expectations of our shareholders. We compete in a mature industry that enables us to generate a considerable amount of cash from our current line of products with well-entrenched brand names. We believe that we should use this cash to expand into the soft drink business. As all our financial projections and analysis indicate, this effort should yield a rate of return that is more than enough to compensate us for the investment and its associated risk."

After giving this executive summary, Bob Burns asked the board for a final decision. "All right, let's vote. All those in favor of entering the soft drink market? Opposed? Great, it's unanimous. Ladies and gentlemen, we're going into the soft drink business."

SUMMARY

Managerial economics is a discipline that combines microeconomic theory with management practice. Microeconomics is the study of how choices are made to allocate scarce resources with competing uses. An important function of a manager is to decide how to allocate a firm's scarce resources. Examples of such decisions are the selection of a firm's products or services, the hiring of personnel, the assigning of personnel to particular functions or tasks, the purchase of materials and equipment, and the pricing of products and services. This text will show how the application of economic theory and concepts helps managers to make allocation decisions that are in the best economic interests of their firms.

Throughout the text, numerous examples will be cited to illustrate how economic theory and concepts can be applied to management decision making. References will also be made to business cases and economic events that have been reported in the popular press. However, a unique feature of this book is a unifying case study of a food and beverage company, Global Foods, Inc. Each chapter begins with a situation in which the managers of this firm have to make key economic decisions. The solutions that end the chapters suggest ways that economic analysis can assist in the decision-making process.

IMPORTANT CONCEPTS

Command process: The use of central planning and the directives of government authorities to answer the questions of *what, how,* and *for whom.* (p. 11)

Economic decisions for the firm: "What goods and services should be produced?"—the product decision. "How should these goods and services be produced?"—the hiring, staffing, and capital-budgeting decision. "For whom should these goods and services be produced?"—the market segmentation decision. (p. 12)

Economics: The study of how choices are made under conditions of scarcity. The basic economic problem can be defined as: "What goods and services should be produced and in what quantities?" "How should these goods and services be produced?" "For whom should these goods and services be produced?" (p. 2)

Economics of a business: The key factors that affect the ability of a firm to earn an acceptable rate of return on its owners' investment. The most important of these factors are competition, technology, and customers. (p. 6)

Managerial economics: The use of economic analysis to make business decisions involving the best use of a firm's scarce resources. (p. 3)

Market process: The use of supply, demand, and material incentives to answer the questions of *what, how,* and *for whom.* (p. 11)

✓ **Opportunity cost:** The amount or subjective value forgone in choosing one activity over the next best alternative. This cost must be considered whenever decisions are made under conditions of scarcity. (p. 10)

Resources: Also referred to as *factors of production* or *inputs,* economic analysis usually includes four basic types: land, labor, capital, and entrepreneurship. This chapter also includes managerial skills as well as entrepreneurship. (p. 9)

✓ **Scarcity:** A condition that exists when resources are limited relative to the demand for their use. In the market process, the extent of this condition is reflected in the price of resources or the goods and services they produce. (p. 9)

Traditional process: The use of customs and traditions to answer the questions of *what, how,* and *for whom.* (p. 11)

QUESTIONS

1. Define *scarcity* and *opportunity cost.* What role do these two concepts play in the making of management decisions?

2. Elaborate on the basic economic questions of *what, how,* and *for whom.* Provide specific examples of these questions with respect to the use of a *country's* scarce resources.

3. Following are examples of typical economic decisions made by the managers of a firm. Determine whether each is an example of *what, how,* or *for whom.*
   a. Should the company make its own spare parts or buy them from an outside vendor?
   b. Should the company continue to service the equipment that it sells or ask customers to use independent repair companies?
   c. Should a company expand its business to international markets or concentrate on the domestic market?
   d. Should the company replace its own communications network with a "virtual private network" that is owned and operated by another company?
   e. Should the company buy or lease the fleet of trucks that it uses to transport its products to market?

4. Define the market process, the command process, and the traditional process. How does each process deal with the basic questions of *what, how,* and *for whom?*

5. Discuss the importance of the command process and the traditional process in the making of management decisions. Illustrate specific ways in which managers must take these two processes into account.

6. Explain the differences between management skills and entrepreneurship. Discuss how each factor contributes to the economic success of a business.

7. Compare and contrast microeconomics with macroeconomics. Although managerial economics is based primarily on microeconomics, explain why it is also important for managers to understand macroeconomics.

8. What do you think is the key to success in the soft drink industry? What chance do you think Global Foods has in succeeding in its new venture into the soft drink market? Explain. (Answer these questions on the basis of the information provided in the chapter as well as any other knowledge you might have about the food and beverage business.)

9. Essentially, what do you think are the changing aspects of the economics (i.e., customers, technology, and competition) of the following industries?
   a. telecommunications
   b. retail merchandising
   c. higher education
   d. aerospace and defense

10. (Optional) Have you been personally involved in the making of a decision for a business concerning *what, how,* or *for whom?* If so, explain your rationale for making such decisions. Were these decisions guided by the market process, the command process, or the traditional process? Explain.

Chapter 2

The Firm and Its Goals

The Situation

Bob Burns looked over the last few numbers provided to him in a consultant's report on the soft drink industry, closed the binder and turned to Nicole Goodman, Global Foods' vice president of marketing. "Looking back, our decision to get into the soft drink industry was a good one, but who would have thought that an industry that showed such strong growth in the early 1990s would start to peak so soon? And also, we should have known that the two leading brands wouldn't stand still while we tried to increase our market share. Coke has been very successful with its Sprite® against Cadbury-Schweppes' 7-Up®, and it seems that they will launch a rival brand to Cadbury's Dr Pepper®. I think we need to get into a growing market.

"An idea occurred to me recently when I was watching the Yankees-Mets baseball game on television. When one of the Yankee players returned to the dugout after hitting a home run, he didn't go to the water cooler, but instead picked up a bottle of water. I already knew that bottled water was the fastest-growing segment of the beverage industry, and statistics I've seen since reinforce this. We must get into this market while it's still growing."

"I hate to say this, Bob, but it may be a case of 'too little, too late,' " said Nicole. "Established companies such as Perrier have been around for a long time; Perrier also owns strong American brands such as Poland Spring, Deer Park, and Calistoga. Evian, which is owned by the French Company, Danone, has also been quite successful in the United States. I am afraid that if we entered the market we would start way behind."

(Continued)

INTRODUCTION

Chapter 1 explained that managerial economics deals primarily with the problem of deciding how best to allocate a firm's scarce resources among competing uses. The best or optimal decision is the one that enables the firm to meet its desired objectives most closely. This chapter will elaborate on the process of making decisions under conditions of scarcity by discussing the goals of a firm and the economic significance of the optimal decision. The appendix to this chapter explains the role of marginal analysis in economic decision making. This appendix also presents a review of the mathematics used in this text to illustrate key economic concepts and methods of analysis.

The major portion of this chapter will be devoted to a discussion of the goals of the firm. However, in order to carry on this discussion sensibly, we must first define and explain the term, *the firm.*

THE FIRM

The traditional (neoclassical) theory of economics defined the **firm** as a collection of resources that is transformed into products demanded by consumers. The costs at which the firm produces are governed by the available technology, and the amount it produces and the prices at which it sells are influenced by the structure of the markets in which it operates. The difference between the revenue it receives and the costs it incurs is *profit.* It is the aim of the firm to maximize its profit.

The preceding theory assumes the existence of the firm. But this leaves the reason for its existence unanswered. Why does a firm perform certain functions internally while it conducts other actions through the market? It appears that the size of the firm is not determined strictly by technological considerations. Then why are some firms very small and others large?

Answers to the preceding questions began to appear in 1937 when Ronald Coase postulated that a company compares costs of organizing an activity internally with the cost of using the market system for its transactions.[1]

---

[1]The seminal work in this area was by Ronald H. Coase in "The Nature of the Firm," *Economica,* 4 (1937), pp. 386–405, reprinted in R. H. Coase, *The Firm, the Market and the Law,* Chicago: University of Chicago Press, 1988, pp. 33–55. Coase was awarded the Nobel Prize in Economics in 1991.

If there were no costs of dealing with the outside market, a firm would be organized so that all of its transactions would be with the outside. However, it is incorrect to assume that the marketplace does not involve any costs. In dealing through the market, the firm incurs **transaction costs.**

Transaction costs are incurred when a company enters into a contract with other entities. These costs include the original investigation to find the outside firm, followed by the cost of negotiating a contract, and later yet, enforcing the contract and coordinating transactions. Transaction costs are influenced by uncertainty, frequency of recurrence, and asset-specificity.[2]

Uncertainty, the inability to know the future perfectly, increases transaction costs because it is not possible to include all contingencies in a contract, particularly a long-term contract. Frequent transactions also tend to make it necessary for explicit contracts to exist.

But probably the most important of these characteristics is asset-specificity. If a buyer contracts for a specialized product with just one seller, and furthermore, if the product necessitates the use of some specialized machinery, the two parties become tied to one another. In this case, future changes in market conditions (or in production technology) may lead to **opportunistic behavior,** where one of the parties seeks to take advantage of the other. In such cases, transaction costs will be very high.

When transaction costs are high, a company may choose to provide the service or product itself. However, carrying out operations internally creates its own costs. A major cost is that, in hiring workers to do the work within the firm, the firm incurs monitoring and supervision costs to ensure that the work is done efficiently. Quite possibly, employees who work for a fixed wage or salary may have less incentive to work efficiently than an outside contractor.

Employers will try to decrease monitoring costs by using incentives to increase employees' output. Among such incentives are bonuses, benefits, and perquisites ("perks"). Another popular incentive is to provide workers with the possibility of stock ownership, using stock options and employee stock plans. Stock ownership is also used to attract new employees. Such employees will, of course, benefit when the company is profitable and its stock increases in value. However, incentives come with a price tag.

The trade-off between external transaction costs and the cost of internal operations can be shown on the simple graph in Figure 2.1. When a company operates at the vertical axis, all of its operations are conducted with the outside. As we move to the right on this graph, the firm substitutes internal for external operations. The cost of external transactions decreases, while the cost of internal operations increases. The total cost is the vertical summation of the two costs, and decreases at first as the company finds that internalizing some operations is efficient. However, as more of the operations are internalized, some efficiency is lost, and the total cost begins to rise again. The company will choose to allocate its resources between external transactions and internal operations so that the total cost is at a minimum, which in this case will occur about midway between the two extremes.

---

[2]Much of this discussion is based on Oliver E. Williamson, "Transaction-Cost Economics: The Governance of Contractual Relations," *Journal of Law and Economics,* vol. 22 (October 1979), pp. 233–61.

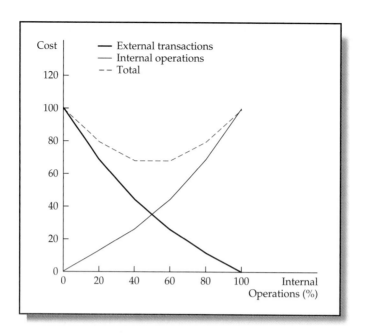

Figure 2.1

If transaction costs for a specific product or service are higher than the costs of carrying on the activity internally, then a company benefits from performing this particular task inhouse. An independent firm may not find it profitable to produce a product if only one or few customers demand it. However, as markets expand, the demand for a product or service, which may have been limited in the past, now expands. This will permit new firms to specialize in activities that previously had to be performed by the firm that needed this task to be performed. Thus new companies and industries come into existence. This is true not only in the case of products, but also for services that at one time were performed by the firm itself and are now produced by independent firms—for example, cleaning services, security services, and cafeterias are often now run by specialized firms. Another example would be the college bookstore that is operated by one of the large companies in the book industry. This idea is actually rather old. It really started with Adam Smith, who stated that "the division of labor is limited by the extent of the market." George Stigler discussed this point in a 1951 article, and concluded that as industries expand, companies that previously had produced everything internally will tend to experience "vertical disintegration."[3] What has happened, of course, is that transaction costs have decreased and that the possibility of "opportunistic behavior" has diminished as well.

While the outsourcing of peripheral, noncore activities has been around for a long time, the outsourcing of a business's core activities is a somewhat more recent but a quickly growing activity. In the past we have seen the outsourcing of private-

---

[3]George J. Stigler, "The Division of Labor is Limited by the Extent of the Market," *Journal of Political Economy*, vol. 59 (June 1951), pp. 185–93.

label or house-brand merchandise. But now the outsourcing of highly technical products and services is widespread.

Thus, for instance, "80% of Kodak's reloadable cameras and all of its digital cameras are sourced in Asia." "Compaq computer makes only about 10% of the computers it sells to consumers." This is a very different situation from that which existed in the earlier part of the twentieth century, when Ford made its own tires, steel, and glass.[4]

At one time, the IBM Corporation's principal and almost exclusive product was computer hardware. This has changed over the past ten years, and today a large part of IBM's business is based on the outsourcing of various computer services by other companies. Its Global Services segment, which is the world's largest information services provider, takes on the responsibility for customers' processes and systems, provides business consulting and e-business implementation, and offers such things as product support, business recovery services, and systems management and networking services. The external revenue of Global Services in the year 2001 was almost $35 billion, or 40.7 percent of IBM's total revenue.[5] That is an increase of about 56 percent since 1996. At the same time, IBM uses outsourcing for much of its hardware production. Many different companies build and assemble components for the company's PCs as well as its large computers. Celestica, Inc., a Canadian company, makes most of IBM's servers.[6] About one third of the revenue of Taiwan's Acer, Inc., comes from shipment of computer equipment to IBM.[7]

Another new venue for outsourcing is human relations. Payroll administration has long been handled by outside firms. Now, some companies use third-party services for recruitment, health care, benefits, pensions, and many other activities. Thus, for instance, in 1999 BP Amoco turned over many of its HR functions to Exult, a Texas firm, with a five-year $600 million contract. And in the fall of 2000, Bank of America contracted with Exult to handle its human relations functions, signing a 10-year $1.1 billion contract.[8]

While outsourcing has tended to be a Western phenomenon, it now appears to be spreading eastward. Japan, in particular, has not been receptive to it in the past. The Japanese, it appears, have been devoted to *monozukuri*, which translates to "making things." However, the Japanese electronics industry, while an extremely strong competitive force throughout the world, has not been significantly profitable. That apparently is a symptom of one of Japan's present economic problems—inefficient use of assets. Even Sony, known to be one of Japan's most progressive companies, earned a rate of return on equity of only 5.5 percent in the fiscal year ending March 31, 2001, compared with a 15 percent rate enjoyed by some major U.S. technological companies.

But Sony is now taking steps to make itself more efficient. In October 2000, it sold one of its plants to the Solectron Corporation, a California company. The new owner of the plant will continue to make products (including car navigation equipment and

---

[4]The above two paragraphs are based on Kerry A. Dolan and Robyn Meredith, "Cover Story," *Forbes,* April 30, 2001, pp. 106–112.
[5]International Business Machines Corporation, *Annual Report 2001.*
[6]Doug Garr, "Inside Out-sourcing," *Fortune,* Summer 2001, pp. 85–92.
[7]"IBM, Taiwan's Acer Will Announce Pact to Deepen Their Ties," *The Wall Street Journal,* June 7, 1999.
[8]Doug Garr, op. cit.

batteries) under the Sony brand name. Since then, Sony has continued to move in the direction of outsourcing. In 2001, it turned over the production of its Play-Station video-game machine to a Chinese company. Also in 2001, it created a subsidiary from 11 of its electronic plants to manufacture some of Sony's most sophisticated products. This, of course, is not the same as farming out production to an independent company; still, it appears to be another step toward Sony's new and greater emphasis on profitability.[9]

Coase and the Internet

When Ronald Coase wrote his article in 1937, he and the rest of the world knew nothing about the advent of the Internet in the last years of the twentieth century. But his contribution to economic theory turns out to have great relevance to today's business transactions over the Internet. If you should surf the Internet and type in the following keywords, "Transaction costs Coase Internet" you will get a large number of hits attesting to today's popularity of Coase's ideas.

The basic idea of the trade-off between the costs of internal operations and external transactions remains as valid as ever. But the revolutionary event that occurred in recent years is that the Internet has caused transaction costs to decrease drastically, making it easier and more efficient for companies to curtail their own operations and farm out much of the work they would have been performing to outside companies that specialize in specific operations.

As mentioned above, transaction costs include the cost of search and investigation, contract negotiations, and coordination or enforcement. How has the Internet impacted these transactions and their costs?

Search and investigation have been made significantly easier. Potential suppliers can be quickly and easily identified. Information on their reliability and credit standing is readily available, and so are evaluations of their financial conditions. "Online clearing houses . . . permit a purchaser to contract for price, quality and delivery dates with few clicks of the mouse," making contracting a much easier task. As far as coordinating costs are concerned, it is now much more simple to follow the location of a shipment as it progresses toward its location, and to take action in real time, if this should become necessary.[10]

While Coase recently stated that he is not paying much attention to e-commerce, he believes that understanding transaction costs in the new economy "enables you to have more specialization and greater production, because you are more efficient. You'll get more small firms as a result, but large firms will also get larger, because they can concentrate on core activities and contract out what they can't do well."[11]

We will discuss this point fully in chapter 12, which is devoted in its entirety to the microeconomics of the new economy.

We end this discussion with the conclusion that a firm will trade off costs incurred in conducting transactions with the outside market with the costs of inter-

[9]Peter Landers, "Why Some Sony Gear is Made in Japan—By Another Company," *The Wall Street Journal*, June 14, 2001.
[10]This section, including the direct quotation, is based on Don Tapscott, David Ticoll, and Alex Lowy, "Internet Nirvana," *eCompany Now*, December 2000, pp. 98ff.
[11]Bob Tedeschi, "Coase's Ideas Flourish in the Internet Economy," *New York Times*, October 2, 2000.

nalizing such transactions in order to minimize the combination of the two. This is consistent with the overall economic goals of the firm, the subject to which we turn next.

THE ECONOMIC GOAL OF THE FIRM AND OPTIMAL DECISION MAKING

Every business has a goal. Most students would assert that the primary goal of a business is to earn a certain amount of profit (i.e., to "make money"), and, in fact, the economic theory of the firm—the foundation on which much of managerial economics rests—assumes that the principal objective of a firm is to maximize its profits (or minimize its losses).[12] Thus, throughout this text, unless otherwise stated, we will assume this same objective, known among economists as the **profit-maximization hypothesis.**

To be sure, there are other goals that a firm can pursue, relating to market share, revenue growth, profit margin, return on investment, technology, customer satisfaction, and shareholder value (i.e., maximizing the price of its stock). It is crucial to be aware of precisely what a firm's goals are. Different goals can lead to very different managerial decisions given the same limited amount of resources. For example, if the main goal of the firm is to maximize market share rather than profit, the firm might decide to reduce its prices. If the main goal is to provide the most technologically advanced products, the firm might well decide to allocate more resources to research and development. The added research and development expenses would most likely reduce the amount of profit the firm earns in the short run but may result in increased profits over time as the company increases its technological lead over its competitors. If the main goal of the firm is to carry a complete line of products and services, it may choose to sell certain products even though they might not be earning a profit.

Given the goal (or goals) that the firm is pursuing, we can say that the **optimal decision** in managerial economics is one that brings the firm closest to this goal. For example, as you will see in chapter 9, to maximize its profit (or minimize its loss), a firm should price its product at a level where the revenue earned on the last unit of a product sold (called *marginal revenue*) is equal to the additional cost of making this last unit (called *marginal cost*). In other words, the optimal price equates the firm's marginal revenue with its marginal cost.

One additional concept should be presented in our discussion of a firm's goals. In economics, a distinction is made between the "short-run" time period and the "long-run" time period. As explained in greater detail in later sections of this text (see chapters 3, 7, and 8), these time periods actually have nothing directly to do with calendar time. During the short run, we assume that a firm can vary the amount of certain resources (e.g., labor hours) but must operate with a fixed amount of at least one of its resources (e.g., factory space). Theoretically, in the long run, a firm is able to

---

[12]As we will see in chapter 9, a firm may lose money in the short run and still be better off than it would be if it were to shut down operations, as long as its losses are less than its fixed costs. However, if it is going to lose money, from an economic standpoint it is optimal to minimize its losses.

vary the quantities of all resources being utilized. In this text, we will look at both short-run and long-run decisions made by the firm. We will assume that a company's goal is to maximize profits both in the short and long run. However, it must be understood that a business will, at times, sacrifice profitability in the short run with the anticipation of maximized long-run profits.

GOALS OTHER THAN PROFIT

Economic Goals

The concept of profit maximization has been attacked as incomplete by many writers. They point out that companies may have other economic objectives, such as those mentioned previously.

For the time being, we will omit discussion of the objective of "value" or "shareholder wealth" maximization and consider some of the other alternatives concerning a company's activity during a single period of time (such as a year). It is readily admitted that profit maximization is a rather vague term. How does a company know that its profits in a given period are the largest they can be? Or, more correctly (from an ex ante, or planning, viewpoint), how does a company know that the actions it is taking in this time frame will result, if all goes as expected, in the greatest possible profit?

Let us look at the objectives set out by a company's chief executive officer (or a committee representing the company's top management). It is not unusual for the CEO or his representatives, having decided on the achievable results for the next fiscal period, to distribute objectives to the various operating heads at the beginning of the planning cycle. Now imagine this memorandum from the firm's CEO to the general manager of one of the company's operating units:

Dear Joe:

We have had a pretty good year in 2002, and we believe that 2003 should be even better.

I am therefore issuing the following objective for your unit in 2003. Take any and all actions that will ensure that your profit is maximized.

Corporate management is confident that you will not disappoint us. We know that the objective we have given you is challenging. We also are convinced that it is achievable.

John, CEO

This memorandum is obviously an extreme simplification, but what is Joe to do with his marching orders to maximize profit? What resources does he have to do this? And how can his performance be measured at the end of the year? What is his maximum profit?

Now let us look at another "objective" memorandum:

Dear Joe,

We have had a pretty good year in 2002, and we expect that 2003 should be even better. We are assigning specific objectives to each of our operating units in such a way that the total result will be a financial posture consistent with our economic and industry forecasts, our available resources, and good increases in productivity. With this in mind, we want you to build your 2003 plan to correspond to the following objectives for your unit:

1. Your revenue should increase by 10 percent from 2002.
2. The profit margin of your unit should increase from 8 percent to 9 percent, and your return on assets should be 10 percent.
3. Your division will receive $10 million of company funds for expansion projects whose minimum internal rate of return should be 12 percent.
4. The head count of your unit can increase by no more than 2 percent.

Corporate management is confident that you will not disappoint us. We know that the objective we have given you is challenging. We also are convinced that it is achievable.

John, CEO

Assuming that this memorandum makes more sense (which it certainly should, for otherwise our point has been lost), does this mean that the company's objective is not really profit maximization at all, but rather a growth rate, a profit margin, or a return on its assets? This is what many writers on this subject say.

Such a conclusion is, however, misleading. Any of these measures in itself is incomplete, and each should be seen as a realistic target consistent with the ultimate objective of maximizing the firm's overall profits. Management, in this example, advised by its expert staff regarding the company's economic environment, competition, technological advances, and market potential, has come to the conclusion that maximum profits can be achieved by the combination of growth and profit measures included in its memorandum.

Thus, the specific objectives assigned to an operating unit are really proxies for the overall objective of profit maximization. The achievement of these proxies is also measurable at the end of the fiscal period; the division executive's performance and contribution toward the company's profits can be evaluated, and rewards in terms of bonuses or incentive plans can then be determined.

Noneconomic Objectives

In this complex world, companies may have objectives that are not strictly economic or at least do not appear to be governed by economic thinking. Indeed, some large companies have published statements of principles that, if accepted at face value, would indicate that making profits is the last thing they strive for. Profits may be mentioned as only one of several objectives, and they may actually be listed last. Furthermore, the statements do not mention any maximum but rather concentrate on such measures as "adequate" or "reasonable" return to stockholders. Such modesty is certainly more palatable to the public. What, then, are some of the guiding principles such companies publish?

1. Provide a good place for our employees to work.
2. Provide good products/services to our customers.
3. Act as a good citizen in our society.

These actions are costly, and at first glance may seem to interfere with profit maximization. However, consider the following: Satisfied employees not only tend to be more productive, but will remain with the company longer, thus decreasing expensive labor turnover. Without satisfied customers, a company will not remain in business. Supporting good causes, such as charitable and other nonprofit organizations, will create goodwill and ultimately potential sales. Therefore, it would be worthwhile for a company to spend resources on such **noneconomic objectives** consistent with increases in revenues and profit. If this is the case, then attaining these objectives is not incompatible with profit maximization, and, indeed, these objectives could be classified as economic.

We could enlarge this discussion of so-called noneconomic objectives, but the point has been made. Today's markets and institutions constrain companies in many ways that did not exist in the past. Therefore, companies must concern themselves with creating employee and customer satisfaction and maintaining social responsibility to a much higher degree than in the past. But these considerations do not contradict the profit maximization principle. If companies were maximizers in the past, under less restrictive conditions, they are still maximizers today but have to operate within the requirements imposed by current standards and the costs that accompany them.

ONCE AGAIN—DO COMPANIES MAXIMIZE PROFITS?

We have discussed some possible alternative objectives to profit maximization and concluded that none of these objectives is necessarily inconsistent with our basic principle. Now let us look at another criticism that has recently been leveled at the view of profit maximization as the primary objective.

The argument is that today's corporations do not maximize at all. Instead, their aim is to "satisfice." To understand this argument, we have to consider two parts of this idea:

1. The position and power of stockholders in today's corporation.
2. The position and power of professional management in today's corporation.

Years ago the owner or owners of a business also managed it. Businesses were predominantly quite small and lent themselves to being operated as individual proprietorships, partnerships, or small, closely held corporations. Modern businesses, particularly medium-sized or large corporations, of course, cannot be managed by the owners, who are the shareholders and number in the thousands or even hundreds of thousands. Many stockholders own only minute pieces of a corporation. Furthermore, stockholders tend to diversify their holdings; thus, they may hold small interests in many different corporations. The argument asserts that most stockholders are not well informed on how well a corporation can do and will be satisfied with an adequate dividend and some reasonable growth. And since they own different stocks, poor performance on one of their holdings may be offset by some of their other assets: the stockholder is more concerned with the portfolio of stocks than with any individual stock. Shareholders may not be capable of knowing whether corporate management is doing its best for them and they actually may not be very concerned as long as they receive what they consider a satisfactory return on their investment—hence **"satisficing."**

Second, in a modern corporation professional managers—the chairman of the board, the president, a group of vice presidents, and other high-level managers—direct the operations of a company. Although they are overseen by a board of directors (which usually includes a large number of insiders), they are responsible for major decision making. It is claimed by a number of writers that managers (who commonly hold a relatively small number of shares) have their own objectives, which do not include maximization of shareholder earnings. Indeed, it is often said that managers tend to be much more conservative—that is, risk averse—than stockholders would be, since their jobs will most likely be safer if they turn in a competent and steady, if unspectacular, performance. They could probably benefit stockholders in the long run by taking some well-calculated risks. However, they may be too cautious to do so, and thus they miss out on opportunities. They fear that they may not survive the reverses that could result from risk taking. If stockholders need only be satisfied, this may be the appropriate way for management to go.

Management's interests may actually be contrary to those of stockholders. For instance, management may be more interested in revenue growth than profits. Why? It has been claimed that management remuneration tends to be a function of revenue size rather than profits. Several studies have been made on this subject, but the evidence is considerably less than overwhelming. Also, company management may be more interested in maximizing its own income, may indulge in various perquisites, and in general may not act in the best interest of the widely dispersed, somewhat disinterested and lethargic stockholder population.[13]

The two sides in this relationship tend to complement one another. The owners of the corporation—the stockholders—are not interested in maximization, or even if they are, they are not well enough informed and have too little power. The corporation's management, whose selfish motives lead them to act in their own favor when stockholder and management goals differ, will manage in a way that serves their interest while keeping the stockholder satisfied with adequate return and moderate growth.

Like all ideas presented by intelligent people, this one probably contains a certain amount of truth. Each of the points seems eminently reasonable and, for all we know, could be valid over limited periods of time. But let us look at some of the realities of life and some recent events in the business world that tend to contradict this argument.

You, the reader of this book, may be among that group of far-flung stockholders owning a hundred shares in a company with millions of shares outstanding.

---

[13]A formal theory dealing with the potential conflicts between shareholders and management has been developed by Michael C. Jensen and William H. Meckling in their article "Theory of the Firm: Managerial Behavior. Agency Costs and Ownership Structure" (*Journal of Financial Economics,* October 1976, pp. 350–60). These conflicts arise whenever managers own less than 100 percent of the stock, which is, of course, the predominant situation in today's large corporation. To ensure that managers act on behalf of the stockholder, the latter will have to incur "agency costs," which are expenditures to monitor managers' actions, to structure the organization in such a way as to limit management's action, and so forth.

However, particularly in the case of large corporations, much of the outstanding stock is held by institutions and in professionally managed accounts. Among these are banks that manage large pension funds, insurance companies with their extensive portfolios, and mutual funds. These organizations employ expert analysts (who are only human and therefore, at least occasionally, make mistakes) who study companies and pass judgment on the quality of their management and their promise for the future. Of course, they deal mostly with stock prices, but after all, stock prices are a reflection of a company's profitability.[14] These analysts make recommendations to their management on which stocks to buy and which to sell. Companies that underperform would be weeded out of these institutional portfolios, with a consequent drop in their stock prices.

Now, what happens when certain stocks tend to underperform in the market? They become targets for takeovers by others. We really do not have to belabor this point, since anyone reading the business sections of daily newspapers or other business publications is very much aware of recent events in the takeover and buyout arenas. In addition to the accumulation of stock and subsequent tender offers by outside financiers, we have also witnessed the existence of proxy fights by dissident large stockholders. Thus, it appears that management in today's corporation is not insulated from outside pressures. Management is constrained to act in agreement with stockholders, who look for increases in stock values and returns and who act to "punish" the managements of those companies that appear to underperform.

Another argument leads to a similar conclusion. Competitive pressures also act to stimulate management to performance. If a company's results lag behind those of competitors, those lethargic stockholders who do not challenge the company directly will tend to sell its shares and turn to those companies providing better returns and better prospects of returns. The price of the company's stock will suffer relative to prices of the others; such a scenario will not go unnoticed in financial markets. Company management will come under the gun to improve performance, and ultimately management may be replaced because of pressure by outside board members, a successful proxy fight, or even a takeover. General Motors, International Business Machines, and Eastman Kodak are just a few examples of companies that replaced their chief executive offices within the last decade. A very vocal and sometimes effective advocate of shareholder rights has been the California Public Employees' Retirement System (Calpers). With more than $150 billion in assets as of August 31, 2001, it has demonstrated that changes in corporate governance can be accomplished.[15]

Management has another, more direct, motivation to act in concert with the objectives of stockholders. Parts—frequently large parts—of an executive's remuneration are tied to performance in terms of operating profits for the corporation or for

---

[14]The connection between profits and stock prices will be examined in the next section, when we expand the maximization principle to include the wealth of stockholders.

[15]Much information about Calpers can be obtained by visiting www.calpers.org or www.calpers.ca.gov. Among the many items on this web site is a "Focus List," which names the companies for which Calpers seeks governance changes. Also, newspaper articles can be detailing Calpers current activities in this area, such as "Calpers Sues Directors of Lone Star Chain, Alleging, 'Self-Dealing'," *The Wall Street Journal*, October 18, 2001, and Joann S. Lublin, "Calpers Will Keep the Heat on Maxxam to Add a Pair of Independent Directors," *The Wall Street Journal*, April 19, 2000.

units supervised by the particular executive.[16] Furthermore, an executive's compensation package is usually enhanced by the issuance of stock options. Since the value of stock options depends on the price of the company's stock, which in turn is a function of the company's profit performance, self-serving company managers may find that their objectives (less than miraculously) coincide with those of the stockholders.

Thus, there appears to be a strong convergence of management and stockholder objectives, contrary to the claims of some well-known writers.

Profit Maximization, Restated

It is readily agreed that the existence of the profit-maximization objective can never be proven conclusively. We must note, however, that lack of financial success by a company is not necessarily a contravention of the principle. The best of plans may go awry, and management's judgment certainly is not error proof. Under certain circumstances, the aim for loss minimization may replace the goal of profit maximization, but this too supports our basic premise. As difficult as it is to point to acts of profit maximization by management, none of the alternative constructions lends itself as well as a yardstick by which to measure business activity. As long as a corporation strives to do better, that is, prefers higher profits to lower profits and lower costs to higher costs, and acts consistently in those directions, the assumption of profit maximization serves as a better basis for judging a company's decisions than any of the other purported objectives. And, incidentally, this "striving to do better" can include a multitude of decisions, including those that lead to a revenue increase greater than a cost increase, a revenue decrease smaller than a cost decrease, or a constant revenue with decreased costs. All of these decisions involve an increase in profits.

However, maximizing profits in the very short term (e.g., one year) can always be accomplished by management. If, for instance, revenue in the coming year is expected to decline, a company can keep up its profits by cutting expenses. If management seeks to do this without an immediate further reaction on revenue, it can eliminate some development projects. The effect of a lack of new products will not be felt right away, but the shortsightedness of this management decision will come home to roost only a few years hence. This is the decision area in which the objective of period profit maximization can be attacked more logically. Profit maximization for one period is an incomplete measure from the viewpoint of a business organization that is expected to operate into the infinite—or at least the foreseeable—future.

MAXIMIZING THE WEALTH OF STOCKHOLDERS

Because period profit maximization is an extremely useful way to look at day-to-day decision making in the firm, we will use it as our model throughout most of this book. However, there is another view of maximization that is usually adopted in finance textbooks and that takes into consideration a stream of earnings over time.

---

[16]The fact that these performance incentives may be tied to near-term profits can create a problem, since the executive's horizon may be shortened. More about this will be discussed later.

This concept includes not only the evaluation of a stream of cash flows; it also considers the all-important idea of the time value of money.[17] Since it is an obvious fact that a dollar earned in the future is worth less than a dollar earned today, the future streams must be discounted to the present. Both the shape of these streams through time and the interest rate at which they are discounted affect the value of the stockholders' wealth today. The discount rate in particular is affected by risk, so risk becomes another component of the valuation of the business. Financial theorists differentiate various types of risk, with the two major types commonly identified as business risk and financial risk.

Business risk involves variation in returns due to the ups and downs of the economy, the industry, and the firm. This is the kind of risk that attends all business organizations, although to varying degrees. Some businesses are relatively stable from period to period, whereas others incur extreme fluctuations in their financial returns. For instance, public utilities (i.e., suppliers of electricity and gas as well as the operating telephone companies) tend to have more stable earnings over time than do industrial companies, particularly those in industries that are highly cyclical (e.g., steel, automobiles, and capital goods), or companies in high-tech fields.

Financial risk concerns the variation in returns that is induced by leverage. *Leverage* signifies the proportion of a company financed by debt. Given a certain degree of leverage, the earnings accruing to stockholders will fluctuate with total profits (before the deduction of interest and taxes). The higher the leverage, the greater the potential fluctuations in stockholder earnings. Thus, financial risk moves directly with a company's leverage.

How do we obtain a measure of stockholders' wealth? By discounting to the present the cash streams that stockholders expect to receive out into the future. Since we know today's price of a company's stock, we can—given the expected dividends to be received by the stockholders—determine the discount rate the investment community applies to the particular stock. This discount rate includes the pure time value of money as well as the premiums for the two categories of risk. The dividend stream is used to represent the receipts of stockholders because that is all they really receive from the company. Of course, a stockholder also looks for a capital gain, but selling the stock at some point involves someone else buying it; thus, this payment represents only a trade, an exchange of funds. However, dividends represent the returns on the stock generated by the corporation. In equation form, we have the following:

$$P = \frac{D_1}{(1 + k)} + \frac{D_2}{(1 + k)^2} + \frac{D_3}{(1 + k)^3} + \cdots + \frac{D_n}{(1 + k)^n}$$

where P = Present price of the stock
D = Dividends received per year (in year 1, year 2, . . . year n)
k = Discount rate applied by the financial community, often referred to as the cost of equity capital of the company

---

[17]Time value of money and discounting of flows will be discussed in much greater detail in the appendix to chapter 13.

If it is assumed that the corporation will have an infinitely long life, and if dividends will remain the same year after year, then the price of each share of stock can be calculated as a perpetuity with the following formula:

$$P = D/k$$

Investors, however, will usually expect dividends to rise. In the case where dividends grow at a constant rate each year, the formula for share price becomes

$$P = D_1/(k - g)$$

where D_1 = the dividend to be paid during the coming year
g = the annual constant growth rate of the dividend expressed as a percentage[18]

Multiplying P by the number of shares outstanding gives the total value of the company's common equity.[19]

A simple example will help clarify the above equation. Assume that a company expects to pay a dividend of $4 in the coming year, and expects dividends to grow at 5 percent each year. The rate at which stockholders discount their cash flows (which is really the rate of return stockholders require to earn from this stock) is 12 percent. There are 1 million shares outstanding. We would expect the price of each share to be:

$$P = 4/(.12 - 0.5) = 4/.07 = \$57.14$$

The value of the company's stock would be $57.14 million. This is the expected market value given the variables that we have assumed. However, this may not be the maximum value the company could achieve. The variables in the equation may have to change. Since k is a function of the company's level of risk (both business and financial), the company may be able to decrease k by lowering the riskiness of its operations or by changing its leverage. It can affect g and D by retaining more or less of its earnings. By retaining a larger portion of its earnings and devoting a smaller portion of its earnings to dividends, the company may be able to increase its growth rate g.

Thus, under this construction, maximizing the wealth of the shareholder means that a company tries to manage its business in such a way that the dividends over time paid from its earnings and the risk incurred to bring about the stream of dividends always create the highest price and thereby the maximum value for the company's stock.

This **wealth maximization** hypothesis tends to weaken even further the management-versus-stockholder argument. Corporate executives, for whom stock options represent a significant portion of remuneration, now have an even greater incentive to aim at results that conform to the objectives of the stockholders.

This is a rather complex if quite obvious development of the maximization principle. As stated previously, we will work primarily with the profit maximization

---

[18]The derivation of these formulas is discussed in greater detail in chapter 13.
[19]The value of a company's equity can also be obtained by calculating the present value of the expected stream of "free cash flows." However, when free cash flow is correctly constructed, it is essentially equal to dividends paid. This subject will be discussed at greater length in chapter 13 when the calculation of the value of corporation is presented.

hypothesis because it is quite sufficient for most of our purposes. We will return to the wealth maximization rule in chapter 13 when we discuss a company's investment and replacement decisions involving expenditures for which the resulting payoffs flow into the corporation over a considerable period of time. In that chapter we will also briefly discuss how the market tends to determine the rate of return it requires from a company (and thus sets the discount rate k, the company's cost of capital). In chapter 14 we will examine the question of risk and uncertainty and attempts to find ways to deal with it.

Market Value Added and Economic Value Added

Various publications have measured the wealth of stockholders by taking the price per share quoted in the stock market pages and multiplying it by the number of shares outstanding.[20] The product is, of course, the current value of the shares, and thus reflects the value of the company accorded to it by the market. But such a measure does not show the wealth that has been created by the company. After all, suppose that the stockholders had contributed more capital than the stock was worth currently. Then, actually, the company would have "destroyed" some of the stockholders' wealth. What is really important is how much the stockholders' investment is worth today relative to what they have contributed to the corporation in originally buying the stock and then having earnings retained by the corporation for reinvestment.

A relatively new measure has become very popular with the financial community as well as many corporations themselves. It is called **Market Value Added (MVA®)** and has been developed by the consulting firm of Stern Stewart.[21] MVA represents the difference between the market value of the company and the capital that investors have paid into the company.

The market value of the company includes the value of both equity and debt. The capital includes the book value of debt and equity on the company's balance sheet plus a number of adjustments that increase the basic number. Among these adjustments is the inclusion of research and development (R&D) expense (which accountants treat as expense). Prior years' R&D is cumulated and amortized over a number of years. Another item that is included is the amortization of goodwill. Thus, in the end, the contributed capital of the corporation will turn out to be larger than merely the book value of equity and debt. While the market value of a corporation will always be positive, the MVA may be positive or negative, depending on whether the market value of the company is greater than the capital which investors contributed. Where a corporation's market value is less than the contributed capital, investors' wealth has actually been "destroyed."

Stern Stewart compiles an annual ranking of 1,000 corporations and their MVA. The most recent results were published in *Fortune* magazine for the year 2001.

[20]See, for instance, *Business Week,* July 9, 2001, pp. 72–90.
[21]This concept was originally introduced in 1990. See G. Bennett Stewart III, "Announcing the Stern Stewart Performance 1,000: A New Way of Viewing Corporate America," *Journal of Applied Corporate Finance,* summer 1990, pp. 38–59.

General Electric ranked first with an MVA of over $312 billion, and Microsoft came in second with $297 billion of value created for its investors. At the other end of the scale (ranking at 1,000th) is AT&T, with a negative value of over $94 billion.[22]

Basically, MVA is a forward-looking measure. If market value reflects the financial markets' appraisal of a company's future cash streams, then MVA represents the financial markets' assessment of the company's future net cash flows (i.e., after subtracting the investments the company must make to achieve those cash streams).

Another measurement developed by Stern Stewart is **Economic Value Added (EVA®).** EVA is calculated as follows:

$$EVA = (Return\ on\ Total\ Capital - Cost\ of\ Capital) \times Total\ Capital$$

Actually, the calculation of return on capital (profit divided by capital) is nothing new. However, EVA subtracts an estimated cost of capital from return. If the resulting number is positive, then the company has earned more than its investors require, and thus will add to investors' wealth. On the other hand, if cost is greater than return, then value is being destroyed.

To avoid distortions created by accounting conventions, Stern Stewart makes numerous adjustments to the return and capital numbers. Actually, EVA could be said to be very much like "economic profits," which are mentioned briefly in the next section of this chapter and are discussed thoroughly in chapter 9. However, when these numbers are calculated they are generally based on past results, and do not necessarily say anything about a company's future profitability. Still, "Stern Stewart says that there is a close correlation between EVA and MVA—if managers improve EVA, the company's MVA is highly likely to improve too."[23]

Another calculation is made in connection with the ranking of these companies. The market value of a company is a function of its future cash flows, as we previously stated. The greater the expected growth, the higher will be the company's value today. Thus, we can ask the following question: how much of the company's value is due to expected growth? To calculate this, it is first assumed that the company's most recent annual earnings will continue to be the same in perpetuity. In other words, the company will not experience any growth. Using the perpetuity formula previously discussed and an appropriate discount rate, the market value of the company is obtained. The result is then subtracted from the company's actual market value, and this difference is then divided by the actual market value. The resulting fraction or percentage is referred to as **future growth rate** (FGV). The higher this percentage, the greater is the proportion of the company's value derived from its expected future growth. While one cannot say with certainty if any particular percentage is appropriate for any company, an extremely high percentage may indicate that the company's market value is unrealistically high, and may indicate that the company is overvalued. We would expect the percentages for old-line companies to be low relative to the new technology companies.[24]

---

[22]David Stires, "America's Best & Worst Wealth Creators," *Fortune,* December 10, 2001, pp. 137–142.
[23]"A Star to Sail By?" *The Economist,* August 2, 1997, p. 54.
[24]David Stires, op. cit. The future growth values are calculated for a large number of companies and the interested reader can make comparisons and decide how realistic these numbers are.

Over the last few years, many companies have begun emphasizing the EVA measure over more traditional measures such as earnings per share and return on equity, as have money managers such as Oppenheimer, Calpers, and others.[25]

ECONOMIC PROFITS

Throughout this chapter we have been using the term *profit* and assumed that it has some kind of meaning. But we have not defined it. We only said that profit—and its maximization—is uppermost in the company owner's and manager's minds. In a way, profit is easy to define. Every company that closes its books annually and whose accountants construct a statement of earnings (whether this company is public so that everybody can see the published statement and its "bottom line," or whether it is private) knows what its profits are. The accountants report the level of profits, and they also affirm that everything in the financial statements has been done in conformance with generally accepted accounting principles (GAAP).

Unfortunately, things are not quite that simple. Profits, as reported on an earnings statement, are not necessarily definitive. Accountants have certain amounts of freedom in recording items leading to the "bottom line."[26] A few examples will suffice:

1. There are different ways of recording depreciation. In the past the straight-line method, the sum-of-the-years'-digits method, the declining balance method, and probably others have been used. Under present tax law the Accelerated Cost Recovery System (ACRS) is most frequently employed.
2. There are various ways of recording inventories, the famous FIFO (first-in, first-out) and LIFO (last-in, first-out) being just two alternatives.
3. Amortization of such items as goodwill and patents can be recorded differently.

This is just a small sample of the better-known alternative treatments by accountants, and any of these are in conformance with GAAP. Moreover, the tax return that a company completes and sends to the IRS may be quite different from the published statement of a public company.

As if the question of what accounting profits really are were not enough, the economist compounds this problem even further. Everybody agrees that profit equals revenue minus costs (and expenses). But economists do not agree with accountants on the concept of costs. An accountant reports costs on a historical basis. The economist, however, is concerned with the costs that a business considers in making decisions, that is, future costs. We will concern ourselves with this concept more thoroughly later in this book, but we must touch on the subject now, albeit briefly. Basically, economists deal with something they call *opportunity costs* or

---

[25]S. Tully, "America's Greatest Wealth Creators," *Fortune*, November 9, 1998, p. 195. The following articles discuss how companies use the EVA concept: "Stern Stewart EVA™Roundtable," *Journal of Applied Corporate Finance*, summer 1994, pp. 46–70; S. Milunovich and A. Tsuei, "EVA® in the Computer Industry," *Journal of Applied Corporate Finance*, spring 1996, pp. 104–15; A. Jackson, "The How and Why of EVA® at CS First Boston," *Journal of Applied Corporate Finance*, spring 1996, pp. 98–103.
[26]Some writers in this field have said that accountants take too many liberties. Professor Abraham Briloff has written a number of books and articles on this subject.

alternative costs: this means that the cost of a resource is what a business must pay for it to attract it into its employ or, put differently, what a business must pay to keep this resource from finding employment elsewhere. To get down to specific examples, we can mention the following:

1. *Historical costs versus replacement costs.* To an economist, the replacement cost of a piece of machinery (and, therefore, the level of periodic depreciation on the replacement cost) is important, whereas an accountant measures cost—and depreciation—on a historical basis.
2. *Implicit costs and normal profits.*
   a. The owners' time and interest on the capital they contribute are usually counted as profit in a partnership or a single proprietorship. But the owners could work for someone else instead and invest their funds elsewhere. So these two items are really costs to the business and not profit.
   b. The preceding item is not relevant in the case of a corporation, since even top executives are salaried employees, and interest on corporate debt is deducted as an expense before profits are calculated. However, the payments made to the owners/stockholders—dividends—are not part of cost; they are recorded as a distribution of profits. But surely a part of the shareholders' return is similar to the interest on debt, since stockholders could have invested their funds elsewhere and require a certain return in order to leave the investment with the corporation. Thus, on this account, corporate profits as recorded by accountants tend to be overstated.

It appears, therefore, that an economist includes costs that would be excluded by an accountant. Indeed, the economist refers to the second category of costs—which are essential to obtain and keep the owners' resources in the business—as **normal profits,** which represent the return that these resources demand to remain committed to a particular firm.

Thus **economic costs** include not only the historical costs and explicit costs recorded by the accountants, but also the replacement costs and implicit costs (normal profits) that must be earned on the owners' resources. In the rest of this book, profits are considered to be **economic profits,** which are defined as total revenue minus all the economic costs we have described in this section.

INTERNATIONAL APPLICATION

The model of a firm's goals discussed in this chapter applies predominantly to firms operating in the United States and possibly the United Kingdom. However, one must ask whether profit maximization or shareholder wealth maximization is also valid for other countries. It is often said that for many reasons (e.g., political, cultural, legal, and institutional), firms in other countries pursue goals that include the interests of other groups, such as labor, community, government, and so on, in addition to interests of stockholders. In some countries, for instance, labor unions are represented on the board of directors. Thus, it may be necessary to consider such interests in our discussions. However, even if such considerations are important, it is possible for us to treat them as constraints on the actions of a firm. Even if profit or shareholder wealth maximization is not the only objective, as long as firms attempt to take actions that will improve their earnings—within specific constraints—our maximization model can still be used.[27] It is important to recognize, however, that multinational firms (e.g., a U.S. parent corporation operating in many different countries through subsidiaries or branches) will encounter restrictions and complications, which they must consider in doing business abroad. We list these and explain them briefly:

1. Foreign currencies and their exchange rates must be considered. Thus, revenues, costs, and other cash flows that are denominated in other currencies must be translated into domestic currencies, and their potential changes must be analyzed for their impact on the business. Under certain circumstances, a profitable activity abroad can become unprofitable from the viewpoint of the domestic parent corporation.

2. Legal differences must be taken into account. Dissimilarities in tax laws can have important consequences on results of transactions between the domestic parent corporation and its foreign subsidiary. Differences in legal systems make the tasks of executives considerably more complex.

3. Most Americans have in the past mastered only their own language and, thus, are often at a disadvantage when dealing with their multilingual counterparts in other countries.

4. The differences in cultural environments influence the defining of business goals and attitudes toward risk. Thus, such differences can greatly affect the way business is conducted.

5. The role of government in defining the rules under which companies operate varies from country to country. While in some countries market competition prevails, in others the political process dictates the behavior of firms in much greater detail.

6. Corporations operating in different countries may be restricted from transferring corporate resources out of the country and may even face the danger of expropriation. This is political risk, which must be included in any economic analysis of a company's prospects.[28]

The points just discussed as well as others must always be considered by companies doing business abroad. While some of the differences may have adverse effects on a company, participation in a global market is a necessity for most large (and even small) firms today. Profitability, and even survival, can depend on a company's entering global markets and competing worldwide.

---

[27]It is interesting to note that, in a recent interview, Heinrich von Pierer, chief executive officer of the German electronics firm Siemens, stressed "German corporate values as concern with quality, reliability and long-term thinking." But he also made the following statement: ". . . if people think that German businesses have an aversion to shareholder value, we are not a very good representative of such companies. . . . To improve profitability and market capitalisation is the main goal." Peter Marsh, "A Conglomerate with an Air of Confidence," *Financial Times,* January 21, 2002.
[28]The preceding points can be found in Eugene F. Brigham, Louis C. Gapenski, and Michael C. Ehrhardt, *Financial Management,* 9th ed., Fort Worth, TX: The Dryden Press, 1999, pp. 1031–32.

SUMMARY

In this text we will generally assume that a firm's short-run and long-run objective is the maximization of its profit or the minimization of its loss. Although a firm can select from a number of other goals, both in the short run and the long run, the assumption of profit maximization provides us with a clear-cut model for explaining how firms can use economic concepts and tools of analysis to make optimal decisions. In presenting these concepts and tools of analysis, a certain amount of mathematics will be employed. Thus, before proceeding to the next chapter, we believe that a brief review of the mathematics used in this text will be helpful. This review is contained in the appendix following this chapter.

---

[29]Corby Kummer, "Carried Away," *New York Times Magazine*, August 30, 1998, p. 40.

IMPORTANT CONCEPTS

Business risk: The variability of returns (or profits) due to fluctuations in general economic conditions or conditions specifically affecting the firm. (p. 40)

Economic cost: All cost incurred to attract resources into a company's employ. Such cost includes explicit cost usually recognized on accounting records as well as opportunity cost. (p. 45)

Economic profit: Total revenue minus total economic cost. An amount of profit earned in a particular endeavor above the amount of profit that the firm could be earning in its next best alternative activity. Also referred to as *abnormal profit* or *above-normal profit.* (p. 45)

Economic Value Added (EVA): The difference between a company's return on total capital and its cost of capital. (p. 43)

Financial risk: The variability of returns (or profits) induced by leverage (the proportion of a company financed by debt). The higher the leverage, the greater the potential fluctuation in stockholder earnings for a given change in total profits. (p. 40)

Firm: An organization that transforms resources into products demanded by consumers. The firm chooses to organize resources internally or to obtain them through the market. (p. 28)

Future growth value (FGV): The value that the market assigns to a company's future growth. (p. 43)

Market Value Added (MVA): The difference between the market value (equity plus debt) of a company and the amount of capital investors have paid into the company. (p. 42)

Noneconomic objectives: A company's objectives that do not appear to be governed by economic thinking but rather define how a business should act. "Acting as a good corporate citizen" is an example of a noneconomic objective. (p. 36)

Normal profit: An amount of profit earned in a particular endeavor that is just equal to the profit that could be earned in a firm's next best alternative activity. When a firm earns normal profit, its revenue is just enough to cover both its accounting cost and its opportunity cost. It can also be considered as the return to capital and management necessary to keep resources engaged in a particular activity. (p. 45)

Opportunistic behavior: One party to a contract seeks to take advantage of the other. (p. 29)

Optimal decision: The decision that enables the firm to meet its desired objective most closely. (p. 33)

Profit-maximization hypothesis: One of the central themes in economics, the claim that a company will strive to attain the highest economic profit in each period. (p. 33)

Satisficing: A concept in economics based on the principle that owners of a firm (especially stockholders in a large corporation) may be content with adequate return and growth since they really cannot judge when profits are maximized. (p. 37)

Transaction costs: Cost incurred by a firm in dealing with another firm, and include the cost of investigation, negotiation, and enforcement of contracts. (p. 29)

Wealth maximization: A company's management of its business in such a manner that the cash flows over time to the company, discounted at an appropriate discount rate, will cause the value of the company's stock to be at a maximum. (p. 41)

QUESTIONS

1. The following is a quote from a *New York Times* article: "If a company makes product donations to the school—computers for instance—then the image of a company goes up as graduate students use the company's products." Does such action square with a company's objective of profit maximization? Discuss.

2. Is the maximization of profit margin (profit as a percentage of total sales) a valid financial objective of a corporation? Discuss.

3. "The growth of consumer information organizations, legal requirements, and warranty requirements has caused significant increases in the cost of customer satis-

faction. Thus it is no longer useful to talk about profit maximization as a company objective." Comment on this quote.

4. Discuss the difference between profit maximization and shareholder wealth maximization. Which of these is a more comprehensive statement of a company's economic objectives?

5. Explain the term *satisfice* as it relates to the operations of a large corporation.

6. Why may corporate managers not specifically aim at profit (or wealth) maximization for their companies?

7. What are some of the forces that cause managers to act in the interest of shareholders?

8. Do you believe that profit (or shareholder wealth) maximization still represents the best overall economic objective for today's corporation?

9. Because of inflation, a company must replace one of its (fully depreciated) machines at twice the nominal price paid for a similar machine eight years ago. Based on present accounting rules, will the company have covered the entire cost of the new machine through depreciation charges? Explain by contrasting accounting and economic costs.

10. How do implicit costs lead to a difference between accounting and economic profits?

11. You have a choice of opening your own business or being employed by someone else in a similar type of business. What are some of the considerations in terms of opportunity costs that you would have to include in arriving at your decision?

12. Various depreciation methods can be used to arrive at an accounting profit number. From the viewpoint of the economist, how should annual depreciation be determined?

13. Do you believe that the profit-maximization model can be applied to the activities of a multinational corporation? Explain.

14. What are transaction costs? How does *opportunistic behavior* tend to increase transaction costs?

15. The outsourcing of important parts of a company's production has been growing in recent years. How would you explain these changes? How has the Internet contributed to these changes?

16. What are some reasons for companies internalizing transaction costs?

17. A company has 2 million shares outstanding. It paid a dividend of $2 during the past year, and expects that dividends will grow at 6 percent annually in the future. Stockholders require a rate of return of 13 percent. What would you expect the price of each share to be today, and what is the value of the company's common stock?

18. Discuss the difference between the calculation of shareholder wealth and the concept of *Market Value Added*. Which of the two would appear to be more meaningful from the viewpoint of a shareholder?

19. The calculation of *future growth value* measures the difference between the actual value of a company and what its value would be if it were not to grow at all. Is this an appropriate measure of a company's earnings growth potential?

Review of Mathematical Concepts Used in Managerial Economics

Economics is the most mathematical of all the social sciences. Indeed, to the uninitiated reader, many academic journals in economics resemble a mathematics or physics journal. Because this text is intended to show the practical applications of economic theory, this presents something of a dilemma. On one hand, the economic theory of managerial decision making has evolved along with the rest of economics to a point where it can be (and usually is) profusely expressed in mathematical terms. On the other hand, industry experience indicates that managers seldom use the more advanced mathematical expressions of economic theory. They do, nonetheless, rely quite often on many of the concepts, graphs, and relatively simple numerical examples that are used throughout this text to assist them in their decision making.

But the dilemma does not end here. Regardless of the role of mathematics in managerial decision making, it certainly serves as an important instructional vehicle for economics professors. Using calculus enables the very concise expression of complex functional relationships and the quick solution of problems involving the optimal allocation of scarce resources. Moreover, students with extensive academic backgrounds or work experience in applied mathematics (i.e., engineers and scientists) often find that they are able to discern the essential nature of an economic problem more easily with equations and calculus than with narratives and tabular examples.

We have resolved the dilemma in the following way. The explanations of economic terms, concepts, and methods of analysis rely primarily on verbal definitions, numerical tables, and graphs. As appropriate, chapter appendixes will present the same material using algebra and calculus. At times, algebra and calculus will be employed in the main body of a chapter. Moreover, problems and exercises at the end of the chapter will give students ample opportunity to reinforce their understanding of the material with the use of algebra and calculus, as well as with tables and graphs.

The authors' experience as teachers indicates that many students have already learned the mathematics employed in this text, both in the main body and in the appendixes. However, some students may have studied this material some time ago and may therefore benefit from a review. Such a review is offered in the balance of this appendix. It is intended only as a brief refresher. For a more comprehensive review, readers should consult any of the many texts and review books on this subject.[30] In fact, any college algebra or calculus text would be just as suitable as a reference.

VARIABLES, FUNCTIONS, AND SLOPES: THE HEART OF ECONOMIC ANALYSIS

A *variable* is any entity that can assume different values. Each academic discipline focuses attention on its own set of variables. For example, in the social sciences, political scientists may study power and authority, sociologists may study group cohesiveness, and psychologists may study paranoia. Economists study such variables as price, output, revenue, cost, and profit. The advantage that economics has over the other social sciences is that most of its variables can be measured in a relatively unambiguous manner.[31]

Once the variables of interest have been identified and measured, economists try to understand how and why the values of these variables change. They also try to determine what conditions will lead to optimal values. Here the term *optimal* refers to the best possible value in a particular situation. *Optimal* may refer to the maximum value (as in the case of profit), or it may refer to the minimum value (as in the case of cost). In any event, the analysis of the changes in a variable's value, often referred to as a variable's "behavior," is almost always carried out in relation to other variables. In mathematics, the relationship of one variable's value to the values of other variables is expressed in terms of a function. Formally stated in mathematical terms, Y is said to be a function of X (i.e., $Y = f(x)$, where f represents "function" if for any value that might be assigned to X a value of Y can be determined). For example, the demand function indicates the quantity of a good or service that people are willing to buy, given the values of price, tastes and preferences, prices of related products, number of buyers, and future expectations. A functional relationship can be expressed using tables, graphs, or algebraic equations.

To illustrate the different ways of expressing a function, let us use the total revenue function. Total revenue (or sales) is defined as the unit price of a product (P) multiplied by the number of units sold (Q). That is, TR = $P \times Q$. In economics the general functional relationship for total revenue is that its value is dependent on the number of units sold. That is, TR = $f(Q)$. Total revenue, or TR, is called the *dependent variable* because its value depends on the value of Q. Q is called the *independent variable* because its value may vary independently of the value of TR. For example, suppose a product is sold for $5 per unit. Table 2A.1 shows the relationship between total revenue and quantity over a selected range of units sold.

---

[30]See, for example, Bodh R. Gulati, *College Mathematics with Applications to the Business and Social Sciences,* New York: Harper & Row, 1978; and Donald and Mildred Stanel, *Applications of College Mathematics,* Lexington, MA: D.C. Heath, 1983.
[31]To be sure, variables in the other social sciences are measurable, but in many instances, the measurement standards themselves are subject to discussion and controversy. For example, psychologists may use the result of some type of IQ test as a measure of intelligence. But there is an ongoing debate as to whether this result is reflective of one's native intelligence or socioeconomic background.

Units Sold (Q)	Total Revenue (TR)
0	$0
1	5
2	10
3	15
4	20
5	25

Figure 2A.1 shows a graph of the values in Table 2A.1. As you can see in this figure, we have related total revenue to quantity in a linear fashion. There does not always have to be a linear relationship between total revenue and quantity. As you will see in the next section, this function, as well as many other functions of interest to economists, may assume different nonlinear forms.

We can also express the relation depicted in Table 2A.1 and Figure 2A.1 in the following equation:

$$TR = 5Q \qquad \textbf{(2A.1)}$$

where TR = Dependent variable (total revenue)
$\quad\;$ Q = Independent variable (quantity)
$\quad\;$ 5 = Coefficient showing the relationship between changes in TR relative to changes in Q

This equation can also be expressed in the general form:

$$Y = a + bX \qquad \textbf{(2A.2)}$$

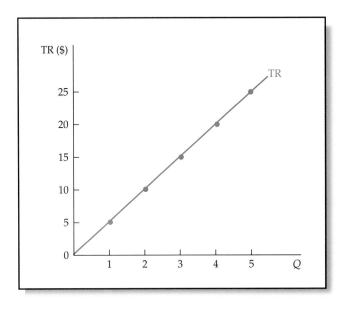

Figure 2A.1
Total Revenue Function

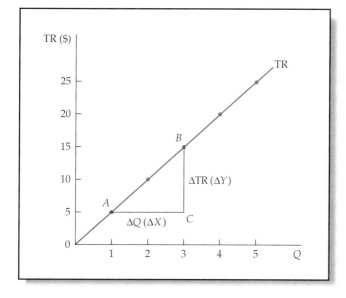

Figure 2A.2
The Slope of the Total
Revenue Line

where Y = Dependent variable (i.e., TR)
      X = Independent variable (i.e., Q)
      b = Coefficient of X (i.e., the given P of $5)
      a = Intercept term (in this case, 0)

In a linear equation, the coefficient b (which takes the value of 5 in our total revenue function) can also be thought of as the change in Y over the change in X, (i.e., $(\Delta Y)/(\Delta X)$). In other words, it represents the slope of the line plotted on the basis of Equation (2A.2). The slope of a line is a measure of its steepness. This can be seen in Figure 2A.1, which, for purposes of discussion, we have reproduced in Figure 2A.2. In this figure, the steepness of the line between points A and B can be seen as BC/AC.

The slope of a function is critical to economic analysis because it shows the change in a dependent variable relative to a change in a designated independent variable. As explained in the next section of this appendix, this is the essence of *marginal analysis*.

THE IMPORTANCE OF MARGINAL ANALYSIS IN ECONOMIC ANALYSIS

One of the most important contributions that economic theory has made to managerial decision making is the application of what economists call *marginal analysis.* Essentially, marginal analysis involves the consideration of changes in the values of variables from some given starting point. Stated in a more formal mathematical manner, marginal analysis can be defined as the amount of change in a dependent variable that results from a unit change in an independent variable. If the functional relationship between the dependent and independent variables is linear, this change is represented by the slope of the line. In the case of our total revenue function, TR = 5Q, we can readily see that the coefficient, 5, indicates the marginal relationship between TR, the dependent variable, and Q, the independent variable. That is, total revenue is expected to change by $5 for every unit change in Q.

Most economic decisions made by managers involve some sort of change in one variable relative to a change in other variables. For example, a firm might want to consider raising or lowering the price from $5 per unit. Whether or not it is desirable to do so would depend on the resulting change in revenues or profits. Changes in these variables would in turn depend on the change in the number of units sold as a result of the change in price. Using the usual symbol for change, Δ (delta), this pricing decision can be summarized via the following illustration:

The top line shows that a firm's price affects its profit. The dashed arrows indicate that changes in price will change profit via changes in the number of units sold (ΔQ), in revenue, and in cost. Actually, each of the dashed lines represents a key function used in economic analysis. ΔP to ΔQ represents the demand function. ΔQ to ΔRevenue is the total revenue function, ΔQ to ΔCost is the cost function, and ΔQ to ΔProfit is the profit function. Of course, the particular behavior or pattern of profit change relative to changes in quantity depends on how revenue and cost change relative to changes in Q.

Marginal analysis comes into play even if a product is new and being priced in the market for the first time. When there is no starting or reference point, different values of a variable may be evaluated in a form of sensitivity or what-if analysis. For example, the decision makers in a company such as IBM may price the company's new workstations by charting a list of hypothetical prices and then forecasting how many units the company will be able to sell at each price. By shifting from price to price, the decision makers would be engaging in a form of marginal analysis.[32]

Many other economic decisions rely on marginal analysis, including the hiring of additional personnel, the purchase of additional equipment, or a venture into a new line of business. In each of these cases, it is the change in some variable (e.g., profit, cash flow, productivity, or cost) associated with the change in a firm's resource allocation that is of importance to the decision maker. Consideration of changes in relation to some reference point is also referred to as *incremental analysis*. A common distinction made between incremental and marginal analysis is that the former simply considers the change in the dependent variable whereas the latter considers the change in the dependent variable relative to a one-unit change in the independent variable. For example, suppose lowering the price of a product results in a sales increase of 1,000 units and a revenue increase of $2,000. The incremental revenue would be $2,000, and the marginal revenue would be $2 ($2,000/1,000).

---

[32]One of the authors was a member of the pricing department of IBM for a number of years. This type of sensitivity analysis involving marginal relationships is indeed an important part of the pricing process. Much more about pricing will be said in later chapters.

FUNCTIONAL FORMS: A VARIATION ON A THEME

For purposes of illustration, we will often rely on a linear function to express the relationship among variables. This is particularly the case in chapter 3, on supply and demand. But there are many instances when a linear function is not the proper expression for changes in the value of a dependent variable relative to changes in some independent variable. For example, if a firm's total revenue does not increase at the same rate as additional units of its product are sold, a linear function is clearly not appropriate. To illustrate this phenomenon, let us assume that a firm has the power to set its price at different levels and that its customers respond to different prices on the basis of the following schedule:

P	Q
$7	0
6	100
5	200
4	300
3	400
2	500
1	600
0	700

The algebraic and graphical expressions of this relationship are shown in Figure 2A.3. As implied in the schedule and as shown explicitly in Figure 2A.3, we have assumed a linear relationship between price and quantity demanded.

Figure 2A.3
Demand Curve

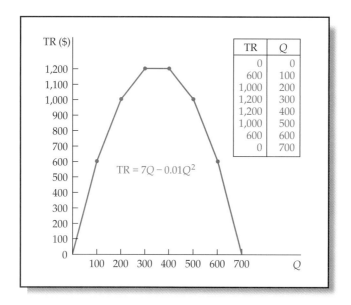

TR	Q
0	0
600	100
1,000	200
1,200	300
1,200	400
1,000	500
600	600
0	700

$TR = 7Q - 0.01Q^2$

Figure 2A.4
Total Revenue

Based on the definition of total revenue as TR = $P \times Q$, we can create a total revenue schedule as well as a total revenue equation and graph. These are all shown in Figure 2A.4.

Since we know that the demand curve is $Q = 700 - 100P$ and TR = $P \times Q$, we can arrive at the values of the coefficient and intercept terms as well as the functional form in a very straightforward manner. First, we need to express P in terms of Q so that we can substitute this relationship into the total revenue equation:

$$Q = 700 - 100P \tag{2A.3}$$

or

$$P = 7 - 0.01Q \tag{2A.4}$$

Substituting the Equation (2A.4) into the total revenue equation gives

$$TR = P \times Q \tag{2A.5}$$

$$= (7 - 0.01Q)Q$$

$$= 7Q - 0.01Q^2$$

As can be seen, a linear demand function results in a nonlinear total revenue function. More precisely, the functional relationship between total revenue and quantity seen here is expressed as a quadratic equation. Basically, this particular functional relationship is obtained whenever the independent variable is raised to the second power (i.e., squared) as well as to the first power. Graphically, quadratic equations are easily recognized by their parabolic shape. The parabola's actual shape and placement on the graph depend on the values and signs of the coefficient and intercept terms. Figure 2A.5 shows four different quadratic functions.

If, in addition to being squared, the independent variable is raised to the third power (i.e., cubed), the relationship between the dependent and independent vari-

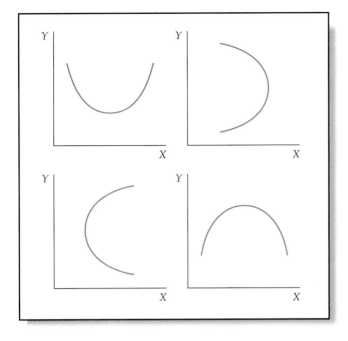

ables is called a cubic function. Figure 2A.6 illustrates different cubic functions. As in the case of quadratic equations, the pattern and placement of these curves depend on the values and signs of the coefficients and intercept terms.

The independent variable can also be raised beyond the third power. However, anything more complex than a cubic equation is generally not useful for describing the relationship among variables in managerial economics. Certainly, there is no

Figure 2A.6
Examples of Cubic Functions

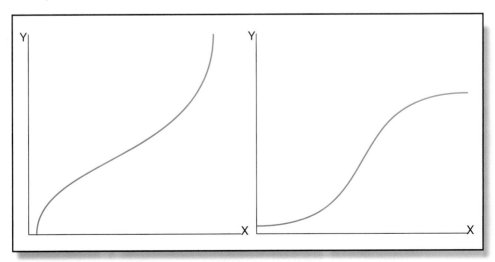

need to go beyond the cubic equation for purposes of this text. As readers will see in ensuing chapters, the most commonly used forms of key functions are (1) linear demand function, (2) linear or quadratic total revenue function, (3) cubic production function, (4) cubic cost function, and (5) cubic profit function. Some variations to these relationships will also be used, depending on the specifics of the examples being discussed.

There are other nonlinear forms used in economic analysis besides those just listed. These forms involve the use of exponents, logarithms, and reciprocals of the independent variables. Simple examples of these types of nonlinear form are shown in Figure 2A.7. These forms are generally used in the statistical estimation of economic functions, such as the demand, production, and cost functions, and in the forecasting of variables based on some trend over time (i.e., time series analysis). More will be said about these particular functional forms in chapters 5, 6, 9, and 10.

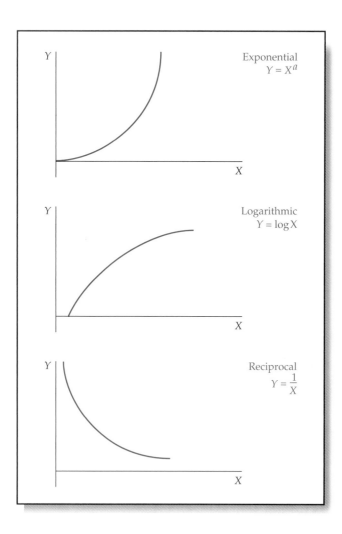

Figure 2A.7
Examples of Selected
Nonlinear Functions

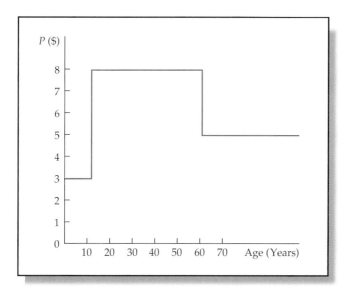

Continuous Functional Relationships

In plotting a functional relationship on a graph, we have assumed that changes in the value of the dependent variable are related in a continuous manner to changes in the independent variable. Intuitively, a function can be said to be continuous if it can be drawn on a graph without taking the pencil off the paper.[33] Perhaps the best way to understand a continuous function is to observe its opposite, a function with discontinuity. Suppose the admission price to an amusement park is established as follows: Ages 1 through 12 must pay $3, ages 13 through 60 must pay $8, and ages 61 and above must pay $5. A graph of the relationship between admission price and age is shown in Figure 2A.8. Notice that there is a jump or break in the graph at the level separating children from adults and the level separating adults from senior citizens. Because of these breaks in the relationship between the independent and dependent variables, this discontinuous relationship is also referred to as a *step function.*

Unless otherwise specified, the functional relationships analyzed in this text are considered to be continuous. Looking back at our example of the demand and total revenue functions, we can see that they indeed indicate a continuous relationship between price and quantity and between total revenue and quantity (see Figures 2A.1 and 2A.4). However, a closer look at the intervals used in the examples might lead you to question the applicability of a continuous function in actual business situations. For instance, let us observe again in Figure 2A.9 the relationship between total revenue and quantity first shown in Figure 2A.4.

The inquiring reader might ask whether or not this relationship, $TR = 7Q - 0.01Q^2$, is in fact valid for points *within* each of the given intervals. For example, if the

---

[33]This particular way of explaining a continuous function is taken from Gulati, *College Mathematics.* To be sure, the author provides a much more rigorous definition of this concept.

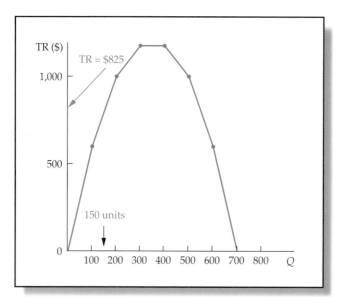

Figure 2A.9
Discrete Intervals in a
Continuous Function: The
Example of Total Revenue

firm sold 150 units, would it earn $825? Even if the answer is affirmative, to be a truly continuous function, the relationship would have to hold no matter how small the intervals of quantity considered.[34] For example, if the firm sold 150.567 units, its revenue would be $827.265.

But at this point, an adjustment to strict mathematics must be tempered with common sense. There are many instances in economic analysis in which continuous functions are assumed to represent relationships among variables, even though the variables themselves are subject to limitations in how finely they can be subdivided. For example, a firm may only be able to sell its product in lots of 100 or, at the very least, in single units. A firm might not want to consider price changes in terms of cents, but only in terms of dollars. In other cases, it might not be a matter of a firm's choice but of what resources are available. For example, suppose we have a function relating persons hired to the output they produce. (In chapter 7, this is referred to as the short-run production function.) Let us further suppose that labor resources are measured in terms of units of people (as opposed to hours, minutes, or even seconds of work time). Many economic activities in business involve variables that must be measured in discrete intervals (e.g., people, units of output, monetary units, machines, factories). For purposes of analysis, we will assume that all of the economic variables are related to each other in a continuous fashion but are valid only at stated discrete intervals.

USING CALCULUS

Calculus is a mathematical technique that enables one to find instantaneous rates of change of a continuous function. That is, instead of finding the rate of change between two points on a plotted line, as shown in Figure 2A.2, calculus enables us

---

[34]According to mathematicians, "A function is said to be continuous over an open interval if it is continuous at *every* point in that interval" (Gulati, *College Mathematics*, p. 505).

to find the rate of change in the dependent variable relative to the independent variable at a particular point on the function. However, calculus can be so applied *only* if a function is continuous. Thus, we needed to establish firmly the validity of using continuous functions to represent the relationships among economic variables.

Our brief introduction to calculus and its role in economic analysis begins with the statement that if all functional relationships in economics were linear, there would be no need for calculus! This point may be made clearer by referring to an intuitive definition of calculus. To quote the author of an extremely helpful and readable book on this subject:

> Calculus, first of all, is wrongly named. It should never have been given that name. A far truer and more meaningful name is "SLOPE-FINDING."[35]

It is not difficult to find the slope of a linear function. We simply take any two points on the line and find the change in *Y* relative to the change in *X*. The relative change is, of course, represented by the *b* coefficient in the linear equation. Moreover, because it is linear, the slope or rate of change remains the same between any two points over the entire range of intervals one wishes to consider for the function. This is shown in the algebraic expression of the linear function by the constancy of the *b* coefficient.

However, finding the slope of a nonlinear function poses a problem. Let us arbitrarily take two points on the curve shown in Figure 2A.10 and label them *A* and *D*. The slope or rate of change of *Y* relative to the change in *X* can be seen as *DL/AL*. Now, on this same curve let us find the slope of a point closer to point *D* and call it *C*. Notice that the slope of the line between these two points is less than the slope between *D* and *A*. (The measure of this slope is *DM/CM*.) The same holds true if we consider point *B*, a point that is still closer to *D*; the slope between *B* and *D* is less than the two slopes already considered. In general, we can state that in reference to the curve shown in Figure 2A.10, the slope between point *D* and a point to the left decreases as the point moves closer to *D*. Obviously, this is not the case for a linear equation because the slope is constant.

To understand how calculus enables us to find the slope or rate of change of a nonlinear function, let us resume the experiment. Suppose we keep on measuring changes in *Y* relative to smaller and smaller changes in *X*. Graphically, this can be represented in Figure 2A.10 by moving point *B* toward point *D*. As smaller and smaller changes in *X* are considered, point *B* moves closer and closer to point *D* until the limit at which it appears to become one and the same with point *D*. When this occurs, the slope or rate of change of *Y* relative to *X* can be represented as point *D* itself. Graphically, this is represented by the slope of a line tangent to point *D*. In effect, this slope is a measure of the change in *Y* relative to a very small (i.e., infinitesimally small) change in *X*. To find the magnitude of the slope of tangency to any point on a line, we need to employ calculus, or more specifically, a concept used in calculus called the *derivative*.

---

[35]Eli S. Pine, *How to Enjoy Calculus*, Hasbrouck Heights, NJ: Steinlitz-Hammacher, 1983. Pine's definition is, of course, a simplification since it leaves out integral calculus. Nevertheless, we recommend this book highly for those who wish a "user-friendly" review of differential calculus.

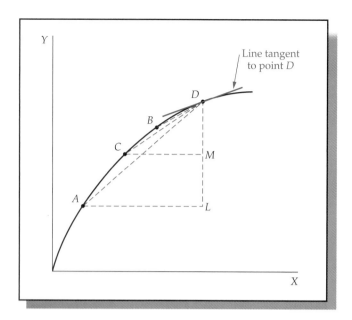

Figure 2A.10
Finding the Slope of a
Nonlinear Function

In mathematics, a derivative is a measure of the change in Y relative to a very small change in X. Using formal mathematical notation, we can define the derivative as

$$\frac{dY}{dX} = \lim_{\Delta X \to 0} \frac{\Delta Y}{\Delta X}$$

This notation can be expressed as, "The derivative of Y with respect to X equals the limit (if such a limit exists) of the change in Y relative to the change in X as the change in X approaches zero."[36] As you can see from the discussion in the previous two paragraphs, the derivative turns out to be the slope of a line that is tangent to some given point on a curve. By convention, mathematicians use d to represent very small changes in a variable. Hence, dY/dX means "changes in Y relative to very small changes in X." For changes between two distinct points, the delta sign (Δ) is used.

Finding the Derivatives of a Function

There are certain rules for finding the derivatives of a function. We shall present in some detail two rules that will be used extensively in this text. The other rules and their use in economic analysis will be only briefly mentioned. Formal proofs of all of these rules are not provided. Interested students may consult any introductory calculus text for this information.

---

[36]The concept of *limit* is critical to understanding the derivative. We have tried to present an intuitive explanation of this concept by considering the movement of point B in Figure 2A.10 closer and closer to point D, so that in effect the changes in X become smaller and smaller. *At the limit*, B becomes so close to D that, for all intents and purposes, it is the same as D. This situation would represent the smallest possible change in X. For a more formal explanation of *limit*, readers should consult any introductory calculus text.

Figure 2A.11
The Derivative of a
Constant Equals Zero

Constants. The derivative of a constant must always be zero. Derivatives involve rates of change, and a constant, by definition, never changes in value. Expressed formally, if Y equals some constant, (e.g., $Y = 100$), then

$$\frac{dY}{dX} = 0$$

The null value of the derivative of a constant is illustrated in Figure 2A.11. Here we have assumed Y to have a constant value of 100. Clearly, this constant value of Y is unaffected by changes in the value of X. Thus, $dY/dX = 0$.

Power Functions. A *power function* is one in which the independent variable, X, is raised to the power of one or more. This type of function can be expressed in general terms as

$$Y = bX^n \tag{2A.6}$$

where $Y =$ Dependent variable
$\quad b =$ Coefficient of the dependent variable
$\quad X =$ Independent variable
$\quad n =$ Power to which the independent variable is raised

The rule for finding the derivative of this type of function is

$$\frac{dY}{dX} = nbX^{(n-1)} \tag{2A.7}$$

Thus, suppose we have the equation

$$Y = 10X^3 \tag{2A.8}$$

The derivative of this equation according to this rule is

$$\frac{dY}{dX} = 3 \times 10X^{(3-1)}$$

$$= 30X^2 \qquad\qquad \textbf{(2A.9)}$$

Thus, at the point where $X = 5$, the "instantaneous" rate of change of Y with respect to X is $30(5)^2$, or 750.

Sums and Differences. For convenience in presenting the rules in the remainder of this appendix, we will use the following notations:

$U = g(X)$, where U is an unspecified function, g, of X
$V = h(X)$, where V is an unspecified function, h, of X

Given the function $Y = U + V$, the derivative of the sum (difference) is equal to the sum (difference) of the derivatives of the individual terms. In notational form,

$$\frac{dY}{dX} = \frac{dU}{dX} + \frac{dV}{dX}$$

For example, if $U = g(X) = 3X^2$, $V = h(X) = 4X^3$ and $Y = U + V = 3X^2 + 4X^3$, then

$$\frac{dY}{dX} = 6X \times 12X^2$$

Products. Given the function $Y = UV$, its derivative can be expressed as follows:

$$\frac{dY}{dX} = U\frac{dV}{dX} + V\frac{dU}{dX}$$

This rule states that the derivative of the product of two expressions (U and V) is equal to the first term multiplied by the derivative of the second, plus the second term times the derivative of the first. For example, let $Y = 5X^2(7 - X)$. By letting $U = 5X^2$ and $V = (7 - X)$, we obtain

$$\frac{dY}{dX} = 5X^2 \frac{dV}{dX} + (7 - X)\frac{dU}{dX}$$

$$= 5X^2(-1) + (7 - X)10X$$

$$= -5X^2 + 70X - 10X^2$$

$$= 70X - 15X^2$$

Quotients. Given the function $Y = U/V$, its derivative can be expressed as follows:

$$\frac{dY}{dX} = \frac{V(dU/dX) - U(dV/dX)}{V^2}$$

For example, suppose we have the following function:

$$Y = \frac{5X - 9}{10X^2}$$

Using the formula and letting $U = 5X - 9$ and $V = 10X^2$, we obtain the following:

$$\frac{dY}{dX} = \frac{10X^2 \times 5 - (5X - 9)\,20X}{100X^4}$$

$$= \frac{50X^2 - 100X^2 + 180X}{100X^4}$$

$$= \frac{180X - 50X^2}{100X^4}$$

$$= \frac{18 - 5X}{10X^3}$$

Applying the Rules to an Economic Problem and a Preview of Other Rules for Differentiating a Function. There are several other rules for differentiating a function that are used in economic analysis. These involve differentiating a logarithmic function and the "function of a function" (often referred to in mathematics as the *chain rule*). We will present these rules as they are needed in the appropriate chapters. In fact, almost all of the mathematical examples involving calculus will require only the rules for constants, powers, and sums and differences. As an example of how these three rules are applied, we return to the total revenue and demand functions presented earlier in this appendix. Recall that

$$TR = 7Q - 0.01Q^2 \tag{2A.10}$$

Using the rules for powers and for sums and differences, we find that the derivative of this *function* is

$$\frac{dTR}{dQ} = 7 - 0.02Q \tag{2A.11}$$

The derivative of the total revenue function is also called the *marginal revenue function* and plays a very important part in many aspects of economic analysis. (See chapter 4 for a complete discussion of the definition and uses of marginal revenue.)

Turning now to the demand function first presented in Figure 2A.3, we recall that

$$Q = 700 - 100P \tag{2A.12}$$

Using the rules for constants, powers, and sums and differences, we see that the derivative of this function is:

$$\frac{dQ}{dP} = 0 - 1(100)P^{(1-1)} \tag{2A.13}$$

$$= -100P^0$$

$$= -100$$

Notice that, by the conventions of mathematical notation, variables such as P that have no stated exponent are assumed to be raised to the first power (i.e., $n = 1$). Thus, based on the rule for the derivative of a power function $(n - 1)$ becomes $(1 - 1)$, or zero.[37]

---

[37]The rule in algebra is that any value raised to the zeroth power is equal to unity.

Therefore, dQ/dP is equal to the constant value 100. Recall our initial statement that there is no need for calculus if only linear functions are considered. This is supported by the results shown in Equation (2A.13). Here we can see that the first derivative of the linear demand equation is simply the value of the b coefficient, 100. That is, no matter what the value of P, the change in Q with respect to a change in P is 100 (i.e., the slope of the linear function, or the b coefficient in the linear equation). Another way to express this is that for a linear function, there is no need to take the derivative of dY/dX. Instead, we can use the slope of the line represented by $\Delta Y / \Delta X$.

Partial Derivatives. Many functional relationships in this text will entail a number of independent variables. For example, let us assume that a firm has a demand function represented by the following equation:

$$Q = -100P + 50I + P_s + 2N \qquad \text{(2A.14)}$$

where Q = Quantity demanded
P = Price of the product
I = Income of customers
P_s = Price of a substitute product
N = Number of customers

If we want to know the change in Q with respect to a change in a particular independent variable, we can take the partial derivative of Q with respect to that variable. For example, the impact of a change in P on Q, with other factors held constant, would be expressed as

$$\frac{\delta Q}{\delta P} = -100 \qquad \text{(2A.15)}$$

The conventional symbol used in mathematics for the partial derivative is the lowercase Greek letter delta, δ. Notice that all we did was use the rule for the derivative of a power function on the P variable. Because the other independent variables, I, P_s, and N, are held constant, they are treated as constants in taking the partial derivative. (As you recall, the derivative of a constant is zero.) Thus, the other terms in the equation drop out, leaving us with the instantaneous impact of the change in P on Q. This procedure applies regardless of the powers to which the independent variables are raised. It just so happens that in this equation, all the independent variables are raised only to the first power.[38]

Finding the Maximum and Minimum Values of a Function

A primary objective of managerial economics is to find the optimal values of key variables. This means finding "the best" possible amount or value under certain circumstances. Marginal analysis and the concept of the derivative are very helpful in finding optimal values. For example, given a total revenue function, a firm might want to find the number of units it must sell to maximize its revenue. Taking the total revenue function first shown in Equation (2A.5), we have

---

[38]An expression such as this is referred to in mathematics as a *linear additive equation.*

$$TR = 7Q - 0.01Q^2 \qquad \text{(2A.16)}$$

The derivative of this function (i.e., marginal revenue) is

$$\frac{dTR}{dQ} = 7 - 0.02Q \qquad \text{(2A.17)}$$

Setting the first derivative of the total revenue function (or the marginal revenue function) equal to zero and solving for the revenue-maximizing quantity, Q^*, gives us[39]

$$7 - 0.02Q = 0 \qquad \text{(2A.18)}$$

$$Q^* = 350$$

Thus, the firm should sell 350 units of its product if it wants to maximize its total revenue. In addition, if the managers wish to know the price that the firm should charge to sell the "revenue-maximizing" number of units, they can go back to the demand equation from which the total revenue function was derived, that is,

$$P = 7 - 0.01Q \qquad \text{(2A.19)}$$

By substituting the value of Q^* into this equation, we obtain

$$P^* = 7 - 0.01(350) \qquad \text{(2A.20)}$$

$$= \$3.50$$

The demand function, the total revenue function, and the revenue-maximizing price and quantity are all illustrated in Figure 2A.12.

To further illustrate the use of the derivative in finding the optimum, let us use an example that will play an important part in chapters 9 and 10. Suppose a firm wishes to find the price and output levels that will maximize its profit. If the firm's revenue and cost functions are known, it is a relatively simple matter to use the derivative of these functions to find the optimal price and quantity. To begin with, let us assume the following demand, revenue, and cost functions:

$$Q = 17.2 - 0.1P \qquad \text{(2A.21)}$$

or

$$P = 172 - 10Q \qquad \text{(2A.22)}$$

$$TR = 172Q - 10Q^2 \qquad \text{(2A.23)}$$

$$TC = 100 + 65Q + Q^2 \qquad \text{(2A.24)}$$

By definition, profit (π) is equal to total revenue minus total cost. That is,

$$\pi = TR - TC \qquad \text{(2A.25)}$$

Substituting Equations (2A.23) and (2A.24) into (2A.25) gives us:

$$\pi = 172Q - 10Q^2 - 100 - 65Q - Q^2 \qquad \text{(2A.26)}$$

$$= -100 + 107Q - 11Q^2$$

---

[39]Henceforth, all optimal values for Q and P (e.g., values that maximize revenue or profit or minimize cost) will be designated with an asterisk.

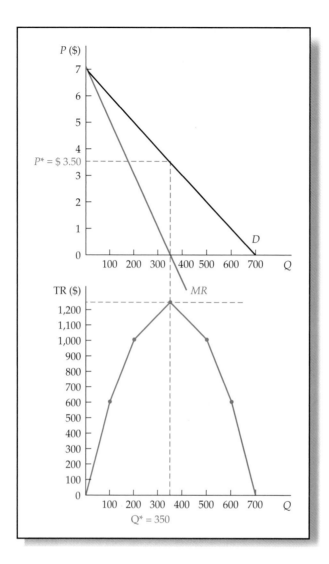

Figure 2A.12
Demand Function, Total
Revenue Function, and
Revenue-Maximizing Price
and Quantity

To find the profit-maximizing output level, we simply follow the same procedure used to find the revenue-maximizing output level. We take the derivative of the total profit function, set it equal to zero, and solve for Q^*:

$$\frac{d\pi}{dQ} = 107 - 22Q = 0$$

$$22Q = 107 \qquad\qquad \textbf{(2A.27)}$$

$$Q^* = 4.86 \qquad\qquad \textbf{(2A.28)}$$

The total revenue and cost functions and the total profit function are illustrated in Figure 2A.13*a* and *b*, respectively.

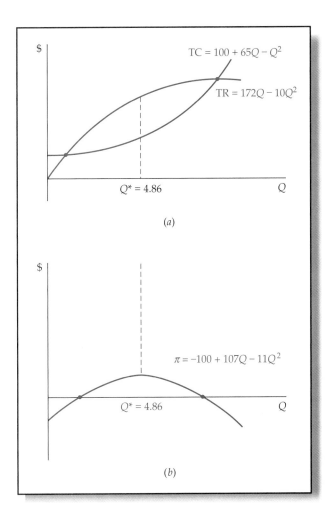

$$TC = 100 + 65Q - Q^2$$

$$TR = 172Q - 10Q^2$$

$Q* = 4.86$

Q

(a)

$$\pi = -100 + 107Q - 11Q^2$$

$Q* = 4.86$

Q

(b)

Figure 2A.13
Total Revenue, Total Cost,
and Total Profit Functions

Distinguishing Maximum and Minimum Values in the Optimization Problem. In economic analysis, finding the optimum generally means finding either the maximum or minimum value of a variable, depending on what type of function is being considered. For example, if the profit or total revenue function is the focus, the maximum value is obviously of interest. If a cost function is being analyzed, its minimum value would be the main concern. Taking the derivative of a function, setting it equal to zero, and then solving for the value of the independent variable enables us to find the maximum or minimum value of the function.

However, there may be instances in which a function has both a maximum and a minimum value. When this occurs, the method described previously cannot tell us whether the optimum is a maximum or a minimum. This situation of indeterminacy can be seen in Figure 2A.14a. The graph in this figure represents a cubic function of the general form $Y = a - bX + cX^2 - dX^3$. Clearly, this function has both a minimum (point A) and a maximum (point C). As a generalization, if we took the first derivative at the four points designated in Figure 2A.14a, we would find that

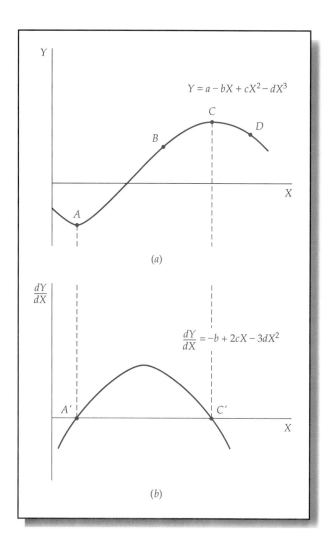

Figure 2A.14
Maximum and Minimum
Points of a Cubic Function

At point A, $dY/dX = 0$.
At point B, $dY/dX > 0$.
At point C, $dY/dX = 0$.
At point D, $dY/dX < 0$.

As expected, the first derivatives of points A and C are equal to zero, reflecting the fact that their lines of tangency are horizontal (i.e., have zero slope). The positive and negative values of the derivatives at points B and D are reflective of their respective upward and downward lines of tangency. However, because *both* points A and C have first derivatives equal to zero, a problem arises if we wish to know whether these points indicate maximum or minimum values of Y. Of course, in Figure 2A.14 we can plainly see that point A is the minimum value and point C is the maximum value. However, there is a formal mathematical procedure for distinguishing a function's maximum and minimum values. This procedure requires the use of a function's *second derivative*.

The second derivative of a function is the derivative of its first derivative. The procedure for finding the second derivative of a function is quite simple. All the rules for finding the first derivative apply to obtaining the second derivative. Conceptually, we can consider the second derivative of a function as a measure of the rate of change of the first derivative. In other words, it is a measure of "the rate of change of the rate of change."[40]

Let us illustrate precisely how the second derivative is used to determine the maximum and minimum values by presenting a graph of the function's first derivative in Figure 2A.14b. As a check on your understanding of this figure, notice that, as expected, the second derivative has a negative value when the original function decreases in value and a positive value when the original function increases in value. But now consider another aspect of this figure. Recall that the second derivative is a measure of the rate of change of the first derivative. Thus, graphically, we can find the second derivative by evaluating the slopes of lines tangent to points on the graph of the *first derivative*. See points A' and C' in Figure 2A.14b. By inspection of this figure, it should be quite clear that the slope of the line tangent to point A' is positive and the slope of the line tangent to point C' is negative. This enables us to conclude the following: At the minimum point of a function, the second derivative is *positive*. At the maximum point of a function, the second derivative is *negative*.[41]

Using mathematical notation, we can now state the *first-* and *second-order conditions* for determining the maximum or minimum values of a function.

Maximum value: $dY/dX = 0$ (first-order condition)

                  $d^2/dx^2 < 0$ (second-order condition)

Minimum value: $dY/dX = 0$ (first-order condition)

                  $d^2/dx^2 > 0$ (second-order condition)

We will now illustrate how the first- and second-order conditions are used to find the profit-maximizing level of output for a firm. Suppose this firm has the following revenue and total cost functions:

---

[40]Mathematics and physics texts often use the example of a moving automobile to help distinguish the first and second derivatives. To begin with, the function can be expressed as $M = f(T)$, or miles traveled is a function of the time elapsed. The first derivative of this function describes the automobile's velocity. As an example of this, imagine a car moving at the rate of speed of 45 miles per hour. Now suppose this car has just entered a freeway, starts to accelerate, and then reaches a speech of 75 mph. The measure of this acceleration as the car goes from 45 mph to 75 mph is the second derivative of the function. Because the car is accelerating (i.e., going faster and faster), the second derivative is some positive value. In other words, the distance (measured in miles) that the car is traveling is increasing at an *increasing* rate. To extend this example a bit further, suppose the driver of the car, realizing that this section of the freeway is closely monitored by radar, begins to slow down to the legal speed limit of 60 mph. As the driver slows down, or decelerates, the speed at which the car is traveling is reduced. In other words, the distance (in miles) that the car is traveling is increasing at a *decreasing* rate. Deceleration, being the opposite of acceleration, implies that the second derivative in this case is negative.

[41]Let us return to the automobile example for an alternative explanation of the second-order condition for determining a function's maximum value. Let us imagine that, at the very moment the car reached 75 mph, the driver started to slow down. This means that at the precise moment the accelerating car started to decelerate, it had reached its *maximum* speed. In mathematical terms, if a function is increasing at an *increasing* rate (i.e., its second derivative is positive), then the moment it starts to increase at a *decreasing* rate (i.e., its second derivative becomes negative), it has reached its maximum value. Similar reasoning can be used to explain the second-order condition for determining the minimum value of a function.

$$TR = 50Q \qquad \text{(2A.29)}$$

$$TC = 100 + 60Q - 3Q^2 + 0.1Q^3 \qquad \text{(2A.30)}$$

Based on these equations the firm's total profit function is

$$\pi = 50Q - (100 + 60Q - 3Q^2 + 0.1Q^3) \qquad \text{(2A.31)}$$

$$= 50Q - 100 - 60Q + 3Q^2 - 0.1Q^3$$

$$= -100 - 10Q + 3Q^2 - 0.1Q^3$$

Notice that this firm's profit function contains a term that is raised to the third power because its cost function is also raised to the third power. In other words, the firm is assumed to have a cubic cost function, and therefore it has a cubic profit function. Plotting this cubic profit function gives us the graph in Figure 2A.15. We can observe in this figure that the level of output that maximizes the firm's profit is about 18.2 units, and the level of output that minimizes its profit (i.e., maximizes its loss) is about 1.8 units.

Let us employ calculus along with the first- and second-order conditions to determine the point at which the firm maximizes its profit. We begin as before by finding the first derivative of the profit function, setting it equal to zero, and solving for the value of Q that satisfies this condition.

$$\pi = -100 - 10Q + 3Q^2 - 0.1Q^3 \qquad \text{(2A.32)}$$

$$\frac{d\pi}{dQ} = -10 + 6Q - 0.3Q^2$$

$$= -0.3q^2 + 6Q - 10 = 0 \qquad \text{(2A.33)}$$

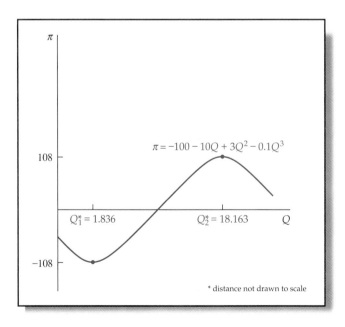

Figure 2A.15
Cubic Profit Function

Note that Equation (2A.33) has been rearranged to conform to the general expression for a quadratic equation. Because the first derivative of the profit function is quadratic, there are two possible values of Q that satisfy the equation.[42]

$$Q_1^* = 1.836 \qquad Q_2^* = 18.163$$

As expected, Q_1^* and Q_2^* coincide with the two points shown in Figure 2A.13. Although both Q_1^* and Q_2^* fulfill the first-order condition, only one satisfies the second-order condition. To see this, let us find the second derivative of the function by taking the derivative of the marginal profit function expressed in Equation (2A.33):

$$\frac{d^2\pi}{dQ^2} = -0.6Q + 6$$

By substitution, we see that at output level 1.836 the value of the second derivative is a positive number:

$$\frac{d^2\pi}{dQ^2} = -0.6(1.836) + 6 = 4.89$$

On the other hand, we see that at output level 18.163 the value of the second derivative is a negative number:

$$\frac{d^2\pi}{dQ^2} = -0.6(18.163) + 6 = -4.89$$

Thus, we see that only Q_2^* enables us to adhere to the second-order condition that $d^2\pi/dQ^2 < 0$. This confirms in a formal, mathematical manner what we already knew from plotting and evaluating the graph of the firm's total profit function: Q_2 is the firm's profit-maximizing level of output.

FIVE KEY FUNCTIONS USED IN THIS TEXT

Five key functions will be used in this text: (1) demand, (2) total revenue, (3) production, (4) total cost, and (5) profit. The following diagrams show the algebraic and graphical expressions for these functions. As can be seen, the demand function is linear, the total revenue function is quadratic, and the production, cost, and profit

---

[42]The economic rationale for cost functions of different degrees is explained in chapter 8. The first derivative of a cubic function is a quadratic function. Such a function can be expressed in the general form

$$Y = aX^2 + bX + c$$

Perhaps you recall from your previous studies of algebra that the values of X that set the quadratic function equal to zero can be found by using the formula for the "roots" of a quadratic equation:

$$X = \frac{-b \pm \sqrt{b^3 - 4ac}}{2a}$$

By substituting the values of the coefficients in Equation (2A.33) (i.e., $a = -0.3$, $b = 6$, $c = -10$) we obtain the answers shown.

functions are cubic. Note that the last three functions all refer to economic conditions in the short run.

1. Demand

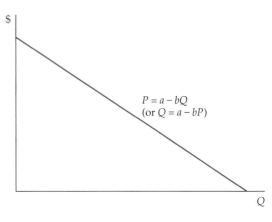

$P = a - bQ$
(or $Q = a - bP$)

2. Total revenue

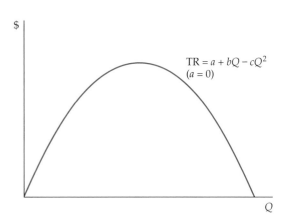

$TR = a + bQ - cQ^2$
$(a = 0)$

3. Production (short run)

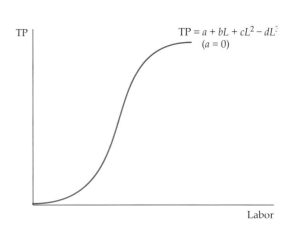

$TP = a + bL + cL^2 - dL^3$
$(a = 0)$

4. Cost (short run)

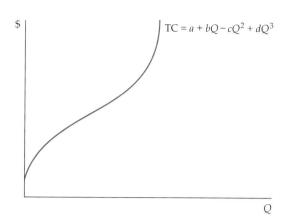

$$TC = a + bQ - cQ^2 + dQ^3$$

5. Profit (short run)

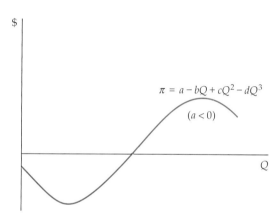

$$\pi = a - bQ + cQ^2 - dQ^3$$

$$(a < 0)$$

SUMMARY

As you proceed with your study of managerial economics and the reading of this text, you will find that the essence of economic analysis is the study of functional relationships between certain dependent variables (e.g., quantity demanded, revenue, cost, profit) and one or more independent variables (e.g., price, income, quantity sold). Mathematics is a tool that can greatly facilitate the analysis of these functional relationships. For example, rather than simply saying that "the quantity of a product sold depends on its price," we can use an algebraic equation to state precisely how many units of a product a firm can expect to sell at a particular price. Moreover, when we engage in a marginal analysis of the impact of price on quantity demanded, we can use the first derivative of this equation to measure the change in quantity demanded relative to changes in price.[43] Furthermore, as shown in this appendix, the precise algebraic

---

[43]In chapter 4, you will see how this first derivative is incorporated into a formula for *elasticity*, a value indicating the percentage change in a dependent variable, such as units sold, with a percentage change in an independent variable, such as price.

expression of the demand function enables us to derive a firm's total revenue and marginal revenue functions. And with the help of calculus, the optimal price and quantity (e.g., the price and quantity that maximize revenue) can be quickly found.

The more data a firm is able to obtain about its key economic functions (i.e., demand, revenue, production, cost, and profit), the more mathematics can be employed in the analysis.

The more that mathematics can be utilized, the more precise a manager can be about such key decisions as the best price to charge, the best markets to compete in, and the most desirable levels of resource allocation. Unfortunately, in the real world firms do not often have the luxury of accurate or complete data with which to work. This is another aspect of decision making and will be discussed in chapters 5 and 6.

QUESTIONS

1. Define the following terms: *function, variable, independent variable, dependent variable, functional form.*
2. Briefly describe how a function is represented in tabular form, in graphical form, and in an equation. Illustrate using the relationship between price and quantity expressed in a demand function.
3. Express in formal mathematical terms the following functional relationships. You may use the general form $Y = f(X)$. However, in each case be as specific as possible about what variables are represented by Y and X. (For example, in the first relationship, advertising is the X variable and could be measured in terms of the amount of advertising dollars spent annually by a firm.)
   a. The effectiveness of advertising.
   b. The impact on output resulting from increasing the number of employees.
   c. The impact on labor productivity resulting from increasing automation.
   d. The impact on sales and profits resulting from price reductions.
   e. The impact on sales and profits resulting from a recession.
   f. The impact on sales and profits resulting from changes in the financial sector (e.g., the stock market or the bond market).
   g. The impact on cost resulting from the use of outside vendors to supply certain components in the manufacturing process.
4. What is a continuous function? Does the use of continuous functions to express economic relationships present any difficulties in analyzing real-world business problems? Explain.
5. Define in mathematical terms the slope of a line. Why is the slope considered to be so important in the quantitative analysis of economic problems?
6. Define *marginal analysis.* Give examples of how this type of analysis can help a managerial decision maker. Are there any limitations to using this type of analysis in actual business situations? Explain.
7. Explain why the first derivative of a function is an important part of marginal analysis.
8. Explain how an analysis of the first derivative of the function $Y = f(X)$ enables one to find the point at which the Y variable is at its maximum or minimum.
9. (Optional) Explain how an analysis of the second derivative of a function enables one to determine whether the variable is a maximum or a minimum.
10. Briefly explain the difference between $\Delta Y/\Delta X$ and dY/dX. Explain why in a linear equation there is no difference between the two terms.

PROBLEMS

1. Answer the following questions on the basis of the accompanying demand schedule.

PRICE	QUANTITY
$100	25
80	35
60	45
40	55
20	65
0	75

   a. Express the schedule as an algebraic equation in which Q is the dependent variable. Plot this on a graph.

   b. Express the schedule as an algebraic equation in which P is the dependent variable. Plot this on a graph.

2. You are given the following demand equations:

$$Q = 450 - 16P$$

$$Q = 360 - 80P$$

$$Q = 1,500 - 500P$$

   a. Determine each equation's total revenue and marginal revenue equations.

   b. Plot the demand equation and the marginal and total revenue equations on a graph.

   c. Use calculus to determine the prices and quantities that maximize the revenue for each equation. Show the points of revenue maximization on the graphs that you have constructed.

3. You are given the following cost equations:

$$TC = 1,500 + 300Q - 25Q^2 + 1.5Q^3$$

$$TC = 1,500 + 300Q + 25Q^2$$

$$TC = 1,500 + 300Q$$

   a. Determine each equation's average variable cost, average cost, and marginal cost.

   b. Plot each equation on a graph. On separate graphs, plot each equation's average variable cost, average cost, and marginal cost.

   c. Use calculus to determine the minimum point on the marginal cost curve.

4. Given the demand equation shown, perform the following tasks:

$$Q = 10 - .004P$$

   a. Combine this equation with each of the cost equations listed in question 3. Use calculus to find the price that will maximize the short-run profit for each of the cost equations.

   b. Plot the profit curve for each of the cost equations.

Chapter 3

Supply and Demand

The Situation

Ross Harris, as a senior purchasing agent responsible for the sweetener used in Global Foods' soft drink product, reported directly to the vice president in charge of purchasing for the entire firm. In two weeks, Ross's firm would be sitting down with the major producers of high-fructose corn syrup (HFCS) to set the price of HFCS for the coming year. Other major soft drink companies would also begin their annual negotiations. Ever since HFCS began replacing sugar (or sucrose) as a sweetener in soft drinks, the major soft drink firms had been negotiating annually with the largest refiners of HFCS on the coming year's price. On balance, the arrangement had worked well for the soft drink industry. Once the price had been determined, soft drink makers were protected from any increase in the spot price for HFCS. Of course, if the price of HFCS fell below the fixed price, the soft drink firms would end up paying more for the product than if they had relied primarily on the spot market for their supply.

This year, however, the major HFCS refiners wanted to change one of the key terms of the pricing agreement. Instead of setting the price on an annual basis, the refiners wanted it to be set every 90 days. "They [the refiners] say they want a more 'market-sensitive' price for their product," Ross's boss explained. "And from the way the spot price of HFCS has been fluctuating in recent years, I don't blame them for this request. As it so happens, most of the agreements have protected us against price increases and have hurt the refiners by preventing them from selling at the higher spot prices."

(Continued)

"Needless to say, this change from an annual to a quarterly agreement puts us in a potentially riskier situation, since we would be able to protect ourselves from possible increases in the price of HFCS for only three months. The management committee does not know whether it is worth 'going to the mat' with the refiners to keep the arrangement on an annual basis. The proposed arrangement may turn out to be beneficial or at least no different from the current one. Ross, I want you and your staff to do a quick but thorough analysis of the situation. Basically, tell us the pros and cons of a quarterly contract."

Meanwhile, Kathy Martinez, whose company was one of the major refiners that processed corn into the HFCS, was given the assignment of preparing a market analysis for corn, the major ingredient of HFCS. This was to be combined with an analysis of the cost of processing the corn into HFCS. The combined report would then be used by her company's negotiating team as supporting material in the firm's efforts to change the contract pricing period from an annual to a quarterly basis. Kathy had only 10 more days in which to complete her portion of the report.

INTRODUCTION

In this chapter, we introduce the basic elements of supply and demand. Although for some of you, this chapter will serve as a review of material covered in an economics principles course, it has been included because it is essential that every reader have a thorough grounding in supply and demand before proceeding to the particulars of managerial economics. There may be situations—such as those described for Ross and Kathy—in which you may be required to conduct or evaluate a study with a considerable use of supply-and-demand analysis. But regardless of how directly this chapter's material may apply to your work, most of the material covered in this book will relate in some way to supply or demand. Indeed, supply and demand can be considered the conceptual framework within which the specifics of managerial economics are discussed.

MARKET DEMAND

The **demand** for a good or service is defined as

> *Quantities* of a good or service that people are ready to *buy* at various *prices* within some given *time period, other factors* besides price held constant.

Note that in this definition "ready" implies that consumers are prepared to buy a good or service both because they are willing (i.e., they have a preference for it) and they are able (i.e., they have the income to support this preference).

Demand can first be illustrated with an example in which we imagine that you, the reader, are part of a simple market experiment. Suppose you were asked to respond to the following survey question: "In a one-week period, how many slices of pizza would you be prepared to buy at the following prices: $2.00, $1.50, $1.00, $.50, and $.05?" Every reader would obviously have his or her own pattern of response. Let us assume that a sample of three readers responds in the following way:

Price (PER SLICE)	Q_{D1}	Q_{D2}	Q_{D3}	Q_{DM}
$2.00	0	2	3	5
1.50	1	2	5	8
1.00	2	2	8	12
0.50	3	3	10	16
0.05	4	4	12	20

As you can see, the combined responses of the three individuals make up the total **market demand** (Q_{DM}) for pizza, the sum of all the individual demands.

Market demand is illustrated with a simple numerical function, as shown in Table 3.1. This table shows a hypothetical demand for pizza. As the price of a slice of pizza falls from $7.00 to zero, the amount that consumers in this market are willing to buy increases from zero to 700 slices. This inverse relationship between price and the **quantity demanded** of pizza is called the **Law of Demand.** There may be instances in which consumers behave in an "irrational" manner by buying more as the price rises and less as the price falls because they associate price with quality. But in the economic analysis of demand, it is assumed that buyers do not associate price with quality and will therefore follow the Law of Demand.

The Law of Demand can be observed in the curve shown in Figure 3.1, derived from the schedule of numbers in Table 3.1. Notice that the curve in this figure slopes downward and to the right, indicating that the quantity of pizza demanded increases as the price falls and vice versa.

A change in the demand for pizza or any other product is indicated by a change in the entire schedule of quantities demanded at a list of prices or a shift in the

Table 3.1
Market Demand for Pizza

Price (PER SLICE)	Q_D
$7.00	0
6.00	100
5.00	200
4.00	300
3.00	400
2.00	500
1.00	600
0	700

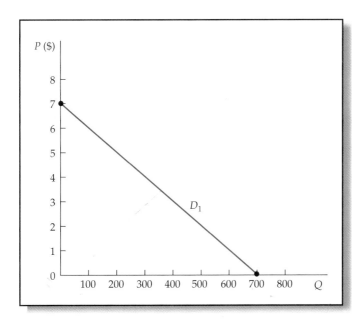

Figure 3.1
Market Demand Curve
for Pizza

demand curve either to the left or to the right. We see these changes in Table 3.2 and Figure 3.2.

To summarize, we can say the following:

Changes in price result in **changes in the quantity demanded** (i.e., movements *along* the demand curve).

Changes in the nonprice determinants result in **changes in demand** (i.e., *shifts* in the demand curve).

This difference can be seen in Table 3.2 in the following manner. At the price of $5 the quantity demanded in the first list of responses (Q_{D1}) is 200. If the price drops to $4, then the *quantity demanded* increases to 300. However, if the *demand* increases to Q_{D2}, then at the price of $5 the quantity increases to 300 and in fact increases by 100 units at each of the prices being offered.

Table 3.2
Different Levels of
Market Demand
for Pizza

PRICE (PER SLICE)	Q_{D1}	Q_{D2}	Q_{D3}
$7.00	0	100	0
6.00	100	200	0
5.00	200	300	100
4.00	300	400	200
3.00	400	500	300
2.00	500	600	400
1.00	600	700	500
0	700	800	600

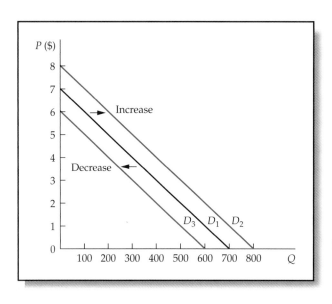

Figure 3.2
Shifts in the Market Demand
for Pizza

Factors that can cause demand to change are called **nonprice determinants of demand.** Following is a list of these determinants and a brief elaboration of their impact on demand.

1. *Tastes and preferences.* Why do people buy things? Marketing professors, corporate market researchers, and advertising executives spend their careers trying to answer this question. Economists use a general-purpose category in their list of nonprice determinants called *tastes and preferences* to account for the personal likes and dislikes of consumers for various goods and services. These tastes and preferences may themselves be affected by other factors. Advertising, promotions, and even government reports can have profound effects on demand via their impacts on people's tastes and preferences for a particular good or service.

2. *Income.* As people's incomes rise, it is reasonable to expect their demand for a product to increase and vice versa. In the next chapter, the possibility of demand moving in the *opposite direction* to changes in income will be discussed.

3. *Prices of related products.* A good or service can be related to another by being a substitute or by being a complement. If the price of a substitute product changes, we expect the demand for the good under consideration to change in the *same direction* as the change in the substitute's price. Consider, for example, what would happen to the demand for software if the price of computer hardware falls, or to the demand for compact discs if the price of CD players falls. It is reasonable to expect that the demand for the two items would *rise* as a result of a *fall* in the price of their respective *complementary* products.

4. *Future expectations.* If enough buyers expect the price of a good or service to rise (fall) in the future, it may cause the current demand to increase (decrease). In markets for various financial instruments (e.g., stocks, bonds, negotiable certificates of deposit, U.S. Treasury bills, etc.) as well as for agricultural commodities and precious metals, expectations of future price changes among both buyers and sellers play an important part in determining the market demand. In most

of these types of markets, speculation among buyers and sellers is an important factor to consider. Buyers and sellers act on a current price of a product not for its immediate consumption but because of the possibility of gaining from some future transaction. (Recall the old adage "buy low and sell high.") In fact, for most of these products, a sizable and growing *futures* market has emerged, in which buyers and sellers conduct transactions for these products at some agreed-upon future date. Naturally, expectations of future price movements have an impact on the supply and demand for the future delivery of a commodity. In turn, movements of futures prices could have an impact on the current (also called "spot") supply and demand for the commodity.

This factor can also affect the demand for consumer and commercial products. For example, the demand for DVD recorders, digital cameras, home entertainment systems, laptop computers, and personal digital assistants was probably not as high as sellers expected when these products were first introduced, because buyers were waiting for their prices to come down at a later time.

5. *Number of buyers.* The impact of the number of buyers on demand should be apparent; as far as sellers are concerned, the more the merrier. What is interesting, nonetheless, is how changing demographics and tastes and preferences within demographic groups can affect the pool of potential buyers for a particular good or service. In other words, sheer numbers (i.e., population) may not be as important as differences within the population. For example, the tracking of the baby boom generation from childhood to adulthood and eventually to retirement age has proven to be a fascinating study for market researchers. One can plainly see the impact on the demand for such items as children's apparel, furniture, and toys during the 1950s and 1960s, when this group was growing up.

As the baby boomers grew into their teen years, the demand for such items as records, stereos, certain types of cars, and admissions to movie theaters went up accordingly. Market researchers are now busy contemplating the impact on the demand for an assortment of goods and services—from health care to retirement condominiums—that will stem from the "graying" of this segment of the population.

We will discuss further how changes in these factors change demand and market price. But first we must introduce the concept of supply. By combining supply with demand, we can conduct a complete analysis of the market, both in the short run and in the long run.

MARKET SUPPLY

The **supply** of a good or service is defined as

> *Quantities* of a good or service that people are ready to *sell* at various *prices* within some given *time period, other factors* besides price held constant.

Notice that the only difference between this definition and that of demand is that in this case the word *sell* is used instead of *buy.* Just as in the case of demand, supply is

Table 3.3
Market Supply
for Pizza

P	Q_{S1}	Q_{S2}	Q_{S3}
$7	600	700	500
6	500	600	400
5	400	500	300
4	300	400	200
3	200	300	100
2	100	200	0
1	0	100	0
0	0	0	0

based on an assumed length of time within which price and the other factors can affect the **quantity supplied.**

Recall that the law of demand states that the quantity demanded is related inversely to price, other factors held constant. On the other hand, the law of supply states that quantity supplied is related *directly* to price, other factors held constant. Thus, any schedule of numbers representing a relationship between price and quantity supplied would show a *decrease* in the quantity supplied as price falls.

Table 3.3 shows a hypothetical supply schedule. Also shown are two additional supply schedules, one indicating a greater supply and the other showing a reduced supply. These schedules are shown as supply curves in Figure 3.3. The supply curve has a positive slope, reflecting the direct relationship between price and quantity supplied.

In analyzing the supply side of the market, it is important to make the distinction between *quantity supplied* and *supply.* The distinction between these two terms is the same as that used for the demand side of the market:

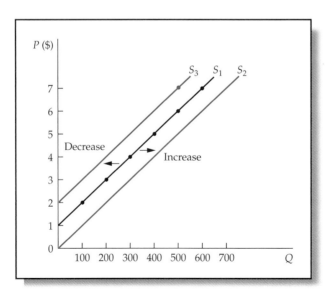

Figure 3.3
Supply Curves for Pizza

Managerial Economics

Changes in *price* result in **changes in the quantity supplied** (i.e., movements along the supply curve).

Changes in *nonprice determinants* result in **changes in the supply** (i.e., shifts of the supply curve).

Just as there are nonprice determinants of demand, there are **nonprice determinants of supply.** A change in any one or a combination of these factors will change market supply (i.e., cause the supply line to shift to the right or the left). Let us briefly discuss each factor to understand why this is expected to happen.

1. *Costs and technology.* The two factors of costs and technology can be treated as one because they are so closely related. *Costs* refer to the usual costs of production, such as labor costs, costs of materials, rent, interest payments, depreciation charges, and general and administrative expenses—in other words, all of the items usually found in a firm's income statement. *Technology* refers to technological innovations or improvements introduced to reduce the unit cost of production (e.g., automation, robotics, and computer hardware and software utilization). Technological changes that result in entirely new products for final consumption are not considered part of this category. These new products would have to be considered in an entirely different market analysis. In any event, unit cost reductions, whether from technological innovations or simply management decisions, will result in an increase in market supply. Increases in the unit cost of production will have the opposite effect.

2. *Prices of other goods or services offered by the seller.* From the consumer's standpoint, any good or service has other goods or services related to it either as substitutes or as complements. From the producer's standpoint, there can also be substitutes or complements for a particular good or service offered in the market. For example, suppose the sellers of pizza notice that the price of hot dogs increases substantially. In the extreme case, they may drop their line of pizza and substitute hot dogs. Or they may at least reduce the amount of resources (e.g., labor and store space) devoted to the selling of pizza in favor of hot dogs. In either case, the market supply of pizza would decrease. If the sellers were already selling two (or more) products, the change in market conditions would prompt them to reallocate their resources toward the more profitable products. (Given this possibility, it may be more appropriate to say that the sellers consider pizza and hot dogs as "competing" products rather than as "substitute" products.)

3. *Future expectations.* This factor has a similar impact on sellers as on buyers; the only difference is the direction of the change. For example, if sellers anticipate a rise in price, they may choose to hold back the current supply to take advantage of the higher future price, thus decreasing market supply. As we discussed in the section on demand, an expected rise in price will increase the current demand for a product.

4. *Number of sellers.* Clearly, the number of sellers has a direct impact on supply. The more sellers, the greater the market supply.

5. *Weather conditions.* Bad weather (e.g., floods, droughts, unusual seasonal temperatures) will reduce the supply of an agricultural commodity. Good weather will have the opposite impact.

With this discussion of supply, we are now able to combine supply with demand into a complete analysis of the market.

MARKET EQUILIBRIUM

Now that we have reviewed the definitions and mechanics of demand and supply, we are ready to examine their interaction in the market. Market demand and supply are compared in Table 3.4 and Figure 3.4.

You can see in both the table and the graph that at the price of $4, the market is cleared in the sense that the quantity demanded (300) is equal to the quantity supplied (300). Thus, $4 is called the **equilibrium price,** and 300 is referred to as the **equilibrium quantity.** Another way to view this market situation is to imagine what would happen if the price were not at the equilibrium level. For example, suppose the price were at a higher level, say $5. At this price, as you can see in Table 3.4 the quantity supplied would exceed the quantity demanded, a condition called a **surplus.** At a lower price, say $3, the situation is reversed: The quantity demanded exceeds the quantity supplied. This situation is called a **shortage.** Both the surplus and the shortage conditions are indicated in Figure 3.4.

In the event of a surplus or a shortage, various competitive pressures cause the price to change (decrease in the case of a surplus, and increase in the event of a shortage). The price thus serves to clear the market of the imbalance. The clearing process continues until equilibrium (i.e., quantity demanded equals quantity supplied) is arrived at. In the case of a surplus, sellers wishing to rid themselves of the extra items offer the product at a lower price to induce people to buy more. At the same time, as the price falls, suppliers are discouraged from offering as much as before. In the case of a market shortage, as the price rises toward the equilibrium level, the market is cleared because the quantity demanded decreases while the quantity supplied increases. In the event of a shortage, sellers try to take advantage of the situation by raising their prices, and people are thus discouraged from buying as much as before. Also, sellers are induced to offer a greater number of items in the market. Both actions serve to clear the market of a shortage.

Table 3.4

Supply and Demand for Pizza

P	Q_D	Q_S
$7	0	600
6	100	500
5	200	400
→4	300	300
3	400	200
2	500	100
1	600	0
0	700	0

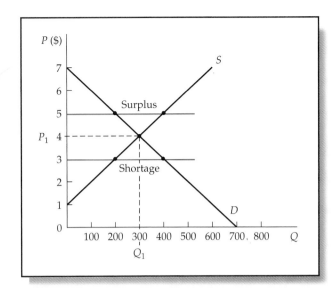

Figure 3.4
Supply and Demand Curves
for Pizza, Indicating Market
Equilibrium

To summarize the material in this section, remember the following definitions:

Equilibrium price: The price that equates the quantity demanded with the quantity supplied; (i.e., the price that clears the market of a surplus or shortage).

Equilibrium quantity: The amount that people are willing to buy and sellers are willing to offer at the equilibrium price level.

Shortage: A market situation in which the quantity demanded exceeds the quantity supplied, *at a price below the equilibrium level.*

Surplus: A market situation in which the quantity supplied exceeds the quantity demanded, *at a price above the equilibrium level.*

COMPARATIVE STATICS ANALYSIS

The model of market demand, supply, and equilibrium price and quantity developed in the preceding sections can now be used to analyze the market. The particular method of analysis we will use is called *comparative statics analysis.* This is a commonly used method in economic analysis and will be used throughout the text. In general, this method of analysis proceeds as follows:

1. State all the assumptions needed to construct the model.
2. Begin by assuming that the model is in equilibrium.
3. Introduce a change in the model. In so doing, a condition of disequilibrium is created.
4. Find the new point at which equilibrium is restored.
5. Compare the new equilibrium point with the original one.

In effect, comparative statics analysis is a form of sensitivity analysis, or what business people often refer to as *what-if* analysis. For example, if we were doing a what-if analysis of a company's cash flow, we would start with a given pro forma income statement adjusted to provide the cash flow for a given period of time. We would then conduct sensitivity analysis by supposing that certain factors changed, such as revenue, cost, or the rate of depreciation. We would then inspect how changes in these factors would change the cash flow of the firm over time. In the same manner, economists conduct a what-if analysis of their models.

The term *statics* alludes to the theoretically stable point of equilibrium, and *comparative* refers to the comparison of the various points of equilibrium. The ensuing sections will explain exactly how comparative statics analysis is used in the analysis of the market.

MODULE 3A

Short-Run Market Changes: The "Rationing Function" of Price

Let us continue with our analysis of pizza. Following the steps involved in comparative statics analysis, we start by assuming that all factors except the price of pizza are held constant, and the various patterns of response to price among buyers and sellers are represented by the supply and demand lines in Figure 3.4. We make a fresh start by redrawing this graph in Figure 3.5. It would also be useful to recall all of the non-price determinants that could affect the demand or supply for a product. They are listed for you in Table 3.5.

As noted in step 2 in the previous section, we begin this analysis in the condition of equilibrium. This is denoted in Figure 3.5 as the point where the supply line intersects with the D_1 demand line (i.e., the price level where quantity supplied is equal to quantity demanded).

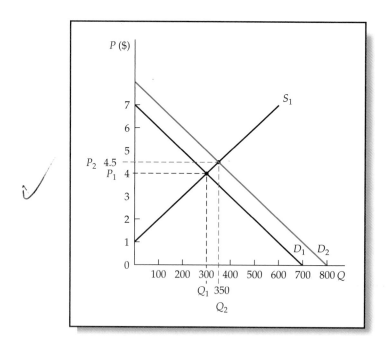

Figure 3.5
Increase in Demand for Pizza and Resulting Impact on Market Equilibrium

Table 3.5
Nonprice Determinants of Demand and Supply

DEMAND	SUPPLY
1. Tastes and preferences	1. Costs and technology
2. Income	2. Prices of other products offered
3. Prices of related products	3. Future expectations among sellers
4. Future expectations among buyers	4. Number of sellers
5. Number of buyers	5. Weather conditions (particularly for agricultural products)

Based on step 3 we introduce a change in one or more of the assumptions made when the model was constructed. Any one or more of the factors shown in Table 3.5 can cause this change. Let us assume that a new government study shows pizza to be the most nutritious of all fast foods and that consumers substantially increase their demand for pizza as a result of this study. In Figure 3.5, this increase is represented by a shift in the demand curve from D_1 to D_2. As you can see, this shift results in a new, higher equilibrium price of $4.50. Notice also that the new equilibrium quantity is greater than the original equilibrium quantity.

The comparison of the new equilibrium point with the original one (step 5 in comparative statics analysis) leads us to conclude that, as a result of a change in tastes and preferences, the price of pizza rises, and so does the quantity bought and sold.

This analysis can be repeated using other possible changes in market conditions (e.g., the price of cheese rises, the price of soft drinks falls). Each time, the same procedure should be followed. If we consider only one possible change at a time, the effects on equilibrium price and quantity can be illustrated as in Figure 3.6. Instead of using specific numbers, we have designated the prices and quantities with the symbols P and Q along with appropriate subscripts. We can summarize the effects shown in the graphs as follows:

An increase in demand causes equilibrium price and quantity to rise. (See Figure 3.6a.)

A decrease in demand causes equilibrium price and quantity to fall. (See Figure 3.6b.)

An increase in supply causes equilibrium price to fall and quantity to rise. (See Figure 3.6c.)

A decrease in supply causes equilibrium price to rise and quantity to fall. (See Figure 3.6d.)

In Figure 3.6 we observe that the shift in demand or supply has in effect created either a shortage or a surplus at the original price P_1. Thus, the equilibrium price has to rise or fall to clear the market. When the market price changes to eliminate the imbalance between quantities supplied and demanded, it is serving what economists call the **rationing function of price.** The term *rationing* is often associated with shortages, but we have defined it to include a surplus situation as well.

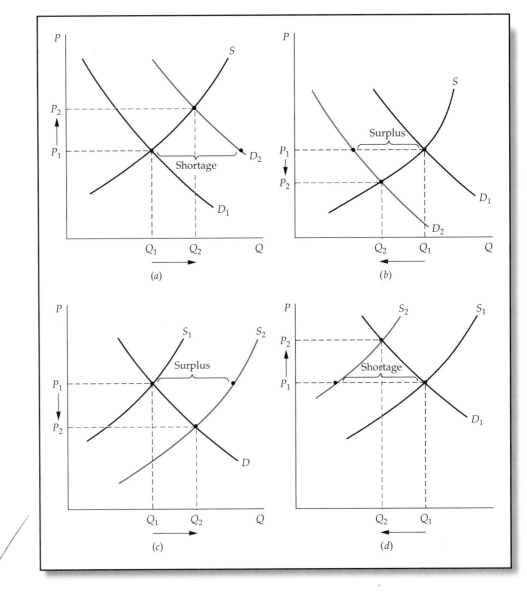

Figure 3.6
Changes in Supply and Demand and Their Short-Run Impact on Market
Equilibrium (the Rationing Function of Price)

Long-Run Market Analysis: The "Guiding" or "Allocating Function" of Price

The comparative statics analysis presented earlier required only that you consider the response of equilibrium price and quantity to a given change in supply or demand. This response was dubbed the "rationing function" of price. Let us consider what might happen as a result of this change in market price. To illustrate this, we shall examine the market for hot dogs, a presumed substitute for pizza. The two markets are represented by the supply and demand diagrams in Figure 3.7.

Now let us assume that at the same time people's tastes and preferences change in favor of pizza, their tastes and preferences become more adverse to hot dogs (e.g., for health reasons). The changes in the demand for the two products are shown in Figure 3.7 by a downward shift in the demand for hot dogs and an upward shift in the demand for pizza (D_1 to D_2). This would cause a shortage in the pizza market and a surplus in the hot dog market. But as we know, the rationing function of price will immediately start to correct these market imbalances. As the price of hot dogs falls, the surplus is eliminated; as the price of pizza rises, the shortage is eliminated. (For the purpose of the analysis, it really does not matter where the price of pizza stands in relation to the price of hot dogs. To simplify matters, we have assumed that the two prices were about equal before the change in tastes and preferences occurred. The point is that after price performs its rationing function, the equilibrium price of pizza will be higher than the equilibrium price of hot dogs in relative terms.)

Now suppose that the prices have indeed changed, and the two markets are once again in equilibrium. What do you suppose will happen next? As you might well imagine, the depressed price of hot dogs will cause the sellers to begin allocating less of their resources to this market. Some may even go out of the business of making or selling hot dogs. On the other hand, the higher price of pizza will induce the allocation of more resources into this market. New pizza stands and restaurants may be opened. Food companies may build new plants to produce frozen pizza for distribution through supermarkets. The effect of these follow-on adjustments to the initial

Figure 3.7
Short-Run and Long-Run Changes in Supply (in Response to an Initial Change in Demand)

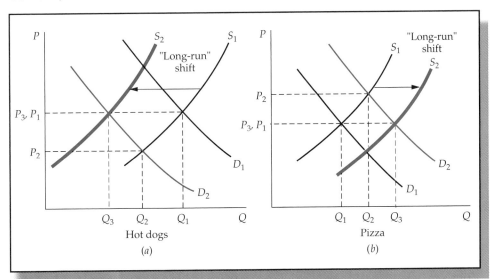

change in equilibrium prices can be seen in the figure as a rightward shift in the supply of pizza and a leftward shift in the supply of hot dogs.

After this "long-run" adjustment is made, equilibrium price and quantity may well return to the levels at which they were before the initial changes in demand took place (i.e., P_3 in each market may be close to or equal to P_1). But the main point is that Q_3 is considerably less than Q_1 in the hot dog market and considerably more than Q_1 in the pizza market. These differences represent the shifting of resources out of the hot dog market and into the pizza market. Several centuries ago, Adam Smith referred to this shifting of resources into and out of markets in response to price changes as the "invisible hand."[1] Another way to express these shifts in supply is that they represent a response to "price signals" sent to the owners of the factors of production. In any event, when resources have been shifted out of the market for hot dogs and into the market for pizza, price is fulfilling its **guiding** or **allocating function.** Defined in a more formal manner, the guiding or allocating function of price is the movement of resources into or out of markets in response to a change in the equilibrium price of a good or service.

The preceding example illustrates a basic distinction made in economic analysis between the "short run" and the "long run." This distinction has nothing to do directly with a specific calendar time. Instead, it refers to the amount of time it takes for sellers and buyers to react to changes in the market equilibrium price. The following descriptions of the short run and the long run will help readers distinguish the two time periods.

1. **Short run**
   a. Period of time in which sellers already in the market respond to a change in equilibrium price by adjusting the amount of certain resources, which economists call *variable inputs.* Examples of such inputs are labor hours and raw materials. A short-run adjustment by sellers can be envisioned as a movement along a particular supply curve.
   b. Period of time in which buyers already in the market respond to changes in equilibrium price by adjusting the quantity demanded for a particular good or service. A short-run adjustment by buyers can be envisioned as a movement along a particular demand curve.

2. **Long run**
   a. Period of time in which new sellers may enter a market or the original sellers may exit from a market. This period is long enough for existing sellers to either increase or decrease their *fixed factors* of production. Examples of fixed factors include property, plant, and equipment. A long-run adjustment by sellers can be seen graphically as a shift in a given supply curve.
   b. Period of time in which buyers may react to a change in equilibrium price by changing their tastes and preferences or buying patterns. (*The Wall Street Journal* and other sources of business news may refer to this as a "structural change" in demand.) A long-run adjustment by buyers can be seen graphically as a shift in a given demand curve.

---

[1] For Smith, the "visible" hand was that of the government, which might try to dictate the allocation of resources among different markets by the command process rather than by the market process.

Another good way of distinguishing the short run from the long run is to note that the rationing function of price is a short-run phenomenon, whereas the guiding function is a long-run phenomenon.

Let us summarize the short-run "rationing function" and the long run "guiding function" of price in terms of our example involving pizza and hot dogs:

1. Changing tastes and preferences cause the demand for pizza to increase and the demand for hot dogs to decrease.
2. The changing demand for the two products causes a shortage in the pizza market and a surplus in the hot dog market.
3. In response to the surplus and shortage in the two markets, price serves as a *rationing* agent by decreasing in the hot dog market and increasing in the pizza market. That is, the short-run response by suppliers of the two products is to change their variable inputs (i.e., movement downward along the supply line in the market for hot dogs, and movement upward along the supply line in the market for pizza).
4. In the *long run*, price fulfills its *guiding* function by causing sellers and potential sellers to respond by increasing capacity or entering the market for pizza and by decreasing capacity or leaving the market for hot dogs (i.e., rightward shift in the supply line for pizza and leftward shift in the supply line for hot dogs).
5. As a result of the shifts in supply, new equilibrium levels of price and quantity are established. The new quantities bought and sold represent shifts in resources out of one market and into the other.

The distinction between short- and long-run changes in the market can also be made in cases that begin with changes in supply rather than in demand. One of the best examples is the case of the Organization of Petroleum Exporting Countries (OPEC) and the world oil market. A complete analysis of this case is beyond the scope of this text. However, the headline of an article in *Newsweek* perhaps best sums up the activities in this market in the decade following the OPEC's major price hike in late 1973: "OPEC, Meet Adam Smith."[2] This reference to the great classical economist Adam Smith pertained to his concept of the "invisible hand," or the guiding function of price.

OPEC conspired to raise the price of oil by limiting production to an amount that would support a price above the current level. The supply-and-demand diagram shown in Figure 3.8 illustrates this action. As we can see, limiting the production of oil can be envisioned as a leftward shift in the supply line to the level where it intersects the demand curve for oil at some designated point above the current market price (i.e., P_2 rather than P_1). The short-run response by consumers to the increase in oil prices was to cut back their consumption of oil. But in the terms specific to our analysis, this reduction can be seen as a decrease in the *quantity demanded* for oil. In other words, the decrease in the supply of oil (i.e., the shift of supply line to the left) prompted a *movement back along the demand curve* for oil.

However, over time consumers began to change their pattern of consumption of oil. They formed car pools, they bought more fuel-efficient cars, they turned their

---

[2]*Newsweek,* October 29, 1984, p. 93.

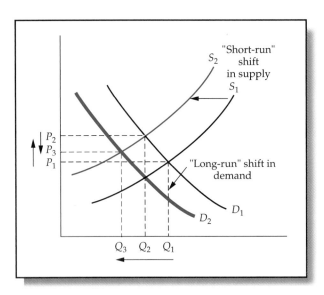

Figure 3.8
Short-Run and Long-Run
Changes in Demand (in
Response to an Initial
Change in Supply)

thermostats down in their homes, and they even tried to follow the new 55 mph speed limit established on highways throughout the country. Industrial users of oil responded by substituting more fuel-efficient machinery as soon as it became cost-efficient to make these changes. The effect of this *long-run* change in the pattern of oil usage was to cause the demand for oil to gradually fall. Graphically, this is represented by a leftward shift of the demand curve for oil from D_1 to D_2. Notice that as a result of this long-run shift in demand, the equilibrium price and quantity fell. As seen in Figure 3.8, the long-run quantity that is bought and sold (i.e., Q_3) was now even less than it was before this decrease in demand took place. This indicates a further shift of resources out of this market.

As in the case of pizza and hot dogs, price fulfilled its short-run rationing function as well as its long-run guiding function. When the supply line for oil first shifted to the left—in large part due to the OPEC conspiracy—a shortage was created. This imbalance forced the market price up to clear the market of this shortage. The higher price served as a signal to buyers to change their consumption pattern for oil, that is, to become more economical in their use of oil.

Thus, price served to reallocate an economy's resources in the sense that the buyer's long-run response was to rely more on resources other than those in the oil market. In fact, a sizable portion of these alternative resources involved the production of goods and services that helped people to reduce their consumption of oil. For example, resources were shifted into the production of fuel-efficient cars and machinery, wood-burning stoves, kerosene heaters, firewood, sweaters, and flannel pajamas.

An additional facet of this long-run, guiding function of price can be observed. In retrospect, OPEC's efforts to raise the world price of oil by deliberately reducing the supply made it possible for non-OPEC oil producers to justify such projects as drilling for oil in the North Sea and Alaska. Moreover, the oil-producing efforts of Mexico were encouraged by the rising oil prices. Over the long run, these additional

Table 3.6
Short-Run and Long-Run Changes in the Market

INITIAL CHANGE (SHORT-RUN TIME PERIOD)	FOLLOW-ON CHANGE (LONG-RUN TIME PERIOD)
Increase in demand causes *price to rise*	*Supply increases* as new sellers enter the market and original sellers increase production capacity
Decrease in demand causes *price to fall*	*Supply decreases* as less profitable firms or those experiencing losses exit the market or decrease production capacity
Increase in supply causes *price to fall*	*Demand increases* as tastes and preferences of consumers eventually change in favor of the product relative to substitutes
Decrease in supply causes *price to rise*	*Demand decreases* as tastes and preferences of consumers eventually change away from the product and toward the substitutes

sources increased the world's supply of oil, putting further pressures on OPEC to limit their supply to keep oil prices from falling.[3]

Because the distinction between short- and the long-run changes in the market is such an essential part of manager's understanding of the workings of the market process, we present one last review of these changes in Table 3.6.

Using Supply and Demand in Forecasting

Chapter 6 is devoted to the topic of forecasting. But we should point out here that a fundamental part of economic forecasting is to understand the nature of the determinants of supply and demand. It is relatively easier to forecast supply than it is to forecast demand. To forecast supply, one essentially needs to assess the current and future capacity of the producers. In manufacturing, this can be done by literally counting the number of factories in operation among suppliers and estimating their capacity utilization rates. The more difficult challenge is to estimate demand. As you will see in chapters 5 and 6, economists rely on statistical analysis of historical data to understand the determinants of demand and to predict the movement of demand based on the estimated relationship between these determinants and the quantity demanded of a particular good or service. But the problem is that it may be difficult to forecast movements in the determinants themselves. For example, in estimating consumer demand, consumer tastes and preferences may shift in sudden or unexpected ways. The demand for capital goods (e.g., machinery, equipment) as well as the raw materials that go into the making of the consumer items (e.g., plastics and

---

[3]The Gulf crisis in 1990 caused a temporary rise in oil prices. As the situation stabilized, oil prices fell to their precrisis level.

paper products) is derived from the demand for final consumer goods. So forecasting their demand is dependent on the vagaries of the demand for consumer goods.

In addition, the demand for specific consumer and capital goods is in many instances sensitive to changes in aggregate demand. For almost a decade, this macro-economic factor was not considered to be very important—at least not in the United States—but quickly became an important determinant of demand with the advent of the recession that began in early 2001. The semiconductor industry provides an excellent example of the importance of understanding the determinants of both supply and demand in trying to forecast market price. It also demonstrates the difficulties of forecasting demand and the impact of the aggregated demand compared with forecasting the supply side of the market. We discuss this in great detail in chapter 16.

SUPPLY, DEMAND, AND MANAGERIAL DECISION MAKING

The forces of supply and demand affect the business decisions of all firms in a competitive market economy. In the extreme case, these forces are the sole determinants of the market price. More will be said about this type of market in chapter 9. But for now, readers should realize that managers operating in this type of market earn a profit by making decisions about the allocation of resources based on their short- and long-run assessment of the movements of supply, demand, and prices. Examples of managers who must make decisions in this market environment are Ross Harris in our "Situation" and the managers who must purchase coffee beans on the world market (see "International Application: What's the Highest Profit Item at Starbucks?" later in this chapter).

There are other types of competitive markets in which firms exercise varying degrees of control over the price of their product. Economists refer to this type of control as **market power.** While supply and demand establish the overall framework in which prices are established, individual firms can exert market power over their price, because of their dominant size in the market or because of their ability to differentiate their product through advertising, brand names, and special features.

When firms do exercise market power, it is important for their managers to understand market demand on two levels. First, there is the overall demand for the product that is offered by all sellers in the market. This is what we have been calling *market demand* throughout this chapter. Second, there is the demand by buyers for the product that is being offered by a particular firm. We can call this the *firm* or *company demand.* Up to this point in the chapter the focus has been primarily on market demand. In this section, we offer several examples of why it is important for managers to understand the firm-specific demand for their product as well as the overall market demand.

In the early 1990s, Gerber, then the leading manufacturer of baby food in the United States, invested about $25 million in the purchase and renovation of a juice plant in Rzeszow, an out-of-the-way town in southern Poland, in order to produce baby food for a market that *The New York Times* described as a "sheer dream." This was because "Polish babies had never sampled the even consistency of specially processed food from a jar." Gerber also spent a considerable amount of time and money training Polish workers to achieve American standards of food quality. (For example, Polish workers had to be constantly monitored for smoking on the factory floor.) But once the manufacturing capacity was in place and the product quality had been established, consumers were not responding as expected.

As it turned out, Polish mothers perceived store-bought baby food as inferior to what they could prepare themselves for their babies. Several women who were interviewed expressed the sentiment that their mothers took the time and trouble to prepare the food for them and they could not conceive of doing anything less for their babies. The statistics tell the story. The annual per baby consumption of prepared food in the United States is 622 jars. In Poland it is 12.[4] Given this unfortunate experience in Poland, it was not surprising to learn that in 1994, Gerber was purchased by Sandoz, a large Swiss multinational pharmaceutical company.

Another good example of a company failing to understand the demand for its product is Schwinn. In the prosperous 1950s and 1960s, Schwinn dominated the bicycle market in the United States. However, starting in the late 1970s, mountain bikes became increasingly more popular. Schwinn completely missed this trend. Besides being unresponsive to this change in demand, Schwinn also did not adequately prepare for changes in the supply side of this market. During this same period of time, lower-priced bikes made in Asian countries began to appear in increasing numbers in bicycle shops and toy stores throughout the United States. This failure to understand and respond to changes in demand and supply led to Schwinn's filing for bankruptcy in 1992. A year later, buoyed by a new management and the protection of Chapter 11, it began to offer a rejuvenated line of bikes, including the popular mountain bike.[5]

In the latter half of the 1990s the new owners of Schwinn repositioned the company as a fitness and recreation company, calling itself "Schwinn Cycling and Fitness, Inc." In so doing, it adjusted to a number of changes in demand for fitness and exercise. In the decade of the 1990s, "working out" for people in their 20s and 30s has become an integral part of their lives starting from college and continuing on to the workplace. Furthermore, aging baby boomers, with their increased discretionary incomes and desire to remain healthy and fit, are a large part of the demand for health club services as well as for exercise equipment that they can use at home.

But at the same time, supply has also increased relative to the demand. There are many more fitness centers and makers of exercise equipment than there were in the past. In an effort to differentiate themselves, manufacturers such as Schwinn are constantly trying to find new types of equipment and exercise routines to offer customers. In addition to its line of road and mountain bikes, the company now produces one of the more popular lines of indoor-stationary cycles. A visit to a typical health club on a Saturday morning will find the "spinning classes"[6] full of stationary bike enthusiasts imagining that they are somewhere on a leg of the Tour de France who are being encouraged to "burn" by a trained leader who is probably also an aerobics instructor.

---

[4]"In Poland, Gerber Learns the Lesson of Tradition," *The New York Times,* November 8, 1993.
[5]"Pump, Pump, Pump at Schwinn," *Business Week,* August 23, 1993, p. 79.
[6]"Spinning" is a registered trademark of Schwinn so other terms are used when other manufacturers' equipment are involved.

Recently, Schwinn has made another business decision in response to the aging baby boomer market. To commemorate 100 years of technical innovation, the company decided to produce the original "Black Phantom," first sold in 1949. This is what the company's Web site had to say about this product:

> Before we could build a single Phantom, we had to build just over a million bucks worth of tools. . . . With their gleaming chrome, integrated headlight, frame mounted horn tank, wide leather saddle and Schwinn Typhoon balloon tires, the original Phantoms represent the emergence of style and sophistication that had never been seen before.[7]

The retail price of this tribute to nostalgia is about $2,500.

One of the lessons learned from the Schwinn case is the need for suppliers to assess the supply and demand conditions in the market, particularly in the long run. Referring back to our supply and demand diagrams, it is one thing to increase the quantity supplied in response to higher demand and prices. It is quite another to commit resources over the long term, thereby causing the supply curve itself to shift. If the higher demand is not sustained, or if too many others enter or add capacity, a company's growth strategy could fail. Already there are at least three other makers of stationary bikes, including sneaker manufacturer Reebok, although Schwinn still has the lead in market share.

In Schwinn's case, going from a nearly bankrupt condition in the early 1990s to one of the most dominant producers of bicycles in the world in less than 10 years required a strong belief that the long-run demand for mountain bikes and exercise equipment would be sustained. It also required management's willingness to spend enough money on research and development and plant and equipment to capture a large part of this growing demand. Because it is a privately held company, it is difficult to find figures to show the extent of their financial success, but in 1997 the company purchased its arch rival, GT, for $90 million. This should be an indication of how well the company is doing.[8]

A recent visit to Schwinn's Web site showed that the company continues to position itself as a "health and fitness company" rather than just one that makes and sells bikes. It even has started a "Fitness Academy" where interested parties can obtain information on health and fitness and can take part in various company-sponsored programs and activities.

INTERNATIONAL APPLICATION: WHAT'S THE HIGHEST PROFIT ITEM AT STARBUCKS?

"Anyone that is able to convince millions of people to spend $3.50 on a cup of coffee is a marketing genius." You have probably heard or read quotes stating something to this effect about Howard Shultz, founder and CEO of Starbucks. The profit margin

[7]Retrieved October 2, 1998, from the Schwinn corporate Web site: www.schwinn.com/collector/bphantom.html.
[8]Some of the details of Schwinn's turnaround strategy were learned in an interview with a Schwinn retail distributor in Brewster, NY, September 1998.

on a "tall, skim latte," is undoubtedly high. But have you ever noticed how prominent the display of beans is in your favorite Starbucks? In any specialty coffee house or retail site, a bag of beans, whole or ground, is also a very high-margin item. If Starbucks sells you a 16 oz. bag of whole or ground coffee beans for $9.99, and up, what does it pay wholesale? Fortunately for companies like Starbucks and unfortunately for coffee growers, not very much, especially in comparison to typical retail prices today.

There are basically two types of beans that become the coffee you drink: robusta and arabica. The former is a lower quality, somewhat bitter type of bean. It currently sells in the world market for about $380 a ton (about $.20 a pound). Arabica is the higher grade bean and it is quoted in commodity markets on a per-pound, rather than per-ton basis. Brazil is the world's largest producer of coffee beans and produces both robusta and arabica. But recently, Vietnam became the world's largest exporter of robusta beans. In recent years there has been an oversupply of robusta beans (thanks in large part to the surge in Vietnam's coffee production). Brazil is not affected as much because falling coffee prices have been cushioned by the falling value of the *real,* the Brazilian monetary unit. (World market prices are quoted and contracts paid for in U.S. dollars.) The country that is being hit hard is Vietnam. The Vietnamese government is trying to convince farmers to reduce their production of robusta and shift to arabica in order to secure better profit margins. But Doan Trieu Nhan, chairman of Vietnam's Coffee and Cocoa Association, said that it is difficult because "We have a policy of democracy in production and commerce. What to plant and what to eradicate depends on the resolution of farmers."

But as you know from reading this chapter, as producers shift from robusta to arabica in search of higher profits, their very actions cause a shift in supply and downward pressures on arabica prices. During 2001, the average price of "C" market coffee (this refers to the benchmark Arabica futures contract that trades in New York) fell by almost 50 percent, from about $.90 a pound to slightly less than $.50 a pound.[9] Costa Rican coffee growers recognized this and are trying to respond accordingly. According to Arnoldo Leiva, vice president of the Specialty Coffee Association of Costa Rica, "[we] cannot compete with countries like Brazil and Vietnam on price. We have to do so on quality." Costa Rican coffee growers began concentrating on producing the highest quality Arabica beans. Moreover, a consortium of six leading coffee growers was formed to sell directly to coffee-roasting importers, thereby eliminating middleman mark-ups. In 2001, Starbucks bought the entire 7,000 bags that this consortium produced for $1.20 a pound. So let us assume a 16 oz. bag of the finest Costa Rican arabica is sold at your local Starbucks for about $10. We figure this to yield a gross profit margin of about 88 percent, slightly lower if you include roasting and packaging. Now you know why you are surrounded by bags of beans at Starbucks.

---

[9]This statistic is cited in "Where coffee is the new wine," *Financial Times,* February 1, 2002. Information and direct quotes for this section come from this article as well as from "Commodities & Agriculture: Vietnam tackles coffee crisis: Plans include reducing acreage and expanding Arabica production," *Financial Times,* January 29, 2002.

The Solution

In his presentation to the management committee, Ross Harris recommended that Global Foods, Inc., acquiesce to the HFCS manufacturers' request to negotiate a pricing and delivery contract on a quarterly basis. "Based on our current projections of demand and supply, we believe that there will be a slight upward trend in HFCS prices in the short run," Ross began. "This means that if we negotiate on a quarterly basis, we may have to pay a bit more for the product, because the negotiated price will reflect the underlying supply and demand conditions in the market. However, if we bought the product in the spot market, we would be operating in an extremely volatile environment. In our business, I strongly believe that continuity of supply and the quality of the product are just as important as the price. By negotiating a contract with the suppliers, we are assured of at least a minimum amount of high-quality product at the contracted price. If we order too much, we can always sell the surplus to other companies in the food industry. If we do not order enough, we can always meet the shortage by purchasing product in the spot market. As you all know, we currently handle our surpluses and shortages of HFCS in this manner. In fact, this is how we know that the product in the spot market is not always of top quality.

In talking to purchasing agents in the rest of the industry and with some of my contacts in the HFCS manufacturing business," Ross continued, "I am convinced that the HFCS companies are very adamant about setting the price on a quarterly basis. The volatility of supply-and-demand conditions in the market for corn has hurt their profit margins in the past, and they want greater flexibility in pricing the final product in order to compensate for the upward movements in the price of corn."

Ross made a final point. "I stated that our projections call for some upward trend in the price of HFCS in the near term. However, if we continue the present arrangement of negotiating the price with our suppliers—even if it is done on a quarterly rather than a yearly basis—we will be helping to preserve a relatively stable market environment in which they can project with greater certainty the future demand for HFCS. This will enable them to better plan for their manufacturing capacity requirements. In *the long run,* this should mean fewer chances of supply bottlenecks, shortages, and higher prices."

The report by Kathy Martinez was short and to the point. The market for corn was found to be typical of markets in which agricultural commodities were bought and sold. She presented a chart showing that these markets are characterized by *price volatility* brought on by frequent changes in supply and demand conditions.

Kathy went on to explain that in the market for corn in the United States, the major factors affecting supply are weather conditions, the output of corn in other countries, and the U.S. government's acreage control program. Another factor is the market for alternative uses for

(Continued)

corn. The supply available for the HFCS market depends on the supply and demand conditions for these alternative uses.

As far as the demand for HFCS is concerned, she noted that the major factor has been the soft drink industry's increasing use of the sweetener as a substitute for sugar. However, soft drink demand is subject to seasonal fluctuations, being the highest in the summer and lowest in the winter. Pricing on a yearly basis does not allow the flexibility to price according to these seasonal fluctuations. In particular, it does not allow prices to be raised in response to the increase in the summer demand for HFCS.

Kathy's report summarized the situation as follows. On the supply side, the price of corn, the major ingredient of HFCS, is very volatile. On the demand side, the major buyers of HFCS are the soft drink manufacturers, the makers of a product that has seen steady long-term growth, subject to seasonal fluctuations. Thus, HFCS manufacturers must try to protect themselves from adverse corn price fluctuations by establishing greater pricing flexibility vis-à-vis the customers responsible for the major part of the demand.

SUMMARY

This chapter has presented the basic elements of supply and demand. We began by introducing the *law of demand* and the *law of supply* and the nonprice factors that affect demand and supply. The law of demand states that, other factors held constant, the quantity demanded is inversely related to price. The law of supply states that, other factors held constant, the quantity supplied is directly related to price. Other factors that affect demand are (1) tastes and preferences, (2) income, (3) prices of related products, (4) number of buyers, and (5) future expectations. Other factors that affect supply are (1) costs, (2) technology, (3) prices of other products that sellers can supply, (4) number of sellers, (5) future expectations, and (6) weather conditions. Both numerical and graphical examples of supply and demand and how they interrelate to determine the equilibrium price and quantity were presented. The appendix to this chapter presents the same material in algebraic terms.

We studied how price serves a short-run rationing function and a long-run guiding function in the marketplace. Price serves a rationing function when it increases or decreases to clear the market of a shortage or surplus caused by a change in market conditions (i.e., a shifting of the supply or demand curve). Price changes serve as a guiding function signaling producers or consumers to put more or less of their resources in the affected markets.

In explaining the rationing and guiding functions of price, we noted the particular way in which economists define the short run and the long run. We also discussed how comparative statics analysis is used to explain the rationing and guiding functions of the price. This technique, involving the comparison of equilibrium points before and after changes in the market have occurred, is a standard way of analyzing problems and will be used throughout this text.

Change in demand: The result of a change in one or more of the nonprice determinants of demand, graphically represented by a *shift* in the demand curve (rightward for an increase in demand and leftward for a decrease in demand). (p. 81)

Change in supply: The result of a change in one or more of the nonprice determinants of supply, graphically represented by a *shift* in the supply curve (rightward for an increase and leftward for a decrease). (p. 85)

Change in the quantity demanded: The result of a change in the price of a good or service, graphically represented by a *movement along* a particular demand curve. (p. 81)

Change in the quantity supplied: The result of a change in the price of a good or service, graphically represented by a *movement along* a particular supply curve. (p. 85)

Demand: Quantities of a good or service that people are ready to buy at various prices, other factors besides the price held constant. Demand can be expressed as a numerical schedule, as a demand curve on a graph, or as an algebraic equation. (p. 79)

Equilibrium price: The price that equates the quantity demanded with the quantity supplied; the price that clears the market of any shortage or surplus. (p. 86)

Equilibrium quantity: The amount that people are ready to buy and sell at the equilibrium price level. (p. 86)

Guiding function of price: Also referred to as the *allocating function of price,* the movement of resources into or out of markets as a result of changes in the equilibrium market price. This is considered to be a long-run function. On the supply side of the market, sellers may enter or leave the market or may vary all of their factors of production. On the demand side, consumers may change their tastes or preferences or find long-lasting alternatives to a particular good or service. (p. 92)

Law of Demand: The quantity demanded depends *inversely* on price. (p. 80)

Long run: A time period in which new sellers may enter a market or sellers already in a market may leave. This time period is sufficient for both old and new sellers to vary *all* of their factors of production. From the standpoint of consumers, the long run provides time enough to respond to price changes by actually changing their tastes or preferences or their use of alternative goods and services. For example, suppose bad weather in Brazil results in an increase in the price of coffee. In the short run, people are expected to buy less coffee because of the higher price. However, in the long run, they may buy even less coffee because the higher price will have prompted them to drink more tea on a regular basis. (p. 92)

Market demand: The sum of all individual demands for a good or service. (p. 80)

Market power: The power to set the market price. (p. 96)

Nonprice determinants of demand: (1) Tastes and preferences, (2) income, (3) prices of related products (i.e., substitutes or complements), (4) future expectations, (5) number of buyers. (p. 82)

Nonprice determinants of supply: (1) Costs, (2) technology, (3) prices of other products that may be produced by a firm, (4) future expectations, (5) number of sellers, (6) weather conditions. (p. 85)

Quantity demanded: The amount that people are ready to buy at a given price. (p. 80)

Quantity supplied: The amount that people are ready to sell at a given price. (p. 84)

Rationing function of price: The increase or decrease in price to clear the market of any shortage or surplus. This is considered to be a short-run function because both buyers and sellers are expected to respond only to price changes. (p. 89)

Shortage: A condition that exists in the market when the quantity demanded exceeds the quantity supplied at a price *below* the equilibrium or market-clearing price. (p. 86)

Short run: A time period in which only those sellers already in the market may respond to a change in market price by using more or less of their variable resources. From the standpoint of consumers, the short run is a period in which they respond only to price changes. As a result of a change in price, consumers may change their tastes or preferences or their use of alternative goods or services. However, in economic analysis, these related changes are considered long-run phenomena. (p. 92)

Supply: Quantities of a good or service that people are ready to *sell* at various prices, other factors besides price held constant. Supply can be expressed as a numerical schedule, as a supply curve on a graph, or as an algebraic equation. (p. 83)

Surplus: A condition that exists in the market when the quantity supplied exceeds the quantity demanded at a price that lies *above* the equilibrium or market-clearing price. (p. 86)

QUESTIONS

1. Define *demand.* Define *supply.* In your answers, explain the difference between *demand* and *quantity demanded* and between *supply* and *quantity supplied.*
2. List the key nonprice factors that influence demand and supply.
3. In defining demand and supply, why do you think economists focus on price while holding constant other factors that might have an impact on the behavior of buyers and sellers?
4. Define comparative statics analysis. How does it compare with sensitivity analysis or what-if analysis used in finance, accounting, and statistics?
5. Define the *rationing function* of price. Why is it necessary for price to serve this function in the market economy?
6. Define the *guiding* or *allocating function* of price.
7. Discuss the differences between the short run and the long run from the perspective of producers and from the perspective of consumers.
8. Explain the difference between shortages and scarcity. In answering this question, you should consider the difference between the short run and the long run in economic analysis.
9. Why do you think it is important for managers to understand the mechanics of supply and demand both in the short run and in the long run? Give examples of companies whose business was either helped or hurt by changes in supply or demand in the markets in which they were competing.
10. "If Congress levies an additional tax on luxury items, the prices of these items will rise. However, this will cause demand to decrease, and as a result the prices will fall back down, perhaps even to their original levels." Do you agree with this statement? Explain.
11. Overheard at the water cooler in the corporate headquarters of a large manufacturing concern: "The competition is really threatening us with their new product line. I think we should consider offering discounts on our current line in order to stimulate demand." In this statement, is the term *demand* being used in a manner consistent with economic theory? Explain. Illustrate your answer using a line drawn to represent the demand for this firm's product line.
12. Briefly list and elaborate on the factors that will be affecting the demand for the following products in the next several years. Do you think these factors will cause the demand to increase or decrease?
   a. convenience foods (sold in food shops and supermarkets)
   b. products purchased on the Internet
   c. fax machines
   d. film and cameras
   e. videos rented from retail outlets
   f. pay-per-view television programing
   g. airline travel within the United States; airline travel within Europe
   h. gasoline
13. Briefly list and elaborate on the factors that will be affecting the supply of the

following products in the next several years. Do you think these factors will cause the supply to increase or decrease?
a. crude oil
b. beef
c. computer memory chips

d. hotel rooms
e. fast food outlets in emerging markets
f. credit cards issued by financial institutions
g. laptop computers
h. PC servers

PROBLEMS

1. The following function describes the demand condition for a company that makes caps featuring names of college and professional teams in a variety of sports.

$$Q = 2{,}000 - 100\,P$$

where Q is cap sales and P is price.
   a. How many caps could be sold at $12 each?
   b. What should the price be in order for the company to sell 1,000 caps?
   c. At what price would cap sales equal zero?
2. Consider the following supply and demand curves for a certain product.

$$Q_S = 25{,}000\,P$$

$$Q_D = 50{,}000 - 10{,}000\,P$$

   a. Plot the demand and supply curves.
   b. What are the equilibrium price and equilibrium quantity for the industry? Determine the answer both algebraically and graphically. (Round to the nearest cent.)
3. The following relations describe the supply and demand for posters.

$$Q_D = 65{,}000 - 10{,}000\,P$$

$$Q_S = -35{,}000 + 15{,}000\,P$$

   where Q is the quantity and P is the price of a poster, in dollars.
   a. Complete the following table.

Price	Q_S	Q_D	Surplus or Shortage
$6.00			
5.00			
4.00			
3.00			
2.00			
1.00			

   b. What is the equilibrium price?
4. The following relations describe monthly demand and supply for a computer support service catering to small businesses.

$$Q_D = 3{,}000 - 10\,P$$

$$Q_S = -1{,}000 + 10\,P$$

where Q is the number of businesses that need services and P is the monthly fee, in dollars.

   a. At what average monthly fee would demand equal zero?
   b. At what average monthly fee would supply equal zero?
   c. Plot the supply and demand curves.
   d. What is the equilibrium price/output level?
   e. Suppose demand increases and leads to a new demand curve:

$$Q_D = 3{,}500 - 10\,P$$

   What is the effect on supply? What are the new equilibrium P and Q?
   f. Suppose new suppliers enter the market due to the increase in demand, so that the new supply curve is $Q = -500 + 10\,P$.
   What are the new equilibrium price and equilibrium quantity?
   g. Show these changes on the graph.
5. The ABC marketing consulting firm found that a particular brand of portable stereo has the following demand curve for a certain region:

$$Q = 10{,}000 - 200\,P + 0.03\,\text{Pop} + 0.6I + 0.2A$$

where Q is the quantity per month, P is price (\$), Pop is population, I is disposable income per household (S), and A is advertising expenditure (\$).

   a. Determine the demand curve for the company in a market in which $P = 300$, Pop $= 1{,}000{,}000$, $I = 30{,}000$, and $A = 15{,}000$.
   b. Calculate the quantity demanded at prices of \$200, \$175, \$150, and \$125.
   c. Calculate the price necessary to sell 45,000 units.
6. Joy's Frozen Yogurt shops have enjoyed rapid growth in northeastern states in recent years. From the analysis of Joy's various outlets, it was found that the demand curve follows this pattern:

$$Q = 200 - 300\,P + 120\,I + 65\,T - 250\,A_c + 400\,A_j$$

where Q = Number of cups served per week
   P = Average price paid for each cup
   I = Per capita income in the given market (thousands)
   T = Average outdoor temperature
   A_c = Competition's monthly advertising expenditures (thousands)
   A_j = Joy's own monthly advertising expenditures (thousands)

One of the outlets has the following conditions: $P = 1.50$, $I = 10$, $T = 60$, $A_c = 15$, $A_j = 10$.

   a. Estimate the number of cups served per week by this outlet. Also determine the outlet's demand curve.
   b. What would be the effect of a \$5,000 increase in the competitor's advertising expenditure? Illustrate the effect on the outlet's demand curve.
   c. What would Joy's advertising expenditure have to be to counteract this effect?

7. Illustrate the example of the world sugar market with supply and demand diagrams. Be sure to show how the relative shifts in supply and demand have led to the reduction in the world price of sugar.

8. Over the past decade, the demand for compact discs (CDs) has dramatically increased. What are some of the causes of this increase in demand? According to supply-and-demand theory, price should rise when demand increases. However, in recent years the average price of a CD has actually fallen. Explain this apparent contradiction between the theory and fact.

9. Suppose a firm has the following demand equation:

$$Q = 1,000 - 3,000P + 10A$$

where Q = quantity demanded
  P = product price (in dollars)
  A = advertising expenditure (in dollars)

Assume for the questions below that P = $3 and A = $2,000.

a. Suppose the firm dropped the price to $2.50. Would this be beneficial? Explain. Illustrate your answer with the use of a demand schedule and demand curve.

b. Suppose the firm raised the price to $4.00 while increasing its advertising expenditure by $100. Would this be beneficial? Explain. Illustrate your answer with the use of a demand schedule and a demand curve.
(Hint: First construct the schedule and the curve assuming A = $2,000. Then construct the new schedule and curve assuming A = $2,100.)

10. A travel company has hired a management consulting company to analyze demand in 26 regional markets for one of its major products: a guided tour to a particular country. The consultant uses data to estimate the following equation (the estimation technique is discussed in detail in chapter 5):

$$Q = 1,500 - 4P + 5A + 10I + 3PX$$

where Q = amount of the product demanded
  P = price of the product in dollars
  A = advertising expenditures in **thousands** of dollars
  I = income in **thousands** of dollars
  PX = price of some other travel products offered by a competing travel company

a. Calculate the amount demanded for this product using the following data:

$$P = $400$$

$$A = $20,000$$

$$I = $15,000$$

$$PX = $500$$

b. Suppose the competitor reduced the price of its travel product to $400 to match the price of this firm's product. How much would this firm have to increase its advertising in order to counteract the drop in its competitor's price? Would it be worth it for them to do so? Explain.

   c. What other variables might be important in helping to estimate the demand for this travel product?

11. Following are three sample equations. Plot them on a graph in which Q is on the vertical axis and P is on the horizontal axis. Then transform these equations so that P is expressed in terms of Q and plot these transformed equations on a graph in which P is on the vertical axis and Q is on the horizontal axis.

   a. $Q = 250 - 10\,P$

   b. $Q = 1{,}300 - 140\,P$

   c. $Q = 45 - 0.5\,P$

12. Use the following equation to derive a demand schedule and a demand curve. What types of products might exhibit this type of nonlinear demand curve? Explain

$$Q = 100P^{-0.3}$$

Appendix 3A

The Mathematics of Supply and Demand

This appendix presents the short-run analysis of supply and demand using algebraic equations and graphs. As you will see, the mechanics of supply and demand can be very concisely expressed in algebraic equations. Furthermore, viewing the demand function in terms of an equation will better prepare you for the next two chapters on demand elasticity and estimation.

The demand function for a good or service can be expressed mathematically as:

$$Q_D = f(P, X_1, \ldots, X_n)$$

where Q_D = Quantity demanded
P = Price
$X_1, \ldots, X_n$ = Other factors believed to affect the quantity demanded

Using pizza once again as our example, let us assume that price and the nonprice factors affect the demand for pizza in the following way:

$$Q_D = -100\,P + 1.5\,P_{hd} - 5\,P_{sd} + 20A + 15\,\text{Pop} \tag{3A.1}$$

where Q_D = Quantity demanded for pizza (pies)
P_{hd} = Price of hot dogs (cents)
P_{sd} = Price of soft drinks (cents)
A = Advertising expenditures (thousands of dollars)
Pop = Percentage of the population aged 10 to 35

Suppose we hold constant all factors affecting the quantity demanded for pizza except price by assuming the values of these nonprice factors to be

P_{hd} = 100 ($1.00 or 100 cents)
P_{sd} = 75 ($.75 or 75 cents)
A = 20 ($20,000)
Pop = 35 (35 percent)

Substituting these values into Equation (3A.1) gives us

$$Q_D = -100\,P + 1.5\,(100) - 5\,(75) + 20\,(20) + 15\,(35) \tag{3A.2}$$

$$= 700 - 100\,P$$

All of the values of the nonprice variables are now included in the constant term, 700. Plotting this equation gives us the demand curve shown in Figure 3A.1.

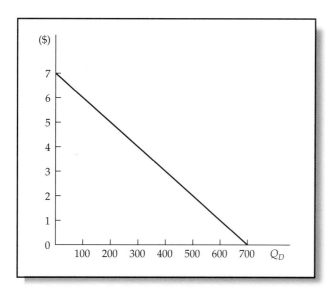

Figure 3A.1
Demand Curve

Those familiar with the graphical presentation of algebraic equations may be puzzled about the way in which economists present the supply and demand equations in graphical form. As a rule, the dependent variable is placed on the vertical or Y axis, and the independent variable is placed on the horizontal or X axis. Given this format, one would expect Q, the dependent variable, to be placed on the vertical axis and P, the independent variable, to be placed on the horizontal axis. However, in this chapter, as well as in the next, Q is placed on the horizontal axis, and P on the vertical axis. It seems that the originator of these diagrams, Professor Alfred Marshall, first presented them in this manner.[10]

Regardless of Marshall's original reasons for reversing the axes, let us simply state that in the analysis of cost, revenue, and profit, the quantity of output is the independent variable. Thus, placing Q on the horizontal axis in the analysis of supply and demand simply prepares us for its subsequent designation as an independent variable.

In the meantime, an adjustment must be made in linking the supply and demand equations to their graphs in order to conform to mathematical convention. In supply-and-demand analysis, whenever an equation such as $Q_D = 700 - 100\,P$ is plotted on a graph, we must do one of two things. If we wish to be consistent with mathematical convention, we must place Q_D on the vertical axis and the P on the horizontal axis. This is shown in Figure 3A.2a. If we wish to follow the usual format in economics, we must rearrange the terms in the equation so that P is expressed in terms of Q_D.

$$Q_D = 700 - 100P$$

$$100\,P = 700 - Q_D$$

[10]Alfred Marshall, *Principles of Economics*, 8th ed., Philadelphia: Porcupine Press, 1920, reprinted 1982, p. 288.

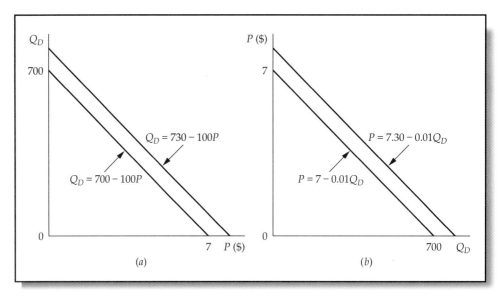

Figure 3A.2
Transforming the Demand Curve

$$P = \frac{700 - Q_D}{100}$$

$$P = 7 - 0.01\, Q_D$$

As such, P is now the dependent variable and can be plotted on the vertical axis. Q_D is now the independent variable and can be plotted on the horizontal axis. This is illustrated in Figure 3A.2b.

Let us review this point by assuming that one of the nonprice factors affecting the quantity demanded for pizza has changed. In particular, suppose the price of hot dogs increases to $1.20. In Equation (3A.2), this would increase the constant or "Y intercept" term from 700 to 730. This, in effect, would cause the demand curve to shift from its original position to the new one shown in Figure 3A.2a. Figure 3A.2b shows the effect of an increase in the price of hot dogs on the transformed demand equation. In this case, the constant term or "Y intercept" increases from 7 to 7.3 and is also shown by a rightward shift in the demand curve.

We now focus on the supply by assuming that the supply equation is the same as the curve used in Table 3.4 and Figure 3.3. This equation can be expressed as:

$$Q_s = -100 + 100\, P \qquad\qquad \textbf{(3A.3)}$$

Once the supply and demand equations are given, there are several ways to find the equilibrium price and quantity. One way is to solve for the supply and demand equations simultaneously. This is done by first setting up the two equations in the following way:

$$Q_D = 700 - 100\ P$$

$$Q_S = -100 + 100\ P$$

We can then eliminate P by adding the equations together. This gives us

$$2\ Q = 700 - 100 \qquad \text{(3A.4)}$$

$$= 600$$

$$Q^* = 300$$

To find the equilibrium price (P^*), we simply return to either the demand or the supply equation, insert the value for the equilibrium quantity, (300), and solve for P. Using Equation (3A.2), this would give us

$$300 = 700 - 100\ P$$

$$100\ P = 700 - 300$$

$$P^* = 4$$

Notice that when we added the supply and demand equations together, we no longer made the distinction between Q_S and Q_D, because in equilibrium $Q_S = Q_D$. In fact, this brings us to the other way in which the supply and demand equations can be used to determine the equilibrium price and quantity. By definition, market equilibrium occurs when the quantity supplied is equal to the quantity demanded. Thus, we can set Equation (3A.2) equal to Equation (3A.3) and solve for the unknown P. That is,

$$700 - 100\ P = -100 + 100\ P$$

$$200P = 800$$

$$P^* = 4$$

And by inserting the value of 4 into either equation, we obtain the equilibrium quantity, 300.

You now have three ways to view the basic elements of supply and demand. First, there are supply and demand schedules, as shown in Tables 3.1, 3.2, 3.3, and 3.4, in which the equilibrium price is found by matching the quantity supplied with the quantity demanded. Second, there are supply and demand diagrams, as presented in most of the figures in this chapter, in which price and quantity are determined by the intersection of the supply and demand curves. Finally, there are supply and demand equations, which enable one to find equilibrium price and quantity by solving for the unknowns in the two equations. For teaching purposes, the use of graphs is favored. But regardless of the manner in which the concepts of supply and demand are presented, there remains the challenge for business decision makers to ascertain the actual supply and demand data for their particular industries and organizations.

Chapter 4

Demand Elasticity

The Situation

Henry Caulfield is the owner-operator of a local "Gas 'n Go" gas station and convenience store. Henry chose to locate his store in an area at least ten minutes away by car from the nearest supermarket or grocery store. For the most part, Henry's business has been quite successful.

Then one day he noticed that a new grocery store was opening just one block away. A month later he noticed that a new convenience store had opened for business less than a three-minute drive away. Henry realized that to maintain the status quo in the face of this new competition, he would have to make some tough decisions about his pricing and promotion policies and the mix of items carried in his store.

The items that he carried were typical of those found in retail establishments of this type, with beer, cigarettes, hot coffee, and soft drinks accounting for about 75 percent of total sales. Soft drinks were by far the best-selling item in his store. Essentially, the retail price of soft drinks was based on the wholesale price plus a mark-up of about 400 percent. Henry recognized that this mark-up was considerably higher than the one used by a supermarket, but he believed that people were willing to pay more for the convenience.

On certain occasions, Henry would offer a particular brand of soft drink at a substantial discount. Regardless of whether he lost

(Continued)

or made money on soft drinks by this action, he found that it helped to attract additional customers into his store, and gasoline sales actually increased. Several people from an adjacent town told him that they waited until they were in the vicinity of his station to fill their tanks because of his discount on soda. Given the public's responsiveness to special discounts on soft drinks and the ability of this product to promote other products, Henry decided to use the pricing of soft drinks as his main weapon against his new competition. Instead of offering a temporary discount, he decided to reduce the price of soft drinks permanently. However, after a month, despite the lower soft drink prices, there was a noticeable decline in his revenue from soft drinks. Henry realized that he would have to reassess his competitive tactic.

THE ECONOMIC CONCEPT OF ELASTICITY

In the previous chapter we studied the idea of demand and discussed the movement along a demand curve (i.e., change in quantity demanded). We found the demand curve to slope downward to the right; this means, of course, that the lower the price, the greater the quantity of the product consumed. We are now going to discuss the question of how sensitive the change in quantity demanded is to a change in price. The measurement of this sensitivity in percentage terms is called the **price elasticity of demand.** Henry Caulfield made implicit use of this concept when he decided to lower his soft drink prices to compete with the new stores in his area. But this is only one of the elasticity measures with which we will concern ourselves in this chapter. We will also cover the concepts of income elasticity, cross-elasticity, and supply elasticity.

In most general terms, we can define **elasticity** as a percentage relationship between two variables, that is, the percentage change in one variable relative to a percentage change in another. In different terms, we divide one percentage by the other:

$$\text{Coefficient of elasticity} = \frac{\text{Percent change in A}}{\text{Percent change in B}}$$

The result of this division is the **coefficient of elasticity.** It is then our task to interpret the coefficient and to determine the effects of the change. The meaning of the size as well as the sign of the coefficient (the coefficient may be negative or positive) will be the focus of our inquiry for the remainder of this chapter. Let us first turn to the most frequently encountered elasticity concept, the price elasticity of demand.

THE PRICE ELASTICITY OF DEMAND

When Henry Caulfield contemplated lowering his price to counteract his new competition, he was dealing with price elasticity of demand. He was determining whether by lowering his prices he would raise his unit sales sufficiently to increase his total revenue.[1]

When we speak of the price elasticity of demand, we are dealing with the sensitivity of quantities bought to a change in the producer's price. Thus, this concept describes an action that is within the producer's (or, in this case, the dealer's) control. Other elasticities to be discussed later are outside the producer's control and may evoke other actions on the producer's part to counteract them.

Demand price elasticity is defined as a percentage change in quantity demanded caused by a one percent change in price. Let us develop this concept mathematically. We can write the expression, "percentage change in quantity demanded" as

$$\frac{\Delta \text{ Quantity demanded}}{\text{Initial quantity demanded}}$$

where Δ (delta) signifies an absolute change. The second part of this relationship, "percentage change in price," can be written as

$$\frac{\Delta \text{ Price}}{\text{Initial price}}$$

Dividing the first expression by the second, we arrive at the expression for the price elasticity of demand:

$$\frac{\Delta \text{ Quantity}}{\text{Quantity}} \div \frac{\Delta \text{ Price}}{\text{Price}} = \frac{\% \Delta \text{ Quantity}}{\% \Delta \text{ Price}}$$

This is the general expression. We turn now to the actual computation of elasticities, and we will describe two methods of obtaining the price elasticity of demand.

MODULE 4A

Measurement of Price Elasticity

Let us begin with **arc elasticity,** the method most commonly used in economics textbooks. The formula for this indicator is

$$E_p = \frac{Q_2 - Q_1}{(Q_1 + Q_2)/2} \div \frac{P_2 - P_1}{(P_1 + P_2)/2}$$

where E_p = Coefficient of arc price elasticity
Q_1 = Original quantity demanded
Q_2 = New quantity demanded
P_1 = Original price
P_2 = New price

The numerator of this coefficient, $(Q_2 - Q_1)/[Q_1 + Q_2)/2]$, indicates the percentage change in the quantity demanded. The denominator, $(P_2 - P_1)/[P_1 + P_2)/2]$, indicates the percentage change in the price.

Notice that the change in each variable is divided by the *average* of its beginning and ending values. For example, if the price of a product rises from $11 to $12, caus-

---

[1]More important, he was wondering whether he would actually increase his profits with this action. However, we are not yet in a position to deal with this question.

ing a fall in the quantity demanded from 7 to 6, the formula gives the following price elasticity coefficient:

$$E_p = \frac{6 - 7}{(7 + 6)/2} \div \frac{12 - 11}{(11 + 12)/2}$$

$$= \frac{-1}{6.5} \div \frac{1}{11.5}$$

$$= \frac{-1}{6.5} \times \frac{11.5}{1}$$

$$= \frac{-11.5}{6.5}$$

$$= -1.77$$

The reason the arc elasticity formula employs the average of the beginning and ending values can be clearly seen. If we had used the beginning values, the coefficient would be

$$Ep = \frac{6 - 7}{7} \div \frac{12 - 11}{11}$$

$$= \frac{-1}{7} \div \frac{1}{11}$$

$$= \frac{-1}{7} \times \frac{11}{1}$$

$$= \frac{-11}{7}$$

$$= -1.57$$

However, suppose the price fell from \$12 to \$11, causing the quantity demanded to rise from 6 to 7 units. Using the beginning values would result in a coefficient of -2 (readers can make this calculation themselves to obtain the answer). Thus, the *same* unit change in price and quantity gives *different* values of elasticity, depending on whether the price increases or decreases.[2] By using the average of the beginning and ending values, we avoid this ambiguity. The price elasticity coefficient is the same whether price increases or decreases.

An additional source of ambiguity arises in the computation of elasticity when we consider changes over different ranges of price and quantity. For example, suppose that the values of price and quantity provided in the preceding analysis are part of the hypothetical demand schedule shown in Table 4.1.

The numbers in this schedule indicate a linear relationship between quantity demanded and price, with a unit change in price resulting in a unit change in

---

[2]The reason for this ambiguity is simply that the base number differs between a percentage increase and a decrease between two numbers. A good example of this can be found in the retail trade. Suppose a company buys a dress wholesale for \$100 and marks it up 100 percent, thereby establishing the retail price at \$200. Suppose in a clearance sale it decides to sell it at cost. This would represent a 50 percent markdown (i.e., from \$200 down to \$100).

Table 4.1

Hypothetical Demand
Schedule

PRICE	QUANTITY
18	0
17	1
16	2
15	3
14	4
13	5
12	6
11	7
10	8
9	9
8	10
7	11
6	12
5	13

quantity over the entire range of the schedule.[3] Suppose we compute the arc elasticity for a price change from $12 to $10 rather than between $12 and $11. Using the arc elasticity formula gives

$$
Ep = \frac{6 - 8}{(8 + 6)/2} \div \frac{12 - 10}{(10 + 12)/2}
$$

$$
= \frac{-2}{7} \div \frac{2}{11}
$$

$$
= \frac{-2}{7} \times \frac{11}{2}
$$

$$
= \frac{-22}{14}
$$

$$
= -1.57
$$

Notice that the coefficient is different from the previously computed value. In fact, for any given value of price, the arc elasticity coefficient will vary depending on the new price's distance from the original price.[4]

To adjust for the ambiguity inherent in the use of the arc formula, economists recommend the use of **point elasticity,** the second of the two ways to compute the elasticity coefficient. This method of computation is expressed as follows (we shall use the Greek letter ε when we are referring specifically to point elasticity):

$$
\epsilon_p = \frac{dQ}{dP} \times \frac{P_1}{Q_1}
$$

---

[3]The algebraic expression of this demand equation is $P = 18 - Q$, or $Q = 18 - P$.
[4]Interested readers should try computing the arc elasticity for changes between $12 and $9, between $12 and $8, and so on. They will find that the arc elasticity decreases as the change in price increases.

Managerial Economics

To compute point elasticity, we employ one of the economist's favorite mathematical devices, the derivative. Students familiar with elementary calculus, or who learned about it in the appendix to chapter 2, will have no difficulty with this expression. The key is that by assuming very small changes (actually, in calculus the change is "infinitesimally small") in price and quantity around some given level, we avoid the problem of the measure of elasticity differing based on the amount of change.

To find the derivative of Q with respect to P (i.e., dQ/dP), we need the algebraic expression of the demand equation. The equation implied in Table 4.1 is $Q = 18 - P$. The derivative of Q with respect to P is -1. Thus, the point elasticity coefficient at \$12 and 6 units is:

$$\epsilon_p = -1 \times \frac{12}{6}$$

$$= -2$$

Actually, whenever the demand equation is linear, the point elasticity formula appears almost too simple because the first derivative of this equation with respect to P is a constant. From a practical standpoint, there is really no need to use calculus for finding the point elasticity of a linear demand function. The first derivative dQ/dP is the same as the (constant) slope of the demand line, $\Delta Q/\Delta P$. Thus, the point elasticity of a linear demand function can be expressed as:

$$\epsilon_p = \frac{\Delta Q}{\Delta P} \times \frac{P_1}{Q_1}$$

Of course, in cases where the demand curve is nonlinear, calculus must be employed to compute point elasticity. For example, consider the following demand curve.

$$Q = 100 - P^2$$

Assuming $P_1 = 5$, then $Q = 75$. Then the point elasticity is

$$\epsilon_p = -2P \times \frac{5}{75}$$

$$= -2(5) \times \frac{5}{75}$$

$$= \frac{-50}{75}$$

$$= -0.67$$

While it is very convenient to use linear demand curves, in reality the shape of the demand curve may be different. In the preceding illustration, price decreases will bring forth smaller increases in quantity. Such a demand curve would take on a concave shape. On the other hand, the demand curve may be convex. (The equation for such a curve would be, for instance, $Q = 10/p^2$.) An example of such a demand curve would occur when, for instance, some quantities would be purchased even at a very high price; in such a case, the demand curve would become almost vertical near the price axis.

So far we have discussed both linear and nonlinear demand curves whose elasticity changes as we move along the curve. However, we could encounter a demand

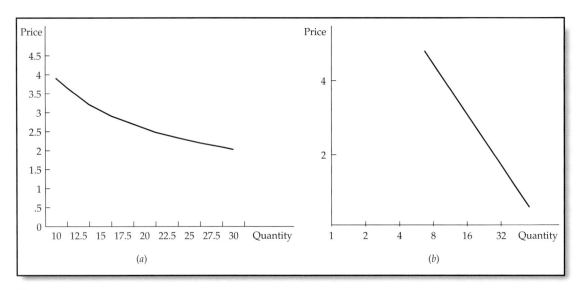

Figure 4.1
Constant Elasticity

curve whose elasticity is constant over its relevant range. Such a curve would be described by the following equation:

$$Q = aP^{-b}$$

a being a constant, and −b representing the elasticity coefficient. This nonlinear equation can be converted to linear by expressing it in logarithms:

$$\log Q = \log a - b(\log P)$$

Such a demand curve would plot as a straight line on double log (or log-log) graph paper, and its elasticity (−b) would be the same at any point on the curve. For example, let the demand equation be $Q = 100P^{-1.7}$. From this equation we can generate the following demand schedule:

Quantity	10	12.5	15	17.5	20	22.5	25	27.5	30
Price	3.875	3.398	3.052	2.788	2.577	2.405	2.260	2.137	2.030

The two graphs in Figure 4.1 illustrate this demand curve. Figure 4.1a shows the curve using the normal arithmetic scales. In Figure 4.1b the scales are transformed into logarithms, and the demand curve plots as a straight line, signifying that the elasticity is constant throughout.[5]

The concept of point elasticity, as well as the use of calculus, will be found to be of particular importance in the next chapter, when the estimation of demand equations will be discussed. However, for now, using discrete changes and the arc elasticity coefficient would appear to be the more realistic thing for Henry Caulfield (and most other practical businesspeople) to do. He may not be familiar with calculus, but

---

[5]We will encounter constant elasticity again in chapter 7 when we discuss the Cobb-Douglas production function.

this certainly does not detract from his business acumen. He is dealing with a concrete problem: how much he will sell if he lowers his price by a discrete quantity (i.e., a certain number of cents). Arc elasticity is perfectly suitable for this problem.

We must realize, however, that in actual business situations, the effects of elasticity may be calculated in simple percentage terms, using the starting price and quantity as base numbers. For instance, a businessperson may state that it is expected that a 10 percent decrease in price will result in a 20 percent increase in quantity, implying that elasticity is -2; as an example, a decrease in price from $10 to $9 will increase quantity sold from 1,000 to 1,200 units. Of course, this would suggest that raising the price from $9 to $10 (an 11.1 percent increase) would decrease quantity from 1,200 to 1,000 units (a decrease of 16.7 percent). The elasticity in this case is -1.5. This asymmetry creates the same problem that we discussed earlier, which was solved by employing arc elasticity. In actual situations, however, we must be realistic and understand that a movement down along the demand curve may not bring about the same results as a movement up along the demand curve. And even more important, we should remember that mathematical refinement may not be the most essential. What is critical to the businessperson faced with a decision is whether a decrease in price will create sufficiently more quantity to improve profits.

Economists, in their neat way, have created categories of elasticity:

1. *Relative elasticity of demand:*

$$E_p > 1 \text{ (in absolute terms)}[6]$$

This occurs when a 1 percent change in price causes a change in quantity demanded greater than 1 percent. The coefficient calculated earlier, 1.77, is a case of relatively elastic demand.

2. *Relative inelasticity of demand:*

$$0 < E_p < 1 \text{ (in absolute terms)}$$

Here the percentage change in price is greater than the corresponding change in quantity. For example, in Table 4.1 as price is lowered from 8 to 7, quantity rises from 10 to 11, giving a coefficient of 0.71.

3. *Unitary elasticity of demand:*

$$E_p = 1 \text{ (in absolute terms)}$$

A 1 percent change in price results in a 1 percent change in quantity in the opposite direction.

These are three common measures of elasticity. But there are also two limiting cases at the extremes of the elasticity scale:

1. *Perfect elasticity:*

$$E_p = \infty \text{ (in absolute terms)}$$

---

[6]Since a demand curve has a negative slope, the coefficient of price elasticity will be negative. However, it is often more efficient to ignore the minus sign and to discuss the elasticity coefficient in absolute terms.

In this case, there is only one possible price, and at that price an unlimited quantity can be sold. The demand curve for $E_p = \infty$ is a horizontal line. We will encounter a demand curve with this shape later, when we discuss perfect competition.

2. *Perfect inelasticity:*

$$E_p = 0$$

Under this condition, the quantity demanded remains the same regardless of price. Such a demand curve may exist for certain products within a particular price range. An example may be the case of salt. Today's price of salt is about 39 cents per pound. If this price were to rise to 49 cents (a significant percentage increase), or fall to 29 cents (a significant percentage decrease), it is very doubtful that the consumption of salt would change at all.

Both of these extreme cases, although possible under certain conditions, will seldom be observed in real life. Still, the two limits should be well understood by every student of economics.

The Determinants of Elasticity

Now that we have described what elasticity is, let us look into the reasons that the demand for some goods and services is elastic, whereas for others it is inelastic. In other words, what determines elasticity? As we look into this question, we must remember that the elasticity for a particular product may differ at different prices. Thus, although the demand elasticity for salt is very low—possibly zero—in the vicinity of its current price, it may not be so inelastic at $5 or $10 per pound.

It is often said—and many use this as a rule of thumb—that demand is inelastic for goods considered to be necessities, and it is elastic for luxury products. For example, the demand for furs, gems, and expensive automobiles is probably more elastic than the demand for milk, shoes, and electricity.

Unfortunately, the luxury/necessity dichotomy is ambiguous. Demand for expensive automobiles may be elastic, but if we consider the demand for Mercedes autos, we will probably find that within the prevailing price range, a movement up or down of several thousand dollars would make relatively little difference to those people who are in the market for this particular kind of car. The probable reason for such inconsistencies is relatively simple: One person's luxury is another person's necessity.

Several important factors that influence demand elasticity are outlined in Figure 4.2, and are discussed in the course of the next few pages.

Probably the most important determinant of elasticity is ease of substitution. This argument cuts both ways: If there are many good substitutes for the product in question, elasticity will be high; conversely, if this commodity is a good substitute for others, its demand elasticity will also be high. The broader the definition of a commodity, the lower its price elasticity will tend to be, since there is less opportunity for substitution. For instance, the demand elasticity for beer or bread will tend to be less than that for a particular brand of beer or for white bread. There are fewer substitutes for bread in general (particularly if we include in this definition other baked products, such as rolls and bagels) than there are for white bread or, even further, a specific brand of white bread. If the price of bread rises (relative to other products), we may consume

- ▶ Ease of substitution
- ▶ Proportion of total expenditures
- ▶ Durability of product
  - ■ Possibility of postponing purchase
  - ■ Possibility of repair
  - ■ Used product market
- ▶ Length of time period

Figure 4.2
Factors Affecting
Demand Elasticity

somewhat less bread than before. However, if the price of brand A white bread rises, while other white bread prices remain the same, then one would expect the quantity of brand A demanded to drop significantly as consumers switch to other brands.

Henry's convenience store was once the only game in town, so to speak. His nearest competitor was relatively distant. Now customers can substitute for Henry's merchandise by walking one block to the grocery store. And since Henry was most likely selling the same soft drink brands as his close competitor, the substitution effect is extremely strong.

Another major determinant of demand elasticity is the proportion of total expenditures spent on a product. Here we can go back to our salt example. The reason for the low elasticity of demand for salt is that the proportion of a consumer unit's (e.g., an individual, a family, and so on) income spent on salt is extremely small. A hefty price increase (e.g., from 39 cents to 49 cents per pound) would probably cause a shrug of the shoulder but would affect consumption of salt very little.

The spending on soft drinks by a typical individual or a family constitutes a larger portion of income than spending on salt. However, in most circumstances, spending on soda still represents a relatively small percentage of a family's income. Thus, we would not expect a change in price to affect the quantity of demand significantly. Still, in households where large quantities of soft drinks are consumed, a price change could have some effect on quantities sold, although it would probably require a substantial change in price to affect purchases significantly.

However, for a product such as a large appliance, the situation may be entirely different. To most families, a clothes washer represents more than a trivial expense, and a price change could have an important impact on purchases. Thus, we expect the demand elasticity for a clothes washer to be considerably greater than that for salt or soft drinks. There is another possible reason for the relatively high demand elasticity of a clothes washer. An appliance purchase may be postponable, since there is commonly a choice between buying and repairing. Faced with a higher purchase price, a consumer may choose to repair the old appliance.[7]

---

[7]The choice between buying and maintaining becomes even more pronounced for the purchase of an automobile. Here, of course, the price and the proportion of a person's income are considerably higher. In this case, there is a third possibility for the consumer: the purchase of a used car. Thus, recalling what we said about substitutability, we can say that the elasticity of demand for cars in general is lower than the demand elasticity for new cars. Of course, it is also possible to purchase a used washing machine, but there is no organized market for these as there is for cars.

Despite the entry of new firms into Henry's market, the geographical size of the market is limited to a relatively small local area. As markets broaden, more and more product substitution becomes possible. Advances in modes of transportation and communication and decreases in their cost have increased the size of markets over time. Thus, the number of substitutes competing for consumers' dollars have increased. Markets have not only widened within national borders, they have more frequently crossed borders, increasing the importance of international trade. Although advances in transportation and communications have been instrumental, an extremely important trend toward freer trade through international trade agreements has undermined artificial barriers (tariffs and quotas). This has increased competition globally and, thus, has increased demand elasticities facing firms. The consumer is the ultimate beneficiary of such trends.

The Effect of Elasticity on Price and Quantity

The response to a change in supply is determined, to a great extent, by the price elasticity of demand. This is of great importance to a businessperson who must be able to adjust its production and prices to a change in economic conditions. Except in the case of perfectly elastic or perfectly inelastic demand, both price and quantity produced will be affected. The extent of the change of each is determined by the price elasticity of demand.

In Figure 4.3, we have charted a demand curve D_1 whose equation is $Q = 27 - 3P$. The equation for the supply curve S_1 is $Q = -5 + 5P$. The resulting equilibrium price is \$4 and quantity is 15 units (point 1).[8] If we chart another, considerably more

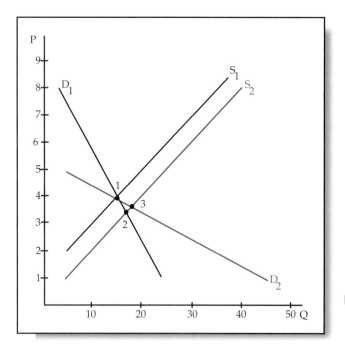

Figure 4.3
Effect of Elasticity on Price
and Quantity

---

[8]The reader can utilize Excel Module 3A, which can be accessed on the companion web site, to calculate the equilibrium point and draw a graph.

elastic, demand curve, D_2, of the form $Q = 55 - 10P$, with the same supply curve, the equilibrium point will be the same, $Q = 15$, and $P = 4$. Now, let us say that supply increases, and the supply curve S_2 is of the form $S = 0 + 5P$. With the new supply curve, the equilibrium points for the two demand curves will no longer be the same. With D_1 the price will be \$3.375 and quantity 16.875 units (point 2). However, with D_2 the result will be $P = 3.667$ and $Q = 18.333$ (point 3). The more elastic demand curve, D_2, has resulted in a smaller price decrease but a larger quantity increase than D_1, the less elastic curve. The reader should try this exercise with the same demand curves, but with a decrease in supply to, say, $Q = -10 + P$. In this case the more elastic demand curve will result in a larger decrease quantity and a small increase in price. Thus, we can see that it is extremely important for a manager to have a good idea regarding the sensitivity of demand to price changes. Making the wrong decision in raising or lowering price in response to changing supply conditions could be disastrous to the manager's company.

The Elasticity of Derived Demand

This section of the elasticity discussion represents a small digression, albeit an important one. So far we have discussed demand elasticity for a final product, that is, a product purchased for consumption, such as soft drinks, a clothes washer, salt, white bread, or beer.

We are now going to look briefly at the demand for items that go into the production of a final commodity, such as materials, machinery, and labor. The demand for such components of a final product is called **derived demand.** In other words, these components are not demanded for their own sake but because there is a demand for the final product requiring them.

The great British economist Alfred Marshall, about whom previous references were made, described four principles governing the elasticity of the derived demand curve.[9] According to Marshall, the derived demand curve will be more inelastic:

1. The more essential is the component in question
2. The more inelastic is the demand curve for the final product
3. The smaller is the fraction of total cost going to this component
4. The more inelastic is the supply curve of cooperating factors

An example will illustrate this concept. Let us consider demand for residential housing (the final product) and the derived demand for one class of labor employed in construction, electricians. After all, the demand for electricians does not exist for its own sake but is due to the demand for housing. Probably all of Marshall's principles apply in this case, but two of them are particularly important. The first is essentiality: You just cannot build a house without employing electricians. Second, the cost of electrical work is probably a relatively small percentage of the entire cost of the house.

Suppose the electricians demand and obtain a substantial wage increase. A contractor may try to cut a few corners with regard to electrical work, but most of it must

---

[9]Alfred Marshall, *Principles of Economics*, 8th ed., Philadelphia: Porcupine Press, reprinted 1982, pp. 319–20.

still be done. Thus, the employment of electricians will not decrease much. The implication here is that the elasticity of demand for electricians is low. Assume that the work of electricians involves 10 percent of the total cost of construction (this cost is probably overstated). A 10 percent wage increase for electricians represents a 1 percent increase in the total cost of construction. This small addition to the total cost will most likely not trigger a price increase and thus will not affect the employment of electricians to any significant extent. If we also consider the probability that the demand for housing is somewhat inelastic and that the supply elasticity of cooperating factors (i.e., other crafts employed on the project) is rather low, we can conclude that the demand elasticity for electricians is relatively low.

These conclusions tend to hold in the short run much more than in the long run. Over a short period of time, employment of electricians will not drop very much. However, given a longer adjustment period, elasticity of demand will rise as people find ways to substitute for the expensive factor, both on the production side and on the consumption side.[10]

Elasticity in the Short Run and in the Long Run

A long-run demand curve will generally be more elastic than a short-run curve. Here "short run" is defined as an amount of time that does not permit a full adjustment by consumers to a price change. In the shortest of runs, no adjustment at all may be possible, and the demand curve over the relevant range may be almost perfectly inelastic. As the time period lengthens, consumers will find ways to adjust to the price change by using substitutes (if the price has risen), by substituting the good in question for another (if the price has fallen), or by shifting consumption to or from this particular product (i.e., by consuming more or less of other commodities).

A good example is the case of energy costs. When heating oil prices shot up in the 1970s, the immediate response by consumers was not great. As time passed, however, consumers adjusted their oil consumption. They became used to lower temperatures around the house and at work. They began to dress more warmly indoors. (Would this result in a higher demand for sweaters? We will look at this particular idea, known as cross-elasticity, later in this chapter.) Over a still longer period, consumers (including one of the authors) converted their homes from oil heat to gas heat. Not only was there conversion, but more newly built homes were equipped with gas heat. In addition, homes up for resale would advertise gas heating to attract potential buyers, and gas-heated homes commanded a premium price. How can we demonstrate this phenomenon graphically?

We can represent this relationship between the short run and the long run using a series of short-run demand curves intersected by the long-run demand curve, as illustrated in Figure 4.4. Each of the short-run demand curves (D_{S1} to D_{S5}) is rather inelastic. Assume that the original position is point a, which represents a price of P_1 and a quantity of Q_1. If the price rises to P_2, consumers will, in the short run, decrease the quantity demanded to point b, at quantity Q_2, a relatively small difference in

---

[10]A very interesting analysis of short- and long-run elasticity effects on the economic power of labor unions can be found in Milton Friedman, *Price Theory: A Provisional Text*, Hawthorne, NY: Aldine, 1962, pp. 155–59.

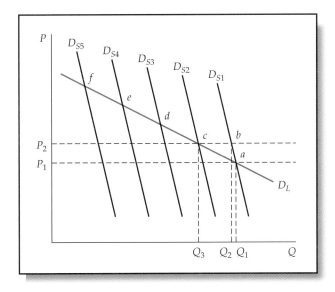

Figure 4.4
Short-Run versus Long-Run
Elasticity

quantity. As time passes, during which consumers adjust to using substitutes, a new short-run demand curve, D_2, will result, and demand will take place at point c, at Q_3, which represents a much larger decrease in quantity. Thus, we can connect points a and c to illustrate the change in quantity demanded in the long run. Then, for constantly increasing prices, we can generate new short-run demand curves, D_{S3}, D_{S4}, and D_{S5}, and connect points d, e, and f to create a long-run demand curve.

In other words, in the short run, price changes increase or decrease the quantity demanded very little, up or down each of the short-run curves. However, over time, adjustment permits movement to another short-run curve, and a long-run demand curve is created. And the long-run demand curve formed from a point on each short-run curve is obviously far more elastic.

The lengths of the short run and the long run depend on how quickly an adjustment can be made. In the case of heating oil, the long run represented several years. But let us return to the case of Henry Caulfield. Once Henry cuts his price (if he decides to do so), the news will probably spread quite quickly around the community. The adjustment from the short run to the long run will probably be a matter of days, or weeks at most.

MODULE 4B
MODULE 4C

Demand Elasticity and Revenue

Demand elasticity in itself is a rather interesting concept. However, if all it meant was the responsiveness of quantity to price change, it could be easily dismissed. But there is an aspect of demand elasticity that is terribly important to Henry Caulfield or any other businessperson in the throes of a pricing decision (in either direction).

There is a relationship between the price elasticity of demand and revenue received. A decrease in price would decrease revenue if nothing else were to happen. But since demand curves tend to be downward sloping, a decrease in price will increase the quantity purchased, and this will increase receipts. Which of the two

	DEMAND		
	ELASTIC	UNITARY ELASTIC	INELASTIC
Price increase	TR↓	$\overline{\text{TR}}$	TR↑
Price decrease	TR↑	$\overline{\text{TR}}$	TR↓

tendencies is stronger? Remember that elasticity is defined as the percentage change in quantity divided by percentage change in price. If the former is larger (and, therefore, the coefficient will be greater than 1 in absolute terms), then the quantity effect is stronger and will more than offset the opposite price effect.

What does that entail for revenue? If price decreases and, in percentage terms, quantity rises more than price has dropped, then total revenue will increase. We summarize the rules describing the relationship between elasticity and total revenue (TR) in Table 4.2.

Let us return to the example of a straight-line demand curve and see what happens to revenue. You will remember that elasticity on such a curve decreases as we move down and to the right. Total revenue and arc elasticity at each price interval are

Table 4.3
Demand Schedule Showing Total Revenue and Elasticity Values

PRICE	QUANTITY	ARC ELASTICITY	REVENUE
18	0		0
17	1	−35.0	17
16	2	−11.0	32
15	3	−6.2	45
14	4	−4.1	56
13	5	−3.0	65
12	6	−2.3	72
11	7	−1.8	77
10	8	−1.4	80
9	9	−1.1	81
8	10	−0.9	80
7	11	−0.7	77
6	12	−0.6	72
5	13	−0.4	65
4	14	−0.3	56
3	15	−0.2	45
2	16	−0.2	32
1	17	−0.1	17
0	18	0	0

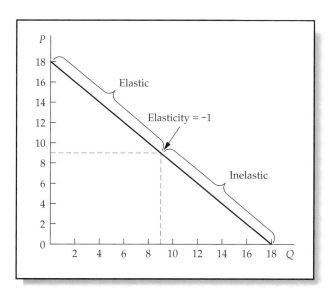

Figure 4.5
The Elasticity–Demand Relationship

calculated in Table 4.3. Figures 4.5 and 4.6 show graphically the relationship between elasticity and revenue. It is obvious that as price decreases, revenue rises when demand is elastic, falls when it is elastic, and reaches its peak (i.e., is level) when elasticity of demand equals 1.

At this point we can formally introduce a term we will use a great deal throughout this book: **marginal revenue.** This concept can be defined as the change in total revenue as quantity changes by one unit.[11]

$$\Delta TR \div \Delta Q$$

Now we can add to the previous table a *marginal revenue* column. This is shown in Table 4.4.[12] Marginal revenue is positive as total revenue rises (and the demand curve is elastic). When total revenue reaches its peak (elasticity equals 1), marginal revenue reaches zero.[13]

Figure 4.7 shows the mathematical and graphic relationship between the demand curve and marginal revenue (MR). It turns out that when the demand curve is described by a straight line, the marginal revenue curve is twice as steep as the demand curve. Under these circumstances, the marginal revenue curve can be drawn by bisecting the distance between the Y-axis (vertical axis) and the demand curve. Of course, at the point where marginal revenue crosses the X-axis

---

[11]Readers with knowledge of calculus will see that we are dealing again with a derivative, dTR/dQ, the derivative of total revenue with respect to quantity.

[12]In this table only a subset of the prices and quantities is shown. This should be sufficient for an understanding of the concept of marginal revenue.

[13]Again, elementary calculus will be of help. As was shown in the appendix to chapter 2, where the mathematics of managerial elasticity was explained, if dTR/dQ equals zero, we can solve for the maximum revenue.

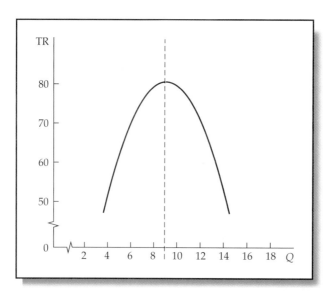

Figure 4.6
The Effect of Elasticity on
Total Revenue

(horizontal axis), the demand curve is unitarily elastic (and total revenue reaches its maximum).[14]

All of this is going through Henry's mind as he is deciding how to counteract his competition. For him to benefit at all from decreasing his price, the demand curve for soft drinks from his store must be elastic. A price cut leading to a decrease in revenue would be self-defeating (or even disastrous). But this is not his only concern. If Henry is a profit maximizer, then it is profit, not revenue, that concerns him. If the demand for his product is elastic, revenue will increase. But as he sells more units, his total cost will, of course, rise. Will the increase in revenue more than offset the additional cost? That is the question uppermost in Henry's mind. Unfortunately, we are not ready to answer at this point. We first have to study production functions and cost functions, and then link demand and cost in chapters 9 and 10.

The Mathematics of Elasticity

It is now time to apply some of the calculus you have learned. Point elasticity was mentioned earlier in this chapter and was said to require the use of differential calculus. The formula for point elasticity was given as

$$dQ/dP \times P/Q$$

For this formula to be employed, the demand curve has to be stated in the form of an equation. The equation for the demand curve represented in Table 4.1 is

---

[14]In mathematical terms, the path from the demand curve to the marginal revenue curve can be traced as follows:

Demand curve:	$P = a - bQ$
Total revenue:	$PQ = aQ - bQ^2$
Marginal revenue:	$dTR/dQ = a - 2bQ$

Figure 4.7
The Relationship between
Demand and Marginal
Revenue

$$Q = 18 - P$$

Therefore, dQ/dP equals -1. This is the slope of the straight-line demand curve.

As stated in the discussion of arc elasticity, elasticity changes along the demand curve (except in the case of constant elasticity discussed previously). So does point elasticity, of course. Thus, the point at which elasticity is measured must be specified. For example, the point elasticity at $Q = 5$ and $P = 13$ is

$$-1 \times 13 \div 5 = -2.6$$

In Table 4.3 the arc elasticity was shown to be -3 in the interval between $P = 13$ and $P = 14$ and between $Q = 4$ and $Q = 5$, and -2.3 in the next interval. Point elasticity, as should be expected, is somewhere between the two arc elasticities. At $Q = 10$ and $P = 8$, the result is

$$-1 \times 8 \div 10 = -0.8$$

We are now in the inelastic section of the demand curve.

Table 4.4
Demand Schedule with
Marginal Revenue Added

Price	Quantity	Total Revenue	Marginal Revenue	Arc Elasticity
13	5	65	9	−3.0
12	6	72	7	−2.3
11	7	77	5	−1.8
10	8	80	3	−1.4
9	9	81	1	−1.1
8	10	80	−1	−0.9
7	11	77	−3	−0.7

We also mentioned the use of calculus in reference to marginal revenue, which was defined as $d\text{TR}/dQ$. For this purpose, we will reverse our demand function so that quantity becomes the independent variable.

Demand:	$P = 18 - Q$
Total revenue:	$\text{TR} = PQ = 18Q - Q^2$
Marginal revenue:	$d\text{TR}/dQ = 18 - 2Q$

At $Q = 5$ and $\text{TR} = 65$, marginal revenue is

$$18 - (2 \times 5) = 8$$

Again, since we are measuring TR at a point rather than over an interval, the result (MR = 8) will be somewhat different from the marginal revenue obtained in Table 4.4, where discrete differences were used in the calculation.

At $Q = 10$, MR $= 18 - (2 \times 10) = -2$. We are now in the area of negative marginal revenue (relative inelasticity on the demand curve), or at a quantity higher than the one that produces maximum revenue.

If we wish to find the point where revenue is maximized, we look for the point at which MR = 0. Thus,

$$18 - 2Q = 0$$
$$18 = 2Q$$
$$9 = Q$$

This result, again, is not the same but is very similar to the number found in Table 4.4, where discrete intervals rather than infinitely small differences were used.

Empirical Elasticities

In the next chapter we will explain how economists estimate demand curves and elasticities from industry and product data. But it may be of interest at this point to reinforce the meaning of price elasticity by mentioning briefly the results of some studies published in recent years.

A study of the demand for coffee estimated the price elasticity to be -0.2 in the short run and -0.33 in the long run.

A study of the demand for kitchen and other household appliances stated that the elasticity was -0.63.

Meals (excluding alcoholic beverages) purchased at restaurants have a high demand elasticity of -2.27.

A study of air-travel demand over the North Atlantic found price elasticity to be -1.2. Furthermore, the elasticity for first-class travel was, as one would expect, considerably lower than that for economy travel, -0.4 and -1.8, respectively. A recent study estimates the price elasticity of passenger travel for the U.S. airline industry to be a high -1.98.

The U.S. Department of Agriculture estimated the price elasticity of a number of farm products. Among them were potatoes at −0.27, butter at −0.62, and peaches at −1.49.

The price elasticity of beer has been estimated at −0.84 and of wine at −0.55.

The price elasticity of white pan bread in Chicago appeared to be −0.69, while for premium white pan bread elasticity was measured at 1.01. This is consistent with the idea that there are more substitutes for premium white pan bread brands than for all white pan bread.

The price elasticity of attendance at English rugby league games was −0.57.

In the short run, demand elasticity for cigarettes in the United States appeared to be −0.4, but it was higher, though still quite low, in the long run at −0.6.[15]

THE CROSS-ELASTICITY OF DEMAND

The previous discussion dealt with the influence of a price change on the quantity demanded of the product subject to the price change. **Cross-elasticity** deals with the impact (again, in percentage terms) on the quantity demanded of a particular product created by a price change in a related product (while everything else remains constant). What is the meaning of "related" products? In economics we talk of two types of relationships: **substitutes** and **complements.**

In Henry Caulfield's case, we are dealing with substitutes. The sodas sold by the new grocery store are substitutes for those sold by Henry. They probably are the same products (same brands) but are sold by different suppliers, and one supplier can be considered a substitute for the other. Of course, there are also substitutes on Henry's own shelves—he stocks different brands of cola, for example.

Much of the time when we consider cross-elasticity we are dealing with similar products (not just different brands of the same product) in a more general sense. Thus, chicken and beef can be considered to be substitutes; a change in the price of chicken will have an effect on the consumption of beef. Other instances of substitutes come to mind easily: coffee and tea, butter and oleomargarine, aluminum and steel, and glass and plastic.

---

[15]A. A. Okunade, "Functional Forms and Habit Effects in the U.S. Demand for Coffee," *Applied Economics,* 24, (1992), pp. 1203–12; H. S. Houthakker and L. D. Taylor, *Consumer Demand in the United States: Analysis and Projections,* 2nd ed., Cambridge, MA: Harvard University Press, 1970, pp. 63, 81; J. M. Cigliano, "Price and Income Elasticities for Airline Travel," *Business Economics,* September 1980, pp. 17–21; Daniel B. Suits, "Agriculture," in Walter Adams and James Brock, *The Structure of American Industry,* 9th ed., Englewood Cliffs, N.J.: Prentice-Hall, 1994, p. 5; D. Heien and G. Pompelli, "The Demand for Alcoholic Beverages: Economic and Demographic Effects," *Southern Economic Journal,* January 1989, pp. 759–69; Bahram Adrangi and Kambiz Raffiee, "New Evidence on Fare and Income Elasticity of the U.S. Airline Industry," *Atlantic Economic Journal,* Vol. 28, Issue 4, December 2000, p. 493; Gregory J. Werden, "Expert Report in United States v. Interstate Bakeries Cop. and Continental Baking Co.," *International Journal of the Economics of Business,* July 2000, pp. 139–48; Fiona Carmichael and Robert Simmons, "Elasticity of Demand for Rugby League Attendance and the Impact of BSKYB," *Applied Economics Letters,* Vol. 6, Issue 12, December 1999, pp. 797–800; Ping Zhan, Corinne Husten, and Gary Giovino, "Effect of the Tobacco Price Support Program on Cigarette Consumption in the United States: an Updated Model," *American Journal of Public Health,* Vol. 90, Issue 5, May 2000, pp. 746–800.

Complements are products that are consumed or used together. Henry sells potato chips, pretzels, and other "munchies" that are consumed together with soft drinks. Other cases of complementary products are peanut butter and jam, stereo sets and CD's, tennis rackets and tennis balls, and personal computers and floppy disks.

The definition of cross-elasticity is a measure of the percentage change in quantity demanded of product A resulting from a 1 percent change in the price of product B. The general equation can be written as

$$E_X = \frac{\Delta Q_A}{Q_A} \div \frac{\Delta P_B}{P_B}$$

Again, we run into a little problem regarding the denominator in this expression, and arc elasticity comes to the rescue:[16]

$$E_X = \frac{(Q_{2A} - Q_{1A})}{(Q_{2A} + Q_{1A})/2} \div \frac{(P_{2B} - P_{1B})}{(P_{2B} + P_{1B})/2}$$

What about cross-elasticity coefficients? First, let us look at the sign. A decrease in the price of the supermarket's soft drinks will cause the quantity of soft drinks sold by Caulfield to decrease. And, of course, if the supermarket raises prices, Caulfield's sales will rise. Thus, the sign of cross-elasticity for substitutes is positive. On the other hand, the coefficient sign for cross-elasticity of complements is negative. For instance, a decrease in the price of CD's could lead to increased purchases of stereo systems.

To measure the strength of the elasticity coefficient, we employ a more arbitrary definition than for demand elasticity. As a rule of thumb in business, two products are considered good substitutes or complements when the coefficient is larger than 0.5 (in absolute terms, since the coefficient for complements is negative).

Empirical Elasticities

Again, it should be useful to briefly mention some study results:

A study of the residential demand for electric energy found the cross-elasticity with respect to prices of gas energy to be low, about +0.13.

Aluminum's cross-elasticity of demand with respect to prices of steel was estimated at about +2.0, and even somewhat higher with respect to copper.

---

[16]The following equation, obtained by arithmetic manipulation, may be easier for some readers:

$$E_X = \frac{(Q_{2A} - Q_{1A})}{(P_{2B} - P_{1B})} \times \frac{(P_{2B} + P_{1B})/2}{(Q_{2A} + Q_{1A})/2}$$

Or, if point elasticity is of interest, the use of calculus gives

$$\frac{dQ_A}{dP_B} \times \frac{P_B}{Q_A}$$

The calculations would proceed similarly to those for demand elasticity.

The cross-elasticity of demand for beef with respect to pork prices was calculated to be about +0.25. With respect to prices of chicken, it was about
+0.12. Both numbers indicate that the products are substitutes, but in
this study, the elasticity coefficients were relatively low.

The cross-elasticity for domestic and imported cigarettes in Taiwan is a
positive 2.78, indicating that they are substitutes.

A study of demand elasticity of kerosene in Indonesia estimated its cross-
elasticity with electricity was only 0.097 in the short run and 0.261 in the
long run. The authors ascribe the low value (during the study period
1957–1992) to the lack of access to electricity in a majority of households.[17]

INCOME ELASTICITY

Before the arrival of his competitors, Henry Caulfield saw his sales grow, not only as
the number of households in the area increased, but also as the household income
level in the area rose. This represents quantity of sales as a function of (i.e., influenced by) consumers' income. As a measure of the sensitivity of this relationship,
economists use the term **income elasticity of demand.** The general expression for
this elasticity is

$$E_Y = \%\Delta Q \div \%\Delta Y$$

where Y represents income.[18] The definition of income elasticity is a measure of the
percentage change in quantity consumed resulting from a 1 percent change in income.

As before, we shall turn to arc elasticity for the actual calculation of income
elasticity:[19]

$$E_Y = \frac{(Q_2 - Q_1)}{(Q_2 + Q_1)/2} \div \frac{(Y_2 - Y_1)}{(Y_2 + Y_1)/2}$$

---

[17]R. Halvorsen, "Residential Demand for Electric Energy," *Review of Economics and Statistics,* 57 (February
1975), pp. 12–18; Merton J. Peck, *Market Control in the Aluminum Industry,* Cambridge, MA: Harvard
University Press, 1961, pp. 31–34; Daniel B. Suits, "Agriculture," in Walter Adams, *The Structure of
American Industry,* 8th ed., New York: Macmillan, 1990, p. 11; Chee-Ruey Hsieh, Teh Wei Hu, and Chien-
Fue Jeff Lin, "The Demand for Cigarettes in Taiwan: Domestic Versus Imported Cigarettes," *Contemporary
Economic Policy,* Vol. 17, No. 2, April 1999, pp. 223–234; Rajindar K. Koshal and Manjulika Koshal,
"Demand for Kerosene in Developing Countries: a Case of Indonesia," *Journal of Asian Economics,* Vol. 10,
Issue 2, Summer 1999, pp. 329–336.

[18]Again, in terms of calculus, this expression could be written as

$$\epsilon_y = \partial Q/\partial Y \times Y \div Q$$

This, of course, expresses the point elasticity. Also, as the reader can see partial derivatives have been
used. As in all other cases of elasticity, the assumption is that only the effect of income on quantity is
being measured, with all other possible variables in the demand relationship, (e.g., price, price of related
products, interest rates, advertising) held constant.

[19]As in the case of the other elasticities, the equation can be rewritten in several different forms. The student can select the equation that is most convenient:

$$E_Y = [(Q_2 - Q_1) \div (Q_2 + Q_1)] \div [(Y_2 - Y_1) \div (Y_2 + Y_1)]$$

$$E_Y = [(Q_2 - Q_1) \div (Q_2 + Q_1)] \times [(Y_2 + Y_1) \div (Y_2 - Y_1)]$$

$$E_Y = [(Q_2 - Q_1) \div (Y_2 - Y_1)] \times [(Y_2 + Y_1) \div (Q_2 + Q_1)]$$

In the case of income elasticity, the coefficient can be either positive or negative. For most products, one would expect income elasticity to be positive. After all, given a rise in income, a person will spend more. Thus, when the coefficient is positive, we refer to the income elasticity as normal. (Later, this definition will be refined in relation to elasticities for "superior" commodities.)

The coefficient of +1 represents another dividing line. As income rises, people can increase consumption of products (and services) proportionally, less than proportionally, or more than proportionally to the income rise. If the expenditure on product A goes up by 10 percent when income goes up by 10 percent, then the income elasticity coefficient equals 1. That is, the proportion of the consumer's income spent on this commodity remains the same before and after the change in income.[20] Suppose a consumer's annual income is $30,000 and spending on clothing is $2,700 per year. If this person's annual income rises by 10 percent to $33,000, and he or she then spends $2,970 annually on clothing—also a 10 percent increase—the proportion of total income spent on clothing remains at 9 percent.

If the income elasticity coefficient is greater or less than 1, the fraction of income spent on the product in question changes more or less than proportionally with income. Products whose income elasticities exceed +1, taking larger portions of consumers' income as incomes increase, are often referred to as "superior" commodities.

Again, a brief review of empirical studies that have estimated income elasticities will illustrate this concept:

Short-run income elasticity for food expenditure has been estimated to be about 0.5 and the elasticity of restaurant meals 1.6. The results show that as incomes rise, spending for food eaten at home increases at a slower rate than income and, thus, takes up a smaller portion of income. On the other hand, the expenditure on restaurant meals rises substantially more rapidly as incomes rise, thus becoming a higher proportion of income.

The short-run income elasticity for jewelry and watches appeared to be 1.0; however, the elasticity in the long run was estimated at 1.6. Apparently, consumers take some time to adjust their demand.

The U.S. Department of Agriculture has estimated income elasticities for a group of farm products, among them eggs at 0.57, butter at 0.37, peaches at 1.43, and peas at 1.05.

The income elasticity for air travel between the United States and Europe was a relatively high 1.9. Recently, the income elasticity for passenger travel with the U.S. airline industry has been estimated at unity.

A study of food demand in Spain, which divided food into six categories, found that only meat had an income elasticity of greater than one, 1.54, thus classifying it as a superior good. The elasticity of fish was 0.81, while fats and oils were the lowest at 0.35.

---

[20]Remember that, by definition, the price of the product remains the same. Thus, it does not matter whether we measure an increase in quantity of the product or in expenditures on the product.

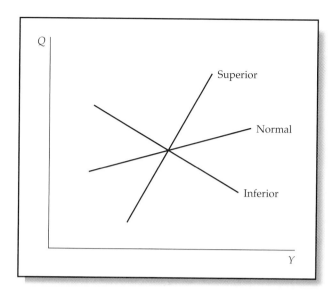

Figure 4.8
Categories of Income
Elasticity

The income elasticity of demand for printing and writing paper in the countries of the European Union was 1.07.[21]

It is possible that the income elasticity coefficient will be less than zero. This would occur if the quantity bought of (or the expenditure on) a product were to decrease absolutely as the result of an increase in income. Although such a result may at first seem implausible, a little reflection will show that such a condition may very well exist. Some products will be demanded by consumers whose incomes are low: but as incomes rise, and consumers feel "better off," they will shift consumption to goods more commensurate with their new economic status. What types of products would be disfavored? The usual examples that economists use are potatoes, pork and beans, and canned luncheon meat.[22] Commodities of this type are usually referred to as **inferior goods.**

So, let us now recapitulate the concept of income elasticity by specifying three categories:

Income elasticity >1: superior goods
Income elasticity ≥ 0, and ≤ 1: normal goods
Income elasticity <0: inferior goods

We can depict these situations graphically as shown in Figure 4.8.

[21]Houthakker and Taylor, *Consumer Demand in the United States*, pp. 62–63, 72. Actually, this study measured the relationship between spending on food and total expenditures, rather than income. Since the proportion of total expenses to income is relatively stable, this substitution does not significantly change results. Daniel B. Suits, "Agriculture," in Walter Adams and James Brock, *The Structure of American Industry*, p. 5; J. M. Cigliano, "Price and Income Elasticities for Airline Travel," *Business Economics*, September 1980, pp. 17–21; Bahram Adrangi and Kambiz Raffiee, "New Evidence on Fare and Income Elasticity of the U.S. Airline Industry," *Atlantic Economic Journal*, Vol. 28, Issue 4, December 2000, p. 493; A. Garcia and J. M. Gil, "Spanish Food Demand: a Dynamic Approach," *Applied Economics*, Vol. 30, Issue 10, October 1998, pp. 1399–1405; M. L. Chas-Amil and J. Buongiorno, "The Demand for Paper and Paperboard: Econometric Models for the European Union," *Applied Economics*, Vol. 32, Issue 8, June 2000, pp. 987–99.
[22]With apologies to consumers at all income levels who happen to like these particular items.

OTHER ELASTICITY MEASURES

We have covered the three most common elasticity measures, but there are others. Elasticity is encountered every time a change in some variable affects quantities. For instance, one thing that Henry could do to counteract his competition is to advertise his products. He might speculate how an increase in advertising expenses would affect his total sales. Thus, **advertising elasticity** can be defined as the percentage change in quantity relative to a 1 percent change in advertising expenses.

Another variable that could have a significant impact on demand—particularly for durable goods—is the interest rate. No one would deny that shifts in mortgage interest rates can cause significant changes in the demand for residential (or nonresidential) construction. Also, the special loan rates offered by automobile manufacturers to customers beginning in the 1980s appear to stimulate car sales, and sales tend to sag when the low rates are terminated.

Elasticity could also be calculated in relation to population size. What is the effect on sales of changes in population? For instance, we could calculate the elasticity of demand for baby carriages as a result of population increases due to the baby boom (and the children of the baby boomers). Or we could investigate the effect of a change in the number of adults (population above the age of 18) on the annual purchases of automobiles (again, as always, holding all other variables constant). And, of course, in Henry Caulfield's case, changes in his community's population will affect his sales. The degree to which sales will be affected is measured by elasticity.

These are just a few examples of possible elasticity calculations. In the next chapter, when we discuss demand estimation, we will see that economists use many variables to explain changes in demand. Although price elasticity, cross-elasticity, and income elasticity are the ones most frequently measured, elasticities can be obtained for a large variety of variables.

ELASTICITY OF SUPPLY

Before we close this chapter, it will be useful to devote a little space to the **price elasticity of supply.** The price elasticity of supply measures the percentage change in quantity supplied as a result of a 1 percent change in price. In other words, this elasticity is a measure of the responsiveness of quantities produced by suppliers to a change in price. In the previous chapter, we developed a supply schedule and a supply curve, and we found that the curve slopes upward and to the right. Thus, the arc coefficient of supply elasticity,

$$E_S = \frac{(Q_2 - Q_1)}{(Q_2 + Q_1)/2} \div \frac{(P_2 - P_1)}{(P_2 + P_1)/2}$$

is a positive number: quantity and price move in the same direction.

The interpretation of the coefficient is the same as for the case of demand elasticity. The higher the coefficient, the more quantity supplied will change (in percentage terms) in response to a change in price.

Again, as in the case of demand elasticity, it is important for a manager to know how supply elasticity affects price and quantity when demand changes. When the supply curve is more elastic, the effect of a change in demand will be greater on quantity than on price of the product. On the other hand, with a supply curve of low elasticity, a change in demand will have a greater effect on price than quantity.

The Solution

Henry Caulfield is no stranger to the economic concept of price elasticity. He has a bachelor's degree in business administration and was doing well as the regional manager of a large supermarket chain when he decided to leave his job and open his own business. Indeed, it was his understanding of price elasticity that prompted him to reduce the soft drink prices as a way of competing against the two new stores in his area. When he had offered special discounts on soft drinks in the past, he noticed that people were very responsive. In fact, Henry had kept a record of the relationship between price and sales, a part of which is shown in Table 4.5. The "special" price was offered as part of the store's "Fourth of July Celebration" sale.

The data indicate an elastic demand for soft drinks at Henry's store. When demand is price elastic, a reduction in price causes total revenue to increase. This was exactly what had happened when Henry had offered his "Fourth of July" celebration special. He was now puzzled because the permanent price reduction did not seem to be having the same positive effect on his total revenue.

Then, in a flash, it dawned on him. One of the most important aspects of demand elasticity—and, for that matter, of any aspect of economic analysis—is the assumption that certain factors are held constant in the examination of the impact of one variable on another. In this case, it was assumed that other factors besides price did not have an impact (or at least not much of an impact) on quantity when Henry had offered the special holiday price for his soft drink. What other factors besides price might now be taken into account?

Table 4.5
Sales Data for 2-Liter Bottles of Soft Drinks

AVERAGE PRICE	AVERAGE WEEKLY SALES	TOTAL REVENUE
Regular Price: $1.89	1,050	$1,985
Special Price: $.89	2,450	2,181

(Continued)

To begin with, last summer Henry did not have any close competitors. Therefore, when he offered his discount, there was no other store nearby to match this price reduction. Obviously, the two new stores were not going to stand by idly watching potential customers go to Henry because he had the lowest price for soft drinks. Therefore, the demand for soft drinks at Henry's store was much less elastic than he thought because he was unable to take away their business. To make matters worse, this "price war" among the three stores might have actually reduced their total soft drink revenues. This is because when all three stores dropped their price, they might well have brought the quantity demanded into the inelastic range of their combined demand curves. (We assume here that the three stores constitute the entire local market for soft drinks.)

But regardless of the reaction of his competitors and the possible impact that all of their price cuts might have had on the degree of price elasticity, there was one simple fact that Henry had completely overlooked. Last year's discount took place in summer, a time when the seasonal demand for this product increases anyway. Thus, when Henry cut the price, the demand for his product had already started to increase and his increased revenue may have been caused by the fact that during this time the demand curve was moving to the right.

One final factor had to be considered. In the past, all of his discounts on soft drinks were "specials" and, therefore, temporary in nature. Consumers knew that they had to take advantage of these specials during a designated period. Since they now realized that the price of soft drinks in Henry's store was permanently lowered, they were in no hurry to buy the product. In other words, Henry had failed to take "future expectations" into account.

Thus, to be able to measure elasticity, Henry would have to separate the effects on unit sales of price from all the other nonprice determinants of demand. Since he had not done this, he had overestimated the degree of responsiveness by his customers to his price reduction. As a result, unfortunately, the reduction in soft drink prices did not provide a solution for Henry. But at least he now understood why it did not.[23] In addition, this analysis reminded Henry never to take for granted that "other factors remain constant." In the real world, conditions are changing all the time, and it is important to factor these changes into the analysis. As a small consolation, Henry realized that the entry of additional suppliers into the market was all part of the economics of running a successful business. After all, if people did not think he was making any money, they would probably not be as willing to start a competing enterprise.

---

[23]Our example may help you to understand an apparent paradox in the pricing of soft drinks in supermarkets. Very often, substantial discounts on soft drinks are offered at all supermarkets during the summer (i.e., "summer specials"). These discounts either may be offered by the soft drink companies to the supermarkets, which then pass them on to customers, or they may be initiated by the supermarkets themselves. Why should they do this at a time when demand is high? After all, economic theory states that an increase in demand causes prices to rise, other factors held constant. What probably happens is that one of the major soft drink companies decides to take market share away from the other major producers by cutting its price. The others quickly follow. The same is true among supermarkets. These price wars can and do occur at any time during the year. It is just that a "summer special" is a good reason to have a sale.

SUMMARY

This chapter has dealt with the important concept of elasticity. In the most general terms, elasticity is defined as the sensitivity of one variable to another or, more specifically, the percentage change in one variable caused by a 1 percent change in another. Several forms of elasticity connected with the demand curve were discussed.

The first was price elasticity of demand: the percentage change in the quantity demanded of a product caused by a percentage change in its own price. Since demand curves slope downward and to the right, the coefficient of price elasticity is negative. If the coefficient is less than -1 (or greater than 1 in absolute terms), demand is said to be elastic. On the other hand, the elasticity coefficient can indicate inelasticity or unitary elasticity.

Elasticity is also tied to total revenue. When demand is elastic, revenue rises as quantity demanded increases; revenue reaches its peak at the point of unitary elasticity and descends as quantity rises on the demand curve's inelastic sector. From the concept of revenue, we developed marginal revenue as the change in revenue when quantity changes by one unit. Marginal revenue is positive at quantities where demand is elastic and becomes negative when the demand curve becomes inelastic.

Next, we explained cross-elasticity, the relationship between the demand for one product and the price of another. Products can be substitutes, and their cross-elasticity is then positive; cross-elasticity is negative for products that are complements.

The third major elasticity concept, income elasticity, measures the sensitivity of demand for a product to changes in the income of the population. Goods and services were defined as superior, normal, and inferior, depending on the responsiveness of spending on a product relative to percentage changes in income.

The examples calculated in the chapter used the method of arc elasticity, which measures changes in both variables over discrete intervals, rather than point elasticity, which deals with change over an infinitely small interval and consequently may require knowledge of elementary calculus.

Several other subtopics appeared in this chapter:

Other elasticities, such as advertising and interest elasticity.
Derived demand, which is the demand for inputs to a final product, and the price elasticity of derived demand.
Supply elasticity, the measure of the sensitivity of quantities produced to the price charged by the producers.

In the next chapter, which discusses methods of estimating demand functions, elasticity concepts will be employed again, and they will reappear in various guises in many of the chapters that follow.

IMPORTANT CONCEPTS

Advertising elasticity: The percentage change in quantity demanded caused by a 1 percent change in advertising expenses. (p. 136)

Arc elasticity: Elasticity which is measured over a discrete interval of a demand (or a supply) curve. (p. 114)

Coefficient of elasticity: The percentage change in one variable divided by the percentage change in the other variable. (p. 113)

Complementary good: A product consumed in conjunction with another. Two goods are complementary if the quantity demanded of one increases when the price of the other decreases. (p. 131)

Cross-elasticity: The percentage change in the quantity consumed of one product as a result of a 1 percent change in the price of a related product. (p. 131)

Derived demand: The demand for products or factors that are not directly consumed but go into the production of a final product. The demand for such a product or factor exists because there is demand for the final product. (p. 123)

Elasticity: The sensitivity of one variable to another or, more precisely, the percentage change in one variable relative to a percentage change in another. (p. 113)

Income elasticity: The percentage change in quantity demanded caused by a 1 percent change in income. (p. 133)

Inferior good: A product whose consumption decreases as income increases (i.e., its income elasticity is negative). (p. 135)

Marginal revenue: The change in total revenue resulting from changing quantity by one unit. (p. 127)

Point elasticity: Elasticity measured at a given point of a demand (or a supply) curve. (p. 116)

Price elasticity of demand: The percentage change in quantity demanded caused by a 1 percent change in price. (p. 113)

Price elasticity of supply: The percentage change in quantity supplied as a result of a 1 percent change in price. (p. 136)

Substitute good: A product that is similar to another and can be consumed in place of it. Two goods are substitutes if the quantity consumed of one increases when the price of the other increases. (p. 131)

QUESTIONS

1. State the general meaning of *elasticity* as it applies to economics. Define the *price elasticity of demand*.

2. Explain the difference between *point elasticity* and *arc elasticity*. What problem can arise in the calculation of the latter, and how is it usually dealt with? In actual business situations, would you expect arc elasticity to be the more useful concept? Why or why not?

3. It has often been said that craft unions (electricians, carpenters, etc.) possess considerably greater power to raise wages than do industrial unions (automobile workers, steel workers, and so on). How would you explain this phenomenon in terms of demand elasticity?

4. Discuss the relative price elasticity of the following products:

   a. Mayonnaise
   b. A specific brand of mayonnaise
   c. Chevrolet automobiles
   d. Jaguar automobiles
   e. Washing machines
   f. Air travel (vacation)
   g. Beer
   h. Diamond rings

5. What would you expect to happen to spending on food at home and spending on food in restaurants during a decline in economic activity? How would income elasticity of demand help explain these changes?

6. Would you expect the cross-elasticity coefficients between each of the following pairs of products to be positive or negative? Why?
   a. Personal computers and software
   b. Electricity and natural gas

c. Apples and oranges
d. Bread and VCRs

7. Why is it unlikely that a firm would sell at a price and quantity where its demand curve is price inelastic?

8. Which products would exhibit a higher elasticity with respect to interest rates, automobiles or small appliances? Why?

9. The immediate effect of gasoline price increases in the aftermath of the Persian Gulf crisis in August 1990 on gasoline consumption was not very significant. Would you expect the consumption of gasoline to be more severely affected if these higher prices remained in effect for a year or more? Why or why not?

10. In December 1990, the federal tax on gasoline increased by 5 cents per gallon. Do you think that such an increase, reflected in the price of gasoline, would have a significant impact on gasoline consumption?

11. Why do you think that whenever governments (federal and state) wish to increase revenues, they usually propose an increase in taxes on cigarettes and alcohol?

12. Could a straight-line demand curve ever have the same elasticity on all of its points?

13. If a demand curve facing a firm is horizontal or nearly so, what does it say about this firm's competition?

14. A company faced by an elastic demand curve will always benefit by decreasing price. True or false? Explain.

15. Discuss the income elasticities of the following consumer products:
   a. Margarine
   b. Fine jewelry

c. Living room furniture
d. Whole lobsters

16. If the income elasticity of tomatoes is estimated to approximate +.25, what would you expect to happen to the consumption of tomatoes as personal income rises?

17. (Read the section called "The market for used automobiles" in Appendix 4A before answering the question.) When prices of used cars dropped about 10% in October 2001, their sales increased by 4.5%. Does this mean that the demand elasticity for used cars is .45?

18. In March 2002 the U.S. Postal Service announced plans to increase first-class postage rates from 34¢ to 37¢ in the summer of 2002. The Service has been losing money. One of the reasons is increased competition from companies such as United Parcel Service and Federal Express. Another reason is the use of faxes and e-mail, as well as electronic bill payment. With this decrease in demand for postal services, why do you think that the Postal Service is seeking a rate increase?

19. A Canadian apparel company, Roots, agreed to provide the U.S. Olympic team at the 2002 winter Olympics with various types of clothing, including berets, for free, and further, to turn over a portion of its profits on sales of this clothing to the U.S. Olympic Committee. The beret became an instant success, and Roots sold a large number of them. What type of elasticity does this arrangement represent?

1. The Acme Paper Company lowers its price of envelopes (1,000 count) from $6 to $5.40. If its sales increase by 20 percent following the price decrease, what is the elasticity coefficient?

2. The demand function for a cola-type soft drink in general is $Q = 20 - 2P$, where Q stands for quantity and P stands for price.
   a. Calculate point elasticities at prices of 5 and 9. Is the demand curve elastic or inelastic at these points?
   b. Calculate arc elasticity at the interval between $P = 5$ and $P = 6$.
   c. At which price would a change in price and quantity result in approximately no change in total revenue? Why?

3. The equation for a demand curve has been estimated to be $Q = 100 - 10P + 0.5Y$, where Q is quantity, P is price, and Y is income. Assume that $P = 7$ and $Y = 50$.
   a. Interpret the equation.
   b. At a price of 7, what is price elasticity?
   c. At an income level of 50, what is income elasticity?
   d. Now assume that income is 70. What is the price elasticity at $P = 8$?

4. Mr. Smith has the following demand equation for a certain product: $Q = 30 - 2P$.
   a. At a price of $7, what is the point elasticity?
   b. Between prices of $5 and $6, what is the arc elasticity?
   c. If the market is made up of 100 individuals with demand curves identical to Mr. Smith's, what will be the point and arc elasticity for the conditions specified in parts a and b?

5. The Teenager Company makes and sells skateboards at an average price of $70 each. Over the past year they sold 4,000 of these skateboards. The company believes that the price elasticity for this product is about -2.5. If it decreases the price to $63, what should be the quantity sold? Will revenue increase? Why?

6. The ABC Company manufactures AM/FM clock radios and sells on average 3,000 units monthly at $25 each to retail stores. Its closest competitor produces a similar type of radio that sells for $28.
   a. If the demand for ABC's product has an elasticity coefficient of -3, how much will it sell per month if the price is lowered to $22?
   b. The competitor decreases its price to $24. If cross-elasticity between the two radios is 0.3, what will ABC's monthly sales be?

7. The Mesa Redbirds football team plays in a stadium with a seating capacity of 80,000. However, during the past season, attendance averaged only 50,000. The average ticket price was $30. If price elasticity is -4, what price would the team have to charge in order to fill the stadium? If the price were to be decreased to $27 and the average attendance increased to 60,000, what is the price elasticity?

8. The Efficient Software Store had been selling a spreadsheet program at a rate of 100 per month and a graphics program at the rate of 50 per month. In September 1990, Efficient's supplier lowered the price for the spreadsheet program, and Efficient passed on the savings to customers by lowering its retail price from $400 to $350. The store manager then noticed that not only had sales of the spreadsheet program risen to 120, but the sales of the graphics program increased to 56 per month. Explain what has happened. Use both arc price elasticity and arc cross-elasticity measures in your answer.

9. Given the demand equation $Q = 1,500 - 200P$, calculate all the numbers necessary to fill in the following table:

P	Q	ELASTICITY		TOTAL REVENUE	MARGINAL REVENUE
		POINT	ARC		
$7.00					
6.50					
6.00					
5.50					
5.00					
4.50					
4.00					
3.50					
3.00					
2.50					

10. Would you expect cross-elasticity between the following pairs of products to be positive, negative, or zero?
    a. Television sets and VCRs
    b. Rye bread and whole-wheat bread
    c. Construction of residential housing and furniture
    d. Breakfast cereal and men's shirts
    Explain the relationship between each pair of products.
11. According to Houthakker and Taylor, the price elasticity of shoes in the United States is 0.7, and the income elasticity is 0.9.
    a. Would you suggest that the Brown Shoe Company cut its prices to increase its revenue?
    b. What would be expected to happen to the total quantity of shoes sold in the United States if incomes rise by 10 percent?
12. A book store opens across the street from the University Book Store (UBS). The new store carries the same textbooks but offers a price 20 percent lower than UBS. If the cross-elasticity is estimated to be 1.5, and UBS does not respond to its competition, how much of its sales is it going to lose?
13. A local supermarket lowers the price of its vanilla ice cream from $3.50 per half gallon to $3. Vanilla ice cream (unit) sales increase by 20 percent. The store manager notices that the (unit) sales of chocolate syrup increase by 10 percent.
    a. What is the price elasticity coefficient of vanilla ice cream?
    b. Why have the sales of chocolate syrup increased, and how would you measure the effect?
    c. Overall, do you think that the new pricing policy was beneficial for the supermarket?
14. The Compute Company store has been selling its special word processing software, Aceword, during the last ten months. Below are shown monthly sales and the price for Aceword. Also shown are the prices for a competitive software, Goodwrite, and estimates of monthly family income. Calculate all the appropriate elasticities, keeping in mind that you can calculate an elasticity measure only when all other factors do not change.

Month	Price Aceword	Quantity Aceword	Family Income	Price Goodwrite
1	120	200	4000	130
2	120	210	4000	145
3	120	220	4200	145
4	110	240	4200	145
5	114	230	4200	145
6	115	215	4200	125
7	115	220	4400	125
8	105	230	4400	125
9	105	235	4600	125
10	105	220	4600	115

15. The demand curve for product X is given as $Q = 2000 - 20P$.
   a. How many units will be sold at $10?
   b. At what price would 2,000 units be sold? 0 units? 1,500?
   c. Write equations for total revenue and marginal revenue (in terms of Q).
   d. What will be the total revenue at a price of $70? What will be the marginal revenue?
   e. What is the point elasticity at a price of $70?
   f. If price were to decrease to $60, what would total revenue, marginal revenue, and point elasticity be now?
   g. At what price would elasticity be unitary?

16. The Transportation Authority in Anytown, U.S.A. raised bus fares from $1 to $1.15 on January 1, 2002. The Authority's statistics show that the number of passengers riding buses decreased from 672,000 in 2001 to 623,000 in 2002.
   a. How much did revenue change?
   b. What is the arc elasticity for bus travel in Anytown?
   c. The answer to b. above would be correct if all conditions (except price) remained the same between 2001 and 2002. Can you think of any other changes that would have affected the result?

17. (Read the section called "A French newspaper and its demand elasticity" in Appendix 4A before answering the question.) What is the arc demand elasticity for the *London Times?* What happened to revenue as a result of the price decrease?

Applications of Supply and Demand

The last two chapters laid the foundation for the student's knowledge of supply and demand and elasticity. Knowing these elements is essential for any further study of economics and is a necessary prerequisite for all the chapters that follow.

Before we discuss the various building blocks that will complete the study of managerial economics, this appendix will endeavor to reinforce the concepts of supply and demand and of elasticity in two ways:

1. Some specific applications of supply and demand will be discussed, including the effects of price controls, excise taxes, and agricultural policies.
2. Various actual situations as reported in the press will be introduced and discussed, and it will be shown that the materials we have just learned can be applied to analyze these situations.

INTERFERENCE WITH THE PRICE MECHANISM

In chapter 3, we discussed the movement toward equilibrium in both the short and long run. A change in demand or supply will call forth actions that will cause equilibrium to occur at a new supply-demand intersection. It was shown that in the short run, price changes will eliminate shortages or surpluses. In the long run, resources in the economy shift from the production of one product to another in response to changes in demand. The shift away from one equilibrium and the move to a new equilibrium will proceed when these movements are permitted to occur freely and are not impeded by any outside interference. Thus, when the supply of corn decreased and price rose so the market cleared at this new price—that is, at the new intersection of supply and demand—there was nothing inhibiting this change from taking place.

However, with present economic institutions, free movement of prices is not always allowed. At least three times in the last 60 years,[24] price controls were imposed in the United States. Prices on various products were set (or fixed at existing levels), and these products could not be sold at prices higher than those prescribed by government. Such a policy is usually referred to as setting a *price ceiling*. If the price ceiling for a product is set at the prevailing equilibrium level, then the ceiling

---

[24]During World War II, the Korean War, and again in 1971.

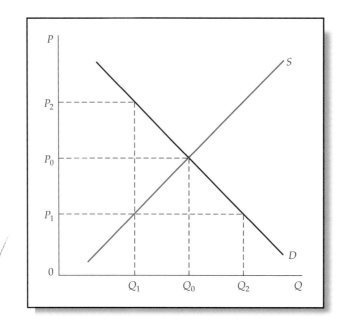

$Q_D > Q_S$
shortage

Figure 4A.1
The Effect of a Price Ceiling
on Supply and Demand

will have no effect (until a change in circumstances dictated a higher price). But if the price were set below the equilibrium price,[25] then, as explained in chapter 3, a shortage would result. In Figure 4A.1, the equilibrium price is P_0 and the quantity sold (and clearing the market) at this price is Q_0. If for some reason the price winds up at P_1 under free-market conditions (i.e., no price controls), the price will rise until the equilibrium price (P_0) is again reached. But if the price is prescribed to be no higher than P_1,[26] the movement toward equilibrium will not take place. Only Q_1 will be supplied while Q_2 is demanded at the lower price, so a shortage of magnitude $Q_1 - Q_2$ will be established. Thus, only the consumers in the interval $0 - Q_1$ will be able to buy this particular product. What will be the result of this forced disequilibrium? Possibly consumers will try to shift their demand to other products, causing a pressure on the other products' prices. And if these products are also price controlled, shortages of these other goods will occur.

There is another possible result. Since only Q_1 units of the product will be supplied at price P_1, these units could be purchased at price P_2 along the demand curve. Consumers would be willing to pay P_2, a price higher than the equilibrium price, P_0, for the limited quantity Q_1. Thus, a strong pressure on the price will be exerted, and somewhere in this process the difference between P_1 and P_2 will be paid to the suppliers.

An example of such a case was the price of automobiles after World War II. A ceiling price below the price level that would have cleared the market was imposed on new

---

[25]It is obvious that a ceiling set above the equilibrium price would be meaningless.
[26]Price ceilings can be enforced by the government imposing fines or even prison sentences on violators. Such punishment would have appeared rather lenient to some of our ancestors. During the times of price controls in ancient Egypt, Greece, and Rome, the death sentence was the penalty for breaking price control laws. The edict of Diocletian in A.D. 301 imposed the death sentence on those selling at prices higher than decreed, as well as on those buying at such prices (Robert L. Schuettinger and Eamonn F. Butler, *Forty Centuries of Wage and Price Controls*, Washington, DC: Heritage Foundation 1979, p. 23).

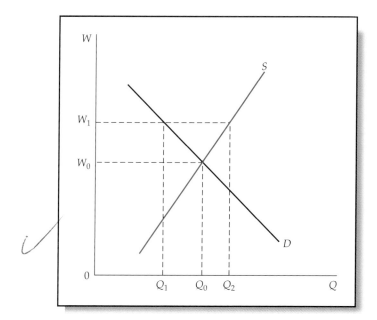

$QS > QD$
surplus

Figure 4A.2
The Effect of a Price Floor
on Supply and Demand

cars. This low price caused automobile manufacturers to limit their production. However, consumers were paying high prices for these cars in the way of a dealer's premium. They may also have received lower trade-in prices on their old automobiles or may have bought their new car as a "used" one, since second-hand cars were not price controlled. The price they actually paid was indeed higher than it could have been if the manufacturers had charged a higher list price.[27] Similarly, where rent ceilings have been imposed many people end up paying a bonus to the superintendent or to a rental agent.

Another example precedes those just discussed by more than 150 years. During the Revolutionary War, the legislature of Pennsylvania imposed limits on prices of goods sold to the military and was thus instrumental in creating extreme shortages of food for George Washington's army at Valley Forge.[28]

On the other side of the price control coin are price floors. In such cases, a price is established below which the product or service may not be sold. An excellent example of a price floor is the legal minimum wage. Employers are not allowed to pay their workers less than the established minimum, and must, therefore, deal with the disturbance to a price equilibrium.[29]

If the equilibrium wage (e.g., per hour) for some unskilled work were to be at level W_0 as shown in Figure 4A.2, but the law stated that a wage lower than W_1 is illegal, then a surplus of labor $Q_1 - Q_2$ would exist. In the absence of the minimum wage law, wages would drop to W_0, and the quantity supplied and demanded of labor would meet at Q_0. Thus, all workers offering themselves for employment at that wage would be hired.

---

[27]Milton Friedman, *Price Theory: A Provisional Text,* Hawthorne, NY: Aldine 1962, p. 18.
[28]Schuettinger and Butler, *Forty Centuries,* p. 41.
[29]Wages are, of course, the price of labor, so it is quite correct to discuss minimum wages under the topic of price floors.

But if the wage cannot fall below W_1, what will happen? The unemployed will look for work elsewhere. If the minimum wage prevails in all types of employment, they would not be able to find work. However, there are still some forms of employment in the United States that are not covered by law. And, a person can become self-employed, in which case minimum wages do not apply.[30]

The effect of increases in minimum wages on employment has been widely studied by economists for many years. In the past, most economists agreed that increases in minimum wages had a negative effect on employment, especially in the case of young and unskilled workers. Unemployment has generally been the highest among teenage workers, many of whom have dropped out of school and acquired few if any skills.[31] However, several recent studies have questioned the traditional findings, concluding that minimum wage increases have not necessarily led to decreased employment.[32] While the new studies cast doubt on the traditional hypothesis, it is much too early to dismiss it. Much additional research is necessary to clarify the effect that increases in minimum wages have on employment.[33]

Several additional points should be made regarding the impact of minimum wages. Even if an increase in the minimum does have a negative effect on employment, workers who remain employed at the higher wage will benefit. The workers can be found in the interval $0 - Q_1$.[34] Second, the short-run effects of an increased legal minimum are probably stronger than the long-run effects. As time passes, the wage levels in the economy will rise (either due to inflation or in real terms), and at some point the minimum wage may approach the free-market equilibrium wage. A third point also appears worth mentioning. Because an increase in the minimum wage must be passed by the legislature (the U.S. Congress in the case of a federal minimum), it is a part of the political process. Legislators may be reluctant to enact a minimum wage increase if it would increase unemployment. Thus, such legislation may be passed only if it would appear to have a minimal effect.

Another example of government controls is in the area of agriculture. We will discuss this subject later.

---

[30]And, at the risk of sounding facetious, the extreme case of self-employment is unemployment.

[31]Among many studies, see, for instance, C. Brown, C. Gilroy, and A. Kohen, "The Effect of the Minimum Wage on Employment and Unemployment," *Journal of Economic Literature,* 20 (June 1982), pp. 487–528; B. S. Frey, W. Pommerehne, F. Schneider, and G. Gilbert, "Consensus and Dissension among Economists: An Empirical Inquiry," *American Economic Review,* 74 (December 1984), pp. 986–94; T. G. Moore, "The Effect of Minimum Wages on Teenage Unemployment Rates," *Journal of Political Economy,* July/August 1971, pp. 897–902. A more recent study that finds negative effects on employment is D. Deere, K. M. Murphy, and F. Welch, "Employment and the 1990–1991 Minimum Wage Hike," *American Economic Review Papers and Proceedings,* 85 (May 1995), pp. 232–37.

[32]See, for instance, D. Card and A. B. Krueger, "Minimum Wages and Employment: A Case Study of the Fast-Food Industry in New Jersey and Pennsylvania," *American Economic Review,* 84 (September 1994), pp. 772–84; D. Card, "Do Minimum Wages Reduce Employment? A Case Study of California, 1987–89," *Industrial and Labor Relations Review,* 46 (October 1992), pp. 38–54; L. F. Katz and A. B. Krueger, "The Effect of the Minimum Wage on the Fast-Food Industry," *Industrial and Labor Relations Review,* 46 (October 1992), pp. 6–21.

[33]A good summary of the recent research and an analysis of various hypotheses regarding the effect of minimum wages on employment is M. Zavodny, "Why Minimum Wage Hikes May Not Reduce Employment," *Economic Review,* Federal Reserve Bank of Atlanta, 83, 2 (second quarter 1998), pp. 18–28.

[34]It is an interesting decision, implicitly made by the U.S. Congress when it passes a law increasing the minimum wage, whether the overall welfare of the country will be increased if some part of the labor force has its wages improved while another part has its income lowered.

THE INCIDENCE OF TAXES

From the viewpoint of the economics of the firm, one important example of applied analysis using supply and demand curves and elasticities is in the area of the incidence or effect of excise taxes on the prices and quantities of products.

An excise tax is a tax imposed as a specific amount per unit of product. It is also sometimes referred to as a specific tax, as compared to a sales tax, which is levied as a percent of the price of the product or service. The federal excise tax on gasoline as of this writing is 18.3 cents per gallon. The sales tax, which is usually collected by states and local communities, in the city of Phoenix, Arizona, for example, is 8.1% of the price of a product. Sales taxes are often referred to as ad valorem taxes. We could discuss the incidence of either ad valorem or specific taxes, but we will choose the latter for our analysis. The principles and applications are similar, but a specific tax provides a simpler and more straightforward illustration.

A numerical example will aid in this exposition. Table 4A.1 shows the demand and supply schedules for a particular product. The equilibrium price is $4. At this price, 15 units will be demanded, and 15 units will be supplied, thus clearing the market.[35] The demand and supply curves are shown in Figure 4A.3a, where an equilibrium at $P = 4$ and $Q = 15$ can be observed.

Now suppose the government imposes an excise tax of $1 per unit, which it will collect from the sellers. The effect is to shift the supply curve up by the unit tax. The shift can be thought of in the following way: Before the enactment of the tax, suppliers offered to sell 20 units at $5. But now, for the producers to obtain $5 per unit, these products will have to be sold at $6 apiece (of which $1 will be remitted to the government).[36] In effect, the production cost for this good has risen by $1 per unit. The last column in Table 4A.1 shows the new supply schedule.

The important question to be asked is what will be the market-clearing price and quantity after the imposition of the new excise tax. An easy answer would be, $1 more than before, or $5. Certainly, the suppliers would prefer not to receive less per unit than they had been getting before the tax. But this is not the correct answer, except in very rare cases.[37] The new intersection will be at $4.50, and the quantity will be 12.5 units.[38]

Thus, sellers will receive only $3.50 per unit after the imposition of the tax, and consumers will be paying 50 cents more than before. In economic jargon, 50 cents of

---

[35]An arithmetic solution can be obtained as follows: the equation of the demand curve for the schedule shown in Table 4A.1 is $Q_D = 35 - 5P$, and the equation for the supply curve is $Q_S = -5 + 5P$. Solving for $Q_D = Q_S$, we obtain

$$35 - 5P = -5 + 5P$$
$$40 = 10P$$
$$4 = P$$

[36]The equation of this new supply curve is $Q_S = -10 + 5P$.
[37]This will occur where the demand curve is perfectly inelastic.
[38]Using our equations,

$$35 - 5P = -10 + 5P$$
$$45 = 10P$$
$$4.5 = P$$

Chapter 4   Demand Elasticity

149

Table 4A.1

Demand and Supply and Tax Incidence

		Quantity Supplied	
Unit Price	Quantity Demanded	Without Tax	With Tax
$6	5	25	20
5	10	20	15
4	15	15	10
3	20	10	5
2	25	5	0
1	30	0	

the tax has been shifted forward to consumers, and 50 cents has been shifted back to the producers. This new equilibrium is shown in Figure 4A.3b.

How the incidence of the tax is distributed between the two parties to the transaction depends on the elasticity of the supply and demand curves. The more elastic the demand curve, the larger will be the portion of the tax that the supplier has to bear. In Figure 4A.4a, we repeat the demand and supply curves previously shown and add a second demand curve, which (before the tax) also intersects the supply curve at $4 and 15 units but at all other points is flatter (more elastic) than the original demand function. In Figure 4A.4b, the tax is added on to the supply curve. With the new demand curve, the equilibrium price is $4.42, and the quantity demanded is just above 12 units.[39]

The effect of the tax on the equilibrium quantity is of significance to the government unit levying the tax. It is obvious that a government setting a new (or increasing an old) excise tax is taking such action to increase its revenue. However, if the demand curve for the particular product is very elastic, the erosion of the revenue base will cut short the amount of revenue the government expects to collect. In the present case, the government would have collected $12.50 in revenue with the original demand curve and only $12.08 for the more elastic demand curve. Had the demand curve been perfectly inelastic (vertical), then not only would the entire tax have been shifted to the consumer, but government revenue would have been $15 because the number of units sold would have remained at 15. Thus, a government would prefer to enact an excise tax on a product with low demand elasticity.[40]

---

[39]The equation for the more elastic demand curve is $Q_D = 43 - 7P$ and the equilibrium price is

$$43 - 7P = -10 + 5P$$
$$53 = 12P$$
$$4.4167 = P$$

[40]You have certainly been subjected to a tax increase in some product you consume, whether it was tobacco, gasoline, or alcohol, to mention just three products on which excise taxes are levied by both federal and local governments. You will probably recall that on the day the tax was increased, the price of say, gasoline, rose by the precise amount of the tax. This is because, first of all, the increase may have been relatively small in comparison to the total price, so that the demand curve may be quite inelastic in this relatively narrow price range. Second, as we have already learned, demand elasticity tends to be lowest in the very short run, so, the tax may be completely (or almost completely) shifted to the consumer at first. But as time passes, there may be a series of small price decreases, or—and this is the more likely scenario in an inflationary environment—prices may not rise as quickly as they otherwise would have.

Managerial Economics

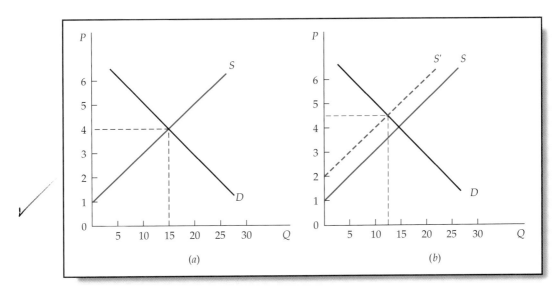

Figure 4A.3
The Influence of an Excise Tax on Supply and Demand

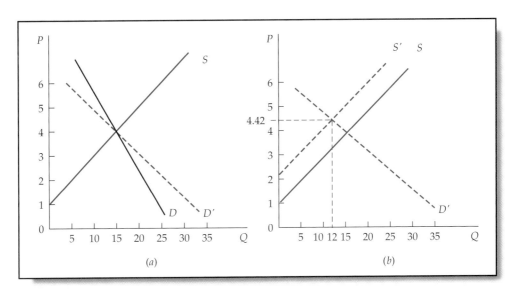

Figure 4A.4
Effect of Demand Elasticity on Equilibrium

Some of the more familiar excise taxes are those on tobacco and alcohol. Because the consumption of these products is not considered desirable by today's standards, tobacco and alcohol are very frequently among the first to be selected when additional taxes are contemplated. All states as well as the federal government impose an excise tax on these two products. In some cases, the amount of the tax on each unit is greater than 50 percent of the total price of the product. Because of the low esteem in which these products are held by a large segment of the population, opposition to the imposition of a tax (or an additional tax) is generally not great (except by the two industries involved). These taxes are often referred to as "sin" taxes. But would it have been attractive to levy such high excise taxes on these two products had the demand curve for them been very elastic? Probably not, because the tax base would have eroded significantly. Therefore, the government unit that wants to achieve what is popularly known as a "revenue enhancement" will find it considerably more favorable to enact an excise tax on products whose demand elasticity in the range of the tax increase is relatively low. Tobacco and alcohol seem to fit this category well. Thus, a government unit can claim to be taxing "undesirable" commodities and at the same time help to maximize its revenue.

Among the many proposals to fight the large federal deficits of the late 1980s was the imposition of a very large tax (as much as 30 to 50 cents per gallon) on gasoline. The popular estimate has been that each cent of tax would decrease the deficit by about $1 billion. However, such calculations may not consider what would happen to the consumption of gasoline over time. The experience with OPEC's price increases in the 1970s and early 1980s shows that the long-run demand curve for gasoline is by no means inelastic.

The elasticity of supply is also important from the viewpoint of tax incidence. From Figure 4A.5, we can see that the effect on the price and quantity is greater the

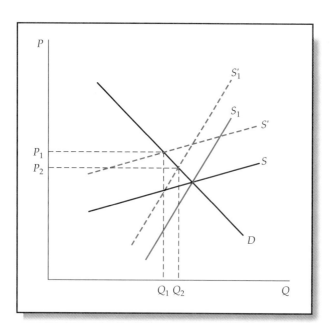

Figure 4A.5
Supply Elasticity and Tax Incidence

higher the elasticity of supply. If supply elasticity is relatively low, the producer will bear the greater burden of the tax.[41]

INTERFERENCE WITH THE PRICE MECHANISM II: AGRICULTURE

It may seem out of place to discuss agriculture in a textbook on managerial economics. But business decisions are not made only in manufacturing or service industries. Farming is a business also, and farmers, whether they own large or small properties, must make decisions that will affect their future. However, owners of agricultural enterprises make their decisions under circumstances quite different from those of other businesspeople. In the United States, for many decades, the federal government has had in place a body of laws designed to help farmers. We will not discuss the philosophy or merits of these long-entrenched policies. Instead, our interest lies in the effect these policies have on prices and the production of agricultural commodities.

Farm incomes in this country, as well as elsewhere, are rather unstable. Both the short-run demand curves and supply curves for food are quite inelastic. Thus, if, for example, some natural disaster decreases the crop of wheat in a given year (i.e., moves the supply curve to the left), the price of wheat will soar. An unexpectedly large crop will drive prices down (and, since the demand curve is inelastic, will bring about a decrease in farm income). On the other side of the coin, since supply curves in agriculture also are inelastic in the short run, a small change in demand will create a significant price response. To protect farmers,[42] the U.S. government has enacted various types of controls.

One of the techniques that has been used is price supports. The government in effect guarantees the farmer that if the entire crop cannot be sold at a stipulated price, the government will buy the unsold (surplus) portion from the farmer. Figure 4A.6a. illustrates this situation.

You will recognize this situation to be almost identical to the price floor discussed earlier. In this case, of course, to relieve the downward pressure on the price of the product, the government takes care of the surplus by buying it up. Assume that the support price is fixed at P_1 whereas the free-market price would have been P_0. Farmers will then be able to sell quantity Q_1 to consumers; however, given the support price, they will produce quantity Q_2, and thus a surplus $Q_2 - Q_1$ will be created. This surplus will be purchased by the government at the support price. The cost to the government is $P_1 \times (Q_2 - Q_2)$, and the farmers' total revenue is $P_1 \times Q_2$. This, of course, is also the total cost to consumers and to the government combined.[43]

---

[41]Again, as in the case of demand, chances are that in the very short run, supply curves will be rather inelastic, as suppliers cannot immediately remove resources from this industry to another pursuit. As time progresses, however, and resources shift out of the affected industry, the supply curve will become more elastic, and both price and production will be affected to a more significant degree.
[42]In the longer run, farm productivity has been rising substantially, moving the supply curve to the right and creating a long-run decrease in farm prices.
[43]The payments to farmers by the government must be obtained through tax revenues: thus, the consumers as well as business pay for that part of the total food bill.

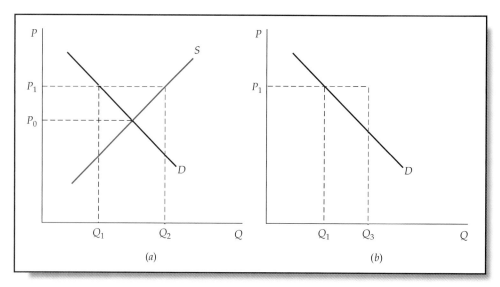

Figure 4A.6
The Use of Price Supports

To reduce the amounts that have to be paid to the farmers, a policy of production controls was instituted. Let us assume that a production quota is at Q_3, as shown on Figure 4A.6*b*: then, the government expenditure will decrease from $P_1 \times (Q_2 - Q_1)$ to $P_1 \times (Q_3 - Q_1)$, and the farmers' income will be $P_1 \times Q_3$.[44]

Another type of policy is the establishment of target prices guaranteed by the government. Such a policy will protect the farmer in the same way as the price support policy; however, instead of selling the product at the supported prices, the producers sell their crops at market prices and collect the difference between the market and target prices for each unit sold from the U.S. government. If we assume the existence of production controls in this case as well, Figure 4A.7 illustrates the results. The price prevailing in the market is now P_2[45] and the quantity sold is Q_3. Price P_2 is, however, less than the target price P_1, and the government will reimburse the farmer the difference between P_2 and P_1 for each of the units sold, or Q_3. Thus, the cost to the government (actually, the taxpayers) is $Q_3 \times (P_1 - P_2)$. In this case, the consumers bought quantities at a lower price than under the price support system of Figure 4A.6*b*), and the government is not forced to become the owner of these farm products and to bear the cost of the storage.

If the target price in Figure 4A.7 is the same as the support price in Figure 4A.6*b*, then the total amount going to the farmers and paid out by the combined forces of consumers and government (not counting storage costs) will be the same, $P_1 \times Q_3$.

---

[44]Actually, to draw the production quota line vertically from the X-axis is not quite correct. At some point, the supply curve drawn in Figure 4A.6*a* will cross the production quota line. Only above that intersection point will the vertical line be effective.
[45]This is not the free-market price, since Q_3 represents the quantity that would be sold under conditions of production controls, a quantity presumably less than would have been produced and sold in the absence of controls.

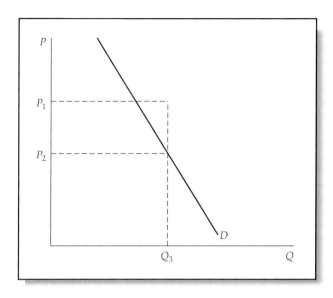

Figure 4A.7
The Effect of Target Prices

But the distribution of the total costs between the government and the consumer will be different, depending on the elasticity of the demand curve. We learned that when total revenue rises in response to a price increase, the demand curve is inelastic. If we concentrate on the total amount paid by the consumer directly for the farm product, we see that with price supports (Figure 4A.6b), the total consumer expenditure is $P_1 \times Q_1$, and with target prices it is $P_2 \times Q_3$. Because P_1 is higher than P_2, then if the area $P_1 \times Q_1$ is larger than the area $P_2 \times Q_3$, the demand curve (in this interval) must be inelastic. To recap, if the demand curve is inelastic, the consumer will pay more under the price support program than under the target price policy. And since the total combined expenditures (government and consumer) are the same under both systems, the government portion of this total cost is larger under the target price system. Since most economists agree that demand curves for most agricultural commodities are inelastic, the target price system would tend to be more expensive for the government.[46]

After many decades of providing financial aid to agriculture, the U.S. Congress enacted the "Freedom to Farm" act in 1996, phasing out agricultural subsidies, while still providing declining payments during a period of transition ending in 2002. However, prices of wheat, soybeans, corn, and other farm products dropped sharply in 1998, caused partially by the Asian economic crisis and ample crops. During the past four years, the government came up with emergency payments and temporary price supports. For example, in August 2001, Congress passed, and the President signed, a $5.5 billion emergency aid bill to prop up farm incomes as commodity prices continued to be low. In late 2001 Congress began to work on a new farm subsidy bill. The "Farm Security and Rural Investment Act of 2002" passed Congress in May 2002, and was signed by the president. The law is expected to cost

---

[46]Storage costs are not being considered in this conclusion. On the other hand, the government may be able at some time to sell some of the stored products and thus recover a part of its original expenditures.

approximately $190 billion over the next ten years. It effectively erased the provisions of the 1996 act.[47]

ACTUAL SITUATIONS

We will now turn to some actual events, reported in newspapers and journals, that can easily be explained using supply-and-demand analysis. Some of these items describe events that took place a number of years ago. These older examples are included because they teach us lessons regarding supply–demand analysis that are really timeless. Together with these, a number of recent examples illustrate how the subjects discussed in the previous two chapters have current applications.

Voluntary Export Restraints

In 1981 the United States and Japan agreed that Japan would limit its exports of cars to the United States to 1,680,000 annually. The limit was later increased but was still considerably below the number that would have been sold in the United States in the absence of this quota. What was the result? The price of Japanese vehicles rose. The effect of such a limitation can be seen in Figure 4A.8a. The original quantity and price of Japanese cars sold in the United States are shown as Q_0 and P_0. The imposition of the "voluntary" export quota on Japan at a limit less than the equilibrium quantity changed the shape of the supply curve. At the level of exports, Q_1, the supply curve becomes vertical, and the demand curve now intersects the supply curve at P_1—a new, higher price.

Given the restriction, the Japanese began to ship their higher-priced models to the United States to satisfy the upper portion of the market. Since the demand for Japanese cars now could not be satisfied, American consumers sought to purchase domestic or other imported automobiles. Such action shifted the demand curve for the rest of the automobile market to the right, as illustrated in Figure 4A.8b, thus increasing the number and the price of vehicles purchased. It was estimated by one economist that new car prices in 1984 were $1,500 higher than they would have been had quotas not been in effect. The additional cost to American consumers was $13 billion. The beneficiaries of this increased cost were the big three automobile manufacturers (to the tune of about $6 billion in higher profits), the autoworkers (about $3 billion in overtime payments), and the American dealers of Japanese cars and the Japanese manufacturers themselves (about $4 billion).[48] Subsequently, Japanese automobile manufacturers began to produce their cars in the United States. In 1985 and thereafter, the U.S. dollar weakened considerably against the Japanese yen. The

---

[47]S. Kilman, "On the Northern Plains, Free-Market Farming Yields Pain, Upheaval," *The Wall Street Journal*, May 5, 1998; S. Kilman, "U.S. Slices Forecasts for Many Farm Prices," *The Wall Street Journal*, August 13, 1998; "Bush Signs $5.5 Billion Farm-Aid Bill to Stabilize Incomes," *The Wall Street Journal*, August 14, 2001; David Rogers, "House GOP Plans Massive Farm-Spending Bill," *The Wall Street Journal*, September 7, 2001; David Rogers, "Aftermath of Terror: Bush Urges Delay on House Farm Bill Citing Cost," *The Wall Street Journal*, October 4, 2001; "United States: Just Plant Dollars; Farm Policy," *The Economist*, October 13, 2001, p. 31; P. Brasher, "Bush Signs, Praises Farm Bill," *Associated Press Newswires*, May 13, 2002.
[48]Yoshi Tsurumi, "They're Merely a Subsidy for Detroit," *New York Times*, December 16, 1984.

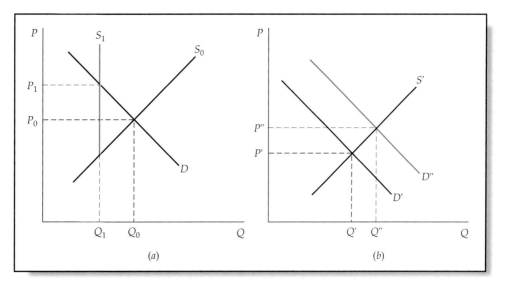

Figure 4A.8
Imposition of Voluntary Export Restraints

prices of Japanese cars in the United States rose significantly, permitting U.S. manu-facturers to continue to increase their prices and enjoy higher profits.[49] But in 1998, with the Japanese yen displaying substantial weakness, it is Japanese cars which appear to have a price advantage.

Economic Consequences of Other Import Restrictions

A 1973 study calculated that the loss to American consumers due to import restric-tions on sugar was $586 million per year. Ilse Mintz estimated that the restrictions raised the price of sugar by 2.57 cents per pound and decreased consumption from 23.2 to 22.4 billion pounds per year. Figure 4A.9 shows this situation. The shaded area representing consumer loss can be calculated as follows:

0.0257×22.4 billion	$575.7 million
$0.0257 \times (23.2 - 22.4$ bill.$) \times 0.5$	<u>10.3</u> million
	$586.0 million

A similar type of study performed in 1977 looked at the consequences of the imposi-tion of import quotas on steel. The study showed that a price increase of $11 per ton of steel and a resulting decrease in steel consumption of 0.9 million tons per year would have cost the consumer over $1 billion per year and would have created a gain of about $870 million for U.S. steel producers. Thus, consumers lose more than U.S. producers gain. A part of the difference would accrue to foreign producers.

---

[49]"Schools Brief," *Economist*, October 25, 1986, pp. 84–85.

Figure 4A.9
Effect of Import Restrictions
on Sugar Demand

Another part is due to the decrease in steel consumption, and another results due to the substitution of high-cost U.S. steel for cheaper foreign steel.[50]

The Demand for Beef

Recently there has been a shift away from beef demand. The result has been an increase in the consumption of seafood, but the main beneficiary of this shift in demand appears to be chicken. Table 4A.2 shows data for these consumption changes over 12 years.

Demand for beef was very high into the early 1970s, and prices kept rising. However, the concern raised about the link between red meat and cholesterol levels was instrumental in putting a check on beef demand. Also, around this same time, chicken producers developed new and convenient chicken products that appealed to the public. Table 4A.2 shows that beef consumption per capita dropped 16 percent from 1975 to 1987, while chicken consumption rose 57 percent. Fish consumption also rose significantly, 26 percent, but considerably less than chicken.

During this period, the U.S. cattle population decreased substantially. As discussed previously, a change in supply is a long-run reaction to changes in demand.[51] More recently, however, the beef industry has begun to take steps that appear to have stopped the demand slide. Actually, there has been some increase in the demand for beef, as the industry has had some limited success with advertising campaigns. In 1987 cattle growers voted to establish a $1-per-animal fund for product and nutritional research and a national advertising campaign. One possible way to combat the demand for chicken is to offer branded merchandise, a method chicken producers have been using for years.

---

[50]Ilse Mintz, *U.S. Import Quotas: Costs and Consequences*, Washington, DC: American Enterprise Institute, 1973; Federal Trade Commission, *Staff Report on the United States Steel Industry and Its International Rivals*, November 1977. Both of these studies are discussed in Edwin Mansfield, *Microeconomics*, 5th ed., New York: W. W. Norton, 1985, pp. 100–103, 509–12.

[51]The discussion in this section is based on the following articles: Marj Charlier, "Beef's Drop in Appeal Pushes Some Packers to Try New Products," *The Wall Street Journal*, August 8, 1985; Marj Charlier, "The U.S. Beef Industry Just Can't Seem to Get the Hang of Marketing," *The Wall Street Journal*, January 4, 1989.

Table 4A.2

U.S. Consumption per Capita, in Pounds

	1975	1987
Beef	88.0	73.4
Chicken	39.9	62.7
Fish	12.2	15.4

The beef industry appears to be rather slow in emulating some of the marketing techniques of the chicken producers, but, according to the research director of the beef council, "there is a sense of emergency that we have to become marketers."[52] These trends are graphically depicted in Figure 4A.10. The original equilibrium of beef prices and production was at the intersection of P_0 and Q_0. As consumer preferences shifted from beef to chicken and fish, the demand curve for beef moved to the left, from D_0 to D_1. Quantities produced were less, and prices declined relatively.[53]

Over time, resources shifted out of beef production. According to the National Cattlemen's Association, the number of beef cattle decreased from 130 million in 1975 to about 110 million in 1985.[54] The shift of resources is shown on Figure 4A.10 as a movement of the supply curve from S_0 to S_1. This action tended to stabilize beef prices during the period.[55] In the last few years, as just described, beef producers have begun to fight back, if not always effectively. The various campaigns mounted by the industry to convince consumers of beef's beneficial qualities are intended to move the demand curve to the right, from D_1 and D_2. Whether the new demand curve will be between D_1 and D_0 or even to the right of D_0 cannot be foreseen. The danger lurking in this effort to increase beef demand was that, given the low level of beef herds,[56] beef prices could soar, thus discouraging consumers. If the supply curve for beef in the short run is rather inelastic, this is what could happen.

What we have described above was the situation prevailing during the 1980's and early 1990's. Despite some efforts by the beef industry, the demand for beef has declined by some 41 percent over the past 25 years. But more recently, the beef industry appears to have learned some lessons from the chicken producers. Now, the industry is spending hundreds of millions of dollars to "reverse a decades-long decline in red meat consumption." Some of the large firms in the industry, such as Hormel Foods, Inc. and IBP, Inc. (now a unit of Tyson Foods, Inc.) are branding their products. One thrust in this effort is to shorten the cooking process by selling branded precooked packaged beef that can then be finished in microwave ovens in a matter of minutes. This is primarily intended to attract families with working

---

[52]Charlier, "U.S. Beef Industry."

[53]Absolute prices of both chicken and beef may have risen due to inflationary factors, which were very strong in the 1970s and early 1980s.

[54]Charlier, "Beef's Drop in Appeal."

[55]Similarly, increases in chicken-producing resources dampened the price effect of the increased chicken demand.

[56]Beef supplies were further depleted in 1988 because of the severe drought.

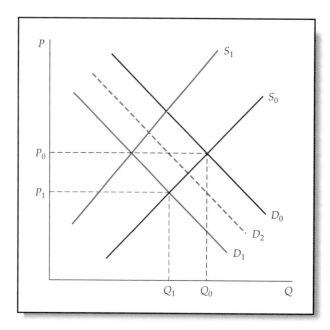

Figure 4A.10
The Downward Shift in Beef Demand

couples that do not have the time to spend several hours preparing dinners. While these meats tend to sell at prices considerably higher than raw meat, the two companies expect to sell about $100 million of their product in 2002. "Within a decade, say some industry officials, microwavable red meats could easily generate $1 billion in sales." But these companies are also producing high-quality steak and chops using their own brand labels for consumers who are not interested in microwaving their meat. In addition, some supermarket chains prefer to sell meats under their own labels, such as Kroger Company's Cattleman's Collection.[57]

Demand for Various Consumer Products

It is a well-known fact that women have significantly increased their participation in the labor force since the end of World War II. After the war, men returned from the armed services, and women, who had taken the men's place in the work force, returned to their traditional pursuits. In 1947, women made up about 28 percent of total employment. Women then began to enter the labor force again, and the proportion of female employment rose to 35 percent by 1965 and to 45 percent by 1987. With the change in women's functions, a change in U.S. living patterns and consumption habits followed. According to a *Wall Street Journal* article, homes in the United States are not quite as clean as they were in the past.[58] Whereas women once spent much of their time as housewives, their acceptance into the labor force has changed this tradi-

---

[57]Scott Kilman, "A Roast Is a Roast? Not in the New Game of Marketing Meat," *The Wall Street Journal*, February 20, 2002.
[58]Betsy Morris, "Homes Get Dirtier as Women Seek Jobs and Men Volunteer for the Easy Chores," *The Wall Street Journal*, February 12, 1985.

tional role. "Sales of scouring powder, mildew removers, floor wax and dishwashing liquid slipped again last year, continuing a 10-year trend," according to Selling Areas Marketing, Inc., a New York-based research company.[59] On the other hand, sales of paper plates and aluminum baking pans have risen significantly. In addition, new time-saving household products have come to the market, and a new service business—maid services—has sprung up.

In the late 1990s, U.S. supermarkets and packaged goods manufacturers faced another shift in consumer demand. With the economy thriving and a significant number of households with working couples, there has been a vast increase in spending on restaurant and take-away meals at the expense of at-home eating. In 1997, it was estimated that away-from-home eating accounted for about 45 percent of total spending on food. The profits of packaged goods manufacturers slipped in 1998. Supermarkets were actually being hit not only by increased restaurant eating but also by competition from discount stores such as Wal-Mart. Many supermarket chains are now trying to compete by having special sections that prepare both hot and cold meals packaged for consumers who do not want to cook meals at home. Usually the profit margin on such meals is greater than on the usual items on grocery shelves, which offsets the decreases in sales of supermarkets' regular merchandise.[60]

A shift in demand patterns also occurred after the events of September 11, 2001. It appears that American consumers turned to "mundane and homey activities and purchases." Among the beneficiaries of the change in the public's mood were stores dealing with old-fashioned crafts like quilting and knitting, and fast foods like pizza and ice cream. On the other hand, there was a decline of business at fancy restaurants. Sales of DVDs and television sets as well as kitchen appliances, such as cooking ranges, were going well.[61]

A French Newspaper and Its Demand Elasticity

In July 1994, the French daily newspaper, *Le Quotidien,* suspended publication. In order to boost its revenue in the face of increasing competition and France's recession, *Le Quotidien* slashed its price from FF6 to FF4. Its circulation increased from 30,000 units to 40,000. But this resulted in a decrease of its revenue from FF180,000 per day to FF160,000. The demand curve turned out to have an arc elasticity of -0.71. A similar action involved a decrease in the price of the *London Times* in September 1993. The price was dropped from 45 to 30 pence, while the daily prices of its competitors remained unchanged. Between August 1993 and May 1994, the *Times'* daily circulation rose from 355,000 to only 518,000, resulting in a decrease in revenue. Again, the demand curve appears to have inelastic.[62]

---

[59]Morris, "Homes Get Dirtier."
[60]Richard Tomkins, "Home Truths for U.S. Grocers," *Financial Times*, August 11, 1998.
[61]Leslie Kaufman and Julian E. Barnes, "Craving a Comfort Zone," *New York Times*, October 10, 2001; Christopher Bowe, "Consumers Turn to the Kitchen in Times of Strife," *Financial Times*, October 16, 2001; and Elliot Spagat, "Retailers Pin Hope on 'Cocooning' TV Buyers," *The Wall Street Journal*, October 18, 2001.
[62]Alice Rawsthorn, "Crisis in French Press May See More Casualties," *Financial Times*, July 6, 1994; R. W. Stevenson, "A Cheaper Times of London Wins Readers," *New York Times*, June 13, 1994.

Controlling Traffic in City Centers

In 1998, Singapore began a new system of controlling traffic in its city center. Motorists must purchase prepaid cash cards and tolls are deducted electronically from this card (which is placed on the car's dashboard). The tolls differ depending on the time of the day a car enters the city. If a car enters the central area without this card, its registration plate will be photographed and a violation notice mailed. The program appears to have been successful. Traffic has decreased by 17 percent during the enforcement period, and the speed at which cars pass through the city center has increased. Singapore is not the only city using this procedure; among others, several Norwegian cities use such cards.[63] A different method to decrease traffic is used in Minneapolis. Here, one of the largest employers, American Express Financial Advisors, is subsidizing the area's bus systems in return for greatly reduced monthly bus tickets for its employees.[64]

Although actions in both Singapore and Minneapolis aim at decreasing rush hour traffic, the two methods have very different effects on the demand for the use of automobiles. In the case of Singapore, the action has increased the cost of travel into the city center, and has caused a movement up along the demand curve, a decrease in the quantity demanded. On the other hand, in Minneapolis, the result is to lower the cost of bus travel, a substitute for car commuting. The demand curve for auto travel will now shift to the left, a decrease in demand.

The effect of these two actions can be illustrated by simple graphs. Assume that the demand for automobile traffic in Singapore is as shown on Figure 4A.11a. If the quantity demanded before the imposition of the toll is at P_0 and Q_0, then after the toll is implemented, the new equilibrium will be at the intersection of P_1 and Q_1. This, of course, as we saw in chapter 3, is a decrease in quantity demanded. Now, let us take a look at the Minneapolis situation. In this case, Figure 4A.11a represents the demand for bus travel. The decrease in bus fares resulting from the financial aid given to the bus systems, will cause a move on the demand curve from P_0 (the price of fares before the decrease) to P_2; this is an increase in quantity demanded from Q_0 to Q_2. Figure 4A.11b depicts the demand for automobile traffic into downtown. Demand curve D_0 represented the demand before the bus fare cuts went into effect. With the decrease in bus fares, the substitution effect will result in a new demand curve D_1, and the demand for automobile travel will decrease from point Q_0 to Q_1.

The Market for Used Automobiles

In the aftermath of the attack on the World Trade Center and Pentagon, Detroit's auto manufacturers and their dealers began to offer 0 percent financing on new cars. This action caused sales of new cars to rise by 35 percent in October 2001. In many cases, people who traditionally purchased used cars, now found new vehicles to be relative bargains. With this surge in new car sales, customers traded in a huge number of old ones, sharply increasing their supply.

---

[63]Sheila McNulty and John Parker, "How to Stop Traffic Jams," *Financial Times,* May 9, 1998.
[64]*The Wall Street Journal,* August 27, 1998.

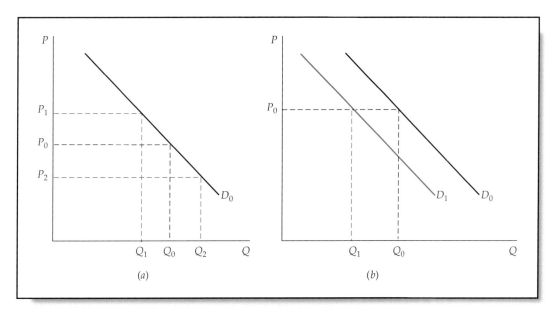

Figure 4A.11
The Effect of Two Different Policies on Automobile Travel

As a consequence, prices on used car lots dropped some 10 percent below the levels prevailing during the summer, while some vehicles dropped as much as 20 percent. In addition, because of the expected decrease in travel, many car rental companies reduced their fleets by 20 to 30 percent, thus adding to the already swollen used car inventories.[65]

The Coffee Glut in Brazil

A very large crop of coffee in Brazil, the world's leading coffee bean grower, as well as in other countries, caused a steep decline in the price of coffee in the year 2001.

Brazil attempted to decrease the supply of coffee by using a "global retention scheme." Brazil was going to keep more than 2 million bags (at 60 kilograms per bag) off the market. However, this plan collapsed in September 2001 when other coffee-producing countries refused to cooperate. In November, Brazil's policy makers planned to introduce another program, under which the government would finance 70 percent of the value of coffee that producers would hold back for a year.

One of the problems that producers in Brazil face is the rather low productivity and thus high cost of coffee production. According to one authority, "at current prices, the break-even point is at 45 bags per hectare (2.471 acres). But in the past year, productivity has averaged 17 bags around here." Many coffee producers have had to seek alternative products, such as soybeans, passion fruit, and grains. It has

---

[65]Sholnn Freeman and Karen Lundegaard, "New-Car Deals Shake Up Market for Used Vehicles," *The Wall Street Journal*, November 16, 2001.

also been estimated that 10 percent of the coffee-growing area has been abandoned since the end of the year 2000, and it is expected that additional land will be left idle by 2002 harvest time.[66]

Ice Cream Prices

In the summer of 2001, consumers were hit by some steep increases in the price of ice cream. The reason was a sharp rise in the price of milk fat, the principal ingredient in ice cream. Manufacturers estimated that "retail prices were up 4 percent from last year, triggering a 3 percent drop in consumption." This would indicate price elasticity to be .75.

The industry blamed the increase on new government regulations that went into effect in January 2000. These regulations apparently tied the cost of milk fat to the price of butter. The price of butter had almost doubled since then due to heavy demand increases. On the other hand, U.S. Department of Agriculture officials ascribed the increase to demand–supply conditions for ice cream, with demand rising in the summer while cows seemingly produce less milk because of the heat.[67]

The French Wine Industry

Over the past several years the French wine industry has been suffering. From 1999 to 2000 alone, exports of French wines have dropped 5.4 percent, and millions of liters of unsold wine are accumulating in French cellars. France's market share in the United States has dropped from 7 percent to 5 percent in the past three years. During this period, sales of producers in California, Australia, and Chile have been rising sharply in the world's important markets of North America, Northern Europe, and Asia. What are the major reasons for this shift in demand from the world's leading wine producers to a group of upstarts in the rest of the world? According to a recent article there are several[68]:

1. French vintners are restricted by the government as to the types of grapes that can be produced in a particular region, and how they are cultivated.
2. They are paid by the amount of grapes they deliver, thus impairing careful growing, and resulting in inconsistent quality.
3. Predominantly, French producers are small, scattered firms (there are about 20,000 of them) that are finding it difficult to compete efficiently with large, new-world companies. Only one French company is among the world's ten largest producers.
4. The many different regional and local labels of French wines make it difficult for consumers (except for connoisseurs) to understand what they are buying, compared to the simple labeling by the new world's large wine producing companies.
5. The dispersed nature of the French wine industry is no match for its large foreign rivals when it comes to marketing and promotion programs. For example,

---

[66]Thierry Ogier, "There's an Awful Lot of Coffee in Brazil," *Financial Times,* November 9, 2001.
[67]" 'Ice Scream': Milk-Fat Prices Raise Cost of Summer Treat" *The Wall Street Journal,* July 24, 2001.
[68]William Echikson and others, "Wine War," *Business Week,* September 3, 2001, pp. 54–60.

U.S. company E. & J. Gallo, the world's largest producer, spent $2.5 million on marketing in England alone, while the entire Bordeaux wine-producing region spent less than half of that amount in 2000.

SUMMARY

As the preceding examples show, it is extremely important that a manager or entrepreneur understand such cause-and-effect relationships. Demand and supply curves move continually in an economic society. It is management's task to identify such movements, to understand their consequences, and to design strategies and tactics to minimize adverse results and take advantage of new opportunities. Knowledge of economic interrelationships is a tool that will assist decision makers in taking these important actions.

Chapter 5

Demand Estimation

The Situation

Jennifer Harrah was assigned the task of developing and testing a statistical model that would help to explain consumer demand for soft drinks. Jennifer worked for a major market research firm that had a worldwide reputation for its work in the "FMCG" (fast-moving consumer goods) sector of the economy. Her firm had just been hired by Global Foods, Inc., to conduct preliminary research into the soft drink market.

As a regular consumer of soft drinks, Jennifer often wondered what affected people's demand for these beverages. Moreover, she had done a case study on Global Foods in graduate school and was looking forward to working with the very company she recalled as very interesting to study at the time. In the study, Global Foods was portrayed as the classic example of a large, multinational company that faced declining profit margins and demand for its products because of the maturity of the markets in which they were being sold. Her class had reached the conclusion that the best way for this company to energize itself was to go into markets where growth in unit sales and profit margins was very high, and that also related to food, its core business.

However, Jennifer was surprised that the company chose soft drinks as its new product line. Her class had decided that microwavable frozen gourmet meals were a logical candidate for the firm's expansion efforts.

(Continued)

In a meeting with the senior partner of her firm and a representative of Global Foods, Inc., Jennifer's assignment was spelled out in greater detail. The partner opened the meeting by saying, "Jennifer, I'm going to put you in charge of the entire project. You decide on the best way to obtain the data, the statistical technique to use to analyze the data, and the most effective way to present the results to our client. Global will give you as much assistance as possible. They have their own internal market research group, but the CEO felt that the use of an outside consultant would give the study more objectivity and credibility. Your only constraint is time. This is a top-priority project for our client. In fact, the CEO wants you to produce the results in three weeks, give or take a few days. Can you do it?"

"This is an assignment made in heaven," Jennifer thought. "An interesting subject, a large, well-known client, an opportunity for interaction with top management, and a major contract for our firm." She waited a bit so as not to seem too eager and then replied, "No problem. The report will be ready in 20 days."

INTRODUCTION

In the previous chapters, we analyzed the demand function from a theoretical standpoint. We showed how each of the determinants of demand—price and the nonprice factors, such as tastes and preferences and income—affects the amount people are willing to purchase of a particular good or service. Hypothetical numerical examples were devised to illustrate the concept of elasticity, a key way in which economists measure the sensitivity of quantity demanded to changes in price and the nonprice determinants of demand. The use of hypothetical data is a convenient way to illustrate the theory. But to put the theory into practice, managers of a firm need to know the true quantitative relationship between demand and the factors that affect it.

What would consumers be willing to pay for a particular good or service? How can we produce a good or service to enable us to sell enough at a certain price to receive an acceptable return on our investment? What impact does advertising have on sales? Can we expect different segments of the market (e.g., by region, income level, occupational category) to react in different ways to our marketing efforts? In short, *"what do consumers really want?"*

For business decision makers, the answer to this question is crucial. We can anticipate that they would be willing to pay considerable sums of money to obtain this information, and, in fact, they do. Many firms have their own market research departments as well as economic research departments. Others hire independent consulting firms, and still others rely on the research arms of their advertising agencies. The leading providers of market research services in the United States are ACNielsen and IRI. ACNielsen also has a strong global presence, while IRI is just starting to expand outside of the United States.

There are a number of ways in which market researchers seek out the "truth" of consumer behavior. They might use the direct approach of a **consumer survey,** either face to face (e.g., stopping people in shopping centers) or by telephone. Perhaps some of you have at some time been a participant in this type of data gathering.

Another direct approach used by market researchers is the focus group. Consumers are asked to attend a group meeting conducted by the researcher, at which various questions are asked regarding a company's goods and services. Company representatives may be present or may choose to observe the proceedings from behind a two-way mirror. The major problem with such direct methods is that consumers often cannot be realistic about how they would act in actual market situations.

To get a more accurate view of the "true" behavior of consumers, market research firms such as ACNielsen also gather data by getting people to participate in consumer panel surveys. Volunteers in this activity are provided with a scanner, which enables them to record all their consumer purchases by reading the bar codes of every item they buy from retail stores. The survey participants then transmit the scanned data to the market research firm on a regular basis via a special modem attached to their home phones.

Technology is making it possible for companies to accumulate, store, and process large amounts of data about consumer behavior. The data are primarily collected with the aid of scanning technology (e.g., bar code readers and point-of-sale [POS] terminals) used at the checkout counters of stores and supermarkets throughout the United States and Western Europe. In most other parts of the world, data on consumer purchases are still done by actual on-site "audits" by market research personnel. However, eventually, it is expected that many more countries, particularly the so-called "Big Emerging Markets" will be using scanning technology.

ACNielsen was recently bought by the VNU, the Dutch company that was cited in chapter 1's "International Applications." A visit to the company's Web site (www.acnielsen.com)[1] will provide readers with a good idea of the kinds of products and services provided by market research companies to their clients, most of whom are large food and beverage companies and other types of fast-moving packaged consumer goods. The site also contains useful articles on current topics in consumer marketing such as B2B exchanges, category management, and global marketing.

Companies such as NCR specialize in providing storage capacity that is measured in "terabits" or trillions of bits of information. IBM recently developed a storage technology that enables the entire contents of the Library of Congress to be stored on a device approximately the size of the head of a pin. Wal-Mart has built a data warehouse of information about what every single one of its customers purchases in every one of its stores every day of the year. The amount of data stored in this warehouse is allegedly second only to that stored by the U.S. government. All of these developments enable statistical analysts to draw on a much richer set of data to estimate consumer demand.

---

[1]At the time we checked its Web site (February 8, 2002), there was an interesting lead story on its home page about the company donation of Homescan panel tools and information to the Sam W. Walton College of Business at the University of Arkansas to "enable students to learn from the same tools and information used by retailers and manufacturers in the consumer packaged goods industry."

The procedure commonly used by economists to estimate consumer demand is **regression analysis.** Besides its application in demand estimation, it is used to estimate production and cost functions (see chapters 7 and 8). It is also used in macroeconomic studies of consumption, investment, international trade, and interest rates. The first section following is an abridged version of the entire chapter's contents, in which we briefly explain what regression analysis is, how to interpret its results, and how to apply the results to management decisions. A more detailed presentation of regression analysis in managerial decision making follows the summary. However, for a comprehensive discussion of this topic, consult a statistics or econometrics text.

A SUMMARY OF REGRESSION ANALYSIS

Specifying the Regression Equation and Obtaining the Data

In estimating the demand for a particular good or service, first determine all the factors that might influence this demand. Suppose we wanted to estimate the demand for pizza by college students in the United States. What variables would most likely affect their demand for pizza? We could start to answer this question by using price and all of the nonprice determinants listed in chapter 3 (i.e., tastes and preferences, income, prices of related goods, future expectations, number of buyers). But it is not always possible or appropriate to include all of these variables in a particular demand analysis. As an example of this, in the demand for pizza, one would not think that "future expectations" would play an important role. Moreover, there may be other variables not specifically considered in the economic theory of demand that may have an impact on pizza purchases. For instance, in this chapter's "solution" we include the average annual temperature as a determinant of the demand for soft drinks.[2]

Ideally, all variables that are believed to have an impact on demand should be included in the regression analysis. In reality, the variables used in regression analysis are based on the availability of data and the cost of generating new data. The two types of data used in regression analysis are **cross-sectional** and **time series.** Cross-sectional data provide information on variables for a given period of time. Time series data give information about the variables over a number of periods of time. For the purpose of illustration, let us assume that we have obtained cross-sectional data on college students by conducting a survey of 30 randomly selected college campuses in the United States during a particular month.

Suppose that we have gathered the following information for each campus from this survey: (1) average number of slices consumed per month by students, (2) average price of a slice of pizza in places selling pizza in and around the campus, (3) annual tuition cost, (4) average price of a soft drink sold in the pizza places, and (5) location of the campus (urban versus suburban or rural). The data obtained from our hypothetical survey are presented in Table 5.1.

The reasons for selecting these variables are based on the economic theory of demand. Therefore, it should be clear why the price of pizza and the price of its

---

[2]However, it could be argued that the climate affects demand via its impact on the "taste and preferences" of consumers.

Table 5.1
Sample Data: The Demand for Pizza

COLLEGE	Y	X_1	X_2	X_3	X_4
1	10	100	14	100	1
2	12	100	16	95	1
3	13	90	8	110	1
4	14	95	7	90	1
5	9	110	11	100	0
6	8	125	5	100	0
7	4	125	12	125	1
8	3	150	10	150	0
9	15	80	18	100	1
10	12	80	12	90	1
11	13	90	6	80	1
12	14	100	5	75	1
13	12	100	12	100	1
14	10	110	10	125	0
15	10	125	14	130	0
16	12	110	15	80	1
17	11	150	16	90	0
18	12	100	12	95	1
19	10	150	12	100	0
20	8	150	10	90	0
21	9	150	13	95	0
22	10	125	15	100	1
23	11	125	16	95	1
24	12	100	17	100	0
25	13	75	10	100	1
26	10	100	12	110	1
27	9	110	6	125	0
28	8	125	10	90	0
29	8	150	8	80	0
30	5	150	10	95	0

Y = Quantity
X_1 = Price of pizza
X_2 = Tuition
X_3 = Price of soft drinks
X_4 = Location

complementary product, a soft drink, were selected for this study. But sometimes a researcher may have to use some creativity in coming up with variables that represent such factors as income and tastes and preferences. Because of the difficulty of finding out the average income of the students (or their families) who attend a particular college, tuition was used as a proxy variable. The location dummy variable is included to find out whether the demand for pizza is affected by the number of available substitutes for pizza. The assumption behind this is that colleges in urban areas may have more eating establishments from which to choose and this might adversely affect the students' demand for pizza.

Using these data, we then express the regression equation to be estimated in the following linear, additive fashion:

$$Y = a + b_1X_1 + b_2X_2 + b_3X_3 + b_4X_4$$

where Y = Quantity of pizza demanded (average number of slices per capita per month)

a = The constant value or Y intercept

X_1 = Average price of a slice of pizza (in cents)

X_2 = Annual tuition (in thousands of dollars)

X_3 = Average price of a 12-ounce can of soft drink (in cents)

X_4 = Location of campus (1 if located in a concentrated urban area, 0 if otherwise)

b_1, b_2, b_3, b_4 = The coefficients of the X variables measuring the impact of the variables on the demand for pizza

Y, or the quantity demanded, is called the dependent variable. The X variables are referred to as the independent or explanatory variables. It is important to note the unit of measurement used for each of the variables. The researcher may choose how to record the data for use in regression analysis. Here we are measuring the prices of pizza and soft drinks in cents and tuition in thousands of dollars. Notice, too, that the unit of measurement for the location variable is quite different from the others. It takes the value of "1" if the campus is located in an urban area and "0" otherwise. By measuring location in this way, the location variable is considered to be a *binary* or *dummy variable*. Given this particular setup of the regression equation and measurement scheme for the variables, we can now estimate the values of the b coefficients of the independent variables as well as the a intercept term by using any one of the many available software packages containing regression analysis.

Estimating and Interpreting the Regression Coefficients

Among the software packages used by economists to conduct a regression analysis of the demand for a good or service are SPSS, SAS, and Micro TSP. To estimate the demand for pizza, we employed the regression function contained in Excel. Although it only contains the basic elements of regression (for example, it does not provide a Durbin-Watson test), we believe it is perfectly suitable for many types of regression analysis that would be conducted in business research. Besides, Excel (and Lotus 1-2-3) is more available in both businesses and colleges and universities than are statistical software packages.

Using the regression function in Excel, we obtained the following estimates for our pizza-demand regression equation:

$$Y = 26.67 - 0.088X_1 + 0.138X_2 - 0.076X_3 - 0.544X_4$$

$$(0.018) \quad (0.087) \quad (0.020) \quad (0.884)$$

$R^2 = 0.717$ Standard error of Y estimate $= 1.64$

$\bar{R}^2 = 0.67$ $F = 15.8$

(Standard errors of the coefficients are listed in parentheses.)

Before interpreting these results, we should first think about what direction of impact changes in the explanatory variables are expected to have on the demand for pizza as evidenced by the signs of the estimated regression coefficients. To put it more formally, we can state the following hypotheses about the anticipated relationship between each of the explanatory variables and the demand for pizza:

Hypothesis 1: The price of pizza (X_1) is an inverse determinant of the quantity of pizza demanded (i.e., the sign of the coefficient is expected to be negative).

Hypothesis 2: Assuming tuition to be a proxy for income, pizza could be either a "normal" or an "inferior." Therefore, we hypothesize that tuition (X_2) is a determinant of the demand for pizza, but we cannot say beforehand whether it is an inverse or a direct determinant (i.e., the sign of the coefficient could be either positive or negative).

Hypothesis 3: The price of a soft drink (X_3) is an inverse determinant of the demand for pizza (i.e., the sign of the coefficient is expected to be negative).

Hypothesis 4: Location in an urban setting (X_4) is expected to be an inverse determinant of the demand for pizza.

Turning now to the regression results, we observe that the X_1 coefficient has a negative sign, and this is exactly what we would expect because of the law of demand. As the price of pizza (X_1) changes, the quantity demanded for pizza will change in the opposite direction. This is what a negative coefficient tells us. The positive sign of the tuition coefficient tells us that tuition costs and quantity of pizza demanded are directly related to each other. Higher tuition costs are associated with a greater demand for pizza, and vice versa. Thus, pizza appears to be a "normal" product. The negative sign of the soft drink price confirms the complementarity between soft drinks and pizza. As the price of a soft drink goes up, college students tend to buy less pizza. The opposite would hold true for a reduction in the price of a soft drink. Finally, the negative sign of the dummy location variable tells us that those students who attend colleges in urban areas will buy about half a slice of pizza per month (i.e., 0.544) less than their counterparts in the suburbs or rural areas.

An interpretation of the magnitudes of the estimated regression coefficients is a bit more involved. Each estimated coefficient tells us how much the demand for pizza will change relative to a unit change in each of the explanatory variables. For example, a b_1 of -0.088 indicates that a unit change in price will result in a change in the demand for pizza of 0.088 in the opposite direction. Price, as you will recall, was measured in cents. Therefore, according to our regression estimates, a 100-cent (or $1.00) increase will result in a decrease in the quantity demanded for pizza of 8.8 (100×0.088). A tuition increase of one unit (in this case $1,000) results in an increase in the quantity demanded for pizza of 0.138. Are these changes and those associated with changes in the price of soft drinks and the location of the college campus substantial or inconsequential?

Researchers who are constantly estimating the demand for a particular good or service will have a fairly accurate idea whether the magnitudes of the coefficients estimated in a particular study are high or low relative to their other work. But if there are no other studies available for comparison, then researchers can at least use the elasticities of demand in order to gauge the relative impact that the explanatory variables have on the quantity demanded.

From our discussion of elasticity in chapter 4, you can see that regression analysis results are ideal for point-elasticity estimation. Recall that the formula for computing point elasticity is

$$\epsilon_x = \frac{dQ}{dX} \cdot \frac{X}{Q}$$

where Q = quantity demanded and X = any variable that affects Q (e.g., price or income). In the case of our estimated demand for pizza, let us assume that the explanatory variables have the following values:

Price of pizza (X_1) = 100 (i.e., $1.00)
Annual college tuition (X_2) = 14 (i.e., $14,000)
Price of a soft drink (X_3) = 110 (i.e., $1.10)
Location of campus (X_4) = Urban area (i.e., $X_4 = 1$)

Therefore, inserting these values into the estimated equation gives us

$$Y = 26.67 - 0.088\,(100) + 0.138\,(14) - 0.076\,(110) - 0.544\,(1)$$

$$= 10.898 \text{ or } 11 \text{ (rounded to the nearest slice)}$$

To compute the point elasticities for each of the variables assuming the preceding values, we simply plug in the appropriate numbers into the point-elasticity formula. The partial derivative of Y with respect to changes in each of the variables (i.e., $\delta Y / \delta X$) is simply the estimated coefficient of each of the variables.

$$\text{Price elasticity: } -0.088 \times \frac{100}{10.898} = -0.807$$

$$\text{Tuition elasticity: } 0.138 \times \frac{14}{10.898} = 0.177$$

$$\text{Cross-price elasticity: } -0.076 \times \frac{110}{10.898} = -0.767$$

With these estimates, we can say that the demand for pizza is somewhat price inelastic and that there is some degree of cross-price elasticity between soft drinks and pizza. Judging from the rather low elasticity coefficient of 0.177, tuition does not appear to have that great an impact on the demand for pizza.

Statistical Evaluation of the Regression Results

Our regression results are based on a *sample* of colleges across the country. How confident are we that these results are truly reflective of the *population* of college students? The basic test of the statistical significance of each of the estimated regression coefficients is called the *t*-**test.** Essentially, this test is conducted by computing a *t*-value or *t*-statistic for each of the estimated coefficients. This is done by dividing the estimated coefficient by its **standard error.**[3] That is:

$$t = \frac{\hat{b}}{\text{standard error of } \hat{b}}$$

As is the common practice in presentations of regression results, the standard errors in our pizza regression are presented in parentheses under the estimated coefficients. Using the **rule of 2,** we can say that an estimated coefficient is statistically significant if the absolute value of the coefficient divided by its standard error is greater than or equal to 2.[4]

It is evident from the preceding regression equation that X_1 (price of pizza) and X_3 (price of soft drinks) are statistically significant because the absolute values of their *t*-statistics are 4.89 and 3.80, respectively. The other two variables, X_2 (tuition) and X_4 (location), are not statistically significant because the absolute values of their *t*-statistics are less than 2.

If the estimated coefficient of a variable passes the *t*-test, we can be very confident that the variable truly has an impact on demand. If it does not pass the *t*-test, then in all likelihood, the variable does not truly have an impact for the whole population of college students. In other words, the regression coefficients are nonzero numbers simply because of a fluke in the sample of students that we took from the population.

In statistical analysis, the best we can hope for is to be very confident that our sample results are truly reflective of the population that they represent. However, we can never be absolutely sure. Therefore, statistical analysts set up degrees of uncertainty. As explained in greater detail later in this chapter, using the rule of 2 generally implies a 5 percent level of significance. In other words, by declaring a coefficient that passes the rule-of-2 version of the *t*-test to be statistically significant, we leave ourselves open to a 5 percent chance that we may be mistaken.

Another important statistical indicator used to evaluate the regression results is the **coefficient of determination** or R^2. This measure shows the percentage of the variation in a dependent variable accounted for by the variation in all of the explanatory variables in the regression equation. This measure can be as low as 0 (indicating that the variations in the dependent variable are not accounted for at all by the variation in the explanatory variables) and as high as 1.0 (indicating that all of the variation in the dependent variable can be accounted for by the explanatory variables). For statistical analysts, the closer R^2 is to 1.0, the greater the explanatory power of the regression equation.

---

[3]In the following equation, the little "hat" (circumflex) over the b is a commonly used notation by statistical analysis to denote a value estimated from sample data.
[4]Readers are reminded that this is only a summary description of the *t*-test. For more details, see the fuller discussion later in this chapter.

In our pizza regression, $R^2 = 0.717$. This means that about 72 percent of the variation in the demand for pizza by college students can be accounted for by the variation in the price of pizza, the cost of tuition, the price of a soft drink, and the location of the college. As explained later in this chapter, R^2 increases as more independent variables are added to a regression equation. Therefore, most analysts prefer to use a measure that adjusts for the number of independent variables used so that equations with different numbers of independent variables can be more fairly compared. This alternative measure is called the adjusted R^2. As it turns out, the adjusted R^2 for this equation is 0.67. Another test, called the **F-test,** is often used in conjunction with the R^2. Interested readers should refer to "The F-Test," later in this chapter for an explanation of this test.

Review of Key Steps for Analyzing Regression Results

We will now review all of the key steps discussed so far in the regression analysis of a demand equation using the following equation:

$$Q = 70 - 10P + 4P_X + 50I$$

$$\qquad\qquad (3) \quad\ (2) \quad\ (30) \qquad \text{(standard errors of the estimated coefficients are noted in parentheses)}$$

$n = 56$

$R^2 = .47$

where Q = the quantity of a product demanded
    P = the price of the product (in cents)
    P_X = the price of a related product (in cents)
    I = per capita income (in dollars)
    n = sample size
    R^2 = adjusted multiple coefficient of determination

Step 1: Check Signs and Magnitudes The negative sign for the P variable indicates an inverse relationship between price and the quantity demanded for the product. A unit *increase* in price (i.e., 1 cent) will cause the quantity to *decrease* by 10 units. A unit *decrease* in price will cause the quantity to *increase* by 10 units. So for example, if price was decreased by $1.00, quantity would increase by 1,000 units.

The positive sign for the P_X variable indicates a direct relationship between the price of a related product and the quantity demanded. This indicates that the related product is a *substitute* for the product in question. For example, if the price of the related product changes by one unit (i.e., 1 cent), then the quantity demanded of the product in question will change by 4 units in the *same direction.*

The positive sign for the I variable indicates that the product is *normal* or perhaps *superior,* depending on the magnitude of the income elasticity coefficient. A unit change in per capita income (i.e., $1,000) will cause the quantity to change by 50 units in the *same direction.*

Step 2: Compute Elasticity Coefficients To compute elasticity coefficients, we need to assume certain levels of the independent variables P, P_X, and I. Let us say they are as follows:

$$P = 100 \text{ (remember, this is 100 cents or \$1.00)}$$

$$P_X = 120 \text{ (also in cents)}$$

$$I = 25 \text{ (this represents \$25,000)}$$

Inserting these values into the previous equation gives us

$$Q = 70 - 10(100) + 4(120) + 50(25)$$

$$Q = 800$$

We now use the formula for point elasticity to obtain the elasticity coefficients. Recall that

$$\epsilon_x = \frac{\delta Q}{\delta X} \cdot \frac{X}{Q}$$

Using this formula, we obtain

$$\epsilon_p = -10 \cdot \frac{100}{800}$$

$$= -1.25$$

$$\epsilon_{p_x} = 4 \cdot \frac{120}{800}$$

$$= .6$$

$$\epsilon_I = 50 \cdot \frac{25}{800}$$

$$= 1.56$$

Step 3: Determine Statistical Significance Using the "rule of 2" as an approximation for the .05 level of significance, we can say that P and P_X are statistically significant because their t values are both greater than 2 (e.g., 3.3 and 2, respectively). I is not statistically significant at the .05 level because its t value is only 1.67.

As an added consideration, we note that the R^2 of .47 indicates that 47 percent of the variation in quantity can be accounted for by variations in the three independent variables P, P_X, and I. While this is not actually an indication of statistical significance, it does show the explanatory power of the regression equation. For cross-section data, this R^2 level can be interpreted as being moderately high.

Implications of the Regression Analysis for Management Decisions

In our experience, the "proof of the pudding" in the business world of any statistical analysis, including regression analysis, is the extent to which the results can help managers to make good decisions. In our pizza example, the results indicate that the price of pizza and the price of its complementary product, the soft drink, are key factors influencing the demand for pizza. Their elasticity coefficients are both less than 1 and both variables' coefficients passed the *t*-test. What does this mean for those in the pizza business? First, it means that they can expect price decreases to lead to decreases in revenue, other factors remaining constant. Therefore, they would probably not want to try lowering price in an effort to increase sales. But they could try lowering the price of soft drinks, with the anticipation that the lower price of the soft drink will attract people to buy the pizza.

In statistical analysis, it is often as important to find out what does *not* pass the *t*-test as much as it is to find out what passes. In our example, we learned that tuition and location do not have statistically significant impacts on pizza demand. Moreover, the magnitudes of their coefficients were relatively small. For managers of national chains such as Pizza Hut or Domino's, this would indicate that they would not have to be very concerned about the type of college (private or public) or its location (urban or rural) in deciding where to open pizza franchises.

We hope that this summary is sufficient for those instructors and readers who simply want a general idea of how regression analysis can be used in business analysis and decision making. For a more detailed discussion, continue with the rest of this chapter.

REGRESSION ANALYSIS

The basic intent of regression analysis is to estimate a quantitative relationship among variables. The first step in this statistical procedure is to specify the regression model (also referred to as the regression equation). The second is to obtain data on the variables specified in the model. The third is to estimate the quantitative impact each of the independent variables has on the dependent variable. The fourth step is to test the statistical significance of the regression results. Finally, the results of the regression analysis may be used as supporting material in the making of business policies and decisions.

Regression analysis involves two basic types of variables: the dependent variable and the independent variables. The latter are also called the *explanatory* variables. As evidenced by its name, the dependent variable is the one whose value depends on the value of some other variable or variables. The dependent variable is the central focus of any regression study and is the variable that researchers try to explain and predict. In the regression analysis of demand, the dependent variable is the quantity demanded of a particular good or service. If only one independent variable is employed in the analysis, we use the term *simple regression.* If more than one independent variable is involved, we use the term *multiple regression.* As you would expect, the independent variables most commonly used in the regression analysis of demand are price, price of related products, tastes and preferences, income, and the number of buyers. For purposes of explanation and illustration, it is much easier to focus on simple regression. After the simple regression model has been developed and explained, we will present the multiple regression model.

The Simple Regression Model

Our discussion of simple regression begins with a formal statement of the relationship we hypothesize to exist between the dependent variable and the independent variable. Stated as a mathematical equation, this relationship is as follows:

$$Y = a + bX + u \tag{5.1}$$

where Y = Dependent variable
X = Independent variable
a = Intercept
b = Slope
u = Random factor

Notice that regression analysis seeks the best *linear* relationship between the dependent variable and the independent variable.[5] Thus, a denotes the intercept of the line and b the slope of the line. Note that another term, u, is included in the formal statement of the regression model. It is usually referred to as the "random" or "error" term. Although its value is not actually a part of the estimated impact of X on Y, its inclusion in the formal regression equation is essential. To understand why, allow us to deviate from the main topic to a brief discussion about the difference between *deterministic* and *probabilistic* models in statistical analysis.

Suppose that you want to develop a simple model of the gasoline consumption of your car, with the dependent variable being the amount of gasoline used and the independent variable being the number of miles traveled. If you knew the number of miles per gallon that your car is able to obtain, it would be a matter of simple arithmetic to quantify this relationship. For example, if your car's gas mileage is 20 miles per gallon and you traveled 100 miles, your consumption would be 5 gallons of gasoline. This relationship can be generalized as $Y = 0.05X$. Figure 5.1*a* shows the deterministic relationship between X and Y.

Now suppose that you decide to measure the relationship between miles traveled and gasoline consumed by recording this information for five separate trips, each 100 miles longer than the last, beginning with a 100-mile trip. As you can imagine, the actual amount of gasoline consumed relative to miles traveled would not conform exactly to what is predicted in the deterministic model. Suppose the actual recorded data are those shown in Figure 5.1*b*. As you can see, the plotting of each trip's mileage along with gasoline consumption actually results in a scattering of points rather than a path of points along a straight line. This implies that other factors besides miles traveled (e.g., weather conditions, traffic patterns, and driving habits) affect gasoline consumption. Our model of gasoline mileage must therefore be restated as $Y = 0.05X + u$, where the value of u accounts for the deviation of the points from the straight line representing $Y = 0.05X$. The variable u represents the factors other than the independent variable that can affect the value of the dependent variable.

We assume in statistical theory that this u factor has a random rather than a systematic impact on the dependent variable. In statistical theory, randomly occurring

---

[5]The application of regression to economic problems generally assumes a linear relationship between the dependent variable and the independent variable(s). In fact, the term linear regression analysis is often used in economic studies. There are more advanced, nonlinear regression techniques that can be used. However, as shown later, economists frequently transform nonlinear relations into equations suitable for linear regression analysis.

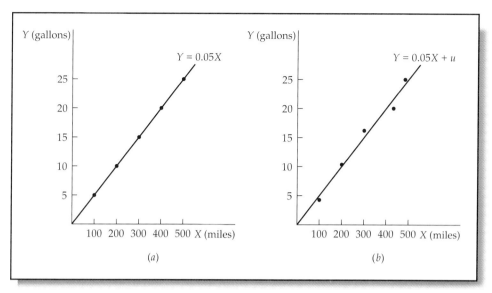

Figure 5.1
Gasoline Consumption Model

events are described in terms of the probability of their occurrence. Hence, the term *probabilistic* is used to describe an equation that contains the random u element. You will see why it is important to understand the nature of a probabilistic model when we arrive at the section discussing the statistical significance of the regression results.

Data Used in Regression Analysis

The data used in regression analysis are divided into two types: cross-sectional and time series. Cross-sectional data provide information on a variable at a given point in time. The different values of the variable represent a cross section of observations of such entities as individuals, groups of individuals, and locations (e.g., county, city, metropolitan area, state, or country). Time series data provide information on one entity over time (e.g., the annual per capita income of a state over a period of 20 years). The pizza examples cited earlier involved cross-sectional data, since information was gathered on a cross section of individuals on campuses at a given point in time (actually, a one-week period). Information on a time series basis might involve tracking the per capital purchase of pizza in a given region of the country relative to its price over a period of time. For example, we could look at the annual per-capita consumption of pizza in the United States.

Estimating the Regression Equation

The estimation of the regression equation involves a search for the best linear relationship between the dependent and the independent variable. Thus, the regression equation we seek to estimate can be expressed as

$$Y = a + bX \tag{5.2}$$

Chapter 5   Demand Estimation

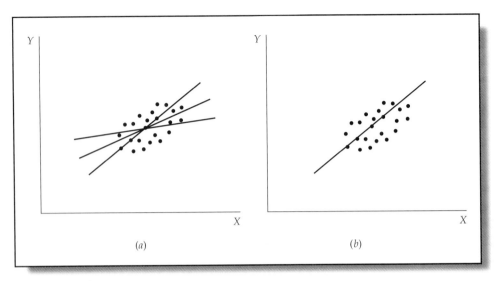

Figure 5.2
Linear Representations of Scatter Plots

where Y = Dependent variable
X = Independent variable
a = Intercept of the line with the Y-axis
b = Slope of the line

The intercept and slope are usually referred to as the *parameters* or **coefficients of the regression equation.**

Figure 5.2 shows a scatter plot of hypothetical data for Y and X. As indicated in part *a* of this figure, any number of lines could be drawn through the scatter plot to represent the relationship between Y and X. In regression analysis, the most common way to estimate the relationship is called the **method of ordinary least squares (OLS).** Essentially, this method requires that a line be drawn through the scatter of points in such a way that the *sum of the squared deviations of each of the points from the line is minimized.* The least squares line is shown in Figure 5.2*b*. An illustration of the least squares method is shown in Figure 5.3.

The actual estimation of the regression line is a relatively simple matter, given the availability of computers and software packages. Many hand-held calculators contain programs or special function keys for estimating simple regression equations. However, when more than one independent variable is used (i.e., multiple regression analysis), the processing power of a computer is required. In any event, those wishing to review the formulas for estimating the equations as well as the mathematical derivations of these formulas may consult a statistics or econometrics text. Using the method of least squares, we arrive at the regression line indicated in Figure 5.2*b*.

Although the method of least squares provides a good linear representation of the scatter of points, there is clearly a difference in fit of the least squares lines shown in Figure 5.4*a* and *b*. Mere observation indicates that Figure 5.4*b* represents a better fit

Managerial Economics

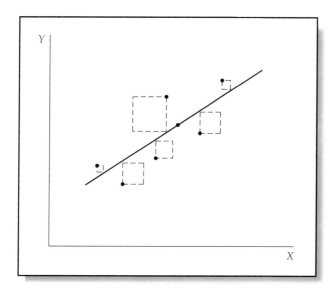

Figure 5.3
Minimizing the Sum of
Squared Deviations

of the regression line through the scatter of points. This is obviously because of the nature of the scatter of points and not because of the way in which the lines were constructed. Both regression lines were drawn in a manner satisfying the least squares criterion. Thus, it would be useful to have some measure of how well a regression line fits the scatter of points.

Figure 5.4
Regression Lines with Different Fits Through the Scattering of Points

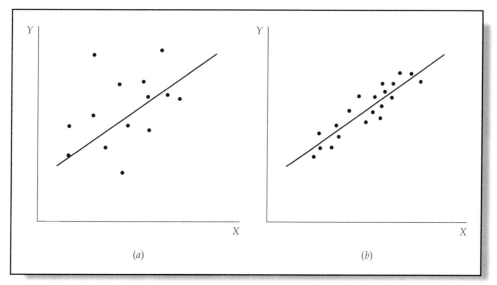

THE COEFFICIENT OF DETERMINATION: A MEASURE OF THE EXPLANATORY POWER OF THE ESTIMATED REGRESSION EQUATION[6]

To explain the meaning of the coefficient of determination, we need to introduce a few concepts and notations used in standard statistics and econometrics texts. Whenever regression results based on sample data are presented, a "hat" (circumflex) is placed over the estimated values:

$$\hat{Y} = \hat{a} + \hat{b}X \qquad (5.3)$$

The hats over Y, a, and b signify that their values are estimated using a sample data set. A reasonable approach to measuring how well this estimated regression equation does in determining the value of Y given the value of X is to compare the values of $\hat{Y}$ with the actual Y values found in the sample.

The scatter plot shown in Figure 5.5 will help to explain this approach. Equation (5.3) represents the estimated regression line through the scatter of points. Let us take one of these points, point A, for purposes of illustration. You can see that the deviation of this point from the regression line is indicated by the distance between A and B in Figure 5.5. If we added up the squared deviations of each of the points from the regression line, we would obtain the smallest possible sum, because the method of least squares was used to estimate the regression line. Thus, in evaluating the fit of this regression line to the scatter plot of actual data, we need some standard of comparison.

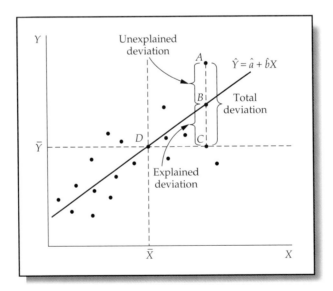

Figure 5.5
Explained and Unexplained Deviations

---

[6]This section draws heavily from the explanation presented in H. Kelejian and W. Oates, *Introduction to Econometrics*, New York: Harper & Row, 1989.

Suppose you were asked to predict the amount of pizza demanded by consumers without the help of a regression equation. Would it not be reasonable to use the mean value (i.e., the arithmetic average) of quantity demanded as the predicted value? Statistical theorists, in fact, use the mean value of the dependent variable (Y) as the basis for comparing the relative "goodness of fit" of the regression line to the scatter of actual data points. In effect, this particular measure answers the question: How much better off are we in using a regression line to predict the value of Y than we are in simply using the mean of Y?

In Figure 5.5, the mean of Y (i.e., $\bar{Y}$) is indicated by the dotted line. The deviation of the regression line from the mean value of Y is indicated by the distance between points B and C. Note that the regression line always passes through the point representing the mean of X and the mean of Y.[7] This is indicated by point D in Figure 5.5. Thus, we observe in Figure 5.5 that the deviation of a sample value of Y from its mean can be divided into two separate components: AB and BC. More formally, we can state the following:

$AC = (Y_i - \bar{Y})$ = Total deviation of the ith sample value of Y from the sample mean

$BC = (\hat{Y}_i - \bar{Y})$ = Explained deviation of Y_i from Y

$AB = (Y_i - \hat{Y}_i)$ = Unexplained deviation of Y_i from $\bar{Y}$

BC is the "explained" deviation of the sample value of Y from its mean because it can be accounted for by the regression line. AB is the "unexplained" portion of the total deviation because its value differs from that estimated by the regression line. If the breakdown between the explained and unexplained components is measured for every observation, and the resulting values are squared (to compensate for positive and negative deviations) and then added together, we arrive at the following relationships:

$TSS = \Sigma(Y_i - \bar{Y})^2$ = Total sum of squares
(sum of the squared deviations of the sample values of Y
from the mean)

$RSS = \Sigma(\hat{Y}_i - \bar{Y})^2$ = Regression sum of squares
(sum of the squared deviations of the estimated values
from the mean)

$ESS = \Sigma(Y_i - \hat{Y}_i)^2$ = Error sum of squares
(sum of the squared deviations of the sample values
from the estimated values)

The abbreviations TSS, RSS, and ESS are commonly used in econometrics books for these relationships, so we will use them here in reference to the total, explained, and unexplained components, respectively, of the variation of the sample values from their mean. To summarize, we can simply say that TSS = RSS + ESS. From these relationships, we can construct a measure of the explanatory power of the regression equation.

---

[7]For the proof of why this always is the case when the method of least squares is used, consult a statistics or econometrics text.

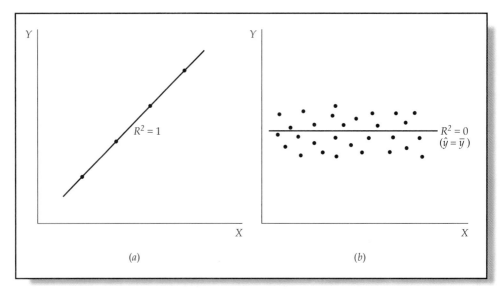

Figure 5.6
The Coefficient of Determination

The most commonly used measure of the explanatory power of the regression equation is called the *coefficient of determination*. The symbol used for this measure is R^2. We define this measure in the following way:

$$R^2 = \frac{\text{RSS}}{\text{TSS}} = 1 - \frac{\text{ESS}}{\text{TSS}} \tag{5.4}$$

If RSS is equal to TSS, this means that the total deviation of Y from its sample mean can be "explained" or accounted for by the equation. This also implies that R^2 is equal to 1. Another way to view this situation is to look at the alternative expression of R^2, $1 - \text{ESS}/\text{TSS}$. If the regression line accounts for the total deviation of Y from its mean, there would be no error sum of squares (i.e., ESS = 0). This means ESS/TSS = 0, and therefore $R^2 = 1$. Figure 5.6a illustrates a situation in which $R^2 = 1$. You can see in this figure that $R^2 = 1$ means that every point on the scatter plot lies on the regression line.

At the other extreme, if the regression line does not account for any of the variation of Y from its mean, R^2 assumes the value of 0. As you can see from the formula, $R^2 = 0$ means that RSS/TSS = 0. Using the alternative formula for R^2, we see that this means ESS = TSS (i.e., ESS/TSS = 1). Such a case would indicate that the mean value of Y is just as useful as the least squares regression line in predicting the value of Y (i.e., $\hat{Y} = \bar{Y}$). Figure 5.6b illustrates this case.

In actuality, R^2 will assume some value between the two extremes of 0 and 1. Clearly, the closer R^2 is to unity, the greater the explanatory power of the regression equation. For example, an R^2 of 0.93 indicates a very good fit of the regression line to the scatter of points (see Figure 5.7a). This statistic indicates that 93 percent of the variation in Y from its mean can be accounted for by the regression equation. An R^2 close to 0 indicates a regression equation with very little explanatory power. For

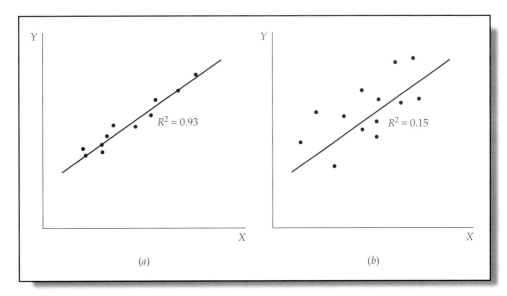

Figure 5.7
Indicator of Regression Line Fit

example, $R^2 = .15$ (i.e., only 15 percent of the variation in Y from its mean is explained) is shown in Figure 5.7b.

Whether a given value of R^2 is considered "high" or "low," or "acceptable" or "unacceptable" in statistical analysis depends on the type of data being used (cross-sectional versus time series), the particular standards of the researcher, and the typical R^2 computed in studies of a similar nature. Studies employing cross-sectional data generally have a lower R^2 than those using time series data. This is because time series data—as would be expected—have a built-in trend element that usually causes the Y and X variables to move closely together over time. It is not uncommon for the estimation of demand using time series data to produce an R^2 of 0.90 or above. Macroeconomic studies of the consumption function usually have an R^2 of 0.95 or more. Ordinarily, if a researcher estimates a regression equation with $R^2 = 0.75$, it means that the regression model has rather strong explanatory power. However, since most consumption function studies produce R^2 values of 0.95 or above, a consumption equation with an R^2 value of 0.75 would have to be considered relatively low.

One further point should be mentioned about R^2. As additional variables are added to the regression equation (i.e., as we move from simple regression to multiple regression), the regression equation, naturally, will "explain" more of the variation in the dependent variable. In fact, it can be shown that the addition of some random number or a variable completely unrelated to the regression model will improve the goodness of fit of the regression equation (i.e., will increase the magnitude of R^2). To compensate for the fact that regression equations with more independent variables tend to have higher R^2 values, we can use a measure called the "corrected" or "adjusted" coefficient of determination, $\bar{R}^2$. This measure is defined as

$$\bar{R}^2 = R^2 - \frac{k}{n - k - 1}(1 - R^2)$$

where k = Number of independent variables

n = Sample size

By observation, you can deduce that in multiple regression R^2 will always exceed $\bar{R}^2$. The difference between the two measures will depend, of course, on the size of the sample (n) and the number of independent variables (k). For a given sample size, $\bar{R}^2$ will show an increasing adjustment downward from R^2 as the number of independent variables increases. Regardless of the number of independent variables in the equation, the amount of downward adjustment from R^2 will decrease as the sample size increases. At any rate, almost all regression software packages automatically compute $\bar{R}^2$ along with R^2.

EVALUATING THE REGRESSION COEFFICIENTS

Up to this point, we have discussed regression analysis in reference to what is called *descriptive statistics*. Data are gathered on two variables, one dependent and the other independent; a line is fitted through the scatter of points representing the values of the two variables; and a measure of how well the line fits the scatter is developed. But to evaluate the usefulness of the results of the regression analysis for making business decisions, we need to enter the realm of *inferential statistics.*

A researcher seeking certain information about some population can attempt to obtain data either on the entire population or on some sample of the population. In just about all cases, a sample from the population is used because of the prohibitive cost of obtaining information on the whole population. Moreover, in many cases it is simply impossible to obtain complete population data. But if a sample is used instead of the population, the researcher must assess the degree to which the results of the sample reflect the population. In other words, it becomes necessary to *make inferences* about the population based on what is known about the sample and to make a judgment about how good these inferences are.

Suppose we are conducting a study of the demand for pizza on a university campus with a student population of 4,500. The variables under study are income and average quantity of pizza slices demanded per month. Suppose further that we are able to obtain information on the entire population of students. This is shown in Table 5.2, where consumers have been divided into 10 groups according to weekly after-tax income, starting with $100 per week and increasing by $20 intervals to $280. The average number of pizza slices purchased per month is shown in the matrix of numbers. To make this illustration as simple as possible, we have assumed that there are 450 student consumers in each of the 10 income categories. For example, reading *down* in the $100 column, we see that 10 students (i.e., one-tenth of 100) buy an average of 10 slices of pizza per month, 30 students (i.e., one-tenth of 300) buy an average of 10.5 slices per month, and so on. (Note the vertical arrow in Table 5.2.) By reading *across* each row, we can observe the number of pizza slices demanded for the nine frequency categories. (Note the horizontal arrow in Table 5.2.) We observe that the

Table 5.2
Number of Pizza Slices Consumed per Month, by Weekly Income

	f	$100	$120	$140	$160	$180	$200	$220	$240	$260	$280
(1)	100	10.0	11.5	13.0	14.5	16.0	17.5	19.0	20.5	22.0	23.5
(2)	300	10.5	12.0	13.5	15.0	16.5	18.0	19.5	21.0	22.5	24.0
(3)	600	10.8	12.3	13.8	15.3	16.8	18.3	19.8	21.3	22.8	24.3
(4)	800	11.2	12.7	14.2	15.7	17.2	18.7	20.2	21.7	23.2	24.7
(5)	900	11.5	13.0	14.5	16.0	17.5	19.0	20.5	22.0	23.5	25.0
(6)	800	11.8	13.3	14.8	16.3	17.8	19.3	20.8	22.3	23.8	25.3
(7)	600	12.2	13.7	15.2	16.7	18.2	19.7	21.2	22.7	24.2	25.7
(8)	300	12.5	14.0	15.5	17.0	18.5	20.0	21.5	23.0	24.5	26.0
(9)	100	13.0	14.3	16.0	17.5	19.0	20.5	22.0	23.5	25.0	26.5
	4,500										

number of pizza slices demanded increases as weekly income increases. For example, in the second row, frequency 300, we see that the 30 individuals (i.e., one-tenth of 300) who have an average weekly income of $100 buy 10.5 slices of pizza per month; the 30 who earn an average of $120 per month buy 12 pizza slices per month, and so on. The most frequently occurring average number of slices for each income category is seen by reading across the row indicated by the frequency of 900. As it turns out, this row also represents the average number of slices of pizza for each income category.

Figure 5.8 shows the distribution of those consumers who earn $200 per week. The entire data set in Table 5.2 is illustrated in Figure 5.9. Notice that we assume that

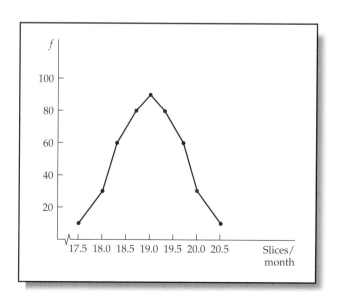

Figure 5.8
Pizza Demand: Distribution
of Consumers Earning $200
per Week

Figure 5.9
Combined Frequency Distributions for Pizza Demand

there is a normal, continuous distribution for each income level. Each distribution has a different mean or expected value, but all have the same variance.

For such population data, the regression line would be

$$Y = 4 + 0.075X \tag{5.5}$$

Now suppose that we select a sample of pizza buyers from this population. As you can well imagine, this sample might indicate a different relationship between income and quantity demanded of pizza. To demonstrate this point, we have drawn a "bird's-eye view" of a portion of Figure 5.9 in Figure 5.10a. Notice that the dense cluster of population points symmetrically placed around the mean of each distribution reflects the normal, bell-shaped distribution that we have assumed to exist for each income level.

The solid line drawn through the scatter of points in Figure 5.10 indicates the true regression line for the population. However, the sample of points selected for a regression study is different from the scatter of points for the population. This would cause the regression equation estimated for the sample to be different from the one for the population. Examples of possible differences between the sample and population regression equations are shown in Figure 5.10b, c, and d. The sample regression equations are represented by the broken lines.

As you can see, a least squares regression line fitted through the sample points in Figure 5.10b would show a positive relationship between income and the demand for pizza. However, because the slope is not as steep as the slope for the population

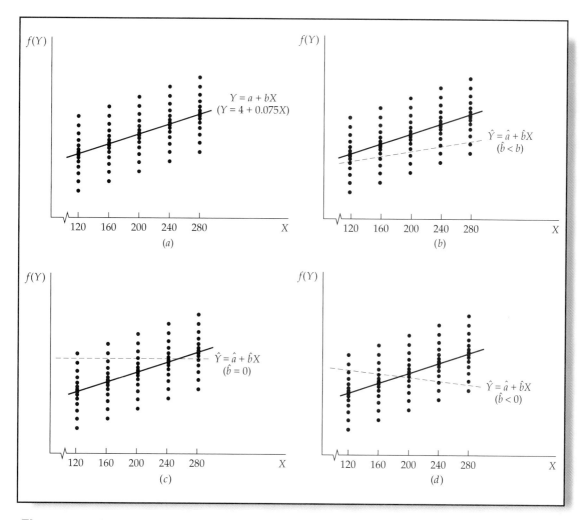

Figure 5.10
Population Regression Line and Three Sample Regression Lines

regression line, the magnitude of this relationship is smaller. The sample shown in Figure 5.10c indicates that no relationship exists between income and the demand for pizza. The sample Figure 5.10d actually shows a negative relationship between income and pizza demand, implying that pizza is an "inferior" product.

In reality, data on the population such as those shown in Table 5.2 are unknown to researchers. All they have to work with are sample data of the type illustrated in Figure 5.10b, c, and d. How confident can a researcher be about the extent to which the regression equation for the sample truly represents the unknown regression equation for the population? The answer to this question is presented in the following section.

A Test for the Statistical Significance of the Estimated Regression Coefficients

The test used to establish, with a certain degree of confidence, that the regression coefficients estimated from sample data are truly reflective of the population is called the test of *statistical significance*. Because this test involves what are called t-values, it is commonly referred to as the **t-test**.

Our explanation of this test begins with a review of the error term, u, introduced at the beginning of this chapter. In statistical theory, it is assumed that this term is randomly distributed about the population regression line in a normal fashion, with its mean being the value of Y given the value of X and with some amount of variance.[8]

As illustrated in Figure 5.10, a random sample taken from the population may produce regression results that are quite different from a regression line fitted through the population. If we repeatedly selected a random sample of a given size from this population and estimated a regression line for each one of these samples, we would generate a large number of sample regression lines (see Figure 5.11). Each of these sample regression lines has its own intercept and slope coefficients, $\hat{a}$ and $\hat{b}$. In statistical theory, it can be shown that if the error term of the population is normally distributed about its regression line with some constant variance (σ_u^2), then repeated sampling will produce a distribution of estimated regression coefficients, $\hat{a}$ and $\hat{b}$, *that are themselves normally distributed with a mean or expected value equal to the population's regression coefficients, and with a variance equal to a number related to the variance of the error term in some systematic fashion.* The following equations express this statement in notational form. Because we are primarily interested in the slope coefficient, we shall focus our attention on b. However, the same statements can be made about the intercept term, a.

$$E(\hat{b}) = b \tag{5.6}$$

$$var(\hat{b}) = \sigma_b^2 = \frac{\sigma_u^2}{\sum (X_1 - \bar{X})^2} \tag{5.7}$$

Equation (5.6) is fairly straightforward. It states that the mean or expected value of the estimated coefficient $\hat{b}$ is equal to b, the true (but unknown) regression coefficient for the entire population. Equation (5.7) states that the variance of the distribution of regression coefficients estimated from a repeated sampling of the population is equal to the variance of the population's error term, u, divided by the sum of the squared deviations of each observed value of X from the mean of X. The verbalization of Equation (5.7) is rather cumbersome, to be sure. But the important thing to keep in mind is that we need to know the variance of the distribution of sample $\hat{b}$ terms to determine the probability of the occurrence of any one particular $\hat{b}$.

Because information about the variance of the population's error term is generally unknown, we resort to the use of an *estimator* of the population variance. In sta-

---

[8]Recall that a normal distribution is the symmetric, bell-shaped curve so often used in statistics. As such, it can be defined by two values, its mean and its variance (or standard deviation, the square root of the variance). The larger the variance, the more "spread out" the normal distribution becomes.

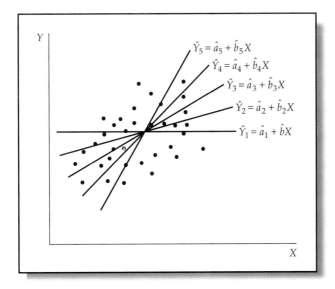

Figure 5.11
Regression Lines Produced
from Repeated Sampling

tistical theory, it can be shown that an unbiased estimator of the variance of the distribution of error terms ($\hat{\sigma}_u^2$) is equal to the *sum of the squared residuals of each of the sample points from the estimated regression line, divided by the sample size minus 2* (i.e., $n - 2$). *Residuals* are the differences between the actual values of Y and those estimated from the regression equation (i.e., Y_i minus $\hat{Y}_i$). Expressed in notational form,

$$\hat{\sigma}_u^2 = \frac{\Sigma \, (Yi - \hat{Y}i)^2}{n - 2}$$

In turn, the unbiased estimator of the variance of the sample b term ($\hat{\sigma}_b^2$) is equal to the estimator of the variance of the error terms divided by the sum of the squared deviations of each observed value of X from the mean of X. In notational form,

$$\hat{\sigma}_b^2 = \frac{\hat{\sigma}_u^2}{\Sigma \, (X_i - \bar{X})^2}$$

We obtain the standard deviation of the distribution of sample $\hat{b}$ coefficients simply by taking the square root of the estimated variance of this distribution. That is,

$$SE_{\hat{b}} = \sqrt{\hat{\sigma}_b^2}$$

As is the custom, we shall refer to standard deviation of the sample regression coefficient as the standard error of the coefficient ($SE_{\hat{b}}$). And, as we are about to show, $SE_{\hat{b}}$ plays a central role in the *t*-test.

In conducting the *t*-test, we start by hypothesizing that the true (but unknown) regression coefficient for the population is a certain value. In statistical analysis, this is called the **null hypothesis.** Typically in economic research, we hypothesize the population's regression coefficient to be 0; that is, there is no relationship between X and Y in the population. The **alternative hypothesis** is that there is indeed a relationship between X and Y. Using conventional statistical notation, we can state the null and alternative hypotheses as:

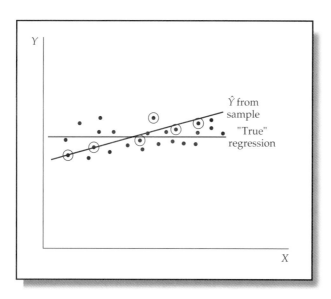

Figure 5.12
False Relationship Indicated
by Sample Regression

$$H_0 : b = 0$$

$$H_a : b \neq 0$$

If the b or slope coefficient is truly 0, as the null hypothesis states, then for the entire population, changes in X would have no impact on Y.

Suppose the true value of b were indeed 0. Would it still be possible to select a sample that showed a relationship between Y and X? Most certainly it would, and Figure 5.12 shows exactly how this could happen. Notice in this figure that the scatter plot of the population is such that a regression line fitted through the points is horizontal (i.e., has zero slope). But suppose the sample that we selected—indicated by the circled points in Figure 5.12—happened to show a positive relationship when a least squares line is fitted through the sample scatter. Based on the results of the regression analysis of the sample data, we would conclude that for the entire population a direct relationship exists between X and Y, when there really is none. This kind of error would be of obvious concern to decision makers. For example, suppose a regression analysis of sales on advertising expenditures mistakenly showed a positive relationship between the two variables and prompted a firm to increase substantially the size of its advertising budget. Since in reality there is no impact of advertising on sales, this decision would lead to a waste of the firm's financial resources.

Earlier, we stated that if the error term of the population regression equation is normally distributed, it can be shown that the estimated sample coefficients are also normally distributed. It can also be demonstrated mathematically that the *standardized deviation* of each sample's estimate from the actual population value has a t-distribution.[9] Figure 5.13 illustrates this point. In Figure 5.13a, we see a normal dis-

---

[9]The t-distribution is a symmetric, bell-shaped distribution that closely resembles the normal distribution. Its precise shape depends on a measure called *degrees of freedom.* In simple regression, there are $n - 2$ degrees of freedom. As the sample size (n) increases, the t-distribution tends toward the standard normal distribution. In the limit, the two become identical.

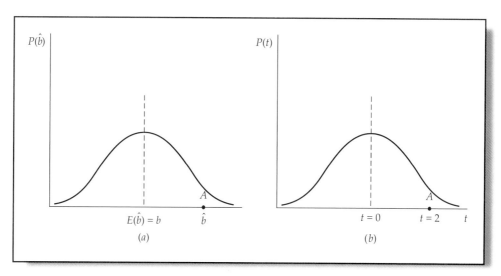

Figure 5.13
The *t*-Distribution

tribution of estimated $\hat{b}$ coefficients with its mid point designating the mean or expected value. The vertical axis of the graph measures the probability of the occurrence of the different values of the estimate $\hat{b}$. Obviously, the mean or expected value of $\hat{b}$ has the greatest probability of occurring. Suppose that the estimated sample coefficient $\hat{b}$ is the one shown by point A in Figure 5.13*a*. What is the probability of such a point occurring? To find the answer to this question, we standardize the differences between any point in the distribution and its expected value. This is done using the following equation:

$$ t = \frac{\hat{b} - E(\hat{b})}{SE_{\hat{b}}} \tag{5.8} $$

This value shows how many *t*-units away from the expected value is the estimated coefficient $\hat{b}$. To interpret this *t*-value, we also need to know the number of **degrees of freedom** (d.f.) involved in this case. For any given sample, d.f. is defined as $n - k - 1$, where n, k, and 1 represent the sample size, the number of independent variables, and the intercept term, respectively. For example, in a regression equation with a sample of 62 observations, there would be 60 degrees of freedom. The probability of the occurrence of value A (converted into 2 units) can now be found with the help of a **t-table**, as shown in Table C.4 in Appendix C at the end of the text. In this table, we see that for 60 d.f., the probability that *t* will have a value of 1.671 or more is about 5 percent. (See column for "one-tail, $a = 0.05$.") Therefore, the probability that *t* will have a value of 2 or more would clearly be less than 5 percent.

After finding the *t*-value for the estimated regression coefficient $\hat{b}$, the researcher must then decide whether to reject the null hypothesis that there is no relationship between X and Y in the population. The standard procedure is to establish what is called the *critical t-value* based on a predetermined point on the *t*-distribution. Usually this point is set at the 0.05 *level of significance*. We can then turn to the *t*-table

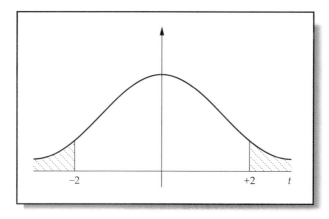

Figure 5.14
Critical *t*-Values for Two-Tail Test, 5 Percent Level of Significance, 60 Degrees of Freedom

to find the critical value of *t* corresponding to this level of significance. For example, the table shows that for 60 degrees of freedom, the range between 2.0 and −2.0 includes about 95 percent of the values of *t*. Another way of saying this is that the chance of obtaining a *t*-value greater than 2.0 or less than −2.0 is about 5 percent or less. Figure 5.14 illustrates the 0.05 level of significance on a *t*-distribution with 60 degrees of freedom. Notice that the values of *t* that are greater or less than the critical *t*-value lie on the two ends or "tails" of the distribution.

The preceding conclusion helps us to understand the rationale for the "rule of 2" often employed by economists in their evaluation of the *t*-test. This rule states that the null hypothesis that $b = 0$ can be rejected if the *t*-value is less than or equal to −2 or greater than or equal to 2. Using the absolute value of *t*, we can state that the null hypothesis can be rejected if

$$|t^*| \geq 2$$

The implication of this rule of thumb is that the 0.05 level of significance is being used to select the critical *t*-value, t^*. As you can see in the *t*-table at the 0.05 level of significance, 2 serves as a useful approximation of the critical *t*-value for about 20 degrees of freedom and above.

A Suggested Classroom Exercise to Illustrate the Use of the t-Test At this point, you may still be a bit puzzled about the notion of a *t*-value and its use in testing the relationship between the sample $\hat{b}$ and the unknown population b, particularly if you are unfamiliar with statistical theory. We will, therefore, present a simple exercise that you may wish to try yourselves or along with your classmates and instructor. This exercise deals with the pizza demand example used earlier.

Cut 45 cardboard squares of equal size. According to Table 5.2, there are nine possible levels of demand for pizza for each income category. Thus, each of the squares is to be given a value ranging from 1 to 9. As shown in the first column of Table 5.2, there should be one square labeled 1, three squares labeled 2, six squares labeled 3, and so on. (Note that we have divided the frequencies in each income category by 100. There are 4,500 observations in the population, but we have reduced the number of squares used to 45 simply for convenience. As long as the relative frequencies are the same, it should not matter whether 45 or 4,500 squares are used in this exercise.)

Place all 45 squares in an envelope. Then select one square for each income category. Be sure to put the square back into the envelope after each selection. By doing this, you are generating a random sample of 10 observations, one for each income category. Because the number 5 occurs most frequently (9 times in this exercise and 900 times in the hypothetical population of student consumers) it is clear that the probability of drawing this number from the envelope is the greatest. In fact, each time a square is selected, there is a 20 percent chance (i.e., 9/45) that the number 5 will be selected. Then combine the number drawn with its income category to determine the corresponding pizza consumption.

Suppose one of these exercises produces the following table of numbers. As a reference to the exercise, the number that was drawn from the envelope is included in parentheses to the quantities demanded for pizza.

AVERAGE QUANTITY OF PIZZA SLICES DEMANDED (Y)	WEEKLY INCOME (X)
10.0 (1)	$100
13.0 (5)	120
15.2 (7)	140
16.0 (5)	160
16.0 (1)	180
18.7 (4)	200
21.2 (7)	220
22.3 (6)	240
22.0 (1)	260
26.0 (8)	280

A scatter plot of these data is presented in Figure 5.15. The regression equation estimated for this sample is

$$Y = 3.27 + 0.078X \qquad\qquad (5.9)$$
$$(0.86)\quad(0.004)$$

Let us now conduct a t-test for the significance of the estimated sample coefficient, $\hat{b}$. Recall that the null and alternative hypotheses can be expressed in the following manner:

$$H_0 : b = 0$$

$$H_a : b \neq 0$$

Clearly, our sample $\hat{b}$ coefficient of 0.078 is greater than zero. Therefore, we must determine the probability of encountering such a sample value from a population whose true value is really zero. We begin by subtracting zero (the hypothesized population value of b) from 0.078 (the estimated sample value, $\hat{b}$), and then we divide this difference by the standard error of $\hat{b}$. By convention, the standard error of an estimated regression coefficient is presented in parentheses under the coefficient. As you can see in Equation (5.9), the standard error of $\hat{b}$ is 0.004, and the standard error of the intercept is 0.86. This procedure is summarized here.

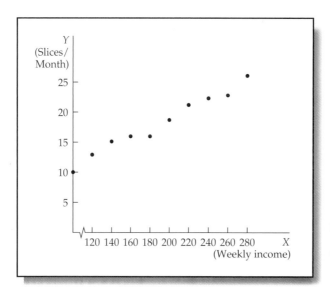

Figure 5.15
Scatter Plot of Sample Data
for Pizza Experiment

$$t = \frac{0.078 - 0}{0.004}$$

(5.10)

$$t = 19.5$$

Equation (5.10) is referred to as the *t*-ratio or the *t*-value.

From the results of the equation, you can see that if the population coefficient, *b*, were truly zero, then 0.078 would lie 19.5 *t*-units away from the mean. Turning to Table C.4 in Appendix C of this text, we see that the probability of encountering such a value is so remote that it is not even included in the chart. However, this table does show that the probability of obtaining a *t*-value (with 8 degrees of freedom) greater than 3.355 or less than −3.355 from a distribution whose mean is zero is one out of one hundred (i.e., 0.01). This implies that the probability of obtaining a value of 19.5 is virtually nil. And so we come to the rather obvious conclusion that the true value of the population coefficient is, in all likelihood, not equal to zero. In terms of statistical theory, we reject the null hypothesis.

In using regression analysis, economists almost always hypothesize the population coefficient to be equal to zero (i.e., $H_0 : b = 0$). However, the value of the unknown population coefficient can be hypothesized to be any value that the researcher desires. For example, suppose that a number of previous studies on the demand for pizza estimated the value of the coefficient of the income variable to be about 0.073. We might then use these previous studies as the justification for hypothesizing that the unknown coefficient is equal to this value:

$$H_0 : b = 0.73$$

$$H_a : b \neq 0.73$$

We find the corresponding *t*-ratio to be

$$t = \frac{0.078 - 0.073}{0.004}$$

$$t = 1.25$$

Suppose we test this hypothesis using the 0.05 level of significance, two-tail test. Turning again to the *t*-table in the appendix, we find a critical *t*-value of 2.306 for a regression with 8 degrees of freedom. Since the *t*-value of 1.25 is not greater than 2.306, we are *not* able to reject the null hypothesis. Once again, this does not mean that we can now say that the population coefficient is indeed 0.073. However, this failure to pass the *t*-test means that we are unable to say with a high degree of certainty that the population value is *not* 0.073. Until future studies indicate otherwise, researchers may want to assume the working hypothesis that the unknown population coefficient is around 0.073.

The t-Distribution and the One-Tail and Two-Tail Tests In using regression analysis for economic and business research, it is standard for the null hypothesis to state that there is no relationship between a particular independent variable and the dependent variable (e.g., $b = 0$). However, researchers usually have a choice as to whether the alternative hypothesis states that the independent variable simply has some impact on the dependent variable (a **two-tail test**) or whether it indicates a positive or a negative impact (a **one-tail test**). In the evaluation of the relationship between income and the quantity demanded for pizza, our alternative hypothesis was that changes in income had an effect on the quantity demanded for pizza; it did not state whether this effect was positive or negative. If we had some *a priori* reason for believing that the effect of income on quantity demanded was either positive or negative, it would be reflected in the alternative hypothesis. For example, if we hypothesized that pizza is a "normal" good, the alternative hypothesis would be that changes in income have a direct relation to changes in quantity demanded. If we hypothesized that pizza is an "inferior" good, the alternative hypothesis would claim an inverse relationship between the two variables. Using the notation we have developed:

If pizza is hypothesized to be a "normal good" (i.e., the income variable's coefficient is positive), then

$$H_0 : b \le 0$$

$$H_a : b > 0$$

If pizza is hypothesized to be an "inferior good" (i.e., the income variable's coefficient is negative), then

$$H_0 : b \ge 0$$

$$H_a : b < 0$$

If income is hypothesized simply to have an impact (either positive or negative) on the demand for pizza, then

$$H_0 : b = 0$$

$$H_a : b \ne 0$$

Summary: Steps in Conducting the t-Test of the Statistical Significance of Estimated Regression Coefficients This has been a rather lengthy discussion of the *t*-test, so it might be helpful to summarize each of the steps involved in carrying out this test.

Step 1: State the hypothesis.

For example, "Pizza is a normal good." (In other words, income is hypothesized to have a direct relation to the demand for pizza.)

Step 2: Restate the hypothesis in terms suitable for statistical testing.

With respect to the preceding hypothesis about income and the pizza,

$$H_0 : b \leq 0$$
$$H_a : b > 0$$

Step 3: Establish a critical level of rejection, and find the *t*-value that corresponds to this level.

For example, for a one-tail test, the 0.05 level, and 8 degrees of freedom (the number we assumed for the pizza analysis), $t^* = 1.86$. Thus, if the *t*-statistic is greater than 1.86, we can reject the null hypothesis at the 0.05 level of significance.

Step 4: Find the *t*-statistic by transforming the difference between the estimated *b* and its hypothesized value, 0.

For example, suppose the estimated coefficient is 2.5 and the standard error of the coefficient is 1.3. Then

$$t = \frac{2.5 - 0}{1.3}$$

$$= 1.92$$

Step 5: Compare the resulting *t*-value with the critical value. Then decide whether to reject the null hypothesis.

In our example, 1.92 is greater than the critical *t*-value of 1.86 for a one-tail test with 8 degrees of freedom. Therefore, we can reject the null hypothesis and state that income has a statistically significant direct impact on the demand for pizza.

MULTIPLE REGRESSION ANALYSIS

Let us begin our explanation of multiple regression by specifying the following *linear; additive regression model* for the demand for pizza:

$$Y = a + b_1 X_1 + b_2 X_2 + b_3 X_3 + b_4 X_4 \tag{5.11}$$

where Y = Quantity of pizza demanded (average number of slices per capita per month)

X_1 = Average price of a slice of pizza (in cents)

X_2 = Annual tuition (in thousands of dollars)
X_3 = Average price of a 12-ounce can of soft drink (in cents)
X_4 = Location of campus (1 if campus is located in a concentrated urban area, 0 otherwise)

Assume as we did in our opening section of this chapter that a regression analysis of cross-sectional data of 30 college campuses yields the following estimated relationship between the quantity demanded for pizza and our selection of independent variables:

$$Y = 26.67 - 0.088*X_1 + 0.138X_2 - 0.076*X_3 - 0.544X_4$$

$$(0.018) \quad\quad (0.087) \quad (0.020) \quad\quad (0.884) \quad\quad \textbf{(5.12)}$$

$$R^2 = 0.717 \quad F = 15.8 \quad n = 30$$

$$\bar{R}^2 = 0.67 \quad \text{Standard error of } Y = 1.64$$

The asterisks indicate statistical significance at the 0.05 level.

In evaluating this equation, we first look at the signs of the estimated coefficients of the independent variables. (We usually ignore the intercept term because by itself this term does not have any economic meaning.) Note that, as expected, the sign of the price variable is negative. The sign of the variable X_2 is positive, indicating that the higher the college tuition, the more pizza is purchased by the students. The sign of X_3, the variable for the price of soft drinks, is negative, indicating that pizza and soft drinks are complementary products.

There is one variable in the equation, X_4, that may seem a bit odd. This is called a *binary* or *dummy variable*. It assumes the value of 1 if the campus is located in a concentrated urban area and a value of 0 otherwise. This type of variable will be explained in greater detail in a later section. However, at this point we can point out that the coefficient of this variable measures the difference in the demand for pizza by students attending colleges or universities in urban areas versus students in institutions located outside of urban areas. As you can see by the magnitude and sign of the X_4 coefficient, the former group is estimated to eat 0.544 less slices of pizza per month than the latter group.

The magnitudes of the coefficients indicate the change in the quantity of pizza demanded relative to a unit change in a particular independent variable *assuming the values of the other variables are unchanged.* This feature of multiple regression analysis is extremely useful in economic and business research because, as you can see, it follows the comparative statics approach to the analysis of problems so commonly used in economic theory. Thus, the equation tells us that, all other factors held constant, a unit (i.e., a one-cent) decrease in the price of pizza will cause the quantity demanded of pizza to rise by 0.088 units. Unless one has actual experience in or prior knowledge about the retail pizza business, it is difficult to judge whether or not the magnitudes of the regression coefficients represent typical patterns of demand for pizza relative to changes in the independent variables. However, as noted earlier, one way to assess these magnitudes is to compute the elasticities of demand with respect to these independent variables. To compute these elasticities, we have to assume a certain starting point for the values of the independent variables. Let us assume the following values:

Price of pizza (X_1) = 100 (i.e., $1.00)
Annual college tuition (X_2) = 14 (i.e., $14,000)
Price of a soft drink (X_3) = 110 (i.e., $1.10)
Location of campus (X_4) = Urban area (i.e., X_4 = 1)

Given these values, we then compute the monthly per-capita demand for pizza to be

$$Y = 26.67 - 0.088\,(100) + 0.138\,(14)$$

$$-0.076\,(110) - 0.544\,(1) \tag{5.13}$$

$$= 10.898 \text{ or } 11 \text{ (rounded to nearest whole slice)}$$

Recall the general formula for point elasticity to be:

$$\frac{\delta Y}{\delta X} \times \frac{X}{Y}$$

We now use this formula to compute the various demand elasticities:

$$\text{Price elasticity: } -0.088 \times \frac{100}{10.898} = -0.807$$

$$\text{Tuition elasticity: } 0.138 \times \frac{14}{10.898} = 0.177$$

$$\text{Cross-price elasticity: } -0.076 \times \frac{110}{10.898} = -0.767$$

The equation has an adjusted R^2 of 0.67. This means that 67 percent of the variation in the dependent variable can be explained by variations in the independent variable. Once again, only those familiar with this type of business can really evaluate the explanatory power of this estimated equation. However, 0.67 is a higher R^2 than is found in most empirical studies of consumer demand that use cross-sectional data.

To conduct the t-test, we first divide the standard errors (cited in parentheses) into their respective coefficients and compare these t-ratios with the appropriate values in Table C.4 in Appendix C. At the 0.05 level of significance, two-tail test, we see that the critical t-value for 25 degrees of freedom is 2.06. Using this critical level, we see that the variables X_1, indicating the price of pizza, and X_3, indicating the price of soft drinks, are statistically significant.

As for the policy implications of these regression findings, suppose you are an entrepreneur who is considering starting a chain of pizza parlors on college campuses across the country. The price inelasticity of pizza implies that you should try to use advertising and promotion instead of price reductions as a means of boosting sales. Moreover, the statistical significance of the coefficient of the price variable would give you a great deal of confidence that you should not try to reduce the price. Although the tuition coefficient did not prove to be statistically significant, the relatively low tuition elasticity of demand might lead you to conclude that the locations of your pizza parlors should not be confined to any particular type of institution of higher education. Based on the fairly high cross-price elasticity between soft drink prices and the demand for pizza, once the pizza parlors are established you might want to consider reducing the price of beverages as a way to boost demand for pizza.

The *F*-Test

There is another test of statistical significance, called the **F-test**, that is commonly used in regression analysis. This test measures the statistical significance of the entire regression equation rather than of each individual coefficient (as the *t*-test is designed to do). Earlier, we stated that R^2 is the measure of the explanatory power of the regression model. In effect, the *F*-statistic is a test of the statistical significance of R^2. The null hypothesis of the *F*-test can be expressed as follows:

$$H_0 : b_1 = b_2 = \cdots = b_k = 0$$

where k equals the number of independent variables in the regression equation.

If the null hypothesis is true, virtually no relationship exists between the dependent variable and the k independent variables for the population, and whatever the value of R^2 (i.e., the proportion of the variation in Y explained by X), it is most probably a chance occurrence in the sampling process.

The *F*-value can be defined as

$$F = \frac{\text{Explained variation}/k}{\text{Unexplained variation}/(n - k - 1)}$$

where the explained variation is $\Sigma(\hat{Y} - \bar{Y})^2$, the unexplained variation is $\Sigma(Y - \hat{Y})^2$, n is the sample size, and k is the number of independent variables. It can also be expressed in terms of the value of R^2:

$$F = \frac{R^2/k}{(1 - R^2)/(n - k - 1)} \tag{5.14}$$

The procedure for using the *F*-value in the *F*-test is similar to the use of the *t*-value in the *t*-test. A critical value for F is established depending on the degree of statistical significance that the researcher wishes to set. Typically, the significance level if set at 0.05 or 0.01. The critical *F*-values corresponding to these acceptance levels are shown in Table C.3 in Appendix C. As can be seen, there are two "degrees of freedom" values that must be incorporated in the selection of the critical *F*-value. One value relates to the numerator of the equation for F, and the other relates to the denominator. Given this background information, we can now interpret the *F*-value for our multiple regression equation for pizza demand. With a sample size of 30 and four independent variables ($n = 30$ and $k = 4$), the *F*-table indicates that at the 0.05 level, the critical *F*-value for 4 and 25 degrees of freedom is 2.76. At the 0.01 level, the critical *F*-value is 4.18.

Because the estimated equation's *F*-value of 15.80 [reported in Equation (5.12)] exceeds both of these critical values, we can conclude that our entire regression model accounts for a statistically significant proportion of the variation in the demand for pizzas. In general, it is fairly easy for a regression model to pass the *F*-test. The null hypothesis, which states that there is no relationship between the dependent variable and *all* of the independent variables, is a rather stringent statement. As long as some of the independent variables in the regression equation truly help to explain the variance in the dependent variable, the *F*-test will more than likely indicate a statistically significant regression model. In fact, it can be seen in Equation (5.14) that for some given sample size and set of independent variables, the higher the R^2, the greater the *F*-value.

Another way to view the general tendency of a regression equation to pass the *F*-test is to recognize that regression models that *do not* pass the test must indeed be inferior. In any event, even if the *F*-statistic indicates the overall statistical significance of the regression model, there is still a need to subject each independent variable to individual testing. For this, we rely on the *t*-test.

THE USE OF REGRESSION ANALYSIS TO FORECAST DEMAND

In addition to helping researchers understand more about the determinants of demand, regression analysis can be used simply as a tool for forecasting. In the next chapter, we will discuss this topic in much greater detail. For now, let us just state that once the regression coefficients have been estimated, arriving at a forecast value of the demand for a particular good or service is simply a matter of assigning values to the independent variables. For example, suppose the regression analysis of time series data resulted in the following estimate of the demand for pizza:

$$Q = 100 - 20P + 100I + 15AD + 10P_{hd}$$

where Q = Demand for pizza (in millions of slices per year)
P = Price of pizza (in cents)
I = Per-capita income (in thousands of dollars)
AD = Advertising expenditures (in millions of dollars)
P_{hd} = Price of hot dogs (in cents)

If we assume that $P = 100$, $I = 5$, $AD = 30$, and $P_{hd} = 125$, our forecast for the quantity of pizza demanded for the coming year will be 300 (million slices). However, when regression analysis is used for forecasting, the same care that was taken in assessing the statistical significance of the individual regression coefficients must be applied. This is because the forecast is based on a sample of data. To take into account that the forecast value of 300 is based on a sample and is therefore subject to a sampling error, we use a measure called the **standard error of the estimate (SEE).** This term is also included as a regular part of the computer printout of any software regression program. As a matter of fact, it can be shown that the standard error of the coefficient ($SE_{\hat{b}}$) is actually derived from the SEE of the regression equation.

According to statistical theory, we can expect that the true (but unknown) value of Y will be within a range determined by the estimated value, plus or minus the product of the standard error of the estimate and the appropriate *t*-value. In notational form,

$$\hat{Y} \pm t_{n-k-1}SEE$$

For example, suppose the estimated regression equation for the pizza demand was generated from a sample size of 27 and had a SEE of 25. Given the previous values, we can say with 95 percent confidence that the actual demand for pizza is 300 $\pm$

2.074 (25), or a range of 248.15 to 351.85.[10] Caution should be exercised when developing the forecast range for the dependent variable of the estimated regression equation. Statistical theory shows that as the given values of the independent variables (e.g., price, income, price of related products) move further away from their mean values, the forecast range widens for any given level of confidence.

ADDITIONAL TOPICS ON THE SPECIFICATION OF THE REGRESSION MODEL

Proxy and Dummy Variables

One of the most challenging aspects of regression analysis (or, for that matter, any type of statistical analysis) is obtaining sample data suitable for use in the analysis. For example, economic theory indicates that "tastes and preferences" is an important determinant of consumer demand. But how do we measure this factor? A researcher who cannot obtain direct information about tastes and preferences may have to use a proxy variable to represent this factor in the regression equation. Level of education and gender of consumers are possible proxy variables for tastes and preferences. Those with higher levels of formal schooling might have different tastes or preferences for a particular good or service. Women might have different tastes or preferences than men. Even differences in residential location might reflect differences in tastes and preferences. For example, the authors have observed that supermarkets in the northeast region of the United States carry a proportionally larger stock and variety of Italian foods than those in other parts of the country. On the other hand, the variety and quantity of Mexican food on supermarket shelves in the Midwest, the Southwest, and on the Pacific Coast are substantially greater than in the Northeast.

In certain instances, for variables such as location and gender to be used in regression analysis, they must be quantified. This can be done by creating a dummy or binary variable, which takes the value of 1 if the unit of observation falls into a particular category and 0 if it does not. For example, we can assign the value of one to a female consumer and zero to a male. In this manner, dummy variables can be created for any nonquantitative factor.

A useful way to consider a dummy variable in a regression equation is as a "shift" factor. For example, in our regression analysis of the demand for pizza by college students, the coefficient of the dummy location variable was estimated to be -0.54. Suppose we graphed the demand equation implied by the values provided in Equation (5.13). This is shown in Figure 5.16. The original demand curve indicates the demand by those students who attend schools outside of urban areas (i.e., $X_4 = 0$). To determine the demand by those students who attend school in urban areas, we

---

[10]According to the t-table, the critical t-value with 22 degrees of freedom (i.e., $n - k - 1$, or $27 - 5$) is 2.074. If a greater degree of confidence were desired, the range of the expected value of the demand for pizza would obviously widen. For example, at the 99 percent confidence level, the critical t-value with 22 degrees of freedom is 2.819.

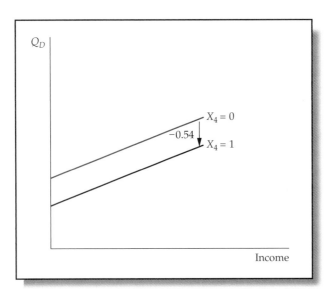

Figure 5.16
Effect of the Dummy Variable

simply assign the value of 1 to the X_4 variable. This gives us the second demand curve shown in Figure 5.16. In effect, the change in X_4 has caused the original curve to shift downward.

Nonlinear Relationships

The method of least squares finds the best linear relationship between the dependent and independent variables. However, in certain instances, economic theory, experience, or simple observation of the scatter plot may lead researchers to suspect that the relationship between the dependent and independent variables is nonlinear. For example, suppose data on income (X) and the demand for restaurant meals (Q_D) for a sample of households yields the scatter plot shown in Figure 5.17a. As you can see, the scatter implies a nonlinear relationship between income and the demand for restaurant meals. Such nonlinear representations are still suitable for estimation with the use of linear regression analysis. For example, we could specify a polynomial regression model in which the independent term, X, is raised to the second as well as to the first degree. Figure 5.17b illustrates this option. We could also specify our regression equation in terms of a power function. Figure 5.17c illustrates this possibility. In either case, the idea is to use the method of least squares to estimate the coefficients of the equations. The usual tests and statistics (e.g., t-test, F-test, R^2) are still used in evaluating the regression results.

When using the power function, we first apply a logarithmic transformation to the original specification. For example, let the original equation be as follows:

$$Q_D = aX^b$$

where Q_D = Demand for restaurant services (number of times a person eats in a restaurant per year)
X = Annual income

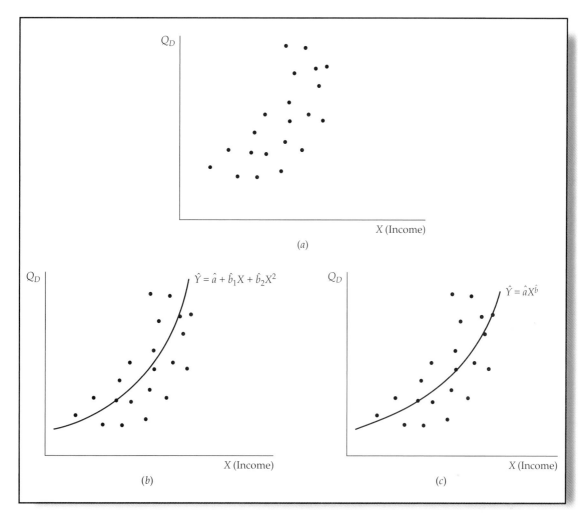

Figure 5.17
Nonlinear Relationships

Taking the log of both sides of the equation gives us the following logarithmic transformation:

$$\log Q_D = \log a + b \log X$$

To perform a regression analysis on this type of nonlinear data, we first find the logs of each of the values of Y and X in the sample data. We then regress $\log Y$ on $\log X$ using the method of least squares. One way in which the transformed regression equation can be evaluated is to compare its R^2 with that of a simple linear equation (i.e., $Q_D = a + bX$). If the R^2 of the transformed power equation is greater than that of the simple linear expression, it would appear that the nonlinear model offers a better explanation for the variance of Q_D.

The use of a *log-linear* equation in regression analysis is particularly appealing for economists because for relatively small changes in X, the estimated coefficient of the log of X can indicate the *percentage change in Y relative to the percentage change in X*.[11] In other words, the coefficients of the transformed variables are in fact measures of the point elasticity of demand with respect to each variable. For example, if the estimated value of b in the preceding equation were 1.2, then we could immediately interpret restaurant dining as a "superior" product because its income elasticity is greater than unity.

PROBLEMS IN THE USE OF REGRESSION ANALYSIS

A full discussion of the problems that may arise in regression is clearly beyond the scope of this chapter and this text. As mentioned at the outset of this chapter, entire textbooks and whole courses ranging from introductory to advanced are dedicated to the study of regression analysis. Nonetheless, we should cite and briefly explain some of these problems so that readers unfamiliar with this topic will gain an appreciation of the real challenges awaiting those who wish to apply regression analysis to business and economic research.

The Identification Problem

The identification problem presents perhaps the greatest challenge to those using regression analysis to estimate the demand for a particular good or service. To explain this problem, let us return to our pizza example. Suppose we had time series data relating the per-capita consumption of pizza with the price of pizza over a 20-year period. The scatter plot of this information is shown in Figure 5.18a. Notice that the scatter tends to slope upward and that a least squares regression estimate would reflect this pattern of relationship. Does this mean that the consumers of pizza behave irrationally and demand more pizza at higher prices? Common sense would balk at such a conclusion, but then why the positive coefficient of the price variable in the demand equation? The alert reader will state that what we have identified as a demand equation is probably some sort of supply equation or perhaps, the result of the movement in *both* supply and demand for pizza over the past 20 years. As can be seen in Figure 5.18b, if the supply remained constant over the past 20 years while demand shifted upward (because of changes in such factors as income, number of buyers, and tastes and preferences over this time period), the regression equation would really be a reflection of the supply curve S_1. If the supply increased but demand increased more than the supply, then the regression estimate would really be a reflection of the intersection of the various S and D curves in Figure 5.18c. Figure 5.18d shows still another possibility. In this case, supply shifts more than demand, so that the estimated regression line is downward sloping and more like what we would expect of a demand curve. Nonetheless, this estimated demand curve is flatter than the true demand curves, which have gradually shifted to the right over the years. Thus, the regression estimate of the relationship between price and quantity

---

[11]For a discussion of the meaning of the coefficients in a log-linear regression equation, see the discussion of the basic mathematics of the Cobb-Douglas function in chapter 7.

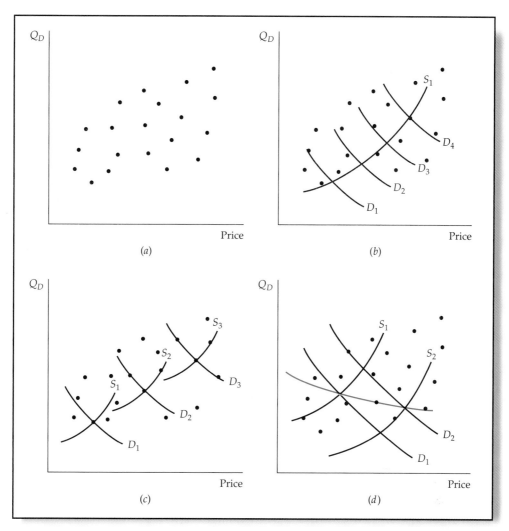

Figure 5.18
The Identification Problem

demanded would be biased in the sense that it would indicate a much greater price elasticity than actually exists in the population of pizza consumers.

There are advanced estimation techniques, such as the methods of *two-stage least squares* and *indirect least squares*, that can help the researcher deal with samples in which the simultaneous shifting of demand and supply takes place. Essentially, these techniques involve the simultaneous consideration of the supply and demand equations with the use of a single regression equation. A discussion of these techniques lies outside the scope of this text. But the principal point to remember is that if the identification problem is not recognized and dealt with by the researcher, the method of ordinary least squares will result in biased estimates of the regression coefficients.

Multicollinearity

One of the key assumptions made in the construction of the multiple regression equation is that the independent variables are not related to each other in any systematic way. If this assumption is incorrect, then each of the estimated coefficients may give a distorted view of the impact of the change in each of the independent variables. For example, suppose a regression model states that the demand for luxury foreign-made automobiles depends on price, income, and education. The latter variable is included because education is a proxy for tastes and preferences, and those with higher levels of education are hypothesized to have a greater preference for luxury foreign cars. But, as you would expect, education and income are closely associated. If their values tend to move up and down together, the least squares method may arbitrarily assign a high value to the coefficient of one variable and a low coefficient value to the other. In effect, if two variables are closely associated, it becomes difficult to separate out the effect that each has on the dependent variable. The existence of such a condition in regression analysis is called *multicollinearity*.

If the regression results pass the *F*-test (the measure of the overall statistical significance of the regression equation) but fail the *t*-test for each of the individual regression coefficients, it is usually a sign that multicollinearity is present in the sample data. Multicollinearity can also be detected by examining the correlation coefficient between two variables suspected of being closely related.[12] As a rule of thumb, correlation coefficients of 0.7 or more provide a basis for researchers to suspect the existence of multicollinearity.

If multicollinearity is a serious problem in the regression analysis, it will tend to introduce an upward bias to the standard errors of the coefficients. This will tend to reduce the *t*-values (which, you will recall, are computed using the standard errors of the coefficients). This makes it harder to reject the null hypothesis and, of course, to identify statistically significant independent variables in the regression model.

It should be pointed out, however, that if the researcher simply wishes to use the estimated regression coefficients as a basis for forecasting future values of the dependent variable, multicollinearity does not pose a serious problem. It is only when the researcher wishes to understand more about the underlying structure of the demand function (i.e., what are the key determinants of demand) that this particular statistical problem should be resolved. Most software packages automatically produce a correlation coefficient matrix for the entire set of independent variables used in the regression equation. A standard remedy for multicollinearity is to drop one of the variables that is closely associated with another variable in the regression equation.

Autocorrelation

Autocorrelation is a problem that is usually encountered when time series data are used. For this reason, it is often referred to as *serial correlation*. Let us use the case of simple regression, involving only the dependent variable Y and one independent variable, X. Essentially, autocorrelation occurs when the Y variable relates to the X

---

[12]The correlation coefficient is a measure of the degree of association between two variables. This measure, denoted r, ranges from a value of -1 (perfect negative correlation) to 1 (perfect positive correlation).

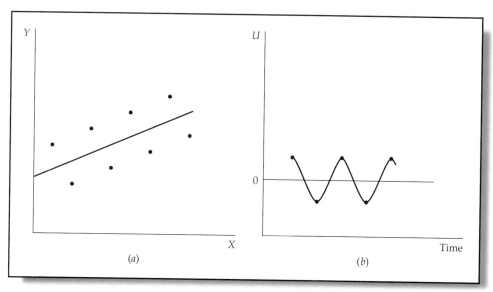

Figure 5.19
Autocorrelation

variable according to a certain pattern. For example, in Figure 5.19*a*, the scatter plot reveals that as *X* increases (presumably over time), the *Y* value deviates from the regression line in a very systematic way. In other words, the *residual term*, or the difference between the observed value of *Y* and the estimated value of *Y* given $X(\hat{Y})$ alternates between a positive and a negative value of approximately the same magnitude throughout the range of *X* values. In fact, if we were to plot these residuals on a separate graph, they would have the pattern shown in Figure 5.19*b*.

One possible cause of autocorrelation is that there are effects on *Y* not accounted for by the variables included in the regression equation. It might also be that the true relationship between *Y* and the independent variable(s) is nonlinear. But regardless of the reason, if autocorrelation is present in the regression analysis, it creates a problem for the validity of the *t*-test. Simply stated, autocorrelation tends to increase the likelihood that the null hypothesis will be rejected. This is because autocorrelation gives a downward bias to the standard error of the estimated regression coefficient ($SE_{\hat{b}}$). Recalling that the *t*-value is defined as $(\hat{b} - b)/SE_{\hat{b}}$, we can see that a smaller $SE_{\hat{b}}$ would tend to increase the magnitude of the *t*-value, other factors held constant. Thus, in the presence of autocorrelation, researchers may well declare that certain independent variables have a statistically significant impact on the dependent variable when in fact they do not. From a policy standpoint, suppose that the estimated coefficient of the advertising variable in a regression model of demand passed the *t*-test when it really should not have. A firm might then be led to increase its advertising expenditures when in fact it should be looking at other ways to expand demand (e.g., through promotions, alternative channels of distribution, or price actions).

It may be difficult to identify autocorrelation simply by observing the pattern of the residuals of a regression equation. A standard test for identifying the presence of this problem is the *Durbin-Watson test*. The Durbin-Watson statistic (i.e., DW) is now routinely calculated in regression software packages and is presented automatically in the computer printout. As in the case of the *t*-test and the *F*-test, there is a Durbin-Watson table listing the critical values of this statistic for a given level of significance (usually the 0.05 level). We have included such a table in the appendix at the back of this text (see Table C.5). As a rule of thumb, if the DW statistic is around 2, there is in all probability no autocorrelation present in the data. Should the DW statistic indicate the presence of autocorrelation, there are certain things a researcher can do to correct the problem. These include transforming the data into a different order of magnitude or introducing leading or lagging data in the time series.

INTERNATIONAL APPLICATION: FOOD IN SPAIN, CIGARETTES IN TAIWAN

It is somewhat difficult to secure actual regression results on consumer demand conducted by companies such as ACNielsen and IRI or by the market research groups of major consumer goods manufacturers. We know that regression is a useful tool for these researchers, but unfortunately, all of their studies are proprietary. Readers should rest assured that many of these actual studies use specifications of regression equations similar to those presented in this chapter. However, many studies conducted by academic researchers are readily available to the general public. We have selected two such studies, mainly because they also give readers an example of studies of consumer behavior outside of the United States.[13]

Example 1: Regression Analysis of Basic Foods in Spain A time series study of the demand for six classes of food for the period 1964 to 1991 in Spain was performed. The six different classifications were:

1. Bread and cereals
2. Meat
3. Fish
4. Milk, dairy products, and eggs
5. Fruits, vegetables, and potatoes
6. Fats and oils

The results show that changes in food demand (in terms of calories consumed) do not depend only on current income and prices but also on lagged values of these variables. Consumers of food in Spain do not immediately adjust their expenditures when incomes or prices change. Rather they appear to show a certain level of inertia.

Of the above six categories, only meat is shown to be a "superior" good, with an income elasticity of 1.54. Among the other five groups, only fruits and vegetables have income elasticity close to unity (.9), while the elasticity of fats and oils is the lowest, at .35. In terms of own price elasticities, meat shows the highest coefficient of

---

[13]We also provide examples of academic studies of cost using regression analysis in chapter 8.

−.8. All the others are also negative; all have *t*-test results that are significantly different from zero. Most cross-elasticities are quite low and not statistically significant, showing that there is no great substitutability among these products. There are a few exceptions, the largest one being fish and meat, whose *t*-test result is significant. The R^2 for the equation is a relatively high .63.[14]

Example 2: Regression Analysis of the Demand for Cigarettes in Taiwan

A recent time-series study investigated the demand for cigarettes in Taiwan, not only as a function of income and price, but also looked into the influence of antismoking campaigns and the impact of the opening of Taiwan's market to imported cigarettes. Data for 30 years (1966–1995) were utilized. The basic estimating equation was written as follows:

$$C_t = a_0 + a_1 P_t + a_2 Y_t + a_3 H_t + a_4 X_t + e_t$$

where C_t = annual cigarette consumption per capita,
P_t = average retail price of cigarettes per pack,
Y_t = disposable income per capita, in 1991 New Taiwan dollars,
H_t = measure of smoke-related health information,
X_t = other determinants,
e_t = random error term, and
a_{0-4} = regression coefficients

In addition, separate demand functions were estimated for domestic and imported cigarettes. The equations used in these calculations were similar to the above, except that one term was added to each equation. In the domestic cigarette demand equation, the price of imported cigarettes was included to measure cross-price elasticity. In the equation for imported cigarettes, the price of domestic cigarettes was included. Two measures of health information were used:

1. Market share of low-tar cigarettes
2. Strongly worded warning labels adopted in 1992. A dummy variable of 0 up to 1991 and 1 thereafter was employed.

Some of the other explanatory variables included lagged consumption, market share of imported cigarettes, and female labor force participation.

The results for the overall model were as follows:

Price elasticity −.5 to −.6
Income elasticity .14 to .22
Low-tar impact −.04

All three of these had statistically significant coefficients at the 1 percent or 5 percent level. The effect of warning labels was also negative but not statistically significant, and the impact of imported cigarettes was positive but only significant at the 10 percent level in some of the models.

---

[14]A. Gracia, J. M. Gil and A. M. Angulo, "Spanish Food Demand: a Dynamic Approach," *Applied Economics*, October 1998, 30(10), pp. 1399–1405.

When domestic and imported cigarettes were considered separately, the results were similar. The cross-price elasticities in both equations were positive, indicating that domestic and imported cigarettes are substitutes. The coefficients of determination for the various models were quite satisfactory. They were approximately .91 for the overall equations and .71 to .88 for the equations in which domestic and imported cigarettes were studied separately.[15]

The Solution

As it turned out, the task of generating a statistical model was not as simple as Jennifer Harrah had anticipated. The key problem was the lack of data. The product was brand new for Global Foods, so there was no historical information that the company could provide for use as time series data in the regression analysis. She could have generated cross-sectional data by conducting a telephone survey, but there simply was not enough time. She was able to find public information on time series data from the government for such items as fruit juices, soft drinks, and beer, but these were aggregated by product type, and no other information besides average price was available. The only data set she could find within the time allowed was part of a market research study conducted in the 1950s by the *National Bottler's Gazette.* This study looked at the per-capita consumption of soft drinks by state, along with the average annual temperature of the state and its per capita income. These figures are shown in Table 5.3.* She conducted a regression analysis of these cross-sectional data using the following model:

$$Q = a + b_1 INC + b_2 TEMP$$

where Q = Per-capita annual consumption of soft drinks
INC = Per-capita annual income
$TEMP$ = Average annual temperature

The results of the computer analysis are shown in Table 5.4. Temperature has a sizable as well as a statistically significant impact on soft drink consumption. Every additional degree of average annual temperature results in an increase in per-capita soft drink consumption by

---

*The authors debated whether to use artificially created data to demonstrate all of the topics presented in this chapter or to use real data, which would limit the application of regression analysis. The latter option was chosen because in actual business situations, the lack of good data is far more limiting than either one's knowledge of statistical analysis or the computing power available to "crunch" the numbers. The soft drink consumption figures from the study by the *National Bottler's Gazette* were originally presented in a market research textbook now out of print. Unfortunately, this text did not cite the date when the figures were obtained.

(Continued)

---

[15]Chee-Ruey Hsieh, Teh-Wei Hu, and Chien-Fu Jeff Lin, "The Demand for Cigarettes in Taiwan: Domestic vs. Imported Cigarettes," *Contemporary Economic Policy,* April 1999, pp. 223–234.

Table 5.3
Soft Drink Consumption, Temperature, and Income by State

STATE	CONSUMPTION OF SOFT DRINKS PER CAPITA	PER CAPITA INCOME (HUNDREDS)	MEAN ANNUAL TEMPERATURE, °F
Alabama	200	$13	66
Arizona	150	17	62
Arkansas	237	11	63
California	135	25	56
Colorado	121	19	52
Connecticut	118	27	50
Delaware	217	28	52
Florida	242	18	72
Georgia	295	14	64
Idaho	85	16	46
Illinois	114	24	52
Indiana	184	20	52
Iowa	104	16	50
Kansas	143	17	56
Kentucky	230	13	56
Louisiana	269	15	69
Maine	111	16	41
Maryland	217	21	54
Massachusetts	114	22	47
Michigan	108	21	47
Minnesota	108	18	41
Mississippi	248	10	65
Missouri	203	19	57
Montana	77	19	44
Nebraska	97	16	49
Nevada	166	24	48
New Hampshire	177	18	35
New Jersey	143	24	54
New Mexico	157	15	56
New York	111	25	48
North Carolina	330	13	59
North Dakota	63	14	39
Ohio	165	22	51
Oklahoma	184	16	82
Oregon	68	19	51
Pennsylvania	121	20	50
Rhode Island	138	20	50
South Carolina	237	12	65
South Dakota	95	13	45
Tennessee	236	13	60
Texas	222	17	69
Utah	100	16	50
Vermont	64	16	44
Virginia	270	16	58
Washington	77	20	49
West Virginia	144	15	55
Wisconsin	97	19	46
Wyoming	102	19	46

4.7 bottles. Using the "rule of 2," we can see that the t-value of 5.70 is clearly significant. The estimated coefficient for the income variable is interesting. First, its negative value indicates that a soft drink is an "inferior" product. Higher levels of income result in lower per-capita consumption, and lower income implies higher consumption. However, the t-value of -1.2 is below the critical t-value. Thus, income cannot be considered a statistically significant determinant of soft drink consumption. The adjusted R^2 of 0.46 indicates that about one-half of the variation in soft drink consumption can be accounted for by the variation in per-capita income and average annual temperature. This is to be expected, considering the fact that cross-sectional data are used and that only two independent variables were incorporated into the equation. Nonetheless, the F-value of 21.37 indicates that the R^2 is statistically significant, because the critical value of F at the 0.05 level with 2 and 45 degrees of freedom is about 3.20.

Jennifer wanted to include price in her regression model. Unfortunately, no time series data were available for price. There were some cross-sectional data on the average prices in different regions of the country, but these data were not suitable for regression analysis, because the prices were basically the same for all regions. Regression analysis requires *variation* in the values of the independent variables. Otherwise, there is no scatter plot to which to fit the regression line.

Table 5.4
Excel Regression Analysis Output

REGRESSION STATISTICS

Multiple R	0.697953501
R Square	0.487139089
Adjusted R Square	0.464345271
Standard Error	49.71283142
Observations	48

ANOVA

	DF	SS	MS	F	SIGNIFICANCE F
Regression	2	105633.7976	52816.9	21.371544	2.98532E-07
Residual	45	111211.4524	2471.366		
Total	47	216845.25			

	COEFFICIENTS	STANDARD ERROR	T STAT	P-VALUE	LOWER 95%	UPPER 95%
Intercept	−54.841134	63.45499732	−0.864252	0.3920329	−182.6460536	72.96379
X Variable 1	−2.20457538	1.825233618	−1.207832	0.2334217	−5.880784437	1.471634
X Variable 2	4.719982058	0.828234444	5.698848	8.722E-07	3.05183233	6.388132

Variable 1 = income per capita
Variable 2 = average temperature

This chapter has presented an introduction to regression analysis, the method most commonly utilized by economists for estimating the demand for goods and services. Actually, this chapter's material is only a small part of econometrics, which is the application of multivariate statistical analysis to economic theory. The primary importance of this chapter is as an aid in understanding how the techniques of regression analysis may be applied to businesses interested in finding out more about the quantitative aspects of the demand for their products. Readers should appreciate the challenge of applying regression analysis and other statistical techniques to business problems because of the difficulty of obtaining accurate and reliable data.

The process of applying regression analysis to the estimation of demand can be summarized in the following steps:

1. Specification of the regression model of demand
2. Collection of the relevant data
3. Estimation of the regression equation
4. Analysis and evaluation of the regression results (e.g., t-test, F-test, R^2), and adjustment or correction for any statistical problems (e.g., multicollinearity, autocorrelation, incorrect functional form)
5. Assessment of regression findings for use in making policy decisions

In a formal econometrics course, most of the emphasis is placed on steps 1, 3, and 4 (i.e., the more technical aspects of this type of statistical analysis). In business, the most important steps are 2 and 5. Powerful computers and sophisticated software packages are available to everyone today at such a reasonable cost that it has become elementary to apply regression analysis to the estimation of demand or any other aspect of business research. The real challenge is to obtain *good* data and to apply judiciously the results of the regression analysis to the managerial decision-making process. In these two areas of regression analysis, no textbook or course can take the place of actual hands-on experience.

IMPORTANT CONCEPTS

Alternative hypothesis: In regression analysis, the hypothesis that stands in contrast to the null hypothesis. It generally states that the true (but unknown) population coefficient is some value other than zero. (p. 191)

Coefficient of determination (R^2): A measure indicating the percentage of the variation in the dependent variable accounted for by variations in some designated independent variable. Its value ranges from 0 to 1. Zero indicates that variations in the independent variable account for none of the variation in the dependent variable. One indicates that 100 percent of the variation in the dependent variable can be accounted for by

the variations in the independent variable. In multiple regression analysis, this measure is referred to as the *multiple coefficient of determination.* (p. 174)

Coefficients of the regression equation: Also referred to as *parameters,* the values that indicate the quantitative impact on the dependent variable of a unit change in an independent variable. The main objective of regression analysis is to estimate the values of these coefficients from a sample of data. For this the method of ordinary least squares is often employed. (p. 180)

Consumer survey: The attempt to obtain data about demand directly by asking consumers about their purchasing habits through such means as face-to-face interviews, focus groups, telephone surveys, and mailed questionnaires. (p. 168)

Cross-sectional data: Data on a particular set of variables for a given point in time for a cross section of individual entities (e.g., persons, households, cities, states, countries). (p. 169)

Degrees of freedom: An adjustment factor that is required in conducting the t-test. This number is found by subtracting the number of independent variables plus 1 from the number of observations in the sample; that is, d.f. $= n - (k + 1) = n - k - 1$. (p. 193)

F-test: A test for the statistical significance of the R^2 value. If this test is passed, a researcher can be quite confident that all of the estimated coefficients of a regression model together are not zero for the population under study. (p. 201)

Method of ordinary least squares (OLS): In simple regression analysis, a method designed to fit a line through a scatter of points indicating values of a dependent variable and an independent variable in such a way that the sum of the squared deviations of the points from the line is minimized. (p. 180)

Null hypothesis: In regression analysis, the hypothesis used in testing for the statistical significance of the estimated regression coefficient. It states that the true (but unknown) regression coefficients for the population are zero. (p. 191)

One-tail test: This refers to the nature of the alternative hypothesis in the t-test. If the alternative hypothesis states that the population coefficient is positive, then the upper tail of the t-distribution is used. If the alternative hypothesis states that the population coefficient is negative, then the lower tail is used. In either case, only one tail is used. (p. 197)

Regression analysis: A statistical technique for finding the best relationship between a dependent variable and selected independent variables.

If one independent variable is used, this technique is referred to as *simple regression.* If more than one independent variable is used, it is called *multiple regression.* (p. 169)

Rule of 2: A general rule of thumb employed by economists in conducting the t-test. Essentially, it states that any t-ratio of 2 or more indicates that the estimated coefficient is statistically significant at the 0.05 level. (p. 174)

Standard error of the coefficient (SE$_{\hat{b}}$): A measure of the deviation of an estimated regression coefficient from the hypothesized value of the true (but unknown) population coefficient. In the t-test, the standard error of a particular estimated coefficient is divided into this coefficient, thereby indicating the t-value. (p. 174)

Standard error of the estimate (SEE): A measure of the deviation of the estimated value of the dependent variable, given the values of the independent variables. In forecasting, the standard error of the estimate is used to develop an interval that contains the true value of the dependent variable, subject to a designated degree of confidence. (p. 202)

t-table: A numerical table indicating the different values of the t-ratio and the frequency of their occurrence in a t-distribution whose mean value is zero. (p. 193)

t-test: A test for the statistical significance of the estimated regression coefficients. If a coefficient passes this test, then a researcher can be quite confident that the value of the true population coefficient is not zero. (p. 190)

Time series data: Data for a particular set of variables that track their values over a particular period of time at regular intervals (e.g., monthly, quarterly, annually). (p. 169)

Two-tail test: A t-test in which the alternative hypothesis states that the population coefficient may be either positive or negative (i.e., it is not zero); that is, either the upper or the lower tail of the t-distribution may be used. (p. 197)

QUESTIONS

1. Explain the difference between time series data and cross-sectional data. Provide examples of each type of data.
2. Would there be any differences in the set of variables used in a regression model of the demand for consumer durable goods (e.g., automobiles, appliances, furniture) and a regression model of the demand for "fast-

moving consumer goods" (e.g., food, beverages, personal care products)? Explain.

3. Explain the difference between a deterministic model and a probabilistic model of the relationship between a dependent variable and one or more independent variables.

4. Briefly explain the meaning of R^2. A time series analysis of demand tends to result in a higher R^2 than one using cross-sectional data. Why do you think this is the case?

5. Overheard at the water cooler: "My regression model of demand is better than the one that the consultant prepared for us because it has a higher R^2. Besides, my equation has three more independent variables and so is more complete than the consultant's." Comment on this statement. Would you agree with the speaker? Explain.

6. Summarize the steps involved in conducting the *t*-test. What is the basis for using the "rule of 2" as a convenient method of evaluating *t*-ratios?

7. Briefly explain the meaning of the *F*-test. Why do you think this test is considered to be more important in multiple regression analysis than it is in simple regression analysis?

8. What is *multicollinearity*? How can researchers detect this problem? What is the impact of this problem on the regression estimates? What steps can be taken to deal with this problem?

9. What is the identification problem? What effect will this problem have on the regression estimates of a demand function? Explain.

PROBLEMS

1. In the first several years of the 1990s, the consumer electronics industry had high hopes for the success of a type of compact disc player that displays sophisticated audio and video programs on a television set. The initial price of this product, which would enable users to scan programs ranging from the complete works of William Shakespeare to a cookbook with more than 450 recipes with color photographs and voiceovers, was set at about $1,000.

   a. Suppose you were asked to conduct market research for this product. Is it possible to use regression analysis for a product such as this, which had never before been on the market? If you believe so, how would you have gone about conducting this research?

   b. As data accumulated about this product's sales, suggest the types of variables that could have been included in a regression analysis of the demand for this new type of CD player.

   c. What does the current popularity of multimedia personal computers, video games, and personal digital assistants, tell you about the difficulties of using regression (or, for that matter, any other quantitative technique) to forecast a product's demand?

2. One of the most difficult tasks in regression analysis is to obtain the data suitable for quantitative studies of this kind. Suppose you are trying to estimate the demand for home furniture. Suggest the kinds of variables that could be used to represent the following factors, which are believed to affect the demand for any product. Be as specific as possible about how the variables are going to be measured. Do you anticipate any difficulty in securing such data? Explain.

DETERMINANTS OF DEMAND FOR FURNITURE	SUGGESTED VARIABLES TO USE IN REGRESSION ANALYSIS
Price	
Tastes and preferences	
Price of related products	
Income	
Cost or availability of credit	
Number of buyers	
Future expectations	
Other possible factors	

3. You are the manager of a large automobile dealership who wants to learn more about the effectiveness of various discounts offered to customers over the past 14 months. Following are the average negotiated prices for each month and the quantities sold of a basic model (adjusted for various options) over this period of time.
   a. Graph this information on a scatter plot. Estimate the demand equation. What do the regression results indicate about the desirability of discounting the price? Explain.

MONTH	PRICE	QUANTITY
Jan.	12,500	15
Feb.	12,200	17
Mar.	11,900	16
Apr.	12,000	18
May	11,800	20
June	12,500	18
July	11,700	22
Aug.	12,100	15
Sept.	11,400	22
Oct.	11,400	25
Nov.	11,200	24
Dec.	11,000	30
Jan.	10,800	25
Feb.	10,000	28

   b. What other factors besides price might be included in this equation? Do you foresee any difficulty in obtaining these additional data or incorporating them in the regression analysis?
4. The maker of a leading brand of low-calorie microwavable food estimated the following demand equation for its product using data from 26 supermarkets around the country for the month of April:

$$Q = -5,200 - 42P + 20P_x + 5.2I + 0.20A + 0.25M$$

$$(2,002) \quad (17.5) \quad (6.2) \quad (2.5) \quad (0.09) \quad (0.21)$$

$$R^2 = 0.55 \qquad n = 26 \qquad F = 4.88$$

Assume the following values for the independent variables:

$$Q = \text{Quantity sold per month}$$
$$P \text{ (in cents)} = \text{Price of the product} = 500$$
$$P_X \text{ (in cents)} = \text{Price of leading competitor's product} = 600$$
$$I \text{ (in dollars)} = \text{Per capita income of the standard metropolitan statistical area}$$
$$\text{(SMSA) in which the supermarket is located} = 5{,}500$$
$$A \text{ (in dollars)} = \text{Monthly advertising expenditure} = 10{,}000$$
$$M = \text{Number of microwave ovens sold in the SMSA in which the}$$
$$\text{supermarket is located} = 5{,}000.$$

Using this information, answer the following questions:
a. Compute elasticities for each of the variables.
b. How concerned do you think this company would be about the impact of a recession on its sales? Explain.
c. Do you think that this firm should cut its price to increase its market share? Explain.
d. What proportion of the variation in sales is explained by the independent variables in the equations? How confident are you about this answer? Explain.

5. A manufacturer of computer workstations gathered average monthly sales figures from its 56 branch offices and dealerships across the country and estimated the following demand for its product:

$$Q = +15{,}000 - 2.80P + 150A + 0.3P_{pc} + 0.35P_m + 0.2P_c$$

$$(5{,}234) \quad (1.29) \quad (175) \quad (0.12) \quad (0.17) \quad (0.13)$$

$$R^2 = 0.68 \qquad \text{SEE} = 786 \qquad F = 21.25$$

The variables and their assumed values are

$$Q = \text{Quantity}$$
$$P = \text{Price of basic model} = 7{,}000$$
$$A = \text{Advertising expenditures (in thousands)} = 52$$
$$P_{pc} = \text{Average price of a personal computer} = 4000$$
$$P_m = \text{Average price of a minicomputer} = 15{,}000$$
$$P_c = \text{Average price of a leading competitor's workstation} = 8{,}000$$

a. Compute the elasticities for each of the variables. On this basis, discuss the relative impact that each variable has on the demand. What implications do these results have for the firm's marketing and pricing policies?
b. Conduct a *t*-test for the statistical significance of each variable. In each case, state whether a one-tail or two-tail test is required. What difference, if any, does it make to use a one-tail versus a two-tail test on the results? Discuss the results of the *t*-tests in light of the policy implications mentioned.
c. Suppose a manager evaluating these results suggests that interest rates and the performance of the computer (typically measured in millions of instructions per second, or MIPS) are important determinants of the demand for workstations and must therefore be included in the study. How would you respond to this suggestion? Elaborate.

6. Deck & Blacker is a maker of small kitchen appliances. Its economist estimates the following demand for toaster ovens using data gathered over 16 quarters

from the ten major retail distributors of its product. This type of sample, which involves the use of cross-sectional and times series data, is referred to as a *pooled sample*. On the basis of this pooled sample of 160 observations, the economist estimated the following equation:

$$Q = 40 - 1.1P + 1.5A + 0.32I + 0.5H + 0.1P_c$$

$$(2.5) \quad (0.9) \quad (0.6) \quad (0.12) \quad (0.17) \quad (0.75)$$

$$R^2 = 0.91 \qquad \text{SEE} = 2.8 \qquad F = 311.43$$

The variables and the values inserted into the equation for purposes of forecasting are as follows:

Q = Quantity demanded, in thousands
P = Price, in dollars = 55
A = Advertising expenditures, in thousands = 20
I = Average household income, in thousands = 31
H = Total number of residential sales, in thousands = 10
P_c = Price of leading competitor, in dollars = 50

a. Should this company try to market its toaster ovens in upscale gourmet shops? Explain.
b. How concerned should this company be about price discounts by its leading competitor? Explain.
c. How effective do you think advertising is for this company?
d. Should this company consider discounting its price in order to gain market share at the expense of its competitors? Explain.
e. Assuming the values of the variables are given, indicate the 95 percent confidence interval of the forecast demand for toaster ovens.

7. You are given the following demand for European luxury automobiles:

$$Q = 1{,}000P^{-0.93} \, P_a^{0.75} \, P_j^{1.2} \, I^{1.6}$$

where P = Price of European luxury cars
P_a = Price of American luxury cars
P_j = Price of Japanese luxury cars
I = Annual income of car buyers

Assume that each of the coefficients is statistically significant (i.e., that they passed the *t*-test). On the basis of the information given, answer the following questions:

a. Comment on the degree of substitutability between European and American luxury cars and between European and Japanese luxury cars. Explain some possible reasons for the results in the equation.
b. Comment on the coefficient for the income variable. Is this result what you would expect? Explain.
c. Comment on the coefficient of the European car price variable. Is that what you would expect? Explain.

Chapter 6

Forecasting

The Situation

Frank Robinson, recently brought into Global Foods, Inc., to build a forecasting department, finds his new position to be very challenging and quite interesting. However, he also knows that forecasting, even in the relatively stable soft drink industry, can be a thankless task. From various forecast requests on his desk, he pulls out the one for the company's lemon-lime soda, Citronade, a brand recently purchased from an older, established company. He has been asked to estimate sales for the next year, and the deadline for his report is nearing. He has annual sales data for the last 11 years, and he also has sales data by quarter. In an industry where sales show considerable increases during the summer months, a forecast that estimates sales for the seasons of the year is very important.[1]

Frank first looks at the annual data, and he quickly computes year-to-year changes. These numbers are shown in Table 6.1. He notices that, although sales were up in each of the years, the percentage growth from year to year appears to have a declining trend. He will have to consider this phenomenon when he makes his forecast.

Quarterly data are shown in Table 6.2. As he looks over these numbers, Frank realizes that he has several busy days ahead of him.

[1]Sales forecasts for a "real" company are usually made on a monthly, not a quarterly, basis. But for the purposes of this text, quarterly data will be utilized. This is done to economize on the quantity of data used. The methods employed in the analysis of the data are identical whether quarterly or monthly figures are employed.

(*Continued*)

Table 6.1
Sales of Citronade (in Thousands of Cases)

Year	Annual Sales	Change	Percent Change
1992	3,892		
1993	4,203	311	8.0
1994	4,477	274	6.5
1995	4,810	333	7.4
1996	5,132	322	6.7
1997	5,407	275	5.4
1998	5,726	319	5.9
1999	6,023	297	5.2
2000	6,360	337	5.6
2001	6,641	281	4.4
2002	6,954	313	4.7

Table 6.2
Quarterly Sales of Citronade, 1989–1999 (in Thousands of Cases)

Year	1st Qtr	2nd Qtr	3rd Qtr	4th Qtr	Total
1992	842	939	1,236	875	3,892
1993	907	1,017	1,331	948	4,203
1994	953	1,103	1,406	1,015	4,477
1995	1,047	1,180	1,505	1,078	4,810
1996	1,124	1,267	1,576	1,165	5,132
1997	1,167	1,340	1,670	1,230	5,407
1998	1,255	1,403	1,766	1,302	5,726
1999	1,311	1,495	1,837	1,380	6,023
2000	1,390	1,565	1,940	1,465	6,360
2001	1,455	1,649	2,026	1,511	6,641
2002	1,536	1,714	2,103	1,601	6,954

INTRODUCTION

One of the authors remembers a poster he saw, many years ago, on the wall of the office of the director of market research of a large manufacturing corporation. It said: "Forecasting is very difficult, especially into the future." One could add: "Accurate forecasting is even more difficult." Certainly, there is a great deal of truth in this statement. But despite the difficulty of forecasting, and forecasting accurately, it is an integral part of our lives. Many of us eagerly watch television weather forecasts or pay heed to the predictions of a favorite stock market guru, knowing only too well how inaccurate they may be. In an even less formal sense we make forecasts when we buy a lottery ticket, bet on a horse, or make a decision whether to carry an umbrella when we leave our house.

In the worlds of business, government, or even nonprofit institutions, forecasting becomes even more important. In a world where organizations and their environments are continually becoming more complex and changes occur more rapidly, decision makers need help in weighing many factors and understanding constantly changing relationships to arrive at decisions whose results have ever-increasing impacts.[2] Utilizing existing resources and acquiring additional resources appropriately requires maximum information about the company's future.

All organizations conduct their activities in an uncertain environment, and probably the major role of forecasting is to reduce this uncertainty. But no forecast, however extensive and expensive, can remove it completely. Managers who use forecasts in their work "need to develop realistic expectations as to what forecasting can and cannot do."[3] "Forecasting is not a substitute for management judgment in decision making; it is simply an aid to that process."[4]

Objectives, Plans, Forecasts

Before we discuss the things that are forecast and methods of forecasting, a brief digression is needed to define and distinguish some business terms.

A business firm operates in such a way as to achieve set objectives. Plans are constructed and implemented to achieve these objectives. Forecasts are used both in setting objectives and in creating plans. Obviously, forecasts are intimately connected with objective setting and planning, but the functions are not identical.

The setting of objectives by a corporation was discussed in chapter 2. Objectives (or goals) are usually stated in terms of revenue or profit growth, profitability or return on investment, and resource growth and deployment. In order that corporate management can set reasonable targets for its objectives, it must have available the relevant forecasts, both for the short and long terms. Thus, corporate management will consult with economists to obtain the best estimates of how the economy will behave over the relevant time period. In addition, management will be interested in the forecast of sales for the company's industry. These forecasts are then utilized in the process of objective setting for the corporation as a whole and for its component parts. Both short-term and long-term objectives will be established. When these objectives are communicated from corporate headquarters to the various profit centers, the process of planning begins.

Corporate planners in all areas—sales, human resources, facilities, manufacturing, finance—will utilize an array of forecasts in constructing the various portions of the plan. Actually, a forecast may show what will happen under certain conditions and assumptions. In such cases, a planner works with these forecasts but also designs actions that may counteract or revise the forecast. If, for example, a forecast

---

[2]The introductory sections of this chapter draw heavily on Steven C. Wheelwright and Spyros Makridakis, *Forecasting Methods for Management*, 5th ed., New York: John Wiley and Sons, 1989.
[3]Ibid., p. 44.
[4]Ibid., p. 30.

shows an unfavorable trend in the sales of a particular product for the next year, the plan may recommend actions that will counteract this prediction. Then, given the new tactics or strategies incorporated into the plan, the original forecast may be superseded by a new, revised forecast, with altered conditions and assumptions.

SUBJECTS OF FORECASTS

Business utilizes forecasting to obtain information about many subjects. In the final analysis, firms are interested in future sales and profits—the bottom line. But to get there, a large number of forecasts may be necessary. In this section of the chapter, we will outline the various categories of forecasts—from the most macro forecasts down to individual series.

The broadest economic forecast series is the gross domestic product (GDP), which describes the total production of goods and services in a country. Actually, some measures are available for the world economy, but these are usually composites of country forecasts. GDP forecasting is usually accomplished with highly complex econometric models that contain hundreds of variables and a huge number of calculations.

There are also forecasts of GDP components, for instance, consumption expenditure, producer durable equipment expenditure, or residential construction, to name just a few. Thus, a company producing heavy machinery would be interested in data on producer durable equipment and a forest products company in construction statistics. Again, such forecasts could be provided to the company by an outside organization specializing in such activities.

A step down from macro forecasting is the industry forecast. The future sales of the soft drink industry as a whole would be included here. Of course, a forecast could also relate to the automobile industry, the steel industry, or any other. In addition, concern may lie with the future sales of a particular product within an industry, such as club soda or compact automobiles.

Finally, the subject of interest may be the sales of a specific product of a specific firm, such as the diet cola of Global Foods' soft drink division.

The preceding discussion of the forecast hierarchy has concentrated on sales forecasts. But the future estimates for a given firm could be for costs and expenses (in total or for various categories), employment requirements, square feet of facilities utilized, or anything else of importance to a company.

Our major emphasis in this chapter will be with forecasting the sales of a particular product of our hypothetical soft drink manufacturer. The forecast of GDP and its constituent parts will be considered to be assumptions underlying the firm's specific product forecast.

Demand Estimating and Demand Forecasting

In the preceding chapter, regression analysis and demand estimation were discussed. There is a great deal of similarity between demand forecasting and demand estimating. Each serves to increase the information available to decision makers. The difference between the two lies largely in the ultimate purpose of the analysis.

The demand estimating technique will be used by a manager interested in probing the effect on the demand (or quantity demanded) of a change in one or more of the independent variables. Thus, a pricing manager may want to know the impact on the sales of the company's club soda as a result of a price change, of a competitor's price changes, or, for example, of a change in the company's advertising expenses.

On the other hand, forecasting puts less emphasis on explaining the specific causes of demand changes and more on obtaining information regarding future levels of sales activity, given the most likely assumptions about the independent variables. Such information is then used in the construction of the company's plan. Indeed, in some cases, to be discussed later in this chapter, forecasting is achieved without the introduction of any causal factors; future sales are predicted solely by projecting the past into the future.

PREREQUISITES OF A GOOD FORECAST

Certain conditions should be met by any good forecast. Unfortunately, this is not always possible.

First, a particular forecast must be consistent with other parts of the business. If you forecast 10 percent growth in the shipments of your product for next year, you must make sure that your manufacturing facilities have sufficient capacity to produce this increased amount, and that the additions to the labor force necessary to produce and sell this increased amount are in the company's plan for next year.

Second, a good forecast should usually be based on adequate knowledge of the relevant past. There are, of course, exceptions to this rule. Sometimes past experience is of no help in predicting future demand. This is the case if conditions have undergone a radical change. Thus, after World War II, forecasts for automobile and appliance sales could not rely on sales data of recent years, since these products were not produced during the country's involvement in the war. Moreover, any sales patterns that held for the prewar years could not be applied, because in 1946, when automobiles again rolled off the production line, the average age of the existing automobile stock was considerably higher than was customary, people had old cars or none at all, returning servicemen and women were new additions to the car market, and many people had saved up large amounts of money during the war years and were ready to spend.

In other instances, there may be no past on which to fall back. This could be the case for a new product or a technological breakthrough. Under these circumstances, analysts' judgments must be injected into the forecasting process. In some cases, "forecasts based purely on the opinions of 'experts' are used to formulate the forecast or scenario for the future."[5]

Third, a forecast should take into consideration the economic and political environment. If significant changes in economic conditions or in political institutions are

---

[5]John E. Hanke, Dean W. Wichern, and Arthur G. Reitsch, *Business Forecasting*, 7th ed., Upper Saddle River, NJ: Prentice Hall, 2001, p. 421. This is another text we recommend for students who are interested in exploring the subject of forecasting in more detail.

expected within the forecast period, these events must be accounted for, since they may have a substantial effect on the future of the business.[6]

One other prerequisite, a rather obvious one, must be added. A forecast must be timely. Sometimes accuracy may have to be sacrificed to achieve timeliness. It serves no purpose to deliver an extremely accurate forecast that is too late to be acted on. As obvious as this point may be, it cannot be stressed strongly enough. Forecasters are often tempted to polish and improve their forecasts. Not only can such embellishment add costs that may not be worth the improvement in accuracy, it may also delay the publication of the estimate. This is particularly important at turning points in the forecast series. If the forecast is published too late to issue a warning, its great accuracy will be worthless.

FORECASTING TECHNIQUES

There are many different forecasting methods. One of the challenges facing a forecaster is choosing the right technique. The appropriate method depends on the subject matter to be forecast and on the forecaster, but we can discuss some of the factors that enter into consideration.[7]

1. The item to be forecast. Is one trying to predict the continuance of a historical pattern, the continuance of a basic relationship, or a turning point?
2. The interaction of the situation with the characteristics of available forecasting methods. The manager must judge the relation between value and cost. If a less expensive method can be used to achieve the desired results, it certainly should be.
3. The amount of historical data available.
4. The time allowed to prepare the forecast. Selection of a specific method may depend on the urgency of the situation.

One other point about forecasting cost and accuracy should be added here. Generally, when the requirements for forecast accuracy are high, more sophisticated and more complex methods may be used. Such methods are, as a rule, more costly. Thus, a manager will authorize greater expenditures when relatively high accuracy is warranted. However, "Empirical studies have shown that simplicity in forecasting methods is not necessarily a negative characteristic or a detriment with regard to forecasting accuracy. Therefore, the authors would advise against discarding simple methods and moving too quickly to replace them with more complex ones."[8]

Forecasting techniques can be categorized in many ways. We will use the following six categories:

---

[6]Taking potential changes in political institutions into account is of importance to multinational corporations, which operate in a large number of foreign countries, probably including those whose political directions are quite unstable and whose governments may be subject to radical changes.

[7]This section relies heavily on Wheelwright and Makridakis, *Forecasting Methods*, pp. 30–31.

[8]Ibid., p. 309. This quote deals with the merits of relatively simple time series methods versus more complex explanatory techniques. "Thus, the evidence suggests that explanatory models do not provide significantly more accurate forecasts than time series methods, even though the former are much more complex and expensive than the latter" (p. 297).

1. Expert opinion
2. Opinion polls and market research
3. Surveys of spending plans
4. Economic indicators
5. Projections
6. Econometric models

As we will see in the following pages, some of the methods can be classified as qualitative, others as quantitative. **Qualitative forecasting** is based on judgments of individuals or groups. The results of qualitative forecasts may be in numerical form but generally are not based on a series of historical data.

Quantitative forecasting, on the other hand, generally utilizes significant amounts of prior data as a basis for prediction. Quantitative techniques can be naive or causal (explanatory). **Naive methods** project past data into the future without explaining future trends. **Causal** or **explanatory forecasting** attempts to explain the functional relationships between the variable to be estimated (the dependent variable) and the variable or variables that account for the changes (the independent variables).

While judgmental (qualitative) forecasting is used frequently, the use of quantitative methods has been growing rapidly. A recent survey by the Institute of Business Forecasting reported that time series models that extrapolate past data into the future were used by 60 percent of the companies surveyed. Causal forecasting models were used by 24 percent of the companies, while judgmental methods were used by only 8 percent. However, this survey also found that in many cases, members of various functions (marketing, production, finance, and sales) of the companies met periodically to review the quantitative forecasts, and "if necessary, overlay[ed] judgment on them to arrive at the final forecast." This was actually done by 78 percent of the companies surveyed.[9] However, a somewhat earlier study of manufacturing companies concluded that judgmental methods are still prevalent in many business organizations. As could be expected, large firms utilized quantitative methods more frequently. Among the more common judgmental forecasting methods used were manager's opinion, jury of executive opinion, and sales force composite. The more frequently used quantitative methods were moving averages, exponential smoothing, and projections. These methods are discussed at length in the remainder of this chapter. The author of the survey found the dominance of judgmental forecasting to be "disheartening to forecasters" as formal approaches have been available for years, and quantitative forecasting has been shown to be more accurate and subject to fewer biases leading to bad forecasts.[10]

Expert Opinion

Various types of techniques fit into the category of expert opinion. Only a limited number will be discussed here.

---

[9]Chamam L. Jain, "Forecasting Practices in Corporate America," *Journal of Business Forecasting Methods & Systems,* Summer 2001, pp. 2–3. Curiously, however, Hanke, Wichern, and Reitsch, *Business Forecasting,* p. 421, state that "research has shown that, when historical data are available, the judgment modification of the forecasts produced by analytical methods tends to reduce the accuracy of the forecasts."
[10]Nada R. Sanders, "The Status of Forecasting in Manufacturing Firms," *Production and Inventory Management Journal,* 38, 2, 1997, pp. 32–37.

One of these methods is called the **jury of executive opinion.** As the name implies, forecasts are generated by a group of corporate executives, who may be sitting around a table discussing the particular subject to be forecast. The members of the panel are experts on the subject matter (representing sales, finance, production, and so on). These panels can be interorganizational (i.e., from different corporations) or intraorganizational (i.e., within one corporation), depending on the breadth of the subject. This technique is used widely and is often quite successful. The major drawback of this approach is that a panel member with a forceful personality but not necessarily the greatest amount of knowledge and judgment may exercise a disproportionate amount of influence.

Another, similar technique involves the solicitation of views of individual salespeople in a company to forecast sales. This approach could have been utilized in the situation outlined at the beginning of the chapter. After all, sales representatives are expected to have a finger on the pulse of the market. The biases inherent in this type of predictive apparatus are, however, obvious. "Often sales people are either overly optimistic or overly pessimistic. At other times they are unaware of the broad economic patterns that may affect demand."[11] The latter problem can be overcome to some extent by informing the respondents of general economic forecasts.

Another popular method of qualitative forecasting, utilized predominantly in predicting technological trends and changes, is the **Delphi method.** This technique was developed at the Rand Corporation in the 1950s. Delphi uses a panel of experts; however, unlike the jury of executive opinion, the participants do not meet to discuss and agree on a forecast. The entire process is carried out by a sequential series of written questions and answers. Although in the past this iterative procedure could be quite time-consuming, the present use of computers and e-mail makes it easy to conduct the entire process in a relatively brief period of time. The reason for separating the experts is to avoid the potential pitfall cited previously.

A relatively early Delphi study was that of Gordon and Helmer, which asked experts to forecast six subjects as far as 50 years into the future: scientific breakthroughs, population growth, automation, space progress, probability and prevention of war, and future weapons systems.[12] To arrive at predictions, the Delphi procedure begins by asking (e.g., by letter) the members selected to reply to a set of questions. In this study, the experts were asked to specify what advances in automation would occur over the next 50 years and to estimate the time period of occurrence. When answers were received, a list of the items was compiled and sent back to the panel for further consideration. Several iterations of this procedure were conducted until the range of choices was narrowed and specific time ranking was established. Finally, a consensus (or convergence of opinion) is obtained. But there is no need for unanimity of opinion; the forecast can include a range of opinions.

The Delphi method has been used to advantage in technological predictions and has been applied in business situations as well. A 1971 study sponsored by Corning Glass investigated trends in residential housing in the ensuing 15 years. Included

[11]Wheelwright and Makridakis, *Forecasting Methods,* p. 242.
[12]T. J. Gordon and O. Helmer, *Report on a Long-Range Forecasting Study,* Rand Corporation, P-2982, September 1964. (Described in Harold Sackman, *Delphi Critique,* Lexington, MA: Lexington Books, 1975, pp. 37–39, 104.)

were forecasts of housing supply and demand, costs, and monetary aspects, among others.[13]

Still, Delphi suffers from many drawbacks: "insufficient reliability, oversensitivity of results to ambiguity of questions, different results when different experts are used, difficulty in assessing the degree of expertise, and the impossibility of predicting the unexpected."[14] Given the long-term nature of Delphi predictions, these criticisms do not appear to differ greatly from those leveled against forecasts in general.

Opinion Polls and Market Research

You are probably familiar with opinion polling, since most of us have at one time or another been subjected to telephone calls or written questionnaires asking us to assess a product—or sometimes a political issue. Rather than soliciting experts, opinion polls survey a population whose activity may determine future trends. **Opinion polls** can be very useful because they may identify changes in trends, which, as we will see later in this chapter, may escape detection when quantitative (both naive and explanatory) methods are used.

Opinion polls are usually conducted on samples of the population. Choice of the sample is of utmost importance, since the use of an unrepresentative sample may give completely misleading results. Further, the questions must be stated simply and clearly in order that they can be easily interpreted by respondents. Often a question is repeated in a somewhat different form so that the replies can be cross-checked.

Market research is closely related to opinion polling. Thorough descriptions of this method can be found in marketing texts. Market research will indicate "not only why the consumer is or is not buying (or is or is not likely to buy), but also who the consumer is, how he or she is using the product, and what characteristics the consumer thinks are most important in the purchasing decision."[15] This information can then be used to estimate the market potential and possibly the market share.

Surveys of Spending Plans

The use of **surveys of spending plans** is quite similar to opinion polling and market research, and the methods of data collection are also quite alike. But while opinion polling and market research usually deal with specific products and are often conducted by individual firms, the surveys discussed briefly here seek information about "macro-type" data relating to the economy.

1. *Consumer intentions.* Since consumer expenditure is the largest component of the gross domestic product, changes in consumer attitudes and their effect on subsequent spending are a crucial variable in the forecasts and plans made by businesses. Firms producing consumer products and services are, of course, affected directly. But companies producing durable equipment will also feel the effect of

---

[13]Selwyn Enzer, *Some Prospects for Residential Housing by 1985,* Institute for the Future, R-13, January 1971. (Cited in Sackman, *Delphi Critique,* p. 99.)
[14]Wheelwright and Makridakis, *Forecasting Methods,* p. 326
[15]Ibid., p. 245.

any changes in this important segment of the economy. Two well-known surveys are reviewed here.

   a. *Survey of Consumers, Survey Research Center, University of Michigan.* This is probably the best known among the consumer surveys conducted. Initiated in 1946, it is conducted monthly. It contains questions regarding personal finances, general business conditions, and buying conditions. The answers to these questions are summarized into an overall index of consumer sentiment and a large number of indexes covering replies to the more detailed questions. Subscribers to this service receive analyses of the most recent surveys as well as a booklet of tables and charts showing trends.

   b. *Consumer Confidence Survey, The Conference Board.* A questionnaire is mailed monthly to a nationwide sample of 5,000 households. Each month a different panel of households is selected. The resulting indexes are based on responses to questions regarding business conditions (current and six months hence), employment conditions (current and six months hence), and expectations regarding family income six months hence. The replies are then summarized monthly into three indexes: the Consumer Confidence Index, the Present Situation Index and the Expectations Index. This survey has been published since 1967.

2. *Inventories and sales expectations.* A monthly survey published by the National Association of Purchasing Agents is based on a large sample of purchasing executives.

3. *Capital expenditure surveys.* In the first two editions of this text we reported on surveys conducted by the U.S. Department of Commerce, the Conference Board, and McGraw-Hill *Business Week.* Unfortunately, detailed surveys of capital expenditures have been discontinued by all three organizations. The Department of Commerce still publishes some historical data on an annual basis.[16]

Economic Indicators

The difficult task of predicting changes in the direction of activity has been discussed previously. Some of the qualitative techniques discussed in the preceding sections are aimed at identifying such turns. The barometric technique of **economic indicators** is specifically designed to alert business to changes in economic conditions.

   The success of the indicator approach to forecasting depends on the ability to identify one or more historical economic series whose direction not only correlates with but precedes that of the series to be predicted. Such indicators are used widely in forecasting general economic activity. Any one indicator series may not be very reliable; however, a composite of leading indicators can be used to predict. Such a series should exhibit a slowing (and an actual decrease) before overall economic

---

[16]While writing the third edition of this book, the authors queried these organizations regarding the existence of the surveys. Our respondent at *Business Week* told us the following: "To my knowledge, there is no capital spending survey that outlines plans for the following year in a detailed way. As an economic analyst, I find this distressing, especially given the rising importance of the fast-growing high-tech sector in assessing the economic impact of business investment. I hope someone will pick up the ball at some point." This situation has not changed as this edition is being written.

activity turns down, and it should start to rise while the economy is still experiencing low activity.

Forecasting on the basis of indicators has been practiced in an informal fashion for many years. It is said that Andrew Carnegie used to assess the future of steel demand by counting the number of chimneys emitting smoke in Pittsburgh. Much of the work of establishing economic indicators was done at the National Bureau of Economic Research, a private organization. Today, economic indicator data are published monthly by The Conference Board in *Business Cycle Indicators.* These monthly data are reported in the press and are widely followed.[17]

There are three major series: leading, coincident, and lagging indicators. As their names imply, the first tells us where we are going, the second where we are, and the third where we have been. Although the leading indicator series is probably the most important, the other two are also meaningful. The coincident indicators identify peaks and troughs, and the lagging series confirms upturns and downturns in economic activity.

Many individual series are tracked monthly in the *Business Cycle Indicators,* but only a limited number are used in the construction of the three major indexes. The leading indicator index contains 10 series, and the coincident and lagging indicators are made up of 4 and 7 components, respectively. All the series making up the indexes are listed in Table 6.3.

It is rather evident why some of the indicators qualify as leading. They represent not present expenditures, but commitments indicating that economic activity will take place in the future. Among these are manufacturers' new orders and building permits. Others are not quite as obvious. But one would expect employers to increase the hours of their work force as they increase production before committing themselves to new hiring. Stock market prices and money supply are usually thought to precede cycles.

The month-to-month changes in each component of the series are computed and standardized to avoid undue influence of the more volatile components. The individual series are then combined to create the index. The index has a base period $1996 = 100$.[18]

In the past, the indexes were published with a lag sometimes exceeding one month. The reason for this was that certain index components were not immediately available. However, some components, for example, stock prices, are available in "real time." In 2001, the Conference Board decided to estimate components that are not obtainable until a later date. The estimates are made using an autoregressive model. As a result of this new procedure, the Conference Board is able to publish the index two to three weeks earlier than before. The index is then revised, when the components previously estimated become available.[19] The Conference Board also computes a diffusion index which tends to indicate the breadth of the indicator index movement.

---

[17]The data can also be accessed on the World Wide Web at www.tcb-indicators.org.
[18]An explanation of the methods to compute, update, and standardize the indexes is available on the web site cited in note 17.
[19]An excellent source of information on the entire subject of economic indicators is *Business Cycle Indicators Handbook,* The Conference Board, 2001.

Table 6.3
Economic Indicators

Leading indicators
1. Average hours, manufacturing
2. Average weekly initial claims for unemployment insurance
3. Manufacturers' new orders consumer goods, and materials
4. Vendor performance, slower deliveries diffusion index
5. Manufacturers' new orders, nondefense capital goods
6. Building permits, new private housing units
7. Stock prices, 500 common stocks
8. Money supply, M2
9. Interest rate spread, 10-year Treasury bonds minus federal funds (%)
10. Index of consumer expectations

Coincident indicators
1. Employees on nonagricultural payrolls
2. Personal income less transfer payments
3. Index of industrial production
4. Manufacturing and trade sales

Lagging indicators
1. Average duration of unemployment
2. Inventories to sales ratio, manufacturing and trade
3. Change in labor cost per unit of output, manufacturing (%)
4. Average prime rate (%)
5. Commercial and industrial loans outstanding
6. Consumer installment credit outstanding to personal income ratio
7. Change in consumer price index for services (%)

How good a forecaster are the leading indicators? To answer this question, we must establish some criteria. First, how many months of change in the direction of the index are necessary before a turn in economic activity is expected? A general rule of thumb is that if, after a period of increases, the leading indicator index sustains three consecutive declines, a recession (or at least a slowing) will follow. On this basis, the leading indicators have predicted each recession since 1948. Second, how much warning do the indicators give (i.e., by how many months do they lead) of the onset of a recession?

The following chart shows the lead times in number of months at both peaks and troughs of the business cycle since World War II[20]:

---

[20]Victor Zarnowitz, "The Record of the U.S. Leading Index and Its Components," *Business Cycle Indicators,* September 2001, pp. 2–4.

CYCLE	PEAK	TROUGH
1948–49	−4	−4
1953–54	−6	−6
1957–58	−23	−2
1960–61	11	3
1969–70	8	7
1973–75	9	2
1980–80	15	3
1981–82	3	8
1990–91	6	2

It is obvious that the lead times vary considerably. So we can sum up by observing that leading indicators do warn us about changes in the direction of economic activity, but they really do not forecast lead times reliably. Additionally, we must be aware of several other drawbacks:

1. In some instances, the leading indicator index has forecast a recession when none ensued. For instance, the index declined for several months in 1966. Although a decline in the growth of the economy (a growth recession) followed, there was no "official" recession.[21]
2. A decline (or a rebound after a decline) in the index, even if it forecasts correctly, does not indicate the precise size of the decline (or rise) in economic activity.
3. The data are frequently subject to revision in the ensuing months. It is not uncommon for a particular month to show a drop in the index only to have the revisions change the direction of the index one or two months later. Thus, the final data may signal a different future from the one suggested by the originally published data.

The preceding criticisms of this forecasting method are certainly significant. But they indicate that this technique should be improved rather than discarded. The existing indicators are reevaluated periodically, and new ones are developed. As the structure of the economy changes, some of the indicators lose their relevance. There have been numerous revisions of the indexes over the years aimed at improving their performance. For instance, in 1996, shortly after the Conference Board took over the publication of the indexes, two components of the leading indicator index were removed, while one series was added. The present index may be overly weighted toward manufacturing activities and neglects service industries, which make up a continuously increasing portion of our economy. The growing importance of international trade and capital flows suggests the inclusion in the index of a series reflecting

---

[21]An "official" recession is pronounced by a panel of economists from the National Bureau of Economic Research, which dates peaks and troughs. As this edition is being written, the panel declared March 2001 to be the beginning of the most recent recession. A look at the leading indicators shows that they appeared to predict the recession with the following changes in the year 2000:

June	−.1	October	−.4
July	−.5	November	−.3
August	−.3	December	−.4
September	0		

these activities. In the meantime, the use of leading indicators has spread to a large number of foreign countries.

In short, despite its drawbacks, the index of leading indicators (and the other two indexes as well) is a useful tool for businesspeople and will continue to be closely watched. As always, reliance on this method must be tempered by the knowledge of its imperfections.

Projections

Earlier in this chapter, we discussed several qualitative methods of forecasting. We then moved to a discussion of economic indicators, a quantitative method. To continue the presentation of quantitative techniques, we now turn to **trend projections,** which we previously identified as a naive form of forecasting. Several different methods will be discussed, but they all have a common denominator: past data are projected into the future without taking into consideration reasons for the change. It is simply assumed that past trends will continue. Three projection techniques will be examined here:

1. Compound growth rate
2. Visual time series projection
3. Time series projection using the least squares method

If annual data are to be forecast, any of these three methods can be used. However, more frequent data, such as monthly or quarterly, may be necessary. If there appear to be significant seasonal patterns in the data, a smoothing method must be applied. The moving-average method of smoothing will be discussed along with the least squares time series projection.

MODULE 6A

Constant Compound Growth Rate   The constant **compound growth rate** technique is extremely simple and is widely used in business situations. When quick estimates of the future are needed, this method has some merit. And, as we will find out, it can be quite appropriate when the variable to be predicted increases at a constant percentage (as opposed to constant absolute changes). But care must be exercised not to apply this technique when it is not warranted.

The most rudimentary application of this method is to take the first and last years of past data, and to calculate the constant growth rate necessary to go from the amount in the first period to the amount in the last. This problem is solved in the same way as if we were to calculate how much a specific sum deposited in an interest-bearing account grows in a certain number of years at a constant rate of interest that is compounded annually. Suppose $1,000 is deposited at the beginning of the year and earns interest at the rate of 7 percent. How much will this deposit be worth at the end of the year? That is easy: $1,000 plus the 7 percent interest. The solution can be expressed in shorthand mathematical notation as follows:

$$E = B + Bi = B(1 + i)$$

where E = Account balance at the end of the year
B = Original deposit
i = Rate of interest

Thus,

$$1,000(1.07) = 1,070$$

Now, if this year-end amount remains in the account for another year, the entire $1,070 will earn interest, of $74.90. Thus, the balance at the end of the second year will be $1,144.90. The second-year balance could have been obtained directly by compounding two years of interest on the original deposit, as follows:

$$1,000 \times 1.07 \times 1.07$$

or

$$1,000 \times (1.07)^2$$

If the deposit is left in the account for any number of years, the ending balance can be found with the following equation:

$$E = B(1 + i)^n$$

where n represents the number of years. If n is large, the calculation can become somewhat complex. Table C.1 in Appendix C to this book will make the computation much easier.[22] To find the amount to which a deposit of $1,000 will grow in 10 years at 7 percent interest, look up the factor in the table and multiply it by 1,000. The factor is 1.9672; therefore, the balance after ten years will be $1,967.20.

Frank Robinson can use the same table to make his projection for Citronade sales. The first period and the last period amounts are known, and the missing number is the growth rate, which, of course, has the same meaning as the interest rate in the preceding example. To solve for the growth rate, the previous formula is revised as follows:

$$(1 + i)^n = E/B$$

Applying this formula to the 1992 and 2002 sales of Citronade from Table 6.1,

$$6,954/3,892 = 1.7867$$

Since there are ten years intervening between the two sales periods, the growth rate can be found by entering the table at ten periods and moving to the right until a number close to 1.7867 is found. At 6 percent, the factor is 1.7908. Thus, the growth rate of Citronade over the last ten years is just under 6 percent.

Can, therefore, next year's sales be estimated at 7,371,000 cases, a 6 percent annual increase? Looking at the year-to-year increases in Table 6.1, Robinson noticed that the growth rate achieved in the early years (through 1996) has not been approached since. Whereas during the first four years of the available data, growth ranged between 6.5 and 8 percent, the second four years registered increases between 5 and 6 percent, and the rise in the last two years was less than 5 percent. Growth has been declining over the ten-year period.

This illustrates a major problem that is frequently encountered when the compound growth rate method of projection is employed. The only two numbers

---

[22]Of course, any number of hand-held calculators will make this computation even easier.

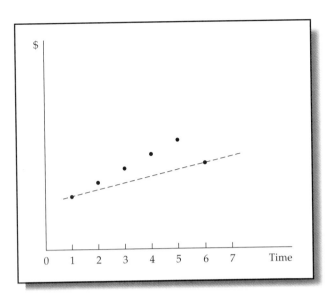

Figure 6.1
An Example in Which the
Constant Compound
Growth Rate Approach
Would Be Misleading

considered in determining the growth rate were the first and the last; any trends or fluctuations between the original and terminal dates are disregarded. Thus, when year-to-year percentage growth is not stable, any estimates based on this result can be misleading.

Figure 6.1 illustrates what may happen. The data plotted in the graph show a strong increase in each year except for the last value, which may have been caused by an exceptional occurrence such as a severe recession or a strike. If the compound growth rate approach is used, any forecast based only on the first and last observations may be quite misleading.

In summary, the compound growth rate (or CGR, as it is popularly known) method can often be useful, particularly when results are required quickly and a rough approximation is sufficient. But its drawbacks are significant and must always be considered.

Visual Time Series Projections A series of numbers is often difficult to interpret. Plotting the observations on a sheet of graph paper (or entering paired data into a computer plotting program) can be very helpful since the shape of a complicated series is more easily discerned from a picture.

Frank Robinson did just that. He had two types of graph paper available to him. One was the familiar kind, with arithmetic scales on both axes, which he used to plot the annual data of Citronade sales, as shown in Figure 6.2. The observations appear to form a relatively straight line. As a matter of fact, one could easily draw a straight line just by putting a ruler through the observations, so that some points fall above and some below the line. Projecting the line to 2003 would give us a fairly good prediction—if the growth, in absolute number of cases, reflects past increases. The reason that a straight line is such a good fit is that the absolute annual increases in sales fluctuate around their mean of 306,000 cases without exhibiting any kind of trend (Figure 6.3).

There is another type of graph paper often used to observe trends—semilogarithmic. This graph has an arithmetic scale along the horizontal axis, but the vertical

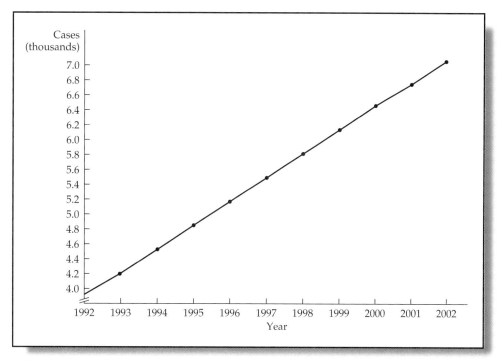

Figure 6.2
Annual Sales of Citronade (1992–2002)

axis transforms numbers into a logarithmic format. Equal distances between numbers on the vertical scale represent a doubling. Thus, the distance between 1 and 2 is the same as that between 2 and 4, between 4 and 8, and so on.[23] In the semilogarithmic format, if observations that exhibit a constant growth rate are plotted, they will fall on a straight line.[24] The data for Citronade, as can be seen in Figure 6.4 where the annual observations are plotted, indicate growth at a decreasing rate. Thus, if Frank Robinson were to base his projections on this line, he would have to continue the curve on its decreasing slope.

---

[23]Incidentally, the point of origin on the vertical axis is 1, not 0.
[24]A simple example will explain why a constant percentage growth rate shows up as a straight line on a logarithmic scale. Assume that the first period's quantity is 100 and that it grows by 20 percent each year. Then translate each number into a common logarithm, and calculate the differences for each series:

Raw Data	Absolute Difference	Logarithm	Difference in Logarithms
100		2.0	
120	20	2.0792	0.0792
144	24	2.1584	0.0792
172.8	28.8	2.2375	0.0791
207.36	34.56	2.3167	0.0792

Although the absolute differences increase, the differences between logarithms remain constant. Thus, if the vertical scale of a graph is shown in terms of logarithms, constant percentage differences will plot as a straight line.

Chapter 6   Forecasting

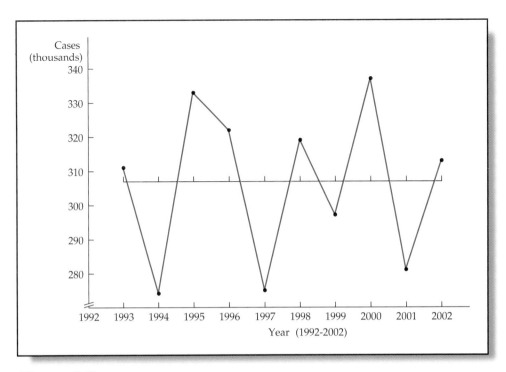

Figure 6.3
Annual Increase in Citronade Sales (1992–2002)

Frank found that the compound growth rate for Citronade sales from 1992 to 2002 was 6 percent. A line representing an annual growth rate of 6 percent in Figure 6.4 is a straight line, since constant growth is assumed. But a projection of the straight line would result in a higher sales estimate for 2003 than if the decreasing year-to-year percentage of growth were taken into consideration.

Thus, a quick estimate of next year's sales can be made by just extending one of the lines that were drawn. If the average of the ten years of absolute growth—306,000—were used, 2003 sales would be 7,260,000 cases, a 4.4 percent increase from the 2000 total of 6,954,000 cases. This would correspond closely to the value produced by extending the line formed by the actual observations in Figure 6.4, which exhibits an increase at a decreasing rate. Using the compound growth rate of 6 percent—plotted as a straight line in Figure 6.4—would indicate sales of about 7,371,000 cases and would, as previously discussed, result in too high an estimate.

Although under some circumstances this type of forecast may be sufficiently accurate, most forecasters would feel that a more detailed estimate—particularly given the seasonal nature of soft drink demand—is essential. Thus, Frank will move on to perform a time series analysis using a least squares equation, and also to identify the seasonal pattern of Citronade sales.

Time Series Analysis In this section we will continue to explore the **time series** method of projection. However, instead of visual estimation, a more precise statistical technique will be employed: the method of least squares. This method was intro-

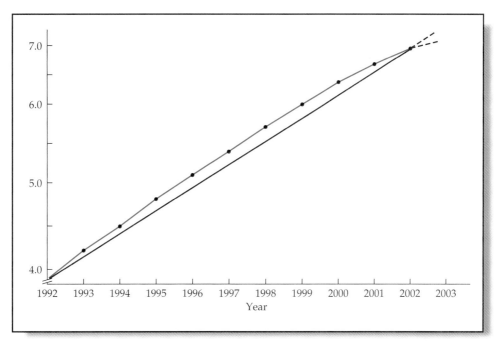

Figure 6.4
Semilogarithmic Graph of Changes in Citronade Sales

duced in the last chapter and was used to estimate demand. Whereas demand estimation requires the use of one or more independent variables, and the interactive relationship between these variables is of great importance, in the context of time series analysis there is only one independent variable: time. Thus, this system of forecasting is "naive," because it does not explain the reason for the changes, it merely says that the series of numbers to be projected changes as a function of time.

Despite the mechanical nature of this type of forecast, time series analysis has much to recommend it:

1. It is easy to calculate. Presently, a large number of software packages on the market will compute the least squares trend line in various ways—linear, curvilinear, or exponential.
2. It does not require much judgment or analytical skill by the analyst. It merely assumes that the pattern of prior periods will repeat into the future.
3. Unlike visual projection, it describes the line that exhibits the best possible fit for past data. In addition, it provides the analyst with information regarding the statistical errors contained in the results and gives an indication of how statistically significant the results are.
4. Finally, except when an absolute turn in the series occurs, the projection based on this method of analysis is usually reasonably reliable in the short run.

The fact that time series analysis does not take into consideration causative factors does not mean that an analyst using this method should not consider additional information about changes in the underlying forces. Any analyst using this naive method of prediction should try to fine tune the conclusions based on information that could alter the results.[25]

When data are collected over a number of periods in the past, they usually exhibit four different characteristics:

1. *Trend.* This is the direction of movement of the data over a relatively long period of time, either upward or downward.
2. *Cyclical fluctuations.* These are deviations from the trend due to general economic conditions. For instance, if one were to observe data for the GDP over time, a long-run upward trend would be evident. Also evident in this series would be movement around that trend as the economy rises more quickly or less quickly (or actually declines).
3. *Seasonal fluctuations.* A pattern that repeats annually is characteristic of many products. Toy sales tend to rise briefly before Christmas. Fashions have spring and fall seasons. In the soft drink industry, the expectation is for higher sales during the warmer periods of the year (i.e., June through September). Thus, time series in which data are collected more frequently than annually (monthly, quarterly) can exhibit seasonal variations.
4. *Irregular.* Departures from the norm may be caused by special events, such as strikes or catastrophes. They occur randomly and do not repeat regularly, if at all, and they certainly cannot be predicted. Actually, these random fluctuations do not have to be caused by any dramatic events. They may just represent "noise" in the series, since events never occur in a completely regular, stable manner.

Thus, time series data can be represented by the following mathematical expression:

$$Y_t = f(T_t, C_t, S_t, R_t)$$

where Y_t = Actual value of the data in the time series at time t
T_t = Trend component at t
C_t = Cyclical component at t
S_t = Seasonal component at t
R_t = Random component at t

The specific form of this equation could be additive:

$$Y_t = T_t + C_t + S_t + R_t$$

Other forms could also exist. The specification most commonly used is the multiplicative form:

$$Y_t = (T_t)(C_t)(S_t)(R_t)$$

Thus, the changes in the actual values (Y_t) are determined by four factors. The task of the analyst is to "decompose" the time series of Y into its four components.

We can now return to Frank Robinson's problem of forecasting Citronade sales not only for the entire year of 2003, but for each of the quarters. This entire procedure is summarized in Table 6.4.

---

[25]It is essential that all changes and alterations are well documented by the analyst so that a trail to her reasoning can be established.

Table 6.4
Citronade Quarterly Sales Analysis

(1) Quarter	(2) Actual	(3) Moving Average	(4) Centered Moving Average	(5) Ratio Actual/ CMA[a]	(6) Adjusted Seasonal Factors	(7) Data Deseason- alized[b]	(8) Trend	(9) Cycle and Irregular[c]	(10) Cycle
1	842				0.889	947.1	940.2	100.74	
2	939				0.991	947.5	959.5	98.75	100.69
3	1,236	973.0	981.2	1.260	1.231	1,004.1	978.8	102.58	99.98
4	875	989.3	999.0	0.876	0.889	984.3	998.1	98.61	100.49
5	907	1,008.8	1,020.6	0.889	0.889	1,020.2	1,017.4	100.28	99.30
6	1,017	1,032.5	1,041.6	0.976	0.991	1,026.2	1,036.7	98.99	100.56
7	1,331	1,050.8	1,056.5	1.260	1.231	1,081.2	1,156.0	102.39	100.19
8	948	1,062.3	1,073.0	0.884	0.889	1,066.4	1,075.3	99.17	99.83
9	953	1,083.8	1,093.1	0.872	0.889	1,072.0	1,094.6	97.94	99.01
10	1,103	1,102.5	1,110.9	0.993	0.991	1,113.0	1,113.9	99.92	99.55
11	1,406	1,119.3	1,131.0	1.243	1.231	1,142.2	1,133.2	100.80	99.93
12	1,015	1,142.8	1,152.4	0.881	0.889	1,141.7	1,152.4	99.07	100.13
13	1,047	1,162.0	1,174.4	0.892	0.889	1,177.7	1,171.7	100.51	99.85
14	1,180	1,186.8	1,194.6	0.988	0.991	1,190.7	1,191.0	99.97	100.50
15	1,505	1,202.5	1,212.1	1.242	1.231	1,222.6	1,210.3	101.01	99.87
16	1,078	1,221.8	1,232.6	0.875	0.889	1,212.6	1,229.6	98.61	100.29
17	1,124	1,243.5	1,252.4	0.897	0.889	1,264.3	1,248.9	101.23	100.22
18	1,267	1,261.3	1,272.1	0.996	0.991	1,278.5	1,268.2	100.81	100.49
19	1,576	1,283.0	1,288.4	1.223	1.231	1,280.3	1,287.5	99.44	100.18
20	1,165	1,293.8	1,302.9	0.894	0.889	1,310.5	1,306.8	100.28	99.57
21	1,167	1,312.0	1,323.8	0.882	0.889	1,312.7	1,326.1	98.99	99.92
22	1,340	1,335.5	1,343.6	0.997	0.991	1,352.2	1,345.4	100.50	99.63
23	1,670	1,351.8	1,362.8	1.225	1.231	1,356.6	1,364.7	99.41	99.96
24	1,230	1,373.8	1,381.6	0.890	0.889	1,383.6	1,384.0	99.97	99.99
25	1,255	1,389.5	1,401.5	0.895	0.889	1,411.7	1,403.3	100.60	100.03
26	1,403	1,413.5	1,422.5	0.986	0.991	1,415.7	1,422.6	99.52	99.87
27	1,766	1,431.5	1,438.5	1.228	1.231	1,434.6	1,441.9	99.50	99.75
28	1,302	1,445.5	1,457.0	0.894	0.889	1,464.6	1,461.2	100.23	99.78
29	1,311	1,468.5	1,477.4	0.887	0.889	1,474.7	1,480.5	99.61	100.14
30	1,495	1,486.3	1,496.0	0.999	0.991	1,508.6	1,499.8	100.59	99.48
31	1,837	1,505.8	1,515.6	1.212	1.231	1,492.3	1,519.1	98.24	99.91
32	1,380	1,525.5	1,534.3	0.899	0.889	1,552.3	1,538.4	100.91	99.84
33	1,390	1,543.0	1,555.9	0.893	0.889	1,563.6	1,557.7	100.38	100.48
34	1,565	1,568.8	1,579.4	0.991	0.991	1,579.2	1,577.0	100.14	99.75
35	1,940	1,590.0	1,598.1	1.214	1.231	1,576.0	1,596.2	98.73	100.29
36	1,465	1,606.3	1,616.8	0.906	0.889	1,647.9	1,615.5	102.00	100.28
37	1,455	1,627.3	1,638.0	0.888	0.889	1,636.7	1,634.8	100.11	100.90

(*Continued*)

Table 6.4
(*Continued*)

(1) QUARTER	(2) ACTUAL	(3) MOVING AVERAGE	(4) CENTERED MOVING AVERAGE	(5) RATIO ACTUAL/ CMA[a]	(6) ADJUSTED SEASONAL FACTORS	(7) DATA DESEASON-ALIZED[b]	(8) TREND	(9) CYCLE AND IRREGULAR[c]	(10) CYCLE
38	1,649	1,648.8	1,654.5	0.977	0.991	1,664.0	1,654.1	100.59	99.69
39	2,026	1,660.3	1,670.4	1.213	1.231	1,645.8	1,673.4	98.35	99.78
40	1,511	1,680.5	1,688.6	0.895	0.889	1,699.7	1,692.7	100.41	99.89
41	1,536	1,696.8	1,706.4	0.900	0.889	1,727.8	1,712.0	100.92	100.41
42	1,714	1,716.0	1,727.3	0.992	0.991	1,729.6	1,731.3	99.90	99.47
43	2,103	1,738.5			1.231	1,708.4	1,750.6	97.59	99.75
44	1,601				0.889	1,800.9	1,769.9	101.75	

[a]Column 2 ÷ Column 4
[b]Column 2 ÷ Column 6 × 100.
[c]Column 7 ÷ Column 8 × 100.

Seasonality   The process of decomposition starts with identifying and removing the seasonal factor from our series of numbers in order to calculate the trend. We will use the method of **moving averages** to isolate seasonal fluctuations.

Column 1:   This column simply represents all the quarters of the 11 years, 1992 through 2002, numbered sequentially.

Column 2:   All the quarterly data, originally shown in Table 6.2, are listed here.

Column 3:   The first step in the deseasonalizing process is to calculate a quarterly average for the first year (i.e., the first four quarters). The result is 973.0, so this number is placed next to quarter 3 in this column. The next number is obtained by moving down one quarter: The first quarter is dropped, the fifth quarter is added, and the average of quarters 2, 3, 4, and 5 is calculated to be 989.3. This number is placed next to quarter 4. The same procedure is then followed for the rest of the quarters. Because of the averaging, the data for the first two quarters and the last quarter are lost.

   The first moving average was placed next to the third quarter. It could also have been placed next to the second quarter. Actually, the average of four quarters belongs between the second and third quarters. This computation is made in column 4.

Column 4:   An average of two adjacent numbers in column 3 is calculated and placed at the third quarter. Because 973.0 in column 3 should have appeared between quarters 2 and 3, and 989.3 should have been between quarters 3 and 4, the average of these two, 981.2, is correctly placed at quarter 3. All centered moving averages are placed in column 4. With this procedure, the next to the last number is now lost.

Table 6.5
Averaging of Seasonal Factors

Year	First Quarter	Second Quarter	Third Quarter	Fourth Quarter	Total
1992			1.260	0.876	
1993	0.889	0.976	1.260	0.884	
1994	0.872	0.993	1.243	0.881	
1995	0.892	0.988	1.242	0.875	
1996	0.897	0.996	1.223	0.894	
1997	0.882	0.997	1.225	0.890	
1998	0.895	0.986	1.228	0.894	
1999	0.887	0.999	1.212	0.899	
2000	0.893	0.991	1.214	0.906	
2001	0.888	0.997	1.213	0.895	
2002	0.900	0.992			
Average	0.890	0.992	1.232	0.889	4.003
Adjusted Average	0.889	0.991	1.231	0.889	4.000

Column 5: We now obtain the seasonal factors. They are the ratios obtained by dividing the actual numbers in column 2 by the centered moving averages of column 4. Observing the numbers in column 5, it can be seen that every fourth quarter, starting with quarter 3 (i.e., quarters 3, 7, 11, and so on), has a factor greater than 1. These quarters represent the summer months (July to September), when soda consumption is at its peak. It can also be seen that data for the second calendar quarters (i.e., quarters 6, 10, 14, and so on) are rather close to 1, while the quarters representing fall and winter are generally below 0.9.

Column 6: To obtain a quarterly seasonal index, we must average the ratios obtained by quarter in column 5. This is done in Table 6.5. The quarterly patterns are quite obvious.[26]

The four averages should add to 4; they do not because of rounding. A minor adjustment must now be made. The results are then transferred to column 6 of Table 6.4.

Column 7: When the actual data of column 2 are divided by the seasonal factors of column 6, the deseasonalized series of numbers in column 7 is obtained. Both the actual and the deseasonalized data have been plotted in Figure 6.5. The latter series, as should be expected, is much smoother than the former.

The first step of the decomposition procedure has now been completed:

$$(T \times C \times S \times R)/S = T \times C \times R$$

---

[26]There appears to be minor downward trend in the third-quarter data. This will be discussed later.

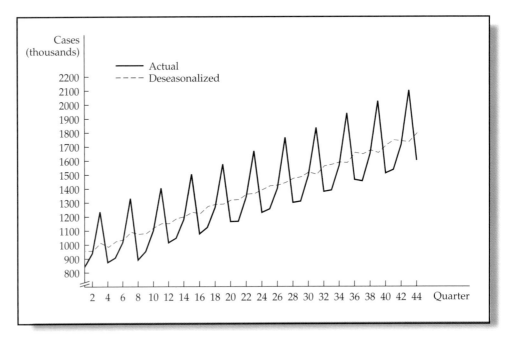

Figure 6.5
Citronade Sales Deseasonalized

The new series has eliminated the seasonality. The next step is to calculate the trend.

The Trend Line Computation of the trend utilizes the least squares method. The dependent variable is the deseasonalized series in column 7 of Table 6.4. The independent variable is time. Each quarter is numbered consecutively; although the initial number usually does not matter, it is easiest and most logical to start with 1. Thus, the consecutive numbers in column 1 of Table 6.4 represent the independent variable.

The form of the equation depends on the shape of the deseasonalized series. A casual observation of the deseasonalized series appears to indicate that a straight line would be most appropriate, but we actually tried three different possibilities:

$$\text{Straight line: } Y = a + b(t)$$

$$\text{Exponential line:[27] } Y = ab^t$$

$$\text{Quadratic line:[28] } Y = a + b(t) + c(t)^2$$

Although all three calculations gave acceptable results, the simplest—the straight line—gave the best statistical answers. Its coefficient of determination (R^2) was .996, and the t-statistic for the independent variable was 103.6—highly significant.

---

[27]This is the equation that would best fit a straight line on a semilogarithmic chart, representing constant percentage growth from period to period.
[28]This equation would fit a curve on a graph with arithmetic scales.

Managerial Economics

The exponential and quadratic equations also had very high R^2s, but their t-statistics were considerably lower (and the squared term in the latter was actually not statistically significant).

The straight-line trend equation was

$$Y = 920.90 + 19.2957t$$

Column 8: Using this equation, we arrive at the trend numbers in column 8.

Column 9: Then, by dividing the data in column 7 by those in column 8, we eliminate the trend from the deseasonalized series. In terms of the fraction used previously,

$$(T \times C \times R)/T = C \times R$$

Thus, only the cycle and random elements remain in column 9, which is in percentage form.

Cycle and Random Elements At this point we could stop the analysis and do a forecast. The data in column 9 fluctuate rather irregularly within a range of about 5 percentage points. Part of this variation is due to random factors, which cannot be predicted and therefore should be ignored. However, there could be some longer business cycle wave in the data. To isolate the cycle, another smoothing operation can be performed with a moving average.

Column 10: The preferred length of the moving-average period cannot be determined except in each individual case. In our illustration we used three periods. If the moving average correctly eliminates the random variations remaining in column 9, then the swings that appear in column 10 should represent a cyclical index.

When the index rises above 100 percent, the indication is that economic activity is strong; the opposite holds for index numbers below 100 percent. The data in column 10 fluctuate very little—less than 2 percentage points. Therefore, no great adjustment is needed here. However, if the indication is that the economy is in a downturn, which may be expected to have some influence on soft drink sales, then a minor forecast adjustment can be made. Such an adjustment can be based on current general forecasts for the economy as a whole or on the latest published leading economic indicators.

Forecasting with Smoothing Techniques Before we leave the section on projections, one other naive method should be mentioned. This method involves using an average of past observations to predict the future. If the forecaster feels that the future is a reflection of some average of past results, one of two forecasting methods can be applied: simple moving average or exponential smoothing.

The smoothing techniques, either moving average or exponential smoothing, work best when there is no strong trend in the series, when there are infrequent changes in the direction of the series, and when fluctuations are random rather than seasonal or cyclical. Obviously, these are very limiting conditions and greatly circumscribe the usefulness of these methods. However, if a large number of forecasts is needed quickly and if the estimates involve only one period into the future, then one of these two techniques can be employed—as long as their drawbacks are well understood by the forecaster.

Moving Average   The average of actual past results is used to forecast one period ahead. The equation for this construction is simply

$$E_{t+1} = (X_t + X_{t-1} + \cdots + X_{t-N+1})/N$$

where E_{t+1} = Forecast for the next period $(t + 1)$
X_t, X_{t-1} = Actual values at their respective times
N = Number of observations included in the average

The forecasts for Citronade, with their strong trend and seasonal patterns, would certainly not lend themselves well to this simple projection method. Instead, a hypothetical example will be used. Twelve observations are shown in the second column of Table 6.6.

The forecaster must decide how many observations to use in the moving average. The larger the number of observations in the average, the greater the smoothing effect. If the past data appear to contain significant randomness while the underlying pattern remains the same, then a larger number of observations is indicated. However, the analyst must remember that more historical data will be needed for the

Table 6.6
Moving Average Forecasting

| | | Three-Month Moving Average | | | Four-Month Moving Average | | | Five-Month Moving Average | | |
| | | | Absolute | Squared | | Absolute | Squared | | Absolute | Squared |
Period	Actual	Forecast	Error	Error	Forecast	Error	Error	Forecast	Error	Error
1	1,100									
2	800									
3	1,000									
4	1,050	967	83	6,944						
5	1,500	950	550	302,500	988	513	262,656			
6	750	1,183	433	187,778	1,088	338	113,906	1,090	340	115,600
7	700	1,100	400	160,000	1,075	375	140,625	1,020	320	102,400
8	650	983	333	111,111	1,000	350	122,500	1,000	350	122,500
9	1,400	700	700	490,000	900	500	250,000	930	470	220,900
10	1,200	917	283	80,278	875	325	105,625	1,000	200	40,000
11	900	1,083	183	33,611	988	88	7,656	940	40	1,600
12	1,000	1,167	167	27,778	1,038	38	1,406	970	30	900
13		1,033			1,125			1,030		
Total			3,133	1,400,000		2,525	1,004,375		1,750	603,900
Mean			348	155,556		316	125,547		250	86,271

Note: Son.e of the squared errors appear to be incorrect; this is so because decimals have been omitted.

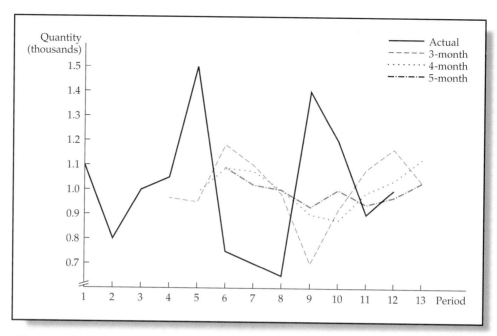

Figure 6.6
Forecasting with Moving Averages

forecast if a large number of past data is to be included in the base. In Table 6.6, three moving averages have been computed—three, four, and five months. The resulting estimates are shown in the forecast columns. For example, the forecast of 967 units in period 4 of the three-month moving average was obtained as follows:

$$E_4 = (X_1 + X_2 + X_3)/N$$

$$= (1,100 + 800 + 1,000)/3$$

$$= 2,900/3 = 967$$

The three forecast columns diverge widely. These variations are shown graphically in Figure 6.6. As more observations are included in the moving average, the forecast line becomes smoother.

Which moving average should be used? One selection method is to calculate the mean error and the mean squared error of the differences between the actual data and the forecast.[29] The series with the smallest squared error would be preferred. In the example of Table 6.6, the five-month moving average minimizes the deviations.

---

[29]The formula for the mean squared error is

$$\frac{\sum_{n=1}^{N} (E_n - X_n)^2}{N}$$

Instead of the mean squared error, we could calculate the root mean squared error by taking the square root of the above equation.

Exponential Smoothing   The moving-average method awards equal importance to each of the observations included in the average, and gives no weight at all to observations preceding the oldest data included. However, the analyst may feel that the most recent observation is more relevant to the estimate of the next period than previous observations. In that case, it is more appropriate to employ the **exponential smoothing** method, which allows for the decreasing importance of information in the more distant past. This is accomplished by the mathematical technique of geometric progression. Older data are assigned increasingly smaller weights; the sum of the weights, if we approached an infinitely large number of observations, would equal 1. All of the complex formulations of the geometric series can be simplified into the following expression:

$$E_{t+1} = wX_t + (1 - w)E_t$$

where w is the weight assigned to an actual observation at period t.

Thus, to make a forecast for one period into the future, all that is needed is the previous period's actual observation and the previous period's forecast. The analyst does not need the extensive historical data required for the moving-average method. The most crucial decision the analyst must make is the choice of the weighting factor. The larger the w (i.e., the closer to 1), the greater will be the importance of the most recent observation. Therefore, when the series is rather volatile and when w is large, the smoothing effect may be minimal. When w is small, the smoothing effect will be considerably more pronounced. This result can be seen in Table 6.7 and Figure 6.7,

Table 6.7
Exponential Smoothing Forecasting

		Smoothing Factor = 0.2			Smoothing Factor = 0.4			Smoothing Factor = 0.8		
Period	Actual	Forecast	Absolute Error	Squared Error	Forecast	Absolute Error	Squared Error	Forecast	Absolute Error	Squared Error
1	1,100									
2	800	1,100	300	90,000	1,100	300	90,000	1,100	300	90,000
3	1,000	1,040	40	1,600	980	20	400	860	140	19,600
4	1,050	1,032	18	324	988	62	3,844	972	78	6,084
5	1,500	1,036	464	215,667	1,013	487	237,364	1,034	466	216,783
6	750	1,128	378	143,247	1,208	458	209,471	1,407	657	431,491
7	700	1,053	353	124,457	1,025	325	105,370	881	181	32,897
8	650	982	332	110,375	895	245	59,910	736	86	7,443
9	1,400	916	484	234,467	797	603	363,779	667	733	536,915
10	1,200	1,013	187	35,109	1,038	162	26,207	1,253	53	2,857
11	900	1,050	150	22,530	1,103	203	41,156	1,211	311	96,528
12	1,000	1,020	20	403	1,022	22	472	962	38	1,434
13		1,016			1,013			992		
Total			2,728	978,180		2,886	1,137,973		3,043	1,442,033
Mean			248	88,925		262	103,452		277	131,094

Note: Some of the squared errors appear to be incorrect; this is so because decimals have been omitted.

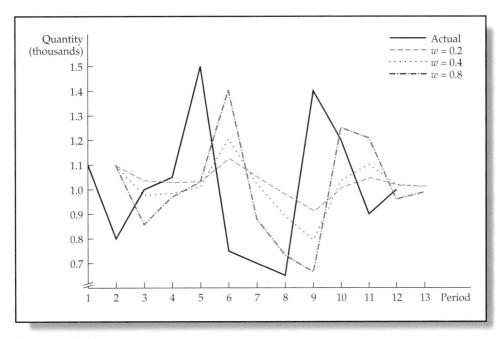

Figure 6.7
Exponential Smoothing Forecasting

where ws of 0.2, 0.4, and 0.8 have been used.[30] Which weights should be used? We can again calculate the mean squared error, as was done in Table 6.7. Using $w = 0.2$ minimizes the error, so this is the best weight for this set of data.

Both of these naive forecasting techniques have their advantages and disadvantages. The simplicity of the methods is certainly an advantage. However, their usefulness is limited to cases where there is an underlying stability (i.e., no trend) with period-to-period random fluctuations. When a trend or a repeating pattern of fluctuations is present, the time series method with deseasonalization is a much better technique to use. In any case, the two methods just discussed should be employed only for extremely short-term estimates—preferably just one period into the future.

Box-Jenkins Forecasting Method Only a brief mention of this sophisticated and fairly complex model will be discussed here. Readers interested in greater detail should consult a business forecasting book.[31]

The Box-Jenkins model, as do time-series analysis and smoothing models, relies on prior observation, rather than exogenous independent variables, to arrive at a forecast. However, it does not assume a specific pattern of prior data. Rather, it permits the choice among a large number of models. Through an iterative procedure, it arrives at the best result, i.e., the one that produces the smallest errors.

---

[30]Note that the forecast for period 2 in each case is the actual observation of period 1. Since there is no forecast for period 1, a forecast must be made up. Any number could have been used, but the actual observation is probably the most logical choice.

[31]For instance, Hanke, Wichern and Reitsch, *Business Forecasting,* chapter 9, or J. Holton Wilson and Barry Keating, *Business Forecasting*, 3d ed., Irwin McGraw-Hill, 1998, chapter 7.

Econometric Models

Up to this point, all of the quantitative forecasting techniques discussed can be classified as naive. In this section of the chapter, our brief discussion will concentrate on models that are termed *causal* or *explanatory*. These **econometric models** were described in detail in chapter 5.

Regression analysis is an explanatory technique. Unlike the case of a naive projection, which relies on past patterns to predict the future, the analyst performing regression analysis must select those independent (or explanatory) variables that are influential in determining the dependent variable. Although simple projection models often give adequate results, the use of explanatory variables in the analysis can enhance the accuracy as well as the credibility of the estimates. Of course, no regression equation will explain the entire variation of the dependent variable, since, in most economic relationships, there are numerous explanatory variables with complex interrelationships. As already explained in chapter 5, the person performing the analysis will have to settle for the inclusion of a limited number of variables, an equation that approximates the functional relationships, and results that explain a significant portion of but not the entire variation in the dependent variable.

The regression methods previously described employ a single equation to make estimates. An analysis estimating the demand for soft drinks was described in the previous chapter. Here we will discuss a few studies of single-equation regression models of demand in which many of the variables are in the form of time series.

Among the many studies of automobile demand, the one written by Daniel Suits[32] is quite interesting. He combined the demand equations for new cars and used cars into one, as follows:

$$\Delta R = a_0 + a_1 \Delta Y + a_2 \Delta P/M + a_3 \Delta S + a_4 \Delta X$$

where R = Retail sales, in millions of new cars
Y = Real disposable income
P = Real retail price of new cars
M = Average credit terms (number of months of the average installment contract)
S = Existing stock, in millions of cars
X = Dummy variable

All of the variables are in terms of first differences; thus, the equation estimates year-to-year changes. The years 1942 through 1948 have been excluded from the time series because of the war years, when no automobiles were produced, and the immediate postwar period, when significant distortions existed in the automobile market.

The dummy variable X takes into account the fact that not all the remaining years in the series can be treated equally. The years 1941, 1952, and 1953 were considered exceptional. The first two were assigned a value of +1, the third a value of −1, and all the other years a value of 0.

Having specified the equation, Suits calculated the coefficients (the *a*s) and tested the results by predicting 1958 new auto sales. "The demand equation predicts a level

[32]Daniel B. Suits, "The Demand for New Automobiles in the United States, 1929–1956," *Review of Economics and Statistics*, August 1958, pp. 273–80.

of sales of slightly less than 6.0 million. This compares favorably with a preliminary estimate of 6.1 million actual sales for the year and stands in sharp contrast with sales forecasts of 6.5 million and over, which were common in the industry at the start of the year."[33]

Another economist studied the demand for computers.[34] He specified the following equation in terms of logarithms:

$$\log(y_t/y_{t-1}) = a_0 - a_1 \log p_t - a_2 \log y_{t-1}$$

where y_t = Stock of computers in year t
$\quad y_{t-1}$ = Stock of computers in year $t-1$
$\quad\quad p$ = Real price of computers

The demand in this equation is measured as the percentage change in the stock of computers from one year to the next.

A further example will be given for coffee demand in the United States.[35] Coffee demand was estimated with the following equation:

$$Q = b_0 + b_1 P_0 + b_2 Y + b_3 P + \sum_{i=1}^{3} b_4 D_i + b_5 T$$

where Q = Per-capita (population over age 16) quantity of coffee
$\quad P_0$ = Real retail price of coffee, per pound
$\quad Y$ = Real per-capita disposable income
$\quad P$ = Real retail price of tea, per quarter pound
$\quad D_i$ = Binary (dummy) variable for quarters of the year
$\quad T$ = Time trend

The authors found that coffee consumption is sensitive to its own price, that there had been a long-term decline in coffee consumption, and that significantly less coffee was consumed during the spring and summer months. The other coefficients did not turn out to be statistically significant. Thus, the consumption of coffee could be estimated from the time trend, from the quarterly changes, and from an assumption made regarding coffee prices.

A last example is a recent one, and represents a demand forecast prepared for a specific product for a specific company. Columbia Gas of Ohio forecasts daily demand by using both time series and regression analysis. Two years of historical data are used to obtain the regression. The time series serves to forecast growth. The forecast is then based on a combination of the regression analysis and the growth rate:

$$Q = (1 + G) \times (a + b_1 T + b_2 P + b_3 W)$$

where Q = daily demand in MDTH (thousand dekatherms)
$\quad G$ = growth rate
$\quad T$ = forecasted temperature

---

[33]Ibid., p. 273.
[34]Gregory Chow, "Technological Change and the Demand for Computers," *American Economic Review*, December 1967, pp. 1117–30.
[35]Cliff J. Huang, John J. Siegfried, and Farangis Zardoshty, "The Demand for Coffee in the United States, 1963–1977," *Quarterly Review of Economics and Business*, 20, 2 (summer 1980), pp. 36–50.

$$P = \text{prior day temperature}$$
$$W = \text{forecasted wind speed}$$
$$a = \text{intercept}$$
$$b_1, b_2, b_3 = \text{coefficients}$$

The R^2 of the regression equation is .983.

This forecast "is used mainly to ensure that scheduled supplies are in balance with forecasted demands over the next five-day period." The company receives a five-day weather forecast twice daily.[36]

In each of these studies, the numerical coefficients (the as and the bs) were obtained by regression analysis. To forecast using these equations, it is necessary, of course, to make estimates of each of the independent variables for the period indicated.[37] Alternative forecasts can be created by assuming different values for each of the independent variables.

An important warning is in order regarding the use of regression equations for forecasting. All the parameters (coefficients) in a regression equation are estimated using past data (whether time series or cross-sectional analysis has been employed). The forecast based on such estimates will be valid only if the relationships between the dependent variable and the independent variables do not change from the past into the future. Literally, a regression equation is valid only within the limits of the data used in it. When we venture outside these limits (i.e., forecast with independent variables outside the range of the past), we are treading on dangerous ground. Still, forecasting with the least squares method is a much-used technique, often employed quite successfully. But its limitations must not be forgotten by the analyst.

Although many forecasting problems can be solved with the use of single-equation regression models, there are instances when one equation is not sufficient. In such cases, economists often turn to multiple-equation systems. Extremely large models used by economists to predict the GDP and its component parts are examples of such models, which may include hundreds of variables and equations.

A single-equation model can be used when the dependent variable can be estimated using independent variables that are determined by events not part of the equation. But what happens when the determining variables are determined by other variables within the model? Then a single equation is insufficient.

In a multiple-equation system, variables are referred to as *endogenous* and *exogenous*. Endogenous variables are comparable to the dependent variable of the single-equation model; they are determined by the model. However, they can also influence other endogenous variables, so they may appear as "independent" (i.e., on the right side of the equation) variables in one or more of the equations. Exogenous variables are from outside the system and are not determined within it; they are truly independent variables.

---

[36]H. Alan Catron, "Daily Demand Forecasting at Columbia Gas," *Journal of Business Forecasting*, Summer 2000, pp. 10–15.

[37]In the case of lagged variables, actual data may be available. See, for instance, y_{t-1}, the stock of computers at the end of the previous year in the equation used in Chow, "Technological Change."

The following is an example of an extremely simple two-equation model of the private economy:

$$C = a_0 + a_1 Y$$

$$Y = C + I$$

where C = Consumption
$\quad Y$ = National income
$\quad I$ = Investment

Here C and Y are endogenous variables. I is assumed (rather unrealistically) to be exogenous, or determined by forces outside the system of equations.

Another simple multi-equation model represents the interrelationships of activities within a firm:

$$\text{Sales} = f(\text{GDP, Prices})$$

$$\text{Cost} = f(\text{Quantity of product, Factor prices})$$

$$\text{Expenses} = f(\text{Sales, Factor prices})$$

$$\text{Product price} = f(\text{Cost, Expenses, Profit})$$

$$\text{Profit} = \text{Sales} - \text{Cost} - \text{Expenses}$$

Here there are five endogenous variables. The exogenous variables are GDP, Quantity of product, and Factor prices. These equations are given in functional form only. The specific forms of the equations would, of course, have to be specified.

Such systems of equations would then be solved to obtain all of the coefficients. The statistical methods used to solve for all the numerical values are beyond the scope of this textbook.

CURRENT FORECASTING PRACTICES IN BUSINESS

In this chapter we have discussed a large array of forecasting methods. In order to see how these methods are applied, we have selected a number of recent articles that describe the techniques employed by various companies or industries. While this is a small sample, it will certainly indicate how business looks at and utilizes forecasting.

Ocean Spray Cranberries

Ocean Spray Cranberries is a grower-owned farming cooperative with $1.5 billion in annual sales. Its headquarters are in Lakeville, Massachusetts. Its forecasting group has seven employees.

Time series models are used predominantly by this organization. The projections are generally based on three years of history. Forecasts are usually made for the current month and the following six months. However, analysts can override the projections if particular events are known to exist, such as promotional plans or advertising.

Three hundred different items are forecast, but when this is broken down across various accounts and geographical area, it results in about 3,000 different forecasts.

Forecasts of new products with no historical data rely on inputs from the marketing and consumer research department.

Causal models are not used very much because independent variables are difficult to find given the disaggregated level of forecasting done by Ocean Spray. The forecasts are utilized by various departments including procurement, supply planning, replenishment planning and corporate revenue planning. Forecasting has resulted in various benefits for the company, including a reduction of inventories from twenty-three to seventeen days.[38]

Pharmaceutical Industry in Singapore

A questionnaire survey was sent to twelve pharmaceutical companies that sell antihypertensive drugs and their distributors, accounting for about 70 percent of total patented drugs sold in Singapore. Fifteen responses were received. The forecasting techniques were somewhat unsophisticated. The most frequent method used was simple extrapolation, followed by market research and personal judgment. The use of quantitative methods was less frequent, "probably due to lack of training in statistics." Not one of the companies responding employed dedicated forecasters; rather, the forecasts were generated by general managers, marketing, sales, finance and operating personnel.

The most important uses of the forecast were in the allocation of resources, strategic planning and the setting of sales quotas. It was reported that the most important determinant of the forecasts were local doctors since in most cases doctors themselves dispense drugs in Singapore.[39]

The Wholesale Industry

Telephone interviews were conducted with 484 wholesale companies in twenty-two cities. The sample included 411 small companies (with fewer than 100 employees) and 73 large companies (with 100 or more employees).

Qualitative methods were used more frequently than quantitative. Managerial judgment was the most popular, followed by percentage of last year's sales, sales force estimates, trend extension, and customer survey. All of the surveyed companies produced annual forecasts; quarterly, monthly, and semiannual forecasts were also prepared by a large number of companies.[40]

E-Commerce

Seven companies from diverse industries were surveyed. Automotive, chemical logistics, transportation, and web-hosting companies were included. Both "pure-play" (companies that conduct business only electronically) and "brick and click"

---

[38]Jack Malehorn, "Forecasting at Ocean Spray Cranberries," *Journal of Business Forecasting Methods & Systems,* Summer 2001, pp. 6–8.

[39]Louis Choo, "Forecasting Practices in the Pharmaceutical Industry in Singapore," *Journal of Business Forecasting Methods & Systems,* Summer 2000, pp. 18–22.

[40]Robin T. Peterson and Minjoon Jun, "Forecasting Sales in Wholesale Industry," *Journal of Business Forecasting Methods & Systems,* Summer 1999, pp. 15–18.

(companies that do traditional business and have begun to move into e-commerce) companies were interviewed.

E-commerce is, of course, relatively new and extremely dynamic. Thus, some companies did not forecast their e-commerce business, because they were new to e-commerce. Others used mostly qualitative forecasting; this should be expected since most of these businesses are new with little or no historical data available. "Qualitative methods capitalize on the judgment, opinions, and intuition of 'experts,' such as company executives, sales people, channel members and industry analysts . . ." However, some quantitative analysis is already in use. Thus, one company uses preliminary orders to forecast, another forecasts market share, while a third projects the next twelve months from a twelve-month history. As more historical data become available the use of quantitative methods will increase. Generally, the forecasts made were relatively short term. Since the e-commerce business is so dynamic "there is not much confidence in a strategic forecast."[41]

Lockheed Martin Aircraft and Logistics Centers (LM-ALC)

LM-ALC is a service-support division of the Lockheed Martin Corporation, its parent. LM-ALC "provides aircraft depot, and maintenance modification support to worldwide customers/fleet." Forecasting is typically done one year in advance, although at some times predictions span over two years. The company utilizes at least five years of historical data in its forecasts. Causal models are also used. Because the company supports products primarily used by the U.S. military, the biggest factor it has to address is the nature of the Congressional budget cycle. The world political-economic environment is, of course, an important determinant of demand. Forecasts are made for about 11,000 parts.[42]

Some Other Forecast Examples

Let us briefly summarize some other, less recent, reports on forecasting practices of several corporations. It should be noted that some of these companies have since combined with or been merged into others. At Bell Atlantic (now Verizon), time-series and regression analyses have been used along with qualitative methods. Rubbermaid (part of NewellRubbermaid) uses various statistical methods, including exponential smoothing and Box-Jenkins. Short-term forecasts as well as one-year forecasts are prepared for some 600 items. Trans World Airlines (now merged into American Air Lines) used a combination of regression and trend models to prepare their annual forecasts, and then converted these into monthly forecasts based on seasonal variations. Brake Parts, Inc. (a division of Dana Corporation) used up to nineteen time-series techniques and causal regression models.[43]

---

[41]Susan L. Golicic, Donna F. Davis, Teresa M. McCarthy, and John T. Mentzer, "Bringing Order out of Chaos; Forecasting E-Commerce," *Journal of Business Forecasting Methods & Systems,* Spring 2001, pp. 11–17. A complete discussion of E-commerce can be found in chapter 12.

[42]Jack Malehorn, "Forecasting at Lockheed Martin Aircraft and Logistics Centers," *Journal of Business Forecasting Methods & Systems,* Fall 2001, pp. 9–10.

[43]These examples were taken from Wilson and Keating, *Business Forecasting,* pp. 2–6. They are summaries of articles published in the *Journal of Business Forecasting* during the 1990s.

INTERNATIONAL APPLICATION: FORECASTING EXCHANGE RATES

In chapter 2, the additional challenges facing a multinational corporation were discussed. Such a corporation must forecast sales, expenses, and cash flows for its operations in different countries. The results from these transactions generated in the home country will depend on the exchange rate between the foreign and domestic currency. Often a company makes substantial investments in foreign operating facilities from which it expects to obtain cash flows. Thus, multinational corporations (MNCs) are vitally interested in forecasting exchange rates in both the short and long run.

A frequently used method to forecast exchange rates for relatively short periods into the future is through the forward rate. In order to understand this, two types of exchange rates must be defined:

1. Spot exchange rate—the price of one currency against another for transactions being completed immediately.
2. Forward exchange rate—the price of one currency against another for a transaction that will occur at some point in the future.

An extremely active exchange market exists, and financial officers can easily ascertain both spot and forward rates for the ten major currencies, which represent a predominant portion of all transactions. One view of the forward rate is that it represents the market's consensus on what the future spot rate should be. Thus, if today's spot rate is $1.494 for 1 British pound sterling, and the 90-day forward rate is $1.485, then one can argue that the market consensus is that the pound will decrease in value by $0.009 relative to the U.S. dollar 90 days hence.

Is the forward rate a good predictor of the spot exchange rate for major currencies? On the average, the forward rate will be equal to the future spot rate; in other words, negative and positive errors in the forecasts will be offset. It can, therefore, be said that the forward rate is an unbiased forecaster of the spot rate. It makes for a best-guess forecast. However, this does not make it an accurate forecast at any one time. Still, for the short run, it is probably as good an estimator as we have. In addition to its lack of accuracy, other shortcomings must be considered:

1. The present exchange rate system does not permit currencies to float freely. Governments interfere in the exchange rate markets when they consider it to be of benefit to their country's economy.
2. While forward rates can be established for relatively long periods into the future (in some cases, they can go out as far as ten years), by far the largest volume of forward contracts is for 180 days or less.
3. Reliable forward markets exist only for currencies of the leading industrial economies of the world.

Longer-term exchange rate forecasts often utilize econometric models. A major problem in constructing these multiple regression models is in finding appropriate reliable independent variables. In most cases, the independent variables are stated in terms of differentials between the domestic and foreign measures, such as:

1. Growth rates of GDP
2. Real interest rates
3. Nominal interest rates
4. Inflation rates
5. Balance of payments

A significant number of complex models is in use today. Here we will use a simple hypothetical model to illustrate the estimate of a relationship between the domestic currency and a foreign currency:

$$E_t = a + bI_t + cR_t + dG_t$$

where E = Exchange rate of a foreign currency in terms of the domestic currency
I = Domestic inflation rate minus foreign inflation rate
R = Domestic nominal interest rate minus foreign nominal interest rate
G = Domestic growth rate of GDP minus the growth rate of foreign GDP
t = Time period
a, b, c, d = Regression coefficients

Such forecasts have all the advantages and disadvantages usually found in the application of regression analysis to economic problems:

1. Which variables should be included?
2. What form should the regression equation adopt?
3. Are accurate measurements of independent variables available? Data may be inadequate for other than the major industrial countries.
4. In order to forecast exchange rates, it may be necessary to forecast the independent variables. And it is not surprising that it may be as difficult to forecast independent variables accurately as it is to forecast the exchange rates themselves.

By now the reader has probably concluded that forecasting exchange rates is not an easy task. But then, no forecasts are easy. The accuracy of exchange rate forecasts has been inconsistent at best. However, this should not deter business people from attempting to make such forecasts. Even if inaccurate, they enhance a manager's knowledge of her environment and provide a manager with insights into the economic variables that affect international decision making.

The discussion of this subject has been limited to its bare essentials. Students interested in studying this topic further can do so by reading one of several textbooks dealing with international financial management.[44]

---

[44]For example, Dennis J. O'Connor and Alberto T. Bueso, *International Dimensions of Financial Management*, New York: Macmillan, 1990. The preceding discussion has drawn on material contained in this book.

The Solution

Frank Robinson is now ready to make his forecast for 2003. He will do it in three steps:

1. He will project the trend for the four quarters of 2003.
2. He will apply the seasonal factors.
3. He may then make an adjustment for cyclical influences.

Since the trend equation is $Y = 920.9 + 19.2957(t)$, his trend forecasts will be as follows:

1st qtr: $920.9 + 19.2957 (45) = 1{,}789.2$
2nd qtr: $920.9 + 19.2957 (46) = 1{,}808.5$
3rd qtr: $920.9 + 19.2957 (47) = 1{,}827.8$
4th qtr: $920.9 + 19.2957 (48) = 1{,}847.1$

Next, each of these results must be multiplied by the seasonal factors:

1st qtr: $1{,}789.2 \times 0.889 = 1{,}590.6$
2nd qtr: $1{,}808.5 \times 0.991 = 1{,}792.2$
3rd qtr: $1{,}827.8 \times 1.231 = 2{,}250.0$
4th qtr: $1{,}847.1 \times 0.889 = 1{,}642.1$

Frank noticed, however, that the seasonal factors in Table 6.5 exhibit some trends over the 11 years. The third-quarter factor has been decreasing and the first- and fourth-quarter factors appear to be rising. To see the effect of these changes, Robinson decides to use the average of the last three observations for each quarter (and adjust to a total of 4, as was done previously). When he applies his new factors to the trend numbers, he obtains the following results:

1st qtr: $1{,}789.2 \times 0.894 = 1{,}599.5$
2nd qtr: $1{,}808.5 \times 0.993 = 1{,}795.8$
3rd qtr: $1{,}827.8 \times 1.213 = 2{,}217.1$
4th qtr: $1{,}847.1 \times 0.900 = 1{,}662.4$

He decides that this last computation is more valid. The last step in his procedure is to evaluate the effect of cycles and random factors. He decides that the cycle's influence on soft drink sales will be neutral in the coming year. Although an estimate of random factors cannot be made, Frank knows that the company has plans to implement a strong advertising campaign on behalf of Citronade during the second quarter of 2003. At this point, however, he does not have sufficient information regarding the effect of advertising on sales. He makes a note to mention that in his report as a possible plus and to try to make some quantitative estimates later.

(Continued)

An additional point deserves attention. We have assumed that the product whose sales Frank is forecasting has been in existence for at least 11 years. Had this been a new flavor, not previously produced, the forecast would have been much more difficult. If competing companies had been selling a similar product in the past, market information would be available in terms of very detailed statistics published by the beverage industry. Frank could then base his forecast on these data and assume some pattern of market penetration for the new brand. If, however, this is a completely new flavor not previously produced in the industry, it may be necessary to conduct market research to establish a base for a forecast. Another method would be to study the sales patterns of other soft drink products from point of introduction and to base the new product forecast on their histories.

Summary

Forecasting is an important activity in many organizations. In business, forecasting is a necessity.

This chapter has summarized and discussed a number of forecasting techniques. Six categories of forecasts were included:

1. *Expert opinion* is a qualitative technique of forecasting based on the judgment of knowledgeable people. Such forecasts can be developed by panels of experts. The Delphi method is another type of expert opinion forecast that is generally applicable in forecasting technological advances.
2. *Opinion polls and market research* are conducted among survey populations, not experts, to establish future trends or consumer responses.
3. *Surveys of spending plans* are concerned with such important economic data as capital expenditures and consumer sentiment. The forecasts are based on replies to questionnaires or interviews.
4. *Economic indicators* are indexes of a number of economic series intended to forecast the short-run movements of the economy, including changes in direction.
5. *Projections*, a quantitative method, employ historical data to project future trends. Usually, no causes for trends are identified. This chapter discussed compound growth rate projections as well as visual and least squares projection techniques.
6. *Econometric models* are explanatory or causal models in which independent variables that influence the statistic to be forecast are identified. Both single- and multiple-equation models were discussed briefly.

The chapter also examined the decomposition of least squares projections into trends, seasonal and cyclical fluctuations, and irregular movements.

One other naive forecasting method was mentioned: forecasting with smoothing techniques. Smoothing techniques fall into two major categories, moving averages and exponential smoothing, and are useful when there are no pronounced trends in the data and when fluctuations from period to period are random.

Causal (explanatory) forecasting: A quantitative forecasting method that attempts to uncover functional relationships between independent variables and the dependent variable. (p. 227)

Compound growth rate projection: Forecasting by projecting the average growth rate of the past into the future. (p. 234)

Delphi method: A form of expert opinion forecasting that uses a series of written questions and answers to obtain a consensual forecast, most commonly employed in forecasting technological trends. (p. 228)

Econometric forecasting model: A quantitative, causal method that utilizes a number of independent variables to explain the dependent variable to be forecast. Econometric forecasting employs both single- and multiple-equation models. (p. 250)

Economic indicators: A barometric method of forecasting in which economic data are formed into indexes to reflect the state of the economy. Indexes of leading, coincident, and lagging indicators are used to forecast changes in economic activity. (p. 230)

Exponential smoothing: A smoothing method of forecasting that assigns greater importance to more recent data than to those in the more distant past. (p. 248)

Jury of executive opinion: A forecast generated by experts (e.g., corporate executives) in meetings. A similar method is to ask the opinion of sales representatives who are exposed to the market on a daily basis. (p. 228)

Moving-average method: A smoothing technique that compensates for seasonal fluctuations. (p. 242)

Naive forecasting: Quantitative forecasting that projects past data without explaining the reasons for future trends. (p. 227)

Opinion polls: A forecasting method in which sample populations are surveyed to determine consumption trends. (p. 229)

Qualitative forecasting: Forecasting based on the judgment of individuals or groups. Also called *judgmental forecasting.* (p. 227)

Quantitative forecasting: Forecasting that examines historical data as a basis for future trends. (p. 227)

Surveys of spending plans: Examinations of economic trends such as capital expenditures, consumer sentiment, and inventory. (p. 229)

Time series forecasting: A method of forecasting from past data by using least squares statistical methods. A time series analysis usually examines trends, cyclical fluctuations, seasonal fluctuations, and irregular movements. (p. 238)

Trend projection: A form of naive forecasting that projects trends from past data. Trend projections usually employ compound growth rates, visual time series, or least squares time series methods. (p. 234)

QUESTIONS

1. Discuss the basic differences among forecasting, planning, and objective setting.
2. Despite the many inaccuracies present in the making of forecasts, forecasting is a very important activity in a large business firm. Why?
3. "The best forecasting method is the one that gives the highest proportion of correct predictions." Comment.
4. Enumerate methods of qualitative and quantitative forecasting. What are the major differences between the two?
5. Discuss the benefits and drawbacks of the following methods of forecasting:
   a. Jury of executive opinion
   b. The Delphi method
   c. Opinion polls
   Each of these methods has its uses. What are they?

6. Here are the numbers for the leading economic indicators as published in 1990:

January	145.4
February	144.1
March	145.4
April	145.2
May	146.0
June	146.2
July	146.2
August	144.4
September	143.2
October	141.5
November	139.7
December	139.5

1982 = 100
Source: U.S. Department of Commerce, Bureau of Economic Analysis, *Survey of Current Business,* March 1991, p. C-1.

What conditions do you think they forecast for 1991?

7. **a.** Why are manufacturers' new orders, nondefense capital goods, an appropriate leading indicator?
   b. Why is the index of industrial production an appropriate coincident indicator?
   c. Why is the average prime rate charged by banks an appropriate lagging indicator?

8. Discuss some of the important criticisms of the forecasting ability of the leading economic indicators.

9. What is meant by "naive" forecasting methods? Describe some of the methods that fall within this category.

10. Manhattan was allegedly purchased from Native Americans in 1626 for $24. If the sellers had invested this sum at a 6 percent interest rate compounded semiannually, how much would it amount to today?

11. The compound growth rate is frequently used to forecast various quantities (sales, profits, and so on). Do you believe this is a good method? Should any cautions be exercised in making such projections?

12. Explain the meaning of *semilogarithmic scale.* When can it be used, and what are its advantages?

13. Describe projections that use either moving averages or exponential smoothing. Under what conditions can these techniques be used? Which of the two appears to be the more useful?

14. How do econometric models differ from "naive" projection methods? Is it always advisable to use the former in forecasting?

15. Which of the following forecasting methods are appropriate for predicting business cycles?
   a. Trend projections
   b. Leading economic indicators
   c. Lagging economic indicators
   d. Survey methods
   Explain.

16. You have been asked to produce a forecast for your company's new product, bottled water. Discuss the kind of information you would look for in order to make this forecast.

17. Why do you think that a survey of planned capital expenditure would be of great importance? (At the time of this writing, several of these surveys have been discontinued.)

18. The following are the monthly changes in the index of leading economic indicators during 2001 and January 2002:

January	+.1	September	−.6
February	+.1	October	+.1
March	−.3	November	+.8
April	−.1	December	+1.3
May	+.6	January 2002	+.6
June	+.2		
July	+.3		
August	0		

What would be your prediction for the U.S. economy in 2002?

19. In an article in the Summer 2000 issue of the *Journal of Forecasting,* Larry Lapide states that executives often believe that "forecasts are always wrong, so why place any focus on demand planning?" Would you agree with this statement?

PROBLEMS

1. If the sales of your company have grown from $500,000 five years ago to $1,050,150 this year, what is the compound growth rate? If you expect your sales to grow at a rate of 10 percent for the next five years, what should they be five years from now?

2. Based on past data, Mack's Pool Supply has constructed the following equation for the sales of its house brand of chlorine tablets:

$$Q = 1,000 + 100t$$

where Q is quantity and t is time (in years), with 1998 = 0.
   a. What is the sales projection for 2003?
   b. The tablet sales are seasonal, with the following quarterly indexes:

Quarter 1	80%
Quarter 2	100%
Quarter 3	125%
Quarter 4	95%

What is the quarterly sales projection for 2003?

3. The sales data over the last ten years for the Acme Hardware Store are as follows:

1993	$230,000	1998	$526,000
1994	276,000	1999	605,000
1995	328,000	2000	690,000
1996	388,000	2001	779,000
1997	453,000	2002	873,000

   a. Calculate the compound growth rate for the period of 1993 to 2002.
   b. Based on your answer to part *a,* forecast sales for both 2003 and 2004.
   c. Now calculate the compound growth rate for the period of 1997 to 2002.
   d. Based on your answer to part *c,* forecast sales for both 2003 and 2004.
   e. What is the major reason for the differences in your answers to parts *b* and *d*? If you were to make your own projections, what would you forecast? (Drawing a graph will be very helpful.)

4. The sales data for the Tough Steel Hardware Company for the last 12 years are as follows:

1991	$400,000	1997	$617,000
1992	440,000	1998	654,000
1993	480,000	1999	700,000
1994	518,000	2000	756,000
1995	554,000	2001	824,000
1996	587,000	2002	906,000

a. What is the 1991–2002 compound growth rate?
b. Using the result obtained in part *a*, what is your 2003 projection?
c. If you were to make your own projection, what would you forecast? (Drawing a graph will be very helpful.)

5. The Miracle Corporation had the following sales during the past ten years (in thousands of dollars):

1993	200	1998	302
1994	215	1999	320
1995	237	2000	345
1996	260	2001	360
1997	278	2002	382

a. Calculate a trend line, and forecast sales for 2003. How confident are you of this forecast?
b. Use exponential smoothing with a smoothing factor $w = 0.7$. What is your 2003 forecast? How confident are you of this forecast?

6. You have the following data for the last 12 months' sales for the PRQ Corporation (in thousands of dollars):

January	500	July	610
February	520	August	620
March	520	September	580
April	510	October	550
May	530	November	510
June	580	December	480

a. Calculate a three-month centered moving average.
b. Use this moving average to forecast sales for January of next year.
c. If you were asked to forecast January and February sales for next year, would you be confident of your forecast using the preceding moving averages? Why or why not?

7. Office Enterprises (OE) produces a line of metal office file cabinets. The company's economist, having investigated a large number of past data, has established the following equation of demand for these cabinets:

$$Q = 10,000 + 60B - 100P + 50C$$

where Q = Annual number of cabinets sold
B = Index of nonresidential construction
P = Average price per cabinet charged by OE
C = Average price per cabinet charged by OE's closest competitor

It is expected that next year's nonresidential construction index will stand at 160, OE's average price will be $40, and the competitor's average price will be $35.
a. Forecast next year's sales.
b. What will be the effect if the competitor lowers its price to $32? If it raises its price to $36?
c. What will happen if OE reacts to the decrease mentioned in part *b* by lowering its price to $37?

d. If the index forecast was wrong, and it turns out to be only 140 next year, what will be the effect on OE's sales?

8. The gross domestic product of the United States, both in current and real dollars, from 1987 to 1998 was as follows:

	CURRENT	REAL (1996 CHAIN)
	($ IN BILLIONS)	
1987	4,743	6,113
1988	5,108	6,368
1989	5,489	6,592
1990	5,803	6,708
1991	5,986	6,676
1992	6,319	6,880
1993	6,642	7,063
1994	7,054	7,348
1995	7,401	7,544
1996	7,813	7,813
1997	8,301	8,145
1998	8,790	8,515

a. Fit a linear (straight-line) trend to each of the data sets.
b. Now fit an exponential trend to these data.
c. Based on both the linear and exponential trend lines, what would have been your GDP (both current and real) forecast for the years 1999 and 2000?
d. Would any of these trend lines be good predictors of GDP? Why or why not?

9. An economist has estimated the sales trend line for the Sun Belt Toy Company as follows:

$$S_t = 43.6 + 0.8t$$

S_t represents Sun Belt's monthly sales (in millions of dollars), and $t = 1$ in January 1998. The monthly seasonal indexes are as follows:

January	60	April	110	July	90	October	110
February	70	May	110	August	80	November	140
March	85	June	100	September	95	December	150

Forecast monthly sales for the year 2003.

10. The U.S. population figures from 1978 to 1997 are as follows (in thousands):

1978	222,585	1985	238,466	1991	252,665
1979	225,055	1986	240,651	1992	255,410
1980	227,726	1987	242,804	1993	258,119
1981	229,966	1988	245,021	1994	260,637
1982	232,188	1989	247,342	1995	263,082
1983	234,307	1990	249,973	1996	265,502
1984	236,348			1997	268,048

a. Calculate the following:
  (1) A linear trend
  (2) An exponential trend
  (3) Compound growth rate
b. Forecast the 1998 and 1999 population figures from your calculations.
c. The actual population figure in 1998 was 270,509 (thousand) and in 1999 272,945 (thousand). Which of the three calculations gave you the best forecast?

11. You have sales for the Walgreen Company (in millions of dollars) and the Gross Domestic Product (in billions of dollars) for the years 1985 to 1999.

WALGREEN SALES		GROSS DOMESTIC PRODUCT	
1985	3,162	1985	4,213
1986	3,660	1986	4,453
1987	4,282	1987	4,743
1988	4,884	1988	5,108
1989	5,380	1989	5,489
1990	6,048	1990	5,803
1991	6,733	1991	5,986
1992	7,474	1992	6,319
1993	8,295	1993	6,642
1994	9,235	1994	7,054
1995	10,395	1995	7,410
1996	11,778	1996	7,813
1997	13,363	1997	8,301
1998	15,307	1998	8,790
1999	17,839	1999	9,269

a. Calculate the following:
  (1) A straight-line trend
  (2) An exponential trend
  (3) A regression with GDP as the independent variable
b. Walgreen's sales in 2000 were $21,207 (000,000) and the 2000 GDP was $9,873 (000,000,000). Which of the three calculations gives the best fit and the best estimate of Walgreen's sales in 2000?

12. The MNO Corporation is preparing for its stockholder meeting on May 15, 2002. It sent out proxies to its stockholders on March 15 and asked stockholders who plan to attend the meeting to respond. In order to plan for a sufficient number of information packages to be distributed at the meeting, as well as for refreshments to be served, the company has asked you to forecast the number of attending stockholders. By April 15, 378 stockholders have expressed their intention to attend. You have available the following data for the last six years for total attendance at the stockholder meeting and the number of positive responses as of April 15:

Year	Positive Responses	Attendance
1996	322	520
1997	301	550
1998	398	570
1999	421	600
2000	357	570
2001	452	650

a. What is your attendance forecast for the 2002 stockholder meeting?

b. Are there any other factors that could affect attendance, and thus make your forecast inaccurate?

13. In the Columbia Gas of Ohio study that forecasted the demand for gas (see p. 251), the company developed the following coefficients for their equation:

Growth rate	.015
Intercept	1376.0
Forecasted temperature	−17.1
Prior day temperature	−3.7
Forecasted wind speed	4.2

Forecast the demand for gas for a day, when the expected average temperature will be 40 degrees, the prior day's average temperature was 37, and the average wind speed is predicted to be 8 miles per hour.

Appendix 6A

Forecasting and the Computer[45]

Forecasting, in particular time series analysis, plays a fundamental role in the world of business and government. Among major topics covered in this chapter, classical decomposition and simple exponential smoothing are just two of the many procedures that forecasters have developed over the years. Simple exponential smoothing (sometimes called Brown's simple exponential smoothing[46]) is appropriate if there is no apparent trend to the data. If the data exhibit some pronounced linear or nonlinear trend, then Brown's method gives poor forecasts. Brown modified this procedure (traditionally called Brown's double exponential smoothing), but the method developed by Holt[47] is considered superior. Holt's method tries to find the equation of the line that fits the data, with more weight on recent observations and less weight on distant past observations. This method has two smoothing equations. The first finds an estimate for the intercept for the trend line, while the second estimates the slope of the trend line. Each equation has its own smoothing constant, and thus the forecaster must find the optimal values for each.

If the time series shows seasonal effects, the classical decomposition method discussed in the text can be used, but a more sophisticated method was developed by Winters.[48] This method is essentially a "superset" of Holt's method. There are three smoothing equations, each with its own smoothing constant. The first two find the intercept and slope of the linear trend line for the data, while the third finds estimates for the seasonal indices. If the data are quarterly, there would be four seasonal factors, monthly data have twelve seasonal factors, and so on. These seasonal indices are used as multiplicative factors in the forecast model. That is, the forecast found by the trend line is tempered by the seasonal index. Once again, the researcher is forced to find the optimal smoothing constants.

Other more sophisticated procedures exist, including the methods developed by Box and Jenkins.[49] This procedure also requires that certain statistical parameters be optimized, and the amount of work to do this becomes prohibitive if done by hand. Because of these issues, researchers can find many forecasting software programs on the market. Traditionally, if you wanted a "top-notch" forecasting program, you would buy a dedicated, standalone product. However, general statistical software

---

[45]This appendix was written by Jack Yurkiewicz, Professor of Management Science, Lubin School of Business, Pace University. The authors are very grateful for Professor Yurkiewicz's contribution.

[46]R. G. Brown, *Smoothing, Forecasting and Prediction of Discrete Time-Series*, Englewood Cliffs, NJ: Prentice Hall, 1962.

[47]C. C. Holt, "Forecasting Seasonal and Trends by Exponentially Weighted Moving Averages," Office of Naval Research, Memorandum 52, 1957.

[48]P. R. Winters, "Forecasting Sales by Exponentially Weighted Moving Averages," *Management Science,* 6 (1960), pp. 324–42.

[49]G. E. P. Box, G. M. Jenkins, and G. C. Reinsel, *Time Series Analysis, Forecasting and Control,* 3d ed., Englewood Cliffs, NJ: Prentice Hall, 1994.

packages have expanded and enhanced their forecasting modules, and some of these rival their standalone counterparts. The advantage of buying a general statistical software package is that the learning curve is small when you jump to the forecasting features. Because most forecasters perform statistical analysis also, the additional cost of the forecasting module could be lower than purchasing a dedicated forecasting program. However, if you want some of the more sophisticated forecasting methods (beyond exponential smoothing and Box-Jenkins procedures, such as spectral analysis or state-space models) then you must buy a dedicated forecasting program that offers these procedures.

Most of the forecasting software currently available offers "ease-of-use" and "ease-of-learning" attributes. You can usually import your data from a spreadsheet (some products make this importation easier than others) and the software will make a time plot automatically. The time plot is usually the first step in the forecasting process, for then the researcher, based on the appearance of the data, can choose an appropriate forecasting technique.

Some programs help the researcher in choosing the most appropriate procedure for the particular time series data. The extent of help offered allows us to categorize forecasting software into three groups. The first category can be called "automatic" software. In these products, the user enters or imports data and asks the program to "analyze" it. Considering various diagnostic tests, the software responds with a "recommended" method that should give the "best" forecasts. If the user concurs with the recommendation, the program will then proceed to find the optimal parameters for the proposed procedure, get the forecasts and corresponding statistics and make forecast plots. Users can manually override the recommended procedure and choose their preferred methodology. The software will then get the optimal parameters for the chosen model and the associated output.

Although it is always prudent to warn users to be leery of using these automatic programs as "black boxes," recently released software has made great strides in the accuracy of their recommendations. The leading software in this category appears to be "Forecast Pro."

The second software category can be called "semiautomatic." The software does not make a recommendation for the methodology best suited for the data. Users must choose the appropriate procedure from a list of procedures available. The program will then find the optimal parameters for the model chosen, make forecasts, and get the appropriate statistics and plots. The user of such software must obviously have a solid knowledge of forecasting and the various associated techniques. Most of the forecast software currently on the market falls into this category, and all of the general statistics programs with forecasting modules are also in this group. A good example of software in this category is "Trends," which is a part of the general statistics program SSPS.

The third software category can best be called "manual." Here the user must specify both the method and the parameters. The program will not find these parameters. Thus, the user must execute many "runs" for a time series, each time noting the corresponding output statistics. The session ends after many iterations, when the user either finds the "best" parameters or becomes tired, whichever comes first. There are few dedicated forecasting or general statistics programs that fall into this category, but because of their limited utility, purchasing them is not recommended.

To help researchers in deciding which software is most appropriate for their needs, *OR/MS Today*, from the Institute for Operations Research and Management Sciences, publishes a survey[50] every two years that describes the currently available forecast software. The survey gives the software's features (automatic, semiautomatic, or manual), methodology available, prices, and other issues. Other forecasting and statistical journals publish similar articles.

---

[50]J. Yurkiewicz, "Forecasting 2000: Predicting What is Best for Your Needs May be a Daunting Task," *OR/MS Today*, February 2000, pp. 58–65.

Chapter 7

The Theory and Estimation of Production

The Situation

The meeting of Global Foods' top production managers must have been important because it was attended by CEO Bob Burns as well as by Jim Hartwell, vice president of manufacturing. Its purpose was to go over the plans for rolling out the company's new bottled water product, "Waterpure." Christopher Lim, manager of the company's largest bottling plant, in St. Louis, Missouri, knew that this product was considered to be the hope of the sagging beverage division. He also suspected that there was going to be more than the usual plans for the bottling operation because of the additional presence of Nicole Goodman, senior VP of marketing.

The meeting began with a few opening remarks by the CEO about the phenomenal growth of the bottled water industry and how and why Global Foods hoped to get into this market. Chris noticed that all but a few of the 15 people at the meeting had their own bottle of water in front of them and thought that this more than any other statistic made the point. Then came the surprise. The opening presentation was given by the senior VP of marketing, not manufacturing.

Nicole Goodman began to make a compelling case for a radical change in the packaging of this product. "You all have seen how Coca-Cola has spent millions of dollars in advertising and packaging in order to focus on the shape of its original glass bottle and how Pepsi-Cola recently changed the look of its label and logo. But packaging can be

(Continued)

270

considered even more important in the market for bottled water, because after all what are we selling?"

"What I propose is that we combine the tradition of Coca-Cola with the design innovation of Pepsi-Cola and a French company that makes another beverage called "Orangina" to create our own distinct packaging. We propose to sell our water in a green glass bottle shaped like a bottle of champagne. To go along with this packaging, we intend to advertise our product as the "champagne of bottled water."

"How original," thought Chris. "I seem to recall that some time ago a beer company used a similar tag line in their advertising. But forget the advertising, doesn't she realize how expensive it is to use glass rather than plastic? There has to be a reason why both Coke and Pepsi don't use glass for most of their bottling, particularly here in the States."

As if in anticipation of Chris's negative thoughts, Nicole continued by saying, "I know some of you might be thinking that this champagne idea is not very original. But our market research indicates that people between the ages of 15 and 35 are the key consumers of bottled water, and so most of our potential customers will be too young to remember that Miller beer commercial. We in marketing realize that it will be you in manufacturing that will actually implement our "creative" ideas. We know that this will present some interesting production challenges in terms of the set-up of the fill lines, the stacking of the cases for shipment and delivery, and so on. But I know you're up to the challenge. We want to begin a pilot program in one of our bottling plants. In consulting with both Bob and Jim, they both recommended strongly that we begin with our bottling plant in St. Louis. Chris, we want you to put together a plan for rolling out our new product in the next quarter."

THE PRODUCTION FUNCTION

Christopher Lim's concerns are certainly justified. No matter how much revenue is generated by the marketing plan, if the cost of production cannot be contained, the company will not be able to earn an acceptable level of profit. In economics, the analysis of cost begins with the study of the production function. The **production function** is a statement of the relationship between a firm's scarce resources (i.e., its **inputs**) and the output that results from the use of these resources. Economic cost analysis can then be seen as the application of a monetary unit such as dollars to measure the value of this input usage in the production process. Therefore, both this chapter on production and the following chapter on cost really deal with the same general topic of economic cost analysis. Because of the length and complexity of this topic, we have divided its presentation into two separate chapters.

In mathematical terms, the production function can be expressed as:

$$Q = f(X_1, X_2 \ldots \ldots X_k) \tag{7.1}$$

where Q = Output

$X_1. \ldots . . X_k$ = Inputs used in the production process

Note that we assume that this relationship between inputs and output exists for a specific period of time. In other words, Q is *not* a measure of accumulated output over time. There are two other key assumptions that you should be aware of. First, we are assuming some given "state of the art" in the production technology. Any innovation in production (e.g., the use of robotics in manufacturing or a more efficient software package for financial analysis) would cause the relationship between given inputs and their output to change. Second, we are assuming that whatever input or input combinations are included in a particular function, the output resulting from their utilization is at the maximum level. With this in mind, we can offer a more complete definition of a production function:

> A production function defines the relationship between inputs and the maximum amount that can be produced within a given period of time with a given level of technology.

For Christopher's company, the Xs could represent raw materials, such as carbonated water, sweeteners, and flavorings; labor, such as assembly line workers, support staff, and supervisory personnel; and fixed assets, such as plant and equipment.

For purposes of analysis, let us reduce the whole array of inputs in the production function to two, X and Y. Restating Equation (7.1) gives us

$$Q = f(X,Y) \tag{7.2}$$

where Q = Output
X = Labor
Y = Capital

Notice that although we have designated one variable as labor and the other as capital, we have elected to keep the all-purpose symbols X and Y as a reminder that any two inputs could have been selected to represent the array.

As stated earlier, in economic analysis the distinction between the short run and the long run is not related to any particular measurement of time (e.g., days, months, or years). Instead it refers to the extent to which a firm can vary the amounts of the inputs in its production process. Thus, a **short-run production function** shows the maximum quantity of a good or service that can be produced by a set of inputs, assuming that the amount of at least one of the inputs used remains unchanged. A **long-run production function** shows the maximum quantity of a good or service that can be produced by a set of inputs, assuming that the firm is free to vary the amount of *all* the inputs being used.

A hypothetical production function with two inputs is displayed in Table 7.1. The numbers in the matrix indicate the amount of output that would result from various combinations of X and Y. For example, the use of 2 units of X and 2 units of Y yields 18 units of output. Adding one more unit of X while holding constant the amount of Y yields an additional 11 units of output ($Q = 29$). Increasing both X and Y by 1 unit yields 41 units of output. The additional 1 unit of X with Y unchanged is considered to be a "short-run" change. An increase in both inputs by 1 unit is a "long-run" change.

Table 7.1
Representative Production Table

UNITS OF Y EMPLOYED	OUTPUT QUANTITY (Q)							
8	37	60	83	96	107	117	127	128
7	42	64	78	90	101	110	119	120
6	37	52	64	73	82	90	97	104
5	31	47	58	67	75	82	89	95
4	24	39	52	60	67	73	79	85
3	17	29	41	52	58	64	69	73
2	8	18	29	39	47	52	56	52
1	4	8	14	20	27	24	21	17
	1	2	3	4	5	6	7	8

UNITS OF X EMPLOYED

A SHORT-RUN ANALYSIS OF TOTAL, AVERAGE, AND MARGINAL PRODUCT

Before we go on to a more detailed analysis of the production function, certain key terms employed throughout this chapter should be clarified. First, economists use a number of alternative terms in reference to inputs and output:

Inputs	Output
Factors	Quantity (Q)
Factors of production	Total product (TP)
Resources	Product

Second, in the short-run analysis of the production function, two other terms besides the quantity of output are important measures of the outcome. They are **marginal product (MP)** and **average product (AP)**. If we assume X to be the variable input, then

$$\text{Marginal product of } X = MP_X = \frac{\Delta Q}{\Delta X}, \text{ holding } Y \text{ constant}$$

$$\text{Average product of } X = AP_X = \frac{Q}{X}, \text{ holding } Y \text{ constant}$$

In other words, the marginal product can be defined as the change in output or **total product** resulting from a unit change in a variable input, and the average product can be defined as the total product (TP) per unit of input used.

The data in Table 7.2 shows a short-run production function. Here we see what happens to output when increasing amounts of input X are added to a fixed amount

Table 7.2

Short-Run Changes in Production Showing Factor Productivity

UNITS OF Y EMPLOYED	OUTPUT QUANTITY (Q)							
8	37	60	83	96	107	117	127	128
7	42	64	78	90	101	110	119	120
6	37	52	64	73	82	90	97	104
5	31	47	58	67	75	82	89	95
4	24	39	52	60	67	73	79	85
3	17	29	41	52	58	64	69	73
2	⑧	⑱	㉙	㊲	㊼	㊾	㊶	㊷
1	4	8	14	20	27	24	21	17
	1	2	3	4	5	6	7	8

UNITS OF X EMPLOYED

of input Y (Y = 2). Table 7.3 restates this information by focusing on the impact on TP, MP, and AP resulting from increases in X, while holding Y constant at 2 units. The impact is also illustrated in the graphs in Figure 7.1. These tables and the figure indicate that the total product is 8 when 1 unit of X is used, it increases to a maximum of 56 when 7 units of X are used, and it decreases to 52 units when unit 8 of the X input is added. Also notice in Table 7.3 that MP begins at 8 units, increases to a maximum of 11, and falls off to an ultimate value of −4. Average product also begins at 8, increases to a maximum of 9.67, and then drops to 6.5 units when 8 units of X are combined with the fixed amount of Y. The pattern of these changes can be seen in Figure 7.1. The total product is plotted in Figure 7.1*a*, and the average and marginal products are plotted in Figure 7.1*b*.

We can observe that when Q, the quantity of the total product, reaches its maximum, MP = 0. We see also that initially (as more units of X are added to the produc-

Table 7.3

Short-Run
Production
Functions, *Q*, MP, AP

VARIABLE INPUT (X)	TOTAL PRODUCT (Q OR TP)	MARGINAL PRODUCT (MP)	AVERAGE PRODUCT (AP)
0	0		
		8	
1	8		8
		10	
2	18		9
		11	
3	29		9.67
		10	
4	39		9.75
		8	
5	47		9.4
		5	
6	52		8.67
		4	
7	56		8
		−4	
8	52		6.5

(a) Total product

Diminishing returns begins to take effect

(b) Average and marginal products

Figure 7.1
Short-Run Production with
$Y = 2$

tion process), MP is greater than AP, and it then becomes less than AP. Furthermore, MP = AP at AP's highest point. Because we are dealing with incremental unit changes in the input, it is difficult to see these points in Table 7.3, but they can be seen clearly in Figure 7.1. In the next section we will have more to say about the pattern of change in Q, AP, and MP and, more important, the reasons for the pattern of change.

The Law of Diminishing Returns

The key to understanding the pattern of change in Q, AP, and MP is the phenomenon known as the **law of diminishing returns.** This law states:

> As additional units of variable input are combined with a fixed input, at some point the additional output (i.e., marginal product) starts to diminish.

Diminishing returns are illustrated in both the numerical example in Table 7.3 and the graph of these same numbers in Figure 7.1. As you examine this information, think "change" as you see the word "marginal." Therefore, the "marginal product" of an input such as labor is the change in output resulting from an additional unit of input. Notice in Table 7.3 that we have placed the marginal product *between* each interval of input and the resulting output. For example, the marginal product of the first unit of input, 8, is placed between 0 and 1 input or between 0 and 8 units of output. Continuing on, we see that marginal product reaches its maximum of 11 between the second and third units of input. It is precisely at this point, 2.5 units of input, that we can say the law of diminishing returns will begin to take effect.[1]

In situations in which it would not be possible to consider intervals of less than one unit, it is necessary to approximate the point at which diminishing returns occurs. Suppose you were a manager who could actually measure and track your employees' marginal product. The first person's MP would be 8, the second one would be 10 and the third person's would be 11. It would be only on the addition of the fourth person that you would realize that the law of diminishing returns had occurred because this person's MP would be less than that of the previous worker. In summary we can say that, given the numbers in Table 7.3, the law of diminishing returns occurs in theory precisely at 2.5 units of input. In practice, a manager would have to add a fourth unit of labor in order to observe the law in action.

There are two key concerns of a practical nature that we advise readers to keep in mind when considering the impact of the law of diminishing returns in actual business situations. First, there is nothing in the law that states *when* diminishing returns will start to take effect. The law merely says that if additional units of a variable input are combined with a fixed input, *at some point*, the marginal product of the input will start to diminish. Therefore, it is reasonable to assume that a manager will only discover the point of diminishing returns by experience and trial and error. Hindsight will be more valuable than foresight. Second, when economists first stated this law, they made some very restrictive assumptions about the nature of the variable inputs being used. Essentially, they assumed that all inputs added to the production process were exactly the same in individual productivity. The only reason why a particular unit of input's marginal product would be higher or lower than the others used was because of the order in which it was added to the production process.

Let us examine more closely the possible reasons for the occurrence of diminishing returns. Essentially, these reasons have to do with the physical limitations of the fixed input and the variable inputs that are added to this fixed input. Suppose that we assume that the numbers in Table 7.3 represent a simple manufacturing situation where the variable input is labor and the fixed input is the factory and its machinery. Suppose that more labor is added to this fixed capital. Clearly when no workers are employed, TP or output is zero. The first worker produces 8 units. Thus, his marginal product (MP) is equal to 8 and his average product (AP) is also equal to 8. When 2 workers are used, their combined efforts yield a total product (TP) of 18. This implies that 2 people working together can produce more than the sum of their efforts working as separate individuals. (AP of one worker = 8 and AP of the two workers = 9.)

---

[1]The idea that diminishing returns will occur at this point is based on an analysis using calculus, in which the first derivative of the total product function, marginal product, is set to zero. The amount of input that fulfills this condition, is then considered the exact point at which marginal product is maximized and the law of diminishing returns will begin to take effect. See Appendix B at the end of this chapter for a complete explanation of this approach.

Moreover, we see that the MP of the second worker is greater than that of the first (MP of second worker = 10, > MP of first worker = 8).

Because it is assumed in economic theory that each worker is equally productive, this must mean that the effect of teamwork and specialization enables additional workers to contribute more than those added previously to the production process, a phenomenon that we can refer to as "increasing returns." But as still more workers are added, there are fewer and fewer opportunities for increasing returns through specialization and teamwork and at some point additional workers result in diminishing returns. Eventually, there may be so many workers relative to the fixed capacity that they may start to interfere with each other's activities. In this case, the additional workers lead to negative marginal returns, causing the total product to decrease. We see this occurring in Table 7.3 when the eighth person is added to the production process. In this case, the old adage "too many cooks spoil the soup" seems to have been realized.

Economists who first thought about the law of diminishing returns relied primarily on deductive reasoning rather than empirical verification to explain the law's existence. It was critical for them to establish this law because it then helped to explain the "Three Stages of Production" and the phenomenon of increasing marginal cost (explained in detail in the next chapter). Furthermore, when this law was established in the nineteenth century, the primary examples used to illustrate its impact on production involved agriculture, with land being the fixed factor of production, and farmers being the variable factors. At some point, it was reasoned, with a fixed amount of land, additional farm workers would result in diminishing amounts of additional harvested output.

To illustrate this law with more contemporary examples, we offer an example based on an actual situation involving a soft drink bottling facility. In addition, we provide two examples related to information technology.

The Sorting of Refillable Glass Bottles In the early days of the soft drink industry, most drinks were packaged in returnable, refillable glass bottles. Now most drinks are packaged in plastic bottles or aluminum cans. But in some parts of the United States (particularly in Michigan) and in many parts of the rest of the world, returnable, refillable bottles are still used extensively.

There are three basic ways to sort and clean the returned bottles: (1) a totally automatic sorting system, (2) a totally manual sorting system, and (3) a hybrid system. The choice of system depends primarily on the anticipated volume of returned bottles. A typical manual sorting area is about 30 feet long and there is usually no room in a plant for expansion. Each sorter requires about 3 feet of space in which to work. A conveyor carrying the returned empties runs along a wall and sorters work from one side of this conveyor.

The standard productivity measure used in a plant is "cases sorted per person-hour." If only one person is sorting bottles, she will not be able to keep up with the flow. The bottles tend to back up, and the system has to stop while the sorter tries to catch up.[2] In an interview with a bottling plant manager, the authors learned that

---

[2]Readers can imagine that this is very much what might happen in stage 1 of the production process. (See next section for Stages of Production.)

typically two sorters per flavor are used.[3] Thus, if five flavors need to be sorted, ten people work at the conveyor belt. These ten sorters take up the maximum length of the sorting area (30 feet) if the recommended amount of 3 feet per person is allocated. The plant manager explained that if more than 10 sorters are used, productivity tends to decrease because the workers start to get in each other's way. Although no quantitative detail was provided, we think that readers can well imagine that at this point, the law of diminishing returns would be starting to take effect, with each additional worker beyond ten sorting less returned bottles than the previously added worker.

> *Fixed input:*   Machinery and working area square footage
> *Variable input:*   People working as sorters

Development of Applications Software

Suppose you are the manager of a team of software engineers that is developing a new program to help companies to make their computer systems compliant with the demands of the year 2000 (often referred to as the "Y2K" problem). Suppose your project management plan calls for writing approximately 500 lines of program code every day in order to reach the objective. You have a team of five programmers each writing about 100 lines of code a day. To speed things up (as January 1, 2000 rapidly approaches), you decide to add more programmers to your team. You notice that the first additional person you add (the sixth member of the team) adds only 90 lines of code and the next person hired after that adds only 80 lines. Assuming that the two additional programmers are equally skilled and work well as team members with the established group, you conclude that the law of diminishing returns must be at work.

> *Fixed input:*   the programming language and the hardware used to
>   develop the applications program
> *Variable input:*   software programmers

Response Time on a Data Network

You are a manager of a data communications network that is responsible for issuing approval codes for a credit card operation. After a credit card is swiped, the data are sent from the merchant's bank to the bank that issued the cardholder the card via the data communications network. The approval code comes back to the merchant within an average of three seconds. The merchants complain that this is too long. Software programmers are put to work to make the adjustments in software that will reduce the average to two seconds. Ten programmers working 10 hours a week for two weeks reduce the response time down to two seconds. Merchants continue to complain and want the average reduced further to one second. As the network manager, you try again with another 10 programmers working the same amount of time as the previous addition of programmers. You find that the same additional time and effort does not yield the desired one-second reduction in response time. You conclude that the law of diminishing returns is at work.

---

[3]Interview with a former student of one of the authors, who used to work as a bottling plant manager for Pepsi-Cola.

Fixed input: the technological infrastructure (i.e., the hardware and bandwidth of the transmission facilities of the physical network and the limits and capabilities of the software)

Variable input: software programmers

In summary, all of these examples illustrate how diminishing returns can be caused by the physical limitations of fixed capital such as machinery and workspace, the technological limitations of computer hardware and software, and the personnel and management problems caused by increasing numbers of people working with a fixed capacity.

The Three Stages of Production in the Short Run

The short-run production function can be divided into three distinct **stages of production.** To illustrate this phenomenon, let us return to the data in Table 7.3 and Figure 7.1. For your convenience, Figure 7.1 has been reproduced as Figure 7.2. As

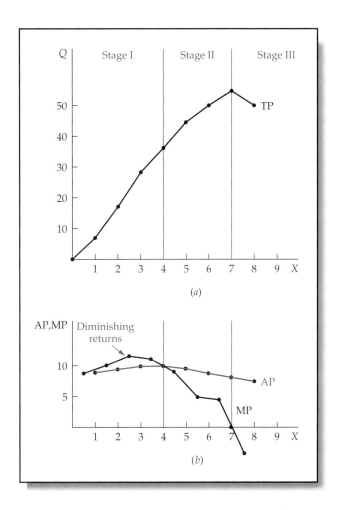

Figure 7.2
The Three Stages of Production

the figure indicates, stage I runs from zero to four units of the variable input X (i.e., to the point at which average product reaches its maximum). Stage II begins from this point and proceeds to seven units of input X (i.e., to the point at which total product is maximized). Stage III continues on from that point. According to economic theory, in the short run, "rational" firms should only be operating in stage II. It is clear why stage III is irrational: the firm would be using more of its variable input to produce less output! However, it may not be as apparent why stage I is also considered irrational. The reason is that if a firm were operating in stage I, it would be grossly underutilizing its fixed capacity. That is, it would have so much fixed capacity relative to its usage of variable inputs that it could increase the output per unit of variable input (i.e., average product) simply by adding more variable inputs to this capacity. Figure 7.3a summarizes the three stages of production and the reasons that the rational firm operates in stage II of the short-run production function.

If you are still not clear about the irrational nature of stage I, there is an alternative explanation. In Figure 7.3b, we have designated two levels of variable input usage: X_1 and X_2. Here we see that the average product is the same whether X_1 or X_2 units of the variable input are used. If output per variable input is the same regardless of which input level is used, the firm should employ X_2 because the total product will be higher.

MODULE 7A
MODULE 7B
MODULE 7C

Derived Demand and the Optimal Level of Variable Input Usage

Given that a firm's short-run production has only one "rational" stage of production (i.e., stage II), we must still determine the level of input usage within stage II that is best for the rational, profit-maximizing firm. To demonstrate how we determine the optimal level of input usage within stage II, we have created another numerical illustration, shown in Table 7.4. In this table we observe that stage II occurs from 60,000 to 80,000 units of total product. In terms of labor input, this stage II ranges from four to eight units of input. But which level of output (or input) usage should we consider to be optimal? In answering this question, note that this table resembles the set up of a spreadsheet program, because MP is placed at the *same* level of output that results from an additional unit of input rather than *between* the two levels of output as shown in Table 7.3. In fact, we have provided you with an Excel exercise so that you can experiment with your own variations of the example shown in Table 7.4.

The answer to this question is based on a concept introduced in chapter 4, derived demand. Recall that the demand for inputs is derived from the demand for their output. In other words, it would do no good for the firm to decide how many units of variable input to use without knowing how many units of output it could sell, the price of the product, and the monetary costs of employing various amounts of the X input.

To see exactly how this works, assume that a firm is operating in a perfectly competitive market for its input and its output. That is, it can sell as many units of the product as it wants as long as it does so at the going market price. Moreover, it can hire as many X inputs as it desires as long as it pays these inputs the going market price (i.e., the competitive wage rate). Note that four new measures are added to Table 7.4:

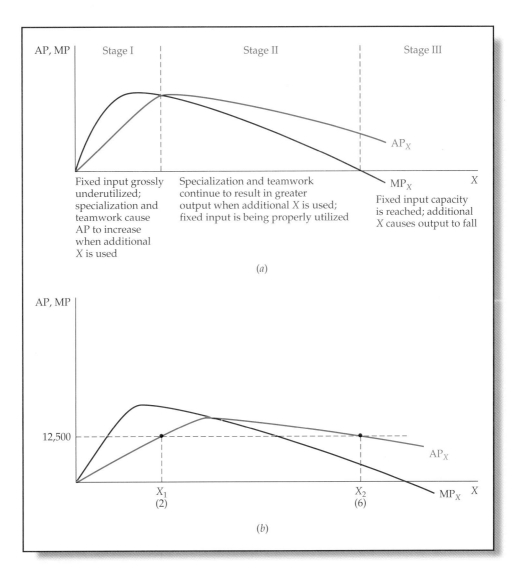

Figure 7.3
Explanation of Production Stages

Total revenue product (TRP): The market value of the firm's output, computed by multiplying the total product by the market price ($Q \times P$).

Marginal revenue product (MRP): The change in the firm's total revenue product resulting from a unit change in the number of inputs used ($\Delta TRP/\Delta X$). It can also be computed by multiplying the marginal product by the product price (MP $\times$ P).

Total labor cost (TLC): The total cost of using the variable input, labor, computed by multiplying the wage rate (which we assume to be some given and constant dollar amount) by the number of variable inputs employed (Wage rate $\times$ X).

Table 7.4
Combining Marginal Revenue Product (MRP) with Marginal Labor Cost (MLC)

LABOR UNIT (X)	TOTAL PRODUCT (Q OR TP)	AVERAGE PRODUCT (AP)	MARGINAL PRODUCT (MP)	TOTAL REVENUE PRODUCT (TRP)	MARGINAL REVENUE PRODUCT (MRP)	TOTAL LABOR COST (TLC)	MARGINAL LABOR COST (MLC)	TRP − TLC	MRP − MLC
0	0		0	0		0		0	0
1	10,000	10,000	10,000	20,000	20,000	10,000	10,000	10,000	10,000
2	25,000	12,500	15,000	50,000	30,000	20,000	10,000	30,000	20,000
3	45,000	15,000	20,000	90,000	40,000	30,000	10,000	60,000	30,000
4	60,000	15,000	15,000	120,000	30,000	40,000	10,000	80,000	20,000
5	70,000	14,000	10,000	140,000	20,000	50,000	10,000	90,000	10,000
6	75,000	12,500	5,000	150,000	10,000	60,000	10,000	90,000	0
7	78,000	11,143	3,000	156,000	6,000	70,000	10,000	86,000	−4,000
8	80,000	10,000	2,000	160,000	4,000	80,000	10,000	80,000	−6,000

Note: P = Product price = $2
W = Cost per unit of labor = $10,000
MRP = $MP \times P$
TLC = $X \times W$
MLC = $\Delta TLC / \Delta X$

Marginal labor cost (MLC): The change in total labor cost resulting from a unit change in the number of variable inputs used. Because the wage rate is assumed to be constant regardless of the number of inputs used, the MLC is the same as the wage rate.[4]

In deriving the figures for these measures in Table 7.4, we have assumed a product price of $2 and a wage rate of $10,000 per unit. Given these figures, you can see that a rational firm would want to hire 6 units of labor. Up to that point it pays for the firm to add more labor because the additional **marginal labor cost (MLC)** to the firm to do so is more than made up for by the additional **marginal revenue product (MRP)** brought in by the sale of the increased output. Beyond that point the firm would pay more in additional labor cost than it would receive in additional revenue.

Can you discern how the demand for the output is incorporated into this analysis, that is, how the demand for the input X is actually derived from the demand for the output? Suppose the market demand increased and drove the market price up to $4. This would increase the market value of the labor input's efforts. In other words,

---

[4]This term is also referred to as *marginal resource cost* (MRC) and *marginal factor cost* (MFC). By assuming that the firm hires workers in a perfectly competitive labor market, we also assume that it can hire as many workers as it chooses at some going market wage rate determined by the supply and demand for this particular type of worker. This would not be the case if the firm were operating in an imperfectly competitive labor market. We will not consider the imperfectly competitive case in this text. Interested readers should consult any economics principles or intermediate microeconomics text for a full discussion on this type of labor market and its impact on the input decisions of the firm.

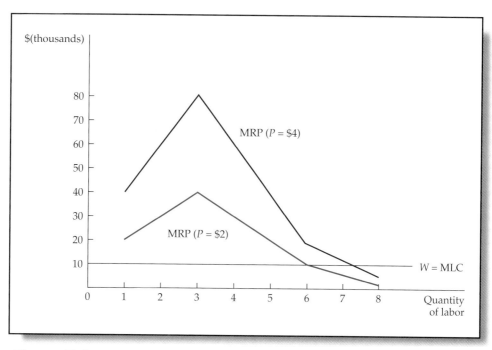

Figure 7.4
The Effect of Increased Market Price on the Demand for Labor

the market value of each additional labor unit's contribution to the total product would double. This increase in the labor input's MRP would then justify the firm's use of a seventh unit of labor. Thus, an increase in the market demand for the output leads to an increase in the demand by the firm for labor input, all other factors held constant. The original figures from Table 7.4 as well as the case in which market price is assumed to increase to $4 are illustrated in Figure 7.4.

We can summarize this relationship between the demand for the output and the demand for the input in terms of the following optimal decision rule:

> A profit-maximizing firm operating in perfectly competitive output and input markets will be using the optimal amount of an input at the point at which the monetary value of the input's marginal product is equal to the additional cost of using that input—in other words, when **MRP** = **MLC**.

The Case of Multiple Inputs (Abridged Version)

The purpose of this section is to present a relatively nonquantitative explanation of optimal input decisions involving two or more inputs. For a complete treatment of multiple inputs using numerical tables, graphs, and algebraic equations, please refer to Appendix 7A at the end of this chapter.

In the example illustrated in Table 7.4, we showed how a firm could use the concept of equalizing at the margin to determine the optimal usage level of a single variable input. This same equalizing concept applies to a situation in which two or more inputs are being considered. In the multiple input case, we must consider the relationship between the *ratio* of the marginal product of one input and its cost to the *ratio* of the marginal product of the other input (inputs) and its (their) cost. Expressed mathematically for "*k*" inputs:

$$\frac{MP_1}{W_1} = \frac{MP_2}{W_2} = \frac{M_k}{W_k}$$

Let us consider the case of a global manufacturing company that has manufacturing facilities in two different countries: a high-wage country and a low-wage country. We can analyze this problem by treating labor in the high wage country as one input and labor in the other country as another input. At first glance, it might seem obvious that a country seeking to minimize its costs and hence maximize its profits should try to manufacture as much as possible in the low-wage country. This would mean using mostly the low-wage labor input. But production theory suggests that the firm should not only look at input costs but also the marginal products of each input *relative* to their respective costs.

Suppose you are the production manager of a company that makes computer parts and peripherals in Malaysia and Costa Rica. At the current levels of production and input utilization in the two countries, you find that:

Marginal Product of labor in Malaysia (MP_{Mal}) = 18
Marginal Product of labor in Costa Rica (MP_{CR}) = 6
Wage rate in Malaysia (W_{Mal}) = \$6/hr.
Wage rate in Costa Rica (W_{CR}) = \$3/hr.

How much would you produce in each manufacturing facility? Because labor is cheaper in Costa Rica, you might be tempted to produce most of your output in that country. However, a closer look at the MP:wage ratios reveals the opposite conclusion. That is,

$$\frac{MP_{Mal}}{W_{Mal}} > \frac{MP_{CR}}{W_{CR}} \quad \text{or} \quad \frac{18}{\$6} > \frac{6}{\$3}$$

This means that at the margin, the last dollar spent on a unit of labor in Costa Rica would yield 2 units of output (6/\$3), while in Malaysia, the last dollar spent would result in three additional units of output (18/\$6). This inequality implies that the firm should begin to shift more of its production away from Costa Rica to Malaysia, until the two ratios are equalized. In theory, this optimal or equilibrium point would occur because as more labor is used in Malaysia, the law of diminishing returns would start to reduce the MP of labor in this country. With less labor being used in Costa Rica, the law of diminishing returns would work in reverse, causing the marginal product of labor in this country to rise. Of course, all this assumes a short-run condition whereby the complementary fixed inputs used along with labor remain constant.[5]

---

[5] Over time, there might be another factor causing the two ratios to begin to equalize. If there are enough companies that see this inequality, their combined increase in demand for labor in Malaysia may start to drive up the wage rate in this country, while a decrease in demand for labor in Costa Rica may slow the rate in increase in wage rates or even cause them to fall. Thus equalizing at the margin could take place because of changes in the values of the denominators of the ratios as well as the value of their numerators.

Once the implication of the basic model is understood, other factors can be brought in. If these factors outweigh the MP-input cost criteria, a company may well modify its decision. For example, despite Malaysia's higher MP/wage ratio, there may be political and economic risk factors to consider. (This was indeed the case when the Malaysian government imposed foreign exchange controls in 1998 by requiring foreign investors to keep their profits in Malaysia for at least one year before they could be repatriated.) On the other hand, Costa Rica is a fairly stable economy with leaders who do not seem to want to impose any such trade and finance restrictions. Its proximity to U.S. markets would also reduce transportation costs. Furthermore, it has a democratic government (with no standing army) and a highly skilled work force with strong English language skills.

THE LONG-RUN PRODUCTION FUNCTION

In the long run, a firm has time enough to change the amount of all of its inputs. Thus, there is really no difference between fixed and variable inputs. Table 7.5 uses the data first presented in Table 7.1 and illustrates what happens to total output as both inputs X and Y increase one unit at a time. The resulting increase in the total output as the two inputs increase is called **returns to scale.**

Looking more closely at Table 7.5, we see for example that if the firm uses 1 unit of X and 1 unit of Y, it will produce 4 units of output. If it doubles its inputs (i.e., 2 units of X and 2 units of Y), it will produce 18 units of output. Thus, a doubling of inputs has produced more than a fourfold increase in output. Proceeding further, we notice that an additional doubling of inputs (i.e., 4 units of X and 4 units of Y) results in more than a threefold increase in output, from 18 to 60. What we are observing in this table is *increasing returns to scale.*

Table 7.5
Returns to Scale

UNITS OF Y EMPLOYED				OUTPUT QUANTITY			
8	37	60	83	96	107	117	127	128
7	42	64	78	90	101	110	119	120
6	37	52	64	73	82	90	97	104
5	31	47	58	67	75	82	89	95
4	24	39	52	60	67	73	79	85
3	17	29	41	52	58	64	69	73
2	8	18	29	39	47	52	56	52
1	4	8	14	20	27	24	21	17
	1	2	3	4	5	6	7	8

Units of X Employed

According to economic theory, if an increase in a firm's inputs by some proportion results in an increase in output by a greater proportion, the firm experiences *increasing returns to scale*. If output increases by the same proportion as the inputs increase, the firm experiences *constant returns to scale*. A less than proportional increase in output is called *decreasing returns to scale*.

You might simply assume that firms generally experience constant returns to scale. For example, if a firm has a factory of a particular size, then doubling its size along with a doubling of workers and machinery should lead to a doubling of output. Why should it result in a greater than proportional or, for that matter, a smaller than proportional increase? For one thing, a larger scale of production might enable a firm to divide up tasks into more specialized activities, thereby increasing labor productivity. Also, a larger scale of operation might enable a company to justify the purchase of more sophisticated (hence, more productive) machinery. These factors help to explain why a firm can experience increasing returns to scale. On the other hand, operating on a larger scale might create certain managerial inefficiencies (e.g., communications problems, bureaucratic red tape) and hence cause decreasing returns to scale. More will be said about the factors that can cause increasing or decreasing returns to scale in the next chapter, when we discuss the related concepts of economies and diseconomies of scale.

One way to measure returns to scale is to use a coefficient of output elasticity:

$$E_Q = \frac{\text{Percentage change in } Q}{\text{Percentage change in all inputs}}$$

Thus,

If $E > 1$, we have increasing returns to scale (IRTS).
If $E = 1$, we have constant returns to scale (CRTS).
If $E < 1$, we have decreasing returns to scale (DRTS).

Another way of looking at the concept of returns to scale is based on an equation that was first presented at the outset of this chapter:

$$Q = f(X, Y) \tag{7.3}$$

Recall in the original specification of this equation that it may include as many input variables as necessary to describe the production process (i.e., i variables). For ease of discussion, we will limit this number to two: X and Y. Now suppose that we increase the amount of each input by some proportion k. For example, if we increase the inputs by 10 percent, $k = 1.10$. If we double the inputs, $k = 2.0$. Of course, Q is expected to increase by some proportion as a result of the increase in the inputs. Let h represent the magnitude of this increase. Expressed in terms of Equation (7.3),

$$hQ = f(kX, kY) \tag{7.4}$$

Using this notation, we can summarize returns to scale in the following way:

If $h > k$, the firm experiences increasing returns to scale ($E_Q > 1$).
If $h = k$, the firm experiences constant returns to scale ($E_Q = 1$).
If $h < k$, the firm experiences decreasing returns to scale ($E_Q < 1$).

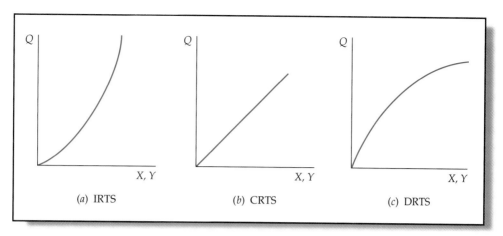

Figure 7.5
Graphic Representations of Returns to Scale

We will illustrate returns to scale with a numerical example. Suppose we have the following production function:

$$Q_1 = 5X + 7Y$$

If we use 10 units of each input, the output will be

$$Q_1 = 5(10) + 7(10)$$

$$= 50 + 70 = 120 \text{ units}$$

Now let us increase each input by 25 percent (i.e., $k = 1.25$). This will give us

$$Q_2 = 5(12.5) + 7(12.5)$$

$$= 62.5 + 87.5 = 150$$

The 25 percent increase in X and Y has led to a proportional increase in output (i.e., 150 is 25 percent more than 120).

We can also illustrate the concept of returns to scale graphically. Figure 7.5 shows the three possible types of returns to scale. In each case, we assume that the inputs (X and Y) are increased by the same proportion; thus, they are both included on the horizontal axis. Obviously, these graphs are idealized representations of returns to scale. In reality, we would not expect the changes in output relative to the changes in inputs to behave in such a smooth and orderly fashion.

THE ESTIMATION OF PRODUCTION FUNCTIONS

Following our examination of demand theory, we turned to the subject of demand estimation. Now it is time to examine another of a managerial economist's important tasks, the estimation of production functions. This section will deal with three major topics. First, we will discuss the possible shapes of production functions. Second, we will discuss the Cobb-Douglas production function, a form which has been commonly used by economists since its introduction in the 1920s. Last, we will look at the data needed for estimation and some of the production function studies published by economists.

The Various Forms of a Production Function

Earlier in this chapter, the short-run production function was introduced. As you remember, the short run is characterized by the existence of a fixed factor to which we add a variable factor. Thus, the simple function, containing just one variable factor and one fixed factor, can be written as follows:

$$Q = f(L)_K$$

where output Q is determined by the quantity of the variable factor L (labor) with the fixed factor K (capital) given.[6]

The theoretical part of this chapter assumed that the production function starts with increasing marginal returns followed by decreasing marginal returns. In other words, all three stages of production are present. This situation is represented by a cubic function:

$$Q = a + bL + cL^2 - dL^3$$

where a is the constant and b, c, and d are coefficients. Figure 7.6a shows the total product line,[7] and Figure 7.6b shows the average and marginal product curves. All three stages of production are present.

It is possible, however, that the data employed in the estimate will exhibit diminishing marginal returns but no stage I. Such an estimate is represented by the quadratic function

$$Q = a + bL - cL^2$$

Figures 7.7a and 7.7b depict total and unit product curves respectively. Both of these graphs show diminishing marginal returns, but increasing marginal returns and thus stage I are absent.[8]

In performing empirical research, it may be possible to identify a linear production function, $Q = a + bL$. This function exhibits no diminishing returns; the total product will be a straight line with slope b, and both the MP and AP lines will be horizontal and equal.[9] Of course, a straight-line production function may hold in some

---

[6]In the prior discussion the letters X and Y designated inputs. This emphasized the production function's generality. Here we will use L (for labor) and K (for capital), since these are the letters that are frequently employed to indicate variable and fixed factors. In long-run analysis, of course, both L and K are variable.

[7]Total product curves should, in theory, be drawn from the origin, since it is most likely that no production would occur in the absence of any variable factor. However, when production functions are estimated using regression analysis, it is probable that the fitted line will have a positive or negative y-intercept. Thus, in the equations which follow we will include the intercept a. It should be noted that this value probably has no economic significance.

[8]If the intercept is present, average product is equal to $a/L + b - cL$. However, if the intercept is omitted, the average product will be a straight line, as shown in Figure 7.7b.

[9]Again, if the intercept is present, the average product will show a decline. If, however, the intercept is omitted, the average product will be horizontal and equal to marginal product.

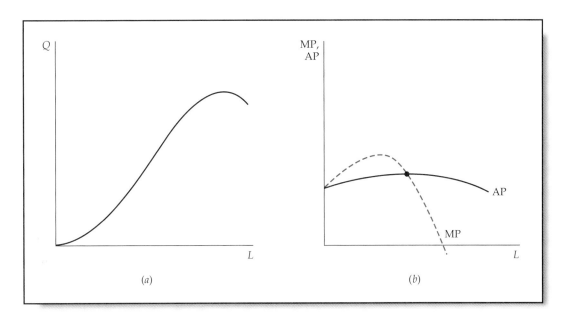

Figure 7.6
Cubic Production Function

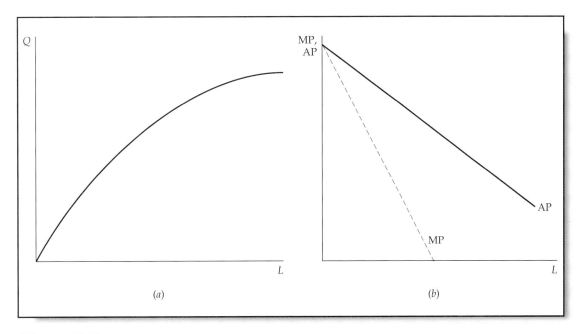

Figure 7.7
Quadratic Production Function

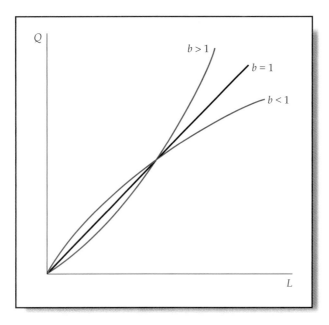

Figure 7.8
Power Production Function

real situations, but given the existence of a fixed factor, constant marginal product should not be expected to prevail over a wide range of quantities produced.

Another form of the production function is the **power function**, which takes the following form:

$$Q = aL^b$$

The shape of this production function depends on the exponent b, as is shown in Figure 7.8.

A major advantage of the power function is that it can be transformed into a linear function when it is expressed in logarithmic terms, making it amenable to linear regression analysis:

$$\log Q = \log a + b \log L$$

The direction of marginal product depends on the size of the exponent b. If $b > 1$, marginal product is increasing; if $b = 1$, it is constant; and if $b < 1$, it is decreasing. It cannot, however, exhibit two directions for marginal product on the same function, as was possible with the cubic equation form. This function is used frequently in empirical work. One reason for its popularity is that it can be readily transformed into a function with two or more independent variables:

$$Q = aX_1^b X_2^c \ldots \ldots X_n^m$$

Using more than one independent variable in a production function is certainly more realistic than limiting the analysis to only one, and when it is assumed that all inputs are variable, we have then moved from short-run analysis to the long run. Indeed, this function can be employed in both analyses. In a simple two-variable model (e.g., labor and capital), the power function permits the estimation of marginal product (e.g., when labor changes and capital remains the same) and of returns to scale (when both variables change).

The Cobb-Douglas Production Function

The **Cobb-Douglas production function** was introduced in 1928,[10] and it is still a common functional form in economic studies today. It has been used extensively to estimate both individual firm and aggregate production functions. It has undergone significant criticism but has endured. "It is now customary practice in economics to deny its validity and then to use it as an excellent approximation."[11] It was originally constructed for all of the manufacturing output (Q) in the United States for the years 1899 to 1922. The two inputs used by the authors were number of manual workers (L) and fixed capital (K). The formula for the production function, which was suggested by Cobb, was of the following form:

$$Q = aL^bK^{1-b}$$

What are the important properties of this function that have kept it popular for more than 70 years?

1. To make this equation useful, both inputs must exist for Q to be a positive number. This makes sense, since total product is a result of combining two or more factors.[12]
2. The function can exhibit increasing, decreasing, or constant returns. Originally, Cobb and Douglas assumed that returns to scale are constant. The function was constructed in such a way that the exponents summed to $b + 1 - b = 1$. (A brief description of the mathematics of the Cobb-Douglas function can be found in Appendix 7B.) However, in later studies, they (as well as other researchers) relaxed this requirement and rewrote the equation as follows:

$$Q = aL^bK^c$$

Under this construction, if $b + c > 1$, returns to scale are increasing and if $b + c < 1$, returns are decreasing.[13] Constant returns exist when $b + c = 1$.
3. The function permits us to investigate the marginal product for any factor while holding all others constant. Thus it is also useful in the analysis of short-run production functions. In the two-factor model discussed here the marginal product of labor turns out to be $MP_L = bQ/L$, and the marginal product of capital is $MP_K = cQ/K$. (The mathematics of this result are shown in Appendix 7B.) Each of the two coefficients will usually be less than 1, and this will mean that they each exhibit diminishing marginal returns. Thus, production takes place in stage II, which is the relevant area of production.

---

[10]C. W. Cobb and P. H. Douglas, "A Theory of Production," *American Economic Review*, 8, 1 (March 1928, suppl.), pp. 139–65. Charles W. Cobb was a mathematician; Paul H. Douglas was an economist, and later a U.S. senator from Illinois.
[11]George J. Stigler, *The Theory of Price*, 4th ed., New York: Macmillan, 1987, p. 153.
[12]If an additive function (such as $Q = a + bL + cK$) were employed, output would still be positive even if one of the two inputs were zero.
[13]Of course, if the function contained more than two factors, the exponents would still have to equal more than one for increasing returns, less than one for decreasing, and one for constant.

4. The elasticity of production is an important concept as discussed in Appendix B of this chapter. In the Cobb-Douglas function, the elasticities of the factors are equal to their exponents, in this case b and c. Thus, the elasticities of labor and capital are constants.
5. Since a power function can be converted to a linear function by using logarithms, it can be estimated by linear regression analysis which makes for a relatively easy calculation with any software package.
6. Although we have limited our discussion to just two input variables (L and K), Cobb-Douglas can accommodate any number of independent variables, as follows:

$$Q = aX_1^b X_2^c X_3^d \ldots \ldots X_n^m$$

7. A theoretical production function assumes that technology is constant. However, the data fitted by the researcher may span a period over which technology has progressed. One of the independent variables in the above equation could represent technological change (a time series) and thus adjust the function to take technology into consideration.

The Cobb-Douglas function has the following shortcomings:

1. The Cobb-Douglas cannot show the marginal product going through all three stages of production in one specification. (A cubic function would be necessary to achieve this.)
2. Similarly, it cannot show a firm or industry passing through increasing, constant, and decreasing returns to scale.
3. There are also important problems with specification of data to be utilized in empirical estimates. These problems will be discussed next.

Statistical Estimation of Production Functions

Let us turn now to a description of the data that would be utilized in empirical estimates of production functions. Later, we will also review some published studies. When the statistical estimate concerns a plant, or group of plants, the data will come from company records—accounting, employment, purchasing, manufacturing, and others.

If only one product is produced in a plant, Q is specified in physical units (e.g., number, tons, gallons). However, if a plant produces a number of different products, and it is not possible to segregate properly the inputs and outputs of the products, estimation becomes considerably more difficult. In such a case, the investigator probably must settle for some measure of value, assigning weights to products depending on the value (in terms of cost or selling price) produced. There are some obvious problems with this procedure. First of all, over time the data will have to be deflated to account for price or cost changes. Second, the price or cost of a product may not be an exact reflection of the inputs combined in the total value. However, until better measurement methods are found, such valuing methods will have to suffice.

Measuring inputs also can vary in the level of difficulty. Inputs should be measured as "flow" rather than "stock" variables, and this is not always possible.[14]

---

[14]Flows measure the usage of services consumed in producing a product, whereas stocks represent the amounts of factors present and available for productive use.

Usually, the most important input is labor. Hours of labor input are probably the best measure for our purposes. Data for direct labor hours are ordinarily available from company records. If they are not, then number of direct workers is the next best choice. However, it must be remembered that number of workers is a stock variable and does not necessarily represent the amount of labor expended in production. For materials, a physical measure is again best. In some cases, such data are readily available (weight of materials consumed, for instance). Of course, since we do not wish to proliferate the number of independent variables, choosing only the most important raw material may be indicated. Alternatively, a combination (by weight or value) may prove to be a viable option. Utilities (electricity, gas, etc.) may also be included; in this case, physical quantities should be fairly easily obtained.

The most difficult input variable is the all-important capital input. How can one measure the use of plant, machinery, and equipment in production? Since different components of plant and equipment are of varying durability and different input intensity, usage per period is very hard to establish. In some cases, periodic depreciation may be an indicator of capital use. However, depreciation as recorded in the company's books is often based on accounting convention or legal requirement. Further, the projected depreciation life of a piece of equipment tends to depend on tax rules, since the firm wishes to take advantage of the fastest write-off permitted for tax purposes. Some capital items, such as land, are not depreciated at all. Unless some rather consistent measurement of capital usage can be designed by the researcher (and this is certainly a formidable task), the common method of measuring capital by the use of a stock variable (e.g., fixed assets) is probably indicated. Obviously, this is not a perfect solution, since the price of these assets depends on when the assets were acquired. Thus, the asset figure must be adjusted by a price index. Should gross fixed assets (i.e., the original cost of all plant and equipment) be used, or net fixed assets (gross assets minus accumulated depreciation)? Again, this is a difficult question. There is no specific answer. The method used must be determined by the investigator as that which is most reasonable (and available) for each specific case.

If the production function estimate is to be accomplished using regression analysis, then we must choose between time series and cross-sectional analysis. The former would be preferable if data have been collected over a period of time in a given plant. However, it would be necessary to make adjustments for inflation if the variables are in monetary (rather than physical) terms. Also, a time variable (or a dummy variable) may have to be employed to account for changes in technology.

Cross-sectional analysis is favored when the data collected cover a number of plants in a given time period. But here again, problems may arise. The various plants may not employ the same level of technology. If the data are in monetary terms, an adjustment for differential price or wage levels at different geographical locations would be necessary.

While a theoretical production function assumes that output is produced at the most efficient input combinations, in reality such an ideal situation is certainly not assured whichever estimating method is used. Ultimately, there is no perfect way to measure and analyze the data. The researcher must choose the most appropriate method.

A Numerical Example of a Cobb-Douglas Production Function
A cross-sectional sample of 20 soft drink bottling plants has been selected. The data are given

for a specific month in 1998. Only two independent variables are used: (1) number of direct workers and (2) plant size. Plants range from 1 to 1.75, based on a size and capacity measure developed by engineers.

Production, the dependent variable, is stated in terms of gallons of product shipped during the period. Table 7.6 contains the data and the results of the analysis.

The Cobb-Douglas function of the form $Q = aL^bK^c$ was applied to the numbers. The regression output in the table shows the results.[15] The regression equation is as follows:

$$Q = 15.14L^{0.66}K^{0.32}$$

R^2 (the coefficient of determination) is quite high, showing that 98 percent of the deviations are explained. The two coefficients are significantly different from zero since they both pass the t-test.[16] The sum of the two coefficients is 0.985. Because this result is so close to 1, it can be assumed that the plants exhibit constant returns to scale. Each of the inputs indicates decreasing marginal returns.

Two Studies of Individual Production Functions In 1967, a study of the production function of the Pacific halibut industry was published. A Cobb-Douglas function appeared to give good results and showed that constant returns are probably the rule in this industry. A "good captain" variable was added—a confidential rating of the management abilities of the captains of the 32 boats in the sample. It was found that good captains made a difference.[17]

A more recent study included management in the production function equation. This study dealt with a sample of plants of a multinational consumer goods manufacturer. Time series and cross-sectional data were combined to obtain 127 observations over eight years (1975–1982). Management was measured as a performance ranking of each plant in terms of three criteria—output goal attainment, cost over- or underfulfillment, and quality level of output. The results showed that the management variable was statistically significant. Another feature of this study was the conclusion that increasing returns existed up to a certain plant size and that decreasing returns resulted at larger sizes.[18]

Aggregate Production Functions

A large proportion of the studies performed using the Cobb-Douglas function did not deal with data for individual firms, but rather with aggregations of industries or even the economy as a whole. Although much of this work has proved to be quite fruitful in describing production functions, the interpretation of the results may not be quite as meaningful as for individual production func-

---

[15]The results were calculated using the Excel regression analysis program. The raw data were transformed into logarithms, and a straight-line regression in logarithms was computed. The constant of 1.18 is a logarithm, and 15.14 is its anti-log.

[16]Labor's t-test is significant at the 1 percent level, and capital's is significant at the 5 percent level.

[17]Salvatore Comitimi and David S. Huang, "A Study of Production and Factor Shares in the Halibut Fishing Industry," *Journal of Political Economy*, August 1967, pp. 366–72.

[18]Robert N. Mefford, "Introducing Management into the Production Function," *Review of Economics and Statistics*, February 1986, pp. 96–104.

Table 7.6

Production Function:
Soft Drink Bottling

TOTAL PRODUCT	LABOR	CAPITAL
97	15	1.00
98	17	1.00
104	20	1.00
120	22	1.00
136	22	1.25
129	25	1.25
145	30	1.25
170	32	1.25
181	35	1.25
166	30	1.50
175	35	1.50
190	38	1.50
212	42	1.50
220	44	1.50
207	45	1.50
228	44	1.75
226	47	1.75
240	52	1.75
270	55	1.75
280	58	1.75

SUMMARY OUTPUT

REGRESSION STATISTICS

R Square	0.980965846
Adjusted R Square	0.978726534
Standard Error	0.020818585
Observations	20

	COEFFICIENTS	STANDARD ERROR	t STAT
Intercept	1.1800154	0.096022924	12.288892
X Variable 1	0.6643702	0.075371367	8.8146228
X Variable 2	0.3214714	0.147006777	2.1867796

tions. When data for the economy as a whole are used, the model must accommodate different technologies and different processes and thus does not represent a specific technological process of a given firm. When the aggregation is done at the level of an industry rather than the overall economy, the assumption of similar technology is more appropriate, but even in such a case many dissimilarities may occur.

Gathering data for such aggregate functions can be difficult. For the economy as a whole, gross national or domestic product—in real terms—could be used to measure output. For specific industries, data from the Census of Manufactures or the production index published by the Federal Reserve Board can be employed. Data for investment and depreciation by industry are also available for the construction of appropriate indexes for the capital variable. The Bureau of Labor Statistics publishes a great deal of data on employment and work hours.

Cobb and Douglas performed their earliest study on U.S. manufacturing in the form of a time series regression for the years 1899–1922. Using the original version of their formula, they obtained the following result:

$$Q = 1.01 L^{0.75} K^{0.25}$$

Other studies used the same technique with similar results.

In 1937, David Durand suggested that the equation should not necessarily limit the results to constant returns to scale.[19] After Durand's article, it was accepted that the exponents in the equation no longer had to equal 1. Douglas corrected the original study and found that the coefficient of labor was reduced to about two-thirds, whereas capital's exponent rose to about one-third. But the sum of the two exponents still summed to about 1, and thus constant returns to scale appeared to prevail.[20]

At about the same time, cross-sectional analysis, rather than time series, came into use, and most of the studies done since then have utilized this technique. The observations were now individual industries in a particular year. Many other studies were conducted on data from the United States, Australia, Canada, and New Zealand. In a majority of these investigations, the sum of the exponents turned out to be very close to 1.

In another study, the author performed a cross-sectional study of 18 industries using data from the Census of Manufactures.[21] The observation units were individual states. Three independent variables were used:

1. Production worker hours
2. Nonproduction worker years
3. Gross book value of depreciable and depletable assets

The dependent variable, Q, was represented by the value added in each industry.

The results showed that the sums of the three exponents in the 18 industries ranged from about 0.95 to 1.11, indicating a span from decreasing to increasing returns. Tests of significance showed that in only 5 of the 18 industries was the sum of the coefficients significantly different from 1. Thus, again, in the majority of cases, constant returns to scale appeared to dominate.

[19]David Durand, "Some Thoughts on Marginal Productivity with Special Reference to Professor Douglas," *Journal of Political Economy*, 45, 6 (December 1937), pp. 740–58.
[20]The history of the Cobb-Douglas function and the major studies were summarized by Douglas himself in his article, "The Cobb-Douglas Production Function Once Again: Its History, Its Testing, and Some New Empirical Values," *Journal of Political Economy*, 84, 5 (October 1976), pp. 903–15.
[21]John R. Moroney, "Cobb-Douglas Production Functions and Returns to Scale in U.S. Manufacturing," *Western Economic Journal*, 6, 1 (December 1967), pp. 39–51.

The Importance of Production Functions in Managerial Decision Making

As stated in the introductory section of this chapter, the production function is an important part of the economic analysis of the firm because it serves as the foundation for the analysis of cost. You will see this in the next chapter. But for managers, an understanding of the basic concepts discussed in this chapter also provides a solid conceptual framework for decisions involving the allocation of a firm's resources both in the short run and in the long run. Another key management principle illustrated in the economic theory of production is planning, discussed in the following subsection.

Careful Planning Can Help a Firm to Use Its Resources in a Rational Manner

In our discussion of the short run, we stated that a firm is expected to have three stages of production. Stage I represents the underutilization of a firm's fixed inputs relative to its variable ones. Stage III represents an overutilization of its fixed inputs relative to its variable ones. Indeed, firms operating in this stage would find their total output *decreasing* as they increased their variable input. The only stage for a rational firm to be in is stage II. Assuming that this information is well known to managers, why would a firm find itself in stage I or III? The answer is, of course, that production levels do not depend on how much a company wants to produce, but on *how much its customers want to buy.*

Suppose we consider the short-run production function shown in Figure 7.9. As we can see, stage II applies to production levels between $Q_1 = 200$ and $Q_2 = 275$. If people want to buy less than 200 units or more than 275 units, for example, then in the short run the firm would be forced to operate in either stage I or stage III.

The information in Figure 7.9 implies that for a firm to avoid having to operate in either stage I or stage III, there must be careful planning regarding the amount of fixed inputs that will be used along with the variable ones. In business, this is often referred to as *capacity planning.* For example, if the firm anticipated that the demand for its product would be in the range of 200 to 275, then the capacity implied in Figure 7.9 is perfect for its needs. However, if a firm forecasts the demand to be greater than 275, it would have to consider increasing its capacity so that stage II would include the higher level of output. By the same token, if the firm forecasts a demand less than 200, it would have to consider decreasing its capacity. These alternative capacity levels are illustrated in Figure 7.10.

Good capacity planning requires two basic elements: (1) accurate forecasts of demand and (2) effective communication between the production and marketing functions (particularly in large organizations, where these functions are often handled by separate work groups). The first element is rather obvious but, as you have seen in chapters 5 and 6, not very easy to achieve. The second element may not be so obvious, especially for those who have not had work experience in large organizations. It is not uncommon for manufacturing people to proceed merrily with their

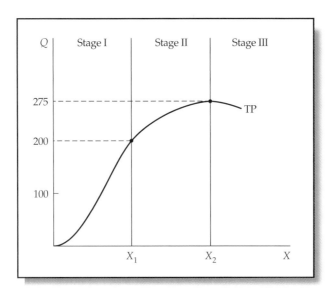

Figure 7.9
Production Stages and
Capacity Planning

production plans on a purely technical basis (i.e., from a strictly engineering point of view) without fully incorporating the marketing plans of those whose main responsibility is to sell the products. It is also quite possible for marketing people to try to sell as many units of the product as possible (as marketing people are supposed to do) without consulting the production people as to whether the firm has the capacity to meet the increase in demand. A full discussion of these problems of management and organization is beyond the scope of this book. However, they are mentioned to underscore the importance for managers of understanding production theory.

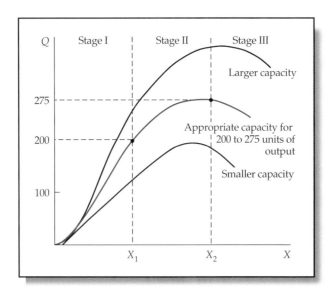

Figure 7.10
Adjusting Capacity Based on
Demand

CALL CENTERS: APPLYING THE PRODUCTION FUNCTION TO A SERVICE

Most production function examples involve manufacturing or agriculture. To illustrate how the concepts in this chapter can be used for a service activity, let us consider the example of a call center. A *call center* is a physical concentration of service representatives providing inbound or outbound communications with a company's customers. Perhaps you have seen pictures of call centers for QVC or LL Bean, in which hundreds of customer service representatives are situated in rows upon rows of cubicles in a large building that appears to be the size of a football field. The earliest call centers were run by the telephone companies themselves, particularly in cases where customer assistance was often required for domestic as well as international calling. As airline, hotel, and car rental businesses began to expand in the 1970s and 1980s, so too did their call center operations. During this time, there was also a tremendous expansion in the credit and charge card industry, and companies such as American Express and banks issuing MasterCard and Visa expanded their call center operations in order to communicate with their growing number of cardholders.

In the 1990s, the number and importance of call centers in the United States dramatically increased due to a combination of lower calling charges stemming from increasing competition among telecommunications companies, rapid growth and intense competition in the finance, retail, travel, and entertainment industries, and breakthroughs in the application of digital technology to voice, data, and video communications. Today, the call center has also become an integral part of multinational business activities.

For purposes of discussion, we will consider the production function of a call center handling inbound calls from customers inquiring about various aspects of their service.[22]

Output: The number of calls handled by customer representatives

In the service industry, the quality of a unit of service may be intrinsically tied to the length of time that it takes to "produce" the service (i.e., the amount of time a call representative spends with a customer). Nevertheless, we will handle this complexity by simply assuming that Q is equal to an incoming call that lasts an average of 300 seconds.

Input: *Labor:* The call center representative

In the United States, there are a number of cities that have established themselves as attractive locations for call centers because they have large pools of qualified labor that are available at wage rates relatively lower than the major metropolitan areas. High on the list of these cities are Sioux Falls, South Dakota, Jacksonville and Tampa, Florida, St. Louis, Missouri, and Salt Lake City, Utah (primarily because of the large concentration of people with foreign language skills).

---

[22]Interviews with representatives from MasterCard International and Bell Atlantic Corporation; "Top 10 Technologies: A New Millennium for the Card Industry," Faulkner and Gray, New York, 1998 pp. 1–5.

Sometime in the year 2000, industry experts believe that improvements in technology and reductions in costs will create the next generation of "Virtual Call Centers." Hardware and software for both information processing and distribution will enable customer service representatives to access information and provide customer support from any location to any customer at any time. To use industry jargon, the ability to provide call center support will be "channel and location–independent." This means that very shortly, if not already, companies will be able to draw on a global pool of labor to work as call representatives. (See also "International Applications: International Call Centers," following this section.)

Input: Capital: Hardware, software, and office facilities

Examples of types of operating systems used by call centers are Windows NT, 2000 and XP, products from vendors such as Novell, Sun, IBM, and HP, and various systems provided by Unisys. These operating systems can be combined with dumb or 3270 terminals or PC workstations. There are a number of emerging technologies and applications software of importance to call center activities, such as Voice Response Unit (VRU) and Automatic Call Distribution (ACD), which automate the switching that route calls to customer service representatives.

Recently, a new technological concept has emerged known as the "Intelligent Center," which shifts the focus of call center activities from answering inbound queries to selling products on both inbound and outbound calls. Key technologies for the Intelligent Center include Computer-Telephony Integration (CTI) and middleware. Imagine you are a typical caller inquiring about the balance on your loan at your bank. Before a representative answers the phone, you are asked to key in your account number. When a representative answers, a window pops up on his or her terminal screen showing your complete financial history. Based on the assessment of your financial condition, the representative may then tell you about the possibility of consolidating all your loans into a home equity loan or of considering the purchase of supplementary life insurance. Many more Internet and Intranet applications will soon be combined with conventional call center operations. So, for example, it will someday be possible for you to type up your application for life insurance and then e-mail it to the bank while talking to its call center representative.

Given these inputs and output, the call center's short-run production function and the three stages of production might be expressed as follows:

$$Q = f(X, Y)$$

where Q = number of 300-second calls
X = variable input (this includes customer services representatives and the complementary hardware such as PCs, desks, and software if site licenses are sold on a per-user basis)
Y = fixed input (this includes the call center building, hardware such as servers and telecommunications equipment, and software site licenses up to the designated maximum number of users)

Using this basic production function, it is possible to consider a number of applications of concepts. The following are offered as examples.

Three Stages of Production: Stage I could be a situation in which there is so much fixed capacity relative to number of variable inputs that many representatives sit around idle, waiting for calls to come in. Stage II could be a situation in which representatives are constantly occupied and callers are connected to representatives immediately after the call is answered or are kept waiting no more than a certain amount of time (e.g., three minutes). If callers are kept waiting for longer than three minutes, the call center manager might consider adding more call center representatives. Stage III could be a situation in which callers begin to experience a busy signal on a more frequent basis or call representatives may begin to experience a slower computer response or more frequent computer "down times." These are all technical manifestations of overloaded computer processing power or transmission capacity (i.e., insufficient bandwidth).

Input Combinations: There are a number of input combinations that could be considered in the operation of a call center. To begin with, there is the location trade-off in which the productivity of call center representatives in two or more locations might be considered relative to the cost of each representative (including wages, training costs, costs associated with turnover rates, etc.). If a global search for the best location is involved, then the further consideration of language skills would have to be made.

Another trade-off involves capital and labor. The cost of upgrading the hardware and software used by each representative could be measured against the number of representatives utilized in the call center. For example, the installation of an automated call distribution system could result in the reduction in the number of representatives working at any time in the center.

Returns to Scale: One can well imagine that a call center would be amenable to increasing returns to scale. This is evidenced by the number of smaller companies who outsource their operations to companies that specialize in call center operations. These "third-party" vendors are able to provide call center services at a lower cost to the company mainly because their size enables them to take advantage of increasing returns to scale.

INTERNATIONAL APPLICATION: INTERNATIONAL CALL CENTERS

 Technology and falling costs of telecommunications have made it economically feasible for call centers to be located anywhere in the world. For example, call center operations have helped to bolster the sagging economy of a small town in Sweden. Over the past several decades, it had been increasingly difficult for this town to keep its young people from leaving in search of gainful employment in urban centers such as Stockholm. But several years ago a sort of "cottage industry" of call centers was established that has provided young people with a chance to earn a decent living without having to move away.[23]

---

[23]Warren Hoge, "Arvidsjaur Journal: Sweden's Frozen North Can Be Balmy for Business," *New York Times,* August 21, 1998.

An article in the *Financial Times* discusses how Salt Lake City has become an attractive site for global call centers. This is because of the high concentration of people in the work force who speak a foreign language, having learned the language while serving their two years of missionary work for the Mormon Church in different parts of the world. But quite often, global call center representatives need to know more than just a foreign language. According to the article, the American representatives who handled the overflow of calls going to a center in the United Kingdom had to be trained in "pounds and pence, spelling differences and place names, not to mention the British sense of humor."[24]

Within recent years, call center operations for the United States and Great Britain have been shifting to India. According to NASSCOM, a technology industry trade group in India, international call center operations will generate $8 billion in revenue by 2008. This growth in call center operations in India parallels the amazing growth in outsourcing activities in many IT (information technologies) activities, particularly software development. One interesting comparison of India's operations with those in Salt Lake City pertains to the accents of the call center operators. In Salt Lake City, American operators were taught to be familiar with the different regional accents in the UK. In India, a number of call center operators go through training in "accent reduction" or are taught to speak with American as well as British regional accents. In addition, they are provided with videos of popular television shows such as "Baywatch" and "Friends" in order to be familiar with American culture.[25]

The Solution

To: Robert Burns, CEO
          Nicole Goodman, SVP of Marketing
          Jim Hartwell, SVP of Manufacturing
From: Christopher Lim, Production Manager
Re: The Economic Feasibility of Packaging in Glass
          Bottles and Key Related Issues

Before beginning plans to bottle and distribute "Waterpure," I feel that I must bring up certain production issues that I was not able to cover at our meeting last week. I have had considerable experience in glass packaging from my previous job as head of bottling for our Latin American beverage division. Glass is a more expensive material than either plastic or aluminum. With the latest slump in aluminum prices and technology developments in plastic, the price differential is widening even further. The reason why glass is so expensive is that it is much heavier and

(Continued)

---

[24]Alan Cane, "Telephone Contact with Customers is Ripe for Outsourcing," *The Financial Times*, September 13, 1996.
[25]"U.S. Dials 1-800-Bangalore; Toll-Free Inquiries Are Increasingly Answered in India," *The Washington Post*, August 5, 2001.

more fragile than these other materials. This causes higher production costs because (1) there are more back injuries to employees (thereby increasing our medical insurance premiums), (2) there is a need for special handling care (e.g., bottle carriers, protective cardboard), (3) breakage occurs, and (4) the greater weight increases the cost of fuel used in transportation.

We use a considerable amount of glass bottles in emerging market countries because the total cost differential between glass and aluminum or plastic is not as great in these countries. For example, because of lower labor costs in South America, we can better afford to use the more labor-intensive process of handling the heavy glass bottles. And the machinery to blow out the plastic pellets into 1- and 2-liter bottles is a lot more expensive in these countries than here in the United States. Furthermore, people in emerging market countries seem to like the idea of receiving their deposit back when returning glass bottles, however small the amount might seem to you to be.

However, a real issue that I think we should address even before devising a packaging, production, and distribution plan is the source of our bottled water. As you know, to be considered "spring water," bottled water must actually come from a spring. The industry has grown so rapidly over the past few years that companies are having a harder time finding good sources of spring water. I have heard of bottled water companies hiring geologists to look for water just as oil companies hire them to look for new sources of oil. Therefore, we should consider the cost of "manufacturing" the product itself—water—before even considering the cost of packaging. I eagerly await your response to the issues raised in this memo.

SUMMARY

The topics in this chapter represent the foundation for the economic analysis of supply. After all, people may be very willing to purchase a firm's product at a certain price, but will the firm be willing to supply the product at this price? The answer to this question begins with the relationship between the firm's inputs and the resulting output, that is, the firm's production function. In the short run, where at least one of the firm's inputs is fixed, we have learned that the firm is subject to the law of diminishing returns and the three stages of production. This means that as additional inputs are added to the fixed input, at some point the additional output (i.e., marginal product) resulting from the additional input will start to diminish. Once this level of production is exceeded, the output per unit of variable input (i.e., average product) will reach a maximum and then start to diminish. The point of maximum average product marks the end of stage I and the beginning of stage II, the stage in which the rational firm should be operating. The use of still more units of variable inputs will eventually cause the total output to decline (i.e., cause MP to assume negative values). By assigning monetary values to both the variable input and the output along with the use of marginal analysis, we were able to determine precisely where in stage II the firm should be operating. A similar analysis can be used to derive the conditions for the optimal use of more than one input. (See Appendix 7B.)

The long-run function, in which a firm is able to vary all of its inputs, was also considered in this chapter. When a firm is able to vary its entire scale of production, it may experience varying returns to scale. That is, the increase in output may be proportional, less than proportional, or greater than proportional to the increase in all of its inputs.

Most studies of production functions have used an exponential expression that results in a monotonically increasing output as inputs are added. This model was introduced by Cobb and Douglas in the 1920s. The original studies utilized the time series method of analysis, but researchers soon switched to cross-sectional regression, which they found more useful. The Cobb-Douglas function permits the investigation of both marginal product in short-run situations (with the presence of a fixed factor) and returns to scale in the long run. It is difficult to summarize the large number of studies conducted over the years, but the results generally indicate that constant returns to scale are the rule in manufacturing industries in the United States as well as in other countries.

In the next chapter, we present an analysis of a firm's cost function. We will then see how a solid background in the economic analysis of production will provide a better understanding of the cost structure of a firm, in both the short and the long runs.

IMPORTANT CONCEPTS (Items with * are discussed in Appendix 7A or 7B)

Average product (AP): The total product divided by the number of units of a particular input employed by the firm. (p. 273)

Cobb-Douglas production function: A power function in which total quantity produced is the result of the product of inputs raised to some power (e.g., $Q = aL^bK^c$). (p. 291)

Inputs: The resources used in the production process. Examples in economic analysis generally involve the inputs *capital* (representing the fixed input) and *labor* (representing the variable input). Other terms used in reference to these resources are *factors* and *factors of production.* (p. 271)

*** Isocost:** A line representing different combinations of two inputs that a firm can purchase with the same amount of money. In production analysis, the isocost indicates a firm's budget constraint. (p. 320)

*** Isoquant:** A curve representing different combinations of two inputs that produce the same level of output. (p. 314)

Law of diminishing returns: A law stating that as additional units of a variable input are added to a fixed input, at some point the additional output (i.e., the marginal product) will start to diminish. Because at least one input is required to be fixed for this law to take effect, this law is considered a short-run phenomenon. (p. 275)

Long-run production function: The maximum quantity of a good or service that can be produced by a set of inputs, assuming that the firm is free to vary the amount of *all* inputs being used. (p. 272)

Marginal labor cost (MLC): The additional cost to the firm of using an additional unit of labor. This is also referred to as *marginal factor cost* (MFC) or *marginal resource cost* (MRC). Labor is used in this term because it is the most commonly used variable input in the economic analysis of production. (p. 282)

Marginal product (MP): The change in output resulting from a unit change in one of the firm's variable inputs. (p. 273)

*Marginal rate of technical substitution (MRTS): Given two inputs X and Y, the marginal rate of technical substitution of X for Y represents the reduction in Y relative to the amount of X that a firm must add to replace Y to maintain the same amount of output. Mathematically speaking, it is represented by the slope of some given isoquant or $\Delta Y/\Delta X$ ($\delta y/\delta x$ for continuous isoquants). (p. 316)

Marginal revenue product (MRP): The additional amount of revenue resulting from the use of an additional unit of a variable input. It can be calculated by taking an input's marginal product and multiplying it by the market price of the product. For example, given some input i, that $MRP_i = MP_i \times P$. (p. 282)

MRP = MLC rule: A rule that guides a firm in its decision about how many units of a variable input it should use relative to its fixed input. The rule states that the firm should employ a particular input up to the point at which the revenue contribution of the additional input is equal to the cost incurred by the firm to employ this particular input. In the case of more than one input, this condition applies separately for every input used by the firm. (p. 283)

Power function: A mathematical function of the form $Y = X^n$, where n is a fixed number and X takes positive values continuously. (p. 290)

Production function: The maximum quantity of a good or service that can be produced by a set of inputs. Production functions are divided into two types: short run and long run. (p. 271)

Returns to scale: The increase in output that results from an increase in all of a firm's inputs by some proportion. If the output increases by a *greater* proportion than the increase in inputs, the firm is experiencing increasing returns to scale. If the output increases by the *same* proportion as the inputs, the firm is experiencing constant returns to scale. Finally, if the output increases by a *smaller* proportion than the increase in inputs, the firm is experiencing decreasing returns to scale. (p. 285)

Short-run production functions: The maximum quantity of a good or service that can be produced by a set of inputs, assuming that the amount of *at least one* of the inputs used remains unchanged as output varies. (p. 272)

Stages of production: In a short-run production function, there are three stages of production. Stage I starts at zero and ends at the point where the firm has reached the maximum level of *average* product. Stage II continues from this point on to the point at which the firm has reached the maximum level of *total* product. Stage III continues from this point on. Economic theory suggests that the rational firm will try to produce in the short run in stage II. In stage I the firm would be underutilizing its fixed inputs, and in stage III it would be overutilizing its fixed inputs. (p. 279)

Total product (TP): The firm's output for a given level of input usage, also referred to as *quantity*, or simply Q. (p. 273)

QUESTIONS

1. Explain the difference between a short-run and long-run production function. Cite one example of this difference in a business situation.

2. Define the *law of diminishing returns*. Why is this law considered a short-run phenomenon?

3. What are the key points in a short-run production function that delineate the three stages of production? Explain the relationship between the law of diminishing returns and the three stages of production.

4. Explain why a firm's adherence to the MRP = MLC rule enables it to find the optimal number of units of a variable input to use in the short-run production process.

5. Define returns to scale. Why is this considered a long-run phenomenon?

6. According to the rule for optimal input usage, a firm should hire a person as long as her marginal revenue product is greater than her marginal cost to the company. It is well known that many compa-

nies have management training programs in which new trainees are paid relatively high starting salaries and are not expected to make substantial contributions to the company until after the program is over (programs may run between 6 to 18 months). In offering such training programs, is a company violating the optimality rule? Explain.

7. Explain the relationship between marginal product and average product. Why can we expect marginal product to equal average product at average product's maximum point?

8. Cite and discuss possible reasons a firm may actually find itself operating in stage I or stage III of the short-run production function.

9. Discuss the problems of measuring productivity in actual work situations. How might productivity be measured for each of the following industries?
    a. Education (e.g., elementary and secondary education, higher education—undergraduate and graduate)
    b. Government (e.g., the Social Security Office, the Internal Revenue Service)
    c. Manufacturing (e.g., soap and toothpaste, computers, heavy machinery)
    d. Finance and insurance (e.g., banks, insurance companies, brokerage houses)

10. For those of you with current or previous work experience, how is (was) productivity measured in your organization?

11. What are the two statistical methods most frequently used to estimate production functions? What are the advantages and disadvantages of each of these two methods?

12. Design a study of a production function for a steel mill and another one for a call center. Which variables would you use, and what statistical method would you select for each function? In general, compare and contrast the production function for a product and one for a service.

Refer to Appendix 7A and 7B to help you answer questions 13–16.

13. What are the properties of the Cobb-Douglas function $Q = aL^bK^{1-b}$. What conceptual change occurs when the equation is changed to $Q = aL^bK^c$?

14. In a power function $Q = aV^b$, how can you tell whether diminishing marginal returns are present?

15. When a Cobb-Douglas function with at least two inputs shows the existence of constant returns to scale, it implies that the marginal product of each input is diminishing. True or false? Explain.

16. Write a production function equation that expresses the existence of diminishing marginal returns. How will this equation differ from one that shows both increasing and decreasing marginal returns?

PROBLEMS

1. Indicate whether each of the following statements is true or false. Explain why.
    a. When the law of diminishing returns takes effect, a firm's average product will start to decrease.
    b. Decreasing returns to scale occurs when a firm has to increase all of its inputs at an increasing rate in order to maintain a constant rate of increase in its output.
    c. A linear short-run production function implies that the law of diminishing returns does not take effect over the range of output being considered.
    d. Stage I of the production process ends at the point where the law of diminishing returns occurs.

2. The Oceanic Pacific fleet has just decided to use a pole-and-line method of fishing instead of gill netting to catch tuna. The latter method involves the use of

miles of nets strung out across the ocean and therefore entraps other sea crea-
tures besides tuna (e.g., porpoises and sea turtles). Concern for endangered
species was one reason for this decision, but perhaps more important was the
fact that the major tuna canneries in the United States will no longer accept tuna
caught by gill netting.

Oceanic Pacific decided to conduct a series of experiments to determine the
amount of tuna that could be caught with different crew sizes. The results of
these experiments follow.

NUMBER OF FISHERMEN	DAILY TUNA CATCH (LB)
0	0
1	50
2	110
3	300
4	450
5	590
6	665
7	700
8	725
9	710

a. Determine the point at which diminishing returns occurs.
b. Indicate the points that delineate the three stages of production.
c. Suppose the market price of tuna is $3.50/pound. How many fishermen
   should the company use if the daily wage rate is $100?
d. Suppose a glut in the market for tuna causes the price to fall to $2.75/pound.
   What effect would this have on the number of fishermen used per boat?
   Suppose the price rose to $5.00/pound. What effect would this have on its
   hiring decision?
e. Suppose the firm realizes that to keep up with the demand for tuna caught
   by the more humane pole-and-line method of fishing, each of its boats must
   catch at least 1,000 pounds of fish per day. Given the preceding data, what
   should it consider doing? Explain.

3. A firm has the following short-run production function:

$$Q = 50L + 6L^2 - 0.5L^3$$

where Q = Quantity of output per week
      L = Labor (number of workers)

a. When does the law of diminishing returns take effect?
b. Calculate the range of values for labor over which stages I, II, and III occur.
c. Assume each worker is paid $10 per hour and works a 40-hour week. How
   many workers should the firm hire if the price of the output is $10? Suppose
   the price of the output falls to $7.50. What do you think would be the short-
   run impact on the firm's production? The long-run impact?

4. The owner of a small car-rental service is trying to decide on the appropriate
   numbers of vehicles and mechanics to use in the business for the current level of
   operations. He recognizes that his choice represents a trade-off between the two

resources. His past experience indicates that this trade-off is as follows **(see Appendix 7A for help in answering this question):**

VEHICLES	MECHANICS
100	2.5 (includes one part-timer)
70	5
50	10
40	15
35	25
32	35

a. Assume the annual (leasing) cost per vehicle is $6,000 and the annual salary per mechanic is $25,000. What combination of vehicles and mechanics should he employ?

b. Illustrate this problem with the use of an isoquant/isocost diagram. Indicate graphically the optimal combination of resources.

5. An American company that sells consumer electronics products has manufacturing facilities in Mexico, Taiwan, and Canada. The average hourly wage, output, and annual overhead cost for each site are as follows:

	MEXICO	TAIWAN	CANADA
Hourly wage rate	$1.50	$3.00	$6.00
Output per person	10	18	20
Fixed overhead cost	$150,000	$90,000	$110,000

a. Given these figures, is the firm currently allocating its production resources optimally? If not, what should it do? (Consider output per person as a proxy for marginal product.)

b. Suppose the firm wants to consolidate all of its manufacturing into one facility. Where should it locate? Explain.

6. The owner of a car wash is trying to decide on the number of people to employ based on the following short-run production function:

$$Q = 6L - 0.5L^2$$

where Q = Number of car washes per hour
L = Number of workers

a. Generate a schedule showing total product, average product, and marginal product. Plot this schedule on a graph.

b. Suppose the price of a basic car wash (no undercoating, no wax treatment, etc.) in his area of business is $5. How many people should he hire if he pays each worker $6/hour?

c. Suppose he considers hiring students on a part-time basis for $4/hour. Do you think he should hire more workers at this lower rate? Explain.

7. The Noble Widget Corporation produces just one product, widgets. The company's new economist has calculated a short-run production function as follows:

$$Q = 7V + 0.6V^2 - 0.1V^3$$

where Q is the number of widgets produced per day and V is the number of production workers working an eight-hour day.

a. Develop a production schedule with V equaling 1 to 10.
b. Calculate average and marginal products.
c. Draw a graph.

8. Suppose Noble's production function (see problem 7) is as follows:

$$Q = 7V - 0.5V^2$$

where Q is the number of widgets produced per day and V is the number of production workers working an eight-hour day.
   a. Develop a production schedule with V equaling 1 to 10.
   b. Calculate average and marginal products.
   c. Draw a graph.
   d. Discuss the difference between the form of the production function in this problem and the form in problem 7. Discuss, among other things, the implications for the three stages of production.

9. The International Calculator Company of China produces hand-held calculators in its plant. It tries to keep the number of workers in the plant constant, so that the only variable factor that can be measured is materials. Over the last seven monthly periods, the data for materials and quantity produced were the following:

MATERIALS	QUANTITY
70	450
60	430
80	460
95	490
77	465
100	550
85	490

   a. Calculate a Cobb-Douglas production function of the form $Q = aM^b$.
   b. Discuss the important properties of your results.
   c. What is the marginal product of materials?

10. The Brady Corporation has 11 plants located around the world. In a recent year, the data for each plant gave the number of labor hours (in thousands), capital (total net plant assets, in millions), and total quantity produced:

CAPITAL	LABOR	QUANTITY
30	250	245
34	270	240
44	300	300
50	320	320
70	350	390
76	400	440
84	440	520
86	440	520
104	450	580
110	460	600
116	460	600

The plants all operate at a similar level of technology, so that a production function can be derived from the data.

    a. Use a Cobb-Douglas production function to calculate a regression, and discuss the important characteristics of your results, such as the form of the equation, R^2, and the statistical significance of the coefficients.

    b. Calculate the estimated production for each plant.

    c. Does the result indicate constant, decreasing, or increasing returns to scale?

    d. What are the elasticities of production of labor and of capital? What is the meaning of the elasticities?

    e. Is the marginal product of labor decreasing? (See Appendix 7B to answer this question.)

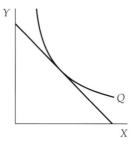

Refer to Appendix 7A and 7B for help in answering problems 11–15.

11. Show what will happen to the following diagram as a result of the changes listed.

    a. The firm's budget increases.

    b. The price of Y decreases.

    c. The price of X decreases.

    d. Y becomes more expensive, and X becomes less expensive.

    e. Technology makes the Y input more productive.

    f. Technology increases the productivity of both inputs by the same proportion.

12. Suppose you are given the following production function:

$$Q = 100K^{0.5}L^{0.5}$$

    a. Use this function to generate the data for the following table:

K									
8									
7									
6									
5									
4									
3									
2									
1									
0	1	2	3	4	5	6	7	8	L

    b. Identify as many isoquants as you can.

    c. Comment on the returns to scale exhibited in this figure. (*Suggestion:* Start by assuming one unit of L and one unit of K are used. Then systematically increase both inputs by some given proportion.)

13. Following are different algebraic expressions of the production function. Decide whether each one has constant, increasing, or decreasing returns to scale.
   a. $Q = 75L^{0.25}K^{0.75}$
   b. $Q = 75A^{0.15}B^{0.40}C^{0.45}$
   c. $Q = 75L^{0.60}K^{0.70}$
   d. $Q = 100 + 50L + 50K$
   e. $Q = 50L + 50K + 50LK$
   f. $Q = 50L^2 + 50K^2$
   g. Based on the answers for the preceding equations, can you make any generalizations about the functional form of a production equation, the relative magnitudes of the coefficients, and the nature of the returns to scale? Explain.

14. Use the production matrix presented to answer the following questions.

Y	8	31	67	101	133	161	184	202	213
	7	30	62	93	122	147	168	184	193
	6	27	54	82	108	130	149	168	163
	5	23	45	69	91	108	126	137	142
	4	17	34	54	72	89	101	108	111
	3	12	25	38	54	65	74	79	79
	2	6	14	24	33	44	54	47	43
	1	3	7	11	17	27	19	16	8
		1	2	3	4	5	6	7	8	X

   a. Determine the returns to scale for this matrix. (Start with one unit of X and one unit of Y.)
   b. Suppose the firm has a budget of $100 and that the price of Y is $20 and the price of X is $10. What is the optimal combination of inputs X and Y for this firm?
   c. Suppose the prices of Y and X are now $10 and $20, respectively. What effect will this have on the firm's optimal input combination?
   d. Illustrate the answers to the preceding questions with the use of an isoquant/isocost diagram.

15. The economist for the ABC Truck Manufacturing Corporation has calculated a production function for the manufacture of their medium-size trucks as follows:

$$Q = 1.3L^{0.75}K^{0.3}$$

where Q is number of trucks produced per week, L is number of labor hours per day, and K is the daily usage of capital investment.
   a. Does the equation exhibit increasing, constant, or decreasing returns to scale? Why?
   b. How many trucks will be produced per week with the following amounts of labor and capital?

LABOR	CAPITAL
100	50
120	60
150	75
200	100
300	150

c. If capital and labor both are increased by 10 percent, what will be the percentage increase in quantity produced?

d. Assume that only labor increases by 10 percent. What will be the percentage increase in production? What does this result imply about marginal product?

e. Assume that only capital increases by 10 percent. What will be the percentage increase in production?

f. How would your answers change if the production function were $Q = 1.3L^{0.7}K^{0.3}$ instead? What are the implications of this production function?

Appendix 7A

The Multiple-Input Case

In this appendix, we examine in greater detail the more general case in which a firm seeks the optimal combination of inputs, rather than simply the optimal level of one particular input. For explanatory purposes, we will address the problem of determining the optimal combination of inputs using the two-input case. Mathematically, there is no problem in considering any number of inputs, but we will use two inputs for ease of graphical illustration. Nonetheless, it should be noted that the decision rule for determining the optimal combination of inputs is the same whether two inputs or more than two are used in the production process.

From the standpoint of economic theory, the two-input case can be considered either a short-run or a long-run analysis, depending on what assumption is made about the nature of the firm's inputs. If we assume that the firm has only two inputs (or, more realistically, that all of its inputs can be divided into two basic categories), then the two-input case must be considered a long-run analysis because, in effect, all of the firm's inputs are allowed to vary. However, if the firm is assumed to have other inputs that are being held constant while the two inputs are being evaluated, then the analysis must be considered short run. Readers should be able to discern from the context of our discussion which case applies for our examples.

To illustrate the two-input case, we will use the data in Table 7.1, reproduced as Table 7A.1. Suppose the firm produces 52 units of output ($Q = 52$). According to the table, the firm can employ the following combinations of inputs Y and X respectively: 6 and 2, 4 and 3, 3 and 4, 2 and 6, and 2 and 8. Together, they form the isoquant shown

Table 7A.1
Representative Production Table Illustrating Isoquants

UNITS OF Y EMPLOYED				OUTPUT QUANTITY (Q)				
8	37	60	83	96	107	117	127	128
7	42	64	78	90	101	110	119	120
6	37	52	64	73	82	90	97	104
5	31	47	58	67	75	82	89	95
4	24	39	52	60	67	73	79	85
3	17	29	41	52	58	64	69	73
2	8	18	29	39	47	52	56	52
1	4	8	14	20	27	24	21	17
	1	2	3	4	5	6	7	8
				UNITS OF X EMPLOYED				

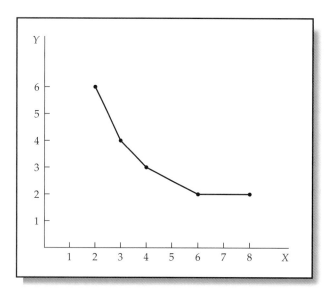

Figure 7A.1
Graph of Isoquant $Q = 52$

in Table 7A.1. An **isoquant** is a curve representing the various combinations of two inputs that produce the same amount of output. Notice that isoquants for $Q = 29$ and $Q = 73$ are also shown in Table 7A.1. The isoquant for $Q = 52$ is plotted in Figure 7A.1.

A continuous production function, in which inputs are assumed to be perfectly divisible, is illustrated in Figure 7A.2. Here the isoquant appears as a smoothed out version of that depicted in Figure 7A.1. Notice that both the discrete and continuous isoquants are downward sloping and convex to the origin.

The latter characteristic means that the slope of the isoquant becomes less steep as one moves downward and to the right. These characteristics pertain to the degree to which the two inputs can be substituted for one another.

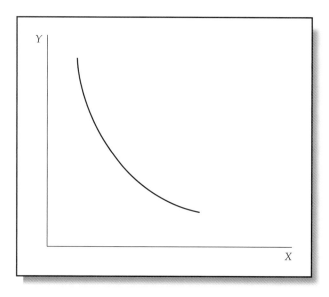

Figure 7A.2
Isoquant for Continuous
Production Function

SUBSTITUTING INPUT FACTORS

The degree of substitutability of two inputs is a measure of the ease with which one input can be used in place of the other in producing a given amount of output. To explain this further, let us use the example of the making of soft drinks. Consider the ingredients listed on the label of a typical soft drink:

> Carbonated water, sugar and/or corn syrup, citric acid, natural flavoring, sodium benzoate as a preservative, and caramel coloring.

Notice that the sweetening component of the recipe is listed as "sugar and/or corn syrup." This implies that the two ingredients are *perfect substitutes* for each other. The linear isoquant shown in Figure 7A.3a depicts the perfect substitutability between the two ingredients. The hypothetical numbers on the X- and Y-axes serve to caution you not to assume that perfect substitutability means the two inputs must be substitutable at a ratio of 1 to 1. In this illustration, the substitution ratio is 2 to 1. That is, 2 grams of sugar can always be substituted for 1 gram of corn syrup, no matter how much sugar or corn syrup is used.

If we divide a soft drink into two components, "natural flavoring" and "all other ingredients," we can illustrate the relationship between these two inputs with the isoquant shown in Figure 7A.3b. Presumably, what gives the soft drink its special flavor is the unique ratio of the flavoring to the rest of the components. The hypothetical numbers in Figure 7A.3b indicate that adding one more part of flavoring without increasing the other contents by five parts will not yield more output. Thus, we see that natural flavoring and the other ingredients are what economists term *perfect complements* to each other, because they must always be used together in some fixed proportion (i.e., one part of flavoring and five parts of the other ingredients).

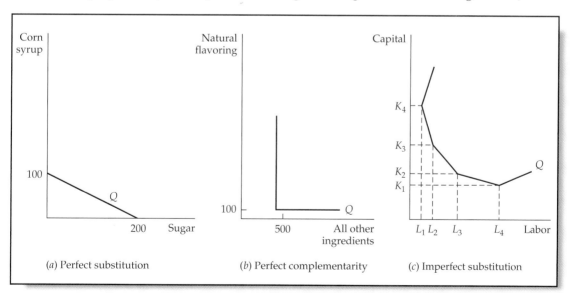

Figure 7A.3
Substitutability of Two Inputs in a Production Function

Between the extremes of perfect substitutability and perfect complementarity lies the case illustrated in Figure 7A.3c. Here labor and capital are *imperfect substitutes* for each other. That is, one can be substituted for the other, but only up to a limit. (As shown in the figure, any addition of labor beyond L_4 units requires more capital rather than less to maintain the level of output at Q.) Furthermore, as more of one input is used in place of the other, it becomes increasingly difficult to substitute. As can be seen in Figure 7A.3c, when the firm is employing L_1 units of labor and K_4 units of capital, it can substitute a relatively small amount of labor for capital and still maintain the same level of output. However, when it is using L_2 units of labor and K_3 units of capital, it must substitute a larger amount of labor to maintain the same level of output. More will be said about imperfect substitution in the next section.

In terms of selecting the optimal combination of inputs, it is clear that the case of imperfect substitutability represents the greatest challenge to the firm. Perfectly complementary inputs must be used together in some fixed proportion. The case of perfectly substitutable inputs is equally trivial. If one input can always be substituted in some fixed amount for another (no matter how much of each input is being used), the only determinant of the optimal combination is input price.

In the case of imperfectly substitutable inputs, the optimal combination depends both on the degree of substitutability and on their relative prices. For example, suppose labor costs much less than capital. Does this automatically mean that the firm should use more labor relative to capital, (i.e., a labor-intensive production process)? No, because the relative productivities of the two inputs also have to be considered. If capital is much more productive than labor, it will benefit a firm to use more capital relative to labor if the difference in productivity more than compensates for the difference in cost.

Before we explain how economists determine the optimal combination of two inputs that are imperfect substitutes, we should explain how the degree of imperfection is measured. The measurement itself is called the **marginal rate of technical substitution (MRTS).** We will consider an example in which we gradually substitute more of the X input for the Y input. Algebraically, the marginal rate of technical substitution of X for Y can be expressed as:

$$\text{MRTS } (X \text{ for } Y) = \frac{\Delta Y}{\Delta X}$$

Notice that the numerator shows the amount of Y that is removed from the production process, and the denominator indicates the amount of X needed to substitute for Y to maintain the same amount of output. Graphically, the MRTS can be represented by moving downward and to the right along any isoquant (Figure 7A.4). Indeed, if we look back at the algebraic expression of MRTS (X for Y), we see that it is the measure of the slope of the isoquant.

To see exactly how MRTS is measured along the isoquant, let us use the discrete case illustrated in Table 7A.1. The different input combinations that can be used to produce 52 units of output are summarized in Table 7A.2. The changes in Y and X as one moves from combination A to E are shown in Figure 7A.5. Moving from combination A to E, we measure the marginal rate of substitution of X for Y as follows:

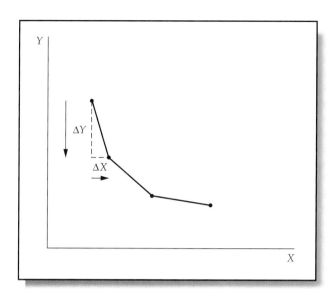

Figure 7A.4
MRTS (*X* for *Y*)

MOVEMENT	MRTS $(X \text{ FOR } Y) = \dfrac{\Delta Y}{\Delta X}$
A to B	$\dfrac{-2}{1}$
B to C	$\dfrac{-1}{1}$
C to D	$\dfrac{-1}{2}$
D to E	$\dfrac{0}{2}$

Notice that because the isoquant is downward sloping, $\Delta Y/\Delta X$, or the MRTS, will always have a negative value. However, in discussing the economic significance of MRTS, it is easier to treat it as a positive value. Therefore, let us for the moment simply drop the negative sign. Thus, for example, the MRTS between A and B becomes: MRTS = 2/1. Between B and C and between C and D, the MRTS values are 1 and 1/2, respectively. Expressed as an absolute value, MRTS can be clearly seen to

Table 7A.2
Input Combinations
for Isoquant $Q = 52$

COMBINATION	Y	X
A	6	2
B	4	3
C	3	4
D	2	6
E	2	8

Chapter 7 **The Theory and Estimation of Production** 317

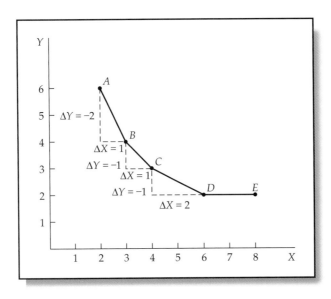

Figure 7A.5
Measuring MRTS along an
Isoquant

diminish as we move from combination A to combination E. Economists refer to this phenomenon as the *law of diminishing marginal rate of technical substitution*. As you might expect, this relates to the law of diminishing returns.

When we move from A to B, we substitute one unit of X for two units of Y. In other words, the loss in output resulting from the use of two fewer units of Y can be made up for by adding one unit of X. When we move from B to C, the loss in output resulting from the use of one fewer unit of Y must be made up for by adding one unit of X. From C to D we see that the loss in output resulting from the use of one fewer unit of Y must be made up for by adding two units of X. Finally, when we move from D to E, we find that rather than substituting X for Y, we must add more units of X to maintain the output level at 52.

Apparently, as we move from A to D, increasingly more X must be added relative to the amount of Y taken out of the production process to maintain the same amount of output. We started out by having to add only one unit of X to replace two units of Y and ended up having to add two units of X to replace one unit of Y. In other words, as more X is used relative to Y in the production process, the productivity of X diminishes relative to Y. This is a result of none other than the law of diminishing returns. Recall that this law states that as additional units of a variable factor are added to a fixed factor, at some point the additional output starts to diminish. If this holds true when one of the inputs is fixed, it must certainly hold when this same input is reduced.

To understand fully why increasingly more of input X is needed to compensate for the loss of a given amount of input Y to maintain the same output, we need to incorporate the concept of marginal product into our analysis. Looking back at Table 7.1 (reproduced as Table 7A.3 for your convenience), we observe that the movement from A to B actually involves two distinct steps. First, input Y is reduced by 2 units (from 6 to 4), resulting in a reduction in output by 13 units (from 52 to 39). This is indicated by the downward-pointing arrow in Table 7A.3. Next input X is added to

Table 7A.3
Representative Production Table

UNITS OF Y EMPLOYED			OUTPUT QUANTITY (Q)					
8	37	60	83	96	107	117	127	128
7	42	64	78	90	101	110	119	120
6	37	52	64	73	82	90	97	104
5	31	47	58	67	75	82	89	95
4	24	39	52	60	67	73	79	85
3	17	29	41	52	58	64	69	73
2	8	18	29	39	47	52	56	52
1	4	8	14	20	27	24	21	17
	1	2	3	4	5	6	7	8

UNITS OF X EMPLOYED

the production process to compensate for the reduction in Y. As can be seen in the table, an additional unit of X is required to restore the output to its original level of 52. This is indicated by the right-pointing arrow in the table.

Recall from an earlier discussion that the marginal product is defined as the change in output relative to the change in some given input. In this case, the movement from A to B in two separate steps reveals that the marginal product of input Y is

$$\frac{\Delta Q}{\Delta X} = \frac{-13}{-2} = 6.5$$

The marginal product of input X is

$$\frac{\Delta Q}{\Delta X} = \frac{13}{1} = 13$$

Proceeding next to combination C and then on to D using the same two-step process gives us the following ratios of the marginal products of X and Y: between B and C, $MP_X/MP_Y = 1$; between C and D, $MP_X/MP_Y = 1/2$.

In reviewing the ratios of the marginal products of X and Y along the isoquant $Q = 52$, you probably have spotted a very important link between the MRTS, the slope of the isoquant, and these ratios. Indeed, they are all equal. More specifically,

$$MRTS = \frac{\Delta Y}{\Delta X} = \frac{MP_X}{MP_Y} \qquad \text{(7A.1)}$$

This equation is illustrated in Table 7A.4.

Because Equation (7A.1) will play an important part in a later section of this appendix, let us briefly explain its derivation. Consider once again the movement along an isoquant between two given points. As illustrated using specific numbers in

Table 7A.4
MP_X/MP_Y in Relation to MRTS (X for Y)

Combination	Q	Y	MP_X	X	MP_Y	MRTS (X FOR Y)	MP_X/MP_Y
A	52	6		2			
B	52	4	13	3	6.5	2	2
C	52	3	11	4	11	1	1
D	52	2	6.5	6	13	1/2	1/2

the previous pages, this movement involves two distinct steps: the reduction in one input (e.g., input Y) and the increase in the other input (e.g., input X). The decrease in the output resulting from a decrease in input Y can be stated as

$$-MP_Y \times \Delta Y$$

The increase in output resulting from an increase in input X can be stated as

$$MP_X \times \Delta X$$

Along the isoquant, the output level must be maintained at a constant level. Thus,

$$\frac{MP_Y}{\Delta Y} = \frac{MP_X}{\Delta X}$$

Rearranging the terms in this equation and remembering that MRTS $= \Delta Y/\Delta X$ gives us

$$MRTS = \frac{\Delta Y}{\Delta X} = \frac{MP_X}{MP_Y}$$

THE OPTIMAL COMBINATION OF MULTIPLE INPUTS

Earlier we stated that the determination of the optimal combination of imperfectly substitutable inputs depends on both their relative prices and on the degree to which they can be substituted for one another. In the previous section, you learned that the degree to which one input can be substituted for another is actually a reflection of the relationship between their marginal products. Therefore, the optimal combination of inputs depends on the relationship between the inputs' relative marginal products and their relative prices. In the case of two inputs, we can state this relationship mathematically as

$$\frac{MP_X}{MP_Y} = \frac{P_X}{P_Y} \tag{7A.2}$$

To demonstrate this relationship we will use **isocost** curves and combine them with the isoquant curves developed in the previous section. First we will rearrange Equation (7A.2) in the following way:

Table 7A.5

Input Combinations for $1,000 Budget

COMBINATION	X	Y
A	0	5
B	2	4
C	4	3
D	6	2
E	8	1
F	10	0

$$\frac{MP_X}{P_X} = \frac{MP_Y}{P_Y} \qquad \text{(7A.3)}$$

In other words, two inputs are combined in the best possible way when the marginal product of the last unit of one input in relation to its price is just equal to the marginal product of the last unit of the other input in relation to its price.

Let us now return to the more formal economic analysis of optimal input combinations by explaining the optimality rule with the use of isoquants and isocost curves. Suppose P_X = $100 and P_Y = $200. Suppose further that a firm has a budget of $1,000 to spend on inputs X and Y. At these prices and this expenditure limit, any of the combinations of X and Y in Table 7A.5 could be purchased.

Algebraically, the budget can be expressed as follows:

$$E = P_X \times X + P_y \times Y \qquad \text{(7A.4)}$$

where E = Total budget allotment for inputs X and Y
P_X = Price of X
P_Y = Price of Y
X = Quantity of input X
Y = Quantity of input Y

In other words, the amount spent for X and Y is equal to the number of units of X multiplied by its price plus the number of units of Y multiplied by its price. In this case,

$$\$1,000 = \$100X + \$200Y \qquad \text{(7A.5)}$$

Using this equation to plot the numbers in Table 7A.5, we obtain the isocost curve shown in Figure 7A.6.

Note that the isocost curve is linear because the prices of the inputs are constant. A few algebraic manipulations of Equation (7A.4) will indicate that the prices of the inputs in relation to each other (i.e., P_X/P_Y) are represented by the slope of the isocost line:

$$E = P_X \times X + P_Y \times Y \qquad \text{(7A.6)}$$

$$P_Y \times Y = E - P_X \times X$$

$$Y = \frac{E}{P_Y} - \frac{P_X}{P_Y} \times X$$

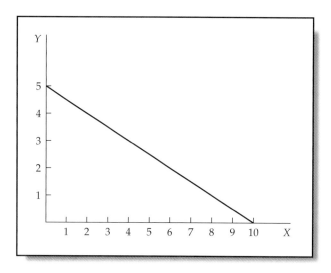

Figure 7A.6
Isocost Curve for Inputs X
and Y

Figure 7A.7 combines the isocost curve shown in Figure 7A.6 and the isoquant shown in Figure 7A.5. Note that the isocost line and the isoquant are tangent to each other between points (4,3) and (6,2). This means that between these two points the slopes of the two curves are identical. Therefore, if the slope of the isocost line is $-P_X/P_Y$ and the slope of the isoquant is $-MP_X/MP_Y$, then between these two points

$$\frac{MP_X}{MP_Y} = \frac{P_X}{P_Y}$$

If we cancel the negative signs on both sides of the equation, we arrive at the optimality rule first stated in Equation (7A.2). Given a budget of $1,000 and the input combinations represented by the isoquant in Figure 7A.7, the firm would employ the optimal combination of inputs if it used either four units of X and three of Y or six units of X and two of Y.

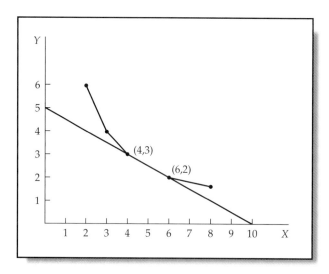

Figure 7A.7
Optimal Combinations of
Inputs X and Y

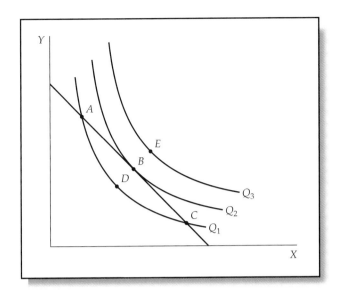

Figure 7A.8
Selecting the Optimal Input
Combination for a
Continuous Production
Function

We are not able to find a unique combination of inputs because we have used a discrete set of input combinations. Graphically, we can show quite easily how the use of a continuous production function enables us to find one optimal input combination. In Figure 7A.8, we have combined the isocost curve with a series of smoothed or continuous production isoquants. Point B represents the firm's optimal combination of inputs. Let us explain why.

To begin with, point D must be ruled out because at that point the firm would not be spending the full amount of its budget allotment. On the other hand, point E represents a combination beyond the limits set by the budget. This leaves points A, B, and C, each representing a combination that can be purchased with the budget allotment. Of these three points, point B represents the best combination because the firm would be producing the maximum amount given its budget limitation.

In terms of the marginal analysis developed previously, we can see that point B is the only one that fulfills the optimality condition expressed in Equations (7A.2) and (7A.3). That is, at point B, the slope of the isocost curve and the slope of the isoquant are identical. (Recall that the slope of a continuous isoquant is measured by the slope of the line tangent to the curve at a particular point.) Therefore, at point B, $MP_X/MP_Y = P_X/P_Y$.

THE OPTIMAL LEVELS OF MULTIPLE INPUTS

By following the optimality condition first presented in Equations (7A.2) and (7A.3), a firm ensures that it will be producing in the least costly way, regardless of the level of output. Therefore, Equation (7A.2) could be more specifically called the condition for cost minimization. But how much output should the firm be producing? The answer to the question, as was the case for a single input, depends on the demand for the product.

As you recall, the decision regarding the number of units of a single input to use was based on the condition $P_X = MCL = MRP_X$. That is, the firm should use the X input up to the point at which its cost (i.e., P_X) just equals the market price of the additional input's efforts (i.e., MRP_X). By the same token, the decision rule for two or more inputs requires that the firm use each input up to the point

$$P_i = MRP_i \tag{7A.7}$$

where P_i = Price of input i
   MRP_i = Marginal revenue product of input i

If the firm is utilizing two inputs (X and Y), its optimality condition is

$$P_X = MRP_X \text{ and } P_Y = MRP_Y \tag{7A.8}$$

We can explain the rationale for the optimality condition with two or more inputs simply by saying that what applies in the case of one input must apply to more than one input. However, there is a more formal explanation in microeconomic theory using several terms and concepts that will not be presented in detail until chapter 9. Nonetheless, following is a brief version of this theoretical explanation.

According to economic theory, the firm that wishes to maximize its profit will always try to operate at the point where the extra revenue received from the sale of the last unit of output produced is just equal to the additional cost of producing this output. In other words, its optimal level of production is at the point where marginal revenue (MR) is equal to marginal cost (MC). In chapter 9, you will learn in much greater detail about the rationale and application of the MR = MC rule. For now, let us simply explain the justification for the rule governing the optimal use of more than one input.

Marginal cost, or MC, is the cost of producing an additional unit of output. Using the terms developed in previous examples in this chapter,

$$MC = \frac{P_i}{MP_i} \tag{7A.9}$$

where MC = Marginal cost of production
   P_i = Price of the input i (i.e., the cost to the firm of using an additional unit of the input i)
   MP_i = Marginal product of the input i

For example, suppose the input used is labor (measured in hourly units), and the price of labor is the wage rate given to the firm under perfectly competitive labor market conditions. Assume a wage rate of $10 per hour. Assume also that a particular hour of labor has a marginal product of 20 units of output. On a per-unit basis, these additional 20 units will cost the firm $0.50 (i.e., $10/20) to produce. In other words, at this point the marginal cost is $0.50.

Let us assume that the firm is operating at the profit-maximizing level of output—in other words, at the point where

$$MR = MC \tag{7A.10}$$

Let us also assume that the firm employs two inputs, X and Y. Substituting Equation (7A.9) into (7A.10) gives

$$MR = \frac{P_X}{MP_X} \text{ for the } X \text{ input} \tag{7A.11}$$

$$MR = \frac{P_Y}{MP_Y} \text{ for the } Y \text{ input} \tag{7A.11}$$

Rearranging terms gives us

$$P_X = MR \times MP_X \text{ and } P_Y = MR \times MP_Y \tag{7A.12}$$

Since $MR \times MP_i = MRP_i$, the firm will be satisfying the optimality condition with that combination of X and Y at which

$$P_X = MRP_X \text{ and } P_Y = MRP_Y \tag{7A.13}$$

In short, the optimal level of multiple inputs occurs when the additional revenue that each input accounts for is just equal to the additional cost to the firm of using each of the inputs. Another way to view this optimality condition is to remember that it is actually derived from the assumption that the firm is already producing at the profit-maximizing level of output (i.e., where MR = MC). This, in turn, implies that the firm is combining its inputs in an optimal fashion. If not, then it could not possibly be maximizing its profit.

Figure 7A.9 illustrates the difference between the cost-minimizing and the profit-maximizing combinations of inputs. You can see that any one of the points along the "expansion path" represents the cost-minimizing combination of inputs X and Y. However, suppose that the MR = MC rule for profit maximization dictates that a firm produce Q_3 units for sale in the competitive marketplace. As you can see, this implies that only one combination of inputs (X_3 and Y_3) should be used. All the other combinations of inputs will be cost-efficient but will not enable the firm to maximize its profits.

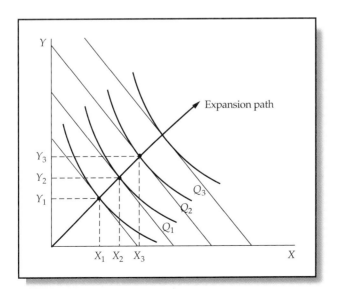

Figure 7A.9
Cost-Minimizing and Profit-Maximizing Input Combinations

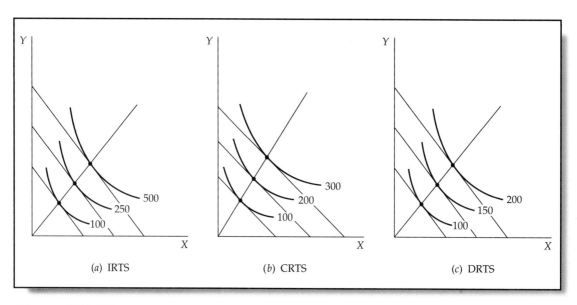

Figure 7A.10
Optimal Input Combinations and Returns to Scale

Incidentally, when returns to scale are measured, economists always assume that the firm is operating with the optimal combination of inputs. In Figure 7A.10, we view returns to scale "from above" rather than "from the side" as we did back in Figure 7.5. In this figure the different levels of output resulting from increases in input are found on a ray from the origin. (This ray is actually the locus of points indicating the optimal combination of inputs for different levels of budgetary constraint.) As implied by the hypothetical numbers assigned to the isoquants, the values of these isoquants in relation to the values of the optimal input combinations indicate whether the firm is experiencing increasing, constant, or decreasing returns to scale.

Expressing the Production Function with the Use of Calculus

In this chapter, we have relied primarily on tables and graphs to illustrate our analysis of the production function. This appendix shows you how calculus can be used in the analysis.

A BRIEF REVIEW OF THE PRODUCTION FUNCTION

The production function expresses the relationship between the output and one or more inputs. The output is referred to either as *total product* (TP) or Q (quantity). We began our analysis of the production function by presenting the relationship between different combinations of two inputs (i.e., labor and capital) and output in a numerical table (see Table 7B.1). As already explained, the production function takes the general form:

$$Q = f(L, K) \tag{7B.1}$$

where Q = Quantity of output
L = Labor (i.e., the variable input)
K = Capital (i.e., the fixed input)

Table 7B.1

Cobb-Douglas Production Function

K	OUTPUT QUANTITY							
8	282	400	488	564	628	688	744	800
7	264	373	456	528	588	644	700	744
6	244	345	422	488	544	600	644	688
5	223	315	385	446	500	544	588	628
4	200	282	346	400	446	488	528	564
3	173	244	300	346	385	422	456	488
2	141	200	244	282	315	345	373	400
1	100	141	173	200	223	244	264	282
	1	2	3	4	5	6	7	8

By stating this general functional form in more specific terms, we have an equation that can be used to generate a tabular model of the production function.

One popular form is the *Cobb-Douglas* production function. It can be stated as follows:

$$Q = AL^aK^b \qquad\qquad \textbf{(7B.2)}$$

Q, L, and K have the same definitions as in Equation (7B.1). The values for A, a, and b determine the actual values in the production table. For example, suppose $A = 100$, $a = 0.5$, and $b = 0.5$. The production function would be

$$Q = 100L^{0.5}K^{0.5} \qquad\qquad \textbf{(7B.3)}$$

This equation can be used to generate the numbers in Table 7B.1.

MARGINAL PRODUCT: THE FIRST DERIVATIVE OF THE TOTAL PRODUCT FUNCTION

As shown in the discussion of isoquants, the marginal product expressed in terms of calculus is the partial derivative of the total product function. We can use the Cobb-Douglas form of the production function shown in Equation (7B.3) to illustrate how the derivative is used to find this marginal product.

Suppose we want to find the marginal product of the fourth unit of labor added to the production process, assuming that we are currently using four units of capital. We simply take the partial derivative of the equation with respect to L, set $L = 4$ and $K = 4$, and find the resulting value of total product:

$$\frac{\delta Q}{\delta L} = 100(0.5)L^{-0.5}K^{0.5}$$

$$= 100(0.5)4^{-0.5}4^{0.5}$$

$$= 50$$

In Table 7B.1 we note that the marginal product of the fourth unit of labor assuming 4 units of capital is 54 (i.e., $400 - 346$). The two values differ because the use of calculus actually enables us to compute marginal product right at the point at which four units of labor are being used, rather than that amount of output resulting from the addition of the fourth unit.

CONVERTING THE COBB-DOUGLAS FUNCTION INTO A LINEAR FORM

1. The Cobb-Douglas function is nonlinear; it is an exponential function. However, it can be converted into a linear function in terms of logarithms:

$$Q = aL^bK^c$$

$$\log Q = \log a + b \log L + c \log K$$

2. The original form of the function was

$$Q = aL^bK^{1-b}$$

This model assumes constant returns to scale. In other words, if both labor and capital inputs are changed by a certain proportion s, Q will also change by s:

$$Q = a(sL)^b(sK)^{1-b}$$

$$= a(s^bL^b)(s^{1-b}K^{1-b})$$

$$= (s^{b+1-b})(Q)$$

$$= s^1Q$$

Thus, the new quantity, Q, will equal the old quantity times s—the proportion by which both L and K changed.

The later version of the function relaxed the requirement of constant returns since it permitted $b + c$ to be less than, equal to, or greater than 1. In this case, the results would be as follows:

$$Q' = a(sL)^b (sK)^c$$

$$= a(s^bL^b)(s^cK^c)$$

$$= a(s^{b+c})(L^bK^c)$$

$$= (s^{b+c})(Q)$$

If $b + c > 1$, then for an input change s, Q will increase by more than s (i.e., increasing returns). If $b + c < 1$, the increase in Q will be less than s (i.e., decreasing returns).

3. The marginal product of a factor is the partial derivative of quantity of output with respect to the factor:

$$MP_L = \delta Q/\delta L$$

$$= abL^{b-1}K^{1-b}$$

$$= abL^bL^{-1}K^{1-b}$$

$$= bL^{-1}Q$$

$$= bQ/L$$

Similarly, the marginal product of capital, MP_K, equals cQ/K or $(1 - b) Q/K$.

4. The elasticity of production measures the sensitivity of total product to a change in an input in percentage terms:

$$E_Q = \frac{\text{Change in } Q\,(\%)}{\text{Change in input }(\%)}$$

or, in the case of labor,

$$\Delta Q/Q \div \Delta L/L = \Delta Q/Q \times L/\Delta L = \Delta Q/\Delta L \times L/Q = \Delta Q/\Delta L \div Q/L$$

$\Delta Q / \Delta L$ is, of course, the marginal product of labor; Q/L is the average product of labor (with capital held constant). Thus, the elasticity of production is equal to the marginal product divided by the average product. It was shown that the marginal product of labor is bQ/L and, as we have just pointed out, the average product of labor is Q/L. Dividing MP_L by AP_L,

$$MP_L/AP_L = bQ/L \div Q/L = bQ/L \times L/Q = b$$

Thus, the elasticity of production for labor is b (and for capital, it is c). These are the original constant exponents of the Cobb-Douglas function. For any percentage increase (or decrease) in the quantity of a factor, holding quantity of the other factor or factors the same, the increase (or decrease) in total product will be a constant percentage. And since the exponents are less than 1, the percent increase in total product is less than the increase in the quantity of the factor.

THE OPTIMAL COMBINATION OF TWO INPUTS

In the main body of this chapter, we showed that if a firm is producing a level of output that maximizes its profit, then it must be using its inputs in such a way that the marginal revenue product of every input used is equal to its price (or cost). In other words, if a firm uses k inputs, then

$$MRP_1 = \text{Cost of input 1}$$

$$MRP_2 = \text{Cost of input 2}$$

$$\cdot$$
$$\cdot$$
$$\cdot$$

$$MRP_k = \text{Cost of input } k$$

Earlier we showed why a rational firm would be using its inputs in the most cost-efficient manner if it combined them in such a way that the ratio of each input's marginal product relative to its price is equal for all inputs used:

$$\frac{MP_1}{P_1} = \frac{MP_2}{P_2} = \cdots = \frac{MP_k}{P_k}$$

In this section, we employ calculus to demonstrate mathematically why this is so. We begin by stating the profit function in the following manner:

$$\pi = TR - TC \tag{7B.4}$$

where π = Total profit
TR = Total revenue
TC = Total cost

By definition, total revenue is equal to price times quantity:

$$TR = P \times Q \qquad \text{(7B.5)}$$

where P = Price of the output
Q = Quantity of output sold

Total cost is equal to the amounts of the inputs used multiplied by their respective prices. Let us assume that the firm is using two inputs, labor and capital, and that their prices are the wage rate and some rental cost of using the capital. Thus, we can say that

$$TC = wL + rK \qquad \text{(7B.6)}$$

where L = Labor
K = Capital
w = Wage rate of labor
r = Rental cost of using capital

Substituting Equations (7B.6) and (7B.5) into Equation (7B.4) gives us

$$\pi = PQ - (wL + rK) \qquad \text{(7B.7)}$$

As you know, the production function can be stated in general terms as

$$Q = f(L, K) \qquad \text{(7B.8)}$$

Substituting this equation into Equation (7B.7) gives us

$$\pi = Pf(L, K) - wL - rK \qquad \text{(7B.9)}$$

To find the level of input that will maximize the firm's profit, we can take the partial derivative of the profit function with respect to each of the inputs, L and K, while holding the other one constant and set each equal to zero:

$$\frac{\delta \pi}{\delta L} = Pf_L - w = 0 \qquad \text{(7B.10)}$$

$$\frac{\delta \pi}{\delta K} = Pf_K - r = 0 \qquad \text{(7B.11)}$$

If we express Equations (7B.10) and (7B.11) in terms of the prices of the inputs, we obtain

$$w = Pf_L \qquad \text{(7B.12)}$$

$$r = Pf_K \qquad \text{(7B.13)}$$

Recall that the definition of the marginal product of a particular input is the change in output with respect to a change in that input. In other words

$$MP_L = f_L \qquad \text{(7B.14)}$$

$$MP_K = f_K \qquad \text{(7B.15)}$$

Recall further that the definition of the marginal revenue product (MRP) is the MP of a particular input multiplied by product price. Thus, Equations (7B.12) and (7B.13) are nothing more than a restatement of the conditions necessary for the optimal use of inputs discussed earlier in the main body of this chapter. That is,

$$Pf_L = \text{MRP}_L = w \qquad \text{(7B.16)}$$

$$Pf_K = \text{MRP}_K = r \qquad \text{(7B.17)}$$

Now that we have established the relationship, we can easily use the same equations and notations to show how the condition necessary for the most cost-efficient combination of inputs is derived. If we divide equation (7B.12) by Equation (7B.13), we obtain

$$\frac{w}{r} = \frac{Pf_L}{Pf_K}$$

The Ps in the denominator and the numerator on the right-hand side cancel out, giving

$$\frac{w}{r} = \frac{f_L}{f_K}$$

Using the definitions of marginal product stated in Equations (7B.14) and (7B.15) and rearranging the terms gives the condition for the most efficient combination of input usage:

$$\frac{\text{MP}_L}{w} = \frac{\text{MP}_K}{r} \qquad \text{(7B.18)}$$

Chapter 8

The Theory and Estimation of Cost

The Situation

Adam Michaels, the Plant Manager at Shayna Soda Company, was going through his daily routine of opening his mail on Monday morning when he came across a marketing flyer from "Lawrence Aluminum Products," a company he had never heard of. The company was in New Jersey, about four hundred miles away from his plant in upstate New York. At first he didn't pay too much attention to it, but then he saw that the base cost of soda cans was almost 30 percent lower than what he was now paying. He read on about the company and was impressed with its offer. The company offered an even higher discount if you integrated with their technology and took advantage of electronic purchase orders. Shayna Soda Company required technological upgrades, so maybe this would be a perfect opportunity to switch both suppliers and computer systems. Adam was always under pressure from Corporate to increase the profitability of its soda production so his excitement on the potential of this change was high.

Adam called in Terry Roberts, the product availability manager, and told her of his discovery. "Terry, this sounds like a great opportunity for us and I want you to investigate this company a little more and let me know what we need to do to get supply from them." Terry did not look excited about the project.

"But Adam," she replied, "what about Kayla Containers? We are their main customer and this could put them out of business."

"Terry, this is a business decision and although I like Kayla Containers, we need to stay in business too. Please get on it, and give me a report by Friday."

(Continued)

Terry went back to her office and picked up the phone to call Lawrence Aluminum Products. She was directed to Joseph Matthews, the Director of Sales. Terry told Joseph who Shayna Soda was and the type of cans that it would need. Lawrence had the right specifications on the can and actually had a little higher grade of quality in the aluminum. She continued to tell of their needs and asked how it would work to get Shayna's logo and artwork on the cans. Joseph explained that they could do the logo and artwork with no problem, but Shayna would need to pay a one time fee to set up the specifications. Moreover, the base price of the cans would go up 10 percent due to the extra coloring and production time. Terry quickly figured that even with the increase, the cost would be lower than Kayla Containers' product.

"OK," Terry continued. "What about delivery?"

"Delivery is no problem," Joseph responded. "We have trucks that deliver in your area once a week. We would get your order in and put it on the next truck going out. And by the way, if you need to change the delivery date and request it in time, we can do it for you but we charge a bit more. If you want our base delivery fee, you must take delivery when we schedule it."

"Is it a flat fee or by the mile?" Terry asked.

"It's by the mile."

Terry began to be concerned with the delivery aspect of the offer. "What about lead time? What do you require?"

"We have a pretty good turn around time, so we only need five days," Joseph replied.

"Five days!" Terry shot back. "That's not great."

"Well, to be honest, most of the time we can give that, but sometimes we may be able to meet your needs sooner, if we know your general plans in advance," Joseph continued. "Ideally, we like to have a monthly forecast. In fact, we can offer you a discount if you integrate with our current technology for submitting forecasts and purchase orders and you make payment through the automated clearing house."

What Joseph was saying now really began to peak Terry's interest because the company was planning on improving its supply chain management anyway, particularly the procurement link of the chain.

"What would be the cost of that?" Terry asked.

"Well, you would need to purchase the software and the necessary support to set it up and integrate it with ours," Joseph stated nonchalantly.

"You don't help with any of the costs?" Terry asked.

"No. That would be your responsibility. But we can refer you to the contractors that helped us and offer any advice along the way. It would be of benefit to you in the long run though. Just think of the efficiencies you could have."

Joseph concluded the conversation by giving Terry all of the numbers to do the necessary calculations. Terry spent the next couple of days figuring out all of the aspects of the calculations.

The Importance of Cost in Managerial Decisions

As the old adage goes, "buy low and sell high." This chapter concerns the part about buying low. Cost has become particularly important in recent years as increasing competitive pressures, changing technology, and customer demand have made it harder for firms to achieve high profit margins by raising their prices. Recall in chapter 1 our discussion of how changing economics forced companies from a "cost-plus" stage to one where "cost management" became preeminent. The most commonly used way to contain or to cut costs over the past decade has been to reduce the number of people on a company's payroll. *Restructuring, downsizing, rightsizing, redundancy,* and *force management* are all terms that have at one time or another been used in reference to this action. In addition, companies have resorted to outsourcing and the relocation of manufacturing facilities to lower-wage countries to reduce their costs.

In 1997 Sara Lee, a company that manufacturers a wide variety of consumer products, including frozen desserts, women's pantyhose, men's underwear, and pork sausages, adopted a cost-cutting strategy that became known in the popular press as "deverticalization." That is, the company began to sell off the basic components of its manufacturing processes, such as textile mills and slaughter houses. In fact, its CEO was quoted as saying that his "role model" was Nike, a company noted for outsourcing the making of its shoes to companies in low-wage Asian countries.[1]

Another common way in which companies have tried to cut costs to remain competitive is to merge, consolidate, and then reduce headcount. It is no surprise that megamergers making the news in recent years primarily involve companies that have been experiencing considerable changes in the economics of their business. Commercial financial services and banks (e.g., Citicorp and Travelers, Bank of America and Nations Bank), pharmaceuticals (e.g., SmithKline and Beecham, Glaxo and Wellcome, Sandoz and Eli Lilly) and telecommunications (e.g., SBC, Pacific Telesis, and Ameritech, now called "SBC"; and Bell Atlantic and GTE, now called "Verizon"). In the oil industry, Exxon merged with Mobil and BP, after merging with Amco, purchased Arco. These mergers clearly will have profound effects on the competitive landscape of the oil industry. Nonetheless, an important reason for these mergers is the cost savings from the economies of scale.[2]

As explained earlier, the economic analysis of cost begins with the production function. We therefore begin the analysis of cost by showing the links between production and cost functions. But before doing so, we review briefly the particular way in which cost is defined and used in economic analysis.

---

[1] Roger Lowenstein, "Intrinsic Value: Remember When Companies Made Things?" *The Wall Street Journal,* September 18, 1997.
[2] For a good overview of the "merger mania" of the late 1990s, see Richard Teitlebaum, "Mergers, Mergers Everywhere, But Do Shareholders Benefit?" *New York Times,* November 29, 1998.

In a typical business organization, cost is generally considered the domain of the accounting department. Its presentation to the outside world (e.g., to bankers, bond holders, investors, and suppliers) is based on generally accepted rules of accounting (GAAP). For purposes of internal analysis and decision making, the definition of cost is based on the concept of relevancy. By definition, a cost is considered to be relevant if it is affected by a management decision. Any cost not affected by a decision is considered irrelevant. Both economists and managerial or cost accountants (as opposed to financial accountants) use the concept of **relevant cost** when analyzing business problems and recommending solutions. Following are some important ways to distinguish between relevant and irrelevant cost.

Historical versus Replacement Cost

Suppose a manufacturer of a video game system has an inventory of $750,000 worth of 16-bit chips left over from a discontinued system. Strong protectionist measures by Congress have created a shortage of these chips, driving their market value up to $1,000,000. Meanwhile, the firm decides to reenter the video game market. (This time, it will manufacture the product in Thailand and will begin production with the leftover inventory of chips.) How much will it cost the firm to use this inventory? Although the **historical cost** is $750,000, the replacement value is $1,000,000. According to the principle of relevant cost, the firm should use the latter figure in computing its cost of reentering the video game market.[3] Let us see why this is so.

If the firm were to decide not to proceed with the project but instead to sell its inventory of chips in the open market, it could receive the full market value of $1,000,000. Therefore, by using the chips, it is forgoing the opportunity to receive $1,000,000 for their sale. Moreover, if it decided to buy chips rather than use its inventory, it would have to pay $1,000,000 for the same quantity that it holds in inventory. The $1,000,000 is the relevant sum because it is the amount that has an impact on the alternatives being considered.

Opportunity Cost versus Out-of-Pocket Cost

Previous discussions pointed out that **opportunity cost** is one of the most important and useful concepts in economic analysis because it highlights the consequences of making choices under conditions of scarcity. We can now use this term in a more specific way to help explain the concept of relevant cost. Opportunity cost, as you recall, is the amount or subjective value that is forgone in choosing one activity over the

---

[3]The recording of the cost of an asset for purposes of financial reporting is subject to generally accepted accounting principles (GAAP), which state that assets and liabilities should be recorded in financial statements at historical cost. Inventories may be reported at historical cost or current market value, whichever is lower. But regardless of the rule set for external reporting, economists and cost accountants (as opposed to financial accountants) recommend that a firm use current market value for internal management decisions.

next best alternative. This type of cost can be contrasted with "out-of-pocket cost." On occasion, economists refer to opportunity cost as *indirect cost* or *implicit cost*, and refer to out-of-pocket cost as *direct cost* or *explicit cost*.

In the case of the company with the inventory of computer chips, we can clearly see that the opportunity cost of using the inventory in its second attempt to penetrate the video game market involves the cost of not being able to resell the inventory for $1,000,000. Seen in this way, this sum is the firm's "relevant opportunity cost." The $750,000 is not relevant because it is not the opportunity cost of going ahead with the project. Incidentally, the firm's out-of-pocket cost of using chips would be the cost of buying additional chips for the production process. For example, if the firm decides that it needs $1,500,000 worth of chips (at current market prices) in the first year of the project's operation, we can infer that this figure consists of $1,000,000 in opportunity cost and $500,000 in additional out-of-pocket cost.

Sunk versus Incremental Cost

Let us evaluate the cost to the firm of using its inventory of chips with a reversal in market conditions. Instead of the firm's inventory increasing in value, suppose something happens to cause its value to fall to $550,000. For example, the introduction of a 32-bit video game system drastically reduces the demand for and price of the 16-bit system. Under these circumstances, how much will it cost the firm to use the inventory for which it originally paid $750,000? To answer this question, we employ the distinction that economists make between *incremental* and *sunk* costs. **Incremental cost** is the cost that varies with the range of options available in a decision. **Sunk cost** is the cost that does not vary in accordance with the decision alternatives. Our computer manufacturer has already paid $750,000 for the chips and can really do nothing about the fact that changes in market conditions have driven the value of the chips down to $550,000. If the firm decides to sell the inventory, it will receive at the most only $550,000. If it decides to go ahead with the project, the incremental cost (i.e., the part of its cost that is affected by the decision) of using the inventory of chips will be $550,000 and not $750,000. And, as you have probably already concluded, the $200,000 difference between these two sums must be considered a sunk cost to the firm. As it turns out, the $550,000 can also be considered the opportunity cost of using the chips instead of selling them. Therefore, in summary, the firm should consider $550,000 to be the relevant cost of using its inventory of chips, because it is an *incremental opportunity cost.*

A dramatic example of the use of incremental and opportunity costs to determine relevant cost is the case of a new technology suddenly rendering the entire inventory of chips obsolete. For example, the introduction of a 64-bit game system would virtually destroy the market for 16-bit games. In this event, no one would want to buy the chips at any price, and the value of this inventory would be reduced to zero. The entire $750,000 investment in inventory would be considered a sunk cost to the firm. Furthermore, since the resale value of the inventory is zero, the firm's use of the chips in its project would not incur an opportunity cost.[4] In economic terms,

---

[4]We will avoid using the term *indirect cost* in reference to opportunity cost because some readers may confuse it with another definition. In manufacturing, *indirect cost* usually refers to the cost of using labor not directly involved in the making of a product (e.g., finance, personnel, research and development, and other support or staff functions).

the chips would represent a "free resource" because there would be no amount forgone with their use in the project. Would the firm be tempted to use the chips simply because of this? Would you want to build a new video game system with obsolete chips? If people will not buy the product, there would indeed be a high opportunity cost in terms of forgone sales.

THE RELATIONSHIP BETWEEN PRODUCTION AND COST

The economic analysis of cost is tightly bound to the economic analysis of production discussed in the previous chapter. As a matter of fact, one can say that the cost function used in economic analysis is simply the production function expressed in monetary rather than physical units. Furthermore, all the limiting assumptions used in specifying the short-run production function apply to the short-run cost function. The only additional assumption needed to determine the short-run economic cost function pertains to the prices of the inputs used in the production process. Here we assume that the firm acts as a "price taker" in the input market; that is, it can hire or use as many or as few inputs as it desires, as long as it pays the going market price for them.

Table 8.1 presents an example of the numerical relationship between production and cost in the short run. The cost of using the variable input is determined by multiplying the number of units by the unit price. In this case, each unit of labor is assumed to be the equivalent of a 40-hour work week. The weekly wage rate is $500. As indicated in the table, when the total product (Q) increases at an *increasing rate*, **total variable cost (TVC)** increases at a *decreasing* rate. When Q increases at a *decreasing* rate, TVC increases at an *increasing* rate. Plotting these numbers on a graph makes

Table 8.1
Relationship between Production and Cost, Short Run

TOTAL INPUT (L)	Q	TVC ($L \times \$500$)	MC ($\Delta TVC/\Delta Q$)	REFERENCE POINT IN FIGURE 8.1
0	0	0		
1	1,000	500	0.50	
2	3,000	1,000	0.25	$A(A')$
3	6,000	1,500	0.16	$B(B')$
4	8,000	2,000	0.25	$C(C')$
5	9,000	2,500	0.50	$D(D')$
6	9,500	3,000	1.00	$E(E')$
7	9,850	3,500	1.42	$F(F')$
8	10,000	4,000	3.33	$G(G')$
9	9,850	4,500	-3.33	$H(H')$

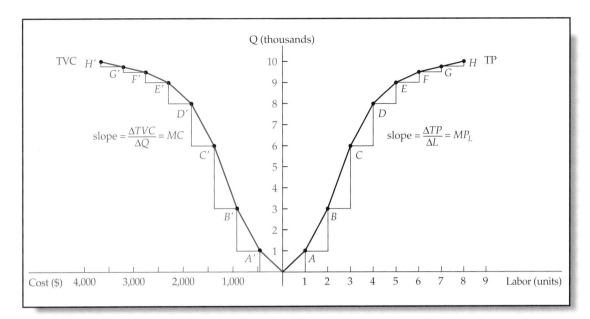

Figure 8.1
Short-Run Production and Cost

it quite apparent that total variable cost is a "mirror image" of total product (Figure 8.1.)

In the previous chapter, the marginal product was defined as the change in total product divided by the change in the amount of the variable input used in the production process. Similarly, the rate of change in total variable cost is called **marginal cost.** Expressed in symbols,

$$MC = \Delta TVC/\Delta Q \text{ or } MC = \Delta TC/\Delta Q$$

Note that marginal cost is either the change in total variable cost or the change in total cost with respect to the change in output. This is because the **total fixed cost** component of **total cost** never changes as output increases. Using marginal cost and marginal product, we can restate the relationship shown in Figure 8.1 in this way: When the firm's marginal product is increasing, its marginal cost of production is decreasing; when its marginal product is decreasing (i.e., *when the law of diminishing returns takes effect*), its marginal cost is increasing.

The relationship between diminishing returns and increasing marginal cost can also be illustrated algebraically. First, assume that the variable input is labor (L), and its unit cost is some given wage rate (W). Now let us start by defining marginal cost as:

$$MC = \frac{\Delta TVC}{\Delta Q} \tag{8.1}$$

Since $TVC = L \times W$, we can say that

$$\Delta TVC = \Delta L \times W \tag{8.2}$$

Substituting Equation (8.2) into Equation (8.1) gives us

$$MC = \frac{\Delta L \times W}{\Delta Q} = \frac{\Delta L}{\Delta Q} \times W \qquad (8.3)$$

Recalling the definition of MP, we know that $MP_L = \Delta Q/\Delta L$. Incorporating this observation into Equation (8.3) gives us

$$MC = \frac{1}{MP} \times W = \frac{W}{MP} \qquad (8.4)$$

Clearly, Equation (8.4) tells us that, assuming a constant wage rate, MC will decrease when MP increases and will increase when MP decreases (i.e., when the law of diminishing returns takes effect).

In economic theory, the relationship between diminishing returns and marginal cost represents a key link between a firm's short-run production function and its short-run cost function because it is the law of diminishing returns that gives the short-run cost function its distinctive nonlinear form. Consequently, as will be seen in ensuing sections of this chapter, the firm's total cost, total variable cost, average cost, average variable cost, and marginal cost functions are all constructed in accordance with this nonlinearity.

THE SHORT-RUN COST FUNCTION

This section deals with the focal point of this chapter: the firm's short-run cost function. A numerical model of the behavior of the firm's short-run cost is shown in Table 8.2. Before commenting on each of the columns in the table, let us review all of the assumptions that economists make in specifying a model of this kind.

1. The firm employs two inputs, labor and capital.
2. The firm operates in a short-run production period. Labor is its variable input, and capital is its fixed input.
3. The firm uses the inputs to make a single product.
4. In producing the output, the firm operates at a given level of technology. (Recall that in our discussion of the short-run production function, we assumed that the firm uses state-of-the-art technology in the production process. The same holds when we talk about short-run cost.)
5. The firm operates at every level of output in the most efficient way.
6. The firm operates in perfectly competitive input markets and must therefore pay for its inputs at some given market rate. In other words, it is a price taker in the input markets.
7. The firm's underlying short-run production function is affected by the law of diminishing returns.

As we proceed in this chapter, you will see why these assumptions are crucial to the understanding of the short-run cost function.

The variables listed in Table 8.2 are defined as follows:

Quantity (Q): The amount of output that a firm can produce in the short run. (*Total product* is also used in reference to this amount.)

Table 8.2
Total and Per-Unit Short-Run Cost

Quantity (Q)	Total Fixed Cost (TFC)	Total Variable Cost (TVC)	Total Cost (TC)	Average Fixed Cost (AFC)	Average Variable Cost (AVC)	Average Total Cost (AC)	Marginal Cost (MC)
0	100	0.00	100.00				
1	100	55.70	155.70	100.00	55.70	155.70	55.70
2	100	105.60	205.60	50.00	52.80	102.80	49.90
3	100	153.90	253.90	33.33	51.30	84.63	48.30
4	100	204.80	304.80	25.00	51.20	76.20	50.90
5	100	262.50	362.50	20.00	52.50	72.50	57.70
6	100	331.20	431.20	16.67	55.20	71.87	68.70
7	100	415.10	515.10	14.29	59.30	73.59	83.90
8	100	518.40	618.40	12.50	64.80	77.30	103.30
9	100	645.30	745.30	11.11	71.70	82.81	126.90
10	100	800.00	900.00	10.00	80.00	90.00	154.70
11	100	986.70	1,086.70	9.09	89.70	98.79	186.70
12	100	1,209.60	1,309.60	8.33	100.80	109.13	222.90

Total fixed cost (TFC): The total cost of using the fixed input K.

Total variable cost (TVC): The total cost of using the variable input L.

Total cost (TC): The total cost of using all of the firm's inputs (in this case, L and K).

Average fixed cost (AFC): The average or per-unit cost of using the fixed input K.

Average variable cost (AVC): The average or per-unit cost of using the variable input L.

Average total cost (AC): The average or per-unit cost of using all of the firm's inputs.

Marginal cost (MC): The change in a firm's total cost (or, for that matter, its total variable cost) resulting from a unit change in output.

The important relationships among these various measures of cost can be summarized as follows:

$$TC = TFC + TVC$$

$$AC = AFC + AVC \ (or \ TC/Q)$$

$$MC = \Delta TC/\Delta Q \ (or = \Delta TVC/\Delta Q)$$

$$AFC = TFC/Q$$

$$AVC = TVC/Q$$

In evaluating the schedule of numbers in Table 8.2, note that as a matter of convenience, we have considered unit changes in output over the range of production

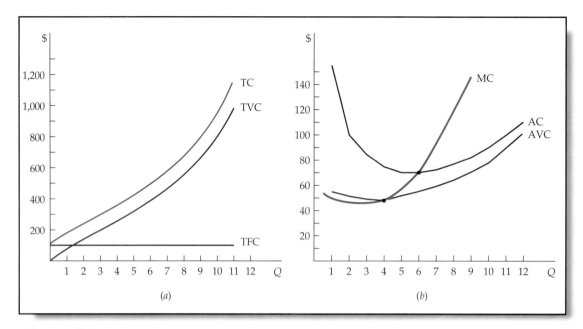

Figure 8.2
Total Cost, Total Variable Cost, Total Fixed Cost, Average Cost, Average Variable Cost, and Marginal Cost

being considered. Since ΔQ will always be equal to 1, we can quickly figure the marginal cost as output increases. For example, the marginal cost of the second unit of output is simply the change in the firm's total cost (or total variable cost) between one unit and two units of production. In Table 8.2, we observe that this amount is $49.90.

As output increases from 0 to 12, observe what happens to the various measures of cost. Total fixed cost, as expected, remains constant at $100 over the range of output. Total variable cost increases at a decreasing rate, but when the fourth unit of output is produced, it starts to increase at an increasing rate. The same is true for total cost. When the numbers are plotted on a graph (see Figure 8.2a), the rate of change in total cost can be seen as the slope of the TC curve. The constancy of fixed cost is depicted by the horizontal line emanating from the corresponding point on the Y-axis.

As for the per-unit cost measures, we see that **average fixed cost (AFC)** declines steadily over the range of production. This is to be expected, because a constant sum of $100 is being divided by the larger amounts of output. **Average variable cost (AVC)** declines, reaches a minimum at four units of output, and then starts to increase. **Average total cost (ATC or AC)** behaves in a similar fashion but reaches its minimum point at six units of output. Marginal cost declines and then starts to increase once the third unit of output is produced.

Notice in Table 8.2 that the values for marginal cost are placed between the output intervals, indicating that this measure of cost shows how total cost changes as a result of a unit change in quantity. For this same reason, marginal cost data are also plotted on a diagram between the output intervals. This particular way of showing marginal cost graphically can be seen in Figure 8.2b, along with the average total cost and average variable cost curves.

Figure 8.2b shows a particular relationship between marginal cost and the two other per-unit cost measures that is not as evident in Table 8.2. Notice that when marginal cost is equal to average variable cost, the latter measure is at its minimum point. (This occurs at four units of output.) When marginal cost is equal to average cost, average cost is at its minimum point. (This occurs at six units of output.) Another way to describe these relationships is to state that as long as marginal cost is below average variable cost, average variable cost declines as output increases. However, when marginal cost exceeds average variable cost, average variable cost starts to increase. The same relationship holds between marginal cost and average total cost. The economic significance of these relationships will be explained in chapter 9. But for now, it is important at least to note these relationships among the different per-unit measures of cost. Summarizing these relationships in abbreviated form:

When MC < AVC, AVC is falling.
When MC > AVC, AVC is rising.
When MC = AVC, AVC is at its minimum point.

To summarize the relationship between marginal cost and average cost, simply substitute AC for AVC.

It is important to understand how the concept of relevant cost can be incorporated into the analysis of short-run cost. Suppose a firm is currently producing six units of output per period and is considering increasing this amount to seven. In deciding whether to produce the seventh unit of output, the relevant cost is the marginal cost. In other words, it is the *change* in total cost and not the total cost itself that must be considered. This is because whether the firm produces six or seven units of output per time period, it still must pay the same amount of fixed cost. By evaluating the change in total cost, the firm automatically excludes fixed cost from consideration.

Increasing Cost Efficiency in the Short Run

As will be seen in chapters 9 through 11, the short-run cost function plays a central part in the economic analysis of production and pricing. For now, we can appreciate the value of this model by considering the ways in which a company might attempt to become more economically efficient. The assumptions listed when the model was specified provide a convenient guide.

To start with, the model assumes that the firm is already operating as efficiently as possible. If we assume that the firm is in fact operating as best it can with state-of-the-art technology, then the only possibility to reduce cost in the short run is for the inputs to decrease in price. If this were to happen, there would be a downward shift in the firm's short-run cost curves. This effect is shown in Figure 8.3a and b. Notice that a reduction in the firm's fixed cost (e.g., a reduction in rental payments) would simply cause the average cost line to shift downward, whereas a reduction in the firm's variable cost (e.g., a reduction in wage rates or raw materials costs) would cause all three cost lines—AC, AVC, and MC—to shift. MC actually shifts downward and to the right.

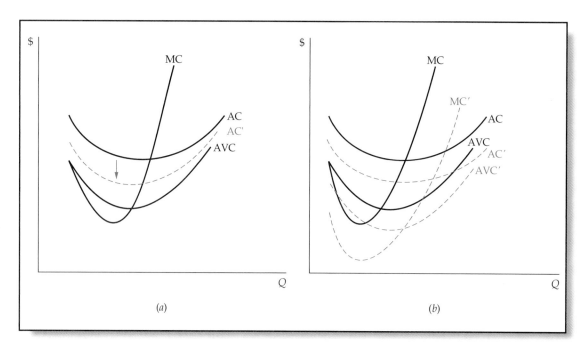

Figure 8.3
Effects on Short-Run Cost Structure of Price Changes in Variable and Fixed Inputs

The purchase of capital equipment was not considered in the discussion because we assumed it to be our model's fixed input. Actually, the addition of capital equipment could be considered a short-run change *if we assume labor to be the fixed input.* For example, a workforce of a certain size might be given additional machinery with which to work. The point is that in the short-run analysis of cost, at least one of the inputs must be held constant.

Alternative Specifications of the Total Cost Function

MODULE 9A

In economic analysis, the most common form of the short-run cost function is the one that has been used thus far in this chapter. That is, the **total cost function** is specified as a cubic relationship between total cost and output. As output increases, total cost first increases at a decreasing rate, and then at some point it increases at an increasing rate. By now you should be well aware that this is due to the underlying relationship between the firm's variable input and the resulting output. Total cost increases at a decreasing rate because the firm is experiencing increasing returns to its variable input. When the law of diminishing returns takes effect, the firm begins to experience decreasing returns to its variable factor, thereby causing its total cost to begin increasing at an increasing rate.

In addition to this cubic form of the cost function, two other important functional relationships between total cost and output are considered in economic analysis. One is a quadratic relationship, and the other is a linear one. These relationships along with the cubic cost function are shown in Figure 8.4. This figure also shows the gen-

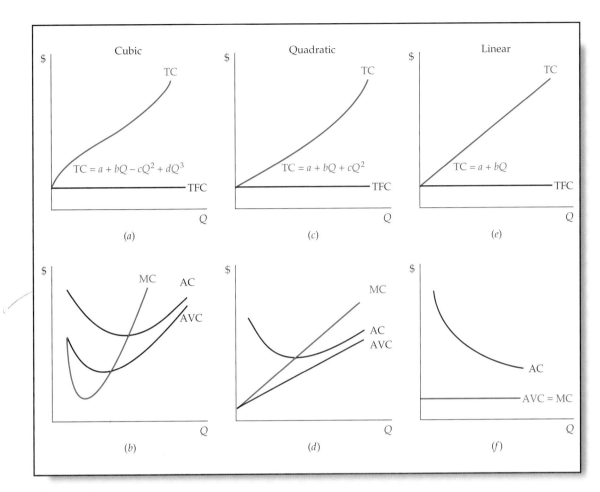

Figure 8.4
Alternative Representations of Total, Average, and Marginal Costs

eral algebraic expressions for the three forms of total cost. These variations can be explained once again by the underlying relationship between the firm's variable input and the resulting output. In Figure 8.4c we can see that the quadratic total cost function increases at an increasing rate from the outset of production. This implies that the law of diminishing returns takes effect as soon as the firm starts to produce. On the other hand, the linear cost function, shown in Figure 8.4e, indicates that total cost increases at a constant rate. Think about this for a moment. What does this mean in terms of the underlying relationship between the firm's variable input and its output? It means that the firm is experiencing neither increasing nor diminishing returns as its variable input is added to its fixed input. Each additional unit of variable input adds the *same* amount of additional output (marginal product) throughout the short-run range of production. Therefore, the change in the total cost relative to the change in output (which, as you recall, is indicated by the slope of the total cost line) is the same throughout the range of output considered.

Chapter 8   The Theory and Estimation of Cost <span></span> 345

Rather than discuss the different specifications of the firm's short-run cost function in terms of total cost, it might be easier and more meaningful to discuss the alternative forms in terms of unit costs, both average and marginal. Thus, instead of referring to total cost "increasing at an increasing rate," we can simply say that the firm's marginal cost is increasing. An increase in total cost at a constant rate means a constant marginal cost. We can also use Figure 8.4 to illustrate this point.

In Figure 8.4b, we see the familiar set of short-run cost curves depicted earlier. As output increases, marginal cost falls, reaches a minimum, and then starts to increase (as the law of diminishing returns takes effect). As it increases, marginal cost intersects with average variable cost and average total cost at their respective minimum points, for reasons explained earlier. In Figure 8.4d, we see that marginal cost increases as soon as production begins, just as we noted when evaluating the slope of the total cost function. As in the case of Figure 8.4b, marginal cost intersects average variable cost and average cost at their minimum points.

In the case of the linear cost function, shown in Figure 8.4f, the horizontal marginal cost line denotes that marginal cost remains constant as output increases. But also witness that marginal cost is equal to average variable cost, unlike the cases in Figure 8.4b and d. To illustrate this relationship, consider the following numerical example. Suppose you are given the following cost function:

$$TC = 100 + 0.50 \, Q \tag{8.5}$$

Assuming the intercept and slope coefficients represent dollar units, this function tells us that the firm's total fixed cost is $100 and its marginal cost is $0.50. That is, each additional unit of production adds $0.50 to the firm's total cost. Omitting the fixed cost component of the equation gives us

$$TVC = 0.50 \, Q \tag{8.6}$$

Recall by definition that AVC = TVC/Q. Dividing Equation (8.6) by Q gives an AVC of $0.50, which is the same as the marginal cost.

The mathematics of this example may seem rather trivial. Nonetheless, it is important to elaborate on this relationship between average variable cost and marginal cost because these two measures of cost are often used interchangeably in the business world. For example, when cost accountants use the term *standard variable cost*, they are usually referring to *both* marginal cost and average variable cost. In so doing, they are assuming that the total cost function is linear, that the firm experiences neither increasing nor diminishing returns in the short run. The importance of these assumptions as well as the role of the linear total cost function in economic analysis will be discussed further in appendices 8B and 9B.

THE LONG-RUN COST FUNCTION

The Relationship Between Long-Run Production and Long-Run Cost

In the long run, all inputs to a firm's production function may be changed. Because there are no fixed inputs, there are no fixed costs. Consequently, all costs of production are variable in the long run. In most work situations, managers of firms make

Table 8.3

Long-Run Cost Function

Scale of Production (Capacity Level)	Total Product (Output/Mo)	Long-Run Total Cost (LRTC)	Long-Run Marginal Cost (LRMC)	Long-Run Average Cost (LRAC)
A	10,000	50,000	$5.00	$5.00
B	20,000	90,000	4.00	4.50
C	30,000	120,000	3.00	4.00
D	40,000	150,000	3.00	3.75
E	50,000	200,000	5.00	4.00
F	60,000	260,000	6.00	4.33

decisions about production and cost that economic theory would consider short-run in nature. For example, they might have to decide how many labor hours are required for a particular project or whether the existing work force requires more machinery to meet increased demand.[5] But from time to time, managers must make long-run production decisions. That is, they must consider possible changes in *all* of the firm's inputs and, hence, changes in all of the firm's cost of operation. Decisions of this kind are considered by economists to be part of a manager's planning horizon.

In explaining the nature of the long-run cost function, we begin with a schedule of numbers showing a firm's long-run cost function in relation to its long-run production function. Unlike the case of short-run cost presented in Table 8.2, the hypothetical numbers in Table 8.3 are based on the assumption that greater amounts of output are the result of increases in *all* of the firm's inputs. Consistent with this assumption, this table implies that the firm would incur no cost if it chose not to produce any output, because in the long run there is no fixed cost.

As output increases, observe that total cost increases, but not at a constant rate. As with the short-run function, the rate of change of the long-run total cost function is called the marginal cost (long-run marginal cost, to be more precise). In looking at the long-run marginal cost column in Table 8.3, we see that this measure at first decreases, then is constant, and finally increases over the range of the output. The numbers in Table 8.3 are plotted on a graph in Figure 8.5. The rate of change in the long-run total cost can be seen by observing the slope of this curve as well as by observing the behavior of the long-run marginal cost curve.

The reason for this particular behavior of the firm's long-run marginal cost (or the rate of change in its long-run total cost) pertains to returns to scale. As explained in the previous chapter, economists hypothesize that a firm's long-run production function may at first exhibit increasing returns, then constant returns, and finally

---

[5]Recall that we stated earlier that the "short run" in economic theory requires only that at least one of the inputs in the production function be held constant. Thus, we can treat the addition of capital equipment as a short-run change if the amount of factory space or the amount of labor, for example, remains unchanged.

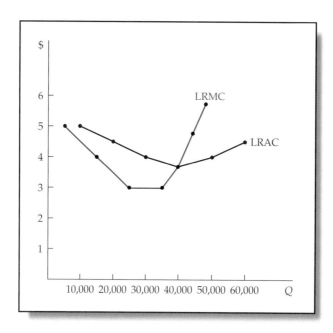

Figure 8.5
Long-Run Average and
Marginal Cost

decreasing returns to scale. This being the case, we would expect a firm's long-run cost to change in a reciprocal fashion.

When a firm experiences increasing returns to scale, an increase in all of its inputs by some proportion results in an increase in its output by some *greater* proportion. Assuming constant input prices over time, this means that if the firm's output increases by some percentage, its total cost of production increases by some *lesser* percentage. The graphs in Figure 8.6 illustrate the reciprocal behavior of long-run cost and long-run production.

It is important to stress that although the long-run cost function appears to exhibit the same pattern of behavior as the short-run cost function, the reasons for their respective patterns are entirely unrelated. The short-run cost function is affected by increasing and diminishing returns, a phenomenon that is assumed to take effect when at least one of the inputs is held constant, and the long-run function is affected by increasing and decreasing returns to scale, a phenomenon assumed to take effect when all of the firm's inputs are allowed to vary. Figure 8.7 serves as a reminder of this distinction.

Economies of Scale

One of the measures of cost in Table 8.3 has yet to be discussed: long-run average cost. This variable is the key indicator of a phenomenon called **economies of scale.** If a firm's long-run average cost declines as output increases, the firm is said to be experiencing economies of scale. If long-run average cost increases, economists consider this to be a sign of **diseconomies of scale.** There is no special term to describe the situation in which a firm's long-run average cost remains constant as output increases or decreases. We shall simply say that such a firm experiences neither econ-

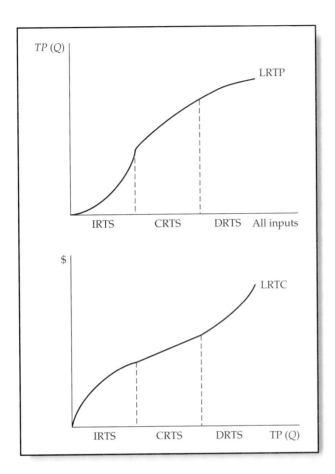

Figure 8.6
Returns to Scale for Long-Run Total Cost and Long-Run Total Production

omies nor diseconomies of scale. Figure 8.8 illustrates a typical U-shaped average cost curve reflecting the different types of scale economies that a firm might experience in the long run.

The primary reason for long-run scale economies is the underlying pattern of returns to scale in the firm's long-run production function. Further evaluation of Table 8.3 indicates that as long as marginal cost is falling, it is less than long-run average cost and in effect pulls the average down—a sure sign of economies of scale. However, once the firm starts to experience decreasing returns to scale, its long-run marginal cost begins to rise. Eventually it becomes greater than long-run average cost, causing LRAC to rise and signifying diseconomies of scale.[6]

---

[6]You should recognize the relationship between LRMC and LRAC to be the same mathematically as the relationship between SRMC and SRAC. That is, regardless of whether a short- or a long-run time period is assumed, when the marginal is below the average, it brings the average down. When the marginal is above the average, it pulls the average up.

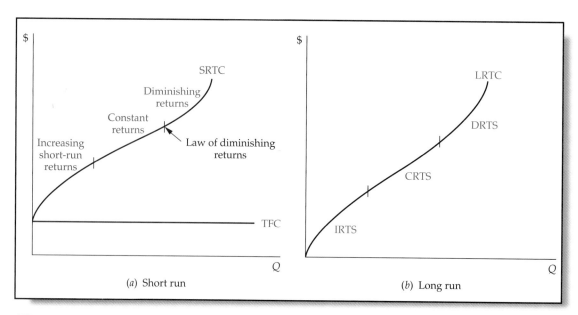

Figure 8.7
Long-Run versus Short-Run Cost Function

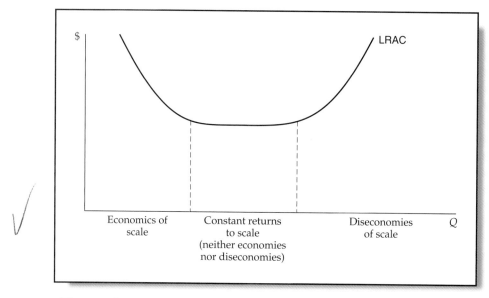

Figure 8.8
Long-Run Average Cost

Scale economies and diseconomies may result from factors besides those relating to returns to scale. These other factors pertain primarily to the prices of the firm's inputs. For example, as the firm's scale of production increases, it may be able to exert some market power over its suppliers and thus receive volume discounts for bulk purchases of raw materials and component parts. Another example involves a firm's use of capital equipment with better *price-performance ratios*. As the firm increases its scale of production, it may be worthwhile to buy more cost-effective machinery whose price and capacity could not be justified at smaller scales of production. Only a few years ago, a typical illustration cited by economists of this type of scale economy was the computer. But with the advent of personal and midsize computers, there are now machines with prices and levels of computing power that are appropriate for firms of all sizes. Furthermore, with the tremendous advances in technology and software, the prices of the machines relative to their computing power (i.e., their price-performance ratios) do not differ much among the various sizes of computers.

We should briefly mention two other factors contributing to economies of scale. First, larger firms may be able to raise funds in capital markets at a lower cost than smaller ones. For instance, a large company may be able to secure short-term funds in the commercial paper market and long-term funds in the corporate bond market, whereas a small company may be able to secure borrowed funds only from a bank. Generally, the interest rates that firms must pay for funds in money and capital markets are less than for bank loans with comparable maturities. Second, a large firm may be able to take advantage of economies resulting from the spreading out of promotional costs. If a firm expands its scale of production, it may not have to expand its advertising budget by the same proportion, if at all. The same can be said about research and development expenditures.

As far as diseconomies of scale are concerned, if the firm's scale of production becomes so large that it begins to affect substantially the total market demand for its inputs, it may start to increase the price of these inputs. A typical case is the expansion of a major employer in a local area with a relatively fixed supply of labor. If the firm's higher scale of production sufficiently increases its demand for labor, it could begin to drive up local wage rates.

Another factor not related to the long-run production function that could cause diseconomies of scale is a firm's transportation costs. As a firm increases the production capacity of a particular manufacturing facility, per-unit transportation cost tends to rise rather than to fall. This is largely because transportation costs involve more than just the delivery of goods from one point to another. In addition, there are handling expenses, insurance and security expenses, and inventory costs (as goods await shipment). Increases in these types of expenses help to increase the total transportation cost to the extent that average transportation cost increases as well. Furthermore, basic delivery expenses may rise at a faster rate than other kinds of cost if the firm has to ship the additional output to farther destinations. Economists hypothesize that eventually the increase in unit transportation cost will more than offset the fall in unit cost due to economies of scale. If this happens, then diseconomies of scale (i.e., rising average total cost) will result. Table 8.4 summarizes the key reasons for economies and diseconomies of scale. Factors that primarily relate to returns to scale are noted with an asterisk.

Table 8.4
Factors Affecting Economies and Diseconomies of Scale

POSSIBLE REASONS FOR ECONOMIES OF SCALE

Specialization in the use of labor and capital*
Indivisible nature of many types of capital equipment*
Productive capacity of capital equipment rises faster than purchase price
Economies in maintaining inventory of replacement parts and maintenance personnel*
Discounts from bulk purchases
Lower cost of raising capital funds
Spreading of promotional and research and development costs
Management efficiencies (line and staff)*

POSSIBLE REASONS FOR DISECONOMIES OF SCALE

Disproportionate rise in transportation costs
Input market imperfections (e.g., wage rates driven up)
Management coordination and control problems*
Disproportionate rise in staff and indirect labor*

*Indicates reason related directly to economies or diseconomies of scale in the long-run production function.

The Long-Run Average Cost Curve as the Envelope of Short-Run Average Cost

Up to now, we have been discussing long-run average cost as part of the firm's planning horizon. That is, the firm is assumed to be free to choose any level of capacity that it wants, because in our theoretical long-run time period, all inputs may vary. However, once a firm commits itself to a certain level of capacity, it must consider at least one of the inputs fixed as it varies the rest. In terms of production cost, this means that once a capacity level is decided on, the firm must work with a short-run cost function. We can illustrate this by returning to the example in Table 8.3.

Suppose that the capacity levels shown in the table represent plants of increasing size. Figure 8.9 shows these capacity levels in relation to each plant's short-run average cost curve. The points labeled *a* through *f* represent the levels of output and average cost shown in Table 8.3. The dotted lines passing through the points indicate the short-run average cost curves that we imagine to exist once the firm has locked into one of the plant sizes represented by the labeled points.

As expected, short-run average cost (SRAC) curves for the larger plants are positioned to the right of the curves for smaller ones, indicating greater production capacity. For example, SRAC B is to the right of SRAC A because plant B is larger than plant A. But, as noted in Figure 8.9, plants with larger capacities are greatly influenced by economies and diseconomies of scale. Because of the impact of economies of scale, plant B's SRAC curve is positioned below as well as to the right of plant A's, so that the minimum point of B's SRAC curve is *lower* than that for A. The same

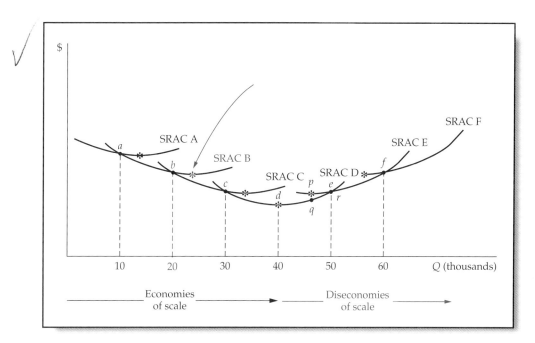

Figure 8.9
Capacity Level and Short-Run Average Cost

can be said for plant C's minimum SRAC in relation to plant B's and for D's in relation to C's. However, because of the impact of diseconomies of scale, plant E's SRAC curve is positioned above and to the right of D's, and plant F's is above and to the right of E's. That is, the SRAC curves of plants larger than plant D have progressively higher minimum average cost points. For reference, the minimum SRAC points for all of the plants are marked in Figure 8.9 with asterisks.

Another important aspect of Figure 8.9 is that none of the labeled dots is at the lowest point of its respective short-run average cost curve *except for the dot representing plant D.* For example, the asterisk marking plant B's minimum short-run average cost depicts a level above the average cost that would be incurred by plant C in the short run for a comparable level of production (see arrow in Figure 8.9). A logical extension of this illustration is the observation that if a firm wants to produce between 20,000 and 30,000 units of output per month, it would be better off utilizing the manufacturing capacity provided by plant C than to try to increase the usage of the smaller plant B. To understand the full economic implication of this observation, it is necessary to take a slight detour in our discussion to explain the particular way in which economists represent plant capacity with the use of short-run average cost curves.

You will recall that the typical short-run average cost curve (based on a cubic total cost function) declines, reaches a minimum point, and then rises as the firm produces more with some fixed amount of input. By definition, economists consider the lowest point of the short-run average cost curve to represent the firm's maximum capacity. Although "maximum capacity" usually denotes the physical limit of production (i.e., a plant simply cannot produce any more output), Figure 8.9 shows that a firm is clearly capable of producing beyond the output level at which average cost is at its

Chapter 8   The Theory and Estimation of Cost   353

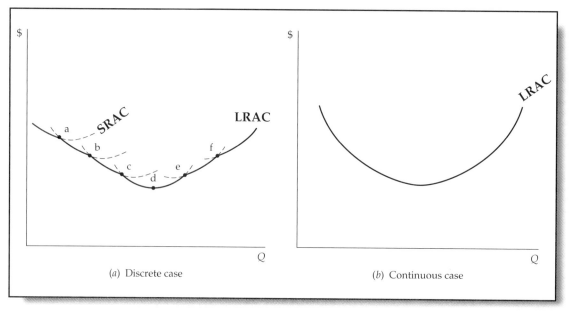

Figure 8.10
Forming LRAC Curve from SRAC Curves

lowest point. Rather than try to figure out the reason for this particular use of the term, just remember that for economists, "maximum plant capacity" coincides with a level of output that costs a firm the least amount per unit to produce in the short run.[7]

Thus, Figure 8.9 shows that over certain ranges of output, a firm is better off operating a larger plant at less than maximum capacity than a smaller plant at maximum capacity. The average cost of production in the larger plant is lower than the lowest possible average cost of production in the smaller plant. What causes this to happen? Economies of scale, of course. Because of this phenomenon, we can expect that over certain ranges of output, the reduction in average cost resulting from the economies of using a larger plant will be greater than the reduction in average cost resulting from operating a smaller plant at its most efficient (the economic "maximum") level of capacity!

As a cautionary note, we should add that once diseconomies of scale take effect, it is better for a firm to operate a plant of a given size beyond its "maximum capacity" than to build a plant of a larger size. We leave it to you to work through a detailed explanation of this observation. Suffice it to say that the reasoning is very similar to the explanation regarding the impact of economies of scale. (If you need help, refer to Figure 8.9, points p, q, and r.)

Looking at Figure 8.9 from another perspective, we can see that the firm's long-run average cost curve is actually the envelope of the various short-run average cost curves. As such, the long-run curve outlines the lowest per-unit costs that the firm will incur over the range of output considered, given the possibility of using plant sizes A through F. Figure 8.10a illustrates this point. As the number of choices of

---

[7]Economists sometimes refer to this point as "minimum efficiency scale," or MES. This term is generally used in industrial organization textbooks.

plant size approaches infinity, the envelope becomes a continuous version of the graph; this version is shown in Figure 8.10b. You should recognize it as the long-run average cost curve first shown in Figure 8.8.

Using Long-Run Average Cost as a Decision-Making Tool: The Importance of Coordinating Production Plans with Market Forecasts

In planning for its long-run capacity, which plant size should a firm choose? Using the schedule of numbers in Table 8.3, we can see that if a firm decides to build plant A, then the lowest per-unit cost of production it can expect is $5. But if it decides to build a plant with greater capacity—for instance, plant C—the potential for reducing per-unit cost is considerable because of economies of scale. Using plant C, the firm could produce its output for as little as $4 per unit. Indeed, this is where accurate forecasts of product demand are needed to help the firm plan for the best plant size. There would be no sense in investing in plant C, for example, if monthly demand is only 20,000. In this case, the smaller plant B would be more suitable. Actually, given the plant size options shown in Table 8.3 and Figure 8.9, we see that it is not necessary for a firm to forecast a specific amount of demand, but it should at least have a good idea of what the range of demand will be in the future. Table 8.5 presents a schedule showing the most appropriate plant size for different ranges of demand and production.

You should recognize that because diseconomies of scale take effect when plant E is used, plant D is appropriate for a wider range of production than the other plants. The penalty for selecting the inappropriate level of capacity is the incurrence of unnecessary cost, whether the actual demand turns out to be above or below the range used as a basis for the firm's decision on long-run production capacity. In Figure 8.11, we can see that if the firm had decided to build plant B and the demand turned out to be 25,000, it would lose on a per-unit basis the amount depicted by the arrow. If demand were such that it required the firm to produce only 5,000 units per month, the firm would suffer a similar type of loss.

As a final comment on long-run cost, it is very easy to put the onus for picking the best level of long-run capacity on the market forecasters. After all, their estimates of future demand should be the main guide for the decision makers who plan production capacity. Nevertheless, the production people in a business could become carried away with considerations of production capacity and efficiency for their own

Table 8.5
Optimal Plant Size According to Expected Demand

Units of Output Produced Based on Expected Demand	Appropriate Plant Size
0 to 10,000	A
10,000 to 20,000	B
20,000 to 30,000	C
30,000 to 50,000	D
50,000 to 60,000	E
60,000 to 70,000 (not shown on graph)	F

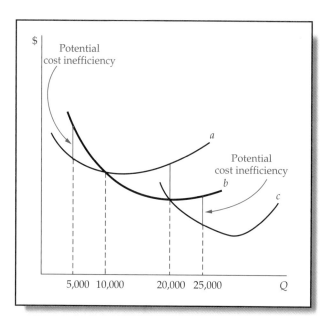

Figure 8.11
Unnecessary Costs Due to
Inappropriate Plant Size

sake (e.g., "let us build a plant of the size that will enable us to benefit substantially from economies of scale") and convince the management to overbuild the company's long-run capacity. Certainly, optimal long-run production decisions require a balanced contribution from both the engineers and the marketing people.

THE LEARNING CURVE

The **learning curve** is a line showing the relationship between labor cost and additional units of output. Its downward slope indicates that this additional cost per unit declines as the level of output increases because workers improve with practice. The reduction in cost from this particular source of improvement is often referred to as the *learning curve effect*.

Specifically, a learning curve is measured in terms of the percentage decrease in additional labor cost each time output doubles. Table 8.6 presents data for an "80 percent" learning curve. Each time the output doubles, the cost of producing the next increment of output decreases to 80 percent of the previous level (i.e., declines by 20 percent). As you can see in this table, the first unit costs $100,000; the second unit costs 80 percent of this amount, or $80,000; the fourth unit costs 80 percent of this amount, or $64,000; and so on. Notice that the percentage reduction is actually with respect to labor hours. However, given some wage rate (in this case, $10/hour), the labor cost decreases by the same percentage. The data in Table 8.6 are plotted in Figure 8.12.

There is a mathematical formula for determining the pattern of reduction in labor cost based on a selected percentage decline. This formula is

$$Y_x = Kx^n$$

Table 8.6
Numerical Example of the Learning Curve

Unit Number	Unit Labor Hours	Cumulative Labor Hours	Cumulative Average Labor Hours	Unit Labor Cost	Cumulative Average Labor Cost
1	10,000	10,000.0	10,000	$100,000	$100,000
2	8,000	18,000.0	9,000	80,000	90,000
4	6,400	31,421.0	7,855.3	64,000	78,553
8	5,120	53,459.1	6,682.4	51,200	66,824
16	4,096	89,201.4	5,575.1	40,960	55,751
32	3,276.8	146,786.2	4,587.1	32,768	45,871
64	2,621.4	239,245.3	3,738.2	26,214	37,382
128	2,097.2	387,439.5	3,026.9	20,972	30,269
256	1,677.7	624,731.8	2,404.6	16,777	24,046

Wage rate = $10/hr.

where Y_x = Units of factor (labor hours) or cost to produce xth unit
K = Factor units or cost to produce kth (usually first) unit
x = Product unit (the xth unit)
n = log S/log 2
S = Slope parameter

For an 80 percent learning curve, the number of direct labor hours required to produce the eighth unit of output is

$$S = .8$$

$$Y_8 = 100,000 \, (8)^{\log.8/\log2}$$

$$= 100,000 \, (8)^{-.322}$$

$$= \frac{100,000}{8^{.322}}$$

$$= \frac{100,000}{1.9535} = 51,200$$

This answer conforms to Table 8.6 and Figure 8.12. You may want to try constructing other learning curves based on different percentages, or refer to learning curve tables in an engineering textbook.

Although the learning curve is expressed in terms of the marginal cost of production, the impact of improving with practice can also be seen in terms of the decline in average cost. Table 8.6 also shows the cumulative labor cost and the cumulative average labor cost of producing various levels of output. As can be seen, the average labor cost also decreases, although not as sharply as the marginal labor cost. In any case, the learning curve effect clearly has an impact on the short-run cost pre-

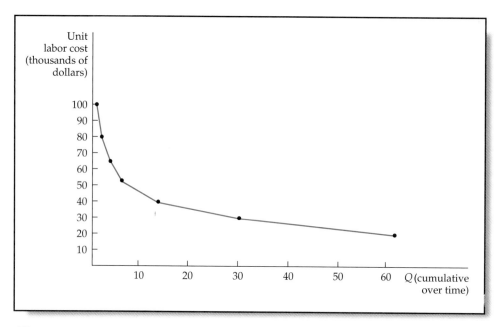

Figure 8.12
An 80 Percent Learning Curve

sented earlier. In particular, the learning curve effect causes the short-run average cost curve to shift downward. This is shown in Figure 8.13.

The Japanese have been frequently cited in academic studies and in the popular press for their use of the learning curve in driving down costs. This is most dramatically shown in their production of computer chips and consumer electronics. Their particular use of the learning curve involves accelerating production experience

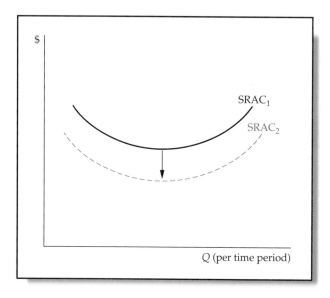

Figure 8.13
Impact of Learning Curve
Effect on Short-Run Average
Cost per Time Period

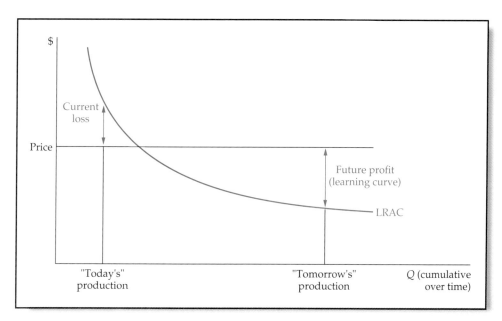

Figure 8.14
Pricing Based on Learning or Experience Curve

through aggressive price-cutting measures. The price cuts enhance sales and give them production experience more rapidly. This in turn helps to drive down costs of production faster. The tactic of learning curve pricing is illustrated in Figure 8.14.

In concluding this section on the learning curve effect, we should note that this phenomenon was first observed in the production of aircraft more than 50 years ago. The reason cited for the learning curve effect was the repetition of tasks performed by workers actually manufacturing the product (e.g., direct labor). Later on, the experience gained from repetition by those indirectly related to the production process (e.g., engineers and researchers) was also included in this phenomenon. Thus, such factors as the development of new process and engineering methods, the substitution of lower-cost materials or processes, and product redesign were also considered as factors causing unit costs to decrease as production levels increased. The recognition of these additional factors prompted the use of the broader term **experience curve.** Today, *experience curve* and *learning curve* are generally used interchangeably. However, some business managers and consultants still prefer to make a distinction between the two terms.

ECONOMIES OF SCOPE

Before summarizing this chapter, we should introduce briefly a concept often used in business but that does not quite fit into the conventional economic theory of cost, namely, **economies of scope.** This term can be defined as the reduction of a firm's unit cost by producing two or more goods or services jointly rather than separately.

The effort by our hypothetical firm Global Foods, Inc., to increase its profits by expanding into the soft drink industry offers a good example of a company seeking to take advantage of economies of scope. The company already has the knowledge, experience, and skills to produce and distribute processed food items and hopes to use these attributes in the production and distribution of soft drinks.

In a sense, the concept of economies of scope is closely related to economies of scale. Engaging in more than one line of business may require a firm to have a certain minimum scale of operation. Another way to view this relationship between scale and scope is to consider that a company's expansion into different lines of business naturally increases its scale of operation.

Economies of scope is a very important concept in the production of services as well as goods. As an example, Fingerhut is a catalog company that specializes in selling products to lower-income households (i.e., below $29,200 per year). The company assumes a higher risk but charges higher prices for their products to compensate for this. In recent years, the increased marketing of credit cards by banks to the same lower-income households that are targeted by Fingerhut have hurt the company's sales. In retaliation, Fingerhut began offering credit cards to its catalog customers through a separate subsidiary, Metris. The key to this company's success is a list of 30 million names that Fingerhut accumulated over the years from its direct mail business. This list contains critical information not generally available through the credit bureaus that issuers of credit cards use, such as occupation, number of children, hobbies, home ownership, and spending and payment patterns. Most important, the list includes 11 million "no-pays" that are purged from every direct mail campaign or solicitation.[8] Thus, we have a good example of how economies of scope is achieved through the sharing of a database between two separate lines of business.

ECONOMIES OF SCALE: THE SHORT RUN VERSUS THE LONG RUN

Economies of scale essentially means that a company's average cost decreases at higher levels of output. In microeconomic theory, *scale* implies a long-run time period. Recall that the economic meaning of *long-run* implies that firms have time to adjust their fixed factors of production. In terms of cost, this means in effect that a firm's "fixed" cost is really "variable" in the long run. Another possible action that a firm could take in the long run is to merge with or acquire another firm or be acquired by another firm. When potential mergers are announced, the CEOs often tell the analysts that one of the benefits is "economies of scale."

From time to time, we have observed that the term *economies of scale* is used in the context of a "short-run" time period. In other words, authors of articles might say that a firm tries to take advantage of economies of scale by operating its plant at or near full capacity. This type of scale economies occurs because in so doing, a firm is

---

[8]Joseph B. Cahill, "Credit Companies Find Tough Rival at Bottom of Consumer Market," *The Wall Street Journal*, December 29, 1998.

spreading out its fixed or overhead costs. This was not the original intention of economic theorists, but we cannot prevent writers from using the term in this way. Therefore, a useful distinction can be made between "short-run economies of scale" and "long-run economies of scale." The reason for the first type of economies is the spreading of fixed cost. The reasons for the second type are all listed in Table 8.4.

SUPPLY CHAIN MANAGEMENT

Supply chain management (SCM) has become a very important way for companies to reduce their costs. Readers will undoubtedly study SCM in great detail in an operations research or production course in an undergraduate or MBA curriculum. Certain elements of SCM pertain either directly or indirectly to managerial economics. As you can see, SCM played a part in the "Situation" that we presented at the beginning of this chapter. Therefore, we now present a brief introduction to the subject.

Supply chain management can be defined as "efforts by a firm to improve efficiencies through each link of a firm's supply chain from supplier to customer." This is done primarily by fostering better communication and cooperation within each link by all parties involved. The goal of SCM is to increase profits primarily by reducing costs. But SCM can also help to increase profits indirectly because a more efficiently operating supply chain can increase customer satisfaction. This in turn may enable firms to charge a premium price or at least help them to retain their customers. Figure 8.15 shows a supply chain for a typical manufacturing company and the efficiencies that SCM hopes to accomplish at each linkage point.

In the most general sense of the term, supply chain management includes all of the firm's internal and external activities required to fulfill its customer's demand. Historically a typical firm, particularly in manufacturing, was a completely vertically integrated entity. U.S. Steel had its own coal mines that eventually fired up its mills. IBM made its own chips (and still does) that go into its computers. But in recent years, much more of a company's activities have been outsourced to other

Figure 8.15
Supply Chain Management

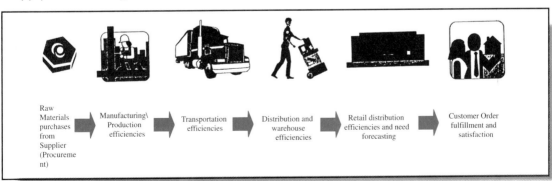

Raw Materials purchases from Supplier (Procurement) → Manufacturing\Production efficiencies → Transportation efficiencies → Distribution and warehouse efficiencies → Retail distribution efficiencies and need forecasting → Customer Order fulfillment and satisfaction

companies.[9] Does Folgers have its own coffee plantations? Does General Motors manufacture antilock brakes or catalytic converters? Have you ever heard of a company called Arima?[10] And herein lies the reason for the increasing importance of SCM among practioners as well as the increasing attention given to it by academic economists. Presumably a firm outsources certain activities to reduce costs. But once the activity is outside the direct control of the firm, there may be certain other costs that may in fact outweigh the cost savings of outsourcing. Let us continue with this discussion by focusing on just one particular aspect of the complete supply chain: the linkage between a raw material and parts supplier (henceforth referred to as the "outside supplier" or "vendor") and a manufacturing company that is purchasing these inputs (henceforth referred to as the "firm" or the "company"). In the context of this particular link, our topic is essentially the "make versus buy" decision that is also discussed in accounting and finance texts, as well as economics texts.[11]

From the perspective of managerial economics, the "make versus buy" decision or the trade-off between cost savings by going outside the firm versus costs incurred by staying inside raises the most fundamental of all questions: What is a firm? Recall our discussion of this question at the very outset of chapter 2, "The Firm and Its Goals." You may also recall that the seminal work on this subject was done by Professor Ronald Coase, who received a Nobel Prize in Economics for this work. Essentially, Coase postulated that a company compares the costs of organizing an activity internally with the cost of using the market system for its transactions. The cost incurred by using resources outside was what he called "transaction costs." These costs include the original investigation to find the outside firm, followed by the cost of negotiating a contract, and later yet, enforcing the contract.

Following Coase's path-breaking work, two other categories of costs of going outside the firm have been identified in addition to transactions costs: coordination costs and information costs.[12] Coordination costs arise because of the uncertainty and complexity of such tasks as timing the deliveries, meeting customer specifications, making alternative payments arrangements, and forecasting needs. Uncertainty exists because it simply may be impossible to plan for or insert in a contractual agreement what to do for every possible case in which an outside supplier is

---

[9]For example, as described in chapter 16, semiconductor companies have significantly increased the outsourcing of the production of wafers and the packaging of chips. Another example is the fact that automobile companies have long been engaged in the outsourcing of many parts of a typical car. (The serious, lengthy, and combative strike of GM workers in 2000 was primarily about workers trying to stop GM's outsourcing of brake production.)

[10]Arima is a Taiwan-based, global company with $1.8 billion in annual sales that makes everything from wafers to battery packs to computer game software for its OEM clients. See *www.arima.com.tw*.

[11]Potentially any or all links of a supply chain could be outsourced in any type of industry. Therefore, supply chain management costs discussed in this section have much broader implications. Think about the supply chain problems that occur when a bank issuing credit cards outsources its direct mail advertising or its billing or even its call centers. Think about what e-Bay is. Some might consider it the ultimate outsourced retail company. Companies that outsource most of their activities have been referred to as "virtual corporations." See our discussion on this in chapter 12.

[12]One could argue that these costs are all part of transactions costs. However, supply chain management experts prefer to use these additional categories. See, for example, Ian Stuart and David McCutheon, "The Manager's Guide to Supply Chain Management," *Business Horizons*, March/April, 2000, pp. 35–44. Some of this section's comments on contracts and supplier relationships were taken from this article.

not able to completely satisfy the firm's requirements. Information costs arise because information is essential to the proper coordination of activities between the firm and its suppliers. For example, to meet the firm's exact specifications, a supplier might require timely and detailed information about a firm's sales. This may mean that a firm has to provide its suppliers with proprietary information. Short of sharing this type of information, the firm must be prepared to sacrifice some efficiency in the supplier's delivery obligations. If this information is shared, there is a certain amount of cost associated with setting up and maintaining the necessary technology platform (e.g., data communications network, logistics software, etc.). As is the case with coordination problems, the need for information flows complicates the relationship between a firm and its outside supplier that also cannot be easily addressed with a contract, no matter how detailed are the terms and conditions.

In the linkage between the firm purchasing the input and the firm supplying the input, one critical indicator of supply chain efficiency is the level of inventory. Ideally, the firm purchasing the input wants to hold no inventory in excess of what it needs to fulfill what its customers demand. Some years ago, Japanese automobile manufacturers became well known for their "just in time" (JIT) inventory control system. What we are talking about is very similar, except we consider JIT to be a part of a bigger picture, i.e., SCM. If anything goes wrong in this linkage, firms purchasing the input will find themselves with more or less inventory than desired. And firms selling the inputs will find themselves with an inventory problem that is a mirror image of the one experienced by firms purchasing its product. As a result, the vendor may be faced with either too much or too little capacity in its production facilities relative to the purchasing firm's mismatch of inventory levels and needs. In all cases, added costs are involved. How should this link of the supply chain be managed in such a way that neither party experiences these problems and added costs?

There are numerous consultants and software products out in the marketplace that promise firms an answer to this question not only for purchasing but for the entire supply chain. This is supposedly what a consultant implies when he or she uses the term *supply chain management* as a buzz-word. Indeed, we can venture to say that all or most major consulting firms have their own supply chain management practice. Moreover, software companies such as Oracle, SAP, PeopleSoft, and Manugistics offer software packages that help companies to become more efficient in some or all aspects of their supply chain. And of course there is a further symbiotic relationship between consultants and software companies. Ideally, they can both do business with a firm wishing to improve its supply chain management. How? The consultants (such as IBM Global Services, EDS, or Accenture) are hired by the firm to implement the software!

If it were easy enough to hire a consultant and implement the right software package, then very few firms would even have problems in the procurement linkage of the supply chain, or for that matter any other linkage in the chain. Yet it is safe to say that many still do. A key reason for this was cited earlier and has to do with a contract. As previously pointed out, no contract between a firm and its vendor can provide contingencies for every possible thing that could go wrong in the business relationship. Moreover, the more money and time involved, the more difficult it is to cover everything. Another reason is the difficulty of forecasting demand. This is exactly what happened in the case of the semiconductor industry supplying chips to hardware manufacturers.[13]

To offset the inherent limitations of a contract, experts suggest that firms develop good working relationships with their suppliers. There are essentially two types of relationships. One type involves the firm and the outside supplier joining together in some sharing of resources. This is often termed a *strategic alliance*. The other type is a less involved relationship which involves the firm utilizing two or more suppliers. This produces *competitive tension* among the suppliers, thereby helping the firm to keep its purchase prices under control.

In our view, the type of relationship that a firm cultivates with its supplier depends on the characteristics of the inputs and the output. Competitive tension relationships are usually more appropriate when standardized inputs and output are involved. For example, a soft drink manufacturer buys high-fructose corn syrup, aluminum cans, or plastic bottles from outside suppliers. Strategic alliances are more useful in cases that involve highly differentiated products. An example would be a high-tech manufacturer of intricate electronic devices that buys highly customized computer chips.[14]

EXAMPLES OF WAYS COMPANIES HAVE CUT COSTS TO REMAIN COMPETITIVE

The consideration of cost in business decisions often evokes mixed feelings among managers. This is because efforts to reduce costs may involve the downsizing of staff, the layoff of workers, reductions in discretionary expenses for such things as training and travel, or the elimination of executive perquisites such as corporate jets. In contrast, efforts to increase revenues involve growth and all of the activities that accompany it (such as new hires, better equipment, new offices, and increases in discretionary spending and perquisites). Yet, from an objective standpoint, it is clear that a dollar saved, given some level of output and revenue, adds as much to the bottom line as an additional dollar of revenue, given some level of output and cost. Following are examples of cost-cutting methods or procedures that firms have implemented in order to remain competitive.

1. *The Strategic Use of Cost*[15]

As we explain in a later chapter of this text (see chapter 10), a firm may choose to use cost leadership as the core of its strategy for competing in the marketplace. In the retail industry, the example that immediately comes to mind is Wal-Mart. In the airline industry, it is Southwest Airlines. Let us

---

[13]See chapter 16 for details. Also, Cisco, the company whose CEO once claimed that his firm could close the books of its multibillion dollar business on the last day of every month because of its sophisticated data network and software, experienced serous inventory problems in the downturn of the technology sector in 2001.

[14]This is exactly the relationship between STMicroelectronics and its major customer Nokia. ST sells chips to Nokia that go into its cell phones. Both work together in the design phase of the chip-making process. See chapter 16 for further details.

[15]For a good historical review of Southwest Airlines' start-up and operations, see Christopher H. Lovelock, "Southwest Airlines," Harvard Business School Case Study #575-060, 1975.

look closer at how this airline used cost leadership as an integral part of its strategy.

Southwest Airlines began in 1967 as a small operation aimed at improving air service between Houston, Dallas-Fort Worth, and San Antonio, Texas. Today it is a formidable competitor in the short-haul (500 miles or less) air transportation market. Indeed, there are now certain routes (for example, Burbank, California to Las Vegas, Nevada) that the major airlines such as American Airlines have withdrawn from since Southwest's entry into the market. Southwest Airlines has achieved this success by being the low-cost provider of short-haul service. Its everyday fares can be as low as one-third of the standard fares charged by the major airlines on short-haul routes.

Among the key cost items that gives Southwest a cost advantage over American and the other major airlines is payroll (it employs nonunion personnel), food (no food is served on short-haul flights), and depreciation (Southwest's fleet is not as new as American's).

It is more meaningful to look at Southwest's cost advantage not as a series of ad hoc cost-cutting measures, but as the consequence of its overall market strategy. When the founders of Southwest Airlines devised their strategy of providing low-priced air transportation in the short-haul market, it anticipated being able to keep costs down by virtue of the very strategy that they selected. By flying only on short-haul routes, Southwest needed only one type of aircraft (the Boeing 737). This meant less training costs for flying and maintenance as well as a lower inventory of replacement parts. Furthermore, short hauls require no in-flight meals. In addition, because it has positioned itself in the minds of its customers as a low-cost provider of air transportation, it can save more money by cutting out services or conveniences that customers generally expect from the major airlines. For example, Southwest does not take reservations, thereby saving money on staff and computer services. Whenever possible, it also uses secondary or alternative airports, thereby avoiding the higher landing fees charged by the major-hub airports.[16]

The cost leadership model has proved to be very resilient in the most recent economic and industry downturn. While all the major airlines were announcing huge losses for 2001, Southwest continued to earn a profit. Furthermore, Southwest's success has prompted other companies to copy this approach, in Europe as well as in the United States. EasyJet in the U.K. and Ryan Air in Ireland have both become successful short-haul European carriers using the same "point-to-point" routing and very low fares to attract leisure travelers. In the United States, JetBlue began by focusing on various routes within New York State.[17]

2. *Reduction in Cost of Materials*

Manufacturers are constantly seeking to cut costs by materials substitution or modification. In the beverage industry, one noticeable example of this is

---

[16]Most of the material in this section was taken from Gene Walden and Edmund O. Lawler, *Marketing Masters: Secrets of America's Best Companies,* New York: HarperCollins, 1993, pp. 17–22.
[17]In spring 2002, JetBlue became a publicly traded company. Its IPO was very successful, but a few months later analysts considered it to be overvalued.

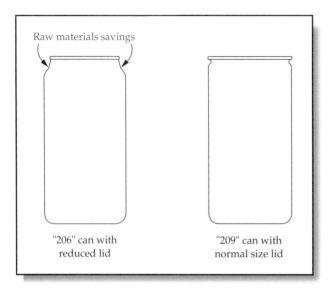

Figure 8.16
Using Reduced-Lid Can to Achieve Raw Materials Savings

"206" can with reduced lid

"209" can with normal size lid

Raw materials savings

the reduction in the size of the lid of a 12-oz. aluminum can. Towards the end of the bottling process, each can on the conveyor belt passes a measuring device called a "fill height detector" that checks if there are at least 12 ounces of liquid in the container. Those with less are discarded. This measuring device shoots a gamma beam about one-quarter inch below the top of the can's lid. Because it is not necessary for the product to be filled to the very top of the can, the lid can be made slightly smaller by crimping the top portion of the can. The savings from the reduction in the aluminum content are considerable, given the millions of cans that are produced each year (Figure 8.16).

3. *Using Information Technology (IT) to Reduce Costs*

From its early beginnings as a tool for the mechanization of routine business tasks such as accounting, IT has played an increasingly greater role in the efforts by companies to reduce costs. The real break-through in using IT to reduce costs began in the early 1990s with *enterprise resource planning* (ERP). SAP, a German company, was one of the first companies to offer services for this tool and continues today to be a leader in the industry. Other companies offering similar products are PeopleSoft and Oracle.

ERP is the industry term for software that enables companies to integrate their planning, scheduling, synchronization, and tracking of the entire chain of their production process. The use of ERP has helped companies to cut costs as well as increase revenues by getting the right products into the hands of their customers in the most timely and efficient way. SAP's web site (*www.sap.com*) provides examples of how companies have saved money by using its products and services. For example, Larry Bergner, vice president of technology for the Earthgrains Company (owner and operator of 39 bakeries and dough plants in the United States, and 8 bakeries and one dough plant in Europe) said that the use of SAP's products "has allowed us to control our disbursements from one central location, giving us better management of our working capital. It's [also] enabled us to streamline our procurement cycle, with an immediate savings of millions of dollars per year."[18] No doubt similar savings also have been achieved by using other companies' ERP products and services.

In more recent years, supply chain management and "B2B" exchanges and other efforts under the general heading of "e-Business" have extended the earlier ERP initiatives. We just discussed SCM in the previous section. B2B and e-Business are discussed in chapter 12. Even more recently, many large, global companies that operate teams of people in "virtual" environments have found that the management of information is a critical part of keeping costs under control. Therefore, software companies and consultants offering products and services such as knowledge sharing or management, document management, and on-line collaborative tools have become very important for companies trying to control their information costs.[19]

4. *Reduction of Process Costs*

Cost savings stemming from the use of ERP has been getting most of the attention in the popular press and the literature on business studies. However, there are also more specific but equally important ways that appropriate software can help to cut costs. More companies are starting to require that their employees use software packages to file travel and expense reports electronically. Studies by American Express found that U.S. companies spent about $175 billion on travel and expenses in 1998 and that the use of electronic filing can cut the cost of processing expense reports from $36.46 per paper report to as low as $7.91.[20]

5. *Relocation to Lower-Wage Countries or Regions*

We have already noted how a number of American companies have decided to relocate to regions or countries where wages are lower to reduce the cost of production. American companies are not the only ones to take this cost-reducing measure. Japanese companies have been relocating to all parts of Southeast Asia. German companies have been moving to Central European countries such as Poland, where wages are less than one-tenth of the average rate in Germany. There are other examples, such as an Austrian company moving to Slovakia and a French company partnering with a German company to manufacture products in Hungary. Furthermore, manufacturing companies are not the only ones who can benefit from the move to lower-wage countries. A thriving software development industry has emerged in India, where American and European companies find that the average wage rate of an Indian programmer is about one-fourth of a comparable person in the United States.[21]

---

[18]Retrieved February 12, 1999 from the World Wide Web: www.sap.com/products/industry/consum/media/earthgr.htm.

[19]Readers interested in all of these special IT topics can obtain current information by reading industry trade journals or specialized periodicals on the subject. We believe *CIO* magazine is one of the best sources for the nontechnical manager.

[20]"Software Is Easing Expense-Form Headaches," *The Wall Street Journal,* December 28, 1998.

[21]See Peter Gumbel, "Western Europe Finds That It's Pricing Itself Out of the Job Market," *The Wall Street Journal,* December 9, 1993; "Europe: The Push East," *Business Week,* November 2, 1994, pp. 48–49. Information about wage rates for Indian software programmers was acquired in an interview in November, 1998 with a representative from Tata, India's largest manufacturing, service, and information technology conglomerate.

6. *Mergers, Consolidations, and Downsizing*

This particular approach to cost cutting was cited earlier in this chapter. We also discuss it briefly in chapter 15. Within the past several years, a number of significant mergers or acquisitions among very large firms have taken place in various industries. For example: Daimler-Benz and Chrysler (auto manufacturers); American Airlines and TWA (airlines); SmithKline Beecham and Glaxo-Welcome, now called "GSK" (pharmaceuticals); and Bell Atlantic and GTE, now called Verizon (telecommunications); and Hewlett-Packard and Compac (computers and IT). Of course, one of the biggest involved AOL and Time-Warner (itself the result of various mergers or acquisitions that involved other giant companies such as Turner Broadcasting). But this merger was not presented as mainly a cost-cutting action. It supposedly was done more to generate increased revenues through the cross-selling of products on the Internet and television and the teaming of content with media distribution.

7. *Layoffs and Plant Closings*

Sometimes companies find it necessary to resort to simply laying off workers and closing down certain operations. The recession that began in the spring of 2001 has triggered numerous layoffs by many companies. Ford and Kodak were among the more prominent companies that had to lay off thousands of its workers.

Although downsizing and restructuring have become practically a way of life for corporate America, they have become much more common in many other parts of the world. Japan, in particular, has been hit hard by this management effort to cut costs. For the Japanese worker, long used to "lifetime employment," this has been very difficult to handle.[22] However, it is gradually becoming more acceptable as an inevitable management tool. The recent success of Renault senior management in the turnaround of Nissan Motors, the company in which it holds a significant equity, is cited as an example of how layoffs can play an important role in the revival of an ailing Japanese company.[23]

INTERNATIONAL APPLICATION: ANOTHER WAY FOR JAPANESE MANUFACTURERS TO REDUCE COSTS

Japanese manufacturers have long had the reputation for being among the most cost-efficient companies in the world. Interestingly enough, the conversion of Western Europe to the euro has provided a good opportunity to reduce costs even further. An article in the *Financial Times* reports that Canon, "one of the world's biggest makers

---

[22]In "Sign of Changed Times: Japan's Jobless Rate Rises to the U.S. Level," *The Wall Street Journal*, December 28, 1998, the author of the article ported that Hoya Corporation, a Tokyo optical glass maker, laid off about one third of its work force through an early retirement program. Those who did not take the program would have faced pay cuts of 30 percent. One unnamed company supposedly ordered its older office workers to chop wood to persuade them to opt for retirement.

[23]"Nissan Returns to Profit," BBC News Service, May 17, 2001.

of cameras and photocopiers, plans to cut its European distribution costs by 20 percent over the next two years."[24] According to the chief of Canon's European operations, Hajime Tsuruoka, the company's cost-cutting strategy "would not be possible without the euro."

Essentially, the euro has prompted a harmonization of prices across Europe and has eliminated the transaction costs associated with different currencies. This essentially means that Canon will be able to reduce by about 50 percent the number of warehouses that it now has all over Europe. There will be economies of scale in having this smaller number of much larger warehouses. Most affected will be the warehouses in smaller countries such as Austria, Norway, and Finland. Warehousing is an important component of cost for Canon in Europe. About 80 percent of its sales in the continent are imported products made in Asia.[25]

The Solution

Terry now needed to put all of the pieces together to figure out if Lawrence Aluminum is really the right way to go. Even before crunching the numbers, she knew she had a somewhat delicate situation to consider. Her company had been doing business with Kayla Containers for many years, and the two companies had developed a close relationship (as well as friendly rivalry in the local softball league). If Shayna Soda stopped ordering from Kayla, Kayla could very easily go out of business. Lawrence is just a start-up, eager to grab new business by "low-balling" its prices. But what if Lawrence went out of business or decided not to source to upstate New York bottlers? Then what would her company do?

With this in mind, she turned to the facts. There was no denying that Kayla Containers had a higher base fee on soda cans, but that included the artwork. Furthermore, Kayla was always willing to change the artwork at no extra cost. Lawrence Aluminum's cans would be more than 20% cheaper in the base fee, but the artwork required an extra one-time fee. Terry took that fee and divided it out for the year to figure what the impact would be on the average cost of the cans for the first year. This fee increased the base cost of the cans another 2%. The cans were still considerably cheaper.

Next Terry considered the delivery charge. Kayla Containers was only 20 miles from Shayna's production plant. The delivery fee for Kayla was basically the same as Lawrence's base fee. But Kayla's fee was for only 20 miles delivery and Lawrence was for 400 miles delivery. In addition, Lawrence charged extra for specific time delivery and could even

(Continued)

---

[24]"Canon sees savings linked to euro," *Financial Times,* February 4, 2002.
[25]Ibid.

require the company to take inventory earlier than it wanted. Terry calculated the average cost of delivery annually using Kayla, and then for Lawrence. Then she also had to determine what the warehouse carrying costs would be for the inventory that would have to be held on early delivery. For each day that the cans were early, Shayna would incur extra costs for having that inventory on the floor. And if the inventory needed to be moved for any reason, than there was a man-hour issue involved. Now the costs really changed. Taking into consideration all these additional costs, Lawrence's base cost now jumped to 8% higher than Kayla.

Terry wanted to immediately run into Adam's office to tell him that Kayla was the better choice, but she first had to make sure that she covered all angles. She admitted that Lawrence Aluminum had a better quality aluminum, but Kay's quality was perfectly acceptable and in fact better than Shayna's corporate minimum requirements. As far as technology was concerned, Terry knew that her company's computer systems needed to be upgraded in order for them to use a sophisticated supply chain management process regardless of which supplier they used.

The technology issue actually proved to be a critical factor in helping Terry to make her decision. She figured that if her company went with Lawrence Aluminum, then it would have to set up its systems according to this new vendor's specifications. Kayla, on the other hand, did not have a sophisticated system in place and in fact was also thinking that it needed to upgrade its system, too. If Shayna stuck with Kayla, then Kayla would have to set up its system in a way that would integrate with Shayna's. It would be the other way around for Shayna if Lawrence Aluminum became the supplier. Terry e-mailed her friend Ryan over at Kayla to see if this would be a good move from Kayla's point of view. As soon as Ryan got her e-mail he picked up the phone to talk to her in person. Given the possibility of losing a major customer and the fact that his company had to improve its systems anyway, there was no question in Ryan's mind that Shayna would work in every way possible to keep Shayna as its customer.

Now Terry was ready. It was Friday and she had all the answers to bring to Adam Michaels. As soon as she walked in, Adam asked, "When are we switching?"

Terry replied confidently, "We're not, we're sticking with Kayla."

SUMMARY

This chapter has been devoted to the analysis of the cost structure of the firm, both in the short run and the long run. In the short-run analysis, it is important to keep in mind that "behind the scenes," the law of diminishing returns causes the firm's marginal cost to increase, and that this increase in turn affects the pattern of behavior of the firm's average variable cost and average total cost. In the long-run analysis, it is important to recognize that certain factors may cause the firm's unit costs to decrease as its scale of operation increases. However, certain other factors may actually cause the unit cost to increase if the scale of operations becomes too large. In addition, other factors such as the learning curve effect and economies of scope must be taken into account in the long-run analysis of cost.

The material that has been covered in this chapter may seem rather mundane because of the great emphasis placed on defining the various cost terms used in economic analysis. However, your patience and thoroughness in reading this chapter will be rewarded when you read the next four chapters. There you will find that the material in this chapter, together with the analysis of demand presented in chapters 3 and 4, forms the core of the economic analysis of the firm. As you will learn, all the decisions involving the production and pricing of goods or services—and, in a much broader sense, the very desirability for a firm to be in a particular line of business—depend on the demand for the particular product, the cost at which the firm is able to provide this product, and the competitive structure of the market in which it is operating.

IMPORTANT CONCEPTS (Items with * are discussed in Appendix 8B.)

Average fixed cost (AFC): The fixed cost per unit of output. (p. 342)

Average total cost (AC or ATC): The total cost per unit of output. (p. 342)

Average variable cost (AVC): The variable cost per unit of output. (p. 342)

Diseconomies of scale: The increase in the unit cost of production as the firm increases its capacity. Like economies of scale, this is considered to be a long-run phenomenon. Among the more important reasons a firm may experience rising unit costs as its scale of production increases are (1) management coordination and control problems and (2) a disproportionate increase in staff in relation to indirect labor. (p. 348)

Economies of scale: The reduction in the unit cost of production as the firm increases its capacity (i.e., increases all of its inputs). It is considered a long-run phenomenon. Among the reasons a firm experiences economies as its scale of production increases are (1) the ability to exact volume discounts from vendors, (2) the ability to utilize more fully specialization and division of labor, (3) the ability to justify the use of certain types of capital equipment or technology appropriate only for very large scales of production, and (4) management efficiencies resulting from an increased span of control at all levels of management. (p. 348)

Economies of scope: The reduction in cost resulting from the joint production of two or more goods or services. (p. 359)

*Engineering cost estimating: A method of estimating long-run costs. Professionals familiar with production facilities calculate optimal combinations of inputs needed to produce given quantities of output. Monetary values are then assigned to obtain cost. (p. 392)

*Estimation of long-run cost functions: Analysis that assumes that all factors, especially capital, are variable. Cross-sectional regression analysis is customarily employed in the estimation. (p. 387)

*Estimation of short-run cost functions: An analysis in which certain factors are assumed to be fixed during the period analyzed. Time series regression analysis is customarily employed in the estimation. (p. 381)

Experience curve: The relationship between the unit cost of labor and all inputs associated with the production process (i.e., both direct labor, such as factory workers, and indirect labor, such as design engineers). (p. 359)

Historical cost: The cost incurred in a past activity (e.g., the purchase price of an asset or the cost of a project incurred up to the point at which a decision is to be made). (p. 336)

Incremental cost: The total cost associated with a particular decision (e.g., the cost of building an additional wing to an office building, the cost of going into the soft drink business). If incremental cost is considered on a per-unit basis, it becomes marginal cost. For example, incremental cost can be considered the change in total variable cost, whereas marginal cost can be considered the change in total variable cost divided by the change in output. (p. 337)

Learning curve: The relationship between the unit cost of labor and the total amount of output produced by labor that is directly associated with the production process (i.e., "direct labor"). Essentially, this concept is based on the principle that one improves with practice. The resulting productivity gains lead to a reduction in the direct labor cost of producing a unit of output. (p. 356)

Marginal cost (MC): The cost to a firm of producing an additional unit of an output. (p. 339)

Opportunity cost: The amount of subjective value forgone in choosing one activity over the next best alternative. (p. 336)

Relevant costs: Costs that are affected by a current decision alternative and that must therefore be taken into account in the decision. Variable costs and incremental costs are considered to be relevant costs. (p. 336)

Sunk cost: A cost incurred in the past that is not affected by a current decision. If a resource has no opportunity cost (i.e., it has no market value in an alternative use), it is considered to be sunk. (p. 337)

Supply chain management: Efforts by a firm to improve efficiencies through each link of a firm's supply chain from supplier to customer. (p. 361)

*Survivorship technique: A method for estimating long-run cost curves. The proportion of total industry output by firms of different sizes is observed over a period of time. That size segment of the industry that gains in proportion of industry output over time is deemed most efficient (lowest cost). (p. 393)

Total cost (TC): The total cost of production, including both total variable and total fixed costs. (p. 339)

Total cost function: Economic analysis considers three basic functional forms of total cost: cubic, quadratic, and linear. The microeconomic theory of the firm relies almost entirely on the cubic function, and break-even analysis generally uses the linear form. (p. 344)

Total fixed cost (TFC): A cost that remains constant as the level of output varies. In a short-run analysis, fixed cost is incurred even if the firm produces no output. (p. 339)

Total variable cost (TVC): The total cost associated with the level of output. This can also be considered the total cost to a firm of using its variable inputs. (p. 338)

QUESTIONS

1. Define and compare the following types of cost:
   a. Sunk cost versus incremental cost
   b. Fixed cost versus variable cost
   c. Incremental cost versus marginal cost
   d. Opportunity cost versus out-of-pocket cost

2. Point out which costs in the preceding question are considered "relevant" and which are considered "irrelevant" to a business decision. Explain why.

3. Explain the relationship between a firm's short-run production function and its short-run cost function. Focus on the marginal product of an input and the marginal cost of production.

4. "If it were not for the law of diminishing returns, a firm's average cost and average variable cost would not increase in the short run." Do you agree with this statement? Explain.

5. Explain the distinction made in economic analysis between the short run and the long run.

6. Define *economies of scale*. How does this relate to returns to scale? Cite and briefly discuss the main determinants of economies of scale.

7. Define *diseconomies of scale*. Cite and briefly discuss the main determinants of this phenomenon.

8. Define *economies of scope.* Is this concept related to economies of scale? Explain.

9. Explain the relationship between the learning curve and a firm's cost function. Would economists consider the learning curve a short-run or a long-run phenomenon?

10. Define the *experience curve.* Compare its impact on a firm's cost function with that of the learning curve.

11. "Because of economies of scale, it is sometimes more cost effective for a firm to operate a large plant at less than maximum efficiency than a small plant at maximum efficiency." Do you agree with this statement? Explain.

12. When a company states its financial results in its annual report, it typically presents its income statement in the following way:

	Revenue
−	Cost of Goods Sold (including some depreciation)
	Gross Profit
−	Selling, General and Administrative Expenses
−	Research and Development
−	Depreciation
	Operating Profit
+/−	Net Interest (income and expense)
	Net Profit before Income Taxes
−	Taxes
	Net Profit after Income Taxes

"Cost of goods sold" includes all costs directly associated with making a product or providing a service. In retail merchandising this cost is essentially the wholesale cost of goods sold.

Discuss the differences between cost of goods sold and the concept of relevant cost used in this chapter. Are there any situations in which selling, general and administrative expenses, or research and development expenses might be considered as part of a firm's relevant costs? Explain.

13. Overheard at the water cooler: "I think our company should take advantage of economies of scale by increasing our output, thereby spreading out our overhead costs." Would you agree with this statement (assuming this person is not your boss)? Explain.

Refer to Appendix 8B for help in answering questions 14 through 16.

14. Discuss the estimation of short-run cost functions. Which regression method is most frequently used, and what are some of the problems a researcher will encounter? What adjustment factors may have to be employed?

15. Discuss the estimation of long-run cost functions. Which regression method is most frequently used, and what are some of the problems a researcher will encounter? What adjustment factors may have to be employed?

16. Comment briefly on the following methods of cost estimation:
   a. Engineering costs
   b. Survivorship principle
   Discuss the strengths and shortcomings of these methods and the circumstances under which each can be applied.

1. Based on your knowledge of the definition of the various measures of short-run cost, complete the table below.

Q	TC	TFC	TVC	AC	AFC	AVC	MC
0	120	—	—	x	x	x	x
1	—	—	—	265	—	—	—
2	—	—	264	—	—	—	—
3	—	—	—	161	—	—	—
4	—	—	—	—	—	—	85
5	—	—	525	—	—	—	—
6	—	—	—	120	—	—	—
7	—	—	—	—	—	97	—
8	—	—	768	—	—	—	—
9	—	—	—	—	—	97	—
10	—	—	—	—	—	—	127

2. Mr. Lee operates a green grocery in a building he owns in one of the outer boroughs of New York City. Recently, a large chemical firm offered him a position as a senior engineer designing plants for its Asian operations. (Mr. Lee has a master's degree in chemical engineering.) His salary plus benefits would be $95,000 per year. A recent annual financial statement of his store's operations indicates the following:

Revenue	$625,000
Cost of goods sold	325,000
Wages of workers	75,000
Taxes, insurance, maintenance, and depreciation on building	30,000
Interest on business loan (10%)	5,000
Other miscellaneous expenses	15,000
Profit before taxes	$175,000

If Mr. Lee decides to take the job, he knows that he can sell the store for $350,000 because of the goodwill built with a steady clientele of neighborhood customers and the excellent location of the building. He would still hold on to the building, however, and he knows he could earn a rent of $50,000 on this asset. If he did sell the business, assume that he would use some of the proceeds from the sale to pay off his business loan of $50,000. He could then invest the difference of $300,000 (i.e., $350,000 − $50,000) and expect to receive an annual return of 9 percent. Should Mr. Lee sell his business and go to work for the chemical company?

In answering this question, also consider the following information:

a. In his own business, Mr. Lee works between 16 and 18 hours a day, six days a week. He can expect to work between 10 and 12 hours a day, five days a week, in the chemical company.

b. Currently, Mr. Lee is assisted by his wife and his brother, both of whom receive no salary but share in the profits of the business.

c. Mr. Lee expects his salary and the profits of his business to increase at roughly the same rate over the next five years.

3. Joe enjoys fishing and goes out about 20 times per year. One day, his wife Sarah told him that fishing is simply too expensive a hobby. "I think that you should stop going fishing," she exclaimed. "I did a little calculation, and I figured that it costs us about $28.75 for every fish that you catch, because you usually catch about 20 fish per trip. Besides, I always end up having to clean them. We would be much better off buying ready-to-cook fish from the local fish market."

Comment on Sarah's remarks. Do you agree with her argument? Explain. (Following below are her cost estimates.)

Boat	$150
(cost = $30,000, usable for 10 years, 20 outings per year)	
Boat fuel	45
Dock fees and insurance for the boat (average per trip)	130
Travel expenses to and from the lake (100 miles @$0.25 per mile: gas, oil, and tires, $0.18, and depreciation and insurance, $0.07)	25
New fishing equipment purchases this year (prorated over 20 trips)	25
Annual fishing license	35
Bait and miscellaneous expenses	50
Food	40
Beverages	35
Traffic fine received on the way to the lake	40
Total cost per trip	$575

4. You are given the following cost functions:

$$TC = 100 + 60Q - 3Q^2 + 0.1Q^3$$

$$TC = 100 + 60Q + 3Q^2$$

$$TC = 100 + 60Q$$

a. Compute the average variable cost, average cost, and marginal cost for each function. Plot them on a graph.

b. In each case, indicate the point at which diminishing returns occur. Also indicate the point of maximum cost efficiency (i.e., the point of minimum average cost).

c. For each function, discuss the relationship between marginal cost and average variable cost and between marginal cost and average cost. Also discuss the relationship between average variable cost and average cost.

5. Decide whether the following statements are true or false and explain why.

a. A decision maker must always use the historical cost of raw materials in making an economic decision.

b. The marginal cost curve always intersects the average cost curve at the average cost's lowest point.

c. The portion of the long-run cost curve that is horizontal indicates that the firm is experiencing neither economies nor diseconomies of scale.

d. Marginal cost is relevant only in the short-run analysis of the firm.

e. The rational firm will try to operate most efficiently by producing at the point where its average cost is minimized.

6. Indicate the effect that each of the following conditions will have on a firm's average variable cost curve and its average cost curve.

    a. The movement of a brokerage firm's administrative offices from New York City to New Jersey, where the average rental cost is lower

    b. The use of two shifts instead of three shifts in a manufacturing facility

    c. An agreement reached with the labor union in which wage increases are tied to productivity increases

    d. The elimination of sugar quotas (as it pertains to those firms that use a lot of sugar, such as bakeries and soft drink bottlers)

    e. Imposition of stricter environmental protection laws

7. You are given the following *long-run* cost function:

$$TC = 160Q - 20Q^2 + 1.2Q^3$$

    a. Calculate the long-run average cost and marginal cost. Plot these costs on a graph.

    b. Describe the nature of this function's scale economies. Over what range of output does economies of scale exist? Diseconomies of scale? Show this on the graph.

Refer to Appendix 8B for help in answering the following problems.

8. Over the last 50 years or so, many studies of cost curves have been published. The results of two of these are summarized here. In each case, interpret the equation and discuss the shapes of the total cost curve, the marginal cost curve, and the average cost curve.

    a. A study of a light plant over a six-month period resulted in the following regression equation:

$$Y = 16.68 + 0.125X + 0.00439X^2$$

    where Y = Total fuel cost
           X = Output

    b. An early study of the steel industry indicated the following results, based on annual data for 12 years.

$$Y = 182,100,000 + 55.73X$$

    where Y = Total cost
           X = Weighted output, in tons

    A time series analysis usually indicates a short-run cost study. Do you believe that a 12-year period is too long? Explain.

9. You have been presented with the following cost data and asked to fit a statistical cost function:

Quantity	Total Cost
10	104.0
20	107.0
30	109.0
40	111.5
50	114.5
60	118.0
70	123.0
80	128.5
90	137.0
100	150.0

a. Plot the data on a graph, and draw a freehand curve that best fits the data.
b. Fit three possible statistical cost functions to the data. Use straight-line, quadratic, and cubic formulas. Do the results confirm the curve you drew in *a?*
c. Discuss the statistical results you obtained in *b.* Include in your discussion R^2, the coefficients, and the statistical significance of the coefficients.
d. If the data represent 10 months of production for one plant of a specific company, would you consider this to be a short-run analysis?
e. How would your answer to part *d* change if you were told that the data represent 10 different plants during a particular month of the year?

10. The economist for the Grand Corporation has estimated the company's cost function, using time series data, to be

$$TC = 50 + 16Q - 2Q^2 + 0.2Q^3$$

where TC = Total cost
$\quad\quad Q$ = Quantity produced per period

a. Plot this curve for quantities 1 to 10.
b. Calculate the average total cost, average variable cost, and marginal cost for these quantities, and plot them on another graph.
c. Discuss your results in terms of decreasing, constant, and increasing marginal costs. Does Grand's cost function illustrate all of these?

11. Discuss the following three cost functions:

$$TC = 20 + 4Q$$

$$TC = 20 + 2Q + 0.5Q^2$$

$$TC = 20 + 4Q - 0.1Q^2$$

a. Calculate all cost curves:
  • Total cost
  • Total fixed cost
  • Total variable cost
  • Average total cost
  • Average fixed cost
  • Average variable cost
  • Marginal cost
b. Plot these curves on graphs.

Chapter 8   The Theory and Estimation of Cost

377

c. Compare the shapes of these curves and discuss their characteristics. (Particularly interesting should be the last cost function, whose shape is often found in engineering cost studies.)

12. The Central Publishing Company is about to publish its first textbook in managerial economics. It is now in the process of estimating costs. It expects to produce 10,000 copies during its first year. The following costs have been estimated to correspond to the expected copies.

a. Paper stock	$8,000
b. Typesetting	$15,000
c. Printing	$50,000
d. Art (including graphs)	$9,000
e. Editing	$20,000
f. Reviews	$3,000
g. Promotion and advertising	$12,000
h. Binding	$22,000
i. Shipping	$10,000

In addition to the preceding costs, it expects to pay the authors a 13 percent royalty and its salespeople a 3 percent commission. These percentages will be based on the publisher's price of $48 per textbook.

Some of the preceding costs are fixed and others are variable. The average variable costs are expected to be constant. While 10,000 copies is the projected volume, the book could sell anywhere between 0 and 20,000 copies.

Using the preceding data,
a. Write equations for total cost, average total cost, average variable cost, and marginal cost.
b. Draw the cost curves for quantities from 0 to 20,000 (in intervals of 2,000).

13. The Big Horn Corporation commissioned an economic consultant to estimate the company's cost function. The consultant collected a large amount of data for a number of years from the books of the corporation and came up with the following equation:

$$TC = 170 + 22Q + 1.5Q^2$$

where TC = Total cost (in thousands)
Q = Quantity produced per period

a. Plot this curve for quantities 1 through 15.
b. Calculate the average total cost, average variable cost, and marginal cost, and plot them on another graph.
c. Discuss your results in terms of decreasing, constant, and increasing marginal costs. Does Big Horn's cost function illustrate all of these?

A Mathematical Restatement of the Short-Run Cost Function

The general form of the short-run cost function is

$$TC = f(Q) \tag{8A.1}$$

where TC = Total cost
      Q = Output

As stated in this chapter, three specific forms of this function are used in economic analysis: the cubic, the quadratic, and the linear. Microeconomic theory relies primarily on the cubic equation because it encompasses the possibility of increasing returns to a factor as well as diminishing returns. The quadratic form of the total cost function implies that only the law of diminishing returns affects the short-run relationship between a firm's output and its variable input. The linear form indicates that neither increasing nor diminishing returns to a factor take place in the short run as the firm uses additional units of its variable input. In this appendix, we use calculus to state the cubic equation, the one most frequently used in economic theory.

Consider the following equation (which, incidentally is the one used to generate the cost data in Table 8.2 and Figure 8.2):

$$TC = 100 + 60Q - 5Q^2 + 0.7Q^3 \tag{8A.2}$$

The total fixed-cost component of this equation is simply the constant term, 100. The balance of the right-hand side gives us total variable cost. The average and marginal costs can be derived from Equation (8A.2) using the definitions provided in the chapter, which are restated in the following equations:

$$\text{Average fixed cost (AFC)} = \frac{TFC}{Q} = \frac{100}{Q} \tag{8A.3}$$

$$\text{Average total cost (AC)} = \frac{TC}{Q} = \frac{100}{Q} + 60 - 5Q + 0.7Q^2 \tag{8A.4}$$

$$\text{Average variable cost (AVC)} = \frac{TVC}{Q} = 60 - 5Q + 0.7Q^2 \tag{8A.5}$$

$$\text{Marginal cost (MC)} = dTC/dQ = 60 - 10Q + 2.1Q^2 \tag{8A.6}$$

Notice that to find marginal cost, we simply took the first derivative of the total cost function stated in Equation (8A.2).

The Estimation of Cost

The literature of empirical economic inquiry deals heavily with estimation of cost curves. This work has its origins with Joel Dean, who wrote the first textbook on managerial economics, and conducted many of the studies, dating back to the 1930s.

As in the case of production functions, we are interested in estimating cost functions both in the short run and in the long run. The purposes of the estimation differ between the two functions. The short-run function helps to define short-run marginal costs and thus assists the manager in determining output and prices. In the long run, the decision that a firm faces involves building the most efficient size of plant. That determination will depend on the existence of scale economies and diseconomies.

Short-run cost functions (like short-run production functions) assume that at least one factor is fixed. Thus, cost is influenced by the quantity produced as changes occur in the variable factor. To estimate such a short-run function, we must find data in which quantity and costs change while certain factors change and others remain fixed. As in the section on production functions, we can make the simplifying assumption that in a two-input model, labor changes while capital remains fixed.

In investigating short-run cost functions using regression analysis, researchers have most frequently employed the time series technique with data for a specific plant or firm over time. It is important that when time series data are collected, the period over which observations are taken is limited to a relatively short span. A major reason is that the size of the plant or firm, as well as technology, should not change significantly during the time interval used in a short-run cost function. To conduct a meaningful analysis, there must be a sufficient number of observations, and there must be variations in production from observation period to observation period.[26] Thus, each observation period, where possible, should be limited to a month, and sometimes even a shorter period (a week or two weeks).

Long-run cost functions—the planning functions—allow for changes in all factors including plant size (or capital investment in general). Time series regression analysis could be used if changes in plant size occurred during the period studied. But such changes would probably occur in limited numbers at certain times, and would not provide a continuous series. For this reason, most studies of long-run cost functions have employed cross-sectional analysis. Observations are recorded in a specific time period (e.g., one year) for a number of different plants of different sizes with different amounts of inputs and outputs. We will discuss short-term and long-term analyses separately.

---

[26]Ideally, these changes in quantities produced should occur under relatively normal circumstances rather than due to some abnormal upheaval. Thus, production cuts because of plant damage or a strike, for instance, may not produce valid data.

Problems and Adjustments

Economic versus Accounting Costs   Most empirical studies of cost functions have utilized accounting data that record the actual costs and expenses on a historical basis. However, decision-making data—economic data—should also include opportunity costs. No amount of adjustment will ever completely reconcile these concepts, but certain corrections can be made.

- Changes in prices of labor, materials, and other inputs must be adjusted so that current prices are used.[27]
- Costs that are not a function of output should be excluded. Because we are dealing with short-run cost functions, fixed costs should not have an influence on pricing or output decisions. Many analysts try to isolate only the direct costs of production, omitting fixed overhead expenses. But care must be taken to include all expenses that vary with output in the cost calculations.
- Closely allied to the previous point is the question of depreciation. Accountants usually record depreciation on a time-related basis. Depreciation is often not related to actual usage but follows accounting convention as adapted to tax rules. If "use" depreciation can be isolated from the accounting data, only that portion should be included in costs. But it must be kept in mind that recorded depreciation is based on the original cost of the equipment, whereas economic depreciation should be based on replacement value.

The problems that arise in the **estimation of short-run cost functions** because of differences between accounting and economic costs are the most difficult to solve. In most cases, some type of compromise is necessary. No definitive advice can be given here to prospective researchers. We can only point out the significant issues and suggest some possibly appropriate adjustments. What is done in the final analysis depends on the data available and the ability of the investigator to make the corrections.

Rate Changes   In addition to inflationary changes in the prices of various inputs, costs can also change due to variations in tax rates, Social Security contributions, labor insurance costs (unemployment insurance or worker's compensation rates), and various benefit coverages that affect costs. Because most of these rate changes are not based on quantity produced, they should be excluded.

Output Homogeneity   The problems encountered in cost estimation are similar to those discussed for the production function. The analysis is easiest when output is relatively homogeneous. If only one product is produced in the plant, the quantity produced (or shipped) can be handled in a rather uncomplicated manner. But if there

---

[27]Since different inputs may incur different relative price changes, some factor substitution may result over time. It can only be hoped that such effects will not be significant, since they are extremely difficult, if not impossible, to remove.

are several products moving through the plant simultaneously, some weighting apparatus must be employed to obtain the quantity produced.[28]

Timing of Costs   In many cases, costs and the service performed to create these costs do not occur at the same time. For instance, a machine that is in use continuously may be scheduled for maintenance periodically. In the airline industry, for example, major maintenance on engines is performed after a given number of flight hours. When such timing differences occur, care must be taken to spread the maintenance costs over the period of machine usage.

Accounting Changes   When a time series analysis using accounting data is performed, it is very important that the researcher ascertain whether changes in accounting methods, such as depreciation methods and recording of development expenses, have occurred during the period included in the study. Such changes must be adjusted to reflect uniformity in the measurements over time.

Given all the warnings about the problems that can be encountered in empirical cost estimation, you may have been persuaded that no useful conclusions can be obtained from such studies. Actually, such difficulties have not turned away many economists. Starting with Dean in the 1930s and continuing until today, economic journals contain many articles investigating statistical cost functions. The studies have also been summarized in articles as well as books.

The Shapes of Short-Run Cost Functions

Earlier in this chapter, three different specifications of cost functions were shown. Each represents a possible shape of the cost curves. The economist, after collecting and adjusting the data, will use one of these specifications to measure the relationship between cost and output. Other statistical functions could be employed (such as the Cobb-Douglas power function), but the three shapes are the ones most frequently encountered in statistical studies.

Figures 8.4*a* and *b* represent the normal theoretical function, which exhibits both decreasing and increasing marginal and average costs. The curves can be drawn in terms of total costs or unit costs. Figure 8.4*a* shows total cost.[29] The mathematical function that describes such a curve is a polynomial function of the third degree, that is, a cubic function:

$$TC = a + bQ - cQ^2 + dQ^3$$

---

[28]If a weighting scheme involving costs or direct inputs for each of the products is utilized, then, in a way, we are employing costs to determine output and then measuring costs as a function of this output. In other words, we are introducing a dependency into the relationship between costs and output, when we are really trying to determine the relationship between the two. This presents a serious problem. But again, as long as accounting and production records of a firm are employed, there is no easy way out of this dilemma.

[29]If only variable costs are estimated, this curve would be the variable cost curve. Theoretically, it should begin at the origin since there are no variable costs when production is zero. However, when the curves are statistically estimated, even if only variable costs are included, the line will most likely intercept the Y-axis at a point other than zero. From the investigator's viewpoint, this is not terribly important, since most of the observations included in the statistical estimate will not be anywhere near zero production. The intercept thus turns out to be meaningless.

where TC = Total cost

      Q = Total output

The negative sign preceding the quadratic term of the equation causes the total cost first to increase at a decreasing rate (decreasing marginal costs). Then the cubic term causes it to increase at an increasing rate (increasing marginal costs). The average and marginal costs shown in Figure 8.4b can be expressed as follows[30]:

$$AC = a/Q + b - cQ + dQ^2$$

$$MC = b - 2cQ + 3dQ^2$$

If the data do not quite fit the cubic function, the quadratic function can be tested. The three equations in this case are as follows:

$$TC = a + bQ + cQ^2$$

$$AC = a/Q + b + cQ$$

$$MC = b + 2cQ$$

As can be seen in Figures 8.4c and d, the shapes of these functions differ substantially from the cubic function. The total cost curve consists of only that section that increases at an increasing rate. Thus, there are no decreasing marginal costs (increasing marginal product) in this construction. This can be seen in Figure 8.4d, where the MC curve is a straight line increasing at all points (i.e., not U-shaped).

A linear total cost function can also be fitted.[31] The three equations take the following form:

$$TC = a + bQ$$

$$AC = a/Q + b$$

$$MC = b$$

Figures 8.4e and f show the curves based on the linear form.[32] Note that the law of diminishing marginal returns has been eliminated. Each additional unit's cost is the constant, b. Thus, this specification of the cost curve exhibits strictly constant marginal costs. This type of analysis does not appeal intuitively to an economist, who knows that if units of a variable factor are continually added to a fixed factor (plant), somewhere at higher production levels unit costs must rise.

These three specifications can fit various types of cost data. But even when a really good set of data is available to the investigator, chances are that the range of observations will be rather limited and will tend to cluster around a midpoint. Very

---

[30]The average cost curve is obtained by dividing TC by Q. To obtain the marginal cost, some elementary calculus is needed. The marginal cost is the first derivative of the total cost function with respect to Q.

[31]In Appendix B of chapter 9, on break-even analysis, we use this function exclusively.

[32]The average total cost curve in this case declines continuously and approaches the marginal cost curve asymptotically. The reason for this, in the formula, is that the first term a/Q, decreases as Q increases and the second term, b, is a constant. If we were dealing exclusively with variable costs, where the a term does not exist (because costs are zero when production is zero), then AVC = b and the marginal and average variable costs equal each other. This, of course, must be true, since if each additional (marginal) unit costs the same, then the average variable cost of each unit does not change and must equal the marginal cost.

seldom will we have data corresponding to near-zero production, and very seldom will data be given for production equaling or exceeding theoretical capacity. Thus, the statistical results economists obtain may not reflect the behavior of costs at the two extremes of the curve. In the following discussion of some of the empirical work that has been performed in the past, we find that this is precisely the case.

A Sampling of Short-Run Cost Studies

There is a large number of cost studies from which we could choose for purposes of illustration. We have selected three studies covering different industries and different time periods. Although some of the estimating procedures have become somewhat more sophisticated over time, the studies all used time series regression analysis.

The Hosiery Mill One of several studies conducted by Joel Dean in the 1930s and 1940s focused on a mill of a large hosiery manufacturer.[33] Its equipment was highly mechanized and its labor skilled.

Data for 54 months from 1935 to 1939 were employed. During this period, the size of the plant did not change, and the equipment remained approximately the same. Production during these months varied from zero to near physical capacity. Direct labor, indirect labor, and overhead costs were included. These costs were adjusted by factor price indexes. Output was a weighted index of individual products, and the weights were based on relative labor costs. The result, using a linear regression form, was

$$TC = 2{,}935.59 + 1{,}998Q$$

where TC = Total Cost
Q = Output, in pairs of hosiery

The results were statistically significant, and the correlation coefficient was 0.973 (and, therefore, the coefficient of determination, R^2, was 0.947).

Quadratic and cubic equations were also calculated but did not show a good fit to the data. Thus Dean's analysis points to the existence of a straight-line total cost curve, a decreasing average total cost curve, and constant marginal costs.

Road Passenger Transport In the United Kingdom J. Johnston collected data from one of the larger transportation companies, with a fleet of some 1,300 vehicles, that operated some 45 million car miles per year.[34] The data were grouped into four-week periods over three years, 1949 to 1952. Production exhibited a marked seasonal pattern, so varying production amounts per period could be observed.

The costs included all the vehicle operations (wages, clothing, gasoline, oil, and tires), maintenance, depreciation (based on mileage), variable overhead, and a minor

---

[33]Joel Dean, *Statistical Cost Functions of a Hosiery Mill*, Studies in Business Administration, 11, 4, Chicago: University of Chicago Press, 1941. This study and others have been reprinted in a volume of Dean's work, *Statistical Cost Estimation*, Bloomington: Indiana University Press, 1976.
[34]J. Johnston, *Statistical Cost Analysis*, New York: McGraw-Hill 1960, pp. 74–86.

amount of fixed overhead. Output was measured in car miles during the period. The data were adjusted by individual price indexes where price changes had occurred.

Again, a straight-line total cost function provided the best fit:

$$TC = 0.65558 + 0.4433Q$$

where Q represents car miles, in millions. The correlation coefficient was 0.95. So, as in Dean's study, the total cost curve was a straight line with constant marginal costs.

Plastic Containers In a study conducted for 10 different products moving through a plant at the same time, 21 monthly observations were taken during the period of January 1966 to September 1967.[35] During this period plant capacity was fixed, and all input prices were also fixed by contract. Only direct costs of labor, machinery, and materials were included, so no allocation problems for overhead items had to be handled. The firm reported wide production fluctuations during the period, with several observations being somewhat above 90 percent of capacity level.

Time series regression analysis was calculated for each of the three functional forms. Again, the straight-line function exhibited the best fit for each of the 10 products. The squared and cubed terms were not statistically significant. Tests to investigate cost interrelationships among the products showed no influence.

The authors also tested for the firm's aggregate cost-output relationship. The total physical output was obtained by weighting each product by its base-period price. Again, the best results were given by a straight-line equation,

$$TC = 56,393 + 3.368Q$$

with the t-test significant at the 1 percent level and the R^2 a respectable 0.89.

Marginal Cost: U-Shaped or Constant?

Each of the three studies just cited concluded that in the short run, the total cost curve is a linear function of production and that the marginal cost is constant. In addition to the hosiery mill, Dean also studied a furniture factory and a leather belt shop. Johnston conducted investigations into a food-processing firm and coal mining, among others. Studies of the steel industry, cement industry, and electric power were also done. Most of these came to conclusions similar to those of the three studies we described briefly. Actually, some of the researchers found decreasing marginal costs to be the rule.

Does that mean that economists should revise their thinking about U-shaped average and marginal cost curves? Although these findings should cause economists to pause and do some additional thinking, the results of these studies—even over the relatively long period of 50 or more years—can be reconciled with the traditional shapes of cost curves:

1. The data employed in most of the studies concentrated on output levels that were limited in range. Thus, even though in some cases production may have

---

[35]Ronald S. Coot and David A. Walker, "Short-run Cost Functions of a Multi-product Firm," *Journal of Industrial Economics,* April 1970, pp. 118–28.

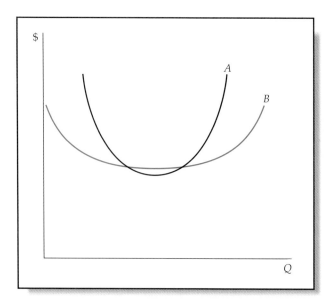

Figure 8B.1
Theoretical versus Realistic
Average Cost Curve

taken place at about 90 percent of capacity, it is quite possible that plants are built and equipped in such a way that unit costs are relatively constant over a fairly long range of outputs. The cost curves that economists draw, as we have seen in this chapter, show very distinct minimum points to show their importance to students of elementary economics. However, the bottom of the curve may represent a fairly wide interval, and unit costs may rise (quite sharply) only when physical capacity is reached. Figure 8B.1 shows an average cost curve (*A*) that most students have seen drawn on blackboards. But curve *B*, which still conforms to the economist's thinking about rising unit costs, may be the one that is more true to life. The minimum point of this curve is not as low as that on curve *A*, but there is a relatively wide range of outputs on curve *B* where costs remain low—lower than for curve *A*. As production fluctuates from period to period, output is more likely to take place on the relatively constant unit cost segment on curve *B* than at curve *A*'s narrowly defined minimum.

2. Many economists explain straight-line cost curves by pointing out that although theory requires capital inputs to be fixed in the short run, they really are not. For instance, when production increases, a firm can easily set up an additional assembly line to keep the fixed/variable input ratio constant. Thus, since the fixed factor is utilized in a fixed proportion with the variable factor, increasing marginal cost will not necessarily occur.

3. Regression analysis is not a perfect tool. If most of the observations fall into an intermediate output range, there may just not be a sufficient number of observations at the extremes to convert a linear fit to a curvilinear one.

Thus, although economists would certainly feel more gratified if empirical work were to confirm their theories, the evidence of the studies is not so overwhelming that an immediate reevaluation of microeconomic theory is necessary. Further, real-life data seem to be consistent with the existence of upward-sloping marginal cost curves. We learned earlier that the upward-sloping short-run supply curve of a firm or industry is based on the existence of an upward-sloping marginal cost curve. The fact that rising demand for a product raises the price and causes an increase in quantity supplied in the short run is evidence of the existence of an upward-sloping supply curve that is theoretically explained by the existence of an upward-sloping marginal cost curve. Thus, despite some of the empirical findings, it appears that corporate managers act as if they were confronted by a marginal cost curve of the kind described by economic theory.

THE ESTIMATION OF LONG-RUN COST FUNCTIONS

The **estimation of long-run cost functions** presents some new challenges. As you will recall, in the economic long run, all costs are variable. That means that capital (plant and equipment), which is ordinarily held fixed in the short run, is now permitted to change. As a matter of fact, it is precisely the goal of long-run cost analysis to trace unit costs for different sizes of plant and different amounts of equipment capacity. Our interest in long-run costs is to investigate the existence of returns to scale.

The question of costs in relation to size is important not only for planning decisions regarding plant or firm expansion. Firms must also consider costs when deciding on potential mergers. Will the synergy of the new units indicate a potential decrease in unit costs as a function of size?

When we speak of the long run, we may imagine that such research requires data for a given plant or firm over a considerable interval of time, so that changes in capacity can be observed. But even if such data are available, it is also important that technology is kept constant over this time period. Such a static situation would be extremely difficult to find.

Therefore, most long-run cost studies have employed cross-sectional regression analysis. This method has several advantages:

1. Observations are recorded for different plants (or firms) at a given point of time. Since different plants generally come in different sizes, the independent variable, quantity of output, can vary over relatively large ranges.
2. Since all observations are taken at a given point in time (e.g., one year), the technology is known and does not change. Under ideal circumstances, each plant will utilize that level of technology, within the known state of the art, that is most efficient for that specific plant. But this ideal is usually not reached, as is explained in the following discussion.
3. Adjusting the various costs for inflation or other price changes is not necessary under cross-sectional analysis. If annual observations are used for the sample of plants, an average figure for costs (e.g., per labor hour or ton of material) will be satisfactory. Only under conditions of very severe inflation—hyperinflation—would the averaging of annual costs become a significant problem, but any studies undertaken under such conditions would surely be of dubious quality in any case.

The use of the cross-sectional technique also creates some difficulties of which the researcher must be well aware. Just a few of these are the following:

1. Inflationary problems may be avoided by abandoning the time series method, but a new problem is introduced. Since the observations are taken from plants (or firms) in different geographical areas, we may encounter interregional cost differences in labor rates, utility bills, material costs, or transportation costs, for example. Adjustments to some common base must be made. But if relative prices of inputs differ, then the combination of inputs in a particular location may be a function of these relative differences. By adjusting prices to a specific benchmark, we may be obliterating the conscious choice made by management in a particular location based on relative prices of different inputs.

2. Although, as stated, the known state of the art for each firm is the same, it is not necessarily true that all plants are, at a given point of time, operating at the optimal level of technology. The assumption that each plant is operating most efficiently for its production level does not necessarily hold. This can be illustrated by drawing the familiar envelope curve. In Figure 8B.2 an envelope curve, *ABC*, is drawn. This long-run average cost curve represents all the optimal points of production. Point *B* is the minimum cost point, which represents the most efficient plant size. If, however, the plants in the sample do not operate at optimal points for any level of production, we may end up with observations along a curve such as *DF*, which will tend to be above the optimal curve, *ABC*, and which indicates not only a level but also a slope quite different from the optimal cost curve. There really is no way to correct for this potential error completely.

3. If accounting data are used to make the estimates, it is very important that the economist verify that there are no significant differences in the way costs are recorded on the firms' books of account. Although different depreciation procedures are the most important cause of discrepancies, varying inventory valua-

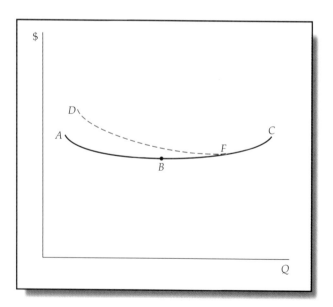

Figure 8B.2
Optimal and Suboptimal
Cost Curves

tion methods and amortization of other expenses can lead to substantial distortions. The best possible adjustments must always be made.

4. Different companies may pay their factors differently. This is most important in the case of labor costs. Total labor costs can comprise varying fractions of wages and benefits (such as vacation time, holidays, and medical care). In some cases, employees may receive part of their income in stock, or stock may be sold to them at a discounted price. The estimator must be certain to include all relevant costs.

A Sampling of Long-Run Cost Studies

As in the case of short-run costs, a large number of inquiries into the properties of long-run costs have been conducted over the last 50 years or so. A small number of these will be mentioned here to provide a flavor of method and results.

Shoe Store Chain In one of the early studies conducted by Joel Dean, the sample comprised 55 metropolitan area shoe stores owned by one firm.[36] "Such units possess the important advantage of being almost identical with respect to records, merchandise, layout, personnel and management methods."[37] Pairs of shoes were the output. Costs were mainly composed of selling expenses (including wages), handling expenses, and building expenses. Corporate allocations were omitted. The study was based on annual data for 1937 and 1938. Quadratic total cost curves gave the best fit for both years, indicating a U-shaped average cost curve and a rising marginal cost curve.

Building Societies In the United Kingdom, building societies are roughly equivalent to savings and loan associations in the United States. Johnston studied 217 such enterprises in the year 1953.[38] The companies were grouped into six size categories based on total annual revenue.

Johnston found that a U-shaped long-run cost curve existed for these enterprises. Cost in this study was measured as a ratio of management expenses to revenue. Middle-size societies were found to have the lowest ratio. However, when Johnston segregated the 217 observations into 149 societies with no branches and 68 with branches, somewhat different results appeared. Most of the firms in the former group were concentrated in the four lower size categories and most firms in the latter group were in the top four. When the nonbranch societies and the branch societies were analyzed separately, the former firms appeared to have a declining cost ratio whereas the companies with branches had a constant ratio. Thus, the appearance of a U-shaped average cost curve and, therefore, economies of scale at the low end and diseconomies of scale at the high end, were the result of two separate underlying patterns.

---

[36]Joel Dean and R. Warren James, *The Long-Run Behavior of Costs in a Chain of Shoe Stores: A Statistical Analysis,* Studies in Business Administration, 12, 3, University of Chicago Press, 1942, reprinted in Dean, *Statistical Cost Estimation,* pp. 324–60.
[37]Ibid., p. 325.
[38]Johnston, *Statistical Cost Analysis,* pp. 103–5.

Electric Utilities   The electric utility industry has been a frequent target of economists studying cost curves. Output is fairly easily defined (electricity produced), and the United States has a large number of independently owned utilities of many different sizes. Since these companies must regularly deal with state regulatory commissions in rate cases, they collect large volumes of data pertaining to costs and revenues. Utilities have also been observed to have constant productivity improvements and technological progress. The study summarized here was performed using 1971 data for 74 utilities.[39] Because the data are for 1971, this study rules out any effects of pollution control equipment on costs.

The major costs were best described by a quadratic function, which led to a U-shaped average cost curve. The cost coefficients were statistically highly significant. The authors identified the intervals for which economies of scale existed and the appropriate minimum cost point. They found that diseconomies of scale appeared beyond moderate firm size. Many earlier studies of utilities found economies of scale throughout the range of observations. This study, as well as another one for the year 1970[40] found the possibility of scale diseconomies in firms of larger size.

Financial Institutions   A more recent article reviewed some 13 studies that attempted to estimate economies of scale and economies of scope for credit unions, savings and loan associations, and commercial banks.[41] Economies of scale are defined as those associated with firm size, whereas economies of scope relate to the joint production of two or more products. "Economies of scale exist if per unit or average production costs decline as output rises. Economies of scope arise if two or more products can be jointly produced at a lower cost than is incurred in their independent production.[42] Each of the studies used a logarithmic function and employed similar measures of economies. The author summarized the results of these 13 studies as follows:

- Overall economies of scale appear to exist only at low levels of output, with diseconomies at larger output levels.
- There is no consistent evidence of global economies of scope.
- There is some evidence of cost complementarities (product-specific economies of scope).
- The results appear to exist generally across the three types of institutions studied as well as across different data sets and product and cost definitions.

Bottling Plants   A few years ago, the authors received access to some confidential cost and production data for more than 30 bottling plants of a large company. The plant sizes and their production varied widely, and thus, the data for a specific time period lent themselves to a cross-sectional regression analysis. It was our aim to investigate the potential existence of an optimum plant size.

---

[39]David A. Huettner and John H. Landon, "Electric Utilities: Scale Economies and Diseconomies," *Southern Economic Journal,* April 1978, pp. 883–912.
[40]L. R. Christensen and W. H. Greene, "Economies of Scale in U.S. Electric Power Generation," *Journal of Political Economy,* 84, 4 (August 1976), pp. 655–76.
[41]Jeffrey A. Clark, "Economies of Scale and Scope at Depository Financial Institutions: A Review of the Literature," *Economic Review,* Federal Reserve Bank of Kansas City, September/October 1988, pp. 16–33.
[42]Ibid., p. 17.

A straight-line total cost function obtained fairly good results. The R^2 equaled 0.62 (quite high for a cross-sectional analysis) and the slope coefficient was statistically significant. Surprisingly, when a cubic function was fitted, the results improved considerably. With the equation $TC = a + bQ + cQ^2 + dQ^3$, we obtained the following answers:

$$R^2 = 0.70 \qquad F\text{-statistic} = 24.87$$

	A	B	C	D
Estimate	0.078	0.891	− 0.096	0.004
t-test		3.653	− 2.240	1.910

The t-tests for coefficients b and c are significant, for d, slightly low. The c coefficient is negative, indicating that the total cost curve would first increase at a decreasing rate and then at an increasing rate—resulting in a U-shaped unit cost curve.

Another piece of data was available—the percentages of canned and bottled sodas. Because the cost of cans was lower than of bottles, we included the percent of canned soda production as another independent variable, with the following results:

$$R^2 = 0.83 \qquad F\text{-statistic} = 37.45$$

	A	B	C	D	E
Estimate	− 0.177	1.316	− 0.146	0.006	− 1.575
t-test		6.358	− 4.229	3.597	− 4.823

All t-tests are now significant and coefficient e, the percentage of can production, has the correct (negative) sign, showing that production costs decrease as the proportion of cans increases.

Granted that we used only data for one period and that we did not refine these data, we still obtained some good results indicating a U-shaped average cost curve and an optimal plant size.

Empirical Long-Run Cost Studies: Summary of Findings Some of the studies just summarized show the possible existence of diseconomies of scale for larger firm and plant size. However, a majority of the empirically estimated functions suggest the existence of scale economies up to a point. As output increases to a substantial size, these economies rapidly disappear and are replaced by constant returns for long intervals of output. Most studies have not found the existence of declining average costs at very large quantities. And findings of diseconomies of scale for high rates of production are rather rare.

Two Other Methods of Long-Run Cost Estimating

The use of regression analysis in long-run (as well as short-run) cost estimating involves the use of accounting data. At the beginning of the discussion of cost estimating, we issued a warning that accounting magnitudes may not correspond to economic measures. However, all the analyses just reviewed employed accounting data and, through various adjustment procedures, attempted to make the numbers correspond more closely to the cost concepts meaningful to the economist. In addition, economists have tried to use methods that are not dependent on numbers drawn from companies' accounting records. Two techniques of analysis will be discussed briefly: the engineering cost method and the survivorship technique.

Engineering Cost Estimates   Engineering costs are based on a thorough understanding of inputs and outputs and their relationships. Knowledgeable professionals will calculate the quantity of inputs needed to produce any quantity of outputs. These calculations are based on optimal assumptions (i.e., the largest output for a given combination of inputs). This is really a production function. From here it is a relatively easy step to apply monetary quantities to the inputs to arrive at costs.

The advantages of such a method are quite obvious. Technology is held constant. There are no problems of inflation. Problems of changing output mix are eliminated. As a matter of fact, such calculations are often made by corporations planning to introduce a new product. While the market research and product forecasting departments concentrate on preparing estimates of sales at different prices, cost estimators in a corporation (engineers and others) prepare estimates of costs for different levels of output. Then members of the pricing department take all the available data and calculate profitability at different prices and levels of output. It is through this process that product prices are obtained.

Although the **engineering cost estimating** technique avoids some of the pitfalls of regression analysis, it suffers from some problems of its own. First of all, the estimates represent what engineers and cost estimators believe cost should be, not necessarily what they actually will be. Since they are really forecasts, calculations may omit certain components that contribute to costs. Further, most of the time, only direct output costs are estimated. Other costs that may be directly associated with the product (such as some portion of overhead and direct selling expenses) are not included, or if they are, it is through some rather arbitrary allocation. Often such estimates are made on the basis of pilot plant operations and do not consider actual production, which may be attended by bottlenecks and other problems, causing costs to differ from those estimated.

Generally, engineering cost estimates will show declining unit costs up to a point and substantially flat unit costs at higher production quantities. The possible existence of diseconomies of scale is usually ignored.

It is quite possible for a study to combine engineering cost estimates for some segments of costs with utilization of accounting data for others. Such an analysis was performed some years ago, when a group of economists at the Transportation Center at Northwestern University published a forecast of aircraft prices.[43] One important step in arriving at the forecast was the calculation of aircraft operating costs. These were computed for a large number of different types of aircraft and utilized both actual data and engineering estimates. Crew salaries were calculated from a number of union contracts and compared with historical data to arrive at an average.

---

[43]Stephen P. Sobotka, Paul G. Keat, Constance Schnabel, and Margaret Wiesenfelder, *Prices of Used Commercial Aircraft*, 1959–1965, Evanston, IL: Transportation Center at Northwestern University, 1959.

Maintenance costs were calculated from a formula supplied by the Air Transport Association. Fuel consumption was obtained from engineering curves produced by aircraft manufacturers and airlines, and reconciled with some actual published data. Other costs (employee benefits, landing fees, liability and property damage insurance) were estimated in similar ways. The resulting curves reflected direct operating costs per aircraft mile for a series of different stage length categories ranging from 0–200 miles to 2,500 miles and over. The resulting cost curves generally exhibited a downward slope up to the limit of the stage length that each of the aircraft could fly nonstop.

Survivorship Principle   A prominent American economist and Nobel Prize winner, George J. Stigler, developed an intriguing method for estimating long-run costs.[44] Stigler felt that the use of accounting data, with all their distortions and subsequent need for adjustments, made the validity of cost estimation based on such data questionable. His method was to observe an industry over time, categorize the firms in the industry by size (measured as a percent of total industry capacity or output), and then arrive at a conclusion regarding cost efficiency based on the relative growth or decline of these size categories. His results for the steel industry (using data for 1930, 1938, and 1951) showed that medium-size firms (defined as between 2.5 percent and 25 percent of industry capacity) appeared to have gained in share of total industry output over the 21-year period, from 35 percent to 46 percent of total, whereas small firms (less than 2.5 percent of capacity) and large firms (actually just one firm, with over 25 percent of capacity) lost market share. Stigler concluded the existence of a U-shaped long-run average cost curve whose path first showed net economies of scale, then constant returns, and finally diseconomies of scale. Figure 8B.3 illustrates Stigler's conclusions.

Economists have continued to use the **survivorship technique** to investigate economies of scale. For example, a later study by R. P. Rogers examined economies of scale in steel manufacturing in the United States. The author measured the distribution of production in conventional steel mills in 1976 and 1987. He classified steel mills into four size categories by their annual capacity (1–1.49 million tons, 1.5–4.5 million tons, 4.5–7.5 million tons, and over 7.5 million tons). He then examined these four categories for the proportion of total capacity in the two years. He found that the 4.5–7.5 MT category increased its market share considerably. The results were consistent with a previous study by D. G. Tarr, who had used the engineering cost approach to estimate the minimum optimal size (MOS) of a steel mill. Tarr had found the MOS plant to be of 6 MT capacity, which is the midpoint of Rogers' findings.[45]

This survivorship principle is intuitively appealing due to its simplicity and avoidance of unreliable data. However, it also suffers some serious limitations. It is of

---

[44]George J. Stigler, "The Economies of Scale," *Journal of Law and Economics*, 1, 1 (October 1958), pp. 54–81.
[45]R. P. Rogers, "The Minimum Optimal Steel Plant and the Survivor Technique of Cost Estimation," *Atlantic Economic Journal*, 21 (September 1993), pp. 30–37; D. G. Tarr, "The Minimum Optimal Scale Steel Plant in the Mid-1970's," *FTC Working Paper*, 3, March 1997; D. G. Tarr, "The Minimum Optimal Scale Steel Plant," *Atlantic Economic Journal*, 12, 2 (1984), p. 122.

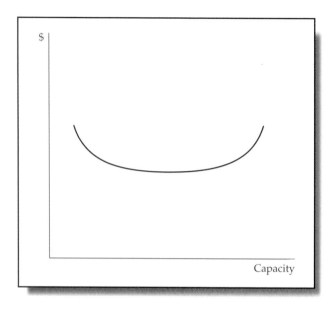

Capacity

no help in measuring costs for planning purposes. It merely tells us which company size appears to be more efficient; it says nothing about relative costs. Further, it implicitly assumes that the industry is highly competitive, so that survival and prosperity are solely a function of efficient use of resources and not of market power or the erection of barriers to entry. Changing technology and inflation over a long span can also cause distortions. As time passes, the structure of an industry can change in such a way that firms of certain size are favored over others.

Moreover, although Stigler's analysis of the steel industry showed a U-shaped cost curve, he could not obtain similar results for the automobile industry, where the survivor cost curve showed declining and constant portions but there was no evidence of diseconomies of scale at high production quantities.

SUMMARY

Accounting data have generally been used to investigate short-run and long-run cost functions. These data present the researcher with a host of problems since the economic and accounting definitions of costs can differ substantially. Also, depending on how the data are collected, adjustments for price changes, geographical differentials, and other variations must be made.

Time series analysis has largely been used to estimate short-run costs, whereas the cross-sectional regression technique appears more suited for long-run cost estimation.

A large majority of these studies have concluded that marginal cost in the short run is relatively constant. In the long run economies of scale predominate at the low end of production, and at higher output, constant returns to scale appear to exist.

The upward-sloping—U-shaped—average and marginal cost curves postulated by economic theory tend to be the exception in empirical findings. Although such results should make economists pause and reexamine some of their theoretical conclusions, the studies have generally been conducted in such a way that the possibility of eventually rising marginal costs and diseconomies of scale cannot be discounted.

Some economists prefer not to use accounting data in their inquiries. Thus, two other methods of cost estimation were briefly described in this appendix. Engineering cost analysis is based on the expert knowledge of the relationship between inputs and outputs and standard costs. It avoids the use of accounting information and does not run into the problem of adjusting for changing technology and inflation. The survivorship method bases its findings on the change in the proportion of total industry output produced by firms of different size categories. It concludes that the more efficient firms will gain share of production at the expense of less efficient ones.

Chapter 9

Pricing and Output Decisions: Perfect Competition and Monopoly

---

The Situation

GLOBAL FOODS

For the job of product manager for the new beverage, "Waterpure," Nicole Goodman, SVP of marketing, did not want a new MBA fresh out of the company's management training program. There was simply too much at stake to entrust the job to a rookie. She firmly believed that the job of bringing the new product to market should be given to a seasoned manager with a proven record of accomplishments. Finding a person with the necessary qualifications from within the company was not going to be easy, because all successful product managers were rapidly promoted to higher management positions. Nicole could have used a "headhunter" firm to find an outside person, but she preferred to give someone within the company a chance to make the project work.

"I've got just the person for you," the executive vice president exclaimed at lunch one day. "There is a real sharp manager over in market research. I think he was the one who did the background study on the soft drink market. It would be nice to give him a chance to put his ideas into practice."

The person recommended for this critical job was none other than Frank Robinson, the head of the forecasting department. (See chapter 6.) In his first meeting with Nicole after being hired, Frank was briefed on the job. "Because this new product is so important to the growth strategy of our firm," Nicole said, "and because of your experience and accomplishments, we decided that we wanted you rather than one of the outside people who were considered for the job.

(Continued)

"One of the first tasks you should pursue is an analysis of the optimal price of this beverage. Tell us what price we should charge to maximize our profit in this new venture. The CEO told us the other day that the Wall Street analysts were questioning our judgment in getting into such a crowded and highly competitive market. We need to prove as fast as possible that we made the right decision, so we want to maximize our profit in this venture in as short a time as possible.

"As always, the management committee has the final say on the price of the new beverage, just as for all our products and services. But don't get discouraged. As I know from the other products that I've managed, pricing is a very useful exercise because it forces one to bring together all the different elements of the business. The market research that you have already done on this product will provide you with a quantitative estimate of the demand as well as a general competitive analysis of the entire beverage industry. Our production people and cost accountants will give you the cost estimates. It will be up to you to put everything together to arrive at a suitable price for 'Waterpure'."

INTRODUCTION

Readers who love to cook may well appreciate the fact that in Chinese cuisine one of the most difficult tasks is the preparation of the ingredients. Once the meats and vegetables are properly sliced and all of the spices are secured, everything is thrown into the wok in a systematic and timely fashion and usually within a minute or two the dish is ready. In a sense, we have been "slicing and dicing" over the past eight chapters and at last we are ready to cook. We have taken you through the definition of economics and managerial economics, the goals of the firm, the market forces of supply and demand, the various types of demand elasticity (own price, cross price, and income), the estimation and forecasting of demand, and the key factors underlying supply (production and cost). We now combine the relevant knowledge from these previous chapters to address one of the most important questions in managerial economics: How do firms establish their prices and output levels in order to achieve their business objective of profit maximization?

The pricing and output decision will actually be answered within the framework of four basic types of markets: perfect competition, monopoly, monopolistic competition, and oligopoly. The distinguishing characteristics of each of the four market types are presented in Figure 9.1A. This chapter deals with pricing and output decisions in perfect competition and monopoly. The pricing and output decisions of firms operating in monopolistic competition and oligopoly markets are analyzed in the next chapter. Perfect competition and monopoly can be considered the two extreme market environments in which a firm competes in terms of **market power**. The concept of market power was introduced back in Chapter 3. But as a reminder, market

Perfect Competition (no market power)
1. Large number of relatively small buyers and sellers
2. Standardized product
3. Very easy market entry and exit
4. Non-price competition not possible

Monopoly (absolute market power subject to government regulation)
1. One firm, firm is the industry
2. Unique product or no close substitutes
3. Market entry and exit difficult or legally impossible
4. Non-price competition not necessary

Monopolistic Competition (market power based on product differentiation)
1. Large number of relatively small firms acting independently
2. Differentiated product
3. Market entry and exit relatively easy
4. Non-price competition very important

Oligopoly (market power based on product differentiation and/or the firm's dominance of the market)
1. Small number of relatively large firms that are mutually independent
2. Differentiated or standardized product
3. Market entry and exit difficult
4. Non-price competition very important among firms selling differentiated products

Figure 9.1A
The Four Basic Market Types

power is simply the power of a firm to establish the price of its products. In **perfect competition,** there are so many sellers offering the same product that an individual firm has virtually no control over the price of its product. Moreover, there is no way for a particular firm to charge a higher price than its competitors because everyone sells a standardized product. Instead, the interaction of supply and demand decides the price for all participants in this type of **market structure**. A firm in this market has no market power and acts only as a **price taker.** All it can do is to decide whether to compete in the market and how much output to produce. In direct contrast to firms in perfect competition, the monopoly firm has a considerable amount of market power. Because it is the only seller in this type of market, it has the power to establish the price at whatever level it wants, subject to possible constraints such as government regulation. It is the consummate **price maker.**

In terms of market power, monopolistic competition and oligopoly are somewhere between the two extremes of perfect competition and monopoly. From a pedagogical standpoint, it is easier to understand and appreciate the particulars of monopolistic competition and oligopoly if there is first a thorough understanding of perfect competition and monopoly. This explains why we first cover perfect competition and monopoly in this chapter and the other two market types separately in the next one. Before proceeding to our first case of pricing and output decisions in perfect competition, let us elaborate further on market structure and the meaning of competition in economic analysis.

COMPETITION AND MARKET TYPES IN ECONOMIC ANALYSIS

The Meaning of Competition

In economic analysis, the most important indicator of the degree of competition is the ability of firms to control the price and use it as a competitive weapon. The extreme form of competition is "perfect" competition. In this market, the competition is so intense and the firms are so evenly divided that no one seller or group of sellers can exercise any control over the price. That is, they are all price takers. A second key measure of competition in economic analysis is the ability of a firm to earn an "above normal" or "economic" profit in the long run. This concept will be described in greater detail in the next section. (Refer back to Chapter 3 for a definition of the "long run.")

Figure 9.1B is a reformatted version of Figure 9.1A. It shows the four market types according to the degree of competition as indicated by the extent of market power and the ability of firms to earn long-run economic profit. A firm in monopolistic competition may have some market power because its product can be differen-

Figure 9.1B
Comparison of Four Market Types by Characteristics Affecting the Degree of Competition

	MARKET TYPE			
MARKET CHARACTERISTICS	PERFECT COMPETITION	MONOPOLISTIC COMPETITION	OLIGOPOLY	MONOPOLY
Number and size of firms	Very large number of relatively small firms	Large number of relatively small firms	Small number of relatively large firms	One
Type of product	Standardized	Differentiated	Standardized or differentiated	Unique
Market entry and exit	Very easy	Easy	Difficult	Very difficult or impossible
Non-price competition	Impossible	Possible	Possible or difficult	Not necessary
KEY INDICATORS OF COMPETITION				
Market power	None	Low to high	Low to high	High
Long-run economic profit	None	None	Low to high, subject to mutual interdependence	High, subject to regulation

tiated from those sold by its competitors. A firm operating in an oligopoly derives its market power from its ability to differentiate its product, its relatively large size, or both.

Market entry and exit most directly affects the ability of a firm to earn economic profit in the long run. In perfect competition, entry into the market is very easy. Therefore, if firms are observed to be earning economic profit, over time the entry of new firms eager to partake in these profits quickly reduces the ability of both incumbents and new entrants to earn economic profit. The same applies to monopolistic competition. This in fact helps us to understand the basis for its name. This market is deemed to be *monopolistic* because product differentiation enables firms to exercise some market power, i.e., to act as price makers. On the other hand it is *competitive* because over time the entry of new firms reduces and ultimately eliminates any economic profit.

In the case of oligopoly, the size and/or the ability to differentiate a product provide firms with considerable market power. Furthermore, because it is relatively difficult to enter this market, there is more opportunity to earn economic profit for an extended period of time. It should be quite obvious why a monopoly is not competitive from the standpoint of economic analysis. Being the only firm, it has the ultimate power to set its price, and its ability to earn economic profit is only constrained by government regulation or perhaps by the introduction of break-through technologies or substitute products from completely different industries.

Non-price competition plays a secondary role in determining the degree of competition in economic analysis. However, we recognize that non-price factors very often come to mind first when people think about how firms compete with one another. Non-price competition involves firms trying to gain an advantage over one another by differentiating their products using such means as advertising, promotion, the development of new products and product features, and customer service. For example, when we consider the competition between Coke and Pepsi, we may think about the amount of money each spends to have well-known entertainers endorse their produces (e.g., Christine Aguilera versus Britney Spears). When we consider the battle between IBM and Sun Microsystems in the computer hardware market, we might consider the speed and reliability of each company's line of servers.

The extent to which buyers and sellers have information about the price of the product as well as the product itself (e.g., product quality, reliability, and integrity) can also be a factor in determining a firm's market power or competitive advantage. For example, have you ever bought an item at a store only to find out the next day that you could have bought it for less at another store? Your first reaction might have been anger at the first store for charging you more. But a store can do this if there are people like you who do not have complete information about the selling prices of the item wherever it is available.[1] Moreover, incomplete information about the product itself may well lead to the exercise of market power among sellers. A general overview of this situation is presented at the end of this text. (See Appendix B: "Asymmetric Information.")

---

[1]This is why economists believe that retail shopping on the Internet helps to make markets more competitive because it makes it easier for potential buyers to compare prices among the sellers.

Examples of Market Types

Perfect Competition The markets for agricultural products (e.g., corn, wheat, coffee, pork bellies), financial instruments (e.g., stocks, bonds, foreign exchange), precious metals (e.g., gold, silver, platinum), and the global petroleum industry provide good examples of this type of market. In each of these markets, the products are standardized commodities, and supply and demand are clearly the primary determinants of their market price.[2] Of course it is precisely because of this that sellers sometimes form cartels in order to raise the price or to keep it from falling. OPEC and the International Coffee Growers Association are good examples of this. As explained in chapter 3, and later in chapter 11, these sellers band together to control price by restricting the supply of their product.

Monopoly Examples of a pure monopoly are not easy to find. Some years ago, good examples could be found among government-sanctioned and regulated monopolies in the telecommunications and gas and electric industries. But these markets have been deregulated and opened up to competition over the past several decades, not just in the United States, but all over the world (see chapter 15). Patent laws sometimes provide companies with temporary monopolies. The pharmaceutical industry can definitely be said to earn economic profit during the time in which its products are protected by patents. There are certain industries in which a company is so dominant that it might be said to exhibit monopolistic status. In the Internet service provider business, AOL Time Warner's market share is greater than the next five largest competitors combined. The dominance of Microsoft in PC operating systems has led to its antitrust problems. In certain situations, a firm may enjoy monopoly status because of its particular surroundings. Simple examples come to mind, such as the only Brazilian barbecue restaurant (*churrascaria*) in town or a "last chance" gas station at the edge of the Nevada desert.

Monopolistic Competition Small businesses, particularly retail and service establishments, provide the best examples of this kind of market. Among them are boutiques, luggage stores, shoe stores, stationery shops, restaurants, repair shops, laundries, and beauty parlors. There are many of them in any given city or area of the city. The start-up capital is relatively low, so it is fairly easy to start these types of businesses. Each one tries its best to stand out among its many competitors by differentiating its product. A Chinese restaurant may attempt to differentiate itself by offering a cuisine from a relatively unknown region of China. A dry cleaner may try to distinguish itself by keeping longer store hours or by having its service clerks greet every regular customer by name as he or she enters. If customers perceive these kinds of differences to be important enough, these retail establishments may be able to charge a higher price than their competitors.

Oligopoly The oligopoly market is generally considered to be the playing field of big businesses. In the United States, a large segment of the manufacturing sector

---

[2]For an excellent review of market conditions in commodities, see "Oversupply and Slackened Demand Vex Commodity Markets," *New York Times,* January 2, 2002.

competes in oligopoly markets. For example, in the manufacturing sector, oil refining, certain types of computer hardware and software, chemicals and plastics, processed foods, tobacco, steel, automobile, copper, and soft drinks can all be considered oligopoly markets. Parts of the service sector also contain good examples of oligopoly markets. For example, airline travel, long-distance telecommunications service, and Internet access are dominated by a relatively small number of very large companies. The names of these oligopoly firms are a prominent part of any listing of large companies based on size of total revenue such as the *Fortune* 500 (American Companies) and the *BusinessWeek* Global 100.

Market Types and Competition in Theory and Reality

The four different market structures discussed above are intended by economists to be a theoretical framework in which to analyze the pricing and output decisions of the firms in these markets. As is the case with all theoretical constructs, the relationship between these four distinct market types and the actual market conditions may vary. Certain markets fit very well into these market types. Others may not exhibit all four characteristics of a particular market type. Still others may evolve over time from one type to another. These differences between theory and reality and the possible blurring of distinctions from one market type to another will be discussed more thoroughly in chapter 10. So now we proceed to examine pricing and output decisions using the four idealized types of markets as a conceptual framework, starting first with perfect competition.

PRICING AND OUTPUT DECISIONS IN PERFECT COMPETITION

The Basic Business Decision

Imagine a firm that is considering entry into a market that is perfectly competitive. If it decides to compete in this market, it will have no control over the price of the product. Therefore, the firm's managers must make a business case for entering this market on the basis of the following questions:

1. How much should we produce?
2. If we produce such an amount, how much profit will we earn?
3. If a loss rather than a profit is incurred, will it be worthwhile to continue in this market in the long run (in hopes that we will eventually earn a profit) or should we exit?

Perhaps even the output decision may seem superfluous. After all, is not the firm so small that it can sell as much as it wants without affecting the market price? Yes, but although the market price does not vary with an individual firm's level of output, the *unit cost* of production most certainly does. Think back to our discussion in chapter 8 about the cost of additional units of output. If we assume that marginal cost rises as output increases (thanks to the law of diminishing returns), then it seems reasonable to expect that eventually the extra cost per unit will exceed the selling price of the product. At this point, it no longer would make sense for a profit-maximizing firm to produce, because each additional unit sold would cost the firm more to produce than the price at which it could sell the product. Much more will be said about this shortly. But the point to emphasize here is that there is indeed a limit as to how much a perfectly competitive firm should produce in the short run. It is up to the firm to determine what this limit is.

Because the perfectly competitive firm must operate in a market in which it has no control over the selling price, there may be times when the price does not fully cover the unit cost of production (i.e., average cost). Thus, a firm must assess the extent of its losses in relation to the alternative of discontinuing production. In the long run, a firm that continues to incur losses must eventually leave the market. But in the short run, it may be economically justifiable to remain in the market, with the expectation of better times ahead. This is because in the short run, certain costs must be borne regardless of whether the firm operates. These fixed costs must be weighed against the losses incurred by remaining in business. It is reasonable to expect that a firm will remain in business if its losses are less than its fixed costs—at least in the short run.

Key Assumptions of the Perfectly Competitive Market

As you are well aware, it is critical to know the assumptions made in the development of an economic model. Let us summarize the key assumptions made in analyzing the firm's output decision in perfect competition.

1. The firm operates in a perfectly competitive market and therefore is a price taker.
2. The firm makes the distinction between the short run and the long run.
3. The firm's objective is to maximize its profit in the short run. If it cannot earn a profit, then it seeks to minimize its loss. (See chapter 2 for a review of the goals of a firm.)
4. The firm includes its opportunity cost of operating in a particular market as part of its total cost of production.

All four assumptions have been discussed earlier, some in greater detail than others. But it might be useful to review certain aspects of these assumptions before proceeding to numerical and graphical examples.

For the economic analysis of a firm's output and pricing decisions to have a unique solution, the firm must establish a single, clear-cut objective. This objective is the maximization of profit in the short run. If the firm has other objectives, such as the maximization of revenue in the short run, the output that it would select would differ from the one based on this model. (See chapter 11, for a discussion of the Baumol revenue-maximization model.)

The consideration of opportunity cost in the cost structure of the firm is vital to this decision-making model. The firm must check whether the going market price enables it to earn a revenue that covers not only its out-of-pocket costs, but also the costs incurred by forgoing alternative activities. A brief numerical example should help to convey this point.

Suppose the manager of a "stop and shop" convenience store wants to own and operate a store of her own. She knows she will have to leave her job and use $50,000 of her savings (currently invested and yielding a 10 percent return). A statement of the projected cost of operating in the first year follows.

Cost of goods sold	$300,000
General and administrative expenses	150,000
Total accounting cost	$450,000
Forgone salary for being a store manager	45,000
Forgone returns from investments (100% return)	5,000
Total opportunity cost	$50,000
Total economic cost (total accounting cost plus total opportunity cost)	$500,000

To keep this example as simple as possible, we did not include depreciation and taxes.

Suppose this budding entrepreneur forecasts revenue to be $500,000 in the first year of operation. From an accounting standpoint, her profit would be $50,000 ($500,000–$450,000). But from an economic standpoint, her profit would be zero, since the revenue would just equal her total **economic cost.** Certainly, there would be nothing wrong with "breaking even" in the economic sense of the term, because this indicates that the firm's revenue is sufficient to cover both its out-of-pocket expense and its opportunity cost. Another way to view this situation is to note that when a firm "breaks even" in the economic sense, it is actually earning an accounting profit equal to its opportunity cost. In other words, if this entrepreneur's annual revenue is $500,000, she will earn an accounting profit that offsets the opportunity cost of going into business for herself. In economic terms, she would be earning a **normal profit.**

The reason for using the term "normal" can be seen in situations in which the entrepreneur's revenue is higher or lower than $500,000. Suppose her revenue is $550,000. In this case, she will earn a profit of $50,000 ($550,000–$500,000). We refer to this sum as "above normal," "pure," or **economic profit** because it represents an amount in excess of the out-of-pocket cost plus the opportunity cost of running the business.

In the case where revenue is less than economic cost, clearly a loss is incurred. However, this **economic loss** might well coincide with a firm earning an accounting profit. For example, suppose our entrepreneur's revenue is $480,000. The economic loss would be $20,000 ($480,000–$500,000), but the accounting profit would be $30,000 ($480,000–$450,000). Table 9.1 summarizes the three scenarios discussed above.

With these assumptions in mind, we are now ready to discuss the decision-making process. Suppose that in determining whether to operate in a particular market at some level of output, the firm is faced with the short-run total cost structure presented in Table 9.2. (For convenience, the cost data are the same as those first presented in Table 8.2.)

Let us assume that the market price is $110. Given this price, the firm is free to produce as much as or as little as it desires. The demand, total revenue, marginal revenue, and average revenue schedules for this firm are shown in Table 9.3. Notice that because the price to the firm remains unchanged regardless of its output level, the total, marginal, and average revenue schedules do not resemble the schedules analyzed in chapter 4. As a price taker, the firm faces a demand curve that is "perfectly

Table 9.1

Normal Profit, Economic Profit, and Economic Loss

	NORMAL PROFIT	ECONOMIC PROFIT	ECONOMIC LOSS
Revenue	$500,000	$550,000	$480,000
Accounting cost	450,000	450,000	450,000
Opportunity cost	50,000	50,000	50,000
Profit	0	$50,000	($20,000)
	Note: Accounting profit for $50,000 equals the opportunity cost of $50,000.	Accounting profit of $100,000 exceeds the opportunity cost of $50,000.	Accounting profit of $30,000 is less than the opportunity cost of $50,000.

elastic." That is, customers are willing to buy as much as the firm is willing to sell *at the going market price*. This special type of demand curve can be seen in Figure 9.2. Moreover, the firm receives the same marginal revenue from the sale of each additional unit of product. This marginal revenue is simply the price of the product. Recall that the price is tantamount to average or per-unit revenue. Hence, a perfectly competitive firm's demand is also its marginal and its average revenue over the range of output being considered. Note in Figure 9.2 that the demand curve is also labeled "AR" and "MR."

Table 9.2

Total and Per-Unit Short-Run Cost

QUANTITY (Q)	TOTAL FIXED COST (TFC)	TOTAL VARIABLE COST (TVC)	TOTAL COST (TC)	AVERAGE FIXED COST (AFC)	AVERAGE VARIABLE COST (AVC)	AVERAGE TOTAL COST (AC)	MARGINAL COST (MC)
0	100	0.00	100.00				
1	100	55.70	155.70	100.00	55.70	155.70	55.70
2	100	105.60	205.60	50.00	52.80	102.80	49.90
3	100	153.90	253.90	33.33	51.30	84.63	48.30
4	100	204.80	304.80	25.00	51.20	76.20	50.90
5	100	262.50	362.50	20.00	52.50	72.50	57.70
6	100	331.20	431.20	16.67	55.20	71.87	68.70
7	100	415.10	515.10	14.29	59.30	73.59	83.90
8	100	518.40	618.40	12.50	64.80	77.30	103.30
9	100	645.30	745.30	11.11	71.70	82.81	126.90
10	100	800.00	900.00	10.00	80.00	90.00	154.70
11	100	986.70	1,086.70	9.09	89.70	98.79	186.70
12	100	1,209.60	1,309.60	8.33	100.80	109.13	222.90

Table 9.3

Revenue Schedules

QUANTITY	PRICE (AR)	TR	MR
0	110	0	
1	110	110	110
2	110	220	110
3	110	330	110
4	110	440	110
5	110	550	110
6	110	660	110
7	110	770	110
8	110	880	110
9	110	990	110
10	110	1,100	110
11	110	1,210	110
12	110	1,320	110

Figure 9.3 compares the perfectly elastic demand curve with the typical downward-sloping linear demand curve used in chapter 4. It also shows the total revenue curves in relation to the two types of demand curves. As is the case with perfect elasticity, a downward-sloping demand curve is the same as the average revenue curve, because P by definition is equal to AR. However, recall that a linear, downward-sloping demand curve is associated with a marginal revenue curve that is twice as steep. In addition, this type of demand results in a nonlinear total revenue curve that reaches a maximum at the point at which marginal revenue equals zero (see Figure 9.3b). In contrast, as shown in Figure 9.3d, there is no limit to the amount of total rev-

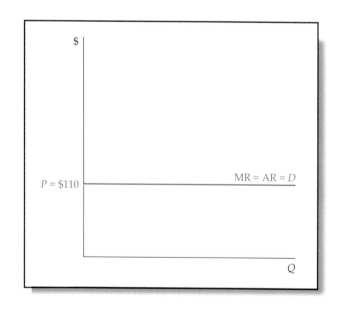

Figure 9.2
Perfectly Elastic Demand
Curve

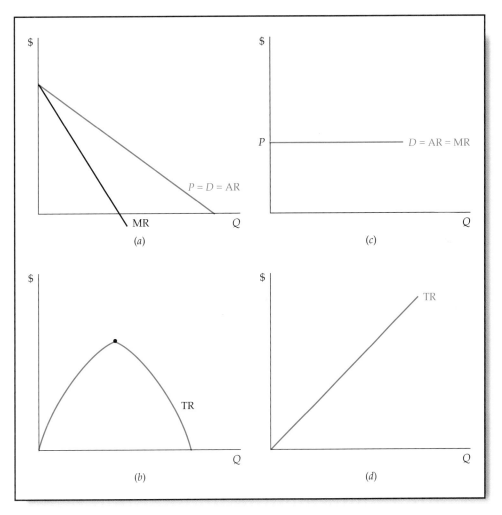

Figure 9.3
Different Types of Demand Curves and Associated Total Revenue Curves

enue that firms can garner in a perfectly competitive market. The more a firm produces, the more revenue it will obtain. The limit to its output is based on revenue in relation to the firm's cost of production, that is, the profit earned at various levels of output.

Armed with its cost and revenue schedules, all that a firm needs to do is to combine the sets of information to find the level of output that maximizes its profit (or minimizes its loss).

MODULE 9A

The Total Revenue-Total Cost Approach to Selecting the Optimal Output Level

The most logical approach to selecting the optimal level of output is to compare the total revenue with the total cost schedules and find that level of output that either maximizes the firm's profit or minimizes its loss. This is shown in Table 9.4 and

Table 9.4
Cost and Revenue Schedules Used to Determine Optimal Level of Output

Quantity (Q)	Price (P)	Total Revenue (TR)	Total Fixed Cost (TFC)	Total Variable Cost (TVC)	Total Cost (TC)	Total Profit (π)
0	110	0	100	0.00	100.00	−100.00
1	110	110	100	55.70	155.70	−45.70
2	110	220	100	105.60	205.60	−14.40
3	110	330	100	153.90	253.90	76.10
4	110	440	100	204.80	304.80	135.20
5	110	550	100	262.50	362.50	187.50
6	110	660	100	331.20	431.20	228.80
7	110	770	100	415.10	515.10	254.90
8	110	880	100	518.40	618.40	261.60
9	110	990	100	645.30	745.30	244.70
10	110	1100	100	800.00	900.00	200.00
11	110	1210	100	986.70	1086.70	123.30
12	110	1320	100	1209.60	1309.60	10.40

Figure 9.4. As can be seen in the table and the figure, this output level is 8, at which the firm would be earning a maximum profit of $261.60. Graphically, this output level can be seen as the one that maximizes the distance between the total revenue curve and the total cost curve. By convention, this point has been labeled Q^*.

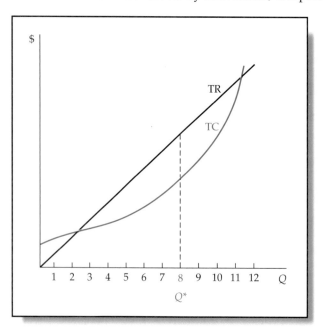

Figure 9.4
Determining Optimal Output from Cost and Revenue Curves—Perfect Competition

The Marginal Revenue-Marginal Cost Approach to Finding the Optimal Output Level

Marginal analysis is at the heart of the economic analysis of the firm. Once we explain how marginal analysis is used by the firm to determine its optimal level of output, we will rely primarily on this type of analysis throughout the rest of this chapter.

Table 9.5 presents the cost and revenue data on a per-unit basis. The marginal revenue and marginal cost columns contain the key numbers the firm must use to decide on its optimal level of output. Let us examine the marginal revenue and the marginal cost associated with additional units of output, starting with zero units. As you can see in Table 9.5, the first unit would result in additional revenue of $110 and cost the firm an additional $55.70 to make. The second unit would add another $110 to revenue and another $49.90 to the firm's total cost. Continuing in this manner, we observe that it would be worthwhile for the firm to produce more as long as the added benefit of each unit produced and sold (i.e., the marginal revenue) exceeds the added cost (i.e., the marginal cost). Because the marginal revenue is equal to the existing market price, it does not change as output increases. However, because of the law of diminishing returns, the firm's marginal cost begins to increase with the fourth unit of output. From that point on, each additional unit of output costs *increasingly more* to produce. Between zero and eight units of output, we observe that marginal revenue exceeds marginal cost. However, production of the ninth unit of output will cost the firm more than the revenue that it would add (MC = $126.90 and

Table 9.5
Using Marginal Revenue (or Price) and Marginal Cost to Determine Optimal Output: *The Case of Economic Profit*

Quantity (Q)	Marginal Revenue (MR = P = AR)	Average Fixed Cost (AFC)	Average Variable Cost (AVC)	Average Total Cost (AC)	Marginal Cost (MC)	Marginal Profit (Mπ)
0	100					
1	110	100.00	55.70	155.70	55.70	54.30
2	110	50.00	52.80	102.80	49.90	60.10
3	110	33.33	51.30	84.63	48.30	61.70
4	110	25.00	51.20	76.20	50.90	59.10
5	110	20.00	52.50	72.50	57.70	52.30
6	110	16.67	55.20	71.87	68.70	41.30
7	110	14.29	59.30	73.59	83.90	26.10
8	110	12.50	64.80	77.30	103.30	6.70
9	110	11.11	71.70	82.81	126.90	−16.90
10	110	10.00	80.00	90.00	154.70	−44.70
11	110	9.09	89.70	98.79	186.70	−76.70
12	110	8.33	100.80	109.13	222.90	−112.90

MR = $110). In Table 9.5, MR = MC actually occurs between eight and nine units of output, but we use eight as the approximate level of optimal output.

Using the relationship between marginal revenue and marginal cost to decide on the optimal level of output is referred to in economics as the **MR = MC** rule. The rule is stated as follows:

> A firm that wants to maximize its profit (or minimize its loss) should produce a level of output at which the additional revenue received from the last unit is equal to the additional cost of producing that unit. In short, MR = MC.

The MR = MC rule applies to any firm that wishes to maximize its profit, regardless of whether it has the power to set the price. However, in the particular case in which the firm has no power to set the price (i.e., it is a price taker), the MR = MC rule can be restated as the **P = MC rule.** This is simply because when a firm is a price taker, its marginal revenue is in fact the going market price. (Refer to Figure 9.3 for an illustration of this.)

Table 9.5 shows that by following the MR = MC rule and producing eight units of output, the firm would earn a profit of $261.60 [8(AR − AC)], which is what we already learned by following the total revenue–total cost approach. Hence, the rule apparently works. Another way to think about MR and MC is in terms of marginal (i.e., additional) profit. If TR − TC is equal to total profit, then MR − MC must be equal to marginal profit. The last column in Table 9.5 indicates the amount of additional profit that would be earned by the firm in producing additional units of output. As you can see, this column is merely the difference between the MR column and the MC column. When MR is equal to MC, marginal profit must be zero. When marginal profit is equal to zero, it indicates that the firm can make no more *additional* profit and therefore should not produce at a higher level of output.

Of course, there is nothing to prevent the firm from producing more or less than eight units of output. As you can see in the last column of Table 9.4, it would still earn a profit if it produced at any of the output levels 2 to 12, but none of these amounts except 8 is the *maximum* that it could earn. Remember that we are now referring to *total revenue* and *total cost*. If the firm were to produce at the level where these two measures are equal, then clearly all it would be doing is earning a "normal" profit.

Although the optimal output level can be found just as easily by using the TR − TC approach, economists rely much more on the MR − MC approach in analyzing the firm's output decision. Essentially, this approach is an extension of the basic analytical technique of "marginal analysis" first introduced in the chapters on demand, production, and cost. Furthermore, the practical implications of this approach are similar to those discussed in these earlier chapters. Very often firms do not have the benefit of complete columns of numbers depicting cost and revenue. Instead, they must rely on actual cost and revenue data at a particular level of output and then conduct sensitivity analysis involving relatively small incremental changes around that level. As will be illustrated in the ensuing sections, "marginal analysis" is much better suited to this situation than "total analysis."

The MR − MC Approach in Graphs   A graphical analysis using the MR − MC approach employs the data in Table 9.5 and is shown in Figure 9.5. Also shown is the

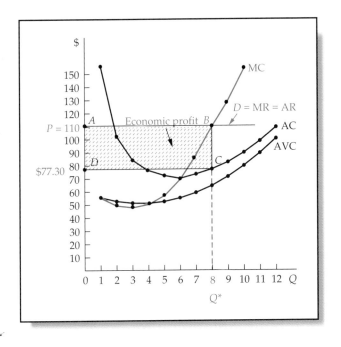

firm's demand curve, a horizontal line intersecting the vertical axis at the level of the given market price of $110. Thus, the demand curve of this price-taking firm is "perfectly elastic." The optimal output level is clearly seen as the level at which the firm's MC line and its MR line (demand line) intersect. The amount of profit earned is represented by the shaded rectangle ABCD. Because these graphs will be utilized in this way throughout the rest of the chapter, it is crucial that you clearly understand their interpretation.

Points on each of the unit cost curves indicate the dollar value of the cost at different levels of output. Therefore, at output level Q^*, the average cost is represented by the distance between point C and the horizontal axis (i.e., CQ^*). It follows that since total cost is average cost multiplied by the quantity of output, it is shown as the area of the rectangle determined by OQ^* and CQ^* (rectangle $ODCQ^*$). In the same manner, we can show that total revenue can be displayed as the rectangle determined by OQ^* and BQ^* (rectangle $OABQ^*$). Therefore, profit (i.e., the shaded rectangle ABCD) can be represented by the difference between the larger rectangle, depicting total revenue, and the smaller one, showing total cost.

Economic Profit, Normal Profit, Loss, and Shutdown

The preceding example assumed that the market price was high enough for the firm to earn an economic profit by following the MR = MC rule. But because the firm is just one of many price-taking sellers in this market, there is no reason to expect that market price will always be this beneficial for the firm. Given the vagaries of supply and demand, it is just as likely that a firm will be faced with prices that result in only normal profit—or worse, in operating losses. Tables 9.6 and 9.7 and Figure 9.6 dem-

Table 9.6

Using Marginal Revenue (or Price) and Marginal Cost to Determine Optimal Output:
The Case of Normal Profit

Quantity (Q)	Marginal Revenue (MR = P = AR)	Average Fixed Cost (AFC)	Average Variable Cost (AVC)	Average Total Cost (AC)	Marginal Cost (MC)	Marginal Profit (Mπ)	Total Profit or Loss (Q[P − AC])
0	71.87						−100.00[a]
1	71.87	100.00	55.70	155.70	55.70	16.17	−83.83
2	71.87	50.00	52.80	102.80	49.90	21.97	−61.86
3	71.87	33.33	51.30	84.63	48.30	23.57	−38.28
4	71.87	25.00	51.20	76.20	50.90	20.97	−17.32
5	71.87	20.00	52.50	72.50	57.70	14.17	−3.15
6	71.87	16.67	55.20	71.87	68.70	3.17	0
7	71.87	14.29	59.30	73.59	83.90	−12.03	−12.04
8	71.87	12.50	64.80	77.30	103.30	−31.43	−43.44
9	71.87	11.11	71.70	82.81	126.90	−55.03	−98.46
10	71.87	10.00	80.00	90.00	154.70	−82.83	−181.30
11	71.87	9.09	89.70	98.79	186.70	−114.83	−296.12
12	71.87	8.33	100.80	109.13	222.90	−151.03	−447.12

[a]If Q = O, firm still incurs a total fixed cost of $100 in the short run.

Table 9.7

Using Marginal Revenue (or Price) and Marginal Cost to Determine Optimal Output: *The Case of Economic Loss*

Quantity (Q)	Marginal Revenue (MR = P = AR)	Average Fixed Cost (AFC)	Average Variable Cost (AVC)	Average Total Cost (AC)	Marginal Cost (MC)	Marginal Profit (Mπ)	Total Profit or Loss (Q[P − AC])
0	58						−100.00
1	58	100.00	55.70	155.70	55.70	2.30	−97.70
2	58	50.00	52.80	102.80	49.90	8.10	−89.60
3	58	33.33	51.30	84.63	48.30	9.70	−79.89
4	58	25.00	51.20	76.20	50.90	7.10	−72.80
5	58	20.00	52.50	72.50	57.70	0.30	−72.50
6	58	16.67	55.20	71.87	68.70	−10.70	−83.22
7	58	14.29	59.30	73.59	83.90	−25.90	−109.13
8	58	12.50	64.80	77.30	103.30	−45.30	−154.44
9	58	11.11	71.70	82.81	126.90	−68.90	−223.29
10	58	10.00	80.00	90.00	154.70	−96.70	−320.00
11	58	9.09	89.70	98.79	186.70	−128.70	−448.69
12	58	8.33	100.80	109.13	222.90	−164.90	−613.56

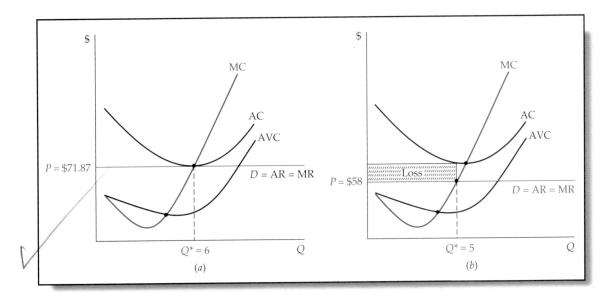

Figure 9.6
(a) Normal Profit and (b) Economic Loss

onstrate these possibilities. To focus on the marginal revenue-marginal cost approach, we include only the per-unit cost data in the tables and figure.

The situation depicted in Table 9.7 and Figure 9.6*b* indicates a loss for the firm. Does this mean that the firm should not be in this market? As you know, in the short run, the firm must bear certain fixed costs regardless of the level of its output. Using the data in Table 9.7, if the firm were to shut down its operations (i.e., if Q = 0), it would still have a fixed cost of $100. Given the market price of $58, we know that the best that a firm can do is to follow the MR = MC rule, produce five units of output, and lose $72.50. But if the firm were to shut down, it would lose $100 because this is the amount of fixed cost that it would incur, whether or not it operates in the short run. Therefore, with a market price of $58, *it would be better for a firm to operate at a loss than to cease its activities in this market.* This is illustrated in Figure 9.7*a*.

Another way to understand this rationale is to compare the firm's total revenue at the $58 price with its total variable cost, assuming a production level of five units. The total revenue is $290 (P × Q), and the total variable cost is $262.50 (Q × AVC). Clearly, this revenue is sufficient to cover the firm's total variable cost. Moreover, the amount left over ($27.50) can be used to pay for a part of its fixed cost. Hence, we can also conclude that as long as a firm's total revenue is greater than its total variable cost (or on a per-unit basis, as long as the market price exceeds average variable cost), it is better to operate than to shut down because at least part of its fixed cost will be defrayed. We refer to the amount by which total revenue exceeds total variable cost as the **contribution margin** (see Figure 9.7*a*). You should also recognize that the portion of fixed cost that is *not* covered by the contribution margin is in fact the amount of the firm's loss (i.e., $27.50 − $100 = −$72.50).

It is not always advisable to operate in the short run at a loss. Suppose the market price fell to $50. In this case, even if the firm followed the MR = MC rule, it would still incur a loss greater than it would have to bear by shutting down. This situation is not

Chapter 9 **Pricing and Output Decisions**

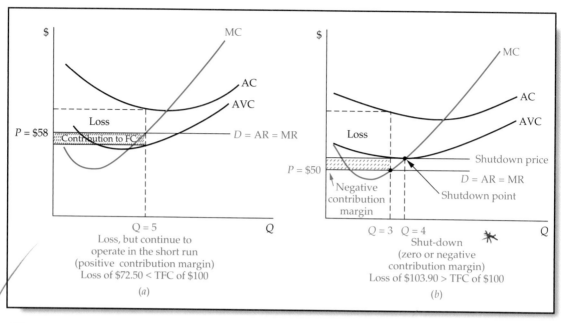

Figure 9.7
Contribution Margin

shown in a separate table but will be discussed in relation to the figures in Table 9.4. By literally following the MR = MC rule, the firm would be led to produce three units of output. But we can see that at this level, the total revenue of $150 ($50 × 3) would not even be enough to cover the firm's total variable cost of $153.90 ($51.30 × 3), resulting in a negative contribution margin of $3.90. Looking at this situation in terms of the firm's loss versus its fixed cost, we can see that its total loss of $103.90 is clearly greater than the fixed cost of $100 that it would incur if it decided to shut down its operations. (As you can see, the firm's loss is the combination of its fixed cost and negative contribution margin.) Thus, given the market price of $50, the firm would be better off by shutting down its operations. This is illustrated in Figure 9.7*b*.

Also shown in this figure is what economists refer to as the **shutdown point.** At this point, the market price is at a level in which a firm following the MR = MC rule would lose an amount just equal to its fixed cost of production. Expressed in another way, this price would result in a zero contribution margin. At the shutdown point, we assume that a firm would be indifferent about operating versus shutting down. However, it would certainly give strong consideration to ceasing to operate in the short run. As you can see, the shutdown point coincides with the point at which the firm's average variable cost is at its minimum.

The Competitive Market in the Long Run

Regardless of whether the market price in the short run results in economic profit, normal profit, or a loss for competing firms, economic theory states that in the **long run,** the market price will settle at the point where these firms earn a normal profit. This is because over a long period of time, prices that enable firms to earn above-normal profit would induce other firms to enter the market, and prices below the normal level would cause firms to leave the market. We just completed a discussion of the rationale for a firm's operating at a loss in the short run. However, in the long run, we assume that firms that are losing money would have to seriously consider leaving the market even if they have positive contribution margins. Recall that in the long run, firms have the time to vary their fixed factors of production. This means that they would have sufficient time to liquidate the fixed assets that account for their fixed costs.

We discussed the long-run adjustment process of entering and exiting firms in chapter 3. The entry of firms shifts the supply curve to the right, driving down market price. The exiting of firms shifts the supply curve to the left, placing upward pressure on market price. A firm's motivation to go into or get out of the market can now be examined in greater detail. There is only one price at which firms neither enter nor leave the market. This, of course, is the price that results in normal profits. The long-run process of entering and exiting firms is illustrated in Figure 9.8.

Figure 9.8*a* shows a hypothetical short-run situation in which the price (determined by supply and demand) is high enough to enable a typical firm competing in this market to earn economic profit. (Viewed in another way, given the market price, the firm's cost structure is low enough to enable it to earn economic profit.) Over time, new firms would enter the market, and the original firms would expand their fixed capacity in response to the incentive of economic profit. This would have the effect of increasing the market supply (shifting the supply curve to the right) and reducing the market price. At the point where firms earn only normal profit, this adjustment process would cease. Figure 9.8*b* shows the opposite case, in which a short-run loss incurred by firms in the market causes firms in the long run to leave the market. This causes price to rise toward the level in which the remaining firms would earn a normal profit.

The concept of a long-run "resting point" may seem a bit unrealistic. As much as we try to use real-world examples to support the theory of managerial economics, it is extremely difficult, if not impossible, to find examples of this principle in action. For one thing, in actual market situations, demand does not remain constant while supply adjusts toward the normal price. Tastes and preferences, the number of buyers, incomes, and prices of related goods are constantly changing. For another, the economic notion of the long run is a theoretical construct, not a period that can be measured in calendar time. If the market price has not reached the normal level, economists can say that the market is still adjusting toward long-run equilibrium. But herein lies the principal relevance of this concept to the real world of business. For business decision makers, the process of *adjustment* toward equilibrium is far more important than the equilibrium price itself.

An understanding of the conditions motivating market entry or exit over the long run should lead the firms to consider the following points:

1. The earlier the firm enters a market, the better its chances of earning above-normal profit (assuming a strong demand in this market).
2. As new firms enter the market, firms that want to survive and perhaps thrive must find ways to produce at the lowest possible cost, or at least at cost levels below those of their competitors.
3. Firms that find themselves unable to compete on the basis of cost might want to try competing on the basis of product differentiation instead.

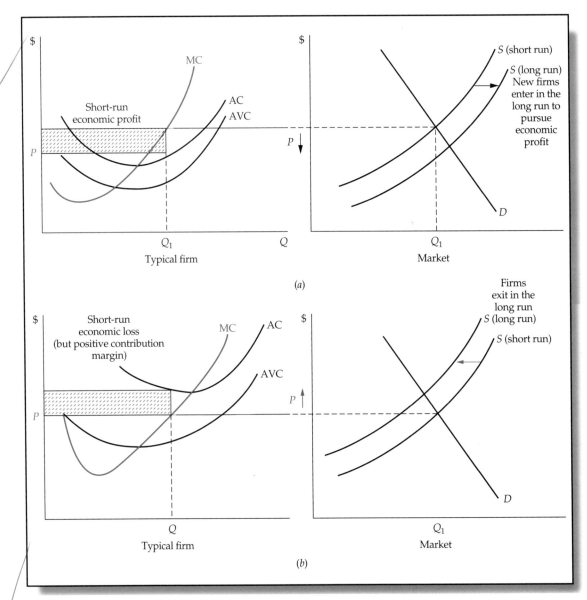

Figure 9.8
Long-Run Effect of Firm's Entering and Exiting the Market

PRICING AND OUTPUT DECISIONS IN MONOPOLY MARKETS

MODULE 9B
MODULE 9C

A monopoly market consists of one firm. The firm *is* the market. Examples are gas and electric utilities and firms selling products under protection of U.S. patent laws. Prior to its breakup in 1984, AT&T was considered one of the largest monopolies in the world. The regional companies that were formed after divestiture still represent monopolies in many of the local calling areas within their respective regions. Most monopolies cited above are closely regulated by government or government-appointed agencies. (A notable exception is companies selling patented products.) Because this regulation severely constrains their ability to choose price and output levels, regulated monopolies are analyzed as a separate group of firms in chapter 15.

In the absence of regulatory constraints, the monopoly stands in counterpoint to the perfectly competitive firm. Firms in perfectly competitive markets have no power to set their prices; the monopoly firm has the power to establish any price that it wishes. If you were responsible for setting the price of a product that you alone were selling in the market, how much would you charge? The layperson's answer is usually "as much as I can" or "whatever the market will bear." On the surface, this answer seems reasonable enough. Unfortunately, it is too simplistic to be of much help to the monopolist. In 1948, when Polaroid first offered its camera, it could have charged any price that it wanted. The original price was $85 (which was a considerable sum at that time), but it could just as well have been $850 or $8,500. The market could have borne those prices because some people probably would have been willing to buy the camera at higher levels. The question is *how many* people would have bought the cameras and *when*. As it turned out, Polaroid offered five cameras for sale on the first day and sold them all in several hours. Who knows how long it would have taken them to sell the five units at $8,500?

The key point is that a monopoly firm's ability to set its price is limited by the demand curve for its product and, in particular, the price elasticity of demand for its product. (Recall that according to the law of demand, people will buy more as price falls and vice versa.) The price elasticity of demand indicates how much more or less people are willing to buy in relation to price decreases or increases. If we assume that the firm's downward-sloping demand curve is linear, we know that as the price of the product falls, the marginal revenue from the sale of additional units falls, reaches zero, and then becomes negative. For purposes of illustration, let us also assume that the firm's marginal cost is constant in the short run. The linear, downward-sloping demand curve, the marginal revenue curve, and the constant marginal cost curve for such a firm are shown in Figure 9.9. Notice that if the firm charges too high a price (e.g., P_1), its marginal revenue will exceed its marginal cost; hence, it will be forgoing some amount of marginal profit (shown by the lighter shade). If the firm sets its price at too low a level, its marginal cost will exceed its marginal revenue, and the firm will experience a marginal loss (shown by the darker shade).

The ability of a monopoly to set its price is further limited by the possibility of rising marginal costs of production. If this is the case, then surely at some point the increasing cost of producing additional units of output will exceed the decreasing marginal revenue received from the sale of additional units. This begins at Q' shown in Figure 9.10.

In conclusion, the firm that exercises a monopoly power over its price should not set its price at the highest possible level. Instead, it should set it at the *right* level. And what is this "right" level? It is the level that results in MR = MC.

To see how the MR = MC rule applies to the monopolist as well as to the perfect competitor, see Table 9.8. Note that the table presents only the cost data relevant to this example. For purposes of comparison, the same cost figures used in the previous

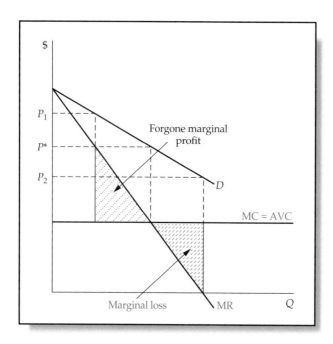

Figure 9.9
Demand, MR, and MC
Curves for a Monopoly

Table 9.8
Using Marginal Revenue and Marginal Cost to Determine Optimal Price and Output: *The Case of Monopoly*

QUANTITY (Q)	PRICE (P)	TOTAL REVENUE (TR)	MARGINAL REVENUE (MR)	AVERAGE TOTAL COST (AC)	TOTAL COST (TC)	MARGINAL COST (MC)	TOTAL PROFIT (π)
0	180	0			100.00		−100.00
1	170	170	170	155.70	155.70	55.70	14.30
2	160	320	150	102.80	205.60	49.90	114.40
3	150	450	130	84.63	253.90	48.30	196.10
4	140	560	110	76.20	304.80	50.90	255.20
5	130	650	90	72.50	362.50	57.70	287.50
6	120	720	70	71.87	431.20	68.70	288.80
7	110	770	50	73.59	515.10	83.90	254.90
8	100	800	30	77.30	618.40	103.30	181.60
9	90	810	10	82.81	745.30	126.90	64.70
10	80	800	−10	90.00	900.00	154.70	−100.00
11	70	770	−30	98.79	1086.70	186.70	−316.70
12	60	720	−50	109.13	1309.60	222.90	−589.60

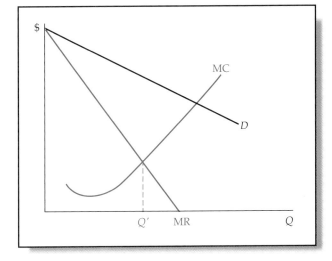

Figure 9.10
Increasing Marginal Costs in
Relation to Decreasing
Marginal Revenue

section for the perfectly competitive firm have been selected.[3] But in this case, we assume that the firm is the "only game in town." Note that the price is not equal to the marginal revenue, because the firm is a price setter and not a price taker. Its demand schedule consists of columns 1 and 2, and the total revenue and marginal revenue schedules are those that normally accompany a downward-sloping demand curve.

Starting from the zero output level, let us consider the price, output, marginal revenue, marginal cost, and marginal profit as additional units of output are produced. You can see that as output increases, the marginal revenue associated with each unit exceeds the marginal cost up to six units. Beyond this level, the firm actually incurs a marginal loss. As the firm moves beyond this level, total profit is still positive, but it is not at its maximum. In other words, by following the MR = MC rule, a profit-maximizing firm would want to produce six units of output per time period. To do so, it would have to set a price of $120.

The way in which the MR = MC rule underlies the monopoly price can perhaps be more clearly seen in a graph. In Figure 9.11, we see that the firm would select P^* because, given the particular demand for the product, this is the price that would prompt customers to buy Q^*. And Q^* is the quantity that the firm would want to produce per time period because this is the amount at which the revenue received from the last unit produced is just equal to its cost (i.e., marginal revenue = marginal cost). With the same graphical references to total revenue and total cost as used in the analysis of perfect competition, we arrive at the measure of total profit as the shaded area *ABCD*.

In a perfectly competitive market, the short-run economic profit enjoyed by the monopoly firm in this example would be vulnerable in the long run to the entry of

---

[3]By maintaining consistency in the cost data, we realize that we are sacrificing some realism because a monopoly would obviously produce more than a perfectly competitive firm. However, this shortcoming can be rectified by simply assuming that each unit of output is the equivalent of a larger number of units (e.g., $Q = 1 = 1,000$).

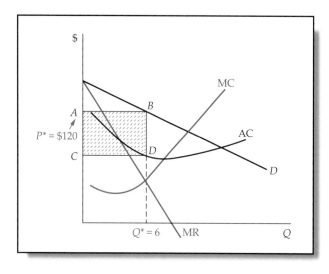

Figure 9.11
Graphical Depiction of MR =
MC Rule for a Monopoly

other firms wishing to earn similar amounts of profit. But because we assume it is a monopoly, this firm would not be subject to such threats in the long run. Nonetheless, the preceding illustration is not meant to give the impression that a monopoly automatically earns economic profit in either the short or the long run. Whether or not it does depends on the demand for its product. For example, a company may have a monopoly on a toy for children that is in great demand and consequently enables it to earn the kind of economic profit illustrated in Figure 9.11. But as the market demand is filled or as children begin to tire of the product, the demand could decline (e.g., the demand curve shifts to the left) to the extent that the firm earns only a normal profit or perhaps even incurs a loss.

Suppose a price-setting firm does not wish to maximize its short-run profit but instead wants to maximize its revenue. Let us explore this possibility using the data in Table 9.8. The price that maximizes the total revenue can be determined simply by observation. As you can see, by charging $90 for its product, the firm will receive the maximum total revenue of $810. You can also see that this revenue-maximizing price is lower than the one that maximizes the firm's total profit (i.e., $90 < $120). This relationship is illustrated in Figure 9.12. This dichotomy between **pricing for profit** and **pricing for revenue** will be discussed in greater detail in chapter 11.

THE IMPLICATIONS OF PERFECT COMPETITION AND MONOPOLY FOR MANAGERIAL DECISION MAKING

After studying this chapter, it might appear to the reader that managers in a perfectly competitive or a monopoly market do not have much of a challenge in deciding on the price and output levels of their firm. In the case of perfect competition, the market price is determined for the managers by the forces of supply and demand. All that they have to do is to decide whether their cost structure will enable their firm to

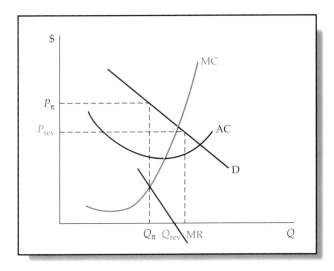

Figure 9.12
Relationship between the
Profit-Maximizing and
Revenue-Maximizing Price
and Quantity

at least earn a normal amount of profit. In the case of monopoly, the fact that the firm has no competition enables its managers simply to follow the MR = MC rule to maximize its profit. We would agree with this view, particularly when the pricing and output challenges of these firms are compared with those in monopolistic competition and oligopoly. This will be evident when reading the next chapter. Nonetheless, as explained earlier, we have presented a detailed analysis of perfect competition and monopoly because those models serve as the basis from which pricing and output decisions in monopolistic competition and oligopoly can be better understood and appreciated. Besides this, we believe that the analysis of firms in perfect competition and monopoly offers lessons to managers that go beyond the routine application of the P = MC or MR = MC rule.

The most important lesson that managers can learn by studying the perfectly competitive market is that it is extremely difficult to make money in a highly competitive market. Indeed, the only way for firms to survive in perfect competition is to be as cost efficient as possible because there is absolutely no way to control the price. Another lesson offered by the perfectly competitive model is that it might pay for a firm to move into a market before others start to enter. This might mean entering a market even before the demand is high enough to support an above-normal price. Spotting these market opportunities and taking the risk of going into these markets are key tasks of a good manager. Of course, the demand may never materialize or the long-run increase in supply might be so great that no one makes any money in this market. But that is all part of the risk that a manager must sometimes take. We will see more of the making of pricing and output decisions in highly competitive markets in the next chapter when we examine the case of monopolistic competition.

In monopoly markets not sanctioned by the government via regulations or patent laws, a monopoly presents a manager with somewhat of a paradox. What happens if the managers of a firm are so successful in beating the competition that the firm in fact becomes a monopoly, or at least one that exercises monopolistic power? Such was the case for IBM, which so dominated the mainframe computer market in the 1960s that in 1969 the Department of Justice instigated an antitrust suit against it to reduce its market power. The suit was eventually dropped in 1982.

Such is currently the case in the antitrust suit against Microsoft. This company, arguably the most successful company in the history of the market economy, was accused by the Department of Justice of violating the Sherman Anti-Trust Act through its domination of the operating system for personal computers and its tie-in of its system with its web browser product. The company settled with the Justice Department in 2001 but its legal problems have continued beyond this settlement. Nine states that have separate suits against the company have refused to settle. European regulators have started looking more closely into possible monopolistic practices in violation of European laws. There is also a potential class-action lawsuit on behalf of U.S. consumers. And in early 2002, AOL Time-Warner instigated a new suit against Microsoft on behalf of its subsidiary, Netscape. (See Chapter 12 for a brief historical background on the development of web browsers.)

Our personal view on this matter is that a number of past examples indicate that changes in the economics of a business (i.e., customers, technology, and competition), eventually break down a dominating company's monopolistic power, no matter how invincible the company might seem (although some might argue that Microsoft will prove to be a major exception). Shortly after the Justice Department dropped the case against IBM, the company began to lose a considerable amount of business as personal computers, workstations, and client server networks became more important than the mainframe in many aspects of computing. Polaroid, the company which even today has a virtual monopoly on its instant developing camera, is no longer the company that it once was, thanks to the one-hour photo developing process, video cameras, and most importantly, digital cameras.

Perhaps one of the best examples of the vulnerability of a monopoly can be found in the pharmaceutical industry. Until the early 1990s, firms in this industry enjoyed among the highest profit margins and returns on equity of all the companies in the *Fortune* 500. However, a number of recent events have started to erode their profitability. To start with, companies that do not have the patent on a drug that treats a particular illness are coming up with what the industry calls "me-too" products. These are drugs that offer a therapy for the same illness but whose chemical compositions are different enough to come under different patents. Furthermore, patents are beginning to run out on a number of highly profitable drugs and generic drugs are entering the market at far lower prices. Finally, those who make the purchasing decisions are exerting much more market power than ever before. It used to be that the majority of purchasers were fee-based private physicians who wrote prescriptions regardless of price, partly because they knew that their patients would be reimbursed by third-party payers such as insurance companies. Now much more of the purchasing decisions are being made by cost-conscious health maintenance organizations, hospital associations, and networks of retail pharmacies.

The key lesson for managers to learn from the many examples of once-powerful monopolies or near-monopolies that have eventually been affected by changing economics is not to be complacent or arrogant and assume that their ability to earn economic profit can never be diminished. This is certainly the case for monopolistic competition and oligopoly, as you will see in the next chapter.

INTERNATIONAL APPLICATION: PERFECT COMPETITION MEANS MORE THAN JUST THE SHIFTING OF SUPPLY AND DEMAND DIAGRAMS

Every morning at dawn, through the winter and spring, the cutters of Cordoba come to the sugar cane fields. They labor with their machetes, each one cutting more than a ton of cane before dusk, taking home $7 for a back-breaking day's work, the same as last year and the year before, with little hope that life will offer more. Their work creates a product that has almost no value: it costs about as much to buy a ton of raw cane in Mexico as it does to buy a ton of refined sugar on the world market. If that makes little economic sense, consider the big picture of Mexico's sugar industry. It is as bitter as the raw smell wafting from the sugar mills. The [sugar] mills are antiques, better suited to the 19th century than the 21st. Yet they produce far more sugar than anyone wants to buy, including the nation's most important customer, the United States. The glut has left Mexico's sugar industry all but bankrupt.[4]

You should be well aware of what happens to firms and their workers when conditions described by the above quote occur in perfectly competitive markets such as the sugar industry. Those firms that cannot earn a profit at the going market price must exit the market. Workers lose their jobs and must try to find work in other industries. This event—abstractly characterized in our diagrams by leftward shifts of the supply curve under the heading of "the guiding function of price"—has presented the President of Mexico, Vicente Fox, with a serious dilemma. If this happens to Mexico's sugar producers, it would have severe consequences for hundreds of thousands of sugar plantation workers, most of whom are poor peasant farmers. (An estimated 2 million people work in Mexico's sugar industry.) But if he uses the power of the government to prevent this from happening, then he would be allocating his country's limited resources to propping up inefficient producers.

It is somewhat ironic that Fox served as Chief Executive of Coca-Cola Mexico prior to becoming the President of Mexico. He is thus fully aware of the economics of the country's sugar industry. As a successful business person and former head of a subsidiary of a company that is a symbol of the market economy throughout the world, he fully recognizes that inefficient companies cannot (and should not be expected to) survive in the face of prolonged excess supply and falling prices. But as a politician and head of his country, he also recognizes that the sugar industry at least provides jobs for millions of workers, no matter how low their pay. Consequently, Fox recently made a move to expropriate half of the nation's mills. To use the concepts discussed in this chapter, we can say that in so doing, he transformed a significant number of firms from perfect competition to a kind

---

[4]Tom Weiner, "In Mexico, Bitterness Is Sugar's Legacy," *New York Times,* December 30, 2001. This entire section is based on the information provided in this article.

of government-owned monopoly. This is in direct contrast to efforts by governments throughout the world over the past decade to privatize their state-owned monopolies.

However, the situation is much more complicated than meets the eye. In the view of many Mexican sugar growers, the United States has been flooding the Mexican market with corn syrup, a cheaper form of sweetener. At the same time, they believe the United States is being as aggressive as possible in keeping Mexican sugar imports out of the country. The American rebuttal to this is exemplified by the views of Jack Roney, an economist at the American Sugar Alliance who believes that this subsidy of inefficient producers will result in huge surpluses that will eventually force Mexico to "dump it on the U.S. market and make it a U.S. problem."

The general view by industry experts who follow the situation as well as many of the plantation owners is that eventually, many of the sugar producers, particularly the smaller ones, will go out of business anyway. Besides, many of the young men who work in the cane fields have started to seek work elsewhere. But the government's efforts should at least reduce the shock of a sudden elimination of large numbers of jobs. In the words of Rodolfo Perdomo Bueno, head of Grupo Perno, a sugar mill founded by his great-grandfather, President Fox's actions have at least avoided a "tremendous social problem." According to Perdomo, if the 27 mills expropriated by the government had been allowed to close, thousands of people would be asking, "How am I going to live, what am I going to eat, what alternative do you give me, what do I do, where do I go? Do I go to the United States?"[5]

The Solution

GLOBAL FOODS

Armed with all the available figures on the estimated cost and demand for "Waterpure," Frank spent the next week trying to come up with an optimal price for the product. The weekly demand for the firm's bottled water product was estimated to be

$$Q_D = 2{,}000 - 1{,}000\,P \tag{9.1}$$

where Q_D = Quantity of 12-ounce plastic bottles (in thousands)
P = Price per container

Based on estimates provided by the bottling plant, Frank expressed the cost function as

$$TC = 150 + 0.25Q \tag{9.2}$$

(*Continued*)

---

[5]Mexico is not the only country that requires government support to help its struggling sugar industry. See Canute James, "Jamaica Struggles to Make Ailing Sugar Industry Pay," *Financial Times*, January 3, 2002.

where TC = Total cost per week (in thousands of dollars)

Q = Output of 12-ounce plastic bottles (in thousands)

To find the optimal price on the basis of the MR = MC rule, Frank first found the total revenue and marginal revenue functions based on the data in Equation (9.1). Expressing this equation in terms of price,

$$P = 2 - 0.001Q \qquad \textbf{(9.3)}$$

and substituting this into the equation for total revenue (i.e., TR = $P \times Q$), he found total revenue to be

$$TR = 2Q - 0.001Q^2 \qquad \textbf{(9.4)}$$

To find marginal revenue, he took the first derivative of this equation and set it equal to the firm's marginal cost. [Based on Equation (9.2), he knew that the firm incurred a constant marginal cost of $0.25 per unit of the product.] He then solved for the quantity (Q^*) that satisfied the equality. Then he found the optimal price by substituting the value of this optimal quantity into Equation (9.3).

$$MR = \frac{d\text{TR}}{dQ} = 2 - 0.002Q \qquad \textbf{(9.5)}$$

$$2 - 0.002Q = 0.25$$

$$Q^* = 875 \ (875,000 \text{ units per week})$$

$$P = 2 - 0.001\,(875)$$

$$P^* = 1.125 \qquad \textbf{(9.6)}$$

$$= \$1.10 \ (\text{rounding to the nearest 10 cents})$$

Figure 9.13 shows Frank's solution on a per-unit basis.

Frank assumed that the main distributors of "Waterpure" would be small retail food establishments, which generally mark up the wholesale price of bottled water by about 100 percent. Therefore, Frank determined the wholesale price that Global Foods could charge the retail stores by simply taking 50 percent of the optimal price of $1.10. For every unit sold, the company would receive $0.55.

Frank then estimated the company's weekly profit from the production and sale of bottled water.

$$TR = \$0.55 \times 875$$

$$= 481.25, \text{ or } \$481,250$$

$$TC = 150 + 0.25\,(875)$$

$$= 368.75, \text{ or } \$368,750$$

$$\text{Total profit} = \$481,250 - \$368,750$$

$$= \$112,500$$

(*Continued*)

Although Frank realized that he had the optimal price for "Waterpure," he also knew that there were already companies with established bottled water products in the market that were selling for about $1.25 a bottle. As the new entrant into the market, should Global Foods go along with the price established by the market leaders or should it try to sell it at a lower price? He was going to have to take this issue up with Nicole Goodman.

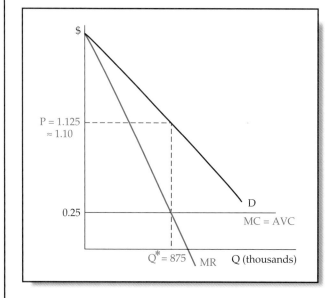

Figure 9.13
Frank's Result for the Optimal Pricing Problem

SUMMARY

This chapter has presented a view of the pricing and output decisions facing firms in two extreme situations. In the case of perfect competition, the firm has virtually no power to set the price and is only able to decide to what extent (if at all) it wants to produce in this market, given the going market price. In the case of a monopoly, the firm *is* the entire market supply. This monopoly of supply gives the firm the power to set any price that it desires. In certain cases, this monopoly power is regulated by the government.

We demonstrated that firms wishing to maximize their short-run profit (or minimize their short-run loss) should establish their price and output levels according to the MR = MC rule. For those firms in perfectly competitive markets, MR is in fact equal to the price that has already been established for them by the forces of supply and demand. For these price-taking firms, the only task is to decide what output quantity results in the matching of the market price (i.e., marginal revenue) and the marginal cost of producing the last unit of its output. For the monopoly firm, following the MR = MC rule involves pricing the product at the level whereby the quantity that people purchase is the amount needed to bring MR in line with MC. We now turn to the cases between the two extremes of perfect competition and monopoly. For these "imperfect competitors," the MR = MC rule is an important part of their pricing decision. However, as we will show, the actions or reactions of their competitors also play a major role in the pricing of their products.

IMPORTANT CONCEPTS

Contribution margin: The amount of revenue that a firm earns above its total variable cost. According to economic analysis, a firm experiencing a loss may continue operating in the short run if it has a positive contribution margin. A firm experiencing a negative contribution margin must shut down its operations because its revenue cannot even cover its variable costs of operations. (p. 413)

Economic cost: All cost incurred to attract resources into a company's employ. Such cost includes explicit cost usually recognized on accounting records as well as opportunity cost. (p. 404)

Economic loss: A situation that exists when a firm's revenues cannot cover its accounting cost as well as its opportunity cost of production. (p. 404)

Economic profit: Total revenue minus total economic cost. An amount of profit earned in a particular endeavor above the amount of profit that the firm could be earning in its next-best alternative activity. Also referred to as *abnormal profit* or *above-normal profit*. (p. 404)

Long run (market analysis): Firms are expected to enter a market in which sellers are earning economic profit. They are expected to leave a market in which sellers are incurring economic losses. (p. 414)

Market power: The power to establish the market price. (p. 397)

Market structure: The number and relative sizes of the buyers and sellers in a particular market. A "competitive" market structure implies that the number of buyers and sellers in a market is large enough that it is difficult, if not impossible, for any one buyer or seller to determine the market price. (p. 398)

Monopoly: A market in which there is only one seller for a particular good or service. There may be legal barriers to entry into this type of market

(e.g., regulated utilities, patent protection). (p. 401)

MR = MC rule: A rule stating that if a firm desires to maximize its economic profit, it must produce an amount of output whereby the marginal revenue received at this particular level is equal to its marginal cost. This implies that those firms with market power must set a price that prompts buyers to purchase this particular level of output. (p. 410)

Normal profit: An amount of profit earned in a particular endeavor that is just equal to the profit that could be earned in a firm's next-best alternative activity. When a firm earns normal profit, its revenue is just enough to cover both its accounting cost and its opportunity cost. It can also be considered as the return to capital and management necessary to keep resources engaged in a particular activity. (p. 404)

P = MC rule: A variation of the MR = MC rule for those firms operating in perfectly competitive markets. In such markets, firms are price takers. Thus, the price they must deal with (which has been determined by the forces of supply and demand) is in fact the same as a firm's marginal revenue. Firms using this rule must also be careful that the price is greater than average variable cost as well as equal to marginal cost (i.e., AVC < P = MC). If a firm cannot operate at the production level where this condition holds, it should shut down its operations. (p. 410)

Perfect competition: A market with four main characteristics: (1) a very large number of relatively small buyers and sellers, (2) a standardized product, (3) easy entry and exit, and (4) complete information by all market participants about the market price. Firms in this type of market have absolutely no control over the price and must compete on the basis of the market price established by the forces of supply and demand. (p. 398)

Price makers: Firms that exercise market power through product differentiation or by being dominant players in their markets. (p. 398)

Price takers: Firms that operate in perfectly competitive markets. (p. 398)

Pricing for profit: The method of pricing that follows the MR = MC rule. (p. 420)

Pricing for revenue: The pricing of a product to maximize a firm's revenue. In this case, the firm would try to price its product to sell an amount of output whereby the revenue earned from the last unit sold would be equal to zero (i.e., MR = 0). Assuming that the firm faces a linear demand curve, the price it establishes to maximize revenue would be lower than the price that would maximize its profit. (p. 420)

✓ **Shutdown point:** The point at which the firm must consider ceasing its production activity because the short-run loss suffered by operating would be equal to the short-run loss suffered by not operating (i.e., the operating loss = total fixed cost). In a perfectly competitive situation, this point is found at the lowest point of a firm's average variable cost curve. If the market price falls to this point, the firm should consider shutting down its operations. Any price lower than this would dictate that the firm should cease its operations. (p. 414)

QUESTIONS

1. What are the main characteristics of a perfectly competitive market that cause buyers and sellers to be price takers? Explain.

2. Explain the importance of free entry and exit in the perfectly competitive market. That is, if free entry and exit did not exist, what impact would this have on the allocation of resources and on the ability of firms to earn above-normal profits over time?

3. "The perfectly competitive model is not very useful for managers because very few markets in the U.S. economy are perfectly competitive." Do you agree with this statement? Explain. Regardless of whether you agree, what lessons can managers learn by studying perfectly competitive markets?

4. Explain why the demand curve facing a perfectly competitive firm is assumed to be perfectly elastic (i.e., horizontal at the going market price).

5. Explain why the demand curve facing a monopolist is less elastic than one facing a firm that operates in a monopolistically competitive market (all other factors held constant).

6. Use the model of perfect competition described in this chapter to explain, illustrate, or elaborate on the following statements.
   a. "Increasing competition from new firms entering the market is good because it means one is in a good business."
   b. "One important difference between an entrepreneur and a manager is that the former gets into a market before demand increases, while the latter gets into the market after the shift."

7. Explain the relationship between $P > AVC$ and a firm's contribution margin.

8. Why do economists consider zero economic profit to be "normal"?

9. "Economic profit" is a theoretical concept used to help explain the behavior of firms in competitive markets. Suggest ways in which this concept can actually be measured.

10. Explain why the $P = MC$ rule is the same as the MR = MC rule for perfectly competitive firms.

11. Explain why a price-setting firm will always set its revenue-maximizing price below the price that would maximize its profit.

12. Provide some examples of business cases that a typical firm must consider. If possible, use current examples reported in the business press.

13. How "perfectly" competitive do you think are the following markets: (1) stock market, (2) bond market, (3) foreign exchange market, (4) world sugar market, and (5) world oil market? Explain.

14. Explain how the concept of "economic profit" might help to explain the rationale for the government's granting of monopo- lies to those firms that protect their product with a patent.

PROBLEMS

For certain questions, consult Appendix 9A.

1. Following is the graphical representation of a short-run situation faced by a perfectly competitive firm. Is this a good market for this firm to be in? Explain. What do you expect will happen in the long run? Explain.

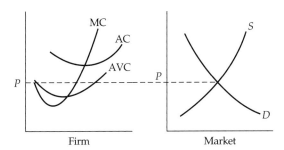

2. Indicate whether each of the following statements is true or false and explain why.
   a. A competitive firm that is incurring a loss should immediately cease operations.
   b. A pure monopoly does not have to worry about suffering losses because it has the power to set its prices at any level it desires.
   c. In the long run, firms operating in perfect competition and monopolistic competition will tend to earn normal profits.
   d. Assuming a linear demand curve, a firm that wishes to maximize its revenue will charge a lower price than a firm that wishes to maximize its profits.
   e. If $P > AVC$, a firm's total fixed cost will be greater than its loss.
   f. When a firm is able to set its price, its price will always be less than its MR.
   g. A monopoly will always earn economic profit because it is able to set any price that it wants to.

3. Kelson Electronics, a manufacturer of VCRs, estimates the following relation between its marginal cost of production and monthly output:

$$MC = \$150 + 0.005Q$$

   a. What does this function imply about the effect of the law of diminishing returns on Kelson's short-run cost function?
   b. Calculate the marginal cost of production at 1,500, 2,000, and 3,500 units of output.
   c. Assume Kelson operates as a price taker in a competitive market. What is this firm's profit-maximizing level of output if the market price is $175?
   d. Compute Kelson's short-run supply curve for its product.

4. A manufacturer of electronics products is considering entering the telephone equipment business. It estimates that if it were to begin making wireless telephones, its short-run cost function would be as follows:

Q (THOUSANDS)	AVC	AC	MC
9	41.10	52.21	30.70
10	40.00	50.00	30.10
11	39.10	48.19	30.10
12	38.40	46.73	30.70
13	37.90	45.59	31.90
14	37.60	44.74	33.70
15	37.50	44.17	36.10
16	37.60	43.85	39.10
17	37.90	43.78	42.70
18	38.40	43.96	46.90
19	39.10	44.36	51.70
20	40.00	45.00	57.10

a. Plot the average cost, average variable cost, marginal cost, and price on a graph.
b. Suppose the average wholesale price of a wireless phone is currently $50. Do you think this company should enter the market? Explain. Indicate on the graph the amount of profit (or loss) earned by the firm at the optimal level of production.
c. Suppose the firm does enter the market and that over time increasing competition causes the price of telephones to fall to $35. What impact will this have on the firm's production levels and profit? Explain. What would you advise this firm to do?

5. This same manufacturer of electronics products has just developed a hand-held computer. Following is the cost schedule for producing these computers on a monthly basis. Also included is a schedule of prices and quantities that the firm believes it will be able to sell (based on previous market research).

Q (THOUSANDS)	PRICE	MR	AVC	AC	MC
0	1,650				
1	1,570	1,570	1,281	2,281	1,281
2	1,490	1,410	1,134	1,634	987
3	1,410	1,250	1,009	1,342.33	759
4	1,330	1,090	906	1,156	597
5	1,250	930	825	1,025	501
6	1,170	770	766	932.67	471
7	1,090	610	729	871.86	507
8	1,010	450	714	839	609
9	930	290	721	832.11	777
10	850	130	750	850	1,011

a. What price should the firm charge if it wants to maximize its profits in the short run?
b. What arguments can be made for charging a price *higher* than this price? If a higher price is indeed established, what amount would you recommend?

Managerial Economics

Explain.

    c. What arguments can be made for charging a *lower* price than the profit-maximizing level? If a lower price is indeed established, what amount would you recommend? Explain.

6. The manufacturer of high-quality flatbed scanners is trying to decide what price to set for its product. The costs of production and the demand for the product are assumed to be as follows:

$$TC = 500{,}000 + 0.85Q + 0.015Q^2$$

$$Q = 14{,}166 - 16.6P$$

    a. Determine the short-run profit-maximizing price.
    b. Plot this information on a graph showing AC, AVC, MC, P, and MR.

7. The demand and cost function for a company are estimated to be as follows:

$$P = 100 - 8Q$$

$$TC = 50 + 80Q - 10Q^2 + 0.6Q^3$$

    a. What price should the company charge if it wishes to maximize its profit in the short run?
    b. What price should it charge if it wishes to maximize its revenue in the short run?
    c. Suppose the company lacks confidence in the accuracy of cost estimates expressed in a cubic equation and simply wants to use a linear approximation. Suggest a linear representation of this cubic equation. What difference would it make on the recommended profit-maximizing and revenue-maximizing prices?

8. Overheard at the water cooler: "The demand and cost estimates that were provided at the meeting are very useful [$Q = 90 - 6.5P$ and $TC = 150 + 3.5Q$]. Unfortunately, what we didn't realize at the time was that our fixed costs were underestimated by at least 30 percent. This means that we'll have to adjust upward our price by at least 30 percent to cover the added fixed cost. In any case, there is no way in the world that we can survive by charging less than $9 for our product."

    a. Comment on this statement. Do you agree with the speaker? Explain. Illustrate your answer with the use of a graph indicating the firm's short-run cost structure.
    b. What price do you think this firm should charge if it wants to maximize its short-run profit?

9. Use the following equation to demonstrate why a firm producing at the output level where MR = MC will also be able to maximize its total profit (i.e., be at the point where marginal profit is equal to zero).

$$P = 170 - 5Q$$

$$TC = 40 + 50Q + 5Q^2$$

10. "In a perfectly competitive market, a firm has to be either *good* or *lucky*." Explain what is meant by this statement. Illustrate your answer with the use of the diagrams shown in Figures 9.5, 9.6, and 9.7.

Appendix 9A

The Use of Calculus in Pricing and Output Decisions

Thus far, we have discussed the firm's pricing and output decisions with the use of tabular and graphical examples. Using both the "total" approach and the "marginal" approach, we arrived at the MR = MC rule for determining the optimal level of output and price for those firms able to exercise market power. As a supplement, we now explain the MR = MC rule with the use of calculus.

To simplify our illustrations, we assume that the firm has a quadratic total cost function, rather than the cubic function used throughout the examples in the previous sections of this chapter.

PERFECT COMPETITION

Suppose that you are the owner and operator of a perfectly competitive firm with the following total cost function:

$$TC = 2,000 + 10Q + 0.02Q^2 \tag{9A.1}$$

Suppose further that the current market price is $25. By definition, TR $P \times Q$, so your total revenue function can be stated as:

$$TR = 25Q \tag{9A.2}$$

Profit (π) is defined as TR $-$ TC. Therefore, using Equations (9A.1) and (9A.2), your firm's profit function can be expressed as:

$$\pi = 25\,Q - (2,000 + 10Q + 0.02Q^2) \tag{9A.3}$$

$$= 25\,Q - 2,000 - 10Q - 0.02Q^2$$

$$= -\,2,000 + 15Q - 0.02Q^2$$

The optimal output level (Q^*) can be found at the point where your firm's marginal profit is equal to zero. In other words, additional units of output should be produced as long as your firm earns additional profit from their sale. Using calculus, the marginal profit can be expressed as the first derivative of the profit function:

$$\frac{d\pi}{dQ} = 15 - 0.04Q \tag{9A.4}$$

Setting Equation (9A.4) equal to zero and solving for the optimal level of output (Q^*),

$$15 - 0.04Q = 0 \tag{9A.5}$$

$$Q^* = 375$$

Returning to the total profit function presented in Equation (9A.3) and substituting Q^* for Q results in the following profit:

$$\pi = -2,000 + 15\,(375) - 0.02\,(375)^2 \qquad \textbf{(9A.6)}$$

$$= \$812.50$$

We conclude that at the price of \$25, the firm will earn maximum economic profit by producing 375 units of output per time period.

An alternative way of finding P^* and Q^* is to set the firm's marginal revenue function equal to its marginal cost function and then solve for Q^*. We already know that $MR = P$. The marginal cost function is the first derivative of the total cost function:

$$MC = \frac{dTC}{dQ} = 10 + 0.04Q \qquad \textbf{(9A.7)}$$

Setting MR equal to Equation (9A.7) and solving for Q^* gives us

$$25 = 10 + 0.04Q \qquad \textbf{(9A.8)}$$

$$15 = 0.04Q$$

$$Q^* = 375$$

Comparison of Equations (9A.8) and (9A.5) provides a useful and concise explanation of the $MR = MC$ rule. As you can see, using this rule is the mathematical equivalent of finding the level of output that maximizes the total profit function.

MONOPOLY

As the manager of a product that only your company sells (e.g., a patent-protected product), suppose you are given the following information:

$$TC = 10,000 + 100Q + 0.02Q^2 \qquad \textbf{(9A.9)}$$

$$Q_D = 20,000 - 100P \qquad \textbf{(9A.10)}$$

You can use the same procedure employed in the case of perfect competition to find Q^* and P^*.

First, determine your marginal revenue function. Because you are a price setter and not a price taker, you cannot assume that $MR = P$. Instead, you must derive the marginal revenue function from your firm's demand function, shown in Equation (9A.10). Because your objective is to find the level of output that will maximize your profit (i.e., Q^*), you must rearrange the terms in the equation so that price depends on the level of output:

$$P = 200 - 0.01Q \qquad \textbf{(9A.11)}$$

By definition, $TR = P \times Q$. So by substitution,

$$TR = (200 - 0.01Q)Q \qquad \textbf{(9A.12)}$$

$$= 200Q - 0.01Q^2$$

The marginal revenue function is the first derivative of the total revenue function:

$$MR = \frac{d\text{TR}}{dQ} = 200 - 0.02Q \qquad \textbf{(9A.13)}$$

From the example of perfect competition, we know that the first derivative of the total cost function is the marginal cost function:

$$MC = \frac{d\text{TC}}{dQ} = 100 + 0.04Q \qquad \textbf{(9A.14)}$$

Thus, the MR = MC rule is adhered to by setting Equation (9A.13) equal to Equation (9A.14) and solving for Q^*:

$$200 - 0.02Q = 100 + 0.04Q \qquad \textbf{(9A.15)}$$

$$0.06Q = 100$$

$$Q^* = 1{,}667 \text{ (rounded to the nearest whole number)}$$

To find P^* we return to Equation (9A.11) and substitute Q^* for Q.

$$P = 200 - 0.01 \,(1{,}667) \qquad \textbf{(9A.16)}$$

$$P^* = \$183.33, \text{ or } \$183$$

At the rounded price of $183, your firm can expect to sell 1,667 units of output per time period and earn an economic profit of $73,333 (rounded to the nearest dollar). From the example on perfect competition, you should be aware of how the profit figure was determined.

* * *

As you can see from the preceding examples, the use of calculus offers a very concise way of explaining the output decision for price-taking firms in perfectly competitive markets and the pricing/output decision for monopoly firms. The same procedures could be applied for those firms in monopolistic competition and even for oligopolistic firms that have clear-cut roles as price leaders in their markets. However, tables and graphs similar to those used in previous sections of this chapter provide the same answers as the calculus method. Our intention is for this appendix to serve as a supplement rather than an advanced treatment of the pricing/output decision.

Appendix 9B

Break-Even Analysis (Volume-Cost-Profit)

The Situation

 October and November of each year are extremely busy months for the department of financial planning at Global Foods, Inc. It is during this period that the financial plan for the next two years is prepared. As is customary in business, greater emphasis is always placed on the first of the two years. Planning data are collected from all departments—covering projected sales, costs, and expenses. After checking as much as possible to ensure reasonability and accuracy, the department consolidates the numbers to obtain a planned income and expense statement. The plans are prepared along profit center lines, usually by specific flavors of the products.

Suzanne Prescott is the senior analyst responsible for the company's new bottled water product, "Waterpure." She and her assistant have worked on this project for two weeks and have completed the profit plan, which she will present to the manager of the financial planning department. The first page of the long and detailed presentation shows the summary income statement for the "Waterpure" profit center for the year 2003 (Table 9B.1).

Suzanne has kept her manager, Dorothy Simon, informed regarding the progress of the plan. As is quite common during a corporate planning cycle, their final discussion has been delayed several times due to late data, changed numbers, and missed schedules. Thus, Suzanne and Dorothy are meeting just one day before the results are to be presented to the company's controller. Dorothy agrees with the method with which the plan has been put together and with the results Suzanne has presented. But she expects that the controller will require additional information. She asks Suzanne whether she has performed a sensitivity analysis calculating profit results if sales were to be 10 percent lower or 10 percent higher than planned. She is also interested in the level of sales at which profit would be zero to establish the "worst case." Suzanne admits that this analysis is incomplete due to lack of time. Since the presentation must be ready the next day, there is not enough time to rework the complete plan to obtain the alternative results. Suzanne will therefore have to devise a method by which she can obtain some good estimates for the "what-if" cases, estimates sufficiently reliable to show the controller. She remembers that in graduate school, she learned a method called break-even or volume-cost-profit analysis. Fortunately, she happens to have a few old textbooks in her office.

(Continued)

Table 9B.1
Income Statement for "Waterpure" Profit Center

	PLAN FOR 2003 ($000)
Sales	$5,000
Cost of sales:	
Materials	800
Labor	1,000
Overhead	950
Total cost of sales	2,750
Gross profit	2,250
Selling and administrative expenses	1,150
Research and development expenses	300
Total expenses	1,450
Net earnings before taxes	$800

INTRODUCTION

The analysis to be described in this appendix is derived from price/output decision making in the short run, which was discussed in the body of chapter 9. **Break-even analysis** (or volume-cost-profit analysis), which is used a great deal in actual business situations, is basically a simplification of the usual short-run analysis in economics. The following are the important elements that go into this analysis:

1. It retains the distinction between fixed and variable costs.
2. Typically it uses a straight-line total revenue curve. Thus, it implicitly assumes the existence of perfect competition since the price is considered to be the same regardless of quantity. (This procedure is followed, however, more for convenience than for theoretical reasons and can be changed.)[6]
3. Probably the most important deviation from the analysis in chapter 9 is that break-even analysis employs a straight-line total variable cost curve. This means that marginal cost and average variable cost are both constants and that marginal and average variable costs are equal to one another. While such an assumption may not seem realistic over large quantity intervals, it may not be

---

[6]It also must be understood that the horizontal (quantity) axis on graphs used in economics tends to measure very large quantity intervals. To claim that exact relationships hold over these long intervals is rather unrealistic. It is done for convenience and ease of exposition. But a firm will generally not consider such wide-ranging alternatives. It is much more likely that a company, given a particular level of production, will try to analyze some limited deviations from that level to, say, 5 to 10 percent higher or 5 to 10 percent lower. In such a limited interval, it is quite possible that a significant price change may not be necessary. Thus, even if the particular firm is not in a perfectly competitive market, a straight-line total revenue curve (i.e., no price change) in the relevant range may be close to reality.

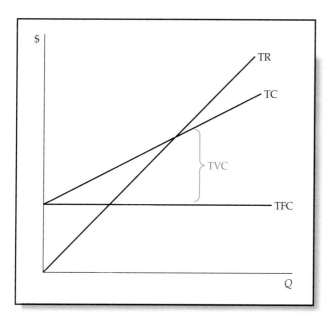

Figure 9B.1
Total Revenue and Cost
Curves (Constant Average
Variable Cost)

unreasonable when a relatively limited range of quantities is considered. The possible existence of constant unit variable costs over a range of quantities has already been mentioned in the discussion of empirical cost estimates.

Figure 9B.1 presents a graph depicting the typical break-even analysis chart.

There are, however, some important differences between customary economic analysis and the break-even method that should not be overlooked.

1. The short-run economic chart shows two points where economic profits are zero, and maximum profit is identified somewhere between these two points. In break-even analysis, there is only one no-profit (break-even) point. As quantities rise beyond this point, profit increases continuously until, presumably, capacity is reached, and no additional quantities of product can be achieved.[7] At this point, costs become infinitely high, and the total cost line would thus cross the total revenue line.

2. There is also a major difference between the objectives of the two analyses. In chapter 9, interest focused on the question of resource allocation—the effect of a price change or a cost change on the quantity produced. In break-even analysis, the question is, What impact does a change in quantity have on variable costs and profit?

3. The third difference lies in the use of the cost concept. Economic costs, as previously discussed, are based on replacement costs and include imputed costs and normal profit. Break-even analysis, as practiced in business, usually relies on accounting costs (often standard costs as used in cost accounting), which include explicit costs only and represent historical data. However, in this case, careful treatment of data could convert accounting data into economic cost data.

---

[7]Because break-even analysis deals with the short run only, capacity does not change.

For instance, as will be shown later, a "required" minimum profit, which can represent the normal profit, can be included in the calculation.

THE BREAK-EVEN POINT

MODULE 9BA
MODULE 9BB

The first of the calculations we will examine identifies the quantity at which the company will just break even—no profit, no loss. But this is not the point where company executives wish the firm to be. The break-even point merely sets the stage to investigate the relationship between quantity of the product, the cost to produce this quantity, and the profit—hence the name *volume-cost-profit* analysis.

The same abbreviations used in previous chapters will be utilized here:

P = Price

TVC = **Total variable cost**

AVC = Average variable cost

TFC = **Total fixed cost**

TC = Total cost

Q = Quantity produced

TR = Total revenue

π = Profit

The very simple equation for profit is:

$$\pi = TR - TC$$
$$= TR - TVC - TFC$$
$$= (P \times Q) - (AVC \times Q) - TFC$$
$$= Q(P - AVC) - TFC$$

To obtain the **break-even point,** total revenue is set equal to total cost:

$$TR = TVC + TFC$$
$$(P \times Q) = (AVC \times Q) + TFC$$
$$(P \times Q) - (AVC \times Q) = TFC$$
$$Q(P - AVC) = TFC$$

Thus, the break-even quantity is

$$Q = TFC/(P - AVC)$$

For example, if P = $5, AVC = $3, and TFC = $20,000,

$$Q = 20,000/(5 - 3) = 20,000/2 = 10,000$$

This result can be checked as follows:

Total revenue (10,000 × $5)	$50,000
Total variable cost (10,000 × $3)	30,000
Total fixed cost	20,000
Total cost	50,000
Profit	$0

Table 9B.2
Break-Even Analysis

VARIABLES

Price per unit	5.00
Variable cost per unit	3.00
Total fixed cost	20000

RESULTS

Break-even quantity	10000
Break-even revenue	50000

UNITS	FIXED COST	VARIABLE COST	TOTAL COST	REVENUE	PROFIT
0	20000	0	20000	0	−20000
5000	20000	15000	35000	25000	−10000
10000	20000	30000	50000	50000	0
15000	20000	45000	65000	75000	10000
20000	20000	60000	80000	100000	20000
25000	20000	75000	95000	125000	30000
30000	20000	90000	110000	150000	40000
35000	20000	105000	125000	175000	50000
40000	20000	120000	140000	200000	60000

If the quantity produced is larger than 10,000 units, a profit will result. If quantity drops below 10,000, the company will incur a loss. Table 9B.2 illustrates the revenue, costs and profits resulting from changes in quantity, and Figure 9B.2 graphs the results.[8]

What happens to the break-even point when one or more of the variables change? An increase in the average variable cost will increase the slope of the total cost curve, and increase the break- even point (a decrease will cause the opposite). A change in the unit price will change the slope of the total revenue curve; a price increase (decrease) will decrease (increase) the break-even point.

An increase (decrease) in fixed costs will cause a parallel shift up (down) in the costs curves and an increase (decrease) in the break-even point.[9]

[8]The table and graph were generated with a Microsoft Excel program.
[9]The reader should substitute new numbers for those shown in Table 9B.2 and Figure 9B.2 and observe the results. Modules 9BA and 9BB will perform this analysis quickly.

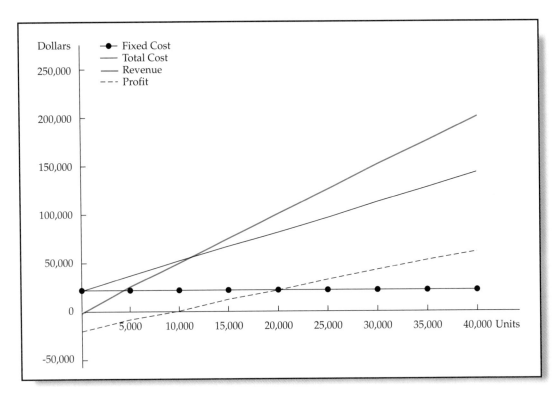

Figure 9B.2
Break-Even Analysis

BREAK-EVEN REVENUE

MODULE 9BC

Under certain circumstances, the product price and the unit variable costs may not be available. This will happen—frequently—when more than one product is produced in a plant. Since each of the different products being manufactured side by side has a different price and a different unit variable cost, it is difficult to utilize the formula of the previous section to establish the break-even point of the plant.

A weighted price and unit cost can be calculated for the products if the various products are produced in constant proportions. If we assume that variable costs are a constant percentage of total revenue, then we can calculate **break-even revenue** directly. Again we are assuming that the relationship between average variable cost and price for each product remains the same and the quantities of the various products are produced in constant proportions. Such an assumption does not appear to be unrealistic for relatively small changes in total revenue.

Starting with the equation that shows revenue at break-even,

$$TR = TVC + TFC$$

we now convert TVC into a constant fraction of total revenue, TVC = $a \times$ TR, where a is a constant less than 1. The break-even total revenue then becomes

$$TR = TFC(1 - a)$$

For example, if TFC = 20,000 and a = 0.6, then break-even TR equals 50,000, which is the same result as obtained previously, since if P = 5, and AVC = 3, a = 0.6 expresses the same relationship.

REQUIRED PROFIT

If the only objective of this analysis were to find the point at which a plant or a company breaks even, not much would be accomplished. For a company to prosper, it must earn profits, not just break even. If a firm has a particular dollar profit objective per period, a small adjustment of the break-even equation will provide the appropriate output measure. A specific, fixed dollar amount of **required profit** can be handled as an addition to fixed cost.

Continuing the illustration that has been used throughout this chapter, if the owners of the firm require a $10,000 profit, the equation is altered as follows:

$$Q_\pi = (\text{TFC} + \text{Profit requirement})/(P - \text{AVC})$$

$$= (20,000 + 10,000)/(5 - 3)$$

$$= 30,000/2 = 15,000$$

where Q_π stands for break-even with profit requirement.

If a specific profit per unit of product is required, this unit profit must be added to the average variable cost. For instance, suppose the company's objective is 40 cents profit per unit. Then AVC is changed to $3.40, and

$$Q_\pi = 20,000/1.60 = 12,500$$

Earlier in this chapter it was stated that the calculation of cost in volume-cost-profit analysis usually involves the use of accounting data. However, the "required profit" concept can easily be interpreted to represent the implied or opportunity costs that economists find crucial to the analysis of the firm. Thus, the profit measure, whether total or per unit, can be the normal profit, which is the minimum amount necessary to cause the owner to continue operating this business.

DEGREE OF OPERATING LEVERAGE

MODULE 9BD

Since volume-cost-profit analysis is concerned with the effect of a change in quantity of product on the profits of a firm, we must develop a method to quantify this effect. Such a method, called **degree of operating leverage (DOL)** is, in fact, a type of elasticity formula. The calculation result is a coefficient that measures the effect a percentage change in quantity has on the percentage change in profit.

$$DOL = \frac{\%\Delta\pi}{\%\Delta Q}$$

The percent change in profit can be written as follows:

$$\%\Delta\pi = \frac{\Delta\pi}{\pi} = \frac{\Delta Q(P - AVC)}{Q(P - AVC) - TFC}$$

The percent change in quantity equals $\Delta Q/Q$. Thus, we obtain the result,

$$DOL = \frac{Q(P - AVC)}{Q(P - AVC) - TFC}$$

To better explain the meaning of DOL, let us use the example of the preceding section. At a production of 15,000 units, profit was $10,000. DOL can now be measured at the 15,000 quantity:

$$DOL = \frac{15,000\,(5 - 3)}{15,000\,(5 - 3) - 20,000} = \frac{30,000}{10,000} = 3$$

DOL = 3 means that, at Q = 15,000, a 1 percent change in quantity will result in a 3 percent change in profit (and a 10 percent change in Q will lead to a 30 percent change in profit). The DOL effect can be seen in terms of an income statement at quantities of 13,500 and 16,500 (a 10 percent decrease and a 10 percent increase):

	Q = 13,500	Q = 15,000	Q = 16,500
Total revenue	$67,500	$75,000	$82,500
Total fixed cost	20,000	20,000	20,000
Total variable cost	40,500	45,000	49,500
Total cost	60,500	65,000	69,500
Profit	$7,000	$10,000	$13,000

At a quantity of 13,500, profit is $7,000, or 30 percent less than at a quantity of 15,000 units. Conversely, at a quantity of 16,500 units, the profit is $13,000, or 30 percent larger.[10]

The importance of the degree of operating leverage is that it reveals to management the effect on profits of a small change in quantity. This construction will hold only, of course, as long as all variables remain the same (i.e., price, average variable cost, and total fixed cost).

The relative sizes of fixed and variable costs influence the level of the DOL coefficient. A plant with high fixed costs and low variable costs will have a higher DOL than a plant with lower fixed costs and higher variable costs. The former plant will also have a higher break-even point. The significance of this relationship is that a firm with high fixed costs—a capital-intensive firm—will usually achieve break-even at a higher quantity, but since it has a higher DOL, its profits will grow at a relatively high rate when production rises above break-even. Its profits will also decline more

---

[10]The degree of operating leverage can be calculated at any point in the profit or loss area. However, it cannot be calculated at the break-even quantity, since a percentage change in profit from zero does not make sense. (The denominator of the DOL formula is zero at break-even quantity.)

quickly during downturns in economic activity, and the firm will become unprofitable at a relatively high point of production (since its break-even quantity will be high). On the other hand, a plant with lower fixed costs and higher variable costs—a labor-intensive plant, perhaps somewhat obsolete—will break even at lower quantities, and its profits will tend to rise or fall less quickly when quantity produced moves up or down.

Thus, the break-even quantity and the DOL can have a very significant influence on a firm deciding whether or not to convert from an old—labor-intensive—manufacturing facility to a more modern, automated (i.e., capital-intensive) plant. For example, using the income statement presented at the beginning of this appendix, let us assume that the average variable costs per unit are $2.75 and total fixed costs are $1,450.[11] The break-even point for a $5 price is easily calculated as 644 units (rounded to the nearest integer).

Now suppose that additional, more up-to-date machinery were installed in the plant, increasing annual fixed costs to $2,000 and driving average variable costs down to $2.25. The break-even point for the modernized plant will have increased to 727 units. Why, then, should the company invest in the new machinery? Since the newly equipped plant enjoys a higher degree of operating leverage, its profits will rise more quickly with increases in production. At some quantity, the modernized plant and the old one will achieve equal profits. In this case, the point of equality is 1,100 units, at which both plants will show a profit of $1,025.[12]

At the production level of 1,100 units, the DOL values for the old and modernized plants are 2.41 and 2.95, respectively. Thus, if more than 1,100 units are to be produced annually in the future, the profit from the modernized plant will be greater. If, however, the quantity is expected to remain at 1,000 units per year as in the company's plan, modernization would not be advisable at this time. The data for the present example are shown in Table 9B.3.

THE USES AND LIMITATIONS OF VOLUME-COST-PROFIT ANALYSIS

Volume-cost-profit analysis is a very useful tool under certain circumstances, but its limitations must be understood. When a corporation prepares its financial plan for the next year or even the next two years, it usually engages in what is referred to as "bottom-up" planning, a process that is not only time consuming but extremely

---

[11]All dollar and unit numbers (except price and variable cost per unit) are in thousands.
[12]This point is calculated as follows:

$$Q(P - AVC_a) - TFC_a = Q(P - AVC_b) - TFC_b$$

where the subscripts a and b denote the old plant and the modernized plant, respectively.

$$Q(2.25) - 1,450 = Q(2.75) - 2,000$$

$$0.5Q = 550$$

$$Q = 1,100$$

The profit for a quantity of 1,100 units is $1,025 for each plant.

Table 9B.3

Break-even and DOL Data for Old versus Modernized Plants

	OLD PLANT	NEW PLANT
Price per unit	5.00	5.00
Variable cost per unit	2.75	2.25
Total fixed cost	1,450	2,000
Break-even quantity	644	727
Break-even revenue	3,222	3,636
Equal Profit		
Quantity	1,100	1,100
Profit	1,025	1,025
Degree of operating leverage at equal-profit quantity	2.41	2.95

detailed. Many parts of the corporate organization contribute data on sales forecasts, prices, manufacturing costs, administrative and marketing expenses, and other measures. Data may be generated from every department in the corporation. Consolidating these data and making various changes in them before bringing a final plan up to top management for approval is a mammoth undertaking. A corporation would not use volume-cost-profit analysis for this type of planning.

The main use of this analysis lies in calculating alternative cases in a restricted period of time. It can also be used to make small, relatively quick corrections. In addition, during early stages of the plan, when detailed data are not yet available, estimates using variable and fixed costs can be used to establish some rough benchmarks for the eventual detailed plan.

However, despite its usefulness, break-even analysis has some important limitations, some of which have already been mentioned.

1. It assumes the existence of linear relationships, constant prices, and constant average variable costs. However, when the effects of relatively small changes in quantity are measured, linear revenues and variable costs are certainly good approximations of reality.
2. It is assumed that costs (and expenses) are either variable or fixed. The existence of fixed costs limits this analysis to the short run. Changes in capacity are ordinarily not considered.
3. For break-even analysis to be used, only a single product must be produced in a plant or, if there are several products, their mix must remain constant.
4. The analysis does not result in identification of an optimal point; it focuses on evaluating the effect of changes in quantity on cost and profits.

A good indication of the usefulness and popularity of break-even analysis is the larger number of web sites that can be found by surfing one of the search engines, and typing in "break-even analysis." Many of these web sites contain information on college courses. Others offer software to calculate break-even points for specific enterprises and activities. Here are just a few of those that we found:

- Delivery services
- Medical facilities
- Various crops
- Home refinancing
- Airline load factors
- Child care facilities
- Car buying versus leasing

AN APPLICATION: THE RESTAURANT INDUSTRY

The following is an illustration of the application of break-even analysis to the restaurant industry. While the numbers that follow are hypothetical, they are based on a survey conducted in conjunction with the National Restaurant Association. The study compared a full-menu restaurant with a fast-food restaurant. Costs and expenses were classified into fixed and variable. It is interesting to note that a large percentage of payroll costs was considered fixed (for skeleton staff necessary to run a restaurant).

	FULL-MENU RESTAURANT	FAST-FOOD RESTAURANT
Revenue	$950,500	$622,100
Fixed cost	445,700	260,700
Variable cost	459,500	280,900
Profit	$45,300	$80,500

From the preceding numbers, several inferences result:

1. The fast-food restaurant has a higher profit margin than the full-menu restaurant, 12.9 percent against 4.8 percent.
2. The break-even points are at revenues of $862,800 and $475,300, respectively.
3. The degree of operating leverage for the full-menu restaurant is 10.8 against the fast-food restaurant's 4.2 at the revenue levels given previously.[13] An increase in the full-menu restaurant's revenue would increase its profits at a much faster rate than a similar revenue increase in the fast-food restaurant's revenue.

Thus, the study concludes that volume-cost-profit analysis "can help you understand your establishment's cost structure, and help improve your decision making by quantifying the effect of specific policy decisions on the bottom line."[14]

---

[13]The formula for the degree of operating leverage is $TR(1 - a)/[TR(1 - a) - TFC]$, where a is the fraction TVC/TR.

[14]Carol Greenberg, "Analyzing Restaurant Performance, " *The Cornell H.R.A. Quarterly,* May 1986, pp. 9–11.

The Solution

To calculate results for "Waterpure" sales of 10 percent more and 10 percent less, Suzanne Prescott needs to make estimates of price per unit, average variable cost, and total fixed cost. She had the production figure and price per case of $5. Breaking up the cost and expense numbers into fixed and variable components was a much more difficult task. Working with her assistant, she arrived at the following estimated breakdown:

Cost of sales ($000)	
Variable materials and labor	$1,800
Variable overhead	500
Fixed overhead	450
Expenses ($000)	
Variable selling and administrative	450
Fixed selling and administrative	700
Fixed research and development	300

Thus, total fixed costs were found to be $1,450, and total variable cost $2,750 or $2.75 per unit.

She calculated the break-even point as follows:

$$\frac{1,450}{5 - 2.75} = 644$$

For the +10 percent and −10 percent she used the DOL equation:

$$\frac{1,000 \, (5 - 2.75)}{1,000 \, (5 - 2.75) - 1,450} = \frac{2,250}{800}$$

$$= 2.8125$$

For every 1 percent change in quantity, profit will change by 2.8125 percent. Thus, if quantity changes by 100 units (i.e., 10 percent), profit will change by 28.125 percent, from its $800 level down to $575 or up to $1,025.

Suzanne proceeded to prepare the presentation chart showing the planned figures, the two 10 percent variations, and the worst case. Table 9B.4 illustrates the results. She is now ready for the next day's meeting with the controller.

(*Continued*)

Table 9B.4
Alternative Plans for Year 2003 ($000)

	BEST ESTIMATE	+10%	−10%	WORST CASE
Quantity	1,000	1,100	900	644
Sales	$5,000	$5,500	$4,500	$3,222
Cost of Sales				
Variable mat. & labor	1,800	1,980	1,620	1,160
Variable overhead	500	550	450	322
Fixed overhead	450	450	450	450
Total cost of sales	2,750	2,980	2,520	1,932
Gross Profit	2,250	2,520	1,980	1,290
Expenses				
Variable selling & admin.	450	495	405	290
Fixed selling & admin.	700	700	700	700
Fixed research & devel.	300	300	300	300
Total expenses	1,450	1,495	1,405	1,290
Net earnings before taxes	$800	$1,025	$575	$(0)

SUMMARY

Break-even (volume-cost-profit) analysis is a simplification of the economic analysis of the firm. It involves several limiting assumptions, such as constant prices and constant average variable costs. Since fixed costs are an essential component of this technique, it is strictly a short-run tool. Yet, despite these simplifications—and possibly because of them—break-even analysis is a very useful aid to an economic or financial analyst. It is, however, necessary to be aware of the method's limitations.

Several specific tools were discussed. The first was the break-even formula itself stated in terms of quantities of production units. If a single product cannot be identified, then a break-even formula for total revenue can be used.

Since the firm's objective is certainly not to break even but to achieve profitability, an equation was developed to identify the required quantity of production, given a lump-sum profit requirement or a profit-per-unit requirement.

To measure the effect of change in quantity on profits, the concept of degree of operating leverage was introduced. This elasticity-like formula measures the relation between a percentage change in quantity sold and a percentage change in profit. This equation was also shown to be useful in comparing two plants employing differing technologies (and therefore having different relationships between fixed and variable costs) or in making decisions on modernizing a plant.

The usefulness of break-even analysis in evaluating alternatives and in making quick corrections was discussed. The limitations in the application of this technique were also pointed out.

Important Concepts

Break-even analysis: Also called *volume-cost-profit analysis,* a simplification of the economic analysis of the firm that measures the effect of a change in quantity of a product on the profits of the firm. (p. 436)

Break-even point: The level of output at which the firm realizes no profit and no loss. (p. 438)

Break-even revenue: The amount of revenue at which the firm realizes no profit and no loss. (p. 440)

Degree of operating leverage (DOL): An elasticity-like formula that measures the percentage change in profit resulting from a percentage change in quantity produced or revenue. (p. 441)

Required profit: Profit that can represent the opportunity cost or the normal profit and that can be incorporated in the break-even formula. A fixed dollar amount of required profit can be handled as an addition to fixed cost; a specific profit per unit of product can be added to the average variable cost. (p. 441)

Total fixed cost (TFC): A cost that remains constant as the level of output varies. In a short-run analysis, fixed cost is incurred even if the firm produces no output. Also referred to simply as *fixed cost.* (p. 438)

Total variable cost (TVC): The total cost associated with the level of output. This can also be considered the total cost to a firm of using its variable inputs. Also referred to simply as *variable cost.* (p. 438)

Questions

1. Although volume-cost-profit analysis uses graphs similar to those used by economists, the analysis differs in content. Discuss these differences.
2. Does the volume-cost-profit method analyze short-run or long-run situations? Why?
3. What is the difference between fixed costs and constant costs?
4. How realistic is the assumption of constant variable unit costs in volume-cost-profit analysis? Does it detract a great deal from the value of this analysis? Explain briefly.
5. What is the effect on break-even quantity of
   a. A decrease in unit price?
   b. A decrease in average variable cost?
   c. A decrease in fixed cost?

   Assume some numbers and illustrate the effect by drawing graphs showing the break-even point.
6. Business risk is usually defined in terms of variations of return (or profit) to a firm due to changes in activity resulting from changes in general economic activity. Can the degree of operating leverage therefore be described as a measure of business risk? Why?
7. Would you expect a company whose production is rather stable from period to period and growing slowly from year to year to have relatively high fixed costs?
8. How would you account for required profit in the break-even formula when
   a. Profit is set as a requirement for a time period (e.g., a year)?
   b. Profit is set as a specific monetary amount per unit?
9. Can the degree of operating leverage be measured at the break-even quantity point? Why or why not?
10. Is volume-cost-profit analysis a good planning tool? Discuss briefly.
11. What are some useful applications of volume-cost-profit analysis?

1. The Automotive Supply Company has a small plant that produces speedometers exclusively. Its annual fixed costs are $30,000, and its variable costs are $10 per unit. It can sell a speedometer for $25.
   a. How many speedometers must the company sell to break even?
   b. What is the break-even revenue?
   c. The company sold 3,000 units last year. What was its profit?
   d. Next year's fixed costs are expected to rise to $37,500. What will be the break-even quantity?
   e. If the company will sell the number of units obtained in part *d* and wants to maintain the same profit as last year, what will its new price have to be?

2. Writers' Pleasure, Inc. produces gold-plated pen and pencil sets. Its plant has a fixed annual cost of $50,000, and the variable unit cost is $20. It expects to sell 5,000 sets next year.
   a. In order to just break even, how much will the company have to charge for each set?
   b. Based on its plant investment, the company requires an annual profit of $30,000. How much will it have to charge per set to obtain this profit? (Quantity sold will still be 5,000 sets.)
   c. If the company wants to earn a markup of 50 percent on its variable costs, how many sets will it have to sell at the price obtained in part *b*?

3. Bikes-for-Two, Inc., produces tandem bicycles. Its costs have been analyzed as follows:

Variable Cost	
Materials	$30/unit
Manufacturing labor	3 hours/unit ($8/hour)
Assembly labor	1 hour/unit ($8/hour)
Packing materials	$3/unit
Packing labor	20 minutes/unit ($6/hour)
Shipping cost	$10/unit
Fixed Costs	
Overhead labor	$50,000/year
Utilities	$5,000/year
Plant operation	$65,000/year
Selling price	$100/unit

   a. Calculate the break-even quantity.
   b. Calculate the break-even revenue.
   c. Develop a chart to show profits at quantities of 2,000, 4,000, 6,000, 8,000, and 10,000.

4. Music Makers Company, a wholesale distributor, is considering discontinuance of its line of tapes due to stiff competition from CDs and other new, technologically advanced recordings. The variable cost of its tapes last year was about 40 percent of its tape revenue, and the allocated fixed cost equaled $100,000 per year. Last year's sales were $250,000, but it is expected that in the future, annual

revenue will drop by 20 percent and variable costs will rise to 50 percent of revenue (because of price reductions). Will tapes still be profitable for the company?

5. The ABC Company sells widgets at $9 each; variable unit cost is $6, and fixed cost is $60,000 per year.
   a. What is the break-even quantity point?
   b. How many units must the company sell per year to achieve a profit of $15,000?
   c. What will be the degree of operating leverage at the quantity sold in part *a?* In part *b?*
   d. What will be the degree of operating leverage if 30,000 units are sold per year?

6. Two companies, Perfect Lawn Co. and Ideal Grass Co., are competing in the manufacture and sale of lawn mowers. Perfect has a somewhat older plant and requires a variable cost of $150 per lawn mower; its fixed costs are $200,000 per year. Ideal's plant is more automated and thus has lower unit variable costs of $100; its fixed cost is $400,000. Since the two companies are close competitors, they both sell their product at $250 per unit.
   a. What is the break-even quantity for each?
   b. At which quantity would the two companies have equal profits?
   c. At the quantity obtained in part *b,* what is each company's degree of operating leverage?
   d. If sales of each company were to reach 4,500 units per year, which company would be more profitable? Why?

7. Elgar Toaster Co. is contemplating a modernization of its antiquated plant. It now sells its toasters for $20 each; the variable cost per unit is $8, and fixed costs are $840,000 per year.
   a. Calculate the break-even quantity.
   b. If the proposed modernization is carried out, the new plant would have fixed costs of $1,200,000 per year, but its variable costs would decrease to $5 per unit.
      (1) What will be the break-even point now?
      (2) If the company wanted to break even at the same quantity as with the old plant, what price would it have to charge for a toaster?
   c. If the new plant is built, the company would want to decrease its price to $19 to improve its competitive position.
      (1) At which quantity would profits of the old and the new plants be equal (assuming the price of a toaster is $20 for the old plant but $19 for the new)? How much would the profit be at this quantity?
      (2) Calculate the degree of operating leverage for each plant at the quantity obtained in part (1).
      (3) If sales are projected to reach 150,000 units per year in the near future, would you recommend construction of the new plant? Why or why not? (Assume that both plants have the capacity to produce this quantity.)

8. The Saline Company produces and sells rock salt. Its annual fixed cost was $10,000. During the past year, the company sold 8,000 bags of its product. It estimates that at this level of sales its degree of operating leverage is 1.5.
   a. How much was Saline's profit last year?
   b. At which level of production would the company just break even?

9. The Amazing Book Co. sells a selection of paperbacks at an average price of $9. Its fixed costs are $400,000 per year and the unit variable cost of each paperback is $4 on average.

a. Calculate the company's break-even quantity.

b. The company's sales target for the year is 100,000 units. What will be its profit?

c. At the beginning of the year the unit variable cost rises to $5. If the company wants to achieve the same profit as obtained in item b, how many books will it have to sell?

d. At the beginning of the year, the company installs new billing equipment. Its fixed costs rise to $450,000. If the company wants to remain on target to sell 100,000 units and preserve the profit obtained in item b, what price will it have to charge per book?

e. An early review of competitive prices forces the company to drop its average price to $8. If it still targets its sales at 100,000 units and will settle for a profit of $50,000, what is the maximum unit variable cost it can afford? (TFC = $400,000)

f. If the average price during the year is $8, the unit variable cost remains at $4, how many books must the company sell to achieve the profit obtained in item b? (TFC = $400,000)

Chapter 10

Pricing and Output Decisions: Monopolistic Competition and Oligopoly

The Situation

In a meeting with Nicole Goodman, Frank Robinson explained the results of his price analysis. "My concern is that we know our optimal price, but do we really know how our competitors are going to react when we launch our product at this price point? Furthermore, I'm not sure the major players really consider us as a threat to their business, at least not yet. Therefore, can we assume that they will take us seriously?"

Nicole agreed, and suggested conducting further research. "One thing that we need is a complete list of prices of the major brands as well as the smaller brands," she began. "I was at a marketing conference in southern California last week and I noticed that the hotel that I stayed in had bottled water with the hotel name on the label in its mini-bar right next to one of the national brands."

"Leave it to California to come out with the trendiest products," Frank retorted.

"Not necessarily," said Nicole. "I heard that private labels are proliferating throughout the country. For example, there is even bottled water with the labels of cities and countries. And you might have heard that even McDonald's has its own bottled water that I understand is selling well in some markets. The other key information that we could use in making our pricing decision is the perception of our product by potential consumers and their view of how much value our product provides them relative to our price. Perhaps it would be worthwhile to hold a few focus groups to find this out."

"Good idea," said Frank. "I'll get on this right away and have a report for you in a couple of weeks."

INTRODUCTION

In this chapter, we examine in detail the pricing and output decisions made by managers in monopolistic competition and oligopoly. Economists also label these markets *imperfect competition.* This is in reference to their relative market power, which you will recall is the economist's main criterion for determining the degree of competition. Perfect competition is, as its name signifies, "perfect" because firms have no market power whatsoever. Monopoly is not competitive at all because the single firm in the market has absolute market power. Monopolistic competition and oligopoly are considered "imperfect" competition, because firms in these markets have the power to set their prices within the limits of certain constraints. This power and these constraints are principal subjects of this chapter.

Table 10.1 provides an overview of the competitive environment by comparing the four market types on the basis of market power, non-price competition, ease of market entry and exit, and the degree of interaction among competitors when making decisions (referred to as **mutual interdependence**). The key characteristic that separates perfect competition from the other three markets is market power. Firms in perfect competition are price takers, while firms in the other three markets are price makers. The key characteristic that separates perfect competition and monopoly from monopolistic competition and oligopoly is non-price competition. Because product differentiation exists in the latter two markets, firms have reason to compete on the basis of other factors besides the price. Market entry and exit are easiest in perfect competition and relatively easy in monopolistic competition. It is not possible in monopoly and could be difficult in oligopoly, depending on how dominant the leading firms are in that market.

In our view, the most challenging aspect of the competitive environment is the presence of mutual interdependence. It is one thing to know how to use optimization techniques such as the MR = MC Rule to set the best price and output levels for the firm. It is entirely another matter when one has to anticipate and judge the possible reaction by competitors to one's decision. The presence of mutual interdependence is the one factor that separates oligopoly from the other markets.

Table 10.1
Overview of Competitive Environment, 4 Market Types

	PERFECT COMPETITION	MONOPOLY	MONOPOLISTIC COMPETITION	OLIGOPOLY
Market power?	No	Yes, subject to government regulation	Yes	Yes
Mutual interdependence among competing firms?	No	No	No	Yes
Non-price competition	No	Optional	Yes	Yes
Easy market entry or exit?	Yes	No	Yes, relatively easy	No, relatively difficult

We begin this chapter with monopolistic competition and show how the MR = ME Rule that was developed in the previous chapter can be used for firms in this industry. We then proceed to oligopoly. Because of its daunting competitive environment, most of this chapter will be devoted to a discussion of the pricing, output, and non-pricing decisions that managers in this type of market must make. The topic of game theory constitutes a good part of this discussion. As you will see, the theory and applications of this very important field of study are ideally suited to the analysis of a mutually interdependent competitive environment. We also bring in the broader topic of business strategy, a vital responsibility for managers, particularly for those whose firms operate in imperfectly competitive markets.

MONOPOLISTIC COMPETITION

Monopolistic competition is a market in which there are many firms and relatively easy entry. These two characteristics are very similar to those of perfect competition. What enables firms to set their prices (i.e., to be monopolistic) is product differentiation. By somehow convincing their customers that what they are selling is not the same as the offerings of other firms in the market, a monopolistic competitor is able to set its price at a level that is higher than the price established by the forces of supply and demand under conditions of perfect competition.

A good example of how product differentiation can turn a product sold in a perfectly competitive market into one in which a seller is able to exercise some degree of market power is the case of the poultry industry. Those readers who live along the east coast will recognize the Perdue brand of chicken. For a number of years, Frank Perdue, owner of the company that bears his name, appeared on television telling people why his chickens were better. ("It takes a tough man to make a tender chicken," was one of his more memorable slogans.) And of course, Perdue chickens were priced higher than the unbranded poultry products sold in the typical supermarket. But in monopolistically competitive markets, entry by newcomers is fairly easy. Soon after Perdue became a well-known brand, along came Bell and Evans as well as Murray chickens. At first, these newcomers could be found primarily in butcher shops and specialty or gourmet food stores. But soon, many supermarkets began to carry these brands.

Perhaps the most successful national campaign to differentiate poultry was conducted by Tyson chicken. Don Tyson, founder of America's leading poultry company, described his company's situation prior to his company's marketing efforts as follows: "My daddy started raising chickens more than 50 years ago. The problem wasn't raising the chickens, it was trying to sell them at prices that seemed to vary every day or every hour."[1]

The solution for Tyson Foods to the problem of price volatility was "further processed value-enhanced poultry." This process of product differentiation began

---

[1]This quote and the rest of the material on Tyson is taken from Gene Walden and Edmund Lawler, *Marketing Masters: Secrets of America's Best Companies*, New York: HarperBusiness, 1993, pp. 12–17.

when Tyson realized that by selling Rock Cornish game hens by the hen and not by the pound, it could maintain its price point even when the price per pound was fluctuating. Once consumers got used to the idea that Tyson's hens were selling for a particular price, they continued to evaluate this price relative to their tastes and preferences, incomes, and the price of competing goods, regardless of what the price per pound happened to be.

In addition to changing the unit used in pricing its poultry, Tyson soon discovered that selling breaded chicken parts enabled it to set prices that were relatively immune to the fluctuating prices of fresh, unprocessed poultry. Then Tyson found that it could vary the seasoning in the breading to fit the particular tastes and preferences of any consumer. In so doing, it also recognized that it could prepare its chicken products to meet the special requirements of large customers such as fast-food and supermarket chains and institutions such as schools and hospitals. These large customers were interested in buying at the lowest possible price, but they were also interested in quality, consistency, and stability of supply. Therefore, Tyson could negotiate long-term price contracts with these large buyers, further protecting itself from the daily vagaries of the perfectly competitive market.

In economic analysis, we assume that the monopolistically competitive firm follows the MR = MC rule in order to maximize its profit (or minimize its loss). Therefore, as a matter of convenience, we employ the same graphical illustration for monopolistic competition that we used for the case of a monopoly market. This is shown in Figure 10.1a.

If the firm is in the situation depicted in Figure 10.1a, that is, if it is earning above-normal profit, then we can expect newcomers to be attracted to this market. The effect of this added competition on the monopolistic competitor can be seen in Figure 10.1b. Notice that the entry of new firms causes the original firm's demand curve to shift downward and to the left. If you are confused by this movement and the movement of the supply curve in the perfectly competitive market, remember that we are talking about this change from the point of view of the *individual firm,* not of the entire market. From an individual firm's perspective, the entry of additional firms in the market would decrease its market share by reducing the demand for its product. The leftward shift in the demand curve serves to illustrate this decline in market share. To be sure, this case assumes that the total market demand remains unchanged while the new firms are entering the market. If the total market demand were increasing while newcomers entered the market, the direction and extent of the shift in demand would be uncertain.

In the long run, economists hypothesize that the same situation would exist for monopolistic competition as for perfect competition: firms would be earning normal profit. If firms either earned above-normal profit or incurred losses, as shown in Figure 10.1c, then the entry or exit of firms, along with the adjustment of fixed capacity by existing firms, would cause each individual firm's demand curve either to increase or decrease until firms in the market earned only normal profit. (See Figure 10.1b.)

Besides the poultry business, some of the best examples of monopolistic competition can be found in the retail trade or in services. Restaurants, grocery stores, dry cleaners, stationery stores, florists, hardware stores, pharmacies, and video rental

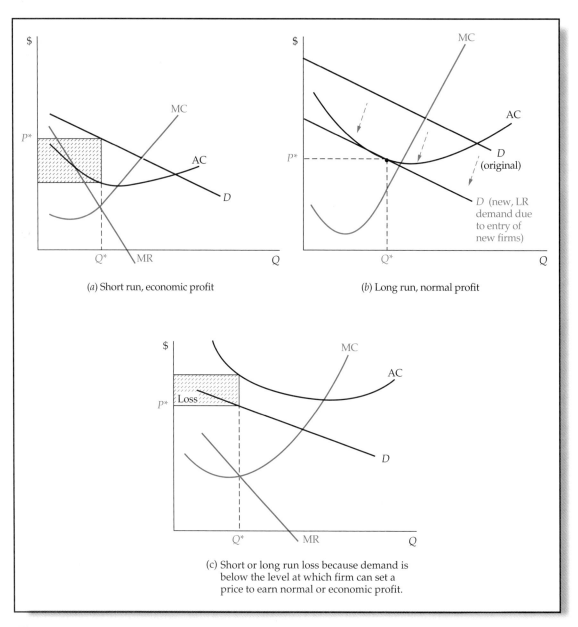

Figure 10.1
Monopolistic Competition

stores are all markets in which entry is fairly easy and the number of sellers is relatively large. In these businesses, owner-managers may use location, "service with a smile," or a slightly different mix of product offerings to differentiate their business. For example, in the previous edition of this text, we noted that throughout the United States, particularly in urban areas, Japanese food (particularly sushi) has really increased in popularity.[2] At that time, we also noticed a growing number of

Chinese restaurants in New York City that were equipped with sushi bars. But the phenomenon of Chinese restaurants offering Japanese sushi reveals another aspect of monopolistic competition that we discussed earlier in our graphical analysis of the short and long run. Differentiation is easy, but so is the entry of newcomers. (This was also pointed out in the example cited earlier about the poultry industry.)

In the never-ending effort to keep new and incumbent competitors at bay, a firm in monopolistic competition must constantly strive to maintain product differentiation. An article that recently appeared in the *New York Times,* goes well beyond our example of Chinese restaurants selling sushi. In "Borscht, Please, With a Side of Sushi," reporter Sarah Kershaw talks about "Russian sushi, Yemeni fried chicken, Taiwanese fish and chips, Japanese spaghetti and Jamaican jerk chicken with chop suey."[3] In addition, the author has discovered Indian-Chinese restaurants in Queens. These restaurants are owned by Chinese who used to live in India and who are supposed to serve Chinese food exactly as it is prepared in India. Want more? Then try Pakistani-Italian and Norwegian-Cantonese in Brooklyn and Korean soul food in Harlem. There are even restaurants that serve Irish-Dominican, Greek-Irish, and Dominican-Italian food. We could go on and on, but the point of the article from our perspective is what immigrant restauranteurs told Mrs. Kershaw: "In the highly competitive world of New York City ethnic food, it pays to branch out, mix, borrow and blend."

OLIGOPOLY

Market Concentration

Oligopoly is a market dominated by a relatively small number of large firms. The products they sell may be either standardized or differentiated. Part of the control that firms in oligopoly markets exercise over price and output stems from their ability to differentiate their products. But market power also comes from their sheer size and market dominance. There are two good sources of information on the degree of concentration that exists in various markets. The Census Bureau's Survey of Manufactures provides a comprehensive account of market share for the major industrial sectors of the U.S. economy.[4] However, it does not always provide the most current data (the most recent survey was conducted in 1997). For more current data as well as market share information on specific brands, we recommend the *Market Share Reporter.*[5]

Table 10.2 presents sample information found in the Census Survey. The Census Bureau classifies industries by level of product specificity. The information that we

---

[2]On international trips taken over the past several years, one of the authors has observed typical supermarkets in London, Paris, and Hong Kong offering a wide array of freshly prepared and packed sushi.
[3]"Borscht, Please, With a Side of Sushi," *New York Times,* December 21, 2001. One of the authors of this text lives in New York, but the other lives in Phoenix. We do not want to slight the good people of Phoenix so we should say that we know at least one ethnic-fusion restaurant in Phoenix. It is called "Chino-Bandito," and we will allow readers to guess what combination of ethnic foods is offered in this establishment.
[4]For a PDF file of the 1997 Survey, go to www.census.govt.
[5]Robert S. Lazich, ed. *Market Share Reporter,* Detroit, The Gale Press, 2002.

Table 10.2

Share of Value of Shipments Accounted for by the 4, 8, and 20 Largest Companies in the 3-, 4-, 5-, and 6-Digit Levels of Beverage and Tobacco Product Manufacturing and Sugar and Confectionary Product Manufacturing

NAICS CODE	INDUSTRY GROUP AND INDUSTRY	COMPANIES	VALUE OF SHIPMENTS ($ MILLIONS)	PERCENT OF VALUE OF SHIPMENTS			HH INDEX
				4 LARGEST	8 LARGEST	20 LARGEST	
311	Food manufacturing	21,958	421,737	14.3	22.0	34.8	91.0
3113	Sugar and confectionary product mfg.	1,556	24,114	41.9	56.4	75.0	580.3
31131	Sugar mfg.	49	7,399	64.4	84.0	95.9	1452.2
311311	Sugarcane mills	34	1,457	56.6	71.4	94.3	1158.7
311312	Cane sugar refining	12	3,209	98.7	99.9	100.0	D
311313	Beet sugar refining	8	2,732	85.0	100.0	N	1997.6
312	Beverage and tobacco product mfg.	2,237	96,971	45.1	59.1	72.7	777.2
3121	Beverage mfg.	2,169	60,896	40.9	52.1	66.0	531.5
31211	Soft drink and ice mfg.	1,008	32,587	45.5	53.6	68.8	743.3
312111	Soft drink mfg.	388	31,376	47.2	55.6	70.9	800.4
312112	Bottled water mfg.	109	785	51.7	64.4	80.3	986.6
312113	Ice mfg.	514	424	24.4	31.3	43.1	302.3

N: Does not apply
D: Data omitted because of possible disclosure.

found in the 1997 report begins at the three-digit level (broadest) and goes to the six-digit level (most specific). In 1997, the Census Bureau introduced a new system for classifying companies called the North American Industry Classification System, or NAICS. Previous to that, the Census Bureau had used the Standard Industrial Classification, or SIC. The categories in the two systems are only about 50 percent compatible with each other, so time comparisons on shifting market shares are difficult to make. Notice that as the product classification becomes more specific, the degree of market concentration among sellers tends to increase. This pattern occurs in many other industries, but not in any consistent or precise manner.

Besides indicating the degree of market concentration by measuring the market share of the top 4, 8, 20, and 50 largest companies, the Census Survey provides a measure of concentration called the Herfindahl-Hirschman (HH) index. The formula for this index is as follows:

$$HH = \sum_{i=1}^{n} S_i^2$$

where n is the number of companies in the industry, and S is the ith company's market share. The HH index is shown for the 15 industries in the last column of Table 10.2. The advantages of the HH index relative to concentration ratios are that

1. It uses the market share information about all the firms.
2. The squaring of individual market shares gives more weight to the larger firms.

The maximum HH index is 10,000—when there is just one firm in the industry. Using the prior example, the HH index will differentiate between an industry, where four firms equally share the total market (HH = 2,500), and an industry where the top firm has 94 percent and the other three 2 percent each (HH = 8,848). According to U.S. Department of Justice Merger Guidelines of 1982, "unconcentrated" markets are defined as those with an HH of less than 1,000. Table 10.2 shows selected markets relating to the soft drink industry.

The *Market Share Reporter,* the other good provider of data on industry concentration that we recommend, is a compendium of information on market share taken from other sources. In fact, for those interested in marketing, it is actually fascinating reading. For example, are you curious what is the leading brand of spaghetti/macaroni? Then turn to page 441 of the 2002 *Market Share Reporter* to find the answer.[6] In keeping with the spirit of our textbook case of "Global Foods," we present in Table 10.3, actual market share information on selected brands in the food and beverage industry as reported in *Market Share Reporter.* Notice that the bottled water market is almost evenly distributed among the top four brands, while the market for Sports Drinks is dominated by one brand, Gatorade.[7]

PRICING IN AN OLIGOPOLISTIC MARKET: RIVALRY AND MUTUAL INTERDEPENDENCE

Whether the sellers in an oligopolistic market compete against each other by differentiating their product, dominating market share, or both, the fact that there are relatively few sellers creates a situation where each is carefully watching the other as it sets its price. Economists refer to this pricing behavior as mutual interdependence. This means that each seller is setting its price while explicitly considering the reaction by its competitors to the price that it establishes.

In the 1930s, economist Paul Sweezy provided an early insight into the pricing dynamics of mutual interdependence among oligopoly firms by developing a **kinked demand** curve model.[8] The basic assumption of the Sweezy model is that a competitor (or competitors) will follow a price decrease but will not make a change in reaction to a price increase. Thus, the firm contemplating a price change may refrain from doing so for fear that quantities sold will be affected in such a way as to decrease profits.

---

[6]No, we will not keep you in suspense. *Market Share Reporter* obtained this information from the *Food Institute Report,* August 7, 2000, p. 4, which in turn got the information from Information Resources Inc. Barilla was the best selling brand, with 8.19% market share, followed by Ronzoni and Mueller's, with 7.10% and 6.9%, respectively.

[7]Readers may recall that in 2000 Coca-Cola intended to purchase Quaker, the owner of Gatorade. Coke's board rebuffed this move. Shortly after this, Pepsi-Cola bought Quaker primarily for the value of this powerful brand.

[8]Paul Sweezy, "Demand Under Conditions of Oligopoly," *Journal of Political Economy,* 47 (1939), pp. 568–73.

Table 10.3
Market Share of Top Four Brands in Selected Food and Beverage Product Categories

PRODUCT CATEGORY AND TOP 4 BRANDS (DATE REPORTED)	PERCENTAGE OF THE MARKET
Tortilla/Tostado Chips (9/10/00)	
Doritos	45.41
Tostitos	25.07
Santitas	4.04
Baked Tostitos	2.43
The rest	23.05
Canned Tuna (12/27/00)	
Star-Kist	40
Chicken of the Sea	22
Bumble Bee Seafoods	20
The rest	18
Meal Replacements (1/1/01)	
Ultra Slim-Fast	42.9
Ensure	13.6
Ensure Plus	8.4
Boost	6.3
The rest	28.8
Bottled Water (4/15/01)	
Poland Spring	7.9
Acquafina	7.8
Arrowhead	5.9
Sparkletts	5.7
The rest (includes such brands as Evian, Dasani, Deer Park, and Crystal Geyser)	72.7
Sports Drinks (5/10/01)	
Gatorade	78.0
Powerade	15.0
All Sport	4.4
The rest	2.6

Source: Market Share Reporter, 2002.

If a firm lowers its price, this may have an immediate impact on the competition. This firm takes its action to increase sales by drawing customers away from the higher-priced competitors, but when competitors realize what is happening (i.e., their sales are declining), they will quickly follow the price cut to maintain their market share. If this firm undertakes the opposite action—a price increase—assuming incorrectly that competitors will follow suit, its sales will drop markedly if competitors fail to do so.

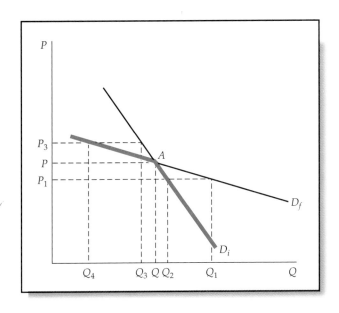

Figure 10.2
Demand Curves for an
Oligopoly Considering a
Price Increase/Decrease

It is easy to demonstrate the "kink" in such a demand curve with the graph in Figure 10.2. Let us assume that the original price and quantity are found at point A. If the firm lowers its price, expecting that quantity demanded will move along the more elastic demand curve D_f and this result materializes, then it will gain a relatively large quantity of additional sales for a relatively small decrease in price. If it lowers its price from P to P_1, it will expect to increase its sales from Q to Q_1. This is the relevant demand curve for the firm if other companies do not retaliate. Our firm would thus gain customers at the expense of competition. However, if competitors do react and match the price cut, our company will increase its sales only to Q_2, along demand curve D_i; this is the relevant demand curve when all companies in the industry decrease their price equally. There will be a relatively small increase in sales, since all prices in the industry are lower, but not nearly as much as the company expected when it reduced its price.

On the other hand, suppose our company decides to raise its price, anticipating that competitors will follow the increase. It thus expects to move along D_i to Q_3 when it boosts its price to P_3. It would thus sustain some loss in sales while benefiting from a significantly higher price. However, suppose its competitors refuse to play along and keep their prices unchanged. The company's situation now becomes more precarious, since its quantity sold drops to Q_4: the demand curve for the firm alone is much more elastic than if all firms raise their prices in unison.

The prospect of being stung by such action will make the company much more loath to change its price from P. From that vantage point, it will appear to the company that the appropriate demand curve is D_i if price is lowered and D_f if the price is increased. The upper portion of D_f and the lower portion of D_i can be seen to form a kinked demand curve around point A; thus, the name of Sweezy's model. These relevant portions of the two demand curves are boldly outlined in Figure 10.2.

Now that we have developed a demand curve for this oligopolist, we can derive a marginal revenue curve as well. This marginal revenue curve will be

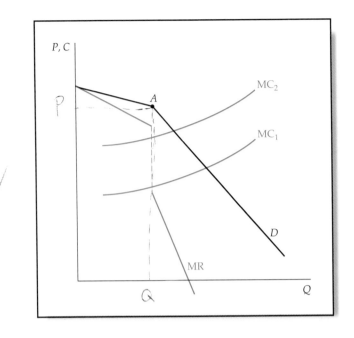

Figure 10.3
The Kinked Demand Curve

discontinuous: there will be a gap at the point where the kink occurs. As we know, a company will maximize its profits at the point where marginal cost equals marginal revenue. The two marginal cost curves drawn in Figure 10.3 both imply the same price and quantity, at point *A*. Thus, a significant change in costs could occur for our firm, but it will not react by changing its price. Actually, the price may remain unchanged even if the demand curve moves to the right or left, as long as the kink remains at the same price level. Hence, it can be concluded that under the circumstances described, a kinked demand curve will result in price rigidities despite changes in demand and cost.

Over the years, the kinked demand curve has been challenged by other economists. In particular, Nobel Prize laureate George Stigler investigated several oligopolistic industries and found little empirical support for Sweezy's model. Stigler found that in these industries, price increases were followed as quickly as were price decreases.[9] Such findings, of course, contradict the existence of the kink. Further, the model does not explain how the price was originally set at the kink. Was it originally set where marginal revenue equaled marginal cost, or was it by some other means, such as tradition?

One commonly held view of how the price at point *A* is determined involves the concept of an industry **price leader.** This is the firm that dares to break out of the pack without fearing the consequences spelled out in the kinked demand model. If this firm decides to raise its price, it assumes all others will follow. If this firm decides

---

[9]George J. Stigler, "The Kinky Oligopoly Demand Curve and Rigid Prices," *Journal of Political Economy,* October 1947, pp. 432–39. Similarly, see Julian J. Simon, "A Further Test of the Kinky Oligopoly Demand Curve," *American Economic Review,* December 1969, pp. 971–75.

Managerial Economics

to lower its price, it assumes the others may follow but will not go even lower, thereby triggering a price war that would hurt the entire industry.

In oligopoly markets in the United States, the role of the price leader is usually assumed by the company with the largest share of the market. For example, General Motors is often the first to announce price increase for the next year's line of cars and trucks. During its reign as the dominant leader in the mainframe computer market back in the 1960s through the mid-1980s, IBM was always the price leader. The "fringe companies" (as economists sometimes refer to the significantly smaller companies in an oligopoly market) generally set their prices about 10 percent lower than the "umbrella price set by IBM." The undisputed champion of the general merchandise retail industry is Wal-Mart. At its 2001 annual shareholders' meeting, the executives at the company stressed that they will continue to be the price leader by maintaining a close watch over its competitors. Tom Coughlin, president and CEO of the Wal-Mart Stores Division, told meeting attendees that the company conducts price checks in 99.8 percent of Kmart stores and 98.7 percent of Target stores every week.[10]

Different companies may take turns setting prices. For example, Coca-Cola and Pepsi-Cola may at different times be the price leader. This rotation in the leadership position indicates that it is not always the largest company that is the first to raise or lower the price. For example, in early 1999, after several years of strong demand, the major airlines decided to raise the price of their full-fare coach seats by about 2 percent. First to make this move was Delta Airlines. When this was first reported in the newspaper, industry analysts were wondering whether the other major airlines would follow. The next day, it was announced that they had.[11] Although Delta is not the leader based on market share, it served as the industry leader in this particular case.

There also may be non-price leaders in an oligopoly market. American Airlines was the first to offer frequent flier points to its passengers. All the other airlines followed suit. It was also the leader in the co-branding of its name with a credit card issuer. The Citibank-American Airlines credit card is the dominant co-branded card in the industry today. Another interesting form of non-price competition and leadership is the practice by pharmaceutical companies of "wining and dining" physicians. Drug company sales representatives often invite doctors to lavish weekend retreats and expensive evenings out. But according to a recent article in the *New York Times*, Merck has instructed its sales representatives that they should "no longer treat doctors to free Broadway plays, weekend trips and other gifts that could be viewed as inappropriate." Other companies may soon be following suit.[12] It appears from this preliminary report, that Merck, the second largest pharmaceutical manufacturer in the United States (after Pfizer) will be the leader in this non-price initiative.

---

[10]Mike Troy, "Wal-Mart Maintains Expansion Strategy," *DSN Retailing Today,* June 18, 2001.
[11]Laurence Zucherman, "Several Major U.S. Airlines Lift Fares Across the Board," *New York Times,* January 30, 1999.
[12]Melody Petersen, "Merck Is Said to Limit Perks in Marketing to Physicians," *New York Times,* January 18, 2002.

Non-Price Competition

The key to the pricing power of firms in monopolistic competition and oligopoly is their ability to differentiate their product so that they are not mere price takers who are subject to the tyranny of supply and demand. All efforts to do so are referred to in economics as *non-price competition*.[13] We have already provided examples of non-price competition in our earlier discussion of monopolistic competition. But we now present this concept in a more formal and systematic manner.

A simple, but useful definition of non-price competition is "any effort made by firms other than a change in the price of the 'product in question'[14] in order to influence the demand for their product." More specifically, these efforts are intended to influence the non-price determinants of demand. Below you will see the non-price determinants of demand (first introduced in chapter 3) and a suggested list of non-price variables that firms might choose to use to compete in monopolistic competition or oligopoly. *Non-price determinants of demand* include any factor other than the price of the good in question that causes the demand curve to shift. They are: (1) tastes and preferences, (2) income, (3) prices of substitutes and complements, (4) number of buyers, and (5) future expectations of buyers about product price. *Non-price variables* include any factor that managers can control, influence, or explicitly consider in making decisions affecting the demand for their goods and services. These variables are (1) advertising, (2) promotion, (3) location and distribution channels, (4) market segmentation, (5) loyalty programs, (6) product extensions and new product development, (7) special customer services, (8) product "lock-in" or "tie-in," and (9) preemptive new product announcements.

Readers might recognize the non-price variables as important tools of marketing. In a typical corporation, the management of these variables (sometimes called the *marketing mix*) is largely the responsibility of the marketing function. A complete discussion of each of these variables is well beyond the scope of this text and in fact would be found in any marketing text. But we will comment briefly on some of these variables in terms of their expected impact on the non-price determinants of demand.

1. **Tastes and preferences:** *Advertising and promotion* are intended to influence tastes and preferences.[15] Very often, advertising and promotional campaigns are tied into the building or support of a brand. A common means of enhancing

---

[13]This somewhat awkward term is an indication of the heavy emphasis in economic analysis of pricing or market power as the basis for competition. In the ordinary language of business, the term to describe the factors discussed in this section would be considered just a part of "competition." Therefore, outside the confines of economic analysis, a "highly competitive market" is assumed to mean price or non-price competition or some combination of both.

[14]The use of the term *product in question* is to remind readers about the difference that we made in chapter 4 between *own-price* and *cross-price* elasticity. Companies may use the price of complements or substitutes to try to stimulate the demand for the product in question. But this is considered to be a form of non-price competition.

[15]One must be cautious about the precise nature of advertising's impact on tastes and preferences. As John Wannamaker, founder of the famous Philadelphia department store, once said, "I believe that half of my advertising is effective, the problem is that I don't know which half."

these campaigns is the use of celebrities as a representative of a brand. Brand advertising and promotion are often combined with *market segmentation.* In this case, rather than try to influence tastes and preferences, firms try to target different market segments in which they believe their products will have the greatest appeal. In recent years, efforts to retain customers over the long term have become as important to firms as those designed to win new customers. Thus, *loyalty programs* such as points given for using a credit card, for mileage traveled on an airline, or for staying at a hotel have been an important means of influencing tastes and preferences.

2. **Income:** Firms cannot affect income. But *market segmentation* is a way for firms to focus on the income levels that they believe will be most likely to buy their products. If they are selling a "superior" product, then they would try to target higher income groups. The opposite would hold if they felt their products were "inferior." (Refer back to chapter 4 for a discussion on the economic meaning of superior and inferior products.) An article in the *Wall Street Journal* pointed out how Volvo (owned by Ford) and Saab (owned by General Motors) have both fallen considerably behind the German and Japanese luxury car brands. In early 2002, they announced that they were going to try to catch up in this market segment by introducing their versions of upscale SUVs.[16]

3. **Prices of substitutes and complements:** Efforts to *lock-in* customers will tend to reduce the effect that changes in the prices of substitutes will have on the products that firms sell. This effort may be fairly aggressive, such as wireless phone companies offering discounts or free mobile phones for long-term contracts but levying a penalty if customers want to get out before the expiration date. On the other hand, this effort may be rather subtle. In effect, Microsoft locks in the use of its PC applications such as Word or PowerPoint through the "network effect." People tend to use these applications because everyone uses them, and this makes the exchange of files much more convenient. AOL's e-mail and Internet services appeal to nontechnical users who become so accustomed to the look and feel of their Web site and e-mail format that they do not want to switch. Also, many are hesitant to change their e-mail addresses. Sometimes, firms resort to product *tie-ins* to increase the sale of complementary products. For example, companies may choose to tie-in the sale of their products with popular Web portals. Just prior to writing this section, one of the authors checked his e-mail on AOL. The first screen that popped up was an offer for Visioneer scanners. Not only was he going to be able to just click "yes" and then be billed in four "easy installments" (the author's credit card information was already known to AOL), but he was told that these products had special software that would make transferring images to his AOL Web site very simple. More is discussed about product tie-ins in the next chapter.

4. **Number of buyers:** Firms also can utilize effective *market segmentation* to increase the number of potential buyers of their product. For example, according to Paul Ballew, a market analyst for General Motors, the richest 20 percent of Americans—those with household incomes over $75,000—now account for 46 percent of new car purchases as compared with only 30 percent in 1995. In

---

[16]"SUVs Swedish Style," *The Wall Street Journal,* January 3, 2002.

the words of Paul Ballew, this represents "a phenomenal structural change in [the auto] industry." He goes on to say that "Your primary vehicle buyer is increasingly a dual-income, 40-something-year-old couple where [at least] one member has a college degree."[17] Firms also can increase the number of potential buyers in the market by expanding their operations beyond their borders. For example, both Wal-Mart and Carrefour (a French retail chain similar to Wal-Mart) have made major investments in China. With the entry of China into the World Trade Organization in 2001, many firms will do the same. It is easy to see why. If we suppose that over the next decade 25 to 30 percent of the Chinese reach a middle income status similar to the rest of the developed world, then we are talking about a consumer market of about the size of the United States or Western Europe. The population of China is currently about 1.3 billion.

5. **Future Expectations:** Firms may attempt to influence the future expectation of customers about product price and availability through such means as early new product announcements. In the days when IBM dominated the mainframe computer market (late 1960s to mid-1980s), it would sometimes announce its intentions of launching a new product at the same time that its competitors launched their products. This did not change future expectations about prices per se. This preemptive announcement tactic was intended to keep its customers from switching to the competitors' new products. This action may not have had a direct impact on the expectations of the future price of a product, but it did have an effect on the demand for the product. Software companies have used this tactic too, prompting wary analysts who wonder whether there actually will be a new product to use the term "vaporware." In some cases, it might be difficult for a company to influence customer expectations. One of the problems that Sears encountered in the late 1980s was that customers realized that it always had sales on selected products and simply waited to purchase these products at that time. Wal-Mart, on the other hand, offered customers "everyday low prices." In the late 1980s, Sears tried switching to an "EDLP" pricing strategy, but unfortunately did not succeed.

6. **Financing Terms and Conditions:** In both consumer and industry markets, sellers can use financing terms and conditions as a way of influencing the demand for their product. This initiative does not quite fit into the set of non-price determinants of demand used in economic theory. But in effect, the use of financing terms and conditions is like changing the price.

Perhaps you have seen advertisements or promotional literature sponsored by electronics stores, furniture stores, or department stores saying "zero interest" or "no monthly payments until next year." This is a way of reducing the price of their products to those who buy on credit without actually lowering the price of the products themselves. Manufacturers of industrial equipment may use the financing arm of the company for this purpose. During the boom years of the telecommunications industry in the previous decade, there were a number of "competitive local exchange carriers" (CLECs) that sprouted up to compete against the incumbent Regional Bell Operating Companies (RBOCs). Much of the equipment sold to them by Lucent was

---

[17]Ibid.

done with the help of Lucent-backed financing. When the technology sector crumbled, a number of these CLECs went bankrupt or failed to meet their obligations to Lucent, thereby causing the company to suffer heavy losses.

American auto manufacturers also have been using easy credit as a way of promoting sales, and they are now being seriously threatened by this tactic.[18] After September 11, the financing subsidiaries of the U.S. automakers used interest-free offers to prop up falling demand. However, low-interest rate financing had been a part of the way American auto makers tried to stimulate sales long before September 11. As *New York Times* reporter Daniel Hakim observes:

> Unlike their foreign rivals, which have developed stables of models that buyers actually will pay more for, Ford and GM have relied more on incentives like low-interest loans and cheap leases to attract customers. The automakers have ponied up billions of dollars to their financing units to make up the difference on the below-market financing.[19]

The problem now is that because of the recession which began in the spring of 2001, the default rate on these loans and leases are expected to rise.

Economic Optimization and Non-Price Competition

We have demonstrated how the MR = MC Rule helps managers to determine the optimal price and output level for their products. As we have also explained, the MR = MC Rule is actually part of a more general economic concept called "equalizing at the margin," which managers can use to help make an optimal decision. (Recall that we used this concept in the determination of the optimal amount of an input and the optimal combination of inputs in a production function; see chapter 7.) Equalizing at the margin also can be used to decide on the optimal expenditure level of a non-price factor that influences a firm's demand. For example, let us consider advertising expenditure. Suppose:

$$MCA = \text{cost of advertising associated with an additional unit of sales of a firm's product}$$

$$= \Delta \text{ total cost of advertising/delta change in quantity demanded}$$

and,

$$MRA = \text{marginal revenue resulting from advertising}$$

$$= \Delta \text{ total revenue/delta quantity minus delta total cost other than advertising/delta quantity}$$

$$= MR - MC \text{ (other than advertising)}.$$

We can therefore say that a firm will increase its advertising expenditure up to the point at which MRA = MRC. Rather than illustrate this with a graph, we will ask you

---

[18]Danny Hakim, "All That Easy Credit Haunts Detroit Now," *New York Times*, January 6, 2002. Shortly after this article appeared, the CEO of Ford announced that the company was going to lay off about 30,000 workers and discontinue four product lines, including the Lincoln Continental.
[19]Ibid.

to suggest how this might be done. (See Problem 11 at end of this chapter.) But for now, just think about a more critical question: How might a manager obtain the *data* to do this calculation? (*Hint:* Refer back to chapter 5.)

Our experience in working with firms on this issue indicates that a number of them utilize the concepts of discounted cash flow and the time value of money. These concepts are explained in detail in chapter 13. However, we will briefly introduce these concepts in the context of this section's subject matter.

Over the past decade, there has been a growing focus among managers, particularly in the market function of a corporation, on the "lifetime" or at least the long-term value of a customer.[20] For example, suppose you are the manager of a wireless telecom company and you and your competition offer free phones to attract customers. These phones may cost up to several hundred dollars. How long does a customer have to use your network in order for you to break even or to make a profit? Suppose you are the manager of a company that issues credit cards? To keep customers from switching to another company, you offer them the chance to get a free airline ticket for a companion if they use your card to buy airline tickets over the next year.

These two examples of promotional efforts involve initial added costs that presumably result in a stream of additional revenue over a long period of time. However, money spent or received over time (e.g., over a 3- to 5-year period) does not have the same value as money spent at the present time, because of a concept called "the time value of money." Therefore, marginal revenue as well as marginal cost has to be adjusted for this time value of money before they can be compared to each other. After adjusting for the time value of money, if marginal revenue exceeds marginal cost, then the promotional effort is justified from an economic standpoint.[21]

The Reality of Monopolistic Competition and Oligopoly: "Imperfect" Competition

In theory, the essential differences between monopolistic competition and oligopoly are the ease of entry into the market, the relative sizes of the sellers, and the presence of mutual interdependence in the pricing of products. Monopolistic competition consists of a large number of relatively small firms who are subject to competitive pressures because of the ease of entry of newcomers into the market and who act independently in setting their prices. Oligopoly consists of a small number of relatively large firms whose size or power in differentiating their products makes it difficult for newcomers to enter the market. But their size and domination of the market also make it imperative for them to watch each other closely in setting their prices.

However, the distinction between monopolistic competition and oligopoly can sometimes be blurred in the "real world." In a market dubbed monopolistic competition, there may well be mutual interdependence in the firms' pricing decisions. In a market considered to be an oligopoly, there may well be situations where newcomers

---

[20]An undocumented, but well-known story, told to one of the authors about Domino's Pizza, serves as a good illustration. Apparently, the employees of the company at one time had banners in their office saying "One customer = $5,000." This was supposedly the average amount that a loyal customer is expected to spend on Domino's Pizza over the course of his or her lifetime.

[21]In our experience, we have found that a number of companies use the term *cost-benefit analysis* or *business case* in reference to optimization analysis using the time value of money.

enter the market fairly easily, particularly if given enough time. Consider the following four examples.

1. *The American Automobile Industry.* The American automobile market is generally acknowledged as an oligopoly market. But a case could be made that it looks more like monopolistic competition than oligopoly. The entry and increasing dominance of Japanese, German, and more recently Korean automakers into the U.S. market, particularly in certain segments of the market (e.g., the Germans and Japanese for luxury cars and family sedans and Koreans for compacts and subcompacts), make it hard to argue that entry is difficult in this market. Moreover, the overwhelmingly large share of the total market enjoyed by the American "Big Three" (one of whom, Chrysler, is now owned by the German company Daimler-Benz), no longer exists. At its peak in the early 70s, General Motors held over 50 percent market share. Today it is down to around 30 percent. Moreover, industry analysts believe Toyota could in fact overtake Daimler-Chrysler very shortly as the third largest seller of cars in the United States.

2. *U.S. Airline Industry.* The deregulation of the U.S. airline industry in the late 1970s was intended to create more competition by allowing new firms to enter various routes and for all airlines to compete on price as well as non-price factors. In other words, deregulation was supposed to have created a market resembling monopolistic competition. But over the past several decades, the industry has become much more concentrated, with the top three U.S.-based carriers (American, United, and Delta) considered the "first tier" and the rest (Northwestern, America West, Continental, and U.S. Air, and TWA) relegated to "second tier" status. American Airlines' purchase of TWA in 2001 has made the industry even more concentrated. United Airlines tried to buy U.S. Air but was stopped by the Federal Aviation Administration. However, the entry into the market of airlines that focus on providing low-cost service on heavily trafficked short-haul routes is more representative of monopolistic competition. Southwest Airlines is a good example of how new entrants can beat out the incumbents. A more recent example is the success of JetBlue in New York and the surrounding states.[22]

3. *Small Retail Establishments Around the World: Monopolistic Competition or Oligopoly.* Small retail establishments are considered by economists to be a classic example of monopolistic competition. They are relatively small, there are many of them, entry is relatively easy, and there are opportunities for them to differentiate their products. However, in certain situations, the competitive environment of these small retail establishments may actually resemble more of an oligopoly than one of monopolistic competition. For example, *within a neighborhood or a mall,* there could be a relatively small number of stores of a certain type that dominate that particular market (e.g., two jewelry stores in a mall, three Japanese sushi restaurants in a town, or two music stores in a city). And as such they may well exhibit the characteristic of price setting by mutual interdependence. Who would argue that a coffee house on one end of a mall does not

---

[22]In the spring of 2002, JetBlue became a publicly traded company.

take into consideration the prices charged by a competitor on the other end of the mall?

Another important trend in retail merchandising is the growing strength of national and global chain stores. These retail giants have seriously hurt the ability of small retail establishments to compete and in many cases have driven them out of business. Good examples of these dominant retail companies are Wal-Mart and "category busters" such as Home Depot, Sports Authority, and Toys R Us and expanding chains such as CVS, Rite Aid, and Walgreens in the retail pharmacy business.[23]

4. *Global Issuers of Credit Cards: Monopolistic Competition or Oligopoly?* On the surface, the credit card industry appears to be an oligopoly dominated by Visa, MasterCard, American Express, and Discover. But a look below the surface reveals that Visa and MasterCard are really associations of financial institutions that issue cards and "acquire" merchants who agree to accept the cards as a means of payment. Visa and MasterCard each have thousands of members, most of whom are banks. This would indicate monopolistic competition. But a still closer look indicates that the card-issuing industry has become increasingly more concentrated. On the basis of card holder receivables (i.e., the amount owed by card holders to issuing financial institutions), the top 10 account for over 60 percent market share. The top 25 have over 80 percent of these receivables. On the merchant side of the business, one company, First Data Corporation, and its partners process and manage the credit card charges of over 40 percent of the establishments who accept general purpose credit cards.

As a way of dealing with the possible blurring of these two types of markets, monopolistic competition and oligopoly are sometimes put together into one category called imperfect competition. We introduced this term at the beginning of this chapter. But let us provide a formal definition of this term just to reinforce our points. Imperfect competition is "a market in which firms are able to exert varying degrees of market power because of their size and/or their ability to differentiate their products from those sold by their competitors."

GAME THEORY AND THE PRICING BEHAVIOR OF OLIGOPOLIES

The economic concepts and tools of analysis that we have used throughout this text are all part of the microeconomic theory of the firm. The basic implication of this theory for managers is that the optimization of their firm's economic situation (i.e., profit maximization or loss minimization) requires that they base their output and pricing decisions on the MR = MC rule. Assuming that a manager has sufficient

---

[23]One of the authors recalled that when he first moved into his town 20 years ago, it had three independently owned and operated by individual pharmacists. His pharmacist knew him and his family by name and would usually find the time to chat at length about sports and town gossip to his customers. All three pharmacies have gone out of business. There is a Rite Aid in the town and two CVS stores in the surrounding towns. The local pharmacist referred to above closed his store after 22 years in business and is now working as a pharmacist for one of the national chains.

information to determine the firm's marginal cost and marginal revenue, this rule can be very useful in practical business situations. This is certainly the case in the perfectly competitive, monopoly, and monopolistically competitive markets.

But the one critical situation in which the MR = MC rule is seriously limited is in a market where pricing and output decisions are made by managers who anticipate or react to the pricing and output decisions of their competitors as they themselves try to determine the optimal level of price and output. The kinked demand model tries to explain why the prices in such markets tend to be very similar for each competitor, but it does not explain how and why this "administered price" is established in the first place.[24]

Over the past decade, managerial economics texts have sought to remedy this by introducing **game theory** into the analysis of pricing and output decisions in oligopoly markets. We believe game theory does add to the understanding of pricing and output decisions in oligopoly markets. We cannot do justice here to the coverage of this material because entire courses and textbooks are devoted to this subject. We can however, explain briefly the essence of this theory and provide a simple example of how the theory might be used to analyze an oligopolist's strategy, particularly in pricing.

Game theory is concerned with "how individuals make decisions when they are aware that their actions affect each other and when each individual takes this into account."[25] This definition should come as no surprise, given that game theory is utilized by economists especially to help them understand mutually interdependent behavior. There are many different types of games, each characterized by a unique set of assumptions concerning such conditions as the number of players, the stakes involved, whether there must be a winner and a loser, and whether the decisions taken are simultaneous or sequential. But regardless of the conditions, the essential idea in game theory is to apply the logic of mathematics to arrive at a "solution," or in economic terms, an "equilibrium."

For example, one of the most well-known and frequently cited games in economics textbooks is one called "Prisoners' Dilemma." This variation is characterized as a *two-person, non–zero-sum, noncooperative game* with a *dominant strategy*. In a *zero-sum game,* one player's gain is the other's loss and vice versa. In a non–zero-sum game, both players may gain or lose, depending on the actions each chooses to take. The noncooperative feature of the game implies that opponents are not allowed to share information with each other. A dominant strategy means that there is one strategy that is best for a person, no matter what the other one does.

The particulars of the prisoners' dilemma are essentially as follows.[26] Two individuals commit a serious crime together and are apprehended by the police. They know that there is insufficient evidence to convict them of the crime. At

---

[24]In the early 1900s, the French economist Cournot developed a mathematical model to explain how a price is determined in a "duopoly" market in which there are just two competitors. However, the model did not take into account the possibility of actions and reactions between the two competing firms.
[25]H. Scott Bierman and Luis Fernandez, *Game Theory with Economic Applications,* Reading, MA: Addison-Wesley, 1998, p. 4.
[26]There are numerous versions of the prisoners' dilemma story. This one is based on Andrew Schotter, *Microeconomics: A Modern Approach,* Reading, MA: Addison-Wesley, 1998, chapter 7, and on J. R. McGuigan, R. C. Moyer, and F. H. Harris, *Managerial Economics,* Cincinnati: South-Western College Publishing, 9th ed., 2002, pp. 532, 568–9.

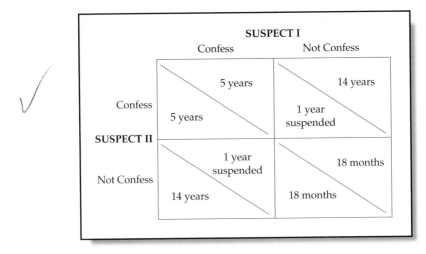

Figure 10.4
Prisoners' Dilemma: Payoff Matrix

worst, they risk being charged and convicted of the less serious offense of loiter-ing near the scene of the crime, which involves a lesser prison sentence. The police interrogate them separately. During this procedure, the suspects are not allowed to communicate with each other. If one suspect confesses, then he will get a mini-mum sentence (that could be suspended) for cooperating with the authorities, while the other will receive the maximum sentence. If both talk, then each will receive a moderate sentence somewhere between the minimum and maximum. Given these conditions, what should each suspect do? Game theory provides the answer.

All solutions in game theory involve what economists call an equilibrium condi-tion. In Prisoners' Dilemma, a stable equilibrium is achieved. It is a stable equilib-rium in that once the suspects have chosen their strategies (in this case, both suspects would choose to confess) neither would want to unilaterally change its strategy.[27] Let us use a numerical illustration to show what the equilibrium situation would look like for each suspect.

Let us assume that the options for each prisoner and the consequences of select-ing each option can be represented in the payoff matrix seen in Figure 10.4. For each suspect, the options are to confess or remain silent. If they both confess, the matrix indicates that they would each receive 5-year sentences. If one confesses and the other remains silent, then the "stool pigeon"[28] would get a 1-year suspended sen-tence, while his tight-lipped partner would receive a 14-year prison term. If they both remained silent, then they would both receive an 18-month sentence.

---

[27]Economists often refer to this as "Nash Equilibrium," after the mathematician John Nash, who first pro-posed this in 1951 and who received a Nobel Prize in Economics for his work in game theory. John Nash is also the focus of the book by Sylvia Nasar, *A Beautiful Mind,* New York: Simon & Schuster, 1998, recently made into an award-winning movie.
[28]We recognize that there are more current terms for this type of person, but we are hoping that we have some readers who on occasion watch a James Cagney movie on television.

Figure 10.5
Oligopoly Pricing Using the Prisoners' Dilemma: Payoff Matrix Model

Game theorists predict that ultimately both suspects would decide to confess, because confessing is a dominant strategy for both of them. To see this, suppose you are suspect 1. If suspect 2 were to choose to confess, which would be your preferred strategy? Given that suspect 2 has confessed, you would prefer confess (5 years sentence) to not confess (14 years sentence). Suppose instead that suspect 2 were not to confess; you would prefer confess (1 year suspended sentence) to not confess (18 months sentence). In both cases, you prefer to confess. With the payoffs as given in this game, confess is a dominant strategy for you. Since the game is symmetric, confess is also a dominant strategy for suspect 2. When both suspects choose not to confess, it is a stable equilibrium because neither would want to change the strategy after the other has chosen his or her strategy.

At this point readers might be wondering what the relationship is between alleged criminals and oligopolistic pricing. Instead of alleged criminals, suppose we use two companies competing in a market for a product in which price is a key consideration in the purchasing decisions of consumers. In place of "confess" or "not confess" we can use the options "high price" and "low price." In place of prison sentences we can use profit.

Figure 10.5 shows two companies, A and B, and the expected profit that each hopes to gain by charging a high or low price relative to the price charged by the other. It is easy to see that real two-company combinations, such as Coca-Cola and Pepsi-Cola, Dell and Gateway, or Miller and Anheuser-Busch, could be used as the A and B companies. As a test of your understanding of the Prisoners' Dilemma, what would be the dominant strategy equilibrium in this version of the game?

If your answer is that both companies would charge the low prices, you would be absolutely right. The low price strategy is a dominant strategy for both firms. However, both firms would prefer to be in the high price/high price situation than in the low price/low price situation. If they both prefer this situation, why was this not the outcome? The problem is that the high price/high price equilibrium is not stable. Once Company B had chosen the high price, Company A would like to change its strategy to the low price. The same holds for Company B; once Company A had chosen the high price, it would like to change its strategy to the low price. Only when both companies have chosen low prices is a stable equilibrium achieved because neither firm would have an incentive to change its strategy on its own. Although the situation in which each company chose high price would be preferred to each choosing the low price, the point of this game is that each would always be thinking of the possibility of the other setting a lower price (i.e., the equivalent of confessing). Therefore, as a sort of "second-best solution," each would choose the more secure situation of the low price, thereby dispensing with the fear of the other gaining an advantage by setting a lower price.

What if we changed the rules to allow them to cooperate? If they could cooperate, they could both choose the high price and both would be better off. This would be *efficient* in that once this equilibrium was achieved there would be no alternative outcome in which at least one player is better off and no player is worse off.[29] But because the rules of the game require noncooperation, the firms end up in an equilibrium that is, from their perspective, suboptimal.

This example shows the value of game theory. By understanding the rules under which players (firms, employers, employees, managers, stock owners, etc.) operate, we can understand why we observe what might be otherwise inexplicable in the marketplace. And, we may even be able to predict outcomes. In a later section, we will look at how managers can use their understanding to strategize, taking advantage of the rules of the game, or working around them, to achieve better results for their firm or even a more efficient result overall. In the remainder of this chapter, we examine four additional examples of games and how they can inform us about market interactions. Two of these examples involve pricing, one involves location, and the fourth involves decisions about output.

Beach Kiosk Game

Let us look at other potential equilibriums to better understand stable and unstable equilibriums. The beach kiosk scenario is a *two-person, noncooperative, zero-sum game.* There are two potential equilibriums in which the players are equally well off, but only one of them is stable. Suppose that two vendors have been granted licenses to provide soft drinks, snacks, and sunscreen to a county beach area that runs north and south for about 200 yards. Every day they roll their kiosks down to the beach and must decide where to set them up. The beachgoers tend to avoid large concentrations and are generally spread out evenly along the beach. They have no preferences for one vendor over the other and will use whichever beach kiosk is nearest. One possibility is for the two vendors to split the market so that one locates 50 yards from the north end and the other locates 50 yards from the south end.

---

[29]Note that this definition of efficiency is not consistent with a welfare maximization concept of efficiency. It is efficient only from the point of view of the players. Others not involved in setting the strategy may be made worse off. For example, consumers facing higher prices would be worse off than if no cooperation were possible and both firms chose the lower price. For this discussion, we choose not to consider whether the outcome of a game is economically efficient or not.

The situation above would not be a stable equilibrium because if the first vendor sets up at 50 yards from the north end, the second vendor can make herself better off by moving closer to the first, perhaps 25 yards further north (midway between the first vendor and the south end). She can then serve a wider portion of the beach, that is, take away some of the other vendor's customers. Likewise, once the second vendor locates at 75 yards from the south end, the first vendor can make himself better off by moving closer to the first vendor, perhaps 12.5 yards further south (midway between the north end and the second vendor). Can you see where this is going and define the Nash equilibrium?

The only stable equilibrium is when both vendors locate next to each other at the midpoint, 100 yards from both the South and from the North ends. Only in this situation will neither vendor have an incentive to move given the location of the other vendor. They will split the market just as when they were located 50 yards from the ends. In this case, neither of the two equilibriums are more *efficient* from the vendors' point of view. However, from the beachgoers' point of view, they would be preferable. Have you ever observed this phenomenon? Consider the location of gas stations or the political rhetoric of the two main American parties in a presidential election year. Is there evidence that they tend to position themselves close together? What additional examples can you provide?

Repeated Games

The beach kiosk example differed from the previous example in that decisions were made across time. Let us see what happens when we bring time into our earlier pricing example by changing the rules somewhat. Suppose our two companies described in Figure 10.5 set prices not just once, but every week for an indefinite period, that is, the game is repeated. How will this change the outcome?

Recall from the players' point of view, the efficient equilibrium is when both charge a high price. But because each has a dominant strategy of choosing a low price, this efficient equilibrium is not achieved. However, when the game is repeated, the threat of retaliation in future periods can offset each firm's incentive to "cheat" by charging a low price while the other firm is charging a high price. In this case, once the high price equilibrium is established, it can potentially be a stable equilibrium.

To see how this works, return to Figure 10.5. Suppose that the high price equilibrium has been established and that each firm receives $400 in revenues in each week. If one firm were to cheat and charge the low price, it would receive $600 in that week, an extra $200. However, the other firm would only be receiving $100 and could retaliate in the next period by also charging the low price. With each firm now charging the low price, for each successive week the firms would earn $200 each. It is apparent that the one-time $200 gain to the first firm would quickly be dissipated by successive weeks in which it earned $200 less than it would have if it had maintained its high price. In repeated games such as this, it is in the interest of each firm to continue with the high price equilibrium and the efficient outcome is achieved.

But there are limits to these rules being able to produce the efficient outcome. What happens if the game is set to end after a certain number of periods? In this case, retaliation for cheating in the last period is not possible and both players will cheat and charge a low price in the last period. But if both players charge a low price in the last period, retaliation is not possible for cheating in the penultimate period, the next-to-last period. Both will then cheat in the penultimate period. But, if both expect low prices in the penultimate period, then retaliation for cheating is not possible for the period just prior to that. As you can see by such chain logic, once the ability to retaliate in the last period is taken away, the threat of retaliation no longer has any teeth for all previous periods and a self-enforcing mechanism for achieving an efficient outcome is not possible.

When is such implicit cooperation (both charging high prices) most likely to occur? We would expect this to occur more in stable industries. In industries in which cost and/or demand function change often, it is difficult to recognize when a firm cheats because what might be a high price in certain circumstances may be a low price when cost and demand have changed. If one firm charges $30 for its product consistent with its understanding of this being a high price, but a second firm perceives the high price to be $40, the second firm may retaliate against what it perceives to be cheating by the first firm. A price war breaks out, and cooperation ceases because of a difference in perception. In addition, when many firms are in the industry, it may be difficult to detect when a rival firm cheats and begins using a lower price. So, the implicit cooperation of a repeated game is more likely to occur in a stable industry with few firms.

Sequential Games and First Mover Advantage

So far, we have discussed decisions made in games as being made simultaneously by the players (in each round, if repeated). However, we can design games in which decisions are made sequentially. In this situation, strategy may differ. Game theory helps us explain observed practices that can be associated with *first mover advantage*.

Suppose that two firms have designed a type of large, specialized printer and are about to go into full-scale production. They must choose and commit to one of two different production processes that vary in their cost schedules and output. One process is more efficient at producing low quantities. The other process is more efficient at producing larger quantities. Suppose that estimated demand and costs are such that the payoff matrix in Figure 10.6 is understood by both firms.

In this example, there is no dominant strategy for either firm. If Firm D were to choose a high output, Firm C would prefer to choose a low output. However, if Firm

Figure 10.6

		COMPANY C	
		HIGH Q	LOW Q
Company D	High Q	(D) 50/50 (C)	(D) 200/75 (C)
	Low Q	(D) 200/75 (C)	(D) 100/100 (C)

D were to choose a low output, Firm C would prefer to choose a high output. Without further information, it is not possible to predict what would happen in this market. Suppose however that one firm, say Firm C, could choose first. In that case, it would be to its advantage to choose the high-output production process and a high output. Then, Firm B would be better off choosing the low-output production process and earning 75 in profits than choosing a high-output and gaining only 50 in profits (unless it considered vengeance—the reduction of the profits of Firm C an additional motive). If Firm C announces its production plans first, it can gain first mover advantage and increase its profits relative to and at the expense of the other firm.

Of course, there also may be gains to moving last. Returning to the beach example, it is to your advantage to position your kiosk second if once established a kiosk cannot be moved. A recent article on the two largest producers in the Arizona copper industry demonstrates this further. At the time of the article, world copper prices had fallen precipitously and the firms were experiencing negative profits from their Arizona mines. Each was trying to decide how much to reduce production. But, as is evident in the article, the firms are interdependent and the actions of one firm will have an effect on what the other firm would like to do. In the words of the article:

> Part of the problem, Moody's says, is the reluctance of producers such as Asarco and Phelps Dodge to appreciably scale back production. While they made modest cutbacks, such as Asarco's move at Mission, they have not taken the sweeping steps some analysts believe are needed to stabilize the industry.
>
> Because it can take months to ramp production back up after a cutback, the two Arizona companies are reluctant to make the first move. A major cutback, such as a mine closing by one of the companies, could leave the other able to take advantage of the resulting higher prices.[30]

These examples of games illustrate how game theory can inform us about observed market pricing, output, or location decision practices in which mutual interdependence exists. We will return to game theory in the final section of this chapter in the context of our discussion about the importance and use of strategy in imperfectly competitive markets.

STRATEGY: THE FUNDAMENTAL CHALLENGE FOR FIRMS IN IMPERFECT COMPETITION

Over the past decade, textbooks in managerial economics have gradually expanded their coverage of strategy. This topic is a principal component of a business curriculum, and entire courses are devoted to its study. There are some important linkages between managerial economics and strategy. Furthermore, within the context of managerial decision making, we believe that no discussion would be

---

[30]"Meltdown Gets Worse for Copper," *Arizona Republic*, October 21, 2001.

complete without some mention of the strategic challenges facing a firm. As the title of this section implies, the decisions pertaining to a firm's strategy are especially critical for managers of firms operating in imperfect competition. Strategic decisions are far less important for perfectly competitive or monopoly firms. The former are price takers and their strategic decisions are confined primarily to whether they want to remain in a market and how best to survive during the downturns of a market. The latter have no competition, so a strategy is not as critical. Strategy becomes a critical part of the manager's responsibility, primarily when firms are price makers and are faced with tough price and non-price competition as well as the threat of new entrants into the market. Such is the case with firms operating in imperfect competition (i.e., monopolistic competition and oligopoly). This is our reason for placing this brief discussion of strategy in this particular chapter of the text.

There are many linkages between managerial economics and strategy because a number of the concepts and tools of analysis used in the making of strategy are rooted in economics.[31] In fact, the two fields of study can be said to be linked almost by definition. In our first chapter, we defined managerial economics as "the use of economic analysis to make business decisions involving the best use of an organization's scarce resources."[32] Textbooks abound with a number of definitions of **strategy**.[33] Here is a composite definition of strategy that we can provide using selected sources: "Strategy is the means by which an organization uses its scarce resources to relate to the competitive environment in a manner that is expected to achieve superior business performance over the long run."

The similarities and differences between managerial economics and strategy can perhaps be best seen by comparing the basic questions that are addressed in the two fields of study. These are the types of questions firms must consider in the study of managerial economics:

1. If we operate in perfect competition, what output level should we set for our product?
2. If we are a monopoly or imperfect competitor, what price (which in turn determines our output level) should we set for our product?
3. If we compete in an oligopoly, what might the reaction of our competitors be to decision #2?
4. Are we prepared to compete as a low-cost producer in the long run as new firms enter the market?
5. If we are not breaking even, should we shut down our operations?
6. How do we make sure that our short-run profit is maximized? If we are losing money, how do we ensure that our losses are minimized?

---

[31]Two excellent texts on strategy written by economics and intended for strategy courses with an economics slant are Sharon M. Oster, *Modern Competitive Analysis*, 3rd ed., New York: Oxford University Press, 1999, and David Besank, David Dranova, and Mark Shanley, *The Economics of Strategy*, 2d ed., New York: John Wiley & Sons, 2000. The latter book has been cited in various other sections of this text and is also used as a reference for this section.

[32]Refer back to chapter 1.

[33]See Besank et al., p. 1 for a list of three definitions of strategy provided by leading academics that are very similar to the one we offer. Also, the introductory section of this book "Primer: Economic Concepts for Strategy," pp. 9–40, provides an excellent survey of the economic foundations of strategy.

7. If we are operating in monopolistic competition or oligopoly, how can we differentiate our products in such a way that we can command a price that is higher than the rest of the competition?

These are the types of questions that firms must consider in the determination of their strategy:

1. What businesses should we be in? (corporate level decision)
2. How should we compete in these businesses: product differentiator or cost leader? (group, division, or product level decision)
3. What are our long run strategic objectives? How do these relate to our short-run tactics?
4. What geographic segments of the market should we focus on? (local, regional, national, and international)
5. What demographic segments of the market should we focus on?[34]
6. What will be the reaction of our competitors to our decisions? Is there a particular advantage to being a first mover in the market?
7. What are our core competencies and how can we use this to our competitive advantage?
8. In making our strategic decisions, how can we best incorporate the changes that are taking place in the total business environment, which includes suppliers, buyers, potential entrants, substitute products in completely different markets, technology, and macroeconomic factors such as the national business cycle and levels of growth and development around the world?

There are more strategic questions that we could add, but this should be sufficient to show the similarities and differences between the study of managerial economics and the study of strategy.

Our coverage of the linkage between managerial economics and strategy is divided into three sections. The first section deals with industrial organization, a branch of economic study that underlies much of the original work on strategy done by Professor Michael Porter. The second section introduces Porter's basic ideas on strategy. The third section provides examples of how game theory can be used in strategic analysis.

Industrial Organization

Industrial organization is the branch of economics that studies ways that firms and markets are organized and how this organization affects the economy from the viewpoint of social welfare (i.e., maximizing the well-being of consumers and producers). An important question that affects this discipline directly relates to managerial economics and the study of the behavior of oligopoly firms. *How, if a all, does industry concentration affect the behavior of firms competing in this industry?*[35] Two approaches to

---

[34]Demographics refers to such well-known characteristics as age, gender, income or education level, and ethnic background or origin. Marketing strategists also use "psychographics," which segments consumers by values and life-styles.
[35]Industry organization specialists who believe that industry concentration does in fact affect the behavior of firms proceed to explore the social welfare implications of this behavior. This part of their work is not within the scope of this text.

the study of industrial organization and to this question in particular have dominated the field. The first, the **structure-conduct-performance (S-C-P) paradigm,** has been predominant since the 1940s until its critics, proponents of the price theory approach, began to challenge it in the 1970s. As so often is the case, the two explanations of industrial behavior were advanced by two of the leading schools of economic thought in the United States, Harvard University and the University of Chicago, respectively. A brief coverage of the two analytical methods follows.[36]

The Structure-Conduct-Performance Paradigm The causality in this theory runs only in one direction. An industry *structure* affects its *conduct,* which in turn affects its *performance.* Hence the label "structure-conduct-performance." We start with structure that is shaped by the demand and supply conditions prevalent in the industry. For instance, if an industry's product demand tends to be inelastic, then market prices would be higher than if demand were more elastic. Growth patterns and substitutability would also affect structure. On the supply side, technology is an important factor. The existence of economies of scale will determine the number of firms, which can operate profitably in the industry.

These basic conditions thus determine industry structure: the number of firms in an industry, conditions of entry, and product differentiation. The structure of the industry then directly influences the way the industry operates—its conduct. Conduct entails primarily pricing strategies and other activities such as advertising, product development, legal tactics, and choice of product, as well as the potential for collusion among companies and mergers, which may further endanger the competitive nature of the industry. "The essence of the structuralist approach is a presumption that industries having fewer (and larger) firms will tend to engage in conduct inconsistent with the norms of perfect competition."[37]

The next step in the S-C-P model is to link conduct to performance. As mentioned, the usual normative standard adopted by economists is the maximization of society's welfare. An industry market with great concentration will fall far short of reaching such a goal. Its performance will be marked by both productive and allocative inefficiencies. Prices will be above marginal costs, the choice and quality of products will not be ideal, technological progress may be slowed down, and ultimately profits will be higher than under competitive circumstances. This high level of profitability arises from the industry's pricing policy and not because of any cost advantages.

We have now connected the three parts of the S-C-P model. A necessary corollary of the results of this approach is that high industry concentration becomes a reason for government intervention proceeding against possible mergers and even trying to deconcentrate industries.

The "New" Theory of Industrial Organization A competing view of industrial organization is offered by a theory stating that there is no necessary

---

[36]The following discussion is based on two texts on industrial organization: Dennis W. Carlton and Jeffrey M. Perloff, *Modern Industrial Organization,* 2d ed., New York: HarperCollins, 1994; and William E. Shugart II, *The Organization of Industry,* Homewood, IL: Irwin, 1990.
[37]Shugart, *The Organization of Industry,* p. 9.

connection between industry structure and performance that uniquely leads to maximum social welfare. It argues that the study of industry organization should utilize and apply microeconomic price theory. Thus, for instance, higher profit levels in more concentrated industries may be caused by economic efficiencies rather than pricing strategies. In other words, a small number of efficient firms can survive better than a larger number of firms that cannot take advantage of economies of scale. In fact, certain industries may not be able to support many firms on an acceptable profit level. Another argument involves the potential for collusion in concentrated industries. George Stigler concluded that while industry concentration makes collusion more likely, collusive agreements (cartels) are inherently unstable because they are expensive to enforce and because participants have incentives to cheat.[38]

A large number of studies examining the links between industry concentration and profits have been produced. The results, particularly in the earlier studies, appear to point to direct correlation between concentration and profit levels. However, the evidence is at best rather weak. Many later studies cast doubt on the earlier results, showing that what appeared to be a link between concentration and profits was actually due to other industry characteristics and often disappeared over the long run. For instance, one researcher found that cost reductions were significantly greater in increasingly concentrated industries, and even though price reductions to consumers were less than cost savings realized, consumers benefited from considerable price advantages.[39]

Another, more recent, addition to the above discussion and the notion that industry profits are not necessarily a function of industry structure is Baumol's theory of "contestable markets."[40] The idea is that performance by firms is ultimately influenced, not by the presence of competition, but by the threat of potential competition. Contestability comes in several forms. An extreme case is perfect contestability, which implies that entry by new firms is free and exit is costless. In such cases, existing firms will not be able to sell their product at prices exceeding marginal costs. Of course, in industries where entry and exit are difficult and costly, such competitive threat would not be present. Still, if outsiders have access to the industry's technology and if assets are nonspecialized so that their costs can be recouped upon exit, such a competitive threat is powerful.

The debate between the advocates of the S-C-P paradigm and the price theory approach has now continued for many years and neither side has gained clear dominance. Market structure is still very important, particularly from a public policy point of view. But other factors must also be considered in deciding what are the important influences affecting social welfare.

---

[38]G. J. Stigler, "A Theory of Oligopoly," *Journal of Political Economy*, 72 (February 1964), pp.44–61. Another argument made by the S-C-P approach is the monopolistic implications caused by tie-in sales. This point is discussed in chapter 11.

[39]S. Peltzman, "The Gains and Losses from Industrial Concentration," *Journal of Law and Economics*, 20 (October 1977), pp. 229–63.

[40]W. J. Baumol, "Contestable Markets: An Uprising in the Theory of Industry Structure," *American Economic Review*, 72 (March 1982), pp. 1–15.

Figure 10.7
The Porter Competitive Framework

Strategy and the Ideas of Michael Porter

In the late 1970s, Michael Porter, an economics professor from the Harvard Business School, began publishing articles on strategy that would have a profound impact on the study of this subject. As with all innovative ideas, his work has been subject to counterarguments and criticism over the years.[41] Nevertheless, many of the terms and concepts that he introduced have become a part of the everyday vocabulary of the business strategist. In our discussion of strategy, we have chosen to limit coverage to his ideas about strategy because they are most directly related to the study of the economics of the firm and industry economics.

Porter did not dwell on theoretical issues about the links between industry structure, business conduct, and performance and whether a concentrated industry structure leads to a misallocation of a country's resources. Instead, he used the concepts of the S-C-P approach to industry economics as the basis for understanding the strategic challenges facing the managers of firms as they seek to maximize their firm's profit. His **"Five Forces" model,** shown in Figure 10.7, illustrates the various factors that affect the ability of any firm in the industry to earn a profit.

If buyers as well as suppliers do not exert much market power and there is little threat from either new competitors or the use of substitute products, firms in the

---

[41]For a good review of Porter's ideas on strategy together with the developments in the entire field of study over the past 30 years, see Henry Mintzberg, Bruce Ahlstrand, and Joseph Lampel, *Strategy Safari: A Guided Tour Through the Wilds of Strategic Management,* New York: The Free Press, 1998.

industry are likely to earn relatively high returns on their investment. An extreme example of this is the market for operating systems software for personal computers . . . as long as you think of Microsoft as *the* company in this industry. It is easy to see the influence of the microeconomic theory of the firm on Porter's ideas when you compare the five forces with the characteristics of the different market types shown earlier in Figure 9.1. For example, "Entry Barriers" is related to "free entry and exit." If it is easier to enter, firms in the industry are less able to exercise market power and hence are less likely to have a relatively high return on investment.

After establishing a model for analyzing the overall profitability of an industry, Porter proceeded to discuss what kind of strategy would enable a specific firm in the industry to earn a return higher than the industry average. This above-average return can be considered akin to "economic" or "above-normal" profit. Porter offers two generic strategies for earning an above-average return on investment. The first is the "differentiation" approach, the second is "cost leadership" approach. There is actually a third approach, in which a firm could exercise either differentiation or cost leadership for a particular market segment rather than for the entire market of potential buyers.

We also can see the influence of the microeconomic theory of the firm in this aspect of Porter's ideas on strategy. The cost leadership approach appears to be based on perfect competition, while the differentiation approach can be seen as related to the case of a monopoly or monopolistically competitive market. Recall that in the perfectly competitive market, all firms are price takers. The only way in which a particular firm in this market can earn an economic profit is to keep its cost structure low enough so that when $P = MC$, there is still a positive difference between P and AC. In our view, this is where Porter came up with the idea of the cost leadership approach.

In the case of monopoly or monopolistic competition, product differentiation results in a downward sloping demand and an MR curve that lies below this demand line. Following the MR = MC rule enables a firm to set a price on the demand line that is higher than its AC, assuming of course that the demand curve itself is high enough to allow this to happen. The extreme case of this was shown in the example of pure monopoly. Not only is the product different, it is unique. In the case of monopolistic competition, the above-normal profit enjoyed by the differentiating firm may be reduced as the entry of firms in the long run shift a firm's demand curve to the left. But Porter would say that those firms that have a solid differentiation strategy would not be affected by the new entrants as much as those who allow their products to be "commoditized."

Strategy and Game Theory[42]

Earlier in this chapter, we studied game theory to see how it can help economists (and policy makers who study industrial organization) better understand the pricing and output decisions of firms competing in oligopoly markets. Game theory also can be applied in a more general way to help managers to analyze their firm's position and to design better strategies in competing as well as cooperating with other firms

---

[42]This section was written by Dr. Shannon B. Mudd.

in the marketplace. Recognizing the differences in the various constraints imposed by the "rules of the game" or by the positions of the individual firms can help managers both to predict the behavior of other firms and to design an appropriate strategy, either in response to their actions or to elicit a preferred response from them. As was evident in the pricing example of Figure 10.5, sometimes the logic of the game may lead players into an inefficient outcome. In order for managers to achieve a preferred outcome, they must try to overcome the logic of the game by designing strategies to get around the rules or by changing the game. Aspects of game theory can inform managerial decision making in many ways. To give a sample of how it can be helpful, two aspects of strategy, commitment and incentives, are examined in the next two sections.[43] The final section describes an overall framework for using the game theory paradigm in designing strategy.

Commitment   In the noncooperative pricing game of Figure 10.5, the players had dominant strategies which led them to the low price equilibrium. They would have both been better off if both had charged the high price. However, the logic of the game made the low price the dominant strategy for both players. Is it possible to break this logic to achieve the better outcome? We saw before how repeating a game could potentially allow the firms to achieve implicit cooperation (e.g., with both charging the higher price). In this section we explore how commitment, explicit or implicit, can be used by firms to achieve preferred outcomes.

In order for commitment to be effective as a strategy, it must be credible because the incentive to cheat is apparent. For example, suppose two firms promise each other to charge high prices for their products. The fact remains that one player can cheat and increase its payoff by charging a lower price. With such an incentive to cheat, how can players' promises be credible?

To make a commitment credible, you must make it in your interest to keep to your commitment. Dixit and Nalebuff provide a list of ways in which this can be done. We discuss three of them[44]:

1. Burn bridges behind you
2. Establish and use a reputation
3. Write contracts

"Burning bridges behind you" is a common form of strategy to make one's commitments credible. A hint of how this works can be gleaned by referring back to the sequential game discussed earlier in this chapter. In that game, firms had to choose between two different production processes: one that was more efficient at low quantities and one that was more efficient at high quantities. Given the profit structure of the example, if one firm could choose first, an announcement of its choice of the higher output production process would leave the second firm with a preferred strategy of producing with the lower output production process. However, simply

---

[43]For a more in-depth discussion of these and other aspects of game theory and strategy, see Avinash Dixit and Barry Nalebuff, *Thinking Strategically: The Competitive Edge in Business, Politics and Everyday Life*, New York: WW Norton, 1991.
[44]The other five are (1) cut off communication, (2) leave the outcome to chance, (3) move in small steps, (4) develop credibility through teamwork, and (5) employ mandated negotiating agents.

announcing its choice may not be sufficient. If the second firm irrevocably commits itself to the high-output production technology, perhaps by licensing the technology or signing a contract with a builder, changing its strategy will clearly be costly. The first firm announced that it is going to employ the high production technology. However, its commitment is not credible. The second firm knows that there is no cost for it to switch to the low-production technology. And, if the second firm is committed to producing a high output, this technology and a low output is not its preferred strategy. By committing itself in an irrevocable way, that is, burning its bridges behind it, the second firm can preempt the move of the first and ensure itself a better outcome for itself.

For the second means of changing the rules of the game, "establish and use a reputation," let us look at an example of how a reputation can make a commitment credible between producers and consumers. Branded soft drinks cost more than store or generic brands. Would you ever expect Coca-Cola to degrade its product by using less consistent production processes? Why not? Coca-Cola has an established reputation for producing soft drinks. It has established its reputation partially by its large advertising expenditures. Why does it spend so much money on advertising? Most people in the United States, if not in the whole world, know what Coke is. So advertising is not providing consumers with information. One interpretation of its advertising expenditures is that it is, in effect, posting a bond. The purpose of spending so much money is to convince you that its product will continue to be what you expect it to be. If it were to cheat and reduce its quality consistency, it would forfeit that bond. Its ability to sell product would be diminished, and all that advertising money would be wasted. By continuing to make huge expenditures to maintain its reputation, it is ensuring that it is in its interest to produce as expected.

A final example of how to make a commitment credible is to write contracts that are irrevocable and can be enforced, for example, through the courts.[45] When punishments for breach of contract are sufficiently severe, the incentive to cheat is dampened. As pointed out by John McMillan, recognition of the importance of enforceable contracts is apparent in the wording of legislation passed by the British Parliament in 1834 when it conferred upon companies the "privilege" of suing and being sued.[46]

While often useful, contracts are not always appropriate. One issue is that in a world in which outcomes are uncertain, it may be difficult to include in the contract clauses to deal with all possible outcomes, that is, contingencies. Returning to the pricing example of Figure 10.5, suppose the two firms could write a contract specifying that each charge a high price and providing penalties to any party that cheats and charges a low price. Consider an extreme case. In the event of a war, prices may rise with a general inflation. A contract between two parties that obligates them to charge what is a high price in normal times may turn out to be a low price in such an inflationary environment. It may be possible to write such a contingency into the contract. But, it is impossible to write into the contract responses to all possible contingencies. The costs of designing such a contract would be enormous, and it is still

---

[45]One possible explanation for the rise of organized crime in Russia was its ability to enforce contracts when the court system was powerless to do so.
[46]John McMillan, *Games, Strategies and Managers: How Managers Use Game Theory to Make Better Business Decisions*, New York: Oxford University Press, 1992, p. 27.

unlikely that all contingencies could be imagined. So, contracts are necessarily incomplete. In addition, there are often legal restrictions on the types of agreements that can be made. In particular, it is illegal in the United States for competitors to discuss pricing.

Commitment is a useful concept in a wide range of business activities. Negotiation is often viewed in a game-theoretic way. Making a "take it or leave" offer in a negotiation can be quite advantageous to you. However, it will only work as a bargaining tool if you are committed to walk away if the offer is not accepted. Of course, most important for its success is that the other party believes your commitment is credible. Reputation, burning bridges behind you, and other means, as in the examples above, can help make such commitments credible.

Incentives In the pricing example of Figure 10.5, each firm has a dominant strategy that leads to an outcome (low price/low price) that is different from the preferred outcome (high price/high price). The U.S. auto and airline industries have faced a similar situation in recent history as they engaged in price wars that were hurting profitability. The problem they faced was how to break the logic of the dominant strategies that each faced.

In both cases, the dominant strategy arose because large numbers of customers were willing to switch from one provider to another when prices were lowered. If it were possible to develop incentives for customers to remain loyal to a single provider, the returns to one firm for lowering its price while others remained at the high price would be diminished, that is, it would change the payoff structure. How did the airlines accomplish this? They instituted frequent flyer programs that encouraged customers to stick to a single airline for their business. This decreased the payoff to other firms of lowering prices because the responsiveness to prices by customers was diminished.

How did the auto industry respond in a similar situation in the early 1990s?[47] At that time, end-of-year rebates and dealer discounts had become entrenched. Competing car manufacturers were stuck with imitating these programs or lose customers to other manufacturers. As customers grew to expect these programs, they tended to delay purchases until the end of the year when they were offered. The auto industry was stuck in a low price equilibrium.

GM came up with a strategy to change the payoffs by offering a credit card that allowed customers who charged purchases to use 5% of their charges, up to $500, to apply toward the lease or purchase of a GM vehicle. The program was incredibly successful for GM. In two months it had opened 1.2 million accounts. In two years it had opened 8.7 million accounts. The GM card program replaced other incentive programs. Because of the nature of the new incentives, GM could decrease its end-of-year rebates and still keep its card holders as customers because other cars were effectively more expensive to them. Because GM decreased its rebate program, other manufacturers could reduce theirs also without worrying about losing as much customer base.

Note that other manufacturers followed GM's lead. When games are thought of as zero-sum, such imitation is expected to diminish the success of the strategy.

---

[47]This example is drawn from Avinash Dixit and Barry Nalebuff, "The Right Game: Use Game Theory to Shape Strategy," *Harvard Business Review,* (July/August), 1995, pp. 58–59.

However, in this case, it was not a zero-sum game. All firms gained because it changed the dynamic of the game and allowed the manufacturers to move to a better outcome, that is, a high price/high price outcome.

Let us look at another example of how the use of incentives can change a game. In general, when one player has more information than another, it can use that information to its advantage. Are there ways for the other players to diminish this advantage? One possibility is to change the rules in a way that provides incentives for players to reveal their information.

A standard example comes from the health insurance industry. Insurance companies make money by pooling risk and charging individuals the expected payout on their insurance claims. However, if they could discern high-risk from low-risk individuals, they would like to extract higher premiums from the high-risk individuals. Individuals necessarily know more about their own health than insurance companies. Is there a way for insurance companies to get individuals to reveal which group they are in? Insurance companies often provide a menu of options to individuals as they choose their health care. A primary feature of these options is a choice of the level of the deductible. High-risk individuals expect to have to pay the full deductible. Low-risk individuals expect to be healthy and do not expect to pay the full deductible on average. Insurance companies can design the pairs of premiums and deductibles offered in such a way that the expected cost of a high-deductible/low-premium plan is lower for low-risk individuals and the expected cost of a low-deductible/high-premium plan is lower for the high-risk individuals. Insurance companies elicit the information on the individual's riskiness by allowing them to self-select into the two different plans. This allows them to charge a higher premium to the high-risk individuals and a lower premium to the low-risk individuals.

A General Framework   The many examples provided so far illustrate two fundamental aspects of game theory: interdependence and uncertainty. First, players are interdependent. There are interactions between your decisions as a manager and the decisions of other people. Decisions that you make as a manager affect other players; decisions that other players make affect you. The second fundamental aspect of the game arises from uncertainty. Actions by other players affect you, but you are not certain what their actions will be, and they may not be certain what your actions will be. This uncertainty arises because other players' actions are not entirely predictable; because information is dispersed, you may not have all the information about the other player's context to help you predict their decision; or the other players may be making decisions without full information. Because of this interdependence and uncertainty, managers must act strategically, that is, make decisions based on what they predict other players are going to do and how those other players are going to react to his or her decision.

The purpose of studying game theory is to equip managers with a paradigm for studying a situation, for predicting players' actions, and for making strategic decisions. The PARTS framework developed by Brandenburger and Nalebuff is one such paradigm.[48] PARTS is an acronym for **P**layers, **A**dded Value, **R**ules, **T**actics, and

---

[48]McMillan, p. 180.

Scope. By examining the game through this paradigm, the authors believe a manager can design a better strategy for his or her personal success as well as for the success of the firm. The basic elements of the paradigm are as follows:

Players: *Who are the players and what are their goals?* For a particular firm, it would be customers, suppliers, and those that produce complementary or substitute products. It could also be people who work for the company. *What are the players' goals?* For example, an individual may not have profit as the primary motive. *What alternative opportunities do they have? How important is it to them to move quickly? Can they make irrevocable commitments?*

Added Value: *What do the different players contribute to the pie?* For success in the business world, the primary question is often not how to take a greater slice of the pie, at the expense of your competitors, but how to take a bigger slice of a bigger pie. Understanding what each player contributes is key. Ideally a strategy will work to raise your value-added, or lower the value-added of the other players.

Rules: *What is the form of competition?* It could be price, output, cost, quality, R&D, marketing, or some combination of these. *What is the time structure of the game?* For example, it could be repeated or sequential. *Does one player face higher costs for a lengthy negotiation than another? What is the information structure of the game? How much do the players know about each others' positions?*

Tactics: *What options are open to the players? Are there possibilities for credible commitments (i.e., those that remove uncertainty)? Can incentives be offered to change the dynamics of the game?*

Scope: *What are the boundaries of the game?* For example, it could be the products, the players, the region or country. *Is it possible these boundaries can be expanded or shrunk?*

The discussion in this section provides an introduction into how game theory can help managers design successful strategies. We encourage you to explore this further in your own reading or in coursework devoted to a more complete discussion of its many aspects. For useful examples of strategic challenges and decisions of firms in the highly competitive and rapidly changing semiconductor industry, see chapter 16.

Concluding Remarks on the Linkages Between Managerial Economics and Strategy

The fundamental link between managerial economics and strategy is the decision regarding the allocation of a company's scarce resources. In this chapter, we also showed how the tools of strategic analysis such as Porter's "Five Forces" model and his "Differentiation versus Cost Leadership" approach are linked to the economic study of industrial organization and the economic models of a firm's behavior in different market settings. The economic study of game theory was also shown to be applicable to the study of strategy. Interested readers can find a thorough discussion of these and many other examples of the linkages between economics and strategy in the textbooks on the subject previously cited.[49]

INTERNATIONAL APPLICATION: STELLA WHO?

We mentioned in the chapter that at times it may be difficult to distinguish between oligopoly and monopolistic competition because it might depend on geographic boundaries (e.g., an entire country vs. a neighborhood) as well as the fact that situations change. Oligopoly markets could evolve into monopolistic competition (such as the U.S. automobile market today) and vice versa (in the early days of the U.S. auto industry, there were hundreds of different auto manufacturers). The shifting distinction between the two types of markets also applies on a global scale. Let us take the market for beer as an example. In the United States, the market for beer is clearly an oligopoly. We are sure that readers are familiar with the products of Anheuser-Busch, America's leading brewer. In 2000, Anheuser Busch had 48.2 percent of the market. Its two leading brands, Budweiser and Bud Light, commanded 16 percent and 16.8 percent of the market respectively. Miller Brewing Company (owned by Philip Morris) had 20.4 percent and Coors Brewing Company had 11.3 percent. So we see that the big three hold about 80 percent of the total U.S. beer market. Interestingly enough, the number four company, Pabst Brewing Company, announced in July 2001 that it would be a "virtual" brewer. It shut down its last brewery and has contracted out production to Miller.[50] As MBA students or upper level business majors, we can well imagine you may on occasion enjoy one of the foreign imports such as Corona, Heineken, Beck's, or Kirin (to go with your sushi). But in 2000, these products made up less than 10 percent of the U.S. market.

When viewed from afar, the global beer market appears to be more monopolistic competition than oligopoly, because it is far less concentrated than the U.S. market. But there is a trend toward greater concentration. According to *Impact*, an industry trade publication, in 1980, the top 10 brewers in the world accounted for 10 percent of beer sales. Twenty years later, that figure is about 35 percent.[51]

It is obvious why the entire beer industry is focusing its attention outside of the United States, particularly in emerging market economies. Growth in population and incomes as well as less government regulations and excise taxes make China and other parts of the Asia-Pacific Region, Central Europe, and Latin America very attractive for brewers. If recent projections are true, China has probably surpassed the United States in total beer consumption. (The country that consumes the most beer per capita on an annual basis continues to be the Czech Republic, with an amazing 175 liters.)

By virtue of its huge share of the U.S. market, Anheuser-Busch is the largest brewer in the world. But the number two position is shared by Dutch brewer Heineken and Belgium's Interbrew. Because of the small populations of their home

---

[49]See Oster as well as Besank et al.
[50]Information taken from *Survey of Alcoholic Beverages and Tobacco,* Standard & Poor's Industry Surveys, September 6, 2001.
[51]Cited in the *Survey of Alcoholic Beverages and Tobacco,* p. 14.

countries, it is obvious that both companies have done well in their global operations. The populations of the Netherlands (16 million) and Belgium (10 million), together are less than that of New York State (19 million) and New Jersey (8 million) combined. But in recent years, Anheuser-Busch has actively pursued markets outside of the United States through a combination of acquisitions, joint ventures, and exports. For example, it recently bought a minority stake in Corona, the leading foreign brand in the United States with 2.7% of the market. Furthermore, Interbrew has recently catapulted itself into the top tier of the world's beer industry with a number of significant acquisitions. Between 2000 and 2001, the company spent about $5.5 billion buying Germany's Beck's and Britain's Whitbread and Bass. This is particularly threatening to Heineken, the other major global competitor, forcing it to reconsider its strategy for growth in the coming years. It has a strong presence in the United States (it follows closely behind Corona with 2.2% of the market) and Europe. However, it needs to consider some blockbuster acquisitions similar to Interbrew's if it intends to maintain its status as one of the top three in the world.[52] By the way, Interbrew's flagship brand is Stella Artois. (But do not worry, this will probably not be on your exam.)

The Solution

A few weeks later Frank again met with Nicole. He recommended selling "Waterpure" for $1.00 instead of the $1.10 suggested by the MR = MC analysis. His focus-group studies showed that people paid more attention to a 25-cent than a 15-cent difference. The average price of the major national brands was $1.25.

"I believe the 25-cent difference will be really noticeable to the consumer," Frank explained. "After all, we're new entrants into the market and we can use this lower price to attract customers away from the competition. At least they'll be more inclined to give our product a try. But we're not going to sell this product as a private label or discount product. According to your marketing plan, Nicole, we're going to be putting a lot of money into advertising to build brand awareness among consumers."

"That's just it, Frank, we are in fact going to be positioning "Waterpure" as a premium product, as good as any other national brand, if not better," Nicole responded. "If we're going to position our product in this way, we have got to use our price in support of this. If we set the price at $1.00 and then decide to raise it to $1.25 after it

(Continued)

---

[52]"Freddy Heineken's Recipe May be Scraped," *Business Week,* January 28, 2002. Heineken must be prepared for a real "dog fight" with Interbrew. At this time, Interbrew is awaiting the results of an offer that Interbrew's basic growth strategy is to buy small and medium-sized breweries in high beer-consuming countries such as the Czech Republic and former Yugoslavian countries. See for example, "Slovenian minnow fights Interbrew tide," *Financial Times,* May 28, 2002.

gains customer acceptance, they may not go along with this increase. We have to use promotion and advertising more than price to build our brand in the marketplace. Why don't we just match the competition's $1.25?"

"It makes sense to me," Frank answered. "The one thing we don't want to do is to trigger a price war. If any of our competitors with established brands decides to match or even beat our lower price, then the whole industry might suffer. As it now stands, I guess we're all doing very well if we can get people to pay more than a dollar for a bottle of water."

"Hey, now I've really got you thinking like a marketing person, Frank. Remember, demand is based on the customer's *perception* of value and not the intrinsic value of the product. If we can use advertising to support the price of $1.25, that's going to be the key to our success. Besides, you're right about a price war—I don't even want to think about starting a price war with the likes of Nestlé, Pepsi, and Coke."*

_____
*Pepsi's main product is Aquafina, a tap water that is purified with triple filtration and a process known as "reverse osmosis." Nestlé's leading bottled brands are Perrier, Deer Park, Poland Spring, and Calistoga. Coca-Cola's brand is Dasani. It also is a major distributor of branded bottle water.

SUMMARY

This chapter examined the pricing and output decisions faced by firms in monopolistic competition and oligopoly. Oligopoly firms have a more challenging task because of mutual interdependence. However, if oligopoly firms are of sufficient size or are very effective in differentiating their products, they may not have as much competition from new market entrants as those firms operating in monopolistic competition. In both types of markets, non-price decisions are an important part of the competitive environment. Game theory is an important tool for analyzing markets in which mutual interdependence exists. The application of elements of this theory to the pricing and non-pricing decisions enables one to gain great insight into the efforts of managers to develop winning strategies for their firms.

IMPORTANT CONCEPTS

Five Forces model: Model developed by Michael Porter that shows the key factors that affect the ability of a firm to earn an economic profit: potential entrants, bargaining power of suppliers, bargaining power of buyers, threat of substitute products or services, and intramarket rivalry. Also referred to as the Porter Competitive Framework. (p. 482)

Game theory: A formal mathematical approach to the study of how individuals make decisions when they are aware that their actions affect each other and when each individual takes this into account. (p. 471)

Kinked demand: A theoretical construction that attempts to explain price rigidities in oligopolistic markets. (p. 459)

Monopolistic competition: A market distinguished from perfect competition in that each seller attempts to differentiate its product from those of its competitors (e.g., in terms of location, efficiency of service, advertising, or promotion). Good examples of this type of market can be found in small businesses, particularly those in the retail trade. (p. 454)

Mutual interdependence: A situation in which each firm in the market sets a price based on its costs, price elasticity, *and* anticipated reaction of its competitors. This type of pricing situation prevails in oligopolistic markets. (p. 453)

Oligopoly: A market in which there is a small number of relatively large sellers. Pricing in this type of market is characterized by mutual interdependence among the sellers. Products may either be standardized or differentiated. (p. 457)

Price leader: One company in an oligopolistic industry establishes the price, and the other companies follow. Two types of price leadership, barometric and dominant, are discussed in chapter 11. (p. 462)

Strategy: The means by which an organization uses its scarce resources to relate to the competitive environment in a manner that is expected to achieve superior business performance over the long run. (p. 478)

Structure-Conduct-Performance (S-C-P) paradigm: An approach to studying industrial economics that states that an industry's structure determines an industry's conduct, which in turn affects the industry's performance. The key factors that shape industry structure are the number of firms in the industry, the conditions of entry and exit, and product differentiation. (p. 480)

QUESTIONS

1. Explain the key difference between perfect competition and monopolistic competition.
2. Assume that firms in the short run are earning above-normal profits. Explain what will happen to these profits in the long run for the following markets.
   a. Pure monopoly
   b. Oligopoly
   c. Monopolistic competition
   d. Perfect competition
3. In certain industries, firms buy their most important inputs in markets that are close to perfectly competitive and sell their output in imperfectly competitive markets. Cite as many examples as you can of these types of businesses. Explain why the profits of such firms tend to increase when there is an excess supply of the inputs they use in their production process.
4. In the short run, firms that seek to maximize their market share will tend to charge a lower price for their products than firms that seek to maximize their profit." Do you agree with this statement? Explain.
5. Explain why it is sometimes difficult to apply the MR = MC rule in actual business situations.

6. Define *mutual interdependence.*
7. Why do oligopolists often rely on a price leader to raise the market price of a product?
8. How does one determine whether a market is oligopolistic? Is it important for managers to recognize the existence of oligopolistic competitors in the markets in which their companies operate? Explain.
9. In the following list is a number of well-known companies and the products that they sell. Which of the four types of markets (perfect competition, monopoly, monopolistic competition, and oligopoly) best characterizes the markets in which they compete? Explain why.
   a. McDonald's—hamburgers
   b. Exxon-Mobil—gasoline
   c. Dell—personal computers
   d. Heinz—ketchup
   e. Procter & Gamble—disposable diapers
   f. Kodak—photographic film
   g. Starbucks—gourmet coffee
   h. Domino's—pizza
   i. Intel—computer chip for the PC
10. This chapter discussed how a game called Prisoners' Dilemma could be used to show

how two competing firms might establish their prices. What other variables besides price might be considered in this particular type of analysis? What are some limitations to using this analysis in actual business situations?

11. Briefly explain the Structure-Conduct-Performance approach to the study of industrial economics.

12. Compare and contrast Porter's Five Forces model with the four basic types of markets first described in chapter 9 in the section, "Market Structure."

13. In May 2002, Philip Morris announced that it was going to sell its Miller Brewing Division to South African Breweries.
    a. What impact do you think this transaction will have on the market structure of the beer industry in the United States? In world markets? Explain.
    b. Using the economic concepts presented in Chapters 8, 9 and 10, discuss possible reasons why both parties agreed to this transaction.

PROBLEMS

1. A group of five students has decided to form a company to publish a guide to eating establishments located in the vicinity of all major college and university campuses in the state. In planning for an initial publication of 6,000 copies, they estimated the cost of producing this book to be as follows:

Paper	$12,000
Research	2,000
Graphics	5,000
Reproduction services	8,000
Miscellaneous	5,000
Personal computer	2,000
Desktop publishing software	500
Overhead	5,500
Binding	3,000
Shipping	2,000

By engaging in this business, the students realized that they would have to give up their summer jobs. Each student made an average of $4,000 per summer. However, they felt that they could keep expenses down by doing much of the research for the book by themselves with no immediate compensation.

They decided to set the retail price of the book at $12.50 per copy. Allowing for the 20 percent discount that retail stores in their state generally required, the students anticipated a per-unit revenue of about $10.00. The director of the campus bookstore advised them that their retail price was far too high, and that a price of about $8.75 would be more reasonable for a publication of this kind.

One of the students, who was a math and statistics major, asked the bookstore manager to provide her with historical data on sales and prices of similar books. From these data, she estimated the demand for books of this kind to be

$$Q = 18,500 - 1,000P$$

Chapter 10   Pricing and Output Decisions

where Q = Number of books sold per year
P = Retail price of the books

a. Construct a numerical table for the retail demand curve, and plot the numbers on a graph. Calculate the elasticity of demand for the interval between $12.50 and $8.00.

b. Do you think the students should follow the store manager's advice and price their book at $8.75? Explain. If you do not agree with this price, what would be the optimal price of the book? Explain.

c. Assuming that the students decide to charge the optimal price, do you think that they should proceed with this venture? Explain.

d. Assuming that the student's demand equation is accurate, offer some possible reasons why the bookstore manager would want to sell the book at the lower price of $8.75.

2. Use the same data presented in problem 1 to answer the following questions:

a. Explain the impact on the optimal price of designating the "miscellaneous" cost item as fixed versus variable. (Hint: Do the pricing analysis assuming miscellaneous is a fixed cost and compare it to an analysis that assumes it is a variable cost.)

b. Under what circumstances do you think the average variable cost would *increase* (as is generally expected in the economic analysis of cost)? Do you think the law of diminishing returns would play a role in increasing AVC? Explain.

c. Under what circumstances do you think the average variable cost would *decrease?* Explain.

3. A firm in an oligopolistic industry has identified two sets of demand curves. If the firm is the only one that changes prices (i.e., other firms do not follow), its demand curve takes the form $Q = 82 - 8P$. If, however, it is expected that competitors will follow the price actions of the firm, then the demand curve is of the form $Q = 44 - 3P$.

a. Develop demand schedules for each alternative and draw them on a graph.

b. Calculate marginal revenue curves for each.

c. If the present price and quantity position for the firm is located at the intersection of the two demand curves, and competitors follow any price decrease but do not follow a price increase, show the demand curve relevant to the firm.

d. Draw the appropriate marginal revenue curve.

e. Show the range over which a marginal cost curve could rise or fall without affecting the price the firm charges.

4. Indicate whether each of the following statements is true or false and explain why.

a. A competitive firm that is incurring a loss should immediately cease operations.

b. A pure monopoly does not have to worry about suffering losses because it has the power to set its prices at any level it desires.

c. In the long run, firms operating in perfect competition and monopolistic competition will tend to earn normal profits.

d. Assuming a linear demand curve, a firm that wishes to maximize its revenue will charge a lower price than a firm that wishes to maximize its profits.

e. In an oligopoly, the firm that has the largest market share will also be the price leader.

f. The demand curve facing a firm in a monopolistically competitive market is more elastic than one facing a pure monopoly.

5. A phenomenon in the retail merchandising of food and clothing in the United States and the United Kingdom is the growing popularity of private-label (also called store-brand) products. These products are priced at a lower level than the premium national brands. Use the concepts of price elasticity and relevant cost to explain the profitability of these products from the point of view of

a. the retail stores that sell these private-label products.

b. the manufacturers of these private-label products.

If you were the manager of a national premium brand, what would you do to fight the growing competition of private labels?

6. Suppose three firms face the same total market demand for their product. This demand is

P	Q
$80	20,000
70	25,000
60	30,000
50	35,000

Suppose further that all three firms are selling their product for $60 and each has about one-third of the total market. One of the firms, in an attempt to gain market share at the expense of the others, drops its price to $50. The other two quickly follow suit.

a. What impact would this move have on the profits of all three firms? Explain your reasoning.

b. Would these firms have been better off in terms of profit if they all had raised the price to $70? Explain.

7. A firm has the following short-run demand and cost schedule for a particular product:

$$Q = 200 - 5P$$

$$TC = 400 + 4Q$$

a. At what price should this firm sell its product?

b. If this is a monopolistically competitive firm, what do you think would start to happen in the long run? Explain.

c. Suppose in the long run, the demand shifted to $Q = 100 - 5P$. What should the firm do? Explain.

8. Suppose there are three firms with the same *individual* demand function. This function is $Q = 1,000 - 40P$. Suppose that each firm has a different cost function. These functions are:

$$\text{Firm 1: } 4,000 + 5Q$$

$$\text{Firm 2: } 3,000 + 5Q$$

$$\text{Firm 3: } 3,000 + 7Q$$

    a. What price should each firm charge if it wants to maximize its profit (or minimize its loss)?

    b. Explain why the answer to the preceding question indicates that two of the firms should charge the same price and the third should charge a higher price.

    c. Which firms will be most vulnerable to a price war? Explain.

9. You and a competing firm are the only sellers of a new product. You are engaged in an intense battle for initial market share. You both realize that the one who captures most of the market share will be the one who spends the most on advertising and promotion. You are the marketing manager and you have up to $1 million for advertising and promotion for all your products. You have to decide how much of your budget you should allocate to the marketing of the new product. Construct a payoff matrix similar to the one shown in Figure 10.5.

Note: Make whatever assumptions that you need about your opponent's spending on advertising and marketing.

10. Professor Michael Porter's generic strategy options for competing are the differentiation approach and the cost leadership approach. The first involves competing by having a better product and the second by having a lower cost than one's competitors. Relate this strategy to the monopolistically competitive model presented in this chapter. In particular, use the diagram in Figure 10.1 to explain the rationale for Porter's generic strategies.

Chapter 11

Special Pricing Practices

The Situation

One of the most difficult challenges in the food and beverage industries is the establishment of effective channels of distribution. Many food-processing and beverage companies rely on food brokers to sell their products to retail outlets such as supermarkets and grocery stores. In the case of bottled water, the product is shipped from the bottling plants to the individual retail establishments. Obviously, there must first be a willingness on the part of these retail businesses to carry a particular product line.

The task of establishing the relationship between Global Foods, Inc. and the retail stores was given to Rebecca James, assistant vice president of marketing of the beverage division. Since the product, "Waterpure," was so new, she found considerable resistance among the major supermarket chains to carrying Global's line of bottled water. Thus far, she had been able to sell relatively small volumes to smaller grocery stores, convenience stores, delicatessens, and sandwich shops. Then she learned that a large catering company that provided food service in major airports all across the country wanted to carry an additional line of bottled water. This firm had put out a request for bids to all the major beverage companies and also to Global Foods. After all, Global had an established reputation in the food business.

(*Continued*)

497

Rebecca was eager to land this major account. But she also realized that her bid would have to be considerably lower than that offered to her present customers. However, this lower price would be more than made up by the potential volume of sales, as well as by the creation of a base from which to further penetrate the market for bottled water. But she was not quite sure how to decide on the price she should recommend. She decided to consult with Philip Olds, an executive in the company's foods service division. Philip had considerable experience in preparing bids on large customer contracts.

INTRODUCTION

In chapters 9 and 10 we discussed output and pricing decisions under different market arrangements. We will now continue this discussion and apply our knowledge to pricing decisions made in specific situations. We will also be confronted by some complications: whereas we have previously assumed that a firm produces only one product, we will now have to allow for the pricing of several products simultaneously. The situations we will encounter in this chapter usually occur under imperfectly competitive conditions.

CARTEL ARRANGEMENTS

Competition is a very tough taskmaster. To survive in competition in the long run, a company must operate at its most efficient (minimum) cost point, and it will earn no more than a normal return. Thus, there is always an incentive for a company to try to become more powerful than its competitors—in the extreme, to become a monopolist. In an oligopolistic type of industry, where there are several powerful firms, it would probably be impossible for one firm to eliminate all the others. So, in order to reap the benefits of a monopoly (i.e., higher profits, stable market shares and prices, and the general creation of a more certain and less competitive environment), it may be advisable for companies in the industry to act together as if they were a monopoly. In other words, they all agree to cooperate with one another; they form a **cartel.** Cartel arrangements may be tacit, but in most cases some sort of formal agreement is reached. The motives for cartelization have been recognized for many years. Indeed, an early recognition can be found in a passage in Adam Smith's famous book: "People of the same trade seldom meet together, even for merriment and diversion, but the conversation ends in a conspiracy against the public, or in some contrivance to raise prices."[1]

---

[1]Adam Smith, *An Inquiry into the Nature and Causes of the Wealth of Nations,* New York: Modern Library, 1937, p. 128.

Cartels were made illegal in the United States with the passage of the Sherman Anti-Trust Act of 1890. Thus, most "official" cartels are found in countries other than the United States. Probably the most famous cartel in existence today is the Organization of Petroleum Exporting Countries (OPEC). But there are others, such as the IATA (International Air Transport Association), to which U.S. airlines can belong. Collusive agreements have existed in the United States as well. One of the most famous cases of price and market share fixing was in the electrical industry and involved General Electric, Westinghouse, and other large corporations. The case was tried and concluded in 1961 and resulted in prison sentences for several executives and large fines. This case, and two more recent ones will be described briefly following a discussion of the characteristics and effects of cartels.

Cartels may not flourish in all oligopolistic markets. Following are some of the conditions that influence the formation of cartels.

1. The existence of a small number of large firms facilitates the policing of a collusive agreement.
2. Geographical proximity of the firms is favorable.
3. Homogeneity of the product makes it impossible for cartel participants to cheat on one another by emphasizing product differences.
4. The role of general business conditions presents somewhat contradictory arguments. Cartels are often established during depressed industry conditions, when companies attempt to forestall what they consider to be ruinous price cutting. However, it also appears that cartels disintegrate as demand for the product falls, and each member thinks it can do better outside the cartel. The cartel may then reestablish itself during the recovery period. Thus, cartels can form or fall apart during either phase of the business cycle.[2]
5. Entry into the industry must be difficult. The case of OPEC is a good example. It is impossible for countries that do not possess the basic resource to begin petroleum production and compete for monopoly profits.
6. If cost conditions for the cartel members are similar and profitability thus will not differ greatly among members, cartels will be easier to maintain. Product homogeneity, mentioned earlier, will contribute to cost uniformity.

The ideal cartel will be powerful enough to establish monopoly prices and earn maximum monopoly profits for all the members combined. This situation is illustrated in Figure 11.1. For simplicity, assume that there are only two firms in this oligopolistic industry. The total industry demand curve is shown in Figure 11.1c. The marginal revenue curve is constructed for this demand curve in the usual manner. Each of the two competitors (illustrated in Figures 11.1a and b) has its respective average total cost and marginal cost curves, which can differ.

The two individual marginal cost curves are then added horizontally, and the result is plotted on the industry graph (MC_T). Industry output will take place where

---

[2]A very cogent description of this phenomenon can be found in George J. Stigler, *The Theory of Price*, New York: Macmillan, 1949, pp. 274–75. Stigler also puts forward the idea that, regardless of the level of business activity, government action in support of such collusion is an important factor in a cartel's success. An important example is the U.S. National Recovery Act (NRA) of the 1930s, later declared unconstitutional by the Supreme Court.

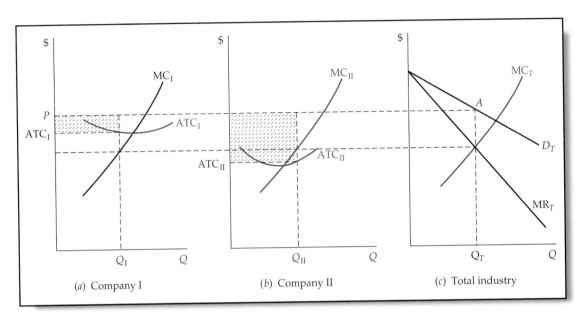

Figure 11.1
The Ideal Cartel

MC_T equals the industry marginal revenue, and the price charged will be found by drawing a vertical line to the demand curve (point A). This is, of course, the classic monopoly situation, and monopoly profits will be maximized at this point.

The next step is to establish how much each of the two companies will sell at this price. In order that the entire industry output be sold, each company will sell that output corresponding to the point at which a horizontal line drawn from the $MC_T = MR_T$ intersection on the industry graph crosses the marginal cost curve of each of the two firms. It can be seen that each of the two firms will produce different quantities and achieve different profits depending on the level of the average total cost curve at the point of production. Generally, the lower-cost company will be the more profitable one (profits for the two companies are shown by the hatched areas in Figure 11.1). This result, although maximizing combined profits, may also be one of the reasons for the subversion of cartels. A very efficient company with low average costs, and most likely with excess capacity under cartel conditions, may find it profitable to cheat by offering its product at a lower price and capturing a larger share of the total business.

Such a cartel may be unstable. Unless strictly enforced, cartels will have a tendency to break down. Secret price cuts may be extremely profitable because (if the product is undifferentiated) the demand curve for an individual firm in a cartel will be quite elastic. Cartel subversion often occurs during slumps in demand, as individual members will be looking to increase their share to avoid significant quantity decreases.

It must also be remembered that collusion is costly. First, there is the cost of forming the cartel. Second, there is a cost of monitoring the actions of the cartel members and of enforcing the rules to minimize cheating. There is also the potential cost of punishment by authorities. Thus, in the end, cartelization may not necessarily be profitable. In short, the additional revenues obtained by cartel members due to collu-

Managerial Economics

sion must exceed the costs just described. We can, therefore, state that while profit maximization is the incentive that leads to collusion, it may also be the cause of a cartel's breakdown.

Cartels often have agreements specifying the market share of each participant. Such allotments may be based on history, or they can be arranged to give each member a certain geographical area. Collusion can also exist in much more informal ways. Thus, physicians within a geographical area coincidentally charge similar fees for their services. Trade associations are often suspected of collecting and conveying information that will lead to the fixing of prices.

Cases of Price Fixing by Cartels

A classic case of price fixing and market sharing ended in February 1961 in a Philadelphia court, when 7 executives of General Electric, Westinghouse, and other companies were sent to prison and fined; 23 others were given suspended sentences and fined; and 29 companies were fined a total of approximately $2 million. Starting shortly after World War II, this conspiracy involved a number of heavy electrical equipment products, such as switching gear, circuit breakers, transformers, and turbine engines. The companies involved pleaded guilty and "no contest" to the federal indictments.

The story of these collusive practices reads like a mystery story.[3] There were meetings in hotel rooms during conventions of the National Electric Manufacturers Association. There were hotel meetings at various locations in which the participants did not register under their company affiliations and recorded trips to other locations in their expense accounts. There were code numbers given to each company. There were telephone calls at the participants' homes and even a conspiratorial round of golf.

A more recent case is that of the Archer-Daniels-Midland Company (ADM), a large agricultural business with annual revenues of approximately $20 billion in 2001. In October 1996, ADM pled guilty to price fixing of two of its products, lysine, a feed supplement, and citric acid, a food additive. Four Asian firms were implicated in the lysine conspiracy, and four European companies were involved in the citric acid case. The price fixing and division of markets was arranged in a series of secret meetings in many locations, including Mexico City, Paris, Tokyo, and Atlanta. ADM was fined a total of $100 million, and in addition paid approximately $90 million to settle customer and stockholder suits.

Two years later, in September 1998, three ADM executives were convicted of participating in the case. One of them was the former vice chairman, Michael Andreas, son of ADM's chief executive officer and his likely successor. He was sentenced to two years in prison and assessed a $350,000 fine. Various civil suits are still in progress in 2001.[4]

---

[3]The description of this case has been obtained from two articles in *Fortune* (April 1961, pp. 132–37 ff, and May 1961, pp. 161–64 ff), and from *The Wall Street Journal,* January 10 and 12, 1962.
[4]N. Millman, "$100 Million Fine in ADM Guilty Plea," *Chicago Tribune,* October 16, 1996; G. Burns, "Three ADM Execs Found Guilty," *Chicago Tribune,* September 17, 1998; S. Kilman, "Jury Convicts Ex-Executives in ADM Case," *The Wall Street Journal,* September 18, 1998; S. Kilman, "Ex-Officials of ADM Given 2 Years in Jail," *The Wall Street Journal,* July 12, 1999; Julie Forster, "A Different Kind of Andreas at ADM," *Business Week,* July 9, 2001, pp. 62–64.

In 1997, the U.S. Department of Justice began to investigate possible collusion in setting buying and selling commissions by two leading art auction houses. The two companies, Sotheby's and Christie's, together controlled 90 to 95 percent of the art auction market. While Sotheby's and Christie's appeared to be active competitors in soliciting business, in 1992 they raised their buyers' commissions to identical rates within six weeks of one another. Then in 1995 they took similar action on sellers' commissions, again within six weeks of one another. In January 2000, Christie's CEO turned over a large number of documents to the Department of Justice, and agreed to cooperate with the Department; in return, he and his firm were granted immunity from prosecution. In February 2001, a federal judge accepted Sotheby's guilty plea to conspiracy to fix prices, and fined the company $45 million. During the same month, a $512 million class-action suit settlement was reached between the two auction houses and some 130,000 buyers and sellers. In addition, Sotheby's settled with a group of shareholders who claimed that the auction house had misled them about the size of their earnings; the amount was $70 million.

In October 2000, the former chief executive officer of Sotheby's, Diana D. Brooks, pleaded guilty to conspiracy to violate antitrust laws, and agreed to cooperate with federal authorities. In May 2001, a federal grand jury indicted both former chairmen, A. Alfred Taubman of Sotheby's and Sir Anthony J. Tennant of Christie's, for collusion. Mr. Taubman was found guilty by a jury in December 2001. He was sentenced to one year and one day in prison and fined $7.5 million in April 2002. Mr. Tennant did not stand trial; he did not leave Britain, his home, and the United States cannot extradite him under British law. Ms. Brooks received no prison term, but was sentenced to home detention, probation, community service and a fine of $350,000.[5]

PRICE LEADERSHIP

When collusive arrangements are not easily achieved, another type of pricing practice may occur under oligopolistic market conditions. This is the practice of **price leadership,** in which there is no formal or tacit agreement among the oligopolists to keep prices at the same level or change them by the same amount. However, when a price movement is initiated by one of the firms, others will follow. Examples of such practices abound. You may have observed that at two or more gasoline stations at the same intersection, prices for each grade of gasoline are either identical or almost the same most of the time. Another example is automobile companies, which in recent years have come up with rebate programs. Surely you have seen advertisements

---

[5]Stories about this case appeared frequently in *The Wall Street Journal* during the period 2000–2001. A few among these were Laurie P. Cohen and Alexandra Peers, "Christie's Davidge Contacted Sotheby's on Pricing," March 20, 2000; Kathy Kranhold, "Judge Backs Guilty Plea from Sotheby's," February 5, 2001; Kathy Kranhold, "Sotheby's $70 million Settlement of Shareholder Suit Is Approved," February 20, 2001; Kathryn Kranhold, "Sotheby's, Christie's Settlement Is Approved by Judge in New York," February 23, 2001; Kathryn Kranhold, "Ex-Chiefs of Sotheby's, Christie's Indicted," May 3, 2001; Kathryn Kranhold, "Sotheby's Chief Is Convicted of Price-Fixing," December 6, 2001; Jerry Markon, "Sotheby's Taubman is Sentenced to Jail Time, Fined $7.5 Million," April 23, 2002. Also see Devin Leonard, "First: Feud? What Feud?" *Fortune Magazine,* March 20, 2000, p. 36, and Joshua Chaffin, "Ex-Sotheby's Chief Avoids Prison for Price-fixing Role," *Financial Times,* April 30, 2002.

offering "$1,000 cash or 3.9 percent financing." One company is usually the first to announce such a program; the others follow in short order. Another case is IBM. For many years, in the 1950s and 1960s, IBM was considered to be the price leader in the computer industry. In fact, IBM's prices were considered to form an "umbrella" for industry pricing. It was said that IBM would establish a price, and since it was the most powerful and preferred manufacturer and thus could command a higher price (an umbrella over the others), its competitors would tend to set their prices at some slightly lower level for similar equipment.

We have just described two major variants of the price leadership phenomenon: barometric and dominant price leadership.

Barometric Price Leadership

There may not be a firm that dominates all the others and sets the price each time. One firm in the industry—and it does not always have to be the same one—will initiate a price change in response to economic conditions, and the other firms may or may not follow the leader. If the **barometric price leader** has misjudged the economic forces, the other companies may not change their prices or may effect changes of a different, possibly lesser, magnitude. If the firm has correctly gauged the sentiment of the industry, all of the firms will settle in comfortably at the new price level. But if this does not happen, the price leader may have to retract the price change, or a series of iterations may be set in motion until a new price level, agreeable to all, is reached. Such a pattern of price changes has been observed in many industries, including automobiles, steel, and paper.

In recent years, the airline industry has furnished several examples of price leadership that was not followed. A recent, almost bizarre, example occurred in August 1998. First, Delta Air Lines and American Airlines raised leisure fares by 4 percent. When Northwest Airlines refused to match the increase, it was rescinded. A few days later, Northwest raised its fares and was matched by the others. Two days later Northwest rescinded the increase, and within a day other airlines followed. Then Northwest raised some of its fares again, only to pull some of them back, and actually decreased leisure fares in some of its markets. Other airlines then realigned their fares with those of Northwest.[6]

Dominant Price Leadership

When an industry contains one company distinguished by its size and economic power relative to other firms, the **dominant price leadership** model emerges. The dominant company may well be the most efficient (i.e., lowest-cost) firm. It could, under certain circumstances, force its smaller competitors out of business by undercutting their prices, or it could buy them out on favorable terms. But such action could lead to an investigation and eventual suit by the U.S. Department of Justice under the Sherman Anti-Trust Act. To avoid such difficulties, the dominant

---

[6]This sequence of fare changes was reported in several issues of *The Wall Street Journal* between August 11, 1998 and the end of August.

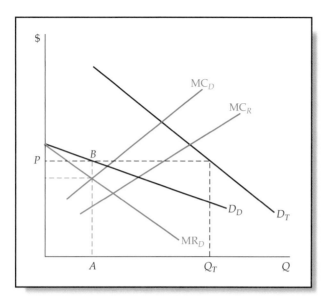

Figure 11.2
Dominant Price Leadership

company may actually act as a monopolist, setting its price at the point where it will maximize its profits, and it will permit the smaller companies to continue to exist and sell as much as they wish at the price set by the leader. The theoretical explanation of the dominant price leadership model is quite straightforward and is presented in all microeconomics textbooks. We will follow its development in Figure 11.2.

The demand curve for the entire industry is D_T. The marginal cost curve of the dominant firm is MC_D, and the sum of all the marginal cost curves of the follower firms is represented by MC_R. The demand curve for the leader, D_D is derived by subtracting at each point the marginal cost curve of the followers from the total demand curve, D_T. The reason is that if the small firms supply the product along their combined marginal cost curve, MC_R, then the dominant firm will be left with product demand shown along D_D. When the leader's marginal revenue curve, MR_D, is drawn in the usual manner, the leader can establish its profit-maximizing quantity at point A, and price at point B. This price is then accepted by the smaller firms in the industry, which will supply the rest of the market at this price. The followers are thus actually faced by a horizontal demand curve at price P.

Such an arrangement is satisfactory to the dominant firm. It maximizes profits and at the same time permits the small firms to exist, thus possibly avoiding legal action. On the other hand, the followers will be able to assure themselves of a piece of the market without inviting the possibility of a price war, which they would most likely lose.

As in the case of cartels, dominant price leadership arrangements tend to break down. As markets grow, new firms enter the industry and decrease the interdependence among the firms. Technological changes may bring changes in pricing, and in the long run the leadership of the dominant firm is likely to erode.

REVENUE MAXIMIZATION

MODULE 11A

Another model of oligopolistic behavior was developed some years ago by the American economist William Baumol.[7] Ignoring interdependence, the **Baumol model** suggests that a firm's primary objective, rather than profit maximization, can be the maximization of revenue, subject to satisfying a specific level of profits. He gives several reasons for this objective, among them (1) a firm will be more competitive when it achieves large size (in terms of revenue) and (2) management remuneration may be more closely related to revenue than to profits.

This situation is depicted in Figure 11.3. The figure shows three solid curves. The total revenue curve is the usual one for a firm in imperfect competition, with revenue increasing at a decreasing rate because the firm is faced by a downward-sloping demand curve.[8] The total cost curve also is no surprise; it indicates first decreasing and then, at higher production levels, increasing marginal cost. The third line represents profits. It is simply the vertical difference between the revenue and cost lines.

If the firm were a profit maximizer (the traditional economic objective), production would take place at point Q_P, where the profit line hits its peak. On the other hand, should the firm be a pure revenue maximizer, equilibrium would occur at output Q_S, where the total revenue curve reaches its peak. This point, as we learned earlier, occurs where demand elasticity is unity (i.e., marginal revenue equals zero).

However, revenue maximization is subject to the constraint that an acceptable profit level exists. This profit will tend to be at a lower level than the maximum achievable. Assuming that this acceptable level is at OP, output will settle at Q_A. This will achieve the highest possible revenue while satisfying the profit requirement. Thus, total revenue will be higher than would have been attained under conditions of profit maximization, but lower than if pure revenue maximization (without a minimum profit constraint) had been pursued.

An interesting implication of this model is the effect of a change in fixed costs. Recall that under conditions of profit maximization in the short run, a change in fixed costs will have no effect on price or quantity, since neither marginal revenue nor marginal cost is impacted, and thus the maximizing requirement of MR = MC will remain the same. However, in the Baumol model, a rise in fixed costs will raise the cost curve and decrease the profit line. Both new lines will be parallel to the old ones. The two broken lines in Figure 11.3 represent this shift. As can be seen, the existence of the profit constraint will cause output to decrease to Q_N. At this lower output, price will be higher.

Baumol's model is an interesting attempt to present an alternative to the traditional maximization hypothesis. Since his model has not been extensively tested, it is difficult to assess its validity. There have been some empirical studies investigating the relationship between executive pay and revenue (as opposed to profits), but no definitive verdict has been obtained. Some of the studies found a more solid relationship between executive pay and revenue, and others appeared to favor a relationship

---

[7]William J. Baumol, *Economic Theory and Operations Analysis,* 3d ed., Englewood Cliffs, NJ: Prentice Hall International Editions, 1972, chapter 13.
[8]Thus, each quantity represents a different price.

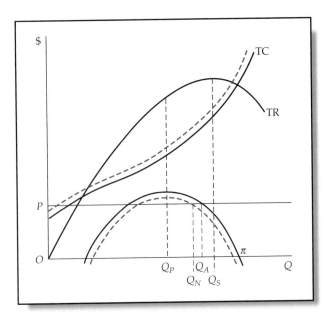

Figure 11.3
Revenue versus Profit
Maximization

with profits. Still others arrived at ambiguous answers. One important question remains: Are corporate owners (stockholders) more concerned—and thus determine the market value of a corporation—with revenue or profitability? In the long run, the most likely answer is the latter. Thus, it is doubtful that Baumol's model, although possibly applicable to some corporate behavior in the short run, will ever replace the traditional profit-maximizing objective.

PRICE DISCRIMINATION

Up to this point, we have assumed that a firm will sell identical products at the same price in all markets. (When the term *identical* is used in this context, it implies that the costs of producing and delivering the product are the same.) But such is not always the case. When a company sells identical products in two or more markets, it may charge different prices in the markets. Such a practice is usually referred to as **price discrimination.** The word *discrimination* here is not used in a normative sense; there is no judgment being made about whether this practice is good or bad. (The term *differential pricing* could be used instead, but the former term has become part of the everyday language of the economist.)

Price discrimination means one of the following:

1. Products with identical costs are sold in different markets at different prices.
2. The ratio of price to marginal cost differs for similar products.

The practice of price discrimination is not an isolated event. It occurs in many familiar situations. Later in this section we will cite a number of common examples. Here we will mention just two, to illustrate each general instance just listed. In the first case, price discrimination exists when an adult and a child are charged different prices for tickets (of the same quality and at the same time) at a movie theater. The latter can be illustrated by the selling of cosmetic items, identical except for names on the labels and the quality of packaging, for vastly different prices at department or specialty stores on the one hand and drug and discount stores on the other. The existence of price discrimination is caused by differing demand conditions, not by differences in cost.

Such discriminating price differentials cannot exist under all circumstances. In fact, two conditions are necessary for such a market arrangement:

1. The two or more markets in which the product is sold must be capable of being separated. Specifically, this includes the requirement that there can be no transfer or resale of the product (or service) from one market to the other. That is, there is no leakage among the markets. Only if the markets are sealed off from one another (by natural or contrived means) will the buyers in the various markets be unable to trade the products among these markets. And only in such a case will the seller be able to charge different prices without the price differential being nullified through competition. If the seller incurs costs in creating separate markets, these costs must be less than the additional revenue obtained from discrimination.
2. The demand curves in the segmented markets must have different elasticities at given prices. Without this condition, price discrimination would be futile.

The reason that companies attempt to engage in price discrimination is that it can enhance profits. From the viewpoint of the consumers of the product, those in the lower-price market may benefit compared to situations where a uniform price is charged. However, consumers in the higher-price market are at a disadvantage.

Economists normally identify three degrees of discrimination. First-degree discrimination is the most profitable for the seller, but it can be enforced only infrequently. Third-degree discrimination, which is not as profitable, is the most commonly observed, and we single it out for brief discussion in the next subsection.

1. First-degree discrimination exists when the seller can identify where each buyer lies on the demand curve and can charge each buyer the price he is willing to pay. Thus, the demand curve actually becomes the marginal revenue curve as faced by the seller. Of course, for the seller—a monopolist[9]—to achieve this advantageous position, it must have considerable information on where each of the buyers can be found on the demand curve, admittedly a herculean amount of market knowledge rarely attained. It is probably almost impossible to find such a pure case in real life, but let us attempt an example. A consumer purchasing a new automobile will generally bargain with the salesperson until they finally agree on a price. If the automobile dealer were clever enough to figure out the highest price that each individual was willing to pay, she could then conclude a deal with each customer at the maximum price (but only if no other dealer offered a lower price). Thus, each price the dealer obtains is on the buyers' demand curve. In reality, automobile dealers (and we must surely be thank-

---

[9]The assumption is usually made that a discriminating seller is a monopolist. But price discrimination also commonly exists in markets where competition is not perfect, not just in pure monopoly markets.

ful for this) are usually not endowed with such omniscience. We could stretch this example to apply to certain personal services such as medical or legal, where different customers (i.e., patients and clients) could be charged different fees based, for example, on their incomes.

2. Second-degree discrimination, although encountered somewhat more frequently than first degree, also is not commonplace in real life. It involves differential prices charged by blocks of services. An example is the way some public utilities price. They will charge the highest unit price (e.g., per kilowatt of electricity) for small quantities (at the top of the demand curve) and lower prices as the rate of consumption per period increases.[10] Thus, again, only if the monopolist seller has a great deal of information about the demand curve will it be able to roughly "skim" the curve and exact higher revenues from its customer set. To be able to engage in second-degree discrimination, a firm must be able to meter the services consumed by the buyers.[11]

3. Third-degree discrimination is by far the most frequently encountered. In this case, the monopolist segregates the customers into different markets and charges different prices in each. Such market segmentation can be based on geography, age, sex, product use, or income, for example.

Third-Degree Discrimination

If the firm can segment markets successfully, it can increase its profits above what they would be if a single price were charged. We will show the pricing results with graphs, and subsequently we will show a numerical example comparing the profitability of differential pricing versus uniform pricing as well as a mathematical solution. As shown in Figure 11.4, the company operates in two markets, A and B. In Figure 11.4a and b, it can be seen that A's demand curve is less elastic than B's. Figure 11.4c shows the horizontal summation of both demand and marginal revenue curves to represent the company's total market.

Because we assume that the products sold in the two markets are homogeneous, we can draw a marginal cost curve for the firm as a whole, as shown in Figure 11.4c. Output will take place at the point where MR = MC. Had a uniform price been charged, it would have been at point C on the aggregate demand curve. However, the firm can increase its profit by differentiating prices between the two markets. By drawing a horizontal line from the MR = MC intersection across the graphs for the two separate markets, we can allocate total production to the two markets. For each market, this will be the point where the horizontal line intersects the marginal revenue curve. Marginal revenue is thus the same for both markets. The price charged in each market can be found by drawing a vertical line at the corresponding quantity to the demand curve. Price will be considerably higher in market A, whose demand elasticity is lower.

---

[10]The price differential here is not related to pricing at peak versus off-peak periods. Such pricing may be related to the cost of producing the service and therefore does not represent discrimination.
[11]Price discrimination can also be achieved by using a "two-part tariff," that is, charging a lump-sum fee and then charging for usage. Thus, buyers with greater demand will pay more. Examples of such charges would be a base fee charged by water and telephone companies.

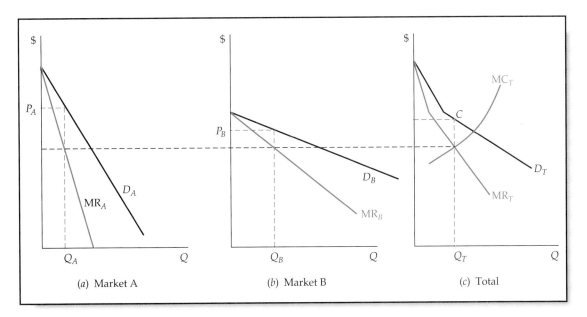

Figure 11.4
Third-Degree Price Discrimination

A numerical example will illustrate third-degree discrimination.[12] Section A of Table 11.1 presents the demand schedule for two markets as well as the combined schedule for the entire market. Assume that fixed costs are $12,000 per period, and that the average variable cost is constant (and consequently so is marginal cost) at $3 per unit.

If the company were to sell at a uniform price in both markets, it would maximize its profits at a price of $18. At that point, its profit would be $10,500. This can be seen in section B of Table 11.1. But if our company can separate the two markets, it can increase its total profit, as shown in sections C and D of the table. If it charges $24 per unit in market A and $12 per unit in market B, its profits will be $12,900 and $300, respectively. Thus, it will be able to increase its profit by $2,700.[13]

Had the company been able to carry out first-degree discrimination and sold to all potential customers at the prices they were willing to pay (with the exception of the last 500 units, which would not have been produced), its profits would have risen to $25,500, as shown in Table 11.2.

---

[12]We have chosen to show a numerical example of price discrimination rather than a mathematical proof. The latter would have been more precise. However, the simpler numerical illustration should be more useful. A brief outline of a mathematical solution is presented in the next subsection.

[13]We have arbitrarily divided the fixed costs equally between the two markets. But this has no effect on the total profits of the company or on the levels of sales in the two markets that will lead to profit maximization. Indeed, we could have omitted the fixed costs altogether, and there would have been no impact, except that the profits would have been $12,000 higher in both cases. Also, it should be noted that the quantity sold in this case is somewhat higher than in the one-price case. This is an inaccuracy caused by using discrete numbers in our demand schedule. Had this case been solved mathematically, using calculus, this inaccuracy would not have arisen.

Table 11.1
Numerical Example of Third-Degree Distribution

A. DEMAND SCHEDULES

PRICE	MARKET A QUANTITY	MARKET B QUANTITY	TOTAL QUANTITY
36	0	0	0
30	475	25	500
24	900	100	1,000
18	1,100	400	1,500
12	1,300	700	2,000
6	1,450	1,050	2,500
0	1,500	1,500	3,000

B. TOTAL MARKET

PRICE	QUANTITY	TOTAL REVENUE	MARGINAL REVENUE	FIXED COST	AVER. VAR. AND MARGINAL COSTS	TOTAL COST	PROFIT
36	0			12,000		12,000	−12,000
30	500	15,000	30	12,000	3	13,500	1,500
24	1,000	24,000	18	12,000	3	15,000	9,000
18	1,500	27,000	6	12,000	3	16,500	10,500
12	2,000	24,000	−6	12,000	3	18,000	6,000
6	2,500	15,000	−18	12,000	3	19,500	−4,500
0	3,000	0	−30	12,000	3	21,000	−21,000

C. MARKET A

PRICE	QUANTITY	TOTAL REVENUE	MARGINAL REVENUE	FIXED COST	AVER. VAR. AND MARGINAL COSTS	TOTAL COST	PROFIT
36	0			6,000		6,000	−6,000
30	475	14,250	30	6,000	3	7,425	6,825
24	900	21,600	17	6,000	3	8,700	12,900
18	1,100	19,800	−9	6,000	3	9,300	10,500
12	1,300	15,600	−21	6,000	3	9,900	5,700
6	1,450	8,700	−46	6,000	3	10,350	−1,650
0	1,500	0	−174	6,000	3	10,500	−10,500

D. MARKET B

PRICE	QUANTITY	TOTAL REVENUE	MARGINAL REVENUE	FIXED COST	AVER. VAR. AND MARGINAL COSTS	TOTAL COST	PROFIT
36	0			6,000		6,000	−6,000
30	25	750	30	6,000	3	6,075	−5,325
24	100	2,400	22	6,000	3	6,300	−3,900
18	400	7,200	16	6,000	3	7,200	0
12	700	8,400	4	6,000	3	8,100	300
6	1,050	6,300	−6	6,000	3	9,150	−2,850
0	1,500	0	−14	6,000	3	10,500	−10,500

Table 11.2

Profits from First-Degree Discrimination

PRICE	QUANTITY		REVENUE
$30	500		$15,000
24	500		12,000
18	500		9,000
12	500		6,000
6	500		3,000
Total revenue			$45,000
Fixed cost		$12,000	
Variable cost (2,500 × $3)		7,500	
Total cost			19,500
Profit			$25,500

A Mathematical Solution for Third-Degree Discrimination We will discuss briefly a simple method to solve for prices and quantities in the presence of third-degree discrimination.

1. Assume that there are two markets, A and B, and the demand curves are straight lines, that is,

$$Q_A = a_A - b_A P_A \text{ and } Q_B = a_B - b_B P_B$$

2. Reverse these equations so that P is the dependent variable:

$$P_A = \frac{a_A}{b_A} - \frac{Q_A}{b_A} \text{ and } P_B = \frac{a_B}{b_B} - \frac{Q_B}{b_B}$$

3. Now calculate total revenue by multiplying by Q:

$$TR_A = \frac{a_A Q_A}{b_A} - \frac{Q_A^2}{b_A} \text{ and } TR_B = \frac{a_B Q_B}{b_B} - \frac{Q_B^2}{b_B}$$

4. Calculate the first derivative of total revenue to obtain marginal revenue:

$$MR_A = \frac{a_A}{b_A} - \frac{2Q_A}{b_A} \text{ and } MR_B = \frac{a_B}{b_B} - \frac{2Q_B}{b_B}$$

5. Now set the marginal revenue equal to the company's marginal cost, which we will assume to be a constant:

$$MR_A = MC \text{ and } MR_B = MC$$

6. Substituting for MR_A and MR_B and solving the two equations gives the quantity sold in each market.

7. From here it is easy to find the contribution profit for the two markets and for the combination of the two. Remember that because MC is a constant, average variable cost is constant also, so that total variable cost can be calculated simply by multiplying AVC (= MC) by the quantity. Fixed cost, if any, can then be subtracted.

8. If we wish to find out what the price would be if a uniform price were charged, we first add the two demand functions found in step 1. We then reverse the resulting equation in terms of price, as in step 2, and obtain marginal revenue. Marginal revenue is then equated to MC, and the price, quantity, and contribution profit are obtained in the same manner as in steps 3 to 7. The quantity sold will be the same as if discrimination existed, but the profit will be lower.

Examples of Price Discrimination

Price discrimination is an extremely common practice encountered in all types of situations. A number of rather common examples follow:

1. In the past, physicians often set their fees in accordance with patient income. In a way, it could be argued that such a fee arrangement was quite equitable: Those who can afford to pay higher prices will do so. However, as stated before, we are not concerned here with the normative aspects of differential pricing. The result of such a practice will still be an increase in the physician's income.

   Presently, medical price discrimination exists in a somewhat different guise. Physicians frequently charge a patient who has health insurance more for the same services than they charge a patient who does not. The difference cannot be explained by the cost incurred by the physician in filing insurance documents. However, the two conditions necessary for differential pricing exist. The elasticities in the two markets (uninsured and insured) are certainly different, and the markets are sealed from each other (either the patient has insurance or does not have it).
2. Very often, products going into the export market will be priced lower than those sold domestically. A major reason for the differential is that international competition is stronger than that faced by the firm in its (frequently sheltered) domestic markets. Thus, demand curves in international markets are more elastic. Japanese electronics and French wines are just two examples of such discrimination.
3. Many pubs and bars have "ladies' hours," and in the past, major league baseball parks had ladies' days on Wednesdays. In both cases, the price for women is lower than that charged their male counterparts.
4. Theaters, cinemas, and sports events often charge lower prices for children occupying equal accommodations as adults. The same arrangement is frequently offered to senior citizens.
5. Public transportation systems commonly offer reduced fares to senior citizens.
6. State universities charge higher tuition fees to out-of-state students, although there is no cost differential to the university between in-state and out-of-state students.
7. Public utilities (electric, gas, telephone) customarily charge higher rates to business customers than to residential customers.
8. University bookstores offer 10 to 15 percent discounts to faculty while charging full prices to students.

9. Individuals can order publications from publishers at lower prices than those charged to libraries and other institutions. Most professional journals are priced in this way.

10. Advancing technology is creating new avenues for practicing price discrimination, as shown in the following two examples:

    a. Last-minute airline ticket buyers can make special deals through the Web site "priceline.com."

    b. New software permits Web-based merchants to identify individual visitors to their Web sites, and to study their shopping behavior. Price-sensitive customers may be offered lower prices. This new approach is a variation on catalog retailers' policies of sending catalogs with different prices to different zip codes.[14]

We leave it to you to think of additional examples.[15] In all of these instances, different prices are charged at the same time. A senior citizen and a person 40 years of age traveling in the subway together will pay different fares. Differential utility charges to business and residential customers are in effect at the same time during the day.

However, there are also price differences that depend on when products or services are consumed:

1. Theaters charge different ticket prices for matinees and evening performances.
2. Theaters charge higher ticket prices on weekends than on weekdays.
3. Daytime telephone rates are higher than nighttime rates.
4. Hotels catering mostly to business travelers charge lower room rates during weekends.

Are these also examples of price discrimination? Many economics texts subscribe to this notion. (Of course, where a firm's costs differ at different times, no price discrimination would be claimed.) However, if these are types of discrimination they do not really belong with the original examples given. After all, movements of a demand curve over time will change the prices of many products without the presence of price discrimination. What appears to be the case here is that weekend theater ticket demand, for example, is considerably higher than demand on a Tuesday or a Wednesday, while the supply curve is essentially vertical. And prices change as demand changes. Whether this qualifies as price discrimination is questionable.

Some Recent Examples of Price Discrimination Practices

It was 1995 when California passed a law banning price discrimination based on gender. The legislation was aimed at retail stores, such as dry cleaners and hair salons, which charged higher prices to women than to men for presumably similar

---

[14]S. Woolley, "I got it cheaper than you," *Forbes,* November 2, 1998, pp. 82–84.

[15]Fare differentials in the airline industry are often mentioned as a prime example of price discrimination. A ticket bought well in advance, whose price is not refundable and which includes a weekend, is usually considerably cheaper than one that does not possess these characteristics. Vacation (elastic demand) and business (inelastic demand) travel are usually differentiated in this manner, and thus it may not be unusual for two travelers to sit next to one another on a plane and be paying vastly different fares. However, there are also differences in cost and risk to the airline between these two different fares, so that the two tickets are really not the same. If the fare differentials occur due to disparities in cost and risk, then this is not an example of price discrimination.

services. However, price differentials still appeared to exist. So in 2001, the California legislature passed a law to further discourage price differentials. In addition to increasing monetary penalties, stores are now required to display prices charged for their 15 most commonly used services. However, differentials due to differences in cost (due to time required or difficulty of service) are still permitted.[16]

In March 2000, McCormick & Co., the leading marketer of spices in the United States, entered into a consent decree with the Federal Trade Commission for violating the Robinson-Patman Act.[17] It was alleged that McCormick charged higher prices to some retail stores than others in return for obtaining greater shelf space at the expense of smaller stores. McCormick commonly demanded as much as 90 percent of a store's shelf space. This practice is usually referred to as "slotting fees," and is a standard way of doing business in grocery stores and some other industries. Thus, this decision could have much wider implications for the future. The consent order did not impose any monetary penalties, but is effective for 20 years.[18]

In 1999, six cigarette vending machine companies filed a $100 million lawsuit against Philip Morris. The suit stated that Philip Morris discriminates against vending machine operators by giving other merchants "rebates, buybacks and other promotional fees that result in lower wholesale cigarette prices."[19]

During the anthrax scare following the events of September 11, 2001, the U.S. Department of Health and Human Services (HHS) negotiated an arrangement to procure the antianthrax medicine Cipro for 95 cents per pill. The retail price of Cipro was $4 to $5 per unit at that time. However, at the same time under another HHS program called "340B," the same medicine was being obtained for about 43 cents a tablet by hospitals and clinics that treat poor people and underserved areas. This arrangement, of course, raised the question of price discrimination. Stephen Schondelmeyer, a professor of pharmaceutical economics at the University of Minnesota, was quoted as saying: "The industry has tried to segment the market into as many sectors as they can that allow them to charge as much as they can in each sector . . . this is called price discrimination."[20]

Pricing in the Hotel Industry: Example of Price Discrimination

Differential room rates have existed in the hotel industry for a long time. However, we will not discuss in this section, for instance, the lower weekend rates that are standard at business hotels or the higher rates charged during the busy season by resort hotels. These intertemporal differences appear to be based on different levels of demand. Here we will be concerned with different rates charged to different customers at the same time (e.g., same day). In the following discussion we must remember an important fact attending the operation of a hotel: A large proportion of the cost of running a

[16]Jim Sanders, "California Lawmakers Pass Bills to Eliminate Retailer Gender Discrimination," *The Sacramento Bee*, September 30, 2001.
[17]The Robinson-Patman Act is discussed briefly in Chapter 15. This law makes it illegal to charge different prices to different customers, unless justified by cost differentials.
[18]Ira Teinowitz, "FTC, McCormick Reach Accord on Slotting Fees," *Advertising Age*, March 13, 2000, p. 75; Tom Weir, "FTC Raises the Ante with McCormick Order," *Supermarket Business*, April 15, 2000, pp. 45–46.
[19]"Machine Cigarette Vendors Sue Philip Morris on Prices," *The Wall Street Journal*, February 4, 1999.
[20]Shankar Vedantam, "HHS' Varying Costs for Cipro Criticized," *Washington Post*, October 26, 2001.

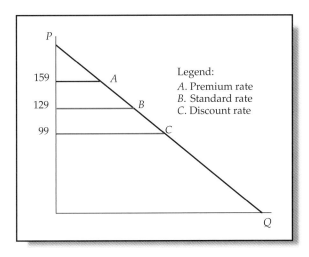

Figure 11.5
First-Degree Discrimination in the Hotel Industry

Legend:
A. Premium rate
B. Standard rate
C. Discount rate

hotel is fixed. The variable cost of renting an empty room is relatively small. "To paraphrase one general manager, 'If I've got a warm body with money standing in front of me and cold sheets upstairs, I want to make a deal. As long as the customer is willing to pay more than my variable cost to clean that room, I'm going to make money.' "[21] Each additional rented room represents incremental revenue.

This situation leads to different types of price discrimination practices in the hotel industry.

Often a hotel will have several different rates, and the actual rate charged to a particular guest will depend on the bargaining skill of the customer and the knowledge of the innkeeper in estimating the highest price the potential patron is willing to pay. Thus, the revenue of the hotel may be found along the demand curve (if the manager is really proficient at estimating the customer's willingness to pay), and the result may approach first-degree discrimination. Figure 11.5 illustrates this situation with potential scenarios for three different prices.

However, the more typical way of discriminating is to segment the market. The simplest method is to separate leisure travelers from business travelers. The demand of the former is certainly more price elastic, since the room price is an important part of the total vacation expense. At the same time, vacation travelers may be willing to make an advance commitment, may stay for a longer time period, and are more flexible in their arrangements. The business travelers' demand is less price elastic; they are much more inflexible in making their arrangements (they must be in a certain place at a certain time); their commitments often cannot be made far in advance; perhaps most important is that they are in most cases not willing to stay over the weekend, when rates are often lowest. Figure 11.6 shows the two demand curves with possible prices.

"As customers have become more sophisticated in manipulating the current pricing system, hotels will eventually be forced to modify their pricing structure." A new

---

[21]Richard D. Hanks, Robert G. Cross, and R. Paul Noland, "Discounting in the Hotel Industry: A New Approach," *The Cornell H.R.A. Quarterly,* February 1992, pp. 15–23. The discussion in this section is based largely on this article. The quote and all that follow also come from this article.

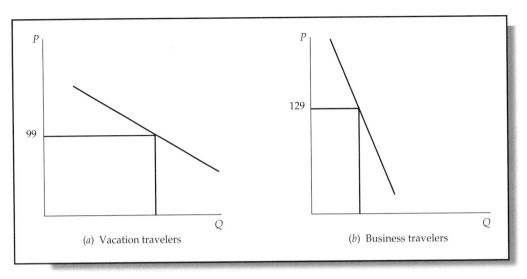

Figure 11.6
Third-Degree Discrimination in the Hotel Industry

approach is being introduced, which will "fence" customers into different rate categories tailored to specific needs so that higher-rate patrons will not be able to "trade down." Among the various methods to segment the customer sets will be the following:

1. Advance reservations and advance purchase
2. Rates differentiated depending on how many days in advance the reservations are made
3. Refundability
4. Flexibility to make changes in arrangements
5. Required time of stay

Hotels will be able to combine and alter these requirements ("fences") depending on the level of demand at any specific time. With these procedures, hotels will be able to penetrate their markets more deeply. However, such a multifaceted program also has its problems. First of all, to carry out this program effectively, hotels must have sophisticated computer-directed reservation systems and must be able to make rapid adjustments to ensure that they do not sell too many rooms at unnecessarily discounted rates. The administration of such a system may require additional staffing and additional costs, and management must be sure that the additional revenue derived from this system more than compensates for this cost.

Tying Arrangements: A Possible Extension of Price Discrimination

A *tying arrangement* (frequently referred to as a *tie-in sale*) exists when a buyer of one product is obligated to also buy a related (usually complementary) product from the same supplier. U.S. antitrust laws take a very dim view of tying arrangements, and a large number of court cases have declared this practice to be illegal. The reasoning behind this is that a firm will use its existing market power in the first (tying) product to suppress previously existing competition in the second (tied) product. The firm will thus extend its monopoly power.

Typically a tying arrangement will involve a major, often durable product and a low-value item that is usually complementary to the former.[22]

The legal argument claiming that tying arrangements cause an extension of monopoly appears flawed. If a company already has market power in the tying product it can maximize its monopoly profit. To tie another product to it may actually dilute its power, in that customers who buy the two complementary products are mainly interested in the total cost of the two products combined. Thus, if a tie-in sale arrangement causes the price of the tied product to increase, it may have to be made up by a decrease in the price of the tying product.

An alternative economic explanation of a tying arrangement is that it is a type of third-degree discrimination. A company may charge identical prices for the tying good. However, purchasers of the tying product may have different levels of demand for its usage. This quantity of demand can be "metered" by the tied product; purchasers who use the product with greater intensity will use a larger quantity of the tied product. Thus, the seller may charge a relatively reasonable price for the major product and collect monopoly profits on the lower-valued complementary product.

One of the more prominent cases in the history of this litigation was the U.S. government suit against IBM.[23] IBM rented its equipment on a monthly basis. All customers paid the same monthly rental whether they used the machine eight hours a day or two hours per week. Those customers who used the equipment with greater intensity had to use a larger number of punch cards. Thus, IBM really had a relatively inexpensive way to separate its customers into those who used the rented machines more intensively and those who used them only sporadically. And it could practice this discrimination even while charging the same unit price for punch cards to all customers. "It is generally agreed that if the tying and tied goods are complementary in demand, then profit maximization under the price discrimination hypothesis will lead the seller to lower the price of the tying good (below the level that would prevail if the good were sold separately) and sell the tied good at a price above its marginal production cost."[24]

While price discrimination is a plausible explanation of tying arrangements, other arguments have been advanced:

1. *Quality control.* Firms have argued that tying arrangements are necessary to ensure the integrity of their product so they do not get blamed if an inferior tied good is used.

---

[22]To illustrate, some of the court cases involving tying arrangements have included riveting machines and rivets, computers and punch cards, camera film and film processing, condominiums and building management services.

[23]*International Business Machines Corporation v. United States*, 298 U.S. 392 (1936).

[24]Meyer L. Burstein, "The Economics of Tie-In Sales," *Review of Economics and Statistics*, 42 (February 1960), p. 69. Much of the preceding discussion is based on William F. Shughart II, *The Organization of Industry*, Homewood, IL: Irwin, 1990, pp. 307–14.

2. *Efficiencies in distribution.* A total lower cost can be attained if there are savings to the company in delivering both products.
3. *Evasion of price controls.* If there is a ceiling price on one of the two products, then selling the second product at a higher price will circumvent price control.

Social Welfare Implications of Price Discrimination

As mentioned previously, U.S. antitrust laws look unfavorably at the practice of price discrimination, which is said to lead to a lessening of competition.

Under monopoly conditions an industry produces a smaller amount of product at a higher price than under competitive conditions. However, as we have seen, under price discrimination of the first and second degree, a company may produce a larger quantity than a single-price monopoly. Given the conditions of first-degree discrimination, the firm will charge prices along the demand curve all the way to the point where demand equals marginal cost. This, of course, results in a larger quantity than produced by a single-price monopoly. A similar situation would hold for second-degree discrimination. Thus, when price discrimination exists, total production may equal that which would exist under competitive circumstances.

In the case of third-degree discrimination, the situation is more ambiguous. As we have seen, as long as the demand curve for the monopolist is a straight downward-sloping line, the quantity produced will be the same under a single-price and a price-discrimination situation. However, under certain circumstances, production under discriminatory pricing may increase. This situation may occur if the demand curve is not a straight line, or if a one-price policy would not be profitable enough for a company to produce the product at all.

In the case of third-degree discrimination, customers in the market with lower price elasticity will pay higher prices, while those in an elastic demand market will pay lower prices than under conditions of a one-price monopoly. The implications here are uncertain, since it is very difficult to weigh the benefits bestowed on the latter compared to the costs imposed on the former as to their effect on total economic welfare. However, there is no question that the sellers in the discrimination case will benefit from the higher prices charged at least in a part of the market, thereby increasing their profits.

NONMARGINAL PRICING

Throughout this text we appear to have assumed that all businesspeople calculate demand and cost schedules, obtain marginal revenue and marginal cost curves, equate marginal revenue with marginal cost, and thus determine their profit-maximizing selling price and production quantity. But how many business owners or managers actually know how to make these calculations? And even if they have the knowledge, how many have the time and, even more important, sufficient information to make such calculations?

In fact, it is often claimed (as discussed in chapter 2) that businesses are really not profit maximizers, that they have other objectives. It has been said that management will seek only satisfactory levels of profit for the owners. The term *satisficing* has been used in this context.[25] Other corporate goals may also be important, such as the achievement of a desired market share, a target profit margin (i.e., percent of profits to revenue), or a target rate of return on assets (profit divided by assets) or on equity (profit divided by stockholder equity).

It also appears that one of the most popular pricing methods, believed to be pervasive throughout industry is the cost-plus or full-cost method, which at first glance seems not to employ the marginal pricing principle at all. It is this subject that we will discuss next.

Cost-Plus Pricing

A researcher questioning a sample of businesspeople on their pricing methods, would probably be told by a majority that they simply calculate the variable cost of the product, add to it an allocation for fixed costs, and then add a profit percentage or markup on top of these total costs to arrive at **cost-plus price**.[26] Thus, for instance, if the direct (variable) cost of a product is $8, its allocated overhead is $6, and the desired markup is 25 percent, the price of the product will be $17.50 (8 + 6 + 0.25 × 14).[27]

Such a calculation appears to be extremely simple, and the whole method is often described as naive. But this apparent simplicity hides some fairly difficult calculations and assumptions:[28]

1. How are average variable costs calculated?
2. How are fixed costs allocated? And why are fixed costs included in the price calculation? Economic theory tells us that fixed costs do not affect price.[29]
3. How is the size of the markup determined? Usually, it is said that the markup should guarantee the seller a "fair profit," or some target profit margin or target rate of return. If this is the case, are demand conditions taken into consideration at all?

We will discuss these problems, and as we go through this analysis we may find that cost-plus pricing and marginal pricing have a lot in common.

In cost-plus pricing, costs, both variable and fixed overheads, are usually calculated at some standard or normal quantity, as is done by accountants. These are historical costs and do not appear to include an opportunity cost. But economic theory tells us that unit costs tend to vary with quantity, and the expected quantities may

---

[25]See Herbert Simon, "Theories of Decision Making in Economics and Behavioral Science," *American Economic Review,* 49 (June 1959), pp. 253–83. This condition usually prevails in large corporations, where professional managers may not act in conformance with the wishes of stockholders. In the textbooks on corporate finance, considerable attention is accorded this subject, which has been named "agency theory." It is based on a famous article by Michael C. Jensen and WIlliam H. Meckling, "Theory of the Firm: Managerial Behavior, Agency Costs, and Ownership Structure," *Journal of Financial Economics,* October 1976, pp. 305–60.

[26]One of the original studies was R. L. Hall and C. J. Hitch, "Price Theory and Business Behavior," *Oxford Economic Papers,* 2 (May 1939), pp. 12–45.

[27]Markup is ordinarily calculated as a percentage of cost. Profit margin is commonly computed as a percentage of price. Thus, a 25 percentage markup is equivalent to a 20 percent profit margin.

[28]It is said that restaurants usually mark up the food cost four times to arrive at the price of a menu item—a very simple calculation indeed.

[29]Only in the Baumol revenue maximization model does fixed cost enter into price determination.

not correspond to those that result.[30] Also, as mentioned, fixed costs should not be used in the determination of prices.

However, if we take these criticisms in turn, the shortcomings of cost-plus pricing may not be as serious as they appear. There is no real reason why accounting costs cannot include some measure of opportunity cost. And even if it is not incorporated, a normal profit (another name for opportunity cost) certainly could easily be included in the markup. Now, it is often said that cost-plus pricing is a long-term concept. If that is the case, then, according to economic theory, all costs are variable; a cost allocation is then an estimate of the additional variable costs in the long run. Further, although economists like to draw nice U-shaped cost curves, it is quite possible that in the longer run the bottom portion of the average cost curve is quite shallow (saucer-shaped) and that over some production range it may appear to be almost horizontal.[31] In that case, as long as a firm is producing in the range at which standard costs are calculated, the problem of costs varying with quantity is obviated. Also, if the curve is relatively horizontal, marginal cost will be identical or almost identical to the average cost in that interval, and pricing on basis of average cost will thus be substantially similar to marginal cost pricing. In addition, economic theory tells us that, under perfect competition, in the long run all but normal profits will disappear. The markup, then, must certainly represent normal profit. It is more likely, however, that competition in the real world is not quite perfect, and the firm will therefore be faced by a downward-sloping demand curve.

This brings us to the question of the demand curve. If a markup is applied to obtain a "fair" profit, the implication is that demand conditions are not taken into consideration. But that would indicate almost complete inflexibility regarding the size of the markup. However, it has been observed in innumerable cases that markup percentages differ among different product lines of the same firm. The fact that a company accepts a lower markup for some products than others indicates that demand conditions and the competitive environment are included in the pricing decision making. As will be shown, the markup percentage tends to vary inversely with demand elasticity. This makes obvious sense: when a firm is faced by very strong competition, the demand curve facing it will tend to be nearly or completely horizontal: under those circumstances, the firm will not be able to afford a very large markup.

---

[30]The accountant's cost for a normal quantity can be shown as one point on the economist's average cost curve:

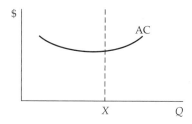

Point X is the "normal" quantity at which costs would be calculated. But other quantities would be produced at different costs.
[31]This situation is consistent with constant returns to scale.

One other important point must be made. Not only will different markups be applied for different product lines of a given firm, but the markup will probably change on a given product from time to time. Such changes could be caused by changing demand or changing cost conditions. When this occurs, a firm will adjust its markup and, thus, its price to meet the new circumstances. Its purpose for such action is most probably to increase or protect its profits. And as long as a firm changes its prices to "do better," (i.e., increase its profit or minimize its loss), it is acting as if it has knowledge of its demand and cost curves: that is, it is acting consistently with marginal pricing.

It is certainly true that businesspeople do not have sufficient knowledge to estimate marginal revenue and marginal cost curves with any degree of accuracy. Thus, cost-plus pricing can be a substitute for marginal pricing in the absence of sufficient knowledge. But given the proclivity for firms to adjust their markups in response to demand and cost conditions in such a way as to improve profitability, profit maximization and cost-plus pricing can be quite compatible.

An Arithmetic Reconciliation of Cost-Plus and Marginal Pricing It can be shown mathematically that under certain circumstances, cost-plus pricing can be consistent with profit maximization (i.e., MR = MC).

Most microeconomics textbooks show the mathematical relationship among price, marginal revenue, and demand elasticity as follows.[32]

$$MR = P\left(1 + \frac{1}{E_p}\right)$$

As profit is maximized when MR = MC, we can rewrite the equation as

$$MC = P\left(1 + \frac{1}{E_p}\right)$$

Further, under certain conditions, marginal cost will equal average cost. Thus, our equation becomes

$$AC = P\left(1 + \frac{1}{E_p}\right)$$

and can then be rewritten as

$$AC = P\left(\frac{E_p + 1}{E_p}\right)$$

---

[32]The equation is derived in the following way: Total revenue (TR) equals price times quantity ($P \times Q$). To obtain marginal revenue, total revenue must be differentiated with respect to quantity:

$$MR = \frac{d\text{TR}}{dQ} = \frac{d(P \times Q)}{dQ} = P \times \frac{dQ}{dQ} + Q \times \frac{dP}{dQ} = P \times 1 + Q \times \frac{dP}{dQ} = P\left(1 + \frac{Q}{P} \times \frac{dP}{dQ}\right)$$

Note that the product inside the parentheses is the reciprocal of elasticity; hence,

$$MR = P\left(1 + \frac{1}{E_p}\right)$$

Remember that demand elasticity has a negative sign.

Chapter 11 Special Pricing Practices

To show how price is based on average cost, we can rearrange the equation as

$$P = AC\left(\frac{E_p}{E_p + 1}\right)$$

Under conditions of cost-plus pricing,

$$P = AC(1 + M)$$

where M stands for the markup percentage. If the two previous equations are comparable, then

$$(1 + M) = \frac{E_p}{E_p + 1}$$

It can be shown that there is an inverse relationship between markup and demand elasticity. For example, if $E_p = -2$, then $(1 + M) = -2/-1 = 2$ and M is therefore 100 percent. If, however, $E_p = -5$, then $(1 + M) = -5/-4 = 1.25$, and markup is only 25 percent. This result is quite reasonable; it indicates that the less elastic the demand curve, the larger the markup will be.

Thus, under the not infrequent conditions where the average cost curve is constant in the relevant range of production, cost-plus pricing may give results identical to those that would be obtained if managers were pursuing profit maximization.

Incremental Pricing and Costing Analysis

We have just discussed the cost-plus method of pricing; it is considered to be a very popular pricing method. We explained that cost-plus pricing and marginal pricing can generally be reconciled. But there are difficulties with implementing marginal pricing in the real world. To do a good job of marginal pricing, a manager would have to have good estimates of the shape of demand and cost curves. Since it may be quite costly and certainly very difficult to estimate marginal quantities, businesses will often use incremental analysis to achieve the objective of profit maximization.

In a way, marginal and incremental analyses are very similar. But while *marginal* implies that we must estimate the revenue and costs created by one additional unit or the additional revenue obtained from one extra dollar of expenses, incremental analysis deals with changes in total revenue and total costs resulting from a particular decision to change prices, introduce a new product, discontinue an existing product, improve a product, or acquire additional machinery or plant. We have already discussed the question of incremental costs in chapter 8.

The important lesson to learn here is that only those revenues and costs that will change due to the decision should be considered. Thus, it is a mistake to include sunk costs in calculating the outcome. Furthermore, if costs such as fixed overhead are already being incurred and will not change (even though accountants may reallocate these costs), they are irrelevant to the decision. On the other hand, if a decision results in a change in revenues or costs of another product (possibly a complementary or substitute good), such an effect must be included in the analysis.

Obviously, this is an important subject to which we are devoting only a small amount of space here. However, incremental analysis is at the heart of the study of long-term investments. This is a subject discussed at greater length in chapter 13.

MULTIPRODUCT PRICING

In economics much of the analysis makes use of simplifying assumptions. For example, we know that very few products in our economy are produced under conditions of perfect competition. Nevertheless, a large portion of our text—and all other economics texts—is devoted to its discussion. There are good reasons for this practice. First, perfect competition is the simplest of the economic models and is thus a good starting point for the discussion of more complex systems. Second, many markets, although not perfectly competitive (i.e., firms are faced by downward-sloping demand curves), can be analyzed as such because their behavior resembles perfect competition closely enough. Any predictions based on this analysis will be sufficiently accurate to obviate the need for more complex models.[33]

Another simplification frequently made in economic theory is assuming that a firm or a plant produces a single product. Up to this point, we have done so in this text. Actually, we first assumed that single products were sold in single markets, and later extended our analysis to operations in more than one market (price discrimination). Now we will provide a brief treatment of **multiproduct pricing,** cases in which a plant or a firm produces two or more products, which are, of course, the norm rather than the exception.

The various products produced by a firm can be independent of one another. This means that neither the demand for nor the cost of one product is affected by the demand for or cost of another product. In such a case, each product will be produced, as usual, at the level where its marginal revenue equals its marginal cost. The analysis can then proceed as if only one good were produced.

In most cases, however, there is some relationship among products produced by one firm. The relationships can exist either on the demand side or the cost side—or both. We can distinguish (at least) four different interrelationships:

1. Products are complements in terms of demand. One company may produce both personal computers and software, or a fast-food restaurant may sell both hamburgers and soft drinks.
2. Products are substitutes in terms of demand: A company may produce different models of a personal computer, or a soft drink company may bottle both cola and lemon-lime soda.
3. Products are joined in production. The extreme case of joint production occurs when two products are produced in fixed (or almost fixed) proportions, such as cattle production, which involves one skin and one carcass per steer.
4. Products compete for resources. If a company making different products that compete for the available resources produces more of one product, it will have to do so at the expense of producing less of other products. The production of different models of the same computer is an example.

Let us now discuss each of these cases.

---

[33]It is the accuracy of the prediction provided by a model that is important to scientists, not the reasonability or realism of the assumptions. This point has been successfully argued by Milton Friedman in "The Methodology of Positive Economics," contained in his *Essays in Positive Economics,* Chicago: University of Chicago Press, 1953, pp. 3–43.

Products Complementary in Demand

When two products are complementary, an increase in the quantity sold of one will bring about an increase in the quantity sold of the other. This may be due to an increase in the demand for product A or a price decrease of product A (bringing about an increase in the quantity demanded). Products may be so closely related that they are bought in fixed proportions. An example is kitchen knives, each of which must be made of one wooden handle and one metal blade. Other complementary products are a personal computer and a keyboard, and still another example is an automobile body and a set of four wheels. Somewhat less fixed in proportion but still closely related products are razors and razor blades, tennis rackets and tennis balls, and computers and software. There are also more remotely related products where the demand for one can easily have a beneficial effect on the demand for the other. For instance, a popular textbook in economics published by a particular company may enhance the sales of a finance textbook by the same publisher.

The important point is that the demand for a product is affected not only by its price, by income, and by tastes, for example, but also very strongly by the prices of related commodities. This subject was discussed in chapter 3, where we defined the determinants of the demand curve in general. Here we will concentrate on the effects of complementary commodities on the revenues of one firm. Thus, if products A and B are complementary, a change in revenue from A will entail a change in the revenue from B. In both cases, profit maximization will occur at the familiar point where the marginal revenue of each product equals its marginal costs. Since each of the demand equations will include the prices of both products, the pricing problem will require the solution of simultaneous equations.

If managers had nice, neat demand and cost functions available for each of these products, they could arrive at the combined profit maximization positions using relatively simple mathematical formulas.[34] However, since in real life the decision maker would most likely not have sufficient data on hand, the maximization process would proceed along a trial-and-error course, where markups (and thus prices) for the products would be adjusted until the optimal combination is reached. Actually, the process would be even more complex in reality, as it is not only the complementary relationship between the firm's two products that has an important influence on the firm's revenue (and profit); competitors' products that are substitutes for our firm's products must also be considered in the process of price setting.

There is another instance in which a company must consider these interrelationships. It is not necessary that a firm produce two related products simultaneously. It

---

[34]For a two-product situation, a manager could calculate the marginal revenue for each of the interrelated products. Because

$$Q_A = f(P_A, P_B) \text{ and } Q_B = f(P_B, P_A)$$

then

$$MR_A = \frac{dTR_A}{dQ_A} + \frac{dTR_B}{dQ_A} \text{ and } MR_B = \frac{dTR_B}{dQ_B} + \frac{dTR_A}{dQ_B}$$

Each of the marginal revenues would be equated to their respective marginal costs simultaneously:

$$MR_A = MC_A \text{ and } MR_B = MC_B$$

may just produce one and be in the process of deciding whether to embark on the production of a complementary product. In calculating the profitability of such expansion, the company must include the increase in sales of and profit earned on the earlier product. If it omitted this positive effect, it would be understating the benefits of the new product. It may decide against the product's introduction when in fact the total profits of the company would increase if the new product were brought to market. As an example, suppose a successful producer of television sets is considering whether or not to introduce a new line of VCRs. In calculating the potential profitability of producing VCRs, the producer must include the possibility of enhanced sales (and profits) from its television line.

Products Substitutable in Demand

A brief treatment of substitutability and pricing will suffice, as this case is extremely similar to that of complements. For substitutes, the effect to be considered is the decrease (increase) in revenue and profits of a second product if quantities bought of the first product rise (fall), either because of changes in demand or changes in price. Examples of such cases abound. Two different sizes of personal computers certainly are substitutes for one another. The different automobile models produced by one manufacturer (sedans versus convertibles, Honda Preludes versus Accords, Chevrolets versus Pontiacs, etc.) are relatively close substitutes, so it is necessary to price them jointly. Another example is Global Foods' soft drink division, which produces cola-type and non–cola-type sodas simultaneously.

Just as in the case of complementary products, substitution can occur when a new product is introduced. Thus, a computer manufacturer developing a new generation of computers must consider the impact that the introduction will have on similar but less advanced products now being marketed.

The analysis of these cases is basically the same as for complementary commodities. The marginal revenue of one product will be a function of the quantities sold of both commodities, and the prices of the two will be found by solving simultaneous equations. However, in this case, the sales of one product will have a negative impact on the sales of the other.

Joint Products with Fixed Proportions

Certain products will be produced together from one set of inputs. In some instances, the two products will be produced in fixed proportions to one another. Although precisely fixed proportions may not occur often in the real world, relative fixity is commonly encountered, particularly in the short run. The example given earlier involved the products of a beef carcass and a hide (only one of each can be obtained from one steer). Other examples are soybean meal and soybean oil, and coconut milk and coconut meat. In many cases, there is a principal product and one or more byproducts.

Assume that products A and B are produced jointly in fixed proportions. Only one cost curve can be constructed in this case. However, the demand curves for the two products are independent (e.g., the demand for coconut meat is not related to the demand for its milk). Thus, the two demand curves and their respective marginal revenue curves can be added vertically to obtain a total demand curve and a total marginal revenue curve. Observe, however, that when one of the separate marginal revenue curves goes negative, it becomes irrelevant to the solution of the problem, because no business would produce at a point where marginal revenue is negative. To the right of this point, the total marginal revenue curve will be coincident with the marginal revenue of the product that is still in the positive range. Production will take place (using our usual maximization rule) where total marginal revenue equals marginal cost. The prices of the two separate products can be found at the quantity indicated on their respective demand curves. Figure 11.7 shows the results. D_A, D_B, MR_A, and MR_B are the demand and marginal revenue curves for the two products, and MR_S represents the vertical summation of the two individual marginal revenue curves. (The summed demand curve is actually irrelevant to the solution of the problem and need not be shown.) As can be seen, MR_S becomes identical with MR_B to the right of the point where MR_A becomes negative.

The curve MC represents the marginal cost of the joint product. Production will take place where marginal cost is equal to MR_S, which is at quantity Q on the graph. The prices charged for the two products will be found on their respective demand curves at P_A and P_B. An interesting aspect of this type of construction is that if the optimal production quantity were to the right (i.e., at higher quantities) of the point where one of the marginal revenue curves (in our case, that for product A) becomes negative, it would become profitable for the company to produce this total amount but not to sell quantities of product A beyond the point where its marginal revenue becomes zero. The company should discard the excess product A.

Another important point is the effect of the change in the demand for one of the two jointly produced products. If the demand for product B rises and the price of B thus increases, there will be a decrease in the price of A (as it will be produced at a lower point on its demand curve).

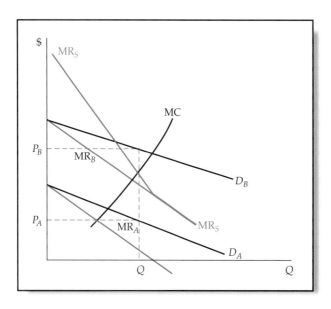

Figure 11.7
Price Determination for
Joint Products Made in
Fixed Proportions

Joint Products in Variable Proportions

When we relax the limitation of fixed proportions, we have the usual case of joint production. Indeed, when two products are produced from similar resources in variable proportions (i.e., if we produce more of one product we must produce less of the other) the situation is not dissimilar to the general case of production of different products with limited resources. We are essentially describing the "guns or butter" situation. Under short-run conditions, there is a given amount of resources with which the two products can be produced.

Figure 11.8 illustrates this situation. Curve I_1 is an isocost curve; the total cost of production is the same at each point. An essential requisite is that the curve be concave to the origin: as more of one product is produced, progressively larger quantities of the other must be given up. The isocost curve shows the alternative quantities of product A and B that can be produced. If the prices of the two products are constant regardless of quantity (i.e., we are implicitly operating under conditions of perfect competition), then a straight-line isorevenue curve can be drawn. At each point on R_1 in Figure 11.8, identical revenue is obtained. To optimize, the company will produce at the point of tangency between the isorevenue and isocost curves (point M in the figure). This represents the highest revenue that the company can attain for a given total cost. If revenue at this point is greater than cost, economic profit will result.

The company could also move from one isocost curve to another (e.g., from I_1 to I_2 to I_3), and consequently from one isorevenue curve to another, representing the use of additional variable resources. Production would take place at the tangency point that results in the largest difference between total revenue and total cost. This point signifies the maximum economic profit the company can achieve. In the long run, these isocost curves would include changes in all resources, including those (such as plant and equipment) that are fixed in the short run. Under conditions of

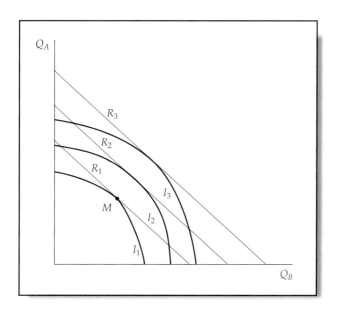

Figure 11.8
Joint Production Using
Variable Proportions

perfect competition, the optimal tangency would occur where total revenue just equals total cost, with no economic profit. At all other points, economic losses would be sustained.

We have limited our discussion to a simple model, utilizing only two products and assuming perfect competition. Much more complex models could be developed, involving more than two products, noncompetitive conditions, and demand interrelationships, for example. The results would be more difficult to obtain, and relatively complicated mathematical models would have to be introduced, but the principles of economic maximization would still apply. Whenever a company takes action in introducing a new product, producing more of one at the expense of another or eliminating a certain commodity from its product line, and when such action is taken to improve its short-run or long-run profitability, the company is guided by the basic principle of equating marginal cost with marginal revenue.

TRANSFER PRICING

In today's complex industrial world, many companies have subdivided their operations into several groups or divisions. As a product moves from its early stages to the point where it is ready to be sold to consumers, it is passed from one operating division of the company to another. In the automobile industry, for example, various auto parts may be produced in different plants and then assembled into the finished product in yet another plant. Computer and peripheral equipment components may be produced in one plant and assembled into different products at other plants. Then, to sell the products, the marketing arm of the company may have to assemble the various individual machines into complete systems.

To continue this analysis, it is necessary to address the notion of *profit center,* a frequently used term that refers to a situation prevalent in large corporations. The management of each division is charged with a profit objective. Thus, each stage of production must measure its costs and then establish a price at which it will "transfer" its product to the next stage. However, if each intermediate profit center were to set its price to maximize its own profit, the price of the final product may not maximize the profit of the company as a whole, which is the appropriate objective. The price set by the division transferring the intermediate product becomes the cost of the division receiving this product. If that price is set too high, this may start a chain reaction resulting in the final product price being higher than the price which would maximize the company's profit. The **transfer pricing** mechanism must be geared toward maximizing total company profit; therefore, the final pricing policy may be dictated centrally from the top of the corporation.

Such processes can be extremely complicated, particularly if there are more than two steps in the transfer process. Further, the intermediate products may be only for internal usage. On the other hand, the producing division may also be selling its product in an external market, and the receiving division may be free to purchase the intermediate product from a competitor, if that would improve the company's profit situation. Let us discuss each of these cases in turn. To simplify matters, we will assume the existence of just two divisions, one that manufactures components (division C), and another that assembles them into the final product and sells it (division A).

No External Markets

If there is no possibility for division A to buy components from a competing firm and no possibility for division C to sell components to other companies, then the two divisions must deal with equal quantities; division C will produce exactly the number of components that will be utilized by division A for assembly and sales. This situation is illustrated in Figure 11.9. The company will be faced by a demand curve for the final product and two marginal cost curves (D, MC_A, and MC_c). The two marginal cost curves, one for each division, will be summed vertically to obtain total marginal cost (MC), and the company will maximize its total profit by equating the total marginal cost with marginal revenue (MR). Production will take place at that intersection (point B), and the price for the final product will be the corresponding price on the demand curve (point A). The quantity sold is Q_t. The transfer price for the intermediate product is P_c.

External Markets

It may be possible for division C to sell its (intermediate) product in a competitive market and for division A to purchase division C's product (an identical product) in a competitive market. In that case, the pricing of the product will proceed as follows:

1. Division C will produce at the point where its marginal cost equals the market price. (Because we are assuming the existence of a competitive market, the demand curve is horizontal, resulting in a uniform price regardless of quantity.)
2. The cost of the intermediate product to division A is the market price. This will be added to division A's marginal cost curve to obtain the total marginal cost for the final product.

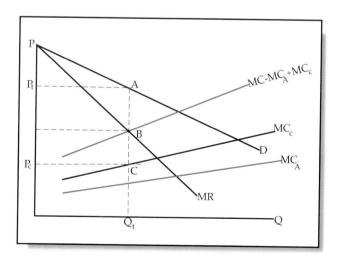

Figure 11.9
Transfer Pricing with No Market for Intermediate Product

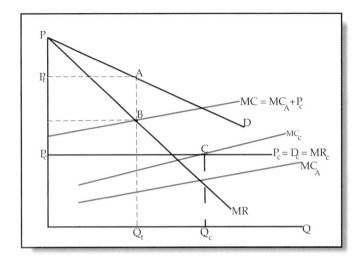

Figure 11.10
Transfer Pricing with Competitive Market for Intermediate Product

3. Production will take place at the quantity where the total marginal cost equals the marginal revenue for the final product.

Figure 11.10 shows a case where there is a competitive market for the intermediate product, and division C produces components in excess of those utilized by the division A. Assume that the market price for division C's product is P_c. The optimal quantity to be produced by C is Q_c, given its marginal cost MC_c. The marginal cost of division C's product to division A is now P_c and the total marginal cost MC equals MC_a plus P_c. The company will sell its product at optimal price P_t at quantity Q_t. Division C will sell quantity Q_c minus Q_t in the competitive market.

Of course, should division C for some reason attempt to price the intermediate product in excess of the market price, then A would buy all of the intermediate product in the external market.

If the optimal output of division C is less than A wishes to buy, then A will turn to the external market for the additional units of the intermediate product it needs to maximize company profits. The graph for this situation would be quite similar to Figure 11.10, and we will leave it to the reader to illustrate this particular situation.

Multinational Transfer Pricing

While transfer pricing presents a domestic company with many problems, the matter becomes even more complex when a multinational corporation is involved, where an internal transfer involves movement across borders. This additional complication arises from the fact that a transfer price may be manipulated in such a way as to transfer funds among countries or to affect a company's income tax liability. A company operating in countries A and B would certainly wish to increase its profit in country A, whose income tax rates are lower, at the expense of profit in high-tax country B. To do this, if the company ships components from its manufacturing facility in A to its assembly plant in B, it would charge very high transfer prices, thus increasing its profitability in A and decreasing its profits in B.[35]

The United States as well as other countries have taken action to prevent such tax evasion by multinational companies. Section 482 of the U.S. Internal Revenue Code gives the IRS the authority to "shift around income and expense figures to arrive at what the government considers a more equitable result."[36] In such cases, the burden of proof is on the taxpayer to prove that the IRS has been incorrect in reallocating income.

The IRS requires that transfer pricing is done on an "arm's length" relationship. The best evidence of such relationship is that prices resemble those that would be established between two independent companies.

Despite the fact that transfer price proceedings have been a prominent activity of the IRS, a recent study estimated that the loss in tax revenues to the U.S. government in the year 2000 was in excess of $44 billion. The largest losses were incurred in our trade with Canada and Japan.[37]

Here are just a few examples of transfer pricing proceedings from the U.S. as well as other countries. In 1994, Japanese tax authorities charged Coca-Cola Japan with a penalty tax of 15 billion yen (approximately $100 million), claiming that brand and royalty payments for three years (to March 1992) transferred by Coca-Cola to its U.S. parent were too high by $36 billion yen.[38]

A case involving a tax dispute over about $140 million occurred in Houston, Texas, in 1997. The case concerned a Mexican manufacturer of transformers, cable wire, and other products, Conductores de Monterrey, and a Houston distributor, Eletex, Inc. In the years 1988 to 1993, the latter incurred such large losses that it reported no taxable income. The question here was whether the two companies were really independent, or whether Eletex was a representative of Conductores.[39] "Multinational companies face $1 billion of tax adjustments following the Australian Taxation Office's latest round of transfer pricing audits." These adjustments related to the audit of 46 companies.[40]

In Canada, in three separate tax disputes, the government alleged that Canadian subsidiaries of European drug companies deducted improperly about $160 million in costs through transfer pricing practices. The chemicals were produced in "rela-

---

[35]The relationship can be shown by the following simple equation

$$\Delta T = Q \times \Delta P \times t_E - Q \times \Delta P \times t_M$$

where ΔT = the change in the total tax bill
Q = the quantity of products shipped by E (exporter) to M (importer)
ΔP = the change in price of the product
t_E and t_M = the tax rates in the exporting and importing countries, respectively.

If $t_E > t_M$, transfer price should be lowered, and if $t_E < t_M$, transfer price should be raised. How much prices can be changed to minimize total tax payments depends, of course, on the level of the transfer price that would be tolerated by the higher tax government. The equation would become more complex if we had included import duties.

[36]C. Carroll, "IRS Targets Local Company in 'Transfer Pricing' Case," *Houston Business Journal*, February 3, 1997.
[37]Simon J. Pak and John S. Zdanowicz, *U.S. Trade with the World*, November 1, 2001.
[38]E. Terazono, "Coca-Cola Faces Tokyo Penalty Tax," *Financial Times*, March 28, 1994.
[39]Carroll, "IRS Targets Local Company."
[40]Fiona Buffini, "Multinationals Hit For $1bn," *Australian Financial Review*, July 21, 2000, p. 11.

tively tax-friendly countries, such as the Bahamas and Ireland." In one of the cases, the government contends that the drug company had paid up to $1,650 per kilogram of ranitidine HCL (an ingredient in an ulcer medicine) made in Switzerland when the price should have been closer to $250.[41]

OTHER PRICING PRACTICES

Price skimming occurs when a firm is the first to introduce a product. It may have a virtual monopoly, and often will be able to charge high prices and obtain substantial profits before competition enters.

In **penetration pricing** a company sets a relatively low price in order to obtain market share.

With **prestige pricing,** demand for a product may be higher at a higher price because of the prestige that ownership bestows on the buyer.

Psychological pricing takes advantage of the fact that the demand for a particular product may be quite inelastic over a certain range but will become rather elastic at one specific higher or lower price. Such a demand curve has the appearance of a step function.

Complete explanations of these pricing practices can be found in many marketing textbooks.

INTERNATIONAL APPLICATION

The Decline of European Cartels

European governments have in the past tolerated and supported monopolies, and while pricing cartels have been illegal, they have flourished. But this situation is currently changing. Where monopolies existed, markets are now opening up.

For instance, in early 1998, when new rules permitted competition with Deutsche Telekom, TelePassport, a small company that discounts telephone services, signed up over 19,000 customers in 20 days. Deutsche Telekom then proceeded to cut its prices to fight this competition. Indeed, it was reported that, by the middle of 1999, prices of domestic long-distance calls had decreased by up to 85 percent. New telephone companies had obtained 35 percent of the long-distance and overseas call markets.

Airline monopolies have also been breaking up. Three small start-up companies have now captured 22 percent of the German market, and in Italy, several new small companies have decreased Alitalia's market share from 90 to 75 percent.

Although changes in the energy sector have been slow, and markets are opening only in 1999, some large consumers had already been able to secure lower electrical rates before that date. Enron Corporation, a Houston, Texas, company has entered

---

[41]Colin Freeze, "Taxman Targets Drug Firms Government Alleges Offshore Purchases Were Inflated to Dodge Canadian Taxes," *The Globe and Mail,* July 7, 2001.

the European market and is selling electricity. Progress may be slow, but freer markets are on the increase in Europe. "Once the ball starts rolling, competitive pressures will make things move very quickly," stated Mark E. Frevert, CEO of Enron's European unit.[42]

The European Carton-Board Cartel

A recent case involving 19 carton-board producers in ten European countries actually resembles the electrical manufacturers' case discussed previously.

In July 1994, the European Commission imposed record fines of $159 million on 19 producers. The cartel involved a market-sharing agreement and orchestrated 6-10 percent price increases each six months during the period from 1987 to 1990. Monthly "social" meetings were arranged at luxury hotels (most frequently in Zurich). "The cartel's members then compared the state of their order books to judge when best to introduce a price increase. Sometimes the big producers agreed on temporary plant stoppages to keep production under control."[43] Fake minutes were drawn up to disguise the business that was transacted.

The European Commission acted after complaints by the industry's customers about the continual price increases during a period of sharp economic downturn. In 1991, officials of the commission staged simultaneous raids on the producers and found private notes documenting the dates and amounts of price increases. One of the companies decided to admit to the conspiracy and aided the probe, which resulted in heavy fines.

The European Vitamin Cartel

In November 2001, the European Commission imposed fines totaling over 850 million euros (approximately $747 million) on 13 pharmaceutical companies for price fixing of vitamins that had spread over nine years. Most of the fine was levied on Roche of Switzerland and BASF of Germany. This decision followed two years after the United States, after a similar investigation, had fined the same two companies an amount exceeding $700. It was said that the companies had "virtually operated as a single company." The cartels met each month or quarter, exchanged sales and price data, and reviewed quotas allotted to each company. In some cases, "participants even prepared an annual 'budget' to adjust sales according to each company's quota."[44]

---

[42]This section is based on T. Peterson, "The Cartels Are Finally Crumbling," *Business Week*, February 2, 1998, p. 52; R. Atkins, "German Phone Call Prices Cut," *Financial Times*, July 9, 1999.

[43]This discussion and quotation are based on Emma Tucker, "Price-fixing Cartel Given Record Fine by Brussels," *Financial Times*, July 14, 1994, and Emma Tucker, "Rise and Fall of a House of Cards," *Financial Times*, July 15, 1994.

[44]Francesco Guerrera and Birgit Jennen, "European Groups Face Record Fines for Roles in Price-fixing," *Financial Times*, November 21, 2001; Francesco Guerrera, "Monti Lashes 'Vitamins AG' Cartel," *Financial Times*, November 22, 2001.

The Solution

 G L O B A L F O O D S

Rebecca James went to see Philip Olds of the food division to solicit his advice on the bid she intended to make for the bottled water supply contract with the large airport catering company.

"One thing is certain," he said. "You have to bid at a price considerably lower than the price at which you sell to small retail stores. These stores have a leeway in how much they can charge their customers, since they are really selling convenience. A small variance in price is not going to change their sales significantly, so they will not stop buying from us as long as our price is not out of line.

"However, your potential new customer intends to give a contract to only one additional supplier, and 10 cents per case will make a large difference when hundreds of thousands of cases are involved. Thus, you will have to shave your markup as much as possible. It may turn out that you will make precious little profit, if any, on this contract."

Philip was telling Rebecca that the demand price elasticity of the large caterer was quite different from that of the small retailers. As a result, Global Foods could sell to these two markets at different prices.

Rebecca is thus confronted with a case of price discrimination. The demand elasticities in the two markets are probably quite different; thus, higher prices can be charged in the market displaying lower elasticity. And the separation of the two markets (i.e., no cross-selling) represents the second important condition for the existence of price discrimination. Another important consideration for Rebecca is that the price to be charged must enable the company to gain a foothold in this large market (penetration or entry pricing).

Back in her office, Rebecca begins to work on determining the price. She assumes that the average cost per case of "Waterpure" for the two customers is the same. Although this is certainly not quite accurate (the large shipments the company will make to the new customer if the bid is won will probably create some cost savings), the unit cost differences probably will not be significant, so her analysis will lose little if she assumes equality.

She estimates the company's usual markup to be about 50 percent. After some additional consideration, and a review of some data for the industry that she obtained, she feels that a 20 percent markup would put the company in a good competitive position.

Before making this recommendation to her boss, she will consult with the finance and accounting departments to determine what, if any, profit would be realized on this transaction. She will, of course, include this analysis with her recommendation. It is quite possible that at this low price profit will be extremely marginal, and she will then have to argue that obtaining a foothold in this market will have beneficial long-run consequences.

(*Continued*)

The decision that she has made has some rather important implications for the estimate of demand elasticities for the two classes of customers. The lower the demand elasticity, the higher will be the markup that a company can obtain. Following the equation developed previously,

$$(1 + M) = \frac{E_p}{E_p + 1}$$

(where demand elasticity is a negative number), an elasticity of 3 conforms to a markup of 50 percent, whereas an elasticity of 6 corresponds to a 20 percent markup. Of course, these numbers are approximations, but such an estimate could be of great help to Rebecca in her attempt to set the proper price.

SUMMARY

This chapter has built on the foundation laid in chapters 9 and 10 by applying the principles of pricing and output to specific pricing situations, most under conditions of imperfect competition. Briefly, we learned the following:

1. Cartels are formed to avoid the uncertainties of a possible reaction by one competitor to price and production actions by another. The firms in the industry agree on unified pricing and production actions to maximize profits. However, as history shows, such arrangements are not always stable.
2. Price leadership exists when one company establishes a price and others follow. Two types of price leadership were discussed: barometric and dominant.
3. Baumol's model describes the actions of a company whose objective is to maximize revenue (rather than profits) subject to a minimum profit constraint.
4. Price discrimination (or differential pricing) exists when a product is sold in different markets at different prices. Third-degree price discrimination is the most common. By charging different prices in separate markets that have demand curves with different price elasticities, a firm can increase its profits over what they would be if a uniform price were charged.
5. Cost-plus pricing appears to be a very common method. However, such pricing does not necessarily imply that marginal principles and demand curve effects are not taken into consideration.
6. Multiproduct pricing was examined, because most firms and plants produce more than one product at the same time. Multiple products produced by one firm can be complements or substitutes, both on the demand side and the supply side. Four possible cases were discussed, and it was shown how application of the marginal principle brings about profit maximization.
7. Several other pricing practices were summarized. One was transfer pricing, which is used to determine the price of a product that progresses through several stages of production within a firm.

IMPORTANT CONCEPTS

Barometric price leadership: In an oligopolistic industry, a situation in which one firm, perceiving that demand and supply conditions warrant it, announces a price change, expecting that other firms will follow. (p. 503)

Baumol model: A model hypothesizing that firms seek to maximize their revenue subject to some minimum profit requirement (i.e., the profit constraint). (p. 505)

Cartel: A collusive arrangement in oligopolistic markets. Producers agree on unified pricing and production actions to maximize profits and to eliminate the rigors of competition. (p. 498)

Cost-plus pricing: Also called *full-cost pricing,* a practice in which prices are calculated by adding a markup to total cost. (p. 519)

Dominant price leadership: In an oligopolistic industry, a firm, usually the largest in the industry, sets a price at which it will maximize its profits, allowing other firms to sell as much as they wish at that price. (p. 503)

Multiproduct pricing: Pricing that reflects the interrelationship among multiple products of a firm that are substitutes or complements. (p. 523)

Penetration pricing: A company charges a lower price than indicated by economic analysis in order to gain a foothold in the market. (p. 532)

Prestige pricing: A perception that charging a higher price will increase quantity sold because of the prestige obtained by the buyer. (p. 532)

Price discrimination: A situation in which an identical product is sold in different markets at different prices. (p. 506)

Price leadership: One company in an oligopolistic industry establishes the price, and the other companies follow. Two types of price leadership are common: barometric and dominant. (p. 502)

Price skimming: The practice of charging a higher price than indicated by economic analysis when a company introduces a new product and competition is weak. (p. 532)

Psychological pricing: The practice of charging, for example, $9.95 rather than $10 for a product in the belief that such pricing will create the illusion of significantly lower price to the consumer. (p. 532)

Transfer pricing: A method to correctly price a product as it is transferred from one stage of production to the next. (p. 528)

QUESTIONS

1. "If a company sets its prices on the basis of a cost-plus calculation, it cannot possibly suffer a loss on its products." True or false? Comment.

2. Price discrimination is often defended on the basis of equity. What is meant by this statement? Comment on its validity.

3. Which products in each pair would tend to have higher markups in a supermarket?
   a. Cigarettes versus tomatoes
   b. Potatoes versus orange juice

4. Many years ago, a neighborhood lunch counter charged 15 cents for a cup of coffee and 15 cents for a buttered hard roll. One day, a customer ordered the two items and was told that the total price was 35 cents. When the customer asked which of the two items had been raised by 5 cents, the owner's condescending reply was, "Which do you think?" In your opinion, which of the two items was affected and why?

5. Differentiate *barometric* price leadership and *dominant* price leadership.

6. Is there a similarity between cartel pricing and monopoly pricing?

7. What conditions are favorable to the formation and maintenance of a cartel?

8. Can government be a potent force in the establishment and maintenance of monopolistic conditions? Name and describe such occurrences.

9. Describe the properties of the Baumol revenue maximization model. Do you consider this to be a good alternative to the profit maximization model?

10. Telephone companies charge different rates for calls during the day, in the evening, and at night or weekends. Do you consider this to be price discrimination?

11. Is cost-plus pricing necessarily inconsistent with marginal pricing?

12. Airline ticket prices may differ with respect to when the ticket is bought, how long a passenger remains on the trip (e.g., over a weekend) and other variables. Are these differences a case of price discrimination?

13. Does cost-plus pricing necessarily ignore the demand curve?

14. Define and describe (giving examples):

a. Transfer pricing
b. Psychological pricing
c. Price skimming
d. Penetration pricing

15. Under what circumstances would a discriminating monopolist produce a more socially optimal quantity than a nondiscriminating monopolist? Is there any situation under which a discriminating monopolist could produce the quantity that would be produced under competition?

16. Why should a government be concerned with the pricing of products that a company transfers to an affiliate in another country?

PROBLEMS

1. There are only two firms in the widget industry. The total demand for widgets is $Q = 30 - 2P$. The two firms have identical cost functions, $TC = 3 + 10Q$. The two firms agree to collude and act as though the industry were a monopoly. At what price and quantity will this cartel maximize its profit?

2. An amusement park, whose customer set is made up of two markets, adults and children, has developed demand schedules as follows:

	Quantity	
Price ($)	Adults	Children
5	15	20
6	14	18
7	13	16
8	12	14
9	11	12
10	10	10
11	9	8
12	8	6
13	7	4
14	6	2

The marginal operating cost of each unit of quantity is $5. (*Hint:* Since marginal cost is a constant, so is average variable cost. Ignore fixed cost.) The owners of the amusement park wish to maximize profits.

a. Calculate the price, quantity, and profit if

(1) The amusement park charges a different price in each market.

(2) The amusement park charges the same price in the two markets combined.

(3) Explain the difference in the profit realized under the two situations.

Chapter 11 Special Pricing Practices

b. (Mathematical solution) The demand schedules presented in problem 2 can be expressed in equation form as follows (where subscript A refers to the adult market, subscript C to the market for children, and subscript T to the two markets combined):

$$Q_A = 20 - 1P_A$$

$$Q_C = 30 - 2P_C$$

$$Q_T = 50 - 3P_T$$

Solve these equations for the maximum profit that the amusement park will attain when it charges different prices in the two markets and when it charges a single price for the combined market.

3. The Bramwell Corporation has estimated its demand function and total cost function to be as follows:

$$Q = 25 - 0.05P$$

$$TC = 700 + 200Q$$

Answer the following questions either by developing demand and cost schedules (*hint:* use quantities from 1 to 14) or by solving the equations.
   a. What will be the price and quantity if Bramwell wants to
   (1) Maximize profits?
   (2) Maximize revenue?
   (3) Maximize revenue but require the profit to be a minimum of $300?
   b. Now assume that the cost function is $TC = 780 + 200Q$ while the demand function remains the same. What will the price and quantity be if Bramwell wants to
   (1) Maximize profits?
   (2) Maximize revenue?
   (3) Maximize revenue but require the profit to be a minimum of $300?
   c. Why are the answers the same in $a(1)$ and $b(1)$ but different in $a(3)$ and $b(3)$?
4. The Great Southern Paper Company has the following marginal cost schedule for producing pulp:

Quantity (tons)	Marginal Cost
1	$18
2	20
3	25
4	33
5	43

Pulp can be bought in the open market for $25 per ton. The marginal cost of converting pulp into paper is $MC = 5 + 5Q$, and the demand for paper is $P = 135 - 15Q$. Calculate the marginal cost of paper if the company produces its own pulp. What is the profit-maximizing quantity? Should the company purchase pulp from the outside or produce it inhouse?

5. The purchase price of Fancy Shoes, sold by Bradbury Footwear Stores, is $30 per pair. The company's economist has estimated the point price elasticity to be -1.8. What price should the company charge if it wants to maximize its profits?

6. An airplane manufacturer has annual fixed costs of $50 million. Its variable costs are expected to be $2 million per plane. If the manufacturer wants to earn a 10 percent rate of return on its investment of $400 million and expects to produce 100 aircraft this year, what will its markup on total cost have to be? If it expects to produce 150 aircraft, what will its markup have to be?

7. Schultz's Orchard grows only two types of fruit—apples and peaches—and over the years it has been able to chart two production levels and the resulting total cost. The figures are shown in the following table, where quantity produced is given in bushels.

Apples	Peaches	Apples	Peaches
900	0	1,400	0
800	200	1,200	300
600	400	900	600
400	500	700	700
250	550	300	850
0	600	0	900
Total cost: $15,000		Total cost: $25,000	

This year it is expected that the price of apples will be $30 per bushel and that of peaches will be $45 per bushel.

What is the best production level at each cost? How much is the profit at each level?

8. The Prestige Office Equipment Company produces and sells different types of office furniture. One of the important items it sells is a high-quality desk. During the past year, Prestige sold 5,000 of these at a price of $500 each. The contribution profit for this line of furniture last year was $700,000.

A consultant suggests that Prestige decrease the price of each desk by $30. In his opinion, another 500 desks could then be sold, and the total profit would be maintained. A trade publication that employs an economist has estimated price elasticity of office furniture (including desks) to be about −1.8.

Assume that the variable unit cost per desk in the coming year will remain the same. Evaluate the consultant's proposal. Be sure to include in your answer the price elasticity assumed by the consultant, as well as the published elasticity estimate.

9. The XYZ Multinational Corporation has manufacturing facilities in country A and an assembly plant in country B. The company ships manufactured units from its plant in A to its assembly plant in B.

a. In April 2002, the company will ship 1,000 units with a production cost of 650 per unit to its plant in country B. Its operating expenses in A are 15,000 for the month. The income tax rate in A is 20% and in B 40%. The company plans to have a transfer price of 100 per unit. The final product can be sold in B for 1400. B's operating expenses are 10,000 during the month. How much will be the combined profits of the two operations in April 2002?

b. Could the company benefit by changing the transfer price to 120?

c. Now, suppose the income tax rate in A is 40% while in B it is 20%. What will the combined profit be if all other numbers are the same as in a. above?

d. What would be the result in c. if the company decreased its transfer price to 900?

Chapter 11   Special Pricing Practices

539

10. The royalties received by an author for writing a college text are frequently set at a rate of about 15 percent of the publisher's book price. This may create a conflict between the goals of a profit-maximizing publisher and those of a royalty-maximizing author. As a student consumer (assuming that you have to pay for your textbooks), whose goal would be more beneficial to you? Why? Demonstrate this situation graphically (assume a downward-sloping demand curve).

11. The Prime Company produces two products, X and Y. They are produced jointly so that for each X manufactured a unit of Y is also produced. The joint cost function is

$$TC = 50 + 2Q + .5Q^2$$

Q represents the number of joint units produced. The demand equations for the two products are the following:

$$Q_x = 100 - P_x$$

$$Q_y = 60 - 2P_y$$

a. How many units should the company produce per period?
b. What price should it charge for each of the joint products?
c. What will be the company's profit per period?
Assume that the company is a profit-maximizer.

Chapter 12

Economic Decision Making in the Twenty-first Century: The "Old" Economics of the "New Economy"

The real obvious difference between New Economy and Old Economy companies is, in the end, does the New Economy have money left in the till to pay the severance?

—Judith Fischer, Managing Director of Executive Compensation Advisory Services, in *Industry Standard* (Quoted in *The American Way,* October 15, 2001, p. 62)

Michelle A. Lemire, 28, moved here [San Francisco] from Denver 18 months ago to join the dot-com revolution. She remained enthusiastic when her first employer went bankrupt. She was undeterred when she was laid off from a second job, and even when told by her third company that she could stay—though it had gone broke—if she agreed not to be paid. Her fourth experience ended practically before it began. Netcentives, an ailing Internet advertising company, hired her this summer and laid her off a week later.

—"Promised Land No Longer: Dot-Commers Who Once Flocked to San Francisco Are Turning Elsewhere." *New York Times,* November 10, 2001, p. C1.

B2B now means 'Back to Banking' and B2C is 'Back to Consulting.'

—Anonymous

The Situation

The mood of the room was grim, to say the least.[1] "It all happened so fast," said Nicole Goodman, Senior Vice President of Marketing. "It seemed like all of a sudden there was a proliferation of our competitors' bottled water products throughout the distribution network of restaurants, fast food establishments, and convenience stores that we had always dominated.

"We immediately investigated the cause of this and found that there is a new B2B company called kwench.com that runs a virtual exchange of raw materials suppliers, bottlers, distributors, and retail outlets." Apparently its business model was resilient enough to withstand the collapse of the dot-coms and it continues to grow, particularly because most of its competitors have gone out of business."

"I don't quite understand how this all works," said CEO Bob Burns. "And if you'll forgive me, I must confess, I'm not the 'high tech' type. In fact, my VCR is still blinking twelve o'clock." This remark was greeted with polite laughter. People in the meeting did not know what was funnier: the CEO not knowing how to set his VCR or the fact that he was still using a VCR rather than a DVD player. But at least his candidness seemed to break the gloomy atmosphere of the meeting.

In any event, Nicole had arranged for A.J. Turner, a senior partner with a high-tech consulting firm, to give a half-hour overview of e business and its implications for Global Foods, especially in the beverage segment, where it was being hurt badly by kwench.com. After listening to his presentation, Nicole stepped in. "OK, it's up to us. How do we want to deal with this new type of competition? Do we start our own B2B exchange? Perhaps we can buy the assets of one of kwench's competitors that failed or is about to go bankrupt. Or maybe we should consider buying kwench?"

Ann Jones, the newly appointed VP of Production, responded first. "Well I think we can rule out buying the assets of one of kwench's competitors. There are really no assets to buy, at least not in the accounting or financial sense of the word. What could they have . . . a bunch of servers, PCs, and databases strapped together by software? With all the dot-coms going out of business, these things could be bought for next to nothing. The real asset is in the knowledge of the people, and we could hire people to do this for us. Maybe a few years ago, when the technology sector and the whole economy were booming, this might have been difficult and expensive. But frankly, the current economic situation makes it much easier and cheaper to recruit these types of skills."

"But do we really need to hire these people into the company?" asked Ted Berry, the VP of Human Resources. After all, we could outsource this to a B2B company. I'm sure that any one of the major consulting or outsourcing companies such as IBM's Global Services, EDS, or Accenture would love to do this for us. Or maybe we could use our

(Continued)

own staff with the support of Oracle and Ariba just like Covisint does."
(Not everyone in the room knew who these companies were or what
they did, but no one asked for fear of appearing to be ignorant.)

"I can see that there is a bit more investigative work that we have to
do before making a decision," said Nicole.

"Yes, but let's not spend too much time on this," replied the CEO.
"kwench has already gotten at least a six-month lead on us, and that's a
lifetime in today's business environment."

"You're absolutely right, Bob," answered Nicole. "A.J., will you and
your firm work with me over the next two weeks to come up with a set
of recommendations?"

Without hesitation, A.J. agreed.

---

[1]The idea for this situation comes from Richard Donkin, "Facing up to a virtual response,"
Financial Times, October 5, 2001. In this article, Donkin talks about how "many traditional companies feel threatened by groups that can quickly assemble teams of experts using the net."

INTRODUCTION

This chapter has two primary objectives. First, it examines the future challenges for
managers in light of the tremendous changes in business practices and life-styles that
have occurred because of the Internet. In fact, the explosion of business activity on
the Internet during the second half of the last decade prompted everyone in the business and academic communities to adopt the term *new economy.* Second, it suggests
ways in which the analytical tools and concepts of the *old economy* can be applied to
the new economy.

In this age of electronic mass communication, we have found that acronyms,
buzzwords, and catchy names or phrases are an essential part of the media "sound
bite." *New economy* is a good example of this. As is often the case with catch phrases,
there is no formal or precise definition of this term. In our review of the literature and
the popular press, we have observed both "macro" and "micro" elements of this
term. But the real essence of the new economy is the rise of the myriad of new *business models* and activities made possible by the Internet and the World Wide Web.
This chapter focuses on the microeconomics of the new economy.[2]

---

[2]From the macro standpoint, writers have used the term *new economy* in reference to the significant
increase in productivity that has occurred in the United States over the past decade. A major reason for
this increase in purported to be the heavy investment in information technology. In turn, as the argument
continued, this productivity increase contributed substantially to the almost decade-long economic
expansion of the American economy without the ill side effect of inflation. Some economists even went
so far as to think that this lengthy expansion heralded the end of business cycles. Of course we know
now that this was a false hope. The booming U.S. economy of the 1990s proved to be no different from
any previous period of expansion. Sometime in early 2000, the economy began to slow down. On
November 14, 2001, *The New York Times* reported that economists determined that the recession had
begun in March 2001.

New business magazines devoted almost exclusively to the new economy began to spring up. Among the more prominent were *Industry Standard* (now defunct), *Business 2.0,* and *Fast Company.* Well-established sources of business news such as the *New York Times* and *The Wall Street Journal* started to run weekly columns on "the new economy." These media, along with the entire community of business practitioners and academics, started using a dizzying array of business acronyms such as B2C and B2B, *broadband, firewalls, portals,* and *Web server application programming interface.* The term *business model* is itself one of the many buzzwords frequently used in a typical discussion of the new economy.[3] Furthermore, thousands of companies eager to strike it rich in this new economy sprang up with exotic, alphanumeric or quirky names such as Akamai (the Hawaiian word for smart) Technologies, i2, Google.com, and Boo.com. So many of these companies had ".com" attached to their name that they were called, appropriately enough, "dot-coms."

The lure of the new economy was that it supposedly offered businesses new ways to make money (i.e., new business models) that were deemed to be fundamentally different from the old economy. For example, a typical new economy business began with the premise that a key success factor was the domination of *marketspace.*[4] But in this case, domination is not necessarily measured in terms of revenue or profit. Such a thought was more for old economy firms. Instead, the idea was to first garner as many "hits" or "eyeballs" as possible and then later to generate revenue and maybe eventually to earn a profit. One of the earliest demonstrations of this is AOL. Very early in the game, it was just one of three major providers of Internet connection service in combination with a homepage that served as a portal to the Internet. To build marketspace, it began giving away its software along with a free one-month trial period for its services. Eventually, it began to generate revenues and profit from its monthly connection charge supplemented by revenue from the sale of advertising space on its Web site. AOL's strategy was so successful that within a few years, it drove Prodigy out of the Internet service providing business and bought out Compuserve.

But not making a profit did not seem to bother the majority of early dot-com entrepreneurs. Instead their idea of making money involved VCs (venture capitalists), "angels" (early investors who provided initial seed money for the venture), "first round," "second round," and "mezzanine" financing, revenue models (not profit models), IPOs (initial public offerings), and "cash burn rates." At the beginning, those dot-coms that did manage to go public rewarded their lucky shareholders with astronomical returns. Their stock prices were selling at levels many hundreds of times greater than their *revenue.* (Because these dot-coms had yet to earn a profit, it made no sense to talk about *price-earnings ratios.* And since they had nega-

---

[3]In our view a buzzword is a term that sounds impressive but has a common or everyday meaning. On a plane flight during the heyday of the dot-coms, one of the authors found himself seated next to a consultant from McKinsey, arguably the world's most prestigious consulting firm. "I've heard the term *business model* used quite a lot these days, but I can't seem to find an official definition of the term. What do you consultants mean when you use this term?" asked the co-author. The McKinsey consultant replied after pausing briefly as if deep in thought, "When we use the term, we mean . . . the way in which a company makes money."

[4]We have found that among the most frequently terms used by consultants are "business model," "road map" and "space."

tive cash flows, it was equally meaningless to consider *price-cash flow ratios*.) But as the dot-coms began to experience serious cash flow problems or simply to file for bankruptcy, investors realized there was still the need to make money the old-fashioned way: by making a profit. And as a result, the Internet stock bubble burst.

A BRIEF HISTORY AND OVERVIEW OF THE INTERNET

"The Internet is a connection of multiple networks. The networks communicate with each other over a suite of standardized protocols, Transmit Control Protocol/Internet Protocol (TCP/IP), in which data is broken up into 'envelopes' called packets."[5] The story of how the Internet developed should be known to most readers. But since it is safe to say that there would be no new economy without it, we will provide a brief history and overview of the Net.[6]

Early Beginnings

In 1969 the Department of Defense's Advanced Research Projects Agency (DARPA) wanted scientists working in different universities around the country to be able to share research information among themselves in a secure and efficient manner. The United States was still in the midst of the Cold War, and DARPA wanted to develop a communications network for these scientists that could withstand a nuclear attack. And so it created the Advanced Research Projects Agency Network or ARPANET. ARPANET used the concept of packet switching developed by the Rand Corporation in 1962. Packet switching has the advantage of allowing packets from multiple computers to share the same circuit. In contrast, circuit switching, the method used in voice telephony, requires a separate connection for each transmission. (Recall on Mother's Day when you try to call mom, you are often greeted with "We're sorry, but all circuits are busy . . ."). Also, in the event of an attack, if certain computers go down, packet switching will automatically reroute data to other computers in the network. This cannot be done for signals carried on a circuit-switched network.[7]

In 1984, with the steady addition of many more network sites, the term *Internet* began to be used. In 1987, the management of the Internet was transferred from the Department of Defense to the National Science Foundation. In 1995, the NSF turned over the management of the Internet backbone to commercial entities. Among them are Sprint, UUNET (now owned by WorldCom), and Cable & Wireless.

---

[5]Annabel Z. Dodd, *The Essential Guide to Telecommunications*, 3d ed., Upper Saddle River, NJ: Prentice Hall, 2001, p. 316.
[6]There are numerous chapters containing a history of the Internet in most books on e-business. For this section, we have relied heavily on two good sources: Dodd, op cit., chapter 8, and Angus J. Kennedy, *The Rough Guide to the Internet*, London: Rough Guides, Inc., 2001, chapter 16.
[7]Sadly, this particular advantage of packet switching over circuit switching was demonstrated when the World Trade Center was attacked on September 11, 2001. A number of financial institutions lost major chunks of their communications because a large part of their voice and data networks relied on circuit switching.

The World Wide Web

The World Wide Web is the first major breakthrough that allowed the explosion of commercial activities on the Internet that we now simply take for granted. It was created in 1989 by Tim Berners-Lee at the European Laboratory for Particle Physics (CERN). Prior to the Web, users of the Internet had to be a lot more "computer literate" than the average user today. In many respects, it is analogous to using the PC with DOS rather than Windows or the Mac. The Web is not a separate part of the Internet. Prior to the Web, the Internet could only handle the transmission of text files. The Web provides a way of simplifying navigation on the Internet. It also enriches Internet content by allowing information to be sent in the form of audio, video, and color graphics.

Web Browsers

The second major breakthrough for commercial activity on the Internet was the Web browser. The browser enabled users to find Web sites without having to be knowledgeable enough to type in special computer commands on their PC. With a browser, users just type in an address or click on a bookmark to find an organization's home page. The U.S. federal government funded the development of the first browser called Mosaic. It was supposed to be *the* standard for browsing on the Net. However, in 1995, Jim Clark of Silicon Graphics and the key developers of Mosaic at the University of Illinois started their own company, Netscape Communications. Their pricing strategy for their browser, Netscape Navigator, was rather unique at the time: they simply gave it away. To be sure, Netscape Navigator was a good product, particularly for commercial applications. But to no one's surprise, it quickly surpassed Mosaic in popularity among Net users. (The strategy of giving the product away and then trying to generate revenue by selling complementary products became a common business model for dot-com companies. The economics of this approach is discussed at later points in the chapter.)

Netscape's browser caught Microsoft by surprise. But as soon as it realized that this was a technology that could disrupt its dominance in the PC software market, the company quickly shifted its resources to the Internet. Within about six months, Microsoft produced its own version of the browser called Internet Explorer. But Microsoft is best known for its marketing rather than its development of technology. In 1996, about a year after Netscape had begun flooding the market with free software, Microsoft negotiated a deal with AOL, the leading ISP (Internet service provider), to use Internet Explorer as its Web browser. Moreover, Microsoft installed its browser on the next version of its operating system, Windows 98. (Interestingly enough, the way in which Microsoft bundled its browser with its Windows operating system became the foundation for the Department of Justice suit against the company. See our discussion of this suit in chapter 15.)

Fearing Microsoft's move to dominate the Internet with its browser, AOL purchased Netscape Communications in late 1998. It now seems that their early concerns about Microsoft were well founded. Analysts and observers of the Internet believe that the battle for Internet dominance is shaping up to be Microsoft vs. AOL Time-Warner.

The Internet Infrastructure

We tend to take for granted that we can e-mail messages using the Internet to anyone anywhere in the world. But do we stop and think what makes this possible? The Internet is not owned or operated by one organization. Instead, it is an arrangement of interconnected networks that spans the globe. Some of the major network service providers in the United States are AT&T, Cable & Wireless, Spring, WorldCom, Genuity, Verio, and Qwest. They interact with foreign network service providers, many of whom are the incumbent telecom companies of their respective countries, to form the worldwide Internet. The actual network hardware (and accompanying software) are developed, manufactured, and sold to these network service providers by such companies as Cisco, Nortel, Lucent (switches and routers), and Corning (fiber optic cable).

For the end user of the Internet, the device of choice is still the PC. Major players such as Dell, Compaq, IBM, and Hewlett-Packard immediately come to mind. Personal digital assistants such as those made by Palm and Mindspring and mobile phones such as those made by Nokia, Samsung, Motorola, and Ericsson will start to become popular ways to access the Net as wireless technology continues to improve.

The Interface Between Service Providers and Users

The different Internet networks themselves need to be connected in a smooth and seamless fashion. The connection of networks with other networks therefore requires *peering* or network access points. In the United States the four peering sites are located in New Jersey, Washington, D.C., Chicago, and San Francisco. These sites are run by private companies, the most prominent of which is WorldCom. In addition, traffic at these peering sites may become bogged down (just as in any freeway interchange), so network service providers such as Genuity, Sprint, and PSINet have started private peering sites.

Another important element of the interface between networks and users is the *content delivery network* (CDN). CDNs make access to Web pages easier by placing them on servers nearer to the users. This enables the content to load faster onto people's PCs. This service is called *caching*. To use the old catalog business as an analogy, it would be similar to L.L.Bean or Lands' End delivering their catalogs to people's homes (or perhaps to local post offices) rather than to have them available only at its stores. There are two types of CDN business models. The first type is a service bureau. It provides caching services to heavy users of the Web. Among them are content providers (e.g., CNN, C-SPAN, and MSNBC-COM), traditional retailers with online services (e.g., Barnes and Noble and Lands' End), and Web portals (e.g., Yahoo! and Excite).

The second type of business model entails the selling of caching hardware and software to organizations who wish to manage this service themselves. Companies such as Inktomi, Nortel, and Cisco will sell these products to network service providers such as AT&T, NT&T (Nippon Telegraph and Telephone), Bell South, and companies that specialize in or provide Web hosting services as one of their lines of business (e.g., Exodus and Intel).[8]

Gateways to the World Wide Web

Internet Service Providers (ISPs)

The primary service offered by these companies is Internet access. In so doing, they also offer e-mail, domain registration, and Web page hosting and design. Leading companies include Genuity, WorldCom, Sprint, AT&T, MindSpring, Road Runner, and NetZero. As essential as their service is to the new economy, they too have been adversely affected by the bursting dot-com bubble. In late 2001, Excite@Home declared bankruptcy and was liquidated in May of that year.

Portals

A portal is the site that greets a customer when they first go online. It is like the virtual version of a mall directory and store greeter. But of course it is much more. The banner ads and headlines with accompanying links can direct customers to other sites in an instant. A portal can be provided by companies who specialize in this type of service, such as Yahoo!, or it can be combined with Internet connection services. The dominant ISP/Portal is AOL Time Warner.

Search Engines

Once the World Wide Web was created, it opened the door for millions of companies and individuals to establish their own Web sites. The problem quickly became one of finding the search engines that would be most helpful to the customer or user. Among the leading search engines are Ask Jeeves, Inc., Northern Light, HotBot, AltaVista, DogPile, LookSmart, and Google.

An important source of revenue for search engines is a fee that they charge companies for advantageous placement in search results. For example, search engine GoTo.com relies very heavily on these fees. Yahoo! charges for listings but only for retail products. (See our later discussion on this source of revenue for Yahoo!). Google (which also happens to be our favorite search engine) does not accept this type of fee but instead licenses its search engine to other companies such as portals (e.g., Yahoo!) and private corporations (for use on their company intranet). Inktomi, another major search engine, provides services to AOL, HotBot, and iWon.

---

[8]The market for caching hardware and services typifies the state of flux of the rest of the Internet industry. Many of the companies that we cite have changed their lines of business or bought or sold other lines of business. In the future, this will probably continue or perhaps these companies will simply go out of business. For example, Nortel's and Cisco's ability to sell caching hardware was made possible by their purchase of Alteon and ArrowPoint respectively. Exodus, a leading "pure play" caching company, was severely affected by the dot-com decline. In late 2001, Cable & Wireless announced its intention of buying the company. In early 2000, Intel tried to diversify away from manufacturing microprocessors for the PC by going into the Web hosting business. In mid-2001, it announced that it was scaling back its original plans to do so.

E-Commerce and E-Business

Along with *new economy, e-commerce* and *e-business* are perhaps the most frequently used terms of the Internet age. And just like the first term, the latter two have no single, agreed-upon definitions. A review of the literature reveals that they have been used in a variety of ways. For example, two university instructors who lecture and consult on technology and business strategy consider e-commerce to encompass both business-to-consumer (B2C) and business-to-business (B2B) activities on the Internet.[9]

A well-respected business consultant with many years of experience first with IBM and later with Deloitte Consultants has this to say about these two "e-terms":

> There are 2.74568 very precise definitions of e-business for every player
> in the field. Mapping the nature, structures, and differences between
> e-Commerce and e-Business has become a subculture all its own . . .
> Here's what we believe is the major difference between e-Commerce and
> e-Business. E-Commerce uses the Internet primarily as a means of conduct-
> ing sales transactions, especially for consumers. E-Business leverages new
> and existing technologies to interact, transact, and collaborate with mem-
> bers of the organization's entire value chain.[10]

TWO FUNDAMENTAL NEW ECONOMY BUSINESS MODELS: B2C AND B2B

B2C

As the term implies, business-to-consumer (B2C) business models utilize the Internet and the World Wide Web to sell goods and services directly to consumers. They stand in contrast to the "brick and mortar" retail establishments who sell their wares in physical locations. The idea of circumventing traditional retail channels by selling goods and services directly to consumers is certainly not new. In fact, one of the first companies to demonstrate the efficiency of direct sales was Sears & Roebuck back in 1911. The Sears Catalog enabled rural residents to bypass country stores that had high prices and limited product lines by ordering directly from Sears through the mail. Farmers were able to buy their farm equipment and supplies, as well as household consumer products ranging from clothing to tombstones from the famed "big book." Eventually, more nimble and focused catalog companies such as L.L.Bean and Lands' End, and specialty retailers such as the Gap and J. Crew, used this same mail order concept and combined it with sophisticated direct-mail strategies, modern call centers, and super-efficient fulfillment operations. They became so successful that they ultimately forced Sears in the late 1980s to abandon its mail order catalog business, one that it had dominated for more than five decades. Ironically, in May, 2002, Sears announced its intention of buying Lands' End.[11]

---

[9]Steffano Korper and Juanita Ellis, *The E-Commerce Book: Building the E-Empire,* San Diego: Academic, 2000, pp. 6–13.
[10]Harry B. DeMaio, *B2B and Beyond: New Business Models Built on Trust,* New York: John Wiley & Sons, 2001, p. 10.
[11]"Recharging Sears," *Time,* May 27, 2002.

Nevertheless, the development of the World Wide Web really enabled retailers to take a quantum leap in direct selling. The benefit-cost equation of selling on the Web seemed so obvious. An "e-retailer" does not require the same kinds of investment in buildings and land needed by traditional retail stores. It would also presumably save money on the cost of preparing, printing, and mailing catalogs. Furthermore, and perhaps most important, "hits" to and orders taken on a company's Web site could be easily tracked, stored (i.e., data warehousing), and analyzed (i.e., data mining).

Amazon.com, a company that we will discuss in detail in a later section of this chapter, was one of the first major B2C companies. But after pure e-commerce retailers such as Amazon.com were established, it was not long before traditional retailers began to realize that they too had to have a presence on the Web. In the words of the popular press, "click and mortar" began to supplement "brick and mortar." Among the major retailers who started their own online operations are Barnes and Noble, Toys r Us, and Wal-mart.

B2B

While the goal of a B2C firm is to provide customers with convenient 24/7 access to goods and services, the goal of a B2B firm is focused more on the reduction of transaction costs within and among businesses. The business model can be far more complicated than the typical B2C model.[12] The term *B2B* simply refers to transactions among businesses conducted on the Internet. But in a broader sense, B2B involves "a much richer combination of cooperative activities, not the least of which is the sharing of data, services, applications, and infrastructure by an ever-widening sphere of partners . . . As the name suggests, B2B is all about interaction, but interaction in the very broadest sense of the term."[13] Along with B2B, consultants have used the term *e-marketplace,* which is defined as "a forum that leverages the Internet to facilitate commerce among business."[14]

A thorough review of e-marketplace activities was conducted by consultants at Booz-Allen & Hamilton.[15] They divided up B2B activity into three ownership models, six basic service offerings, and 24 traditional segments. We provide a summary of their findings on ownership models and service offerings. Interested readers will find the original article well worth reading.

OWNERSHIP MODELS

Type I: The Independent or "Pure Play" E-Marketplace

Description: Provides an independent forum where all the different types of firms involved in the sale of particular products or services can interact with each other online.

---

[12]Transaction costs within and among firms are a critical part of the issue of whether a firm should be a unified, vertically and horizontally integrated entity or a network of individual firms each selling their products and services to each other. Refer back to our discussion of outsourcing and the ideas of Ronald Coase in chapter 2.
[13]Harry DeMaio, pp. 24–25.
[14]Tim Laseter et al. "B2B Benchmark: Winners and Losers in Electronic Exchanges," *Strategy + Business,* Booz-Allen & Hamilton, 4th Quarter, 2001, p. 33.
[15]Ibid., pp. 33–42.

Example: AutoTradeCenter.com. It describes itself as "the automotive industry's leading B2B remarketing company. ATC provides the most technologically advanced Internet tools with industry-proven marketing in the management and redistribution of pre-owned vehicle inventories. ATC markets its services to captive finance companies, financial institutions, fleet/lease companies, and dealers. The ATC 'suite of services' incorporates the marriage of Internet technology, vehicle remarketing, land based operations, and partnering. We deliver 'end to end' solutions that are industry proven, giving buyers and sellers a real competitive edge."[16]

Remarks: This is the first type of e-marketplace that was established. It has been in existence since 1996. This is also the most common type of ownership type, comprising 92 percent of the 2,233 publicized e-marketplaces that were surveyed by Booz-Allen.

Type II: The Consortium

Description: This type consists of various industry players, including competitors. They have joined forces to create an online forum for the exchanges of goods and services.

Examples: Some of the bigger and more well-known B2B consortia are Aeroxchange (Aerospace), Covisint LLC (Automotive), Trade-Ranger (Energy), and Transora (Consumer Goods). Let us look closer at Transora, because it is directly related to the challenges faced by our "Global Foods." Transora bills itself as "the leading global e-marketplace for the consumer packaged goods (CPG) industry. Transora offers an integrated array of collaborative solutions to eliminate inefficiencies throughout the supply chain to deliver breakthrough value."[17] It was founded in early 2000 at a meeting of e-business leaders. As of late 2001, 58 leading global CPG companies have signed on as members of this exchange. Among them are such giants as Coca-Cola, Procter & Gamble, Unilever, Mars, Kraft Foods and Nabisco, and Colgate-Palmolive. These members invested a total of $240 million for the start up of this e-marketplace.

Remarks: Booz-Allen consultants found a total of 92 of these consortium-owned exchanges. Although this represents only five percent of the total in their survey, they believe these types of exchanges have great potential because of the "deep pockets" of their membership.

Type III: The Private Network

Description: This type of e-marketplace is operated for the exclusive use of a single owner and actually was formed as an extension of the owner's in-house system of supply-chain management.

---

[16]ATC homepage: www.autotradecenter.com ATC was founded in 1997. In July 2000, *Forbes* rated it among the "Best on the Web."

[17]www.transora.com, home page.

Examples: Two of the most dominant merchandisers in the world, Dell and Wal-mart, provide excellent examples of this type of e-marketplace ownership. Dell's private network facilitates online transactions among its suppliers, itself, and its corporate customers. Its online catalog (see below on e-marketplace services) is its most important service. Wal-mart could have joined a consortium (such as WorldWide Retail Exchange, LLC, or GlobalNetXchange LLC), but instead formed its own private exchange by moving its supply chain management system, SupplierLink, to the Internet. Its over 10,000 suppliers are now able to obtain online information about sales and inventory levels in every Wal-Mart store. For itself, Wal-mart intends to use the expanded functionality now available on the Internet to "consolidate purchasing worldwide, create global collaboration, establish real-time information flows, bring suppliers online to compete for contracts and negotiate better deals."[18]

Remarks: Private networks are the newest e-marketplace type. They pose the biggest threat to types I and II because companies that have their own e-marketplaces may not be as willing to devote the resources necessary to support the independents or the consortia.

Basic E-Marketplace Services

Booz-Allen consultants identified six core services offered by the three types of e-marketplaces discussed above. They are listed and briefly discussed below.

1. *Information Exchange.* This is the most basic type of service. It does not cost very much and helps to build a sense of community among the participants in the e-marketplace.
2. *Digital Catalogs.* The value of this service is clear. Sellers save money on design, printing, and distribution costs. Buyers have real-time 24/7 access to prices and availability of all the products being offered. Ariba and Commerce One are two leading providers of the software to implement and maintain these catalogs for an electronic exchange.[19]
3. *Online Auctions.* The software to handle online auctions is relatively inexpensive (starting as low as $50,000). However, this service obviously tends to reduce the profit margins of the sellers.
4. *Logistics Services.* This involves the facilitation of the physical flow of goods and services within the firm and among the firm and its suppliers and customers. Therefore, it is much more difficult than simply the transfer of data.
5. *Supply Chain Planning.* Sales and production forecasting is a major part of this type of service. Manugistics Group, Inc. and i2Technologies are the major providers of the software to e-marketplaces that offer this type of service.
6. *Design Collaboration.* This type of service enables original equipment manufacturers (OEMs) to work directly with their first-tier suppliers by enabling them to share design workloads via the Internet.

---

[18]Ibid.
[19]See www.ariba.com and www.commerceone.com.

A B2C or B2B firm may be a technologically sophisticated operation, but first and foremost, it is a business. And the managers of this business are bound to reckon with the economic fundamentals presented in our text. In this section, we examine the economic concepts and tools of analysis that we consider most helpful to those trying to understand the dot-com experience. (The chapters that cover this topic in the text are noted in parentheses.)

The Goals of a Firm (chapters 2 and 11)

In the beginning, the primary goal of the typical B2C dot-com was to build market share or at the minimum "mindshare." Market share implies revenue. Curious Internet surfers who log onto a firm's Web site and start clicking through to product offerings are no different from window shoppers. They may "hit" and they may "click" but they do not spend. But for dot-coms, this build up of mindshare was considered to be almost as good as real money because their primary goal was to build brand equity as well as general consumer awareness of online shopping.

Mindshare and market share became so important for many dot-com entrepreneurs that some seemed to scoff at the idea of profit. And as long as investors believed in what they were trying to do, everything was fine. In some cases, the stock market valuations of certain companies would rise as their quarterly losses increased. As long as their "top line" or at least their reported Web site "hits" rose, dot-com investors did not seem to mind the losses. Consequently, the dot-coms kept right on investing millions in technology, Web site design, development, and maintenance, and even more millions on advertising and promotion.

The collapse of the dot-coms vindicates those who steadfastly maintained the traditional economic view that the long-run goal of a firm is to make a profit, although in the short run it may not be the case. Even the Baumol revenue model, discussed earlier in chapter 11, hypothesizes that firms seek to maximize their revenues *subject to earning a certain minimum profit.*

Estimation and Forecasting of Demand (chapters 5 and 6)

It seems ludicrous now to think about how sure the dot-com entrepreneurs were about the demand for their online services. They were so enthralled with the new economy hyperbole that they apparently did not fully anticipate that the growth in demand would not be sufficient to provide them with a positive cash flow. Moreover, their overconfidence in market potential, coupled with the stock market's astronomical valuations in their stock, made them lax in business fundamentals such as cost management and control. To be fair, we should note that economic techniques of demand estimation and forecasting are difficult to apply in the case of new products, because there is no historical data. And e-business was so new that it was also difficult to find comparable products to use as proxies in the analysis. Because of this lack of historical evidence of past demand for online products and services, their forecast of soaring future demand was just a function of their imagination.

Price Elasticity (chapter 4)

The relationship between the quantity demanded and price is fundamental to the economic understanding of demand. One would expect that because revenue was so important to the dot-com start-ups, they would at least have had some notion of the price elasticity of demand for their products. But once again, since their businesses were new, there was no precedent to go by. Furthermore, their experience also reinforces what we cautioned earlier: sometimes, in the real world, managers must learn about the price elasticity of their products through trial and error. Now that many dot-coms have learned (often the hard way) about the market response to price changes, we can make some observations about price elasticity in the new economy.

What complicates the situation for the dot-coms, particularly the B2C types, were their selection of business models (also referred to more specifically as *revenue models*). Once on the Internet, access to a firm's Web site is free. Therefore, the challenge for B2C dot-coms was to figure out a way to charge for their products or services as well as to determine the right price points. It was easier for some dot-coms than for others. In the late 1980s and early 1990s, AOL was fairly even in market share with the two other major providers of private online services, Compuserve and Prodigy. Then with the advent of the World Wide Web and Netscape Navigator, AOL transformed itself into an Internet service provider and portal.

What enabled AOL to break away from its two major rivals was its decision to launch a mass giveaway campaign for its proprietary software needed to get onto the Net. Once it got a PC user to choose AOL and its software, it charged a price based on minutes of usage. A few years later, it initiated a flat fee of $21.95 for unlimited usage. It later increased this to $23.90 without a significant fall in demand.

Cross-Price Elasticity and Pricing Tactics (chapter 4 and 11)

Because the Internet is an open network, the pricing tactics for dot-coms are particularly challenging. One way in which portals and search engines have dealt with this is to offer free services and then try to generate revenue by selling banner ad space and assessing "click through" fees. The former effort is similar to periodicals that offer low-priced or free subscriptions while selling advertising space. The latter effort, however, is new and is made possible because of the Internet. Also, companies may try to bundle their free and paid services or products together in a complete package. AOL did this by offering its software free but then charging for using its portal and Internet connection services. This is akin to the McDonald's "Happy Meal" whereby a "free" toy is combined with the high profit margin beverage and fries and lower margin burger.

The offering of a low-priced or free item used to entice (or require) the purchase of higher priced ones aptly illustrates the concept of cross-price elasticity of complementary products. The greater the degree of complementarities or cross-price elasticity, the more successful is this pricing tactic. In fact, Microsoft got itself into trouble with the Justice Department by aggressively bundling its Web browser with its operating system.

Break-Even Analysis and Operating Leverage (chapter 9, Appendix B)

The straightforward application of break-even analysis and the concept of operating leverage help to explain why so many of the dot-com retail firms failed. Recall that operating leverage refers to the proportion of a firm's fixed cost to its total cost. A high fixed cost combined with a low variable cost (high operating leverage) means that a firm has to sell a high volume of its product in order to break even. But once it does, its profit increases relatively quickly. The opposite is true for firms with a low operating leverage. All other factors being equal, they do not have to sell as much as high operating leverage companies in order to break even, but the profit earned beyond that point increases more slowly. Initially, it appeared that compared with their "brick and mortar" counterparts, certain B2C firms had certain distinct advantages in their break-even structure.

Let us take, for example, portals and Internet service providers. The three main revenue-generating products of portals are advertising space on their homepage, connections to other sites, and priority placements on search engine listings. In all three cases, the sponsoring companies rather than the end users are expected to pay. Companies pay to have banners advertising their products. They also may be required to pay every time a user clicks onto another Web site (i.e., "click-through" revenue). And finally, companies may pay a portal to have their names listed among the first every time a search engine request is related to what they do. But regardless of who pays, the point is that the variable (or marginal) cost of providing these services is zero or very close to it. This same extremely low variable cost applies to Internet connection services. Assuming that the ISP has the capacity, the cost of an additional connection or e-mail service is practically nothing.

For online retailers, the variable cost is not as low as it is for portals and Internet service providers. But it was felt that online retailers still had an advantage over traditional retailers because they did not have to invest in and operate actual stores. This meant that if all other factors held constant, the online retailers had similar variable costs but lower fixed costs than traditional stores.

Unfortunately for these types of dot-coms, the reality of their break-even structure turned out to be quite different from what was expected. Essentially, here is what happened.

1. Fixed costs turned out to be higher than expected. Although the dot-com retailers did not have stores, they found that they still required warehouses to store their inventory. Both types of assets became very costly. Two examples of this are e-Toys and Amazon.com. E-Toys is out of business[20] and Amazon is still trying to earn a profit. Another type of fixed cost that grew beyond expectations was advertising and promotional spending. Recall that a key element of the dot-com business model was to start out by generating brand equity and mindshare. Huge sums of money were spent on traditional print and media ads to try to accomplish this. This type of fixed overhead was too much, given the slim contribution margins being earned.

---

[20]In mid 2001, traditional toy retailer Kaybee bought the remaining assets of e-Toys, including its Web site and brandname.

2. Variable costs turned out to be higher than expected. In addition, pricing to adequately cover unit variable costs turned out to be more difficult than expected. We have already discussed some of the problems pertaining to the pricing of dot-com products and services. We will elaborate further on the variable cost problem in our discussion of Amazon.com, Webvan, and Peapod.com presented below. In any case, these two factors mean that the contribution or gross profit margin was lower than planned, certainly lower than the level needed to cover the unexpectedly high fixed costs.

3. Handling and distribution costs turned out to be greater than expected. For a retailer, this type of cost is a major part of the total variable cost of doing business. One of the reasons for this is that online grocers such as Webvan required special machinery to assist their warehouse workers in selecting the products by each online customer. Another reason was the added cost of handling returned items.

THE APPLICATION OF OLD ECONOMY CONCEPTS TO NEW ECONOMY BUSINESSES

A good way to appreciate how fundamental economic concepts can be used to analyze new economy firms is to review the experiences of specific dot-com firms. For this discussion we have selected Amazon.com, Yahoo!, and online grocers Webvan and Peapod.com.

Amazon.com

When Amazon.com was launched in 1995, founder and CEO Jeff Bezos envisioned the company to be "the bookseller to beat all booksellers."[21] At first, investors believed wholeheartedly in his vision. From its initial trading price of about $2 per share, the stock rose to over $80 in the next two years.[22] By late 2001, the stock had dropped back down to close to its starting level. As of late 2001, the company had yet to report a profit.

As reported in the already cited article on Amazon.com in *Fortune,* sometime in 2000, a shareholder of the company asked Bezos in a public forum the following question: "Can you tell me what it is exactly that I own?" The article in *Fortune* goes on to relate just how pertinent that question still continues to be.

Early in its life, the two most relevant economic concepts for the firm were operating leverage and price elasticity. To begin with, in order to draw shoppers away from traditional bookstores, Amazon offered significant discounts (20–30 percent) on popular books. The assumption was that the combination of cross-price elasticity (between Amazon and old economy rivals such as Barnes and Noble) and own-price elasticity (simply attracting people to buy more books because of the lower price)

---

[21]"Can Amazon Be Saved?" *Fortune,* November 26, 2001, pp. 156–58.
[22]Up to late 2001, Amazon stock has split twelve times. These figures are expressed on the most recent split-adjusted basis.

would eventually provide Amazon with a dominant share of the retail book market. This pricing decision seemed to work as revenue from book sales began to climb. (Remember at this early stage of B2C businesses, Amazon had to contend with people's reluctance to shop online. Amazon is indeed one of the pioneer dot-coms instrumental in helping people to overcome their initial concerns about the security and reliability of online transactions and the actual delivery of products.)

But soon after take off, the original Amazon.com business model revealed an inherent weakness. The whole idea of an online retail store is to save money on the fixed costs of "brick and mortar." This means inventory and warehouses as well as stores. Amazon soon realized that it could do without the latter but not the former. In exchange for the publishers holding the inventory, Amazon had to pay full or close to full wholesale prices for the book that its customers had ordered online. When combined with their already discounted retail prices, this meant that their profit margins on books sold were squeezed even further. And so it decided to invest in warehouses and inventory. This of course meant that its fixed costs would be higher.

With a higher overhead, there is the need for higher volumes of sales in order to clear the higher break-even point. This, as you well know from your understanding of operating leverage, is an essential lesson of break-even analysis. In order to increase sales volume, Amazon decided to expand its product offerings beyond just books. Click onto its Web site and you will see the following at the top the general product categories of what it sells: health and beauty products, electronics, toys and games, music CDs, DVDs, and so forth. Amazon was no longer a book store. It had transformed itself into a consumer goods store closer to a traditional store such as Kohl's or Wal-Mart, than to Barnes and Noble or Borders. The economics of this transformation proved to be just as daunting as the original business model. More product line offerings led to more inventory "SKUs" (stock keeping units), which in turn led to more warehouses and special equipment to help manage the storage and distribution. Sales continued to grow but Amazon still was not able to show a positive bottom line.

Then at the public meeting in 2000 referred to above, Bezos' answer to the stockholder's query seemed to surprise the entire audience. "What you own is what we like to think of as an incubator for e-commerce companies that can start companies at lower costs and more quickly than any other company in the world."[23] After the meeting, he began to explain to the investment community that being an "incubator" entailed making contractual arrangements with other dot-coms such as drugstore.com, living.com, Audible, and Greenlight.com (an online auto sales company). Each had agreed to pay a fee for being featured on perhaps Amazon's greatest asset: its highly trafficked Web site. Some critics then began to dismiss this new approach as being simply an online mall. But from an economic standpoint, this new line of business appeared to be attractive because it did not require the added cost of more inventory and physical infrastructure. Finally, this fee-based approach would enable Amazon to grow its top line without excessive cost increments, and Amazon could have its long-awaited positive bottom line.

A year later, in 2001, the "online mall" yielded disappointing results. Many of the dot-coms that Amazon had signed up had gone out of business. Moreover, they had

---

[23]"Can Amazon Be Saved?", p. 156.

paid Amazon in their stock rather than in cash. With so many dot-coms out of business, the chances of signing up new companies is very slim. So this has prompted Bezos to again try something different to get the company on its "path to profitability." He has decided to transform Amazon from a dot-com incubator to a service company similar to IBM Global Services or EDS. The company will now run all or part of the e-commerce operations of traditional retailers such as Target, Circuit City, and Borders. It will also sell their products on the company Web site. If these corporate customers so desire, Amazon will run their warehouse and distribution operations and even their Web sites. And so it appears that in 2001, Amazon has decided to become both a B2B and B2C company. Critics are once again as dubious about this new business model as they were with the previous changes. Once again, they do not think that the simple arithmetic of revenue minus expenses will yield a positive number. Even when taking into account the bear market of 2001, Amazon's stock stands as a clear reflection of these doubts.

Yahoo!

Let us review the origin of Yahoo! in the company's own words:

> Yahoo! began as a student hobby and evolved into a global brand that has changed the way people communicate with each other, find and access information and purchase things. The two founders of Yahoo!, David Filo and Jerry Yang, Ph.D. candidates in Electrical Engineering at Stanford University, started their guide in a campus trailer in February 1994 as a way to keep track of their personal interests on the Internet. Before long they were spending more time on their home-brewed lists of favorite links than on their doctoral dissertations. Eventually, Jerry and David's lists became too long and unwieldy, and they broke them out into categories. When the categories became too full, they developed subcategories . . . and the core concept behind Yahoo! was born.[24]

Unlike Amazon.com, Yahoo! has proven that its version of a new economy business model can be profitable. The company began operations in 1995 and started to earn a profit by the third quarter of 1998. By combining a Web site offering of search engine and directory services, news, shopping, and online classified ads, it has managed to garner roughly 200 million visitors a month onto its global network of 24 international sites in 13 languages. With such a base of visitors, it has been able to generate a stream of revenue from advertising and sponsorships sufficient to more than cover its total cost of operations. But Yahoo's business model has not been immune to the bursting of the dot-com bubble in mid-2000. For four straight quarters up to the third quarter of 2001, the company has suffered losses. In late 2001, the company's stock was trading at $8 a share, down from a previous 52-week high of $173.[25]

About 80 percent of the company's revenue comes from advertising. The collapse of dot-com advertising revenue resulted in a 44 percent decline in third quarter 2001

---

[24]Yahoo Web site homepage.
[25]Yahoo's opening day stock price was about $2.75 on a split equivalent basis. Its all-time high was $250 back on January 4, 2000. On September 27, 2001, it had sunk to about $8.00 a share.

revenue from the same period the year before. Because Yahoo has such a high operating leverage (i.e., there is relatively little variable cost associated with providing additional advertising space), the sharp decline in revenue has caused considerable damage to the company's bottom line. In 2000, Yahoo's net profit was $70.8 million. Net *loss* for 2001 was $92.8 million. While Yahoo's current problems can be explained using the concept of cost structure and operating leverage, its ability to come up with solutions for these problems are related more to the concept of price elasticity.

To begin with, the 200 million people who visit the Yahoo! Web site go through the "free admission" gate. Yahoo! is not an Internet service provider like AOL Time Warner. Moreover, once on the site, these visitors can use any number of services available free of charge, such as information searches, Web hosting, and classified advertising. The collapse of ad revenue from dot-com companies has exposed the weakness of this business model. Now, newly appointed CEO Terry Semel has said that his goal is to create more paid service offerings so that advertising charges represent 76 percent of the company's total revenue by the end of 2001 and 50 percent by year end 2004. A key issue now becomes: How will people react when they are charged for services that they have become accustomed to receiving for free?

There is a number of pricing initiatives that Yahoo! has announced it will take. Among them are charging a fee for streaming video, charging a fee for listing items for sale on its auction service, charging for being a top listing on search engine queries, and forcing users of its Web site hosting service who use more than 3 gigabytes of data transfer space to migrate to one of its paid Web-hosting services.

At first, it might seem that demand elasticity is irrelevant to the company's efforts to generate fee income for premium services. When the price goes from zero to a positive number, revenue automatically increases. Nonetheless, the *amount* of incremental revenue that Yahoo will be able to generate with more paid services may well determine its ability to sustain future profits, given the company's relatively high fixed cost structure. Unfortunately, the Wall Street analysts have been very skeptical about Yahoo's plans to diversify its revenue stream with paid services. Speaking in reference to Yahoo's plan to charge the heavy users of its Web-hosting storage space, media analyst Jordan Rohan commented that, "Yahoo's trying to improve its business model, and at the margin it can do so by charging high-intensity users for that intensity. It would make sense that they would charge more for people that have more saved, but it doesn't win any friends."[26] He went on to say that, "If there is a free competitor that's widely known by consumers, then paid services will fail . . ." From the standpoint of investors in the company, he had this to say: "It's hard to get people [i.e., investors] excited about premium services when there are no proven businesses that have made it work."

Rohan is not alone in this way of thinking. In reference to Yahoo's plans to charge for streaming video, Mark Mooradian, an analyst at Jupiter Media Metrix, said, "It's an extremely imprudent time to start charging for random entertainment products on the Web (although music is probably the exception). Companies haven't been able to convince people that virtually any content is worth paying for, and the market right now is in no way signaling that consumers are ready for that."[27]

---

[26]"Yahoo to Freeze some GeoCities Sites," CNET News.com, September 10, 2001.
[27]"Yahoo set to charge for Streamed content" CNET News.com, October 29, 2001.

Overall, analysts seemed to be rather cool to Yahoo's prospects as of late 2001. "As we had anticipated, the company came in ahead of our estimates and the Street's consensus," said Derek Brown, equity analysis at W. R. Hambrecht. "On the other hand, I think that there's not enough upside to warrant significant investor enthusiasm." Jordan Rohan added, "The problem is they're only marginally profitable. While operating metrics in terms of usage and audience growth is impressive, the monetization of that growth remains to be proven."[28]

One final concern about Yahoo's plans to diversify its revenue stream: The amount of the service units purchased when migrating from free to paid services could have an indirect, but very significant, effect on a company's profit. For example, in 2001, Yahoo! announced that it would begin charging visitors to its French site for listing items for sale. Ninety percent of its users later abandoned the site.[29] If Yahoo! visitors around the world react in a similar way to all of these paid services, it may begin to have a negative effect on its advertising revenue. With fewer "clicks and eyeballs," Yahoo may not be able to sustain its advertising rates, just as can happen with magazines and newspapers that experience a decline in the number of readers or subscribers.

Webvan and Peapod.com

One of the most heralded breakthroughs in e-commerce was the online grocery store. Very few people like to spend their free time shopping for food and personal and household necessities. Would it not be wonderful if consumers could simply order these goods online and then have them shipped to their door step?

Two leading dot-coms representing slightly different business models were Webvan and Peapod.com. Both companies enabled shoppers to order goods on their Web sites. But Webvan delivered goods from their own warehouses while Peapod.com formed strategic alliances with supermarkets and fulfilled orders by using its partners' inventory.

Marketing Professor Nirmalya Kumarisa provided the following assessment of online grocers in early 2001:

> Online grocery retailing has turned out to be more challenging than anyone imagined. Initially, there was great euphoria as Peapod, Homegrocer, Webvan, Streamline and Priceline all rushed into this marketspace. On its first day of trading in November 1999, Webvan achieved a market capitalization in excess of $8 billion. Since then the stock has fallen by 97% and its current market capitalization is about $200 million, which is less than the company's cash reserves! It is anticipated that Webvan will run out of cash in the second quarter of this year. At least Webvan is still surviving. In contrast, Peapod has been acquired by Ahold [a Dutch company that is one of the world's largest supermarket chains]. Homegrocer has been acquired by Webvan. Streamline has gone bust and Priceline has withdrawn from the grocery sector.[30]

[28]"Yahoo rises as Semel touts gains" CNET News.com, July 12, 2001.
[29]"Yahoo!" Hoover's News and Commentary, November 15, 2001.
[30]Nirmalya Kumarisa, "Can Online Grocery Retailing Ever Be Profitable? Lessons from the Bleeding Edge of e-Commerce," *Perspectives for Managers*, IMD, No. 78, February 2001, p. 1.

While finishing the draft of this chapter, we logged on to the Webvan site to check on its status. What we found was "Web Page Not Found," which some humorists have called the "e-business tombstone." Webvan had gone out of business in August 2001.

According to Professor Kumarisa, the basic problem with the online grocery store business model is that the "industry gross margins are too low to cover the additional costs of delivering the last mile to the consumer and consumers are unwilling to pay the full costs of filling their orders."[31] He states that the typical supermarket gross profit margin is about 25 percent. He goes on to say that the average online order is $100, thereby providing a gross profit of $25. For this, the online supermarket has to pick out the goods that the consumer would ordinarily do himself and transport the products to the consumer's home. The cost of an average online order for picking and packing 50 items were found to be between $5 to $15. Estimated transportation cost was found to be about $200/day. For Webvan, 20 deliveries a day was considered to be a good number. If we use this figure, then we could add another $10 of cost per order.

Using these simple numbers, we can see that based on 20 orders of $100 each, the online company just about breaks even with each sale! (That is, the up to $25 in picking and transportation cost could very well offset the $25 gross profit.) If the online company charges for the delivery service, what price can it charge? How much would you be willing to pay for this convenience? Here Professor Kumarisa states that consumers do not perceive the value of the delivery service to be greater than $5 to $8 and therefore, delivery charges by the online grocers tended to fall within this range. This might appear to be the mark-up that is needed to carry the online grocer to profitability, but as the salesman on the late-night infomercial says, "Wait, there's more!"

Retail dot-coms like the online grocers incurred huge marketing costs in order to establish market presence and brand name, as well as fixed staff expenses for Web masters, HTML programmers, and other assorted technical support. (Recall the many Super Bowl commercials that were sponsored by dot-coms in 1998 and 1999.) Furthermore, if an online grocer such as Webvan carried its own inventory, then it would have to make an investment in warehouses, special inventory-picking equipment, and the inventory itself. The deprecation of the capital investment further increases overhead expenses. If, like Peapod.com, it chose to buy the inventory from already established brick and mortar supermarkets, then its gross profit margin would be lower because of the higher cost of goods sold. Either way, the bottom line is reduced (or perhaps we should say the negative bottom line is expanded).

WHITHER THE NEW ECONOMY? FUTURE CHALLENGES FOR MANAGERS

While it is true that new economy entrepreneurs finally learned the hard way about the importance of fundamental economic concepts such as supply, demand, production, and cost and profit, it is also true that old economy managers learned that the commercial and technological promises of the new economy cannot be ignored. For

---

[31]Ibid.

example, perhaps the most successful of all old economy CEOs is Jack Welch, recently retired head of GE. In 1998 he had an epiphany about the importance of the new economy and quickly made it a top priority to transform GE into an "e-company." He began by mandating that all of the company's senior executives take on a mentor within the firm who could teach them all about the Internet. The only requirement, other than knowledge, was that the selected individual be under the age of 25. Today, GE is considered to be a leader in using the Internet to manage its internal supply chain and its relationships with its suppliers and customers. In so doing, it has reportedly saved many millions of dollars in cost.

In addition to old economy companies adopting aspects of the new economy, there are some new economy dot-coms that are surviving or actually doing rather well. For example, e-Bay was profitable in 2000 and has reported profits throughout the end of the third quarter in 2001.[32] Amazon.com anticipates reporting a profit on a "pro-forma" basis for 2001, although on a normal basis, it is still losing money.[33] Near the end of the *New York Times* article from which the quote at the beginning of this chapter was taken, the reporter states the following:

> This is not to say that there are no dot-com companies left. Many Internet companies and software start-ups continue to operate, having cut back their budgets to try to survive. A few are even thriving. And no one here disputes that the Internet is here to stay, or that it has contributed to fundamental shifts in lifestyles and business practices.[34]

So while the current situation for dot-com companies is very bad, the long-term one could still be promising, particularly if their managers have learned from the experiences of the dot-com pioneers. In the meantime, old economy companies will continue to incorporate the Internet and its related technologies and applications into their business strategy and tactics.

CONCLUSION

Undoubtedly, the Internet and the World Wide Web have and will continue to change the way we live and work. And already the term "new economy" may be passé not only because of the burst in the recent dot-com bubble, but because all of the consumer services and ways of doing business made possible by Internet business applications are no longer "new" but simply business as usual.

In providing this brief overview of the new economy, our main purpose has been to show that many of the "old" or traditional economic concepts and tools are relevant and useful in understanding and analyzing the challenges that managers face in "marketspace" as well as the marketplace. One news item that appeared at the time of the writing of this revision perhaps best underscores this point. A November 15, 2001, front-page headline of the *New York Times* announced, "Wall Street's Internet-Stock Star Calls It Quits."

---

[32]See an excellent article on e-Bay in *BusinessWeek,* December 3, 2001.
[33]*Pro forma* in this case means "after adjusting for extraordinary expenses."
[34]*New York Times,* November 10, 2001. For a good review of some of the "survivors," see "Seven Habits of Highly Persistent Dotcoms," *Business 2.0,* November 2001, pp. 87–94.

Henry Blodget of Merrill-Lynch, along with Morgan Stanley's Mary Meeker (once called the "Queen of the Net"), used to be considered the top analysts of Internet stocks. According to the article in the *Times*, Blodget graduated from Yale in the early 1980s with a degree in history and aspired to be a journalist. After a brief stint as a fact checker for *Harper's Magazine*, he got a job as a junior analyst for CIBC Oppenheimer and followed Internet stocks for that firm. In December 1998, he made one call that would catapult him to fame and fortune: He declared that Amazon.com's stock was worth $400 a share. At that time Amazon.com was considered to be the "El Dorado" of e-commerce and its stock was already selling for $240 a share. Just about that time, Jonathan Cohen, Merrill's Internet analyst, predicted that Amazon would fall to $50. Investors heeded Blodget's advice and drove Amazon's shares well past his target valuation. Shortly after this, Blodget replaced Cohen as Merrill's Internet analyst.

Several years later, Blodget's shine began to tarnish as the Internet stock bubble burst. Many of the companies that he had advocated as "buys" either went bankrupt or saw their stock falling to as low as $1 a share. Robert Olstein, who manages the $1 billion Financial Alert fund in Purchase, New York, considered Blodget's departure as the "belated end of an era on Wall Street in which all of these great salesmen and great storytellers rose to the top." As he put it, "Blodget had good concepts, but the numbers didn't work. *This is a numbers business as well as a concepts business*" [emphasis added].[35]

The Solution

Nicole met with A.J. right after the meeting. "I think I should tell you that what you want me to do is more of a marketing than a technology assignment," cautioned A.J. "I could easily spend the next two weeks hammering out the technical pros and cons of a Web-based supply chain management system or the launching of a private B2B network. But what we really have to determine is: What is the market potential for the types of products being sold by kwench? Given the estimated demand for these products, would there be sufficient volumes and profit margins for you to justify your investment in the technology required to develop-ment your e-business capabilities? But to be honest, you and your marketing staff are more qualified to do this."

"This is a breath of fresh air," Nicole thought to herself, "here's a consultant that actually admits that the client knows more than he does."

(Continued)

---

[35]The story behind Blodget's departure from Merrill was taken from *The New York Times,* November 15, 2001, p. 1. However, we should not worry too much about Mr. Blodget. He reportedly received a $2 million severance package and has contracted with a publisher to do a book on the Internet stock bubble. Then he is considering, among other pursuits, to go into hedge fund management.

"You're right," responded Nicole. "If there is one lesson to be learned from the collapse of the dot-coms, it is the danger of spending a whole lot of money to have the latest and greatest e-business technology platform and then not have the demand to justify all that capital investment. My staff will work with you on this and let's come up together with a proposal to Bob."

At the meeting held two weeks later, A.J. deferred to Nicole to begin the presentation to Bob. She opened with a review of the market for beverages that were noncarbonated and contained no fruit juice or alcohol. She broke down this category into three basic types: sports drinks such as Gatorade, new-age drinks such as flavored green tea, and bottled water. "We are already well established in bottled water and there is no way we can catch up with Pepsi's Gatorade and Coke's Powerade," she concluded. "Kwench's products are of the new age variety. This type of beverage became very fashionable about 5 or 6 years ago but it is so trendy that the demand might be too volatile. For example, new-age drinks were synonymous with the boom years of the 1990s. Maybe consumers are a lot more subdued given the recession and what happened on September 11. Perhaps we should consider going into this market, but in doing so, I don't think we should try to match kwench's business model. In my view, there is nothing wrong with launching a new age drink with old economy methods. Let me now turn the meeting over to A.J., who will spell out more of the details."

"Yes, Bob, I concur 100% with Nicole's assessment of the situation," A.J. began. "But the money part for the technology is not that critical. We could partner with companies such as Ariba and Commerce One and they could help us set up a private B2B exchange without much of an up-front cost. But when we did a business case using a three-year time horizon, we found that the middle and worst-case scenarios yielded a negative NPV or an internal rate of return that was below your firm's cost of capital.[36] Only when we assumed a high top line growth of sales on this type of product were we able to come up with a rate of return that was above your hurdle rate. One key factor that affected our cash flow forecast was the tremendous amount of money that we know we would have to spend to build up our own brand of new age drink. But let me offer a completely different perspective on this issue: It is not so much whether you want what kwench has as much as it is what kwench wants what you have!"

"I know you're going to explain this statement," Bob responded. "But you've really peaked my curiosity on this."

"Okay, Bob, this is how I see it," A.J. continued. "By its ingenious use of the Internet, kwench.com was able to develop and sell a trendy new age drink that has really caught on in the market. But who it sells

---

[36]For further information on the importance of NPV analysis, see chapters 13 and 14.

(*Continued*)

through, not *to*, is the key. When all is said and done, all they have are certain upscale restaurants, gourmet food shops, and maybe a few sandwich shops and delis. In order to achieve real volume, they need to have a bigger presence in the supermarkets, fast-food chains, and convenience store chains. And these are the distribution channels that Global Foods dominates.[37] Why don't you establish a joint venture with kwench.com whereby you offer—at a price—your distribution channels to kwench. You could even sell your supply chain management system to help them monitor their inventory, and by the way, why not offer them—again at a price—your warehouses?"

"But if we have all this know-how, why don't we just start our own new-age drink and do it all ourselves?" asked Bob.

"Your own marketing team has done work on this point and can answer your question. But why don't I give you the short answer and you can check with them for the backup data. It does not make economic sense to do it all ourselves because building a brand from scratch is not easy and can be very expensive. Given the anticipated volume of sales, we don't think the benefit of keeping all the revenue ourselves will outweigh all the added promotion and advertising expenses."

"Okay, I assume that my team did all of its homework on this. Your plan does sound like a great idea, A.J.," Bob exclaimed. "It is ironic that we're going to sell our 'old economy' competencies to a 'new economy' upstart."

"Thanks, Bob," replied A.J. in a very modest tone. "But I must confess that the original idea for this came from Nicole."

---

[37]The idea for this solution came from reading about a proposed joint venture between Coca-Cola and Procter & Gamble. The goal of this alliance was for P&G to use the power of Coca-Cola's distribution channels to help P&G sell its snack products such as its Pringles potato chips in exchange for various offerings from P&G to Coke. However, in late 2001, the two companies announced that they were backing off from the deal.

Chapter 13

Capital Budgeting

The Situation

 George Kline is the manager of Global Foods' capital planning department. He is responsible for analyzing projects that require extensive expenditures and whose payoffs occur over a significantly long period of time—capital budgeting projects. When the analysis is completed, George and his staff of five make presentations up the company hierarchy—to the treasurer (George's boss) and the vice president of finance. If the proposal is large enough, it may finally have to be approved by the Corporate Management Committee (a group composed of top executives).

George has in front of him two new project proposals that require extensive analysis by his staff. The first is the proposed expansion of company activities into a new geographical region. Global is investigating the possibility of entering a new region where its soft drink and bottled water products have not been marketed previously. Potential annual sales for this area have been estimated at 100,000,000 cases. A 4 percent annual increase in total consumption is forecast. The market research people have estimated that, given an extensive advertising campaign, the first year's market share could reach 1 percent, and it may grow to some 5 percent four years later.

For the company to compete in this new area, it must establish a plant. An unused, somewhat obsolete bottling plant is available in the area for $5 million. The total costs of rebuilding and renovating the plant and purchasing and installing the new equipment are expected to amount to $2 million. During the first year, the company will incur

(Continued)

566

expenses of recruiting a new workforce. Just before production starts in year two, there will be an extensive advertising and promotion campaign. These expenses are estimated at $750,000.

If Global Foods actually achieves a 1 percent share of the market, it will sell 1 million cases. Each case sells for $5. Production costs will be $2.50 per case. General and administrative expenses will be $650,000 during the first year. Of this amount, $500,000 is fixed; the remainder is a function of quantity. Distribution and selling expenses will be 60 cents per case. Advertising expenses will be 5 percent of sales.

The cost of rebuilding and renovating the plant will be depreciated over 31 1/2 years. The remainder, $1 million (for new machinery, etc.), will be depreciated over seven years using the modified accelerated cost recovery system (MACRS). The purchase cost of the plant is to be allocated as follows: 10 percent for land, 50 percent for building, and 40 percent for equipment. The same methods of depreciation will be used. (Land is not depreciable.)

Global also expects that it will have to increase the size of its working capital by $750,000, to cover the additional inventory, accounts receivable, and cash for transactions.

The analysis will span seven years, including the first year of expenditures and six years of operations. This is a relatively conservative assumption—if the company cannot make a viable business of this plant over a seven-year time period, it would consider the operation too risky to undertake. Two other important pieces of information needed to complete the analysis are the following:

The company's marginal income tax rate (federal, state, and local) is 40 percent.
The cost of capital for this project will be 15 percent.

The second project George must consider is replacing an old depalletizing machine, which, although still in good working condition, is relatively slow and expensive to operate. A new machine will increase revenue and decrease operating and maintenance expenses. The total annual benefit from this will amount to $18,000.

A new machine will cost $100,000 and is conservatively expected to last ten years. The old machine has a present book value of $10,000. If properly maintained, it can be made to last another ten years. At that point it will have no market value. If sold today (there is a market for used depalletizers), it would have a cash value of $12,000.

The remaining depreciation life of the old machine is two years; it is being depreciated on a straight-line basis. The new machine will be depreciated over seven years, also using the straight-line method.

The company's income tax rate is 40 percent. The required rate of return (cost of capital), as this project is less risky than the expansion project, is 12 percent.

In chapter 2, we discussed the question of profit maximization as an objective of the firm. In all the chapters that followed we explicitly assumed that firms were actively pursuing this objective. We dealt with a firm's action during a specified period of time, such as a year, a month, or a day.[1] For example, a demand curve and revenues flowing to the firm were defined in terms of quantities per year; costs were stated in term of quantities produced for the same period. Even when we discussed long-term relationships, such as the long-run cost curve (the envelope curve), where each point on the horizontal (quantity) axis represented a plant of a different size, we did not concentrate on how the firm changed from a smaller to a larger plant. It was merely accepted that at each point on the horizontal axis, different quantities were produced by plants of different capacities.

To increase production over time, a firm must invest in new capacity. Even for a firm to maintain level capacity, it must replace worn-out equipment and plant. Such action also involves investment of resources.

A company's decision to commit funds to obtain revenues not only in the current period, but also in future periods, has not yet been analyzed. A brief reference regarding the consideration of expenditures to obtain payoffs over a considerable period of time in the future was made in chapter 2, in the section on maximizing the wealth of stockholders. We are now prepared to discuss decisions leading to this maximization criterion.

The subject of capital budgeting is generally taught in courses in finance. Large portions of basic and more advanced courses are devoted to this topic, and in some schools the finance curriculum includes a one-semester course in capital budgeting. However, the principles of capital budgeting also are properly a part of microeconomic theory extended to multiperiod problems. The application of incremental and marginal analysis will be encountered in this chapter just as in all the previous ones. Thus, it is not only desirable to include a chapter on this subject, but it is essential to make this book a complete treatment of managerial economics.

The Capital Budgeting Decision

Capital budgeting describes decisions where expenditures and receipts for a particular undertaking will continue over a period of time. These decisions usually involve outflows of funds (expenditures) in the early periods (sometimes just one expenditure will be made at the beginning of a project, as for the purchase of a new machine), and the inflows (revenues) start somewhat later and (it is hoped) continue for a significant number of periods.[2]

---

[1]The only exception was the discussion of the learning curve, which was defined over a given production run, regardless of the time involved.

[2]Note that the term *flows*, meaning inflows or outflows, is being used in this chapter. In capital budgeting decisions, the quantities considered are the actual expenditures and receipts of cash, not quantities adjusted by accounting conventions, such as accruals. Cash flows are quite objective—either cash goes out or it comes in—and there are no allowances made for when revenues and expenses are recognized in the company's books of account.

The following figure is a simple illustration of the components to be considered in making capital budgeting decisions. The figure shows one outflow at the beginning of the project and five inflows in subsequent periods. This model could represent the purchase of a new machine that will last five years and provide new revenues (or savings, if it decreases the cost of production) during that time. We could have shown an example with outflows occurring during, say, the first three years. Such outflows could represent a company's decision to build a new plant and equip it with new machines. Such a large investment could easily occur over a period of three years, and revenues would not start until the fourth year or even later.[3]

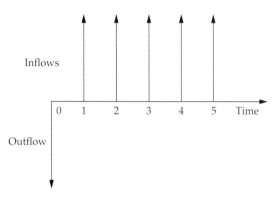

Types of Capital Budgeting Decisions

Now that we have described the general characteristics of a capital budgeting decision, we can list types of projects that fit this category.

Expansion of facilities. Growing demand for a company's products leads to consideration of a new or additional plant. Planning for other new facilities, such as sales offices or warehouses, would also be included here. George Kline's first project is an expansion proposal.

New or improved products. Additional investment may be necessary to bring a new or changed product to the market.

Replacement. Replacement decisions can be of at least two types: (1) replacement of worn-out plant and equipment or (2) replacement with more efficient machines of equipment that is still operating but is obsolete. George's second proposal falls in this group.

Lease or buy. A company may need to decide whether to make a sizable investment in buying a piece of equipment or to pay rental for a considerable time period.

Make or buy. A company may be faced with deciding whether to make a significant investment to produce components for its product or whether to forgo such investment and contract for the components with

---

[3]The replacement problem and the expansion proposal of the "Situation" are examples of these two types of projects.

a vendor. Outsourcing, which has become extremely important during the past decade or so, was discussed in chapter 2 and elsewhere.

Other. The preceding list is certainly not complete, since a capital budgeting problem exists whenever initial cash outflows and subsequent cash inflows are involved. For instance, an advertising campaign or an employee training program would lend itself to the same method of analysis. Also, as we pointed out in chapter 10, a customer retention program can be seen as a form of capital budgeting.

Safety or environmental protection equipment. Such investments may be mandated by law and therefore are not necessarily governed by economic decision making. However, if there are alternate solutions, capital budgeting analysis may be helpful in identifying the most cost-efficient alternative.

TIME VALUE OF MONEY

If a capital budgeting problem simply involved the subtraction of outflows from inflows, the mechanics of obtaining a solution would be extremely easy. However, because the various flows occur at disparate times in the future, we must adjust these numbers to make them equivalent. Differences in the values of the flows are based on the **time value of money.**

All this term really means is that a dollar today is worth more than a dollar tomorrow. For example, if you were offered a choice between a gift of $100 today and the same amount one year from now (the receipt of both amounts being certain), you would most likely select the first alternative. If you were to take the $100 today and put it in a bank paying 5 percent interest, you would have $105 a year from now; thus, the $100 today would be equivalent to $105 a year later. As long as you have an opportunity to earn a positive return on your funds over the one-year period, a dollar today and a dollar a year from now are not equivalent. Some people would conclude that this phenomenon is due to the presence of inflation, that is, a decrease in the value of the purchasing power of money over time. But inflation is not a necessary condition. Certainly, during a period of rising prices, nominal interest rates will be higher than during times of price stability. However, even when inflation is absent, funds that are saved and invested will earn interest for their owner.

Thus, to put cash flows originating at different times on an equal basis, we must apply an interest rate to each of the flows so that they are expressed in terms of the same point in time. In capital budgeting calculations, cash flows are usually brought back from various points in the future to the beginning of the project—time zero. It is then said that all cash flows are discounted to the present to obtain a present value. This is a useful convention, although we could discount or compound the flows to any date.

Those of you who have had previous exposure to the mechanics of compounding and discounting will be able to move immediately into the discussion of the solution of capital budgeting problems that follows. However, those of you who are unfamiliar with the calculations or whose memory on this subject is somewhat hazy will benefit from reading Appendix 13A at the end of this chapter.

METHODS OF CAPITAL PROJECT EVALUATION

Various methods are used to make capital budgeting decisions, that is, to evaluate the worth of investment projects. Two methods that have been used for many years will be mentioned only briefly. They are the payback method and the accounting rate of return method. Although they are still often used in the business world, they have generally been judged to be inadequate.

The **payback** method calculates the time period (years) necessary to recover the original investment. The **accounting rate of return** is the percentage resulting from dividing average annual profits by average investment.[4] Among the many drawbacks of these methods is the fact that neither applies the criterion of the time value of money in its computations.[5] Readers who are not familiar with these two measures and are interested in learning about them will find more lengthy descriptions in any basic corporate finance textbook.

The two methods that do discount cash flows to a present value are **net present value (NPV)** and **internal rate of return (IRR).**[6] Both of these techniques satisfy the two major criteria required for the correct evaluation of capital projects: use of cash flows and use of the time value of money.

Net Present Value

The net present value (NPV) of a project is calculated by discounting all flows to the present and subtracting the present value of all outflows from the present value of all inflows. In simple mathematical terms,

$$NPV = \sum_{t=1}^{n} \frac{R_t}{(1 + k)^t} - \sum_{t=0}^{n} \frac{O_t}{(1 + k)^t}$$

where t = Time period (e.g., year)
n = Last period of project
R_t = Cash inflow in period t
O_t = Cash outflow in period t
k = Discount rate (cost of capital)

Some of these terms must be explained further. Inflows are shown from period 1 to period n; however, inflows may not occur in all periods. Should the project under consideration be the construction of a plant, the time elapsed before the first shipment of product, and thus the first inflow, may not occur until period 3, for example. Remember that in George Kline's expansion project, inflows will not begin until the second period.

---

[4]Note that the accounting rate of return uses profits, rather than cash flows, in its calculation.
[5]Another version of payback, the discounted payback method, utilizes time value of money calculations. But it does not consider cash flows received after the payback period has been reached.
[6]A third calculation method using discounted cash flows is called the *profitability index* or *index of present value*. This is a derivative of the other two methods and will not be discussed in this text. You should refer to any of the leading textbooks in managerial finance.

Outflows are shown starting in period 0 (i.e., at the very beginning of the project). Indeed, the only outflow may occur in period 0 if the proposal being evaluated is the purchase of a machine that will begin to produce cash inflows upon installation. The depalletizing machine is a case in point. On the other hand, the expansion proposal considered by Kline will have outflows in periods 0 and 1.

Thus, the two terms have been generalized to allow for inflows and outflows throughout the life of the project, even though flows of one kind or the other may not occur in all periods.

The **discount rate,** k, is the interest rate used to evaluate the project. This rate represents the cost of the funds employed (the opportunity cost of capital) and is often called the **cost of capital.** It can also be referred to as the *hurdle rate,* the *cut-off rate,* or the *minimum required rate of return.*[7]

To illustrate the net present value method, we will use a simple numerical example. A proposed capital budgeting project requires one initial investment of $100 today. Its expected life is 5 years, and the annual cash inflows will be $25, $35, $40, $40, and $30 in years 1 through 5, respectively. The cost of capital at which the cash flows will be discounted is 14 percent. The relevant amounts are as follows:

Inflows		
Year 1	25 × 0.8772	$21.93
2	35 × 0.7695	26.93
3	40 × 0.6750	27.00
4	40 × 0.5921	23.68
5	30 × 0.5194	15.58
		$115.12
Outflow, year 0		100.00
Net present value		$15.12

All the estimated cash inflows have been brought back (discounted) to the present at the 14 percent cost of capital and then added. (The factors by which each of the cash flows is multiplied have been obtained from Table C.1c in Appendix C at the end of this text.) The total present value of cash outflows is deducted. In this case, there is only one outflow occurring at period 0 (now); thus, no discounting is necessary. The net present value equals $15.12. Should this proposal be accepted?

The answer is yes. The net present value for this program is positive. Stated somewhat differently, if we add all the cash inflows discounted at the cost of capital and deduct the cash outflow, we still have something left over. We expect to earn more than the cost of capital (i.e., the cost of financing this project). The proposal earns what the suppliers of capital require plus an additional amount.

We have arrived at the NPV rule for evaluating capital budgeting programs. If the NPV is positive, the project is financially acceptable. If NPV is negative, rejection is indicated. If NPV is exactly zero, this proposal is just earning the cost of capital; we

---

[7]The term *cost of capital* often applies to the overall average cost of funds for a corporation. This cost may differ from the rate used for a specific division of the company or for a particular capital budgeting proposal. One of the major reasons for the difference is risk (both business and financial risk). Thus, the corporation's cost of capital represents an average for the whole entity, but specific areas of the business may be more or less risky than the average and thus require higher or lower discount rates. Thus, the discount rate may differ from area to area or project to project within the same company.

are on the borderline. However, since the return just equals the required rate of return, the project appears to be acceptable.[8]

Internal Rate of Return

Internal rate of return (IRR) is the second of the two methods we will discuss that discounts cash flows. However, rather than looking for an absolute amount of present-value dollars, as in the NPV analysis, we solve for the interest rate that equates the present value of inflows and outflows:

$$\sum_{t=1}^{n} \frac{R_t}{(1 + r)^t} = \sum_{t=0}^{n} \frac{O_t}{(1 + r)^t}$$

or

$$\sum_{t=1}^{n} \frac{R_t}{(1 + r)^t} - \sum_{t=0}^{n} \frac{O_t}{(1 + r)^t} = 0$$

The r term in the equations is the internal rate of return—the unknown variable for which we solve. Actually, the IRR solution is only a special case of the NPV technique; the internal rate of return of a project is the discount rate that causes NPV to equal zero (which occurs when the project is just earning its cost of capital).

The calculation of the IRR can be easily accomplished with a hand-held business calculator or a computer (using, for instance, an Excel function), and this is what most people do. However, for our purposes, we will use the tables in Appendix C at the back of the text. In this case, the calculation may become rather cumbersome. Unless all cash inflows are uniform and there is only one outflow (in which case we can simply employ the annuity formula), it is necessary to find the answer by trial and error. One must first choose an applicable interest rate—and this may be no more than an educated guess—and then iterate until the correct answer is obtained.

Turn to the example used before. We found in the NPV analysis that, with a 14 percent cost of capital, net present value is positive ($15.12), so the internal rate of return must be greater than 14 percent. We will first try 18 percent (again using the factors in Table C.1c):

Inflows		
Year 1	25 × 0.8475	$21.19
2	35 × 0.7182	25.14
3	40 × 0.6086	24.34
4	40 × 0.5158	20.63
5	30 × 0.4371	13.11
		$104.41
Outflow, year 0		100.00
Net present value		$4.41

---

[8]This case is similar to one encountered previously, in chapter 9. Production takes place at the point where marginal cost equals marginal revenue. If discrete quantities are involved, the cost of the "last" unit produced is the same as the revenue received from it; it earns no economic but only normal profit. In capital budgeting, the situation is really the same: the "last" proposal that would be accepted is the one that just earns the rate required by the suppliers of capital.

As the result is still positive, we will choose a higher discount rate, 20 percent:

Inflows		
Year 1	25 × 0.8333	$20.83
2	35 × 0.6944	24.30
3	40 × 0.5787	23.15
4	40 × 0.4823	19.29
5	30 × 0.4019	12.06
		$99.63
Outflow, year 0		100.00
Net present value		$− 0.37

NPV is now negative; 20 percent is too high. Thus, the result lies somewhere between 18 percent and 20 percent. It is readily seen that the IRR is much closer to 20 percent than to 18 percent, because $−0.37 is much nearer to 0 than is $4.41. A more precise answer can be obtained using linear interpolation; this would result in an internal rate of return of about 19.8 percent.

The accept/reject criterion for the internal rate of return is based on a comparison of the IRR with the cost of capital of the project. Although the cost of capital is not used in the calculation of the IRR, it is still an all-important component of decision making. If the internal rate of return is larger than the cost of capital—the required rate of return—of the proposal, it signals acceptance. If IRR < k, the proposed project should be rejected. If IRR = k, although it could be said that decision makers would be indifferent on whether to undertake the project, an argument can be made that the project is earning its cost of capital and therefore should be accepted at the margin.

MODULE 13A

NPV versus IRR

Two methods have just been described that conform to the criteria specified for a valid capital budgeting decision. Is one preferred over the other, or are the two equally valid?

In a large majority of cases, either NPV or IRR can be used with confidence. These two tests of investment worth give consistent accept/reject indicators. In other words, when

$$NPV > 0, IRR > k$$

$$NPV = 0, IRR = k$$

$$NPV < 0, IRR < k$$

Thus, either of the two measures gives the correct answer. In some cases, however, problems may arise.

When **independent projects** are being analyzed, both IRR and NPV criteria give consistent results. "Independent" implies that if a company is considering several projects at the same time, they can all be implemented simultaneously as long as they pass the NPV or IRR tests, and as long as funds are not limited. The adoption of one independent project will have no effect on the cash flows of another. For example, the two proposals on George Kline's desk are independent. Global Foods can expand into a new territory and replace the depalletizing machine at the same time. The acceptance of one proposal does not preclude executing the other.

However, proposals may be **mutually exclusive.** This occurs when two solutions for a particular proposal are offered, only one of which can be accepted. Suppose Global decides to acquire a new depalletizer. At this point, sales representatives from two manufacturers of these machines descend upon the company, and each offers a new version. But the company needs only one depalletizer. If both NPV and IRR are calculated, inconsistent recommendations can result. NPV analysis may suggest purchase of machine A, but IRR indicates machine B. Such disparate signals can occur if one or both of the following conditions are present:

1. The initial costs of the two proposals differ.
2. The shapes of the subsequent cash inflow streams differ; for instance, one alternative may have large early inflows with the other exhibiting increasing inflows over time.

The reason for the differences between IRR and NPV results is the implicit reinvestment assumption. In the NPV calculation, as inflows occur, they are automatically assumed to be reinvested at the cost of capital (the project's k). The IRR solution assumes reinvestment at the internal rate of return (the project's r).

Conflicting accept/reject signals may not occur frequently in capital project analysis, but they do occur and they may cause the analyst some anxious moments.

An Example As mentioned previously, conflicting results can be caused by a difference in project size. Table 13.1 shows such a case. Two mutually exclusive projects are presented. Project A involves an original outlay of $1,500; its cash inflows are $580 per year for four years. Project B (which is a substitute for A) is somewhat less expensive—only $1,000—but the four cash inflows are also smaller, at $400 each. Each project has a four-year life and no salvage value. Proceeding in the normal way, we find that the IRR of project B is higher than that of project A—21.9 percent against 20.1 percent. If we were to go no further, basing our choice on a comparison of IRRs, project B would be selected. But if we perform an NPV calculation (at the company's cost of capital of 15 percent), project A tops B's NPV by $14 (i.e., $156 against $142). The IRR tells us to adopt project B, but if we want to maximize net present value, we should implement project A.

To resolve this dilemma, we calculate the NPV and IRR for an "incremental" (or *delta*) project. That is, we take the differences between the two project cash flows and create a delta project. If we undertake A rather than B, we must incur an additional original cash outflow (at $t = 0$) of $500 and receive in turn additional cash inflows of $180 for each of the next four years. Such a project, evaluated separately, would have an NPV of $14 and an IRR of 16.4 percent. This means that the additional outlay of $500 provides an incremental positive NPV ($14) and an internal rate of return (16.4 percent) that exceeds the 15 percent cost of capital. Thus, both criteria indicate that the additional investment of $500 is worthwhile. It follows that the NPV rule, which suggested project A, was the correct indicator, and that project A should be chosen over project B.

Figure 13.1 illustrates the relationship between the two projects. At the bottom of Table 13.1, the two projects have been evaluated at six different discount rates, and

Table 13.1
Two Mutually Exclusive Projects that Differ in Size

PROJECT	$t = 0$	$t = 1$	$t = 2$	$t = 3$	$t = 4$	$t = 5$
A	(1,500)	580	580	580	580	0
B	(1,000)	400	400	400	400	0
Cost of capital			15.0%			

	Internal Rate of Return		Net Present Value
Project A	20.1%		156
Project B	21.9%		142

Delta Project						
(A − B)	(500)	180	180	180	180	0
Internal rate or return	16.4%		Net Present Value			14

Project Evaluation as Several Discount Rates

	0.00%	5.00%	10.00%	15.00%	20.00%	25.00%
Project A	820	557	339	156	1	(130)
Project B	600	418	268	142	35	(55)

their respective NPVs have been plotted on the graph. When the discount rate is 0, the NPV is merely the sum of all the cash flows (for project A, − 1,500 + 580 + 580 + 580 + 580 = 820). This is shown on the vertical axis. On the horizontal axis, the projects' NPVs become 0 at their respective IRRs (20.1 percent for A and 21.9 percent for B). The two projects' NPVs cross at $111, at a discount rate of 16.4 percent, which is the IRR of the incremental project. To the left of this intersection, project A's NPV exceeds that of project B's, which creates a conflict, since project B's IRR (21.9 percent) is always higher than project A's (20.1 percent). Had the cost of capital been higher than 16.4 percent, project B would have been preferred under both methods, since it also would now have the higher NPV.

The second instance when the two measures may give conflicting rankings occurs when the shapes of the cash inflow streams differ significantly. Although the initial outlays for both mutually exclusive projects may be the same, one of the projects has a cash flow pattern that starts slowly and builds up, whereas the other has cash inflows that are initially large but decline over time. Readers can verify that this is so by entering data into Module 13A and calculating results.

Another problem that may occur concerns the case of nonconventional cash flows. Conventional cash flows occur when cash outflows are followed by a series of cash inflows for the remainder of the project's life. In other words, over time, there is only one change from negative flows (outflows) to positive (inflows). But suppose there are two or more changes. If a project starts with a cash outflow followed by a series of cash inflows, and then ends up with a cash outflow (i.e., two changes in sign), two different rates of return will result. Such an answer is obviously not satisfactory. If NPV analysis is used, a single answer will be obtained.

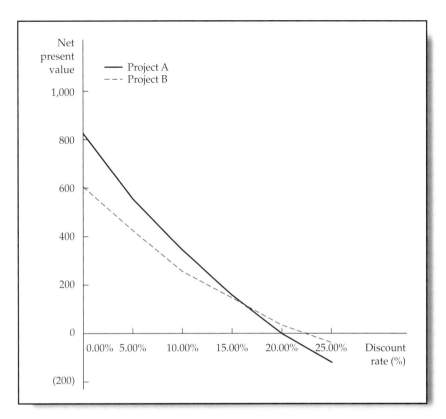

Figure 13.1
Net Present Value Profiles for Projects of Different Size

Writers of financial and economic literature almost unanimously recommend NPV as the theoretically more correct measure. A full explanation of the reasons for this choice would be quite long. For the purpose of our limited exposition of this subject, let us mention just briefly two arguments:

1. The financial objective of the firm is the maximization of stockholder wealth, and the NPV method is more applicable to this end. Projects with the largest NPVs will add up to the highest present value for the business.
2. The NPV reinvestment assumption, at k, appears to be more realistic in most cases than reinvestment at r of a particular project.[9]

---

[9]There is a method that has gained favor and that corrects some of the problems encountered with the internal rate of return. It is called the *modified internal rate of return* (MIRR) and is calculated by discounting, at the cost of capital, all cash outflows to year zero and compounding all inflows to the end of the project. The discount rate that equates the sum of the ending values to the sum of the beginning values is the MIRR. Using this method reinvests the cash flows at the cost of capital. Also, the possibility of obtaining more than one solution (nonconventional cash flows) is eliminated. However, accept/reject signal conflicts with NPV can still occur. For a longer explanation, see Eugene F. Brigham, Louis C. Gapenski, and Michael C. Ehrhardt, *Financial Management: Theory and Practice*, 9th ed., Fort Worth, TX: Dryden, 1999, pp. 440–41.

Capital Budgeting in Practice

For many years, a number of surveys has been conducted to examine how companies perform their capital budgeting analyses. In the past, the primitive methods—payback and the accounting rate of return—were by far the more popular. This is still the case with small companies, where the more sophisticated methods (IRR and NPV) take second place. According to these studies, companies that employed discounted cash flow methods favored the use of the IRR rather than NPV. Why? Businesspeople—especially nonfinancial managers—are much more comfortable making their judgments by looking at percentages. The NPV number, a dollar figure, is not readily recognizable.

When the numerous surveys of capital budgeting methods over the past 30 years or so are examined, it is obvious that the use of the more sophisticated evaluation methods—IRR and NPV—has increased significantly. A recent study of 392 companies showed that 76 percent of those surveyed used the IRR "always or almost always," while 75 percent used the NPV method. The payback came in third with 57 percent. This study also distinguished between large and small companies. Among the large companies, the emphasis on discounted cash flow analysis was even greater. Payback was relatively more prominent among the smaller firms. Large firms were defined as those with annual sales greater than $1 billion dollars.[10]

Another recent survey told a somewhat different story. This study covered 232 small manufacturing companies. The definition of "small," however, was different from the one used in the study described above: companies with sales of less than $5 million per year and with fewer than 1,000 employees. Obviously, the companies surveyed here were considerably smaller than those of the one discussed previously. The payback method and the accounting rate of return were the primary methods employed, by 43 percent and 22 percent of the firms, respectively. The IRR was the primary method in 16% and the NPV in 11%.[11]

In summary, as one looks at the numerous surveys that have been conducted over the last 30 or so years, there is an unmistakable significant upward trend in the use of the more sophisticated capital budgeting analysis methods.

CASH FLOWS

MODULE 13B
MODULE 13C

Up to this point the discussion has concentrated on the methods and mechanics of the capital budgeting process. Cash flows were assumed and put into the appropriate formulas for processing. The term *cash flow* has been used in abundance but has not been explained thoroughly.

When confronted with a capital budgeting proposal, the analyst's most difficult task is to enter the best estimates of cash flows into the analysis. Since all of the inflows and outflows are in the future, their amounts and timing are uncertain. Some of them can be assessed with relative certainty. For instance, if a replacement pro-

---

[10]John R. Graham and Campbell R. Harvey, "The Theory and Practice of Corporate Finance: Evidence from the Field," *Journal of Financial Economics*, 61 (2001), pp. 1–53.
[11]Stanley Block, "Capital Budgeting Techniques Used by Small Business Firms in the 1990s," *The Engineering Economist*, Summer 1997, pp. 289–302.

posal is being considered, the cost of the new machine has probably been established. But as the analyst tries to assess future annual benefits and costs, the amount of uncertainty increases.

In most cases, capital budgeting analysts do not generate the inputs for the model. They obtain the estimates from other parts of the organization, such as market research, marketing, manufacturing, engineering, or service. There will be market forecasts, price estimates, and cost and expense forecasts. These data have to be examined for potential bias. Market forecasts may be too high, since the people who prepare them are interested parties. Costs often are underestimated. In general, estimated cash flows tend to be optimistic and must be adjusted to make them more realistic.[12]

The person organizing the data must understand the following points:

1. All revenues and costs must be stated in terms of cash flows.
2. All cash flows should be incremental. Only those flows that will change if the proposal is accepted should be recorded. For example, ongoing overhead costs, part of which may be allocated to the project under consideration, should be ignored.
3. Sunk costs do not count. Costs incurred prior to the time the project is being evaluated and that cannot be recouped should be omitted from consideration.
4. Any effect on other parts of the operation must be taken into account. If the introduction of a new diet soda will have an adverse impact on sales of current soft drinks, this amount must be subtracted from the cash flows planned for the new product. On the other hand, impact may be positive. For example, if the company also sells alcoholic beverages, the introduction of a "light" tonic could enhance sales of the company's gin. These are, of course, examples of the familiar cases of substitutes and complements. Some idea of the size of cross-elasticities of demand is needed to estimate these impacts. Cost impacts must also be considered.
5. Generally, in capital budgeting analysis, interest paid on debt is not considered. Since interest is included in the discount rate, showing it as a cash outflow would amount to double-counting.

Types of Cash Flows

Cash flows come in many varieties. Some of the most common and important types are discussed next.

Initial Cash Outflows   Cash flows occur at the inception of the project. If a new machine is installed, this represents a one-time outflow. But initial outflows can also be spread over a period of time, as mentioned previously.

Operating Cash Flows   When a new project goes on line, it begins to generate cash inflows (revenues). Of course, it also generates cash outflows (costs and expenses), which must be subtracted from the inflows. In the early years of opera-

---

[12]Stephen W. Pruitt and Lawrence J. Gitman, "Capital Budgeting Forecast Biases: Evidence from the *Fortune* 500," *Financial Management,* Spring 1987, pp. 46–51.

tions, outflows can exceed inflows; thus, the annual net outflow can continue even after the initial investment stage.

So far this exposition is relatively simple. But one of the expenses that accountants record in the income statement of a company is depreciation (and amortization). Obviously, this is not a cash flow; it is a bookkeeping entry to show that the value of the plant and equipment is declining. The actual cash flow occurred when the plant was built and the machinery purchased, and it was recorded as such in the capital investment analysis. If we were living in that ideal society with no income tax, we would simply ignore depreciation in calculating cash flows.

But because income taxes are a fact of life, they must be considered in the treatment of depreciation. The after-tax profit reflects the deduction of depreciation. But since depreciation did not result in a cash outflow, it has to be added back to the after-tax profit to obtain net cash flow.

An example will illustrate this procedure. If cash sales during a period are $100, cash costs and expenses are $50, depreciation of buildings and equipment is $20, and the income tax rate is 40 percent, then net cash flow for the period will be $38:

Sales	$100
Costs and expenses	50
Depreciation	20
Total costs and expenses	$ 70
Net profit before tax	30
Income tax	12
Net profit after tax	$ 18
Depreciation	20
Net cash flow	$ 38

For each of the periods (years), operating cash flows have to be calculated and the results discounted to the present.

Additional Working Capital In the case of an expansion proposal, in addition to new plant and equipment, increased working capital may be required. Inventories may be larger, accounts receivable may grow, and more cash may be needed to finance the transactions engendered by the growth in operations. Investing in working capital is a cash outflow that is similar in nature to an investment in brick and iron. We must account for it. However, there may not be a periodic write-down (i.e., depreciation) for such investments in the plan. When the proposed project comes to the end of its life, inventories will be used up, accounts receivable will be collected, and the additional cash will no longer be needed. So the same amount that was expended at the beginning of the program may be returned at the end—with one big difference: The cash outflow occurs at or near the beginning of the operations, whereas the inflow of the same amount occurs at the end and must be discounted to the present.

The ending amount of working capital may actually be less than the original investment since some accounts receivable may turn out to be uncollectible and some inventory may become obsolete. The actual loss on this decrease in working capital can be deducted from the cash flows for a tax benefit.

Salvage or Resale Values At the end of the project's life, a machine that has been completely depreciated (i.e., has an accounting book value of zero) may turn out to have a residual resale value or some scrap value. If cash can be obtained for it, a cash inflow will result.

But care must be exercised in including this cash flow. If the market value is greater than the book value, a profit will result, with inevitable tax consequences. Thus, if a fully depreciated piece of equipment is expected to bring in $5,000 in resale value at the end of the project life, and if the tax rate is 40 percent, then the actual cash flow will be only $3,000, since $2,000 must be paid in taxes. The formula for computing the cash flow in such a case is

$$SV - (SV - BV)\ T$$

where SV = Salvage or resale value
   BV = Book value
      T = Tax rate

Noncash Investment Sometimes a new project involves an investment that does not require a cash flow. For instance, suppose an old, fully depreciated machine is standing on the factory floor. This machine is not needed for present production requirements. But then a new expansion proposal is accepted, allowing this old machine to be utilized. Does it represent a cash outflow? Yes, if the machine has a salvage value; no, if it has no market value at all. Thus, as in all cases of capital budgeting decisions, the alternatives have to be considered.

COST OF CAPITAL

In each of the capital budgeting decisions described, a certain cost of capital was assumed. Its derivation has not been explained. Much space is usually devoted to this subject in finance textbooks—an entire chapter or more. Such an exposition is beyond the scope of this text. However, a brief explanation of this important concept is essential.

To invest in capital projects, a company must obtain financing. Financing, of course, comes from different sources. There is debt, either short-term or long-term. Then there is equity. A company may retain earnings, which then become part of its equity, or it can issue new shares. Each type of financing must be paid for; each has its cost. It is these costs that establish a company's cost of capital. When all of the costs have been identified, they are combined to arrive at an average cost of capital for a given debt/equity mix.[13]

Debt

The cost of debt is the easier to explain. It is simply the interest rate that must be paid on the debt. But since interest expense is tax deductible, the actual cost of the debt to the company is the after-tax cost. The expression for the cost of debt is

---

[13]Admittedly, there are other financial instruments with which a company obtains funds, such as preferred stocks or convertible bonds. However, this short description will limit itself to debt and common equity.

Which interest rate should be used? If a company already has debt outstanding, it pays a certain rate. But the rate being paid on past debt is not relevant. What is important to the company in measuring its cost of capital is the interest it would have to pay if it were to borrow today. Thus, the present rate being charged in the market for the kind of debt the company would issue (e.g., life to maturity, risk category) determines the company's cost of debt.

MODULE 13D

Equity

The cost of equity is more difficult to obtain. A large body of literature exists on this subject, and there are different methods to arrive at this cost. Two of these will be described here.

The Dividend Growth Model   The cost of equity is determined by the population of stockholders. Because the stockholders expect to receive dividends (D) plus a selling price (P_n) for the shares in the future, the price they are willing to pay for the stock today (P_0) is determined by discounting the future cash flows to the present at the rate of return (k_e) the stockholders require to buy the stock:

$$P_0 = \sum_{t=1}^{n} \frac{D_t}{(1 + k_e)^t} + \frac{P_n}{(1 + k_e)^n}$$

The stockholders will sell the shares at time n to new stockholders, who again may hold the stock for a limited period before selling it to other stockholders, and so on. Since the buying and selling of the stock merely represent an exchange and thus cancel out, the net cash flow from this stock is the dividend, which will continue over an infinite period of time if it is assumed that the corporation will live in perpetuity. The equation showing an infinite stream of dividends can be written as

$$P_0 = \sum_{t=1}^{\infty} \frac{D_t}{(1 + k_e)^t}$$

The dividend does not have to be the same in each period. An assumption, referred to as the **dividend growth model,** is often made that the dividend will grow at a constant rate (g) forever. The equation then converts to[14]

$$P_0 = \frac{D_0(1 + g)}{(1 + k_e)} + \frac{D_0(1 + g)^2}{(1 + k_e)^2} + \cdots + \frac{D_0(1 + g)^n}{(1 + k_e)^n}$$

which can be simplified to

$$P_0 = \frac{D_1}{k_e - g}$$

Because it is the cost of capital that we seek, the equation can be written in terms of k_e as

---

[14]D_0 represents the most recent dividend paid, and thus $D_0(1 + g) = D_1$; D_1 is the dividend expected to be paid during the next period.

$$k_e = \frac{D_1}{P_0} + g$$

Thus, this construction states that the cost of equity capital (k_e) equals the dividend in year 1 divided by today's stock price—the dividend yield—plus the expected growth rate in the dividend. This formula is often referred to as the Gordon model, so named for Myron J. Gordon, an economist who has done a great amount of work in this area and who is credited with a major role in developing this model.[15]

The dividend growth model just presented is generally applicable when a company reinvests the earnings that have not been paid out as dividends. If a company issues new stock in the financial markets, it incurs an additional cost. The proceeds from the sale of the stock will be less than the current market price, P_0. The cost of underwriting the issue must be taken into consideration. If these costs, often referred to as *flotation costs, f*, are expressed as a percentage of P_0, the Gordon model converts to

$$k_0 = \frac{D_1}{P_0(1 - f)} + g$$

Obviously, the cost of external equity capital will be higher for newly issued stock than for retained earnings.[16]

While the Gordon model formula appears rather simple, it requires a forecast of growth. Forecasts, as we have found out, are always tenuous. Thus, the calculation of the cost of capital can be only as good as the estimates entered into it.

The Capital Asset Pricing Model (CAPM)

The **capital asset pricing model** had its birth in the 1960s.[17] It is based on the principle that there is a relationship between risk and return. The more risky the investment, the higher will be the required return. Only a brief description of this model will be given here.

An important conclusion of this model is that the required rate of return[18] on a stock is a function of the volatility (market risk) of its returns relative to the return on

---

[15]See, for instance, Myron J. Gordon, *The Investment, Financing, and Valuation of the Corporation,* Homewood, IL: Irwin, 1962.

[16]The assumption of constant growth may not always be realistic. For a variable growth rate, the growth rate must be estimated for each period and the entire equation solved for k_e. For example, in the case of a company that expects rapid growth at first, then a slowdown, and finally some "normal" constant growth, the equation becomes somewhat complicated:

$$P_0 = \sum_{t=1}^{n} \frac{D_t}{(1 + k_e)^t} + \frac{D_{n+1}}{k_e - g}\left[\frac{1}{1 + k_e}\right]^n$$

where n = Number of years of nonconstant growth
g = Expected annual growth rate during the constant growth period
D_t = Dividend expected in each year t of the nonconstant growth period
D_{n+1} = Dividend in first period of constant growth

For additional information on this construction, see any finance textbook, for instance, Brigham, Gapenski, and Ehrhardt, *Financial Management*, pp. 339–42. This method of calculation will be employed later in this chapter, in the section, "The Value of a Corporation."

[17]See, for instance, William F. Sharpe, "Capital Asset Prices: A Theory of Market Equilibrium under Conditions of Risk," *Journal of Finance*, 19 (September 1964), pp. 425–42.

[18]The rate of return for a period is defined as

$$\frac{\text{Dividend} \pm \text{change in stock price}}{\text{Stock price at the beginning of the period}}$$

a total stock market portfolio. This volatility is referred to as *beta* (β) and is calculated by regression analysis. The variability of the individual stock's return is the dependent variable, and the variability of the market return is the independent variable. The higher the volatility of the individual stock's return compared to the market return, the higher the beta. A beta of 1.0 signifies that the stock's return is as volatile as the market's. If the beta is greater than 1.0, the stock's return is more variable and, therefore, the stock is more risky; the reverse situation holds when beta is less than 1.0.

One other item is included in this model, the riskless interest rate. The riskless rate is usually represented by interest paid on U.S. Treasury securities. The beta coefficient is used to arrive at the risk premium of the individual stock relative to the difference between the average return for the market portfolio and the riskless rate.

The required rate of return on an individual stock is calculated as follows:

$$k_j = R_f + \beta\,(k_m - R_f)$$

where k_j = Required rate of return on stock j
$\quad\ R_f$ = Risk-free rate
$\quad\ k_m$ = Rate of return on the market portfolio

This model has experienced immense popularity—and also criticism. Although it provides a logical explanation of maximizing behavior under conditions of risk, it suffers, as does the Gordon model, from difficulties of obtaining the relevant data. Probably one of the most serious objections is that the model tries to predict the present and future costs of equity capital with past data. It assumes, therefore, that the past relationship between stock return and market return will continue into the future. This, of course, is a shortcoming of all forecasts made using regression analysis.

Another criticism of CAPM lies in the fact that betas are not always stable. They vary depending on the time period used in making the analysis, and they are affected by the specific statistical method used. Thus, again, the cost-of-capital estimate is only as good as the data used in the computation and the method used. It is obvious that there is much work yet to be done to improve the estimates of the equity cost of capital.

The Weighted Cost of Capital

MODULE 13E

Despite the fact that the measurements of the components of capital costs are not entirely satisfactory, they are the best available at the present, and they are used in obtaining an overall cost of capital of the firm. This is achieved by weighting the various costs by the relative proportion of each component's value in the total capital structure.

A question arises at this point. Should the weights be based on book values (i.e., the numbers on the balance sheet) or market values? The answer is market values, since they reflect the actual values of the various components today, and the prices the securities would command if new financing is needed.

If debt makes up 20 percent and equity 80 percent of a company's financial structure, and their respective costs are 6 percent and 14 percent, the weighted cost of capital is

$$0.2\,(0.06) + 0.8\,(0.14) = 0.012 + 0.112 = 0.124 = 12.4 \text{ percent}$$

Since the cost of debt capital is usually lower than that of equity, this formula would indicate that a company can decrease its cost of capital (and thus increase the value of the firm) by increasing the ratio of debt to equity. This is misleading, however. As the proportion of debt increases (i.e., as leverage rises), the financial community will view the company as more risky. Consequently, the cost of both components, debt as well as equity, will rise, causing the weighted average to rise also. There is probably some point where the combination of components is optimal, and where the weighted cost of capital of a particular firm is at a minimum.

THE CAPITAL BUDGETING MODEL

In the arena of corporate decision making, capital budgeting is an application of the marginal revenue-marginal cost principle. Figure 13.2 illustrates this principle.

Assume that a company is faced with a menu of seven independent capital budgeting proposals. The capital planning department has analyzed each of them and has calculated the internal rate of return, which is the evaluation technique the company uses. In Figure 13.2, the projects have been ranked by IRR from highest to lowest. Each proposal is represented by a bar; its height represents the IRR, and the width indicates the size of the investment. If a line were drawn connecting the tops of the bars and then smoothed, it would resemble a marginal revenue curve. In this case, it would be a curve representing the internal rate of return on successive doses of investment—a marginal investment opportunity curve.

Figure 13.2
The Capital Budgeting Decision

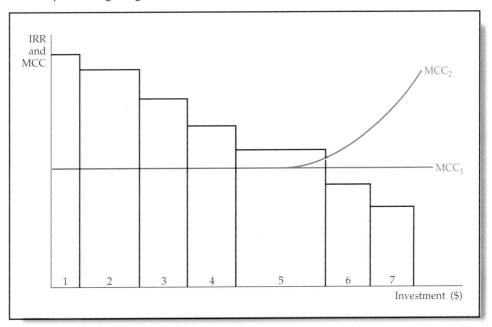

The marginal cost curve is based on the cost of capital. In Figure 13.2, two possible constructions of the cost of capital curve are shown. The first, a horizontal line (MCC_1), implies that a company can obtain the funds it needs at a set cost.

In the more likely case, as a company requires additional funds (i.e., moves from left to right on the graph), it will be forced to pay higher costs. We have already said that obtaining new equity carries a higher cost of capital than retained earnings. If a company has large requirements for investment funds, and after using up its retained earnings it must look to the outside equity market for additional financing, the marginal cost of capital will rise at that point. If the company's debt–equity ratio is considered optimal, the company will increase its debt proportionally to maintain it. As the company increases its borrowing, it will most likely be required to pay increasing interest rates for additional amounts of debt capital.

Thus, as the costs of both debt and equity rise, the marginal weighted cost of capital will show an increase as the corporation increases its demand for capital funds. Hence, it is considerably more realistic to draw the weighted marginal cost of capital as a rising curve (MCC_2), particularly after the capital budget of a certain size is reached.

The company will reach the optimal investment budget at the point where the marginal investment opportunity curve and marginal cost of capital curve intersect. This is, of course, the principle that was applied in the one-period case. In the example shown in Figure 13.2, the conclusion is that projects 1 through 5 should be accepted, and those with lower IRRs (projects 6 and 7) should be rejected.

The illustration shown here is a great simplification. A menu of projects will not usually be put on the table at one time. Projects typically arrive at the capital planning department at various times, and the proposals have to be evaluated one at a time. However, this simplification should be sufficient to show that capital budgeting is indeed an application of the marginal principle.

There is one other important point that must be made. We have just concluded that in order to arrive at an optimal capital budget, a company will accept all projects with positive NPV's (an exception, capital rationing, is discussed in the next section). However, if a firm operates in a competitive market, then in the long run, all NPV's will be reduced to zero. This is consistent with our discussion of competition in chapter 9, where we concluded that in a long-run equilibrium firms will earn only their normal profit. Of course, in reality, continuous changes in demand and supply conditions may prevent a static long-run equilibrium from ever being reached. Nevertheless, competitive forces will require companies to continue to innovate to maintain their market advantage or to attempt to create noncompetitive (monopolistic) conditions to produce economic profits—and positive NPV's—in the long run.

CAPITAL RATIONING

The marginal rule indicates that the company should invest in every project whose IRR exceeds the marginal cost of capital or whose net present value is positive. However, some corporations impose an absolute limit on capital spending during a particular interval, and not all projects that pass the IRR or NPV test will be accepted.

Table 13.2

Investment Choices under Capital Rationing

PROJECT	ORIGINAL INVESTMENT	NET PRESENT VALUE
A	$50	$25
B	70	30
C	20	25
D	30	10
E	80	30

This situation, referred to as **capital rationing** occurs when management may not be willing to obtain external financing. There are various reasons for such a practice. For instance, there may be a reluctance to incur increasing levels of debt. Alternatively, management may not wish to add to equity in fear of diluting control. Thus, under capital rationing conditions, a company may have to reject otherwise acceptable projects to remain within its expenditure limit.

Assume that a corporation has evaluated five independent capital projects, with the results shown in Table 13.2. Each of the projects has a positive net present value and therefore should be undertaken under the usual rule. To embark on these five projects, the company would have to incur cash outflows of $250 and would obtain a net present value of $120.

However, the management of this firm has decreed that only $100 will be spent on capital projects at this time. Which projects should it select? To create the most value it can under the circumstances, it will choose the combination of projects that will give the highest net present value within the spending constraint. This leads to the selection of projects A, C, and D. These three projects together will require an outlay of just $100 and will have a combined net present value of $60. No other combination of projects within the $100 spending constraint will achieve a net present value as high as $60.

Although the imposition of capital rationing does not appear to be rational maximizing behavior, it nevertheless occurs quite frequently. The final judgment on capital rationing is that it does not permit a company to achieve its maximum value.

THE VALUE OF A CORPORATION

We have just learned how to calculate the present value of a project given cash inflows and outflows over a period of time, and discounting these to the present using a discount rate, the cost of capital.

A similar method of computation can be employed to value a corporation as a whole. Of course, if the corporation's stock trades on a stock exchange and its debt is composed of publicly owned bonds, its market value can easily be established from published data. However, assume that you are one of the founders of a relatively small private corporation. You and the other owners are now planning to carry out an "initial public offering" (usually referred to as an IPO). How would you go about estimating what your company is worth?[19] To come up with some kind of a reasonable value figure, you will have to estimate your cash inflows and outflows several years into the future. To do a complete valuation job, it would be necessary to project your income statements and balance sheets. We will try to condense our procedure here by selecting the essential data we will need to make our computation without constructing complete financial statements.

To accomplish our objective we must start with the concept of **free cash flow.**[20] Free cash flow consists of funds that would be available to investors from operating cash flows after we subtract investments in working capital and fixed assets needed to operate and grow the company. These terms are defined as follows:

1. Operating cash flow = EBIT $\times$ (1 − T) + Depreciation
   where EBIT = Earnings before interest and tax (also frequently called operating profit)
   T = Tax rate
2. New investment in operating working capital represents the annual increases in certain parts of current assets. In general, this would include increases in cash, accounts receivable, and inventories minus increases in accounts payable and accrued expenses.
3. Increases in fixed assets are increases in land, property, and equipment before subtracting depreciation (i.e., the gross increases in fixed assets).

Let us construct a simple example to illustrate the valuation method. Assume that in 2002, the following were the relevant numbers (in $000):

EBIT	$60
Depreciation	20
Operating working capital	80
Gross fixed assets	120

Your company expects to have rather rapid growth during the next three years because of a new product you are bringing to the market. You expect, however, that after three years your competition will have caught up with you. Because you are not certain what new products you will introduce then, you make the conservative judgment that your company's free cash flow will increase at 6 percent per year for the foreseeable future. To calculate the free cash flow for the years 2003, 2004, and 2005, you have estimated the following:

	2003	2004	2005
EBIT	$90	$110	$125
Depreciation	30	35	40
Operating working capital	110	135	155
Gross fixed assets	160	190	220

---

[19]The reader should notice that in calculating the value of this company we will use the nonconstant growth model, discussed in note 16 of this chapter.
[20]Free cash flow was mentioned briefly in chapter 2. Free cash flow is essentially the same as dividends, which were used to calculate the value of the common stock in that chapter. The following discussion has benefited from Brigham, Gapenski, and Ehrhardt, *Financial Management*, chapter 9.

EBIT and depreciation give us the two components of free cash flow. To calculate the other two, we must compute the year-to-year changes to obtain the cash outflow arising from an increase in those investments. Thus,

	2003	2004	2005
Operating working capital	$30	$25	$20
Gross fixed assets	40	30	30

We expect the income tax rate to be 40 percent in each of the years. Now we are ready to calculate the free cash flows for the three years:[21]

	2003	2004	2005
EBIT $\times$ (1 − T)	$54	$66	$75
+ Depreciation	30	35	40
− Increase in operating working capital	30	25	20
− Increase in gross fixed assets	40	30	30
Free cash flow	$14	$46	$65

The next step is to calculate the present value of the free cash flows. At this point we must establish the discount rate—the cost of capital. We estimate it to be 12 percent. Therefore, the present value of the above three cash flows at the end of 2002 will be the following (again using data from Appendix Table C.1c):

Year 2003	14 $\times$ .8929	$12.5
2004	46 $\times$ .7972	36.7
2005	65 $\times$ .7118	46.3
Total		$95.5

Now we must account for the cash flows after the first three high-growth years. We had assumed previously that we would expect the normal long-term growth rate in free cash flow to be 6 percent. We can use the constant growth formula (Gordon model) to give us the answer. If free cash flow grows by 6 percent in 2006, then it will amount to 65 $\times$ 1.06 = $68.9. As the cost of capital is 12 percent and the growth rate is 6 percent, our calculation will proceed as follows:

$$68.9/(0.12 - 0.06) = 68.9/(0.06) = 1148.3$$

The answer is the present value of all future cash flows at the beginning of year 2006 (or the end of 2005). To bring this amount back to the end of 2002, we must discount the amount for three years, or 1148.3 $\times$ .7118 = 817.4. The last step is to add the present value of the first three years to the present value of the growing perpetuity: 95.5 + 817.4 = 912.9.

---

[21]It is quite common for a new, small, and growing company to have negative free cash flows in its early years. Even though its EBIT is positive, it will have substantial cash outflows as it builds up its working capital and fixed asset base. To simplify matters, we have assumed positive free cash flows in each year.

We have thus estimated the total value of your business to be $912,900. But as one of the owners of the business, you are interested in how much you could receive for your stock. We must now deduct any bank debt and long-term debt that you have on your balance sheet. Suppose that you had borrowed $300,000. Then the estimate of your stock value is $612,900. Let us assume that you and the other present owners wish to retain 20 percent of the stock ownership of the firm. This means you could expect to obtain $490,320 from your IPO.

Some cautions are in order. The result that we calculated is extremely sensitive to all the estimates we had made for cash flows, tax rates, and discount rates. The final results could differ substantially from our calculations. It would most likely be useful to do one or more additional calculations, using more optimistic and pessimistic assumptions, to help establish a range of potential outcomes.[22]

You would perform a similar calculation, if instead of an IPO, you were to consider a buyout offer by a large established firm in your industry. You would then be interested in determining the price at which you would be willing to sell your company. Again it would be useful to make several calculations to arrive at a desirable selling price. Further, if the acquiring firm should be able to achieve some synergies from taking over your firm, then the value of your company could be higher. That firm certainly made calculations similar to yours, and because of the synergies, they may have arrived at a higher figure. Thus, after you have bargained with the large firm, you may end up with a larger amount. And if you were lucky enough to have two large firms competing to acquire you, you may indeed strike a good bargain.

INTERNATIONAL APPLICATION: CAPITAL BUDGETING IN A MULTINATIONAL CORPORATION

The capital budgeting process, as we have seen, is often quite complicated. Investment proposals are analyzed carefully, and then approvals must be obtained by management to implement these projects, particularly when the potential expenditures are large.

While this is true when proposals are confined to the company's domestic operations, the process becomes even more complex when a multinational corporation considers an investment in one of its foreign subsidiaries. Corporations invest in foreign countries for many reasons. A corporation may be able to take advantage of lower production costs. The higher sales will permit a corporation to spread fixed costs (e.g., research and development). Because a company may be excluded from exporting its product due to various import restrictions, it protects its foreign markets if it can produce abroad. These and many other reasons have caused U.S. corporations to go international. Of course, making foreign investments may also carry considerable risk, which we will discuss in our next chapter. Here we consider only the complications that are inherent in making investments across national borders.

Since it is the domestic parent company that pays dividends to the stockholders, the parent will expect that at least some part of the foreign subsidiary's cash flow will

---

[22]Sensitivity analysis calculations are discussed in detail in chapter 14.

be repatriated to the domestic company. However, in some cases, the foreign country may not permit a free flow of cash abroad. If this blockage is temporary, and the subsidiary has an opportunity to make an investment in its own country, then the effect may not be great or may even be advantageous. However, if it is more or less permanent, then this will decrease the cash flows to the parent. In some cases, taxes are imposed by the subsidiary's country when it remits dividends to its parent.

Income tax rates probably differ in the two countries. The foreign subsidiary pays a tax on its income. Usually this tax will be credited against the taxes the parent must pay on the income and dividends generated by the subsidiary. If the parent's tax is higher than the subsidiary's, the parent will have to pay this additional tax to its tax authority, thus decreasing the net cash flow it receives.

Various other cash flows can be obtained by the parent from its subsidiary. Frequently, there are licensing fees that must be remitted. Second, the parent may export certain components that the subsidiary will incorporate in its final product. These charges must be paid for; the transfer price of these components probably includes a profit to the parent, which must be accounted for in its income tax reports.

The differences in inflation rates and changes in currency exchange rates also may have a significant effect on the cash flows between the two organizations.

All of these events will most likely cause the cash flows from a project to the parent to be different from those received by its subsidiary. Thus, when the present values of the project are calculated both from the point of view of the parent and the subsidiary, substantial differences may occur. It may not be at all extraordinary for the net present value of a project to be positive to the subsidiary and negative to the parent.

Which of the two results should prevail? Theoretically, the parent's cash flows and net present value should determine the decision whether to invest. After all, it is the parent's cash flow that is used to pay shareholder dividends, and the net present value generated by the parent is instrumental in creating shareholder value. Thus, while it is important to analyze projects at the subsidiary's level, the parent's result should determine the final decision.[23]

A recent study of multinational company capital budgeting practices uncovered some interesting results. This study surveyed 146 companies with total annual sales ranging from $1 billion to over $50 billion. The median sales figure was $2.89 billion, with foreign sales of 34 percent of total sales. The median number of countries in which the companies had foreign operations was 19; some companies operated in more than 50 countries. Maximization of shareholder wealth was the primary goal of 54 percent of the firms. You will remember that we had said above that the cash flow of the parent company should be the determining factor in the evaluation of foreign projects. However, this study showed that 61 percent of the firms evaluated the subsidiaries' results primarily while only 39 percent made decisions on the basis of cash flows to the parent. The author of the study states that "[f]rom a normative viewpoint, this is a less than satisfactory circumstance."[24]

---

[23]This section has benefited greatly from materials contained in David K. Eiteman, Arthur I. Stonehill, and Michael H. Moffett, *Multinational Business Finance*, 9th ed., Boston: Addison-Wesley, 2001, pp. 408–409; and Dennis J. O'Connor and Alberto T. Bueso, *International Dimensions of Financial Management*, New York: Macmillan, 1990, pp. 431–42.

[24]Stanley Block, "Integrating Traditional Capital Budgeting Concepts into an International Decision-Making Environment," *The Engineering Economist*, 45 (2000), pp. 309–325.

MODULE 13F

GLOBAL FOODS

The Solution

PROJECT 1: EXPANSION PROPOSAL

George Kline is now ready to put some numbers together. He ascertains that the market forecast of 100 million cases pertains to Global's first year of production, and the 4 percent assumed growth rate will apply thereafter. Since the market research people expect, rather optimistically, that market share will grow to 5 percent after four years, George sets market share at 2, 3, and 4 percent respectively, for the interim years. He calculates the seven-year MACRS depreciation for the equipment using the midyear convention as required by the 1986 tax law. (Generally, under this law, only one-half of the first year's depreciation can be taken in the first year and one-half at the end. Thus, if a piece of equipment is depreciated on a seven-year basis, it will actually be depreciated over eight years. The depreciation percentages used in this example are 14 percent, 25 percent, 17 percent, 13 percent, 10 percent, 9 percent, 9 percent, and 3 percent.) Depreciation will start in year 2; thus, the equipment will not be fully depreciated at the end of six years; nor will the buildings. George assumes that the remaining book values will represent the market value at the end of year 7 and will be shown as cash inflows at that point. He also decides that of the original $750,000 cash outflow for working capital, 80 percent will be recovered as cash at the end of year 7 (some accounts receivable will not be collectible, and some inventory will be obsolete). The 20 percent loss will be tax deductible.

George now prepares his worksheet, shown in Table 13.3. The column labeled "Constant" contains the parameters established originally. (These constant parameters can be changed if different assumptions are to be used. A change in one of these will alter the entire line. This technique will be used in chapter 14 when we examine how any change in the assumptions will affect the results.) Most of the numbers in this table are self-explanatory, but a few comments should help. The start-up expense of $750 is tax deductible; thus, the cash outflow is $450. The cost of the plant is $3.5 million (50 percent of the purchase price plus $1 million for renovation). The cost of equipment is $3 million (40 percent of the original purchase price plus $1 million for new machinery). Land ($500,000) is assumed not to appreciate.

When the cash flows are obtained and discounted at the 15 percent required rate of return, the resulting NPV is a positive $3,553,000. The internal rate of return is 24.2 percent—considerably above the required rate.

George can therefore recommend the acceptance of this expansion project. However, since all of the cash flows are estimates into the future, there is probably considerable uncertainty about their accuracy. We will revisit this project in chapter 14 and will show how risk and uncertainty can be accommodated in our analysis.

(*Continued*)

Table 13.3
Expansion Project ($000)

	CONSTANT	YEAR 0	YEAR 1	YEAR 2	YEAR 3	YEAR 4	YEAR 5	YEAR 6	YEAR 7
Total market	4.0%			100,000	104,000	108,160	112,486	116,986	121,665
Market share (%)				1.0	2.0	3.0	4.0	5.0	5.0
Company sales (qty)				1,000	2,080	3,245	4,499	5,849	6,083
Expenditures		(5,000)	(2,000)						
Working capital			(750)						
Start-up expense	(750)		(450)						
Sales	5.00			5,000	10,400	16,224	22,497	29,246	30,416
Product cost	2.50			2,500	5,200	8,112	11,249	14,623	15,208
Distribution cost	0.60			600	1,248	1,947	2,700	3,510	3,650
G&A expense (fixed)	500			500	500	500	500	500	500
G&A expense (variable)	3.0%			150	312	487	675	877	912
Advertising expense	5.0%			250	520	811	1,125	1,462	1,521
Depreciation (plant)	3,500			111	111	111	111	111	111
Depreciation (equipment)	3,000			420	750	510	390	300	270
Total cost & expenses				4,531	8,641	12,478	16,749	21,384	22,173
Net earnings before taxes				469	1,759	3,746	5,748	7,863	8,244
Income tax	40%			188	704	1,498	2,299	3,145	3,298
Net earnings after taxes				281	1,055	2,248	3,449	4,718	4,946
Add: depreciation				531	861	621	501	411	381
Operating cash flow				812	1,916	2,869	3,950	5,129	5,327
Remaining values									
Land									500
Plant									2,833
Equipment									360
Working capital	80.0%								660
Total cash flow		(5,000)	(3,200)	812	1,916	2,869	3,950	5,129	9,681
Net present value	15.0%								3,553
Internal rate or return									24.2%

PROJECT 2: DEPALLETIZER REPLACEMENT

The original cash outflow at time 0 is $100,000. But if the investment in the new machine is made, the old one will be sold for $12,000. Since its book value is only $10,000, there would be profit from the disposal of used equipment of $2,000. The tax rate being 40 percent, the company would have to pay income tax of $800 on this profit; so the cash inflow from the sale of the old depalletizer would be $11,200.

The annual increase in operating cash flows would be $18,000. The new machine would be depreciated over seven years straight-line. The annual depreciation would, therefore, be $14,286. The annual operating cash flow statement would be as follows:

Revenue less cost	$18,000
Depreciation	14,286
Net profit before taxes	$3,714
Income tax	1,486
Net profit after taxes	$2,228
Depreciation	14,286
Net cash flow	$16,514

Original investment at $t = 0$	$-100,000
Cash proceeds from old machines at $t = 0$	11,200
Annual cash flow from operations, years 1–7, at PV of annuity factor, 7 years at 12%:	
16,514 × 4.5638	75,363
Annual operating cash flows, years 8–10:	
Year 8 10,800 × 0.4039	4,362
Year 9 10,800 × 0.3606	3,894
Year 10 10,800 × 0.3220	3,478
Depreciation of old machines forgone:	
5,000 × 0.4 × 1.6091	-3,380
Net present value	$-5,083

These cash flows would occur during the first seven years of operations. In years 8–10, there would be no depreciation tax shield. Thus, the annual operating cash flows would be:

Revenue less cost	$18,000
Income tax	7,200
Net cash flow	$10,800

One additional piece of information must be included. If Global Foods had kept the old machine, it would be depreciated in years 1 and 2 at $5,000 annually. Since the tax rate is 40 percent, Global would save $2,000 each year in taxes—a cash inflow. If the old machine is sold, this

(Continued)

depreciation tax shield will no longer be available. Consequently, the cash flows would be decreased by the present value of the two after-tax depreciation deductions.

Now the proposal can be put together: The IRR calculation would have given us 10.5 percent.

The result is a negative net present value (and an IRR less than the cost of capital). Acquisition of the new depalletizer is not indicated at this time. This is the recommendation the capital planning department will make. However, the decision could be reconsidered if any of the cash flow estimates should change.

Summary

In this chapter we expanded the economic concept of profit maximization to multi-period projects.

Capital budgeting involves the evaluation of projects in which initial expenditures provide streams of cash inflows over a significant period of time. The process of evaluating capital proposals includes the following:

1. Estimating all incremental cash flows resulting from the project
2. Discounting all flows to the present
3. Determining whether a proposal should be accepted

Two methods were recommended for evaluating capital budgeting proposals—net present value and internal rate of return. These two criteria were compared as to their validity. It was found that, from a theoretical viewpoint, net present value is the more valid. However, there is much to recommend the use of IRR, and business, in fact, favors this technique. In most cases, both methods lead to the same answer.

The concept of the cost of capital was then developed, and methods of arriving at a weighted cost of capital were discussed.

Finally, using the economist's marginal revenue–marginal cost approach, it was shown that, to maximize its total value, a firm should accept any project whose IRR exceeds the marginal cost of capital.

Important Concepts

Accounting rate of return: Also known as the *return on investment* (ROI) or *return on assets* (ROA), a method for evaluating capital projects. It is obtained by dividing the average annual profit by the average investment. (p. 571)

Capital asset pricing model (CAPM): A financial model specifying relationships between risk and return. An important part of the CAPM is the development of beta, which measures the market

risk of a security and is a necessary ingredient in determining a stock's required rate of return. (p. 583)

Capital budgeting: An area of business decision making that concerns undertakings whose receipts and expenses continue over a significant period of time. (p. 568)

Capital rationing: The practice of restricting capital expenditure to a certain amount, possibly resulting in the rejection of projects that have a positive net present value and should be accepted to maximize the company's value. (p. 587)

Cost of capital: Also often referred to as the required rate of return, the hurdle rate, or the cut-off rate, the rate of return a company must earn on its assets to justify the using and acquiring of funds. (p. 572)

Discount rate: The rate at which cash flows are discounted. It is the required rate of return or cost of capital. (p. 572)

Dividend growth model: A method to arrive at the value of a security. Given the price of the security, it calculates the company's cost of equity as the dividend divided by the current stock price plus the growth rate in dividends (assumed to be constant). It is an alternative method to CAPM in calculating the equity cost of capital. (p. 582)

Free cash flow: Funds that are available for distribution to investors. It includes operating cash flow after taxes minus (plus) increases (decreases) in operating working capital and fixed assets investment. (p. 588)

Independent projects: A situation in which the acceptance of one capital project does not preclude the acceptance of another project. (See *mutually exclusive projects.*) (p. 574)

Internal rate of return (IRR): One method of evaluating capital projects by discounting cash flows. The IRR is the interest rate that equates the present value of inflows with the present value of outflows, or, in other words, causes the net present value of the project to equal zero. (p. 571)

Mutually exclusive projects: A situation in which the acceptance of one project precludes the acceptance of another. (p. 575)

Net present value (NPV): A method of evaluating capital projects in which all cash flows are discounted at the cost of capital to the present and the present value of all outflows is subtracted from the present value of all inflows. (p. 571)

Payback: A method of evaluating capital projects in which the original investment is divided by the annual cash flow. It tells management how many years it will take for a project's cash inflows to repay the original investment. (p. 571)

Time value of money: Very basically, this means that a dollar today is worth more than a dollar tomorrow, because today's dollar will earn interest and increase in value. (p. 570)

QUESTIONS

1. What is the objective of capital budgeting?
2. Name five types of decisions that utilize the capital budgeting method.
3. Define the *time value of money.*
4. How is net present value calculated? What is the decision rule for net present value?
5. How is the internal rate of return calculated? What is the decision rule for IRR?
6. The relationship between net present value and the internal rate of return is such that the IRR of a project is equal to the firm's cost of capital when the NPV of the project is $0. True or false? Explain.
7. Under which circumstances can the NPV and IRR calculations lead to conflicting results? What is the major reason for the difference? Which of the two methods is preferable? Why?
8. What are the major types of cash flows to be included in a capital budgeting analysis? Describe each.
9. Why is depreciation important in the analysis of a capital budgeting proposal?
10. Should a reallocation of fixed costs from other projects to the project being analyzed be included in the project's cash flows, if there is no net increase in cash outflow to the company? Why or why not?
11. You are analyzing a potential capital investment project involving a new product. As you are compiling all the relevant data for your analysis, you are informed of an expenditure that occurred during the prior year. The marketing research department of your company conducted an assessment of the demand for this new product. The cost of this research was

$100,000 and was part of the company's expenses during the previous year. Is this relevant to your present analysis? Why or why not?

12. How does the market value of an old piece of equipment affect an equipment replacement decision?

13. How is the company's optimal capital budget determined? Does the decision-making process in this case resemble the procedure used in determining the price and quantity of output? How?

14. How is the weighted cost of capital determined?

15. Discuss the two methods by which the costs of equity can be determined.

16. Define *beta*. How is it used to compute the required rate of return on a company's stock (the equity cost of capital)? An investment publication recently estimated the beta of Dominion Resources (a large electric utility company) to be .5, while the beta of Hewlett-Packard (a computer and printer manufacturer) was 1.2. Why is there such a large difference between the betas of the two companies? Which would you expect to have the higher required rate of return on its common stock?

17. Why is capital rationing not considered to be rational maximizing behavior?

PROBLEMS

1. Jay Wechsler agrees to purchase a car from a local dealer, the Con Car Co. The purchase price is $15,000. Jay has the cash to pay the entire amount and wants to do so. Con's sales manager uses the following argument to convince him to finance the car: "All we require is a down payment of $3,000. Then you can borrow the $12,000 from our finance company at 12 percent. You will make monthly payments of $266.93 for five years (60 months), a total of $16,015.80. If you do that, you get to keep your $12,000. Now suppose you keep this money in a money market account that pays you 8 percent compounded quarterly. In five years the $12,000 will grow to $17,831.40. That means that you will be better off by $1,815.60 than if you pay the $12,000 in cash."

Assume that all the numbers are correct. Does the offer sound too good to be true? Why? (This is an argument often used by automobile dealers. One of the authors encountered it not too long ago.)

2. Your firm has an opportunity to make an investment of $50,000. Its cost of capital is 12 percent. It expects after-tax cash flows (including the tax shield from depreciation) for the next five years to be as follows:

Year 1	$10,000
Year 2	20,000
Year 3	30,000
Year 4	20,000
Year 5	5,000

a. Calculate the net present value.
b. Calculate the internal rate of return (to the nearest percent).
c. Would you accept this project?

3. You own a large collection of fine wines. You now decide that the time has come to consider liquidating this valuable asset. However, you predict that the value of your collection will rise in the next few years. The following are your estimates:

YEAR	TODAY	1	2	3	4	5	6
Value ($000)	70	88	104	119	132	142	150

   If you assume your cost of capital to be 10 percent, when should you sell your collection to maximize your NPV?
4. The Glendale Construction Company is considering the purchase of a new crane. Its cost would be $500,000. If it were to make the purchase, the company would sell its old crane, which still has a book value of $100,000 and which it could probably sell in the second-hand market for $70,000. If the tax rate is 40 percent, what would be the actual cash investment in the new crane?
5. As capital investment analyst for the Parkhurst Printing Corporation, you have been asked to evaluate the advisability of purchasing a new printing press to accommodate projected increases in demand. This new machine is expected to last five years, and you will be calculating the cash flows of the project for that period.

   The purchase price of the press is expected to be $140,000; in addition, it will cost $10,000 to install it. The press will be depreciated on a straight-line basis over five years to a zero salvage value. However, it is expected to have a market value of $10,000 at the end of five years.

   The press is expected to generate the following cash revenues and cash costs and expenses:

	YEAR 1	YEAR 2	YEAR 3	YEAR 4	YEAR 5
Cash revenue	$50,000	$80,000	$80,000	$80,000	$40,000
Cash cost and expense	25,000	40,000	40,000	40,000	20,000

   Because of increased production, additional working capital of $15,000 will be needed at $t = 0$ (today) and will be returned at the end of the project (five years from now). The income tax rate is 40 percent, and the company's cost of capital is 12 percent. Calculate the net present value. Should the press be purchased?
6. The Gillmore Corporation is analyzing a new investment project. Cash flows for all the project years are being calculated. The following items, all pertaining to year 5, are directly associated with this project:

Sales	$800,000
Manufacturing costs (including $40,000 of depreciation)	380,000
Selling expenses (including $20,000 of depreciation)	170,000
Research & development expenses	50,000
	(Continued)

Fixed expenses reallocated from other products	15,000
Purchase of equipment	30,000
Sales of old equipment	10,000
Increase in working capital	35,000
Income taxes paid (on profits from this project)	45,000

Calculate the cash flow in year 5 to be used in the computation of the present value of this investment.

7. The Thunderbird Quick Delivery Company needs a truck and is evaluating two alternatives for meeting its needs for the next ten years.

Choice A: Buy a used Ford truck for $6,000. It will be depreciated straight-line over a 5-year life to a salvage value of zero. However, it is expected that the truck will be sold after 4 years for $800. At this point, another used Ford truck will be bought for $12,000. It will last six years and will have no market value at the end of this period. This truck will also be depreciated over 5 years on a straight-line basis.

Choice B: Buy a new Chevrolet truck for $16,000. The truck will last the entire ten years and will have a market value of $1,000 at the end. Again, 5-year straight-line depreciation will be used.

Other information: Income tax rate   34%
                   Cost of capital   12%

Which of the two choices is preferable?

8. Marriner Manufacturing is evaluating an expansion project expected to have a life of 20 years. You are given the following information:

   a. Land must be bought at a cost of $100,000. It is expected that it will be worth $200,000 at the end of 20 years, and that it can be sold at that price.
   b. A building, costing $100,000, will be bought and will be depreciated straight-line over 20 years to a salvage value of zero. However, it is estimated that the market value of the building at the end of 20 years will be $40,000.
   c. Equipment will be purchased for $200,000 and will be depreciated straight-line over seven years to a salvage value of zero. The actual market value of the equipment at the end of 20 years is expected to be zero.
   d. The project will require additional working capital of $50,000 initially (at t=0). The entire amount is expected to be recovered at the end of year 20.
   e. Net earnings before taxes (after depreciation) are expected to be $100,000 in year 1, and are expected to grow at 4% per year until the project terminates at the end of year 20.
   f. The tax rate (both ordinary and capital gains) is expected to be 40%.
   Compute the cash flow expected to be generated in year 20.

9. The Colgate Distributing Company has the choice of furnishing its sales representatives with a car or paying a mileage allowance for the use of the representatives' own cars. If the company furnishes the car, it will pay all expenses connected with it, including gasoline for business mileage. The estimates are as follows:

Cost of car: $15,000
Estimated life: Four years
Depreciation method: Straight-line over four years (assuming no salvage value)

Expected sales value of car at end of four years: $2,500
Estimated annual operating costs:

Gasoline	$900
License and insurance	600
Garaging	300
Maintenance	
Year 1	250
Year 2	350
Year 3	450
Year 4	600

If the sales representatives use their own cars, the company will reimburse them at 35 cents per mile; the company estimates that each representative will drive 18,000 miles per year for business purposes. The company's cost of capital is 10 percent, and its income tax rate is 40 percent.

Should the company buy cars for its sales representatives or pay them a mileage allowance? Use the NPV method in your calculation.

10. The Manchester Tool Company is considering the replacement of an existing machine by a more efficient machine. The new machine costs $1,200,000 and requires installation costs of $150,000.

The present machine is four years old. It originally cost $800,000 and is being depreciated straight-line over ten years to a zero salvage value. Its market value today is $400,000. It can be used for the next six years; at that time, its market value will be zero.

The new machine has an expected life of six years and will be depreciated on a straight-line method over five years to a salvage value of zero. However, it is expected to have a market value of $200,000 at the end of six years.

The new machine will reduce operating costs by $250,000 per year. The company's income tax rate is 40 percent, and its cost of capital is 9 percent. Would you recommend that the old machine be replaced?

11. A company's common stock is currently selling at $40 per share. Its most recent dividend was $1.60, and the financial community expects that its dividend will grow at 10 percent per year in the foreseeable future. What is the company's equity cost of retained earnings? If the company sells new common stock to finance new projects and must pay $2 per share in flotation costs, what is the cost of equity?

12. Harvey Corporation's stock price today is $40. The most recent annual dividend it paid was $2. You estimate that the company's equity cost is 10 percent. If you expect the company's dividends to increase at a constant rate, what do you expect the growth rate to be?

13. A company has 1,000,000 shares of common stock outstanding, and the current market price is $50 per share. The company has also issued 20,000 bonds ($1,000 maturity value each), which are presently selling in the market at $980 each. The bonds are selling at a yield of 11 percent; the company expects to pay a dividend of $3 per share in the coming year, and the dividend is expected to grow at 8 per-

cent per year. The company is in the 40 percent tax bracket. What is the weighted cost of capital?

14. A company has a beta of 1.3. The risk-free interest rate today is 8 percent, and the return on a market portfolio of stocks is 14 percent. (Therefore, the market risk premium is 6 percent, the difference between the market return and the risk-free return.)

   a. What is the required return (equity cost) on the company's stock?
   b. If the risk-free rate rises to 9 percent, what will be the required rate of return on the company's stock?
   c. If the beta of this company were 0.8, what would be its required rate of return?

15. Two mutually exclusive alternatives, projects C and D, have the following investments and cash flows:

	Project C	Project D
Investment at period $t = 0$	$40,000	$40,000
Cash inflow at $t = 1$	10,000	20,500
Cash inflow at $t = 2$	10,000	20,500
Cash inflow at $t = 3$	47,000	20,500

   a. Calculate the net present value and internal rate of return of each project. The company's cost of capital is 12 percent.
   b. Which of the two projects would you accept? Explain.
   c. Sketch the two projects' NPV profiles.

16. The Berkshire Resort Hotel has planned several improvement projects. However, it has decided to restrict its capital expenditures to $340,000 during the next year. The following are the projects it has on its drawing board:

	Original Investment	Net Present Value
Additional tennis court	$ 20,000	$ 5,500
Kitchen renovation	50,000	14,000
New children's playground	60,000	12,500
New bungalows	100,000	22,500
New golf clubhouse	120,000	32,500
Olympic-size swimming pool	140,000	45,000
New theater arena	150,000	40,000

Which projects should it undertake?

Appendix 13A

Calculations for Time Value of Money

In this appendix, a brief explanation of the computation of the time value of money is given for readers not familiar with this subject. Modern technology has made these calculations very easy. Many computer programs have built-in time-value functions, and a large assortment of hand-held calculators will solve these problems using special keys. However, some people who use these methods do not understand the rationale for the answers and merely accept the results.

At the other extreme, the calculations could be made using exponentials and/or logarithms. Such a procedure may provide a thorough learning experience, but it is tedious and time consuming. Compound interest tables have been developed to provide a relatively easy tool for solving time-value problems. They will be found in Appendix C at the end of this book. Here we will walk through four types of calculations, each representing one of the four tables.

THE FUTURE VALUE OF A SINGLE SUM

MODULE
13AA

If you deposit $1,000 in a savings account that pays 7 percent interest annually, and you do not withdraw this interest, the original amount will keep growing. (In real life, bank interest is usually compounded more frequently than once a year, but annual compounding will be assumed here. In other words, the 7 percent will be credited to the account once a year, at the end of the year.) One year later, $70 of interest will be added to the account, making the total balance $1,070. In mathematical terms, this occurrence can be written as follows: If i equals the annual interest rate, then the amount of interest paid in one year equals A times i, where A is the original amount deposited. Thus, B, the ending balance in the account, will be

$$B = A + (A \times i) \quad \text{or} \quad B = A(1 + i)$$

In the present case, this will compute as

$$B = 1{,}000(1 + 0.07) = 1{,}000(1.07) = 1{,}070$$

Now, if the $1,070 is left in the account for another year, interest will be paid on the $1,070:

$$B = 1{,}070(1.07) = 1{,}144.90$$

We could also find the answer in the following way:

$$B = 1{,}000 \times 1.07 \times 1.07 = 1{,}144.90$$

This expression simplifies to $1{,}000\ (1.07)^2$. Thus, in general terms,

$$FV = PV(1 + i)^n$$

where FV = Future value
    PV = Present value
    i = Rate of interest
    n = Number of periods over which compounding takes place

Table C.1a in Appendix C at the end of this book presents the $(1 + i)^n$ factors for a large number of periods and interest rates. Thus, if you wish to find out how much your original $1,000 will grow in eight years, you can look it up by moving down the leftmost (period) column to 8 and then moving to the right until you hit the 7 percent column. You will obtain an answer of 1.7182. Substituting into the general formula,

$$FV = 1,000(1.7182)$$

$$= 1,718.20$$

This table can also be used if you know the beginning and ending amounts and want to find the rate of interest it took to go from the first to the last amount. The formula for future value can be easily transformed to solve for the interest rate. If we refer to the number that appears in the table as "factor," then

$$FV = PV \text{ (Factor)}$$

$$Factor = FV/PV$$

Assume that you are saving for a particular purpose. You put aside $1,000 today and want to have $2,000 five years from now:

$$Factor = \frac{2,000}{1,000}$$

$$= 2$$

To find the answer, enter the table at five periods and move to the right until the number nearest to 2 is reached. This happens at 15 percent, where the $(1 + i)^n$ factor equals 2.0114. Thus, you would have to earn approximately 15 percent interest to double your amount in five years.[25]

This type of calculation is employed frequently to obtain compound growth rates, a very popular concept in business.

THE FUTURE VALUE OF AN ANNUITY

MODULE 13AB

In the previous section we dealt with the compounding of a single sum. But suppose that a uniform amount is set aside each period (e.g., each year), and we want to know how much will be in the account after several years.

For example, suppose five annual deposits of $500 each will be made to an account paying 7 percent annually, starting a year from now. What will be the amount at the end of five years? A simple diagram will illustrate:

---

[25]If more exact results are needed, linear interpolation should be used. We will not explain interpolation here. An explanation can be found in any basic mathematics text.

The first $500 will collect interest for four years, the second for three years, and so on. This problem could be solved by making all the separate calculations and adding the items:

$$FV_a = A(1 + i)^{n-1} + A(1 + i)^{n-2} + \cdots + A(1 + i)^0$$

where FV_a = Future value of the annuity
A = Annuity

This expression simplifies to

$$\frac{(1 + i)^n - 1}{i}$$

Again, a table has been constructed to ease the effort involved in this calculation. Table C.1b in Appendix C shows the *sum of an annuity*. For the question posed here the answer is:

$$FV_a = A \text{ (Factor)}$$
$$= 500 \text{ (5.7507)}$$
$$= 2,875.35$$

where "factor" is found in Table C.1b.

The preceding calculation solves for the future value of the annuity. But suppose we have a problem stated in the following form:

To finance the college education of a just-born child, the parents expect they will need $200,000 18 years from now. They believe that they can earn 7 percent on their savings. How much should they put aside each year? The future-value formula can be transposed to solve for the annuity, *A:*

$$A = FV_a/\text{Factor}$$
$$= 200,000/33.999$$
$$= 5,883$$

The parents will have to deposit $5,883 per year to have $200,000 in 18 years.

Table C.1b presents factors for ordinary annuities, which means that the first payment is made at the end of the first period and the last payment occurs on the final date. But suppose the payments are to start right now, and the last payment will occur at the beginning of the last period. Such a series of payments is usually referred to as an *annuity due*, and the diagram for such an arrangement, using data from the first example of this section, is:

Table C.1*b* can still be applied, with one small change. The ordinary annuity factor in Table C.1*b* must be multiplied by $(1 + i)$. With interest again at 7 percent, the "annuity due" factor becomes 5.7507 times 1.07, or 6.1532. Thus, the result is

$$FV_a = 500(6.1532)$$

$$= 3,077$$

Note that the amount accumulated at the end of five years is considerably larger than in the first example. The reason? Each of the contributions has an extra year to compound.

PRESENT VALUE OF A SINGLE SUM

MODULE 13AA

Suppose you are to receive a sum of $500 three years from now on. You would like to receive the money today, and you would be willing to accept less, as an amount deposited today with interest would grow to a larger sum in three years. The question can be stated as follows: How much money accepted today would be equivalent to $500 three years from now? That depends, of course, on the rate of interest you earn on your money. As with our previous example, let us use a 7 percent interest rate.

Remember from our discussion of compounding a single sum that FV = PV $(1 + i)_n$. We are now attempting to solve the opposite problem: we know the future value and wish to find the present value. Therefore,

$$PV = \frac{FV}{(1 + i)^n}$$

Because

$$\frac{1}{(1 + i)^n} = (1 + i)^{-n}$$

this simple equation can be written as

$$PV = FV (1 + i)^{-n}$$

The number can be found in Table C.1*c*. We look up the three-year factor at 7 percent and find it to be 0.8163. Thus,

$$PV = 500 (0.8163)$$

$$= 408$$

Incidentally, the present-value factors (Table C.1*c*) are reciprocals of the future-value factors (Table C.1*a*). Thus, if you have only one of these tables available, you can still do both future- and present-value calculations. For the preceding case, if only Table C.1*a* were available, the solution would be as follows:

$$FV = PV (1 + i)^n$$

$$PV = \frac{FV}{(1 + i)^n}$$

$$= \frac{500}{1.225}$$

$$= 408$$

PRESENT VALUE OF AN ANNUITY

**MODULE
13AB**

Suppose that instead of receiving just one amount in the future, you expect to receive a series of uniform payments annually for four years starting a year from now (an ordinary annuity), or, as an alternative, you can receive a lump sum today. The single amount that would be equivalent to the annuity again depends on the interest rate you can earn. Assume that you are to receive four annual payments of $2,000. This is illustrated as follows:

The solution could be obtained by calculating the present value of each payment using Table C.1c and totaling the results. The first $2,000 would be discounted one year, the second two years, and so on. Using Table C.1d, however, avoids this time-consuming method. The factors contained in this table already include the discounting and summation of all the individual numbers. Thus, if the interest rate to be used is 8 percent, then

$$PV_a = A \text{ (Factor)}$$

$$= 2,000 \text{ (3.3121)}$$

$$= 6,624$$

where "factor" is found in Table C.1d. You would be indifferent between receiving a sum of $6,624 today and a series of four annual payments of $2,000.

The preceding calculations apply to an ordinary annuity. If the first payment is to be received today, a relatively simple adjustment must be made to the factors of Table C.1d.

A very relevant example of the present value of an annuity due is the case of a state lottery. You certainly have seen a banner headline such as "John P. Oliver Wins $5 Million in the Lottery." True, Mr. Oliver will receive $5 million (before he pays his taxes), but not all at one time. State lotteries frequently pay the winners in 20 equal installments; the first payment is received today and the other 19 are received annually starting one year from today. To convert the calculation to an annuity due, the ordinary annuity factor in Table C.1d must be multiplied by $(1 + i)$. For 20 payments of $250,000 each, using an 8 percent interest rate, the 20-year factor is 9.8181 which, when multiplied by 1.08, becomes 10.6035. The calculation is as follows:

$$PV_a = A \text{ (10.6035)}$$

$$= 250,000 \text{ (10.6035)}$$

$$= 2,650,875$$

Obviously, this amount is much less than the $5 million that was announced as Mr. Oliver's winning ticket. Still, more than $2.5 million dollars is not that bad.

There is one more exercise that should be examined in this section. Suppose we know the present value of the annuity and the interest rate, but the annuity payment is unknown. Assume that you wish to borrow $20,000 to be paid back over five years in equal installments at an interest rate of 9 percent. What will your annual payments be? The factors in Table C.1d are again applicable, but we must reverse the formula:

$$PV_a = A \text{ (Factor)}$$

$$A = \frac{PV_a}{\text{Factor}}$$

$$= \frac{20,000}{3.8897}$$

$$= 5,142$$

MORE FREQUENT COMPOUNDING

All of the preceding examples were in terms of years—annual compounding. But compounding may occur more frequently. Banks advertise that they compound interest on savings accounts quarterly, monthly, or even daily. The more frequent the compounding, the greater the effect of the time value of money.

In the first section of this appendix, compounding of a single sum was discussed. The formula was

$$FV = PV (1 + i)^n$$

If compounding occurs more often than n—for instance, m times n—then the compounding formula is revised as follows:

$$FV = PV (1 + i/m)^{mn}$$

Suppose a deposit of $10,000 pays an annual interest rate of 8 percent compounded semiannually, and the time elapsed is five years. The equation would be:

$$FV = 10,000 (1 + 0.08/2)^{5 \times 2}$$

$$= 10,000 (1.04)^{10}$$

$$= 10,000 (1.4802)$$

$$= 14,802$$

If compounding had been annual, the resulting amount would have been lower: 10,000 (1.4693) = 14,693.

On the other hand, with quarterly compounding:

$$FV = 10,000 (1.02)^{20}$$

$$= 10,000 (1.4859)$$

$$= 14,859$$

The more frequent the compounding, the larger will be the future value.

BOND VALUES AND PERPETUITIES

MODULE
13AC

One more application of present-value calculations will be discussed here. A corporate or government bond pays periodic interest and then repays the face value on the maturity date. Interest payments are generally fixed for the life of the bond and are expressed as a percentage of the face value. Whether market interest rates rise or fall during the life of the bond, the periodic interest paid will not change. However, the price of the bond will change so that the yield corresponds to the interest rate paid in the market for bonds of a similar risk class and length of life.[26]

As an example, we will take a bond with a face and maturity value of $1,000 (the usual amount in which bonds are denominated). It will mature in 20 years (it was originally a 30-year bond, issued ten years ago), and the stated interest rate is 8 percent. Thus, the annual interest payment is $80.[27]

Interest rates have risen recently, and today bonds with 20-year maturities yield 10 percent. But because the interest payment of $80 per year on the bond cannot be changed, the market value of the bond (the price someone would be willing to pay for it today) will have to decline. This situation is quite obvious. If bonds are now yielding 10 percent, a potential buyer of a $1,000 bond would require $100 of annual interest. The bond in our example pays $80 per year, with a final payment of $1,000 at maturity. To obtain its value when the current market yield is 10 percent, we compute the present value of a 20-year annuity of $80 at a 10 percent discount rate and add to it the present value of the maturity value, $1,000, also discounted to the present at 10 percent:

$$P_0 = 80\ (8.5136) + 1,000\ (0.1486)$$

$$= 681 + 149 = 830$$

At $P_0 = 830$, representing the market price of the bond today, and a yield of 10 percent to maturity, this bond is equivalent to a bond selling today for $1,000 that pays $100 annually and will mature 20 years hence at $1,000.

Had interest rates dropped to 6 percent, the bond of our example, still paying $80 a year, would rise in price above its maturity value:

$$P_0 = 80\ (11.4699) + 1,000\ (0.3118)$$

$$= 918 + 312 = 1,230$$

Perpetual bonds do not exist in the United States. However, they have been issued elsewhere, for example, in the United Kingdom. Such bonds never mature, but they promise to pay a stated interest amount forever. If

$$P_0 = \text{Price of the bond today}$$

$$I = \text{Annual interest paid}$$

$$i = \text{Market interest rate}$$

---

[26] The riskier, or less safe, a bond, the higher will be the interest that the market will require. The longer the length of life of the bond, the higher will be the required interest, under normal circumstances.
[27] Bond interest is usually paid semiannually, but for this example, annual payments are assumed.

then

$$i = \frac{I}{P_0}$$

and

$$P_0 = \frac{I}{i}$$

If the bond pays $80 a year and the market rate is 8 percent, the price of the bond today will be its face value of $1,000. However, should the market rate of interest for bonds of this type rise to 10 percent, the bond paying $80 per year will be worth

$$P_0 = \frac{80}{0.1} = 800$$

A bond selling for $800 and paying $80 a year yields precisely 10 percent in perpetuity.

Fluctuations in bond prices will be greater for any change in the market interest rate, the longer the period to maturity. The price of a bond that matures one year hence will not decrease much when market interest rates rise. On the other hand, the price of a perpetuity will fluctuate very significantly with changes in market interest yields.

Chapter 14

Risk and Uncertainty

The Situation

When George Kline completed his analysis of the expansion proposal, he concluded that the company's plan for extending its activities into a new geographical region was desirable.[1] He had calculated a net present value that was positive and, consistently, an internal rate of return that exceeded the required rate of return (cost of capital).

He discussed his findings with his immediate manager, the company's treasurer. The treasurer agreed that the estimates used were the best available, and that even if some of them turned out to be overly optimistic, the project would still be acceptable. However, he indicated management's awareness that expanding into new, relatively untested territory was a rather perilous undertaking. He believed that more should be done to examine the economic risk characteristics of the project. Therefore, he asked George to perform additional risk analyses. George informed him that there are various techniques available, some of which involve statistical concepts. The treasurer suggested that George keep his analysis on a relatively simple level, but that it should be extensive enough that the vice president of finance and others who will be present when the proposal is presented can be comfortable with this important decision.

---

[1]See "Solution" in chapter 13.

INTRODUCTION

This chapter would be unnecessary if we were living in a world of perfect knowledge, where all future events could be determined with complete certainty.

Throughout this text, all quantities have been treated as if they were certain. Demand curves showed specific quantities that would be sold at specific prices. Cost curves showed definite dollar amounts of costs for specific quantities. In the preceding chapter, on capital budgeting, the various estimates of cash flows for projects were treated as if they were known with certainty. In the real world, of course, most future events are not known with any degree of certainty. Managers must make decisions daily, relying on estimates they believe are reasonably reliable but by no means certain. Dealing with uncertainty and recognizing that future results may differ from well-constructed plans is a reality in the business world.

Although risk or uncertainty was not explicitly considered in the calculation of cash flows in the preceding chapter, there were several references to risk. For example, the replacement project was evaluated at a lower discount rate than the expansion project because the latter was considered to be more risky. Risk and uncertainty also played an important role in chapter 6, on forecasting. In this chapter, the meaning of the words *risk* and *uncertainty* will be explained, and the various methods of incorporating these concepts into economic analysis will be explored.

RISK VERSUS UNCERTAINTY

In economic or financial theory, the two terms **risk** and **uncertainty** have somewhat different meanings, even though they are often used interchangeably.[2] Although no future events are known with certainty, some events can be assigned probabilities, and others cannot. Where future events can be defined and probabilities assigned, we have a case of risk. Thus, for instance, a company's sales manager estimates that next year's sales of diet cola have a 25 percent probability to be 5 million cases, a 50 percent probability to be 6 million, and a 25 percent probability to be 7 million. If there is no way to assign any probabilities to future random events, we are addressing pure uncertainty. Even though this distinction is theoretically important, many writers omit it as a matter of convenience. We will follow this practice.

How are probabilities obtained? There are at least two ways. In the terminology of economist Frank Knight, probabilities can be classified as *a priori* or *statistical*.[3] The former can be obtained by repetition. Thus, if a true two-sided coin is flipped an infinite number of times, tails will come up on half the tosses and heads on the other half. When two dice are thrown, there are 36 possible combinations of numbers.

---

[2]An early discussion of this distinction can be found in Frank H. Knight's *Risk, Uncertainty and Profit* (Boston: Houghton Mifflin, 1921, reprinted as no. 16 in a series of reprints by the London School of Economics and Political Science). Knight made the distinction as follows: "The essential fact is that 'risk' means in some cases a quantity susceptible of measurement, while at other times it is something distinctly not of this character . . . It will appear that a 'measurable' uncertainty, or 'risk' proper, as we shall use the term, is so far different from an unmeasurable one that it is not in effect an uncertainty at all" (pp. 19–20).

[3]Ibid., pp. 224–25. The names *objective* and *subjective* probabilities, respectively, can also be used.

Because there are six ways to obtain a 7, we can say that a 7 should appear on average once every six throws, if the two dice were thrown an infinite number of times. Instead of throwing the coin or dice an infinite number of times, we can specify the frequency based on general mathematical principles.

In everyday business, a priori probabilities cannot be specified. To assign probabilities to various outcomes, businesspeople must rely on statistical probabilities. These may be obtained empirically, based on past events. For instance, if a particular event has occurred once every ten times in the past, a 10 percent probability would be assigned to it. If probabilities of future events are assigned based on the past, then we are assuming that the future is a mirror of the past (which in itself could be construed to be an a priori judgment). Alternatively, probabilities obtained from past events can be adjusted to reflect changed expectations for the future.

SOURCES OF BUSINESS RISK

Before discussing how risk should be treated in economic analysis, it is important that we first explain the reasons a businessperson faces an uncertain future. What are some of the sources of business risk?

First, there are general economic conditions. Firms face rising and declining phases of business cycles. Some success can be attained in forecasting economic fluctuations, but the timing of changes and the volatility of economic activity are never known with certainty. Moreover, the effects of movements in general economic activity on a specific firm or a specific product are not known ahead of time. Thus, a firm does not have the ability to completely prepare for these changes.

In addition to uncertainty with respect to the economy as a whole, there are fluctuations in specific industries, which are at least as uncertain and may not always coincide with those of the overall economy.

Further, the actions of a company's competition are certainly not known perfectly. Closely related to competitive actions are changes in technology. If a competitor effectively introduces an improved product, sales of a particular company or even an industry may suffer. For instance, the introduction of DVDs has cut greatly into the demand for videotapes. Many travelers now book trips and hotel reservations over the Internet with a resulting decrease in travel agent business (in fact, airlines offer discounts to travelers who book over the Internet), and instant messaging on the Internet has impacted the business of telephone companies. On the other hand, a firm's own technological breakthrough may bring about considerably increased sales.

The vagaries of consumer demand create another source of risk for the businessperson. Successful products of one year or one season may become the discarded, unwanted items of the next. It is easy to find examples of such products. "Tickle-Me-Elmo" dolls—hot items for a year—met their demise. The fashion industry is notorious for changes in styles from one year to another; changes in the styles of women's shoes are a good example. And over the past few years, the popular sport of roller-skating has been replaced by roller-blading.

Not all sources of uncertainty stem from the demand side. In the process of decision making, a company must also consider costs and expenses. When estimates of future expenditures are made, the company cannot be sure what the prices of its factors of production will be (unless they are stipulated in contracts into which a company has entered). Thus, the prices of materials, such as sugar, corn starch, and flavorings, can change, and so can the costs of electricity and other services. Labor costs and the cost of benefits are also subject to change unless union contracts are in existence.

It is easy to see that almost any future business event is attended by uncertainty. Both revenues and costs per period as well as the length of life of a product are uncertain. Obviously, this greatly complicates the jobs of managers.

THE MEASURES OF RISK

When outcomes are uncertain, two measures that take risk into consideration are used.

First, not just one outcome but a number of outcomes is possible. Each potential result will have a **probability** attached to it. In making estimates of a future cash inflow, for example, the analyst must decide on the probability of each possible result and construct a probability distribution.

A **probability distribution** describes, in percentage terms, the chances of all possible occurrences. When all the probabilities of the possible events are added up, they must total 1, because all possibilities together must equal certainty. Thus, we may assign probabilities to various possible cash flows as shown in Table 14.1.

The interpretation of Table 14.1 is as follows: We estimate that possible cash flows from a project during the coming year will be $3,000, $4,000, $5,000, $6,000 or $7,000. Which of the five possible flows actually occurs will depend, for instance, on general economic conditions, the conditions in the industry, and the action of the competition. If all factors are favorable to the project, the cash flow will be $7,000; if unfavorable conditions prevail, the cash flow will be only $3,000. One of the other outcomes will emerge if some factors work to our benefit and others are unfavorable. Table 14.1 can also be translated into a bar chart, shown in Figure 14.1.

The assigned probabilities indicate that there is only a 10 percent chance that all the unfavorable predictions will materialize. Similarly, there is only one chance in ten (i.e., 10 percent) that all of the favorable conditions will prevail. It is much more likely that some favorable and some unfavorable influences will ensue. Therefore, the probabilities for the intermediate cash flows are the highest.

Table 14.1
Probability Distribution for Cash Inflows

CASH INFLOW	PROBABILITY
3,000	0.1
4,000	0.2
5,000	0.4
6,000	0.2
7,000	0.1

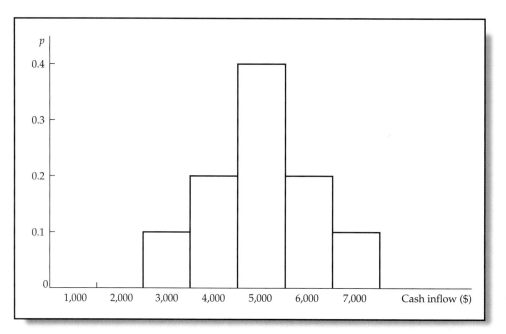

Figure 14.1
Bar Graph of Data from Table 14.1

Once we have established a probability distribution, we are ready to calculate the two measures used in decision making under conditions of risk.

MODULE 14A

Expected Value

From the numbers given in Table 14.1 we calculate a single value, the **expected value** of possible outcomes. The expected value is simply the average of all possible outcomes weighted by their respective probabilities.

$$\overline{R} = (3{,}000 \times 0.1) + (4{,}000 \times 0.2) + (5{,}000 \times 0.4) + (6{,}000 \times 0.2) + (7{,}000 \times 0.1)$$

$$= 300 + 800 + 2{,}000 + 1{,}200 + 700$$

$$= 5{,}000$$

where $\overline{R}$ represents the expected value. The generalized expression for expected value is as follows:

$$\overline{R} = \sum_{i=1}^{n} R_i p_i$$

where $\overline{R}$ = Expected value
R_i = Value in case i
p_i = Probability in case i
n = Number of possible outcomes

Table 14.2

Calculation of Standard Deviation for Table 14.1

R_i	p_i	$(R_i - \bar{R})$	$(R_i - \bar{R})^2$	$(R_i - \bar{R})^2 p_i$
3,000	0.1	−2,000	4,000,000	400,000
4,000	0.2	−1,000	1,000,000	200,000
5,000	0.4	0	0	0
6,000	0.2	1,000	1,000,000	200,000
7,000	0.1	2,000	2,000,000	400,000
				1,200,000

$$\sigma = \sqrt{1,200,000} = 1,095$$

Now that the weighted average—the expected value—has been obtained, we can determine the second measure, the one that specifies the extent of the risk.

The Standard Deviation

In economics and finance, risk is considered to be the dispersion of possible outcomes around the expected value. The greater the potential differences from the average, the greater the risk. Thus, to measure risk, we must find some yardstick that reflects the variation of possible outcomes from this average. A concept prominent in elementary statistics is used for this purpose—the standard deviation.[4]

The **standard deviation** is the square root of the weighted average of the squared deviations of all possible outcomes from the expected value:

$$\sigma = \sqrt{\sum_{i=1}^{n} (R_i - \bar{R})^2 p_i}$$

where σ is the standard deviation. For the example in Table 14.1, the standard deviation is calculated in Table 14.2.

What is the meaning of a standard deviation of 1,095? First of all, since our probability distribution is symmetric, there is a 50 percent chance that the outcome will be larger than the expected value and a 50 percent chance that it will be less. The chance of a particular outcome occurring depends on how many standard deviations it is removed from the mean. Based on statistical theory describing the normal curve (which will be discussed more fully later), about 34 percent of all possible occurrences will be within one standard deviation of the mean, on each side of the mean, 47.7 percent within two standard deviations, and 49.9 percent within three standard deviations. Thus, given the expected value of 5,000 and standard deviation of 1,095, we conclude the following: There is 34 percent probability that the cash flow will fall between 5,000 and 5,000 − 1,095, or 3,905. In other words, there is a 16 percent probability that our cash flow will be 3,905 or lower. Further, because two standard deviations are equal to 2,190, there is a 2.3 percent probability (50 percent–47.7 percent)

---

[4]If you wish to review the concept of standard deviation more thoroughly, any college statistics textbook can be consulted. See, for instance, Mark L. Berenson and David M. Levine, *Basic Business Statistics: Concepts and Applications,* 7th ed., Upper Saddle River, NJ: Prentice Hall, 1999.

Table 14.3
Data for Project 2

R_i	p_i	$(R_i - \bar{R})$	$(R_i - \bar{R})^2$	$(R_i - \bar{R})^2 p_i$
2,000	0.10	−3,000	9,000,000	900,000
3,500	0.25	−1,500	2,250,000	562,500
5,000	0.30	0	0	0
6,500	0.25	1,500	2,250,000	562,500
8,000	0.10	3,000	9,000,000	900,000
				2,925,000

$$\bar{R} = 5,000$$

$$\sigma = \sqrt{2,925,000} = 1,710$$

that the cash flow will be 2,810 or lower. And it is almost certain that the cash flow will not fall below 1,715 (5,000 minus three standard deviations, or 3,285). The same reasoning leads us to conclude that chances are almost nil that the cash flow will exceed 8,285. There is a 16 percent probability that it will exceed 6,095, and so on.

The combination of the expected value and the standard deviation aids in making a decision between two projects. Suppose that we have to choose between project 1 (shown in Tables 14.1 and 14.2) and another, called project 2. Data for project 2 are shown in Table 14.3 and Figure 14.2 is the bar chart for this project.

Since the expected values of the two proposals are identical, the decision will be made on the basis of the standard deviation. Project 2, with the greater standard

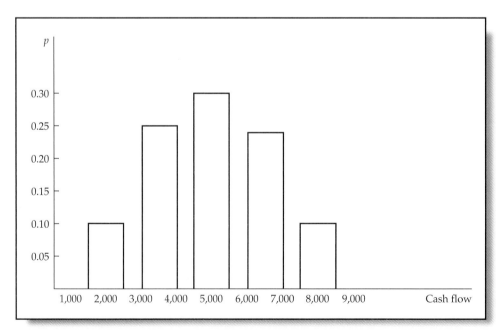

Figure 14.2
Bar Graph of Data from Table 14.3

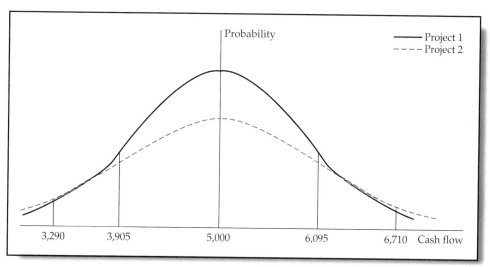

Figure 14.3
Continuous Distributions for Projects 1 and 2

deviation (1,710), is the riskier of the two. Generally, businesspeople are averse to risk; therefore, project 1, which has the lower risk, would usually be accepted.

Discrete versus Continuous Distributions and the Normal Curve

The frequency distributions that have been discussed so far are known as discrete.[5] The potential outcomes have been limited to just five numbers for each of the two projects. However, it is quite likely that other outcomes could occur—for instance, 4,679 or 6,227. If all possible outcomes are considered, we have a continuous distribution. The possible outcomes on a continuous distribution are often described by a bell-shaped curve, referred to as a *normal curve.* It is only on this type of curve that the properties of the standard deviation previously explained apply strictly. The two normal curves, shown in Figure 14.3, peak at the center, at the expected value, and are symmetrical on either side. Actually, the curves approach but do not reach zero at either end of the X-axis. Curves of this kind are called *asymptotic.*

With projects 1 and 2 drawn as continuous standard normal probability functions, project 1 exhibits a tighter curve, whereas project 2's curve is spread out over a much larger horizontal distance. Since project 1's standard deviation is 1,095, 34 percent of the area under its curve is between 5,000 and 3,905 (and also between 5,000 and 6,095). For project 2, whose standard deviation is 1,710, 34 percent of the area under the curve can be found between 5,000 and 3,290 (and also between 5,000 and 6,710).

The probabilities for any other range of numbers can be easily obtained from a table of values of the areas under the standard normal distribution function (see

---

[5]They are also symmetrical, which means that the observations to the left and to the right of the mean have the same probabilities and the same deviations from the mean.

Table C.2 in Appendix C at the end of this text). If, in assessing project 1, we wish to find the probability that the cash flow will be between, for example, 3,200 and 5,000, we can apply the following formula:

$$Z = \frac{X - \bar{R}}{\sigma}$$

where Z = Number of standard deviations from the mean
X = Variable in which we are interested

Thus,

$$Z = \frac{3,200 - 5,000}{1,095} = \frac{-1,800}{1,095} = -1.64$$

The quantity 3,200 is 1.64 standard deviations below the mean. Looking up 1.64 in Table C.2, we find the value to be 0.4495. Thus, the probability that the cash flow will be between 3,200 and 5,000 is 45 percent. Since the left half of the normal curve represents 50 percent of all probabilities, we can also state that the chance of the cash flow being below 3,200 is 5.0 percent.

The Coefficient of Variation

When the expected values of two projects are equal, or at least close to one another, the standard deviation is a proper measure of risk. But since the standard deviation is an absolute measure, it may not serve our purposes if the two projects being compared have divergent expected values. For example, compare the two following hypothetical projects:

	EXPECTED VALUE	STANDARD DEVIATION
Project A	100	30
Project B	50	20

Project A has both the larger expected value and the larger standard deviation.

Since the expected values of the two projects are so dissimilar, an absolute measure of risk may not give an adequate answer. In such cases, another concept is introduced, the **coefficient of variation,** which measures risk relative to expected value. The simple formula for the coefficient of variation is

$$CV = \sigma/\bar{R}$$

For the two projects,

$$CV_A = 30/100 = 0.30$$

$$CV_B = 20/50 = 0.40$$

The coefficient of variation is greater for project B. Thus, despite the fact that project A's standard deviation is higher in absolute terms, its relative risk is lower. Since project A's expected value is greater and relative risk is smaller, project A is preferable.

The coefficient of variation will provide a satisfactory solution in most cases. However, when it does not, the businessperson will have to make a choice based on the perception of whether the risk is worth the potential return.[6]

CAPITAL BUDGETING UNDER CONDITIONS OF RISK

So far the discussion of expected value and risk has been limited to the results of one period only. However, the assessment of risk is even more important when plans span a term of several years. So we now turn to the question of how to deal with a capital investment proposal in which an initial outlay of funds promises to return cash flows over some period into the future. In chapter 13 the analysis of capital projects was discussed, but risk was not considered explicitly.

The first task is to calculate the net present value of the expected values obtained in each year, or the expected net present value. For a three-year project with one initial investment, we can use the following equation:

$$\overline{NPV} = \frac{\overline{R}_1}{1 + r_f} + \frac{\overline{R}_2}{(1 + r_f)^2} + \frac{\overline{R}_3}{(1 + r_f)^3} - O_0$$

or, in more general terms,

$$\overline{NPV} = \sum_{i=1}^{n} \frac{\overline{R}_t}{(1 + r_f)^t} - O_0$$

where $\overline{NPV}$ = Expected net present value
$\overline{R}_t$ = Expected values of the annual cash inflows
O_0 = Initial investment
r_f = Risk-free interest rate

It should be noted that the expected cash flows are discounted at the riskless interest rate. Since risk is considered separately (in calculating the standard deviation), discounting at a rate that includes a risk premium could result in double-counting risk.[7]

---

[6]The economic theory of the marginal utility of money can also provide a way to incorporate risk in decision making. Although such an approach is quite elegant, it is somewhat doubtful that it can be utilized in most practical situations. To apply this approach, one would have to know the utility function of the decision maker, or of the stockholders the decision maker represents. This appears to be a rather monumental task. However, in the final analysis, it is the decision maker's perception of risk that determines the shape of the utility function. Thus, the decision is a subjective one. For a more detailed explanation of utility, see for example, Haim Levy and Marshall Sarnat, *Capital Investment and Financial Decisions*, 5th ed., Hertfordshire, England: Prentice Hall International, 1994, p. 221 ff. This exposition is based on the famous work of John Von Neumann and Oskar Morgenstern, *Theory of Games and Economic Behavior*, 2d ed., Princeton, NJ: Princeton University Press, 1953.

[7]Actually, the use of the proper discount rate is subject to some controversy. In discounting at the risk-free rate, we have followed the method recommended in several books, Levy and Sarnat, *Capital Investment*, pp. 243–44; and James C. Van Horne, *Financial Management and Policy*, 11th ed., Upper Saddle River, NJ: Prentice Hall, 1998, pp. 166–68. However, other authors suggest that the company's (or the specific unit's or project's) risk-adjusted discount rate is more appropriate.

Table 14.4
Capital Budgeting Under Risk

EXPECTED VALUE

	Year 0	Year 1		Year 2	
		p	R	p	R
	-500	.2	300	.25	400
		.6	500	.50	500
		.2	700	.25	600
$\bar{R}$			500		500

$$r_f = 0.05$$
$$\overline{NPV} = 500/1.05 + 500/1.05^2 - 500$$
$$= 476 + 454 - 500 = 430$$

STANDARD DEVIATION

	Year 1				Year 2		
p	$(R - \bar{R})$	$(R - \bar{R})^2$	$(R - \bar{R})^2 p$	p	$(R - \bar{R})$	$(R - \bar{R})^2$	$(R - \bar{R})^2 p$
.2	-200	40,000	8,000	.25	-100	10,000	2,500
.6	0	0	0	.50	0	0	0
.2	$+200$	40,000	8,000	.25	$+100$	10,000	2,500
			16,000				5,000

$$\sigma = \sqrt{16,000/1.05^2 + 5,000/1.05^4}$$
$$= \sqrt{14,512 + 4,114} = \sqrt{18,626} = 136$$

The standard deviation of the present value is

$$\sigma = \sqrt{\sum_{t=1}^{n} \frac{\sigma_t^2}{(1 + r_f)^{2t}}}$$

where σ = Standard deviation of NPV

σ_t = Standard deviation of each year's cash flow

Note that the exponent in the denominator of the expression is $2t$. Thus, the first year's σ will be discounted at $(1 + r_f)^2$, the second at $(1 + r_f)^4$, and so on.

A simple numerical example will conclude this section. Table 14.4 shows that for a two-year project with a cash flow distribution and probabilities as specified, and with an initial investment of $500, the expected net present value is $430, and the standard deviation is 136. From these results we can conclude that chances are almost zero that NPV will be less than 22 (430 minus three standard deviations of 136) or more than 838 (430 plus three standard deviations of 136).

The preceding calculations are generally valid when the cash flows over the years are independent, that is, if in the case depicted in Table 14.4, the results in year 2 are not influenced by those of year 1.

Two Other Methods for Incorporating Risk

Two other techniques of accounting for risk are commonly used. Both of these make the risk adjustment within the present-value calculation (without the use of the standard deviation), so that the final result is just one number: the net present value adjusted for risk. The two methods are

1. The **risk-adjusted discount rate (RADR),** in which the risk adjustment is made in the denominator of the present-value calculation
2. The **certainty equivalent,** in which the numerator of the present-value calculation is adjusted for risk

The Risk-Adjusted Discount Rate (RADR)

RADR is probably the most practical risk adjustment method and is the one most frequently used in business. In fact, we employed this technique in chapter 13 in the discussion of the cost of capital. The discount rate at which capital project flows are discounted to the present comprises two components, the riskless (or risk-free) rate, r_f, and the risk premium, RP:

$$k = r_f + RP$$

The risk-free rate is, in the ideal sense, the pure time value of money. Since such a rate is very difficult—if not impossible—to establish, it is usually represented by yields on short-term U.S. Treasury securities.[8] The risk premium represents a judgment as to the additional return necessary to compensate for additional risk.

For example, assume that the risk-free rate is 6 percent, but that a corporation uses a cost of capital of 10 percent for projects thought to carry average risk. The risk premium is 4 percent. However, that does not mean that each part of the company should always use the 10 percent discount rate. A company may be composed of divisions with different levels of risk. Suppose a company is made up of two divisions of similar size: the Sure division (for instance, a supermarket) and the Risk division (a high-tech operation). If these had been separate companies, their risk-adjusted discount rates would have been 8 and 12 percent respectively. These discount rates should be used rather than the average 10 percent for the company as a whole. If the average were to be used, the company's resources may be misallocated. For instance, a Sure division project with an IRR of 9.5 percent would have been rejected, while a Risk division project with an IRR of 11 percent would have been accepted. If the correct adjusted discount rates had been used, the Sure division project would have been accepted (its IRR is higher than its discount rate, and NPV is positive), while the Risk division project would have been rejected. Additionally, different projects within a division should often be evaluated at different discount rates. Suppose the Risk division is analyzing two projects, the development of a new product and the replacement of some inefficient equipment. Obviously, the former

---

[8] Of course, even the shortest of U.S. Treasuries, the three-month bill, includes an inflation factor in its yield.

should be discounted at a higher rate than the latter because of the different levels of risk.

Of course, it must be recognized that developing risk-adjusted discount rates involves a large amount of judgment. But even if such adjustments are necessarily judgmental, they are very important. Companies with staffs capable of such refinements have developed some methods for differentiating discount rates.[9]

Certainty Equivalents

In calculating the risk-adjusted discount rate, the inclusion of risk in the calculation of present value is accomplished by altering the discount rate or the cost of capital, that is, the denominator of the discounting equation.[10] Another technique for including risk in the calculation of present values is to work through the numerator of the cash flow fraction; that is, the cash flow itself is adjusted to account for risk. Basically, this is accomplished by applying a factor to the cash flow to convert a risky flow into a riskless one. Since, as was said before, businesspeople tend to be risk-averse, they are expected to prefer a smaller cash flow that is certain (risk-free) over one that is attended by risky conditions. To accomplish this, the risky cash flow must be reduced by some amount, or multiplied by a number smaller than 1. We will refer to this adjustor as the *certainty equivalent factor.*

However, assigning a size to the certainty equivalent factor is fraught with at least as many problems as estimating the risk premium. But when all is said and done, the size of the certainty equivalent factor depends on the decision maker's attitude toward risk. Thus, if she decides that a specific risky cash flow (or the expected value of the risky cash flow) of $500 is equivalent to a risk-free cash flow of $450, the certainty equivalent factor, a_t, equals 0.9:

$$0.9 \times 500 = 450$$

So, for each risky cash flow, R_t, a certainty equivalent factor is assigned. If risk increases as a function of time, the certainty equivalent factors will decrease as we move into the future. For instance, a project could have the following cash flows and certainty equivalent factors:

Period	R_t	a_t	$a_t R_t$
1	100	0.95	95
2	200	0.90	180
3	200	0.85	170
4	100	0.80	80

---

[9]See, for instance, Benton E. Gup and Samuel W. Norwood, III, "Divisional Cost of Capital: A Practical Approach," *Financial Management,* spring 1982, pp. 20–24. See also Grenville S. Andrews and Colin Firer "Why Different Divisions Require Different Hurdle Rates," *Long Range Planning,* 20, 5, 1987, pp. 62–68.
[10]In other words, the discounted cash flows can be expressed as follows:

$$PV = \sum_{t=1}^{n} \frac{\overline{R}_t}{(1 + r_f + RP)^t}$$

The risk is included in the formula by increasing the denominator for higher levels of RP.

The risk-free cash flows, $a_t R_t$, are obviously smaller than the risky flows, R_t, as would be expected for a risk-averse investor. These risk-free cash flows are then discounted at the risk-free interest rate to obtain the present value of the cash flows.

RADR versus Certainty Equivalents

Two methods of accounting for risk without specifically calculating a standard deviation have just been presented. Which of the two is preferable? The certainty equivalent technique appears to be more sophisticated and is often recommended by people in academia. Businesspeople prefer RADR, which is by far the more frequently used technique. The reason for this preference is fairly obvious. It is considerably easier to make a rough estimate of the cost of capital than to specifically calculate each cash flow's certainty equivalent factor. However, it can be shown that the two methods arrive at identical results if the calculations and adjustments are made in a consistent manner.

The present value of a risky cash flow discounted at the risk-adjusted discount rate can be written as follows:

$$\frac{R_t}{(1 + k)^t}$$

On the other hand, the present value of a risk-adjusted cash flow discounted at the risk-free rate is:

$$\frac{a_t R_t}{(1 + r_f)^t}$$

If the two discounted cash flows are to be equal, then:

$$\frac{R_t}{(1 + k)^t} = \frac{a_t R_t}{(1 + r_f)^t}$$

$$a_t = \frac{(1 + r_f)^t}{(1 + k)^t}$$

Thus, the certainty equivalent factor is equal to $(1 + r_f)$ divided by $(1 + k)$, each term raised to the appropriate power. It must be noted that, in this solution, a_t decreases over time while k remains constant. This implies that given a constant k, risk increases over time. If this is the case, then using a constant k is appropriate. However, there may be other cases in which risk does not grow with time. Therefore, an analyst should be aware that using a constant RADR may penalize longer-term projects that in fact do not exhibit higher risks.

SENSITIVITY ANALYSIS

MODULE 14B

Sensitivity analysis is a very pragmatic way to estimate project risk. It involves identifying the key variables that affect the results (the NPV of a project or its internal rate of return), and then changing each variable (and sometimes a combination of variables) to ascertain the size of the impact.

Table 14.5
Expansion Project: Sensitivity Analysis Worksheet ($000)

	CONSTANT	YEAR 0	YEAR 1	YEAR 2	YEAR 3	YEAR 4	YEAR 5	YEAR 6	YEAR 7
Total market	4.0%			100,000	104,000	108,160	112,486	116,986	121,665
Market share (%)				1.0	2.0	3.0	4.0	5.0	5.0
Company sales (qty)				1,000	2,080	3,245	4,499	5,849	6,083
Expenditures		(5,000)	(2,000)						
Working capital			(750)						
Start-up expense	(750)		(450)						
Sales	5.00			5,000	10,400	16,224	22,497	29,246	30,416
Prod. & distrib. cost	3.10			3,100	6,448	10,059	13,948	18,133	18,858
Variable expenses	8.0%			400	832	1,298	1,800	2,340	2,433
Fixed costs				1,031	1,361	1,121	1,001	911	881
Total cost & expenses				4,531	8,641	12,478	16,749	21,384	22,172
Net earnings before taxes				469	1,759	3,746	5,748	7,863	8,244
Income tax	40%			188	704	1,498	2,299	3,145	3,298
Net earnings after taxes				281	1,055	2,248	3,449	4,718	4,946
Add: depreciation				531	861	621	501	411	381
Operating cash flow				812	1,916	2,869	3,950	5,129	5,327
Remaining values									
Land									500
Plant									2,833
Equipment									360
Working capital	80.0%								660
Total cash flow		(5,000)	(3,200)	812	1,916	2,869	3,950	5,129	9,680
Net present value	15.0%								3,552
Internal rate of return									24.2%

To explain and illustrate the concept of sensitivity analysis, we will utilize the data that were presented in Table 13.3 of the previous chapter. However, we will simplify the worksheet by combining product and distribution costs, which are a function of the number of cases shipped; by combining expenses, which are a percentage of dollar revenue; and by combining all the fixed costs. This is shown in Table 14.5.

We must now decide which of the lines in the projected cash flow statement will have the greatest impact on results. The following four items are probably key factors:[11]

1. Number of cases sold
2. Sales price
3. Product and distribution costs
4. Variable expenses

---

[11]We could have included a fifth variable, terminal values. We leave this calculation to the reader. Would variations in terminal values have an important effect on your final results?

Table 14.6

Results of Sensitivity
Analysis: Expansion
Project (NPV in $000)

CHANGE (%)	SALES	SALES PRICE	COST	VARIABLE EXPENSES
+40	7,524	15,731	−4,655	2,493
+30	6,531	12,687	−2,603	2,758
+20	5,538	9,642	−552	3,023
+10	4,545	6,597	1,500	3,287
0	3,552	3,552	3,552	3,552
−10	2,559	507	5,604	3,817
−20	1,567	−2,537	7,656	4,082
−30	574	−5,582	9,708	4,347
−40	−419	−8,627	11,760	4,611

Because the amount of capital expenditures is fairly certain, fixed costs will not be used as a test variable.

Next, a decision must be made on the range of the changes in the variables. The changes will be tested at 10 percent intervals between − 40 percent and +40 percent. Admittedly, these are very wide ranges, and the extremes would represent very serious deviations from the best estimates. However, using such wide ranges is quite useful in pointing out by how much the forecasters would have had to miss their estimates to convert a positive NPV into a negative one. Furthermore, should a particular percentage point in between appear to be important for the analysis, it could easily be computed and added to the table of numbers. The results are summarized in Table 14.6.

Of the four variables selected for closer scrutiny, sales price appears to have the most serious impact. NPV turns negative if the price per case drops by a little over 10 percent. Of course, this will occur only if production and distribution costs do not decrease concurrently. But there is no reason that they should, unless the price decrease follows a cost decrease. Prices could decline for other reasons, such as intense competition.

Because a large amount of variable costs and expenses can be saved if sales quantities do not come up to the best estimate, a drop in sales of about 35 percent below estimated levels would have to occur before NPV would become negative. On the other hand, an increase of between 10 and 20 percent in production and distribution costs would make the NPV unacceptable. An error in the estimate of the relationship of variable expenses to revenue would not have a significant impact on net present value.

One other analysis should also be performed: the effect of an error in the assumed discount rate. Fifteen percent was the risk-adjusted rate that was employed. Since the internal rate of return on the project was 24.2 percent, it would take an increase of more than 9 percentage points to reverse the recommendation. That appears to be too large a margin to occur within any reasonable assumptions.

Sensitivity analysis is commonly used in business. Its outcomes can be displayed in a simple and straightforward manner. It permits analysts (and their managers) to evaluate each of the important variables and to examine the trade-offs among them. It can easily utilize a spreadsheet program to generate alternative results quickly.

SIMULATION

Although the sensitivity analysis technique is popular with business, it does not make use of probability distributions. There is one method that does: simulation. In **simulation analysis,** each of the key variables is assigned a probability distribution. Thus, for instance, the sales variable of our previous example could be given the following distribution:

DEVIATION FROM ESTIMATE VALUE (%)	PROBABILITY	CUMULATIVE PROBABILITY
−30	0.1	0.1
−15	0.2	0.3
0	0.4	0.7
+15	0.2	0.9
+30	0.1	1.0

The column of cumulative probabilities indicates that there is a 10 percent chance that sales will be 30 percent lower than the base case. Furthermore, the probability is 30 percent that sales will be at least 15 percent below the base case, 70 percent that sales will not exceed the base estimate, and so on. Similar distributions would be estimated for the other important variables.

The device of random numbers is used to "simulate" a possible outcome. Suppose a random number generator with numbers from 1 to 100 is utilized. For this case, we can assign numbers from 1 to 10 to represent the −30 percent case. Any number between 11 and 30 (which has a 20 percent chance of being drawn) would stand for a −15 percent sales situation. All numbers between 31 and 70 would represent 0 percent deviation (the base case estimate) and so on.

We will also assign probability distributions to the other three variables considered to have significant impacts on net present value. The next step is to generate a random number for each of these four key variables, obtain the appropriate values, and calculate an NPV figure. This process will then be repeated a large number of times, each time generating another NPV figure. The NPVs thus generated will form a probability distribution and also enable the analyst to calculate a standard deviation as well as a z-statistic.[12]

To show how each NPV can be obtained, we will calculate one iteration with the distributions shown in Table 14.7. Suppose the random numbers generated turn out to be 24, 37, 69, and 29, respectively. These numbers are associated with sales 15 percent below expectations, sales price and costs at expected values (i.e., 0 percent deviation), and variable expenses 5 percent below the best estimates. They result in a net present value of 2,175 and an internal rate of return of 20.9 percent. If we repeat this operation a large number of times—say one thousand—we will obtain a frequency distribution of NPVs. Such a procedure appears to be very time consuming and cum-

---

[12]The simulation procedure discussed here is based on a technique introduced by David B. Hertz in "Risk Analysis in Capital Investment," *Harvard Business Review,* January–February 1964, pp. 95–106, and "Investment Policies that Pay Off," *Harvard Business Review,* January–February 1968, pp. 96–108.

Table 14.7
Simulation Analysis

Sales:					
Deviation from expected value (%)	−30	−15	0	+15	+30
Probability	0.1	0.2	0.4	0.2	0.1
Cumulative probability	0.1	0.3	0.7	0.9	1.0
Sales price:					
Deviation from expected value (%)	−20	−10	0	+10	+20
Probability	0.1	0.25	0.3	0.25	0.1
Cumulative probability	0.1	0.35	0.65	0.90	1.0
Production and distribution costs:					
Deviation from expected value (%)	−10	−5	0	+5	+10
Probability	0.1	0.15	0.5	0.15	0.1
Cumulative probability	0.1	0.25	0.75	0.9	1.0
Variable expenses:					
Deviation from expected value (%)	−10	−5	0	+5	+10
Probability	0.1	0.2	0.4	0.2	0.1
Cumulative probability	0.1	0.3	0.7	0.9	1.0

bersome. However, thanks to the existence of computers, a large number of iterations can be obtained quickly and effortlessly.

Simulation can be a good tool for decision making. However, the illustration used here is severely simplified and may not be sufficient for the solution of complex business problems. In obtaining the preceding solution, we made at least two assumptions that may have omitted some important relationships among the variables. First, we assumed that the deviations obtained with the use of random numbers remain the same in each year for which estimated cash flows were calculated. This need not be the case. A set of different random number calculations for each year may have been more appropriate. With the use of a computer, such calculations could have been taken care of quite efficiently.

Even more important, it has been assumed here that the four variables are statistically independent. It is much more likely that the various factors are interrelated. For example, a shortfall in market demand may have a negative effect on the price of each case of soft drinks. An unexpected increase in sales may have an effect on costs: in the short run, cost per unit may rise as plant employees work overtime at increased wages. If such interdependencies actually exist, they must be included in the simulation model. Such a model would, of course, be considerably more complex. A large number of estimates relating to these relationships would have to be made. And even though such a model would present the manager with a significant amount of useful information, the final decision, as in all cases, would still have to be based on the decision maker's judgment. In other words, no amount of data and information will substitute for mature business thinking.

One other method for making decisions under conditions of risk is the **decision tree.** This technique is especially suitable when decisions have to be made sequentially, for instance, if a decision two years hence depends on the outcome of an action undertaken today. Such decision making can be extremely complex, and the use of a tree diagram facilitates the process because it illustrates the sequence in which decisions must be made. It also compares the values (e.g., net present values) of the various actions that can be undertaken.

The best way to explain the technique is to use a relatively uncomplicated example. To manufacture a new product, a company must decide whether to buy a larger, more expensive, and more productive machine or a smaller, less expensive, and less productive one. If the demand for this new product turns out to be at the high end of the forecast, the purchase of the larger machine may turn out to be profitable; the smaller machine does not possess sufficient capacity to produce large quantities efficiently, and its purchase would require an additional machine to be purchased to satisfy the high demand. On the other hand, should the optimistic forecast turn out to be wrong, then the larger machine, if it were the one originally acquired, would not be used to capacity. The smaller machine, in this case, would be able to produce the quantities needed efficiently and profitably.

Such a scenario could be played out over several years, but we will assume that the life of this project, as well as of the machines, is just two years. The market and cash flow forecasts have been put together, and the decision tree analysis can begin. To simplify our task here, and also to save steps involving familiar calculations, we will assume that all flows occurring in the future (i.e., years 1 and 2) have already been converted to present values.

Table 14.8 shows all the probabilities and forecasts, and Figure 14.4 illustrates the decision tree with the resulting calculations. The first step in the analysis is to set up all the "branches" of the decision tree. As we move from left to right on the diagram, we are faced with decision points (e.g., acquire the large machine versus the small machine) and with chance events (e.g., the probabilities are 50/50 that the demand will be high/low). On the diagram, decision points are designated with squares and chance events with circles. When the entire tree is completed, the procedure is to move back from right to left, calculate the value of each branch, and where appropriate combine or eliminate branches.

Starting in the upper right, if the large machine is acquired and year 1 demand is high, there is a 75 percent probability that the second-year (present-value) cash flow will be $500 and a 25 percent probability that it will be $100. The expected value is, therefore, $400. If the first-year demand is high, cash flow will be $150 in year 1, so the present value of the cash flow of years 1 and 2 combined will be $550. If first-year demand is low, the expected value of the second set of branches will be $−37.50 (0.25 × 300 + 0.75 × −150). The cash flow in year 1 when demand is low is $−50, so the present value of the two cash flows combined will be $− 87.50. As the probabilities are 50/50 that first-year demand will be high/low, the present value of cash flows, if the large machine is purchased, is $231.25 (0.5 × 550 + 0.5 × −87.50). Now the original investment of $250 must be deducted, and the result is an NPV of $−18.75.

Table 14.8

Decision Tree Inputs

DEMAND FORECASTS		
Year 1:	High 50%	Low 50%
Year 2:		
If year 1 is high:	High 75%	Low 25%
If year 1 is low:	High 25%	Low 75%

COST OF MACHINE	
Large $250	Small $150

CASH FLOWS (PRESENT VALUES)

If large machine is acquired:

Year 1:

    If demand is high: $150

    If demand is low: $−50

Year 2:

  If year 1 demand is high:

    If demand is high: $500

    If demand is low: $100

  If year 1 demand is low:

    If demand is high: $300

    If demand is low: $−150

If small machine is acquired:

Year 1:

    If demand is high: $100

    If demand is low: $30

Year 2:

  If year 1 demand is high and second machine is acquired:

    If demand is high: $400

    If demand is low: $80

  If year 1 demand is high and second machine is not acquired:

    If demand is high: $250

    If demand is low: $120

  If year 1 demand is low:

    If demand is high: $150

    If demand is low: $0

If the small machine is acquired, a decision must be made at the end of year 1 if demand in that year is high: Should a second machine be purchased? If first-year demand is high and the second machine is acquired, then the present value of the year 2 cash flow is $320 ($0.75 \times 400 + 0.25 \times 80$). If the second machine is not acquired, the cash flow is $217.50 ($0.75 \times 250 + 0.25 \times 120$). Since it would cost $150 to obtain the second small machine, the NPV of the former result is only $170 compared to $217.50. Therefore, the decision at this point would be not to expand productive capacity. We put an X over the "additional machine" branch in the tree to sig-

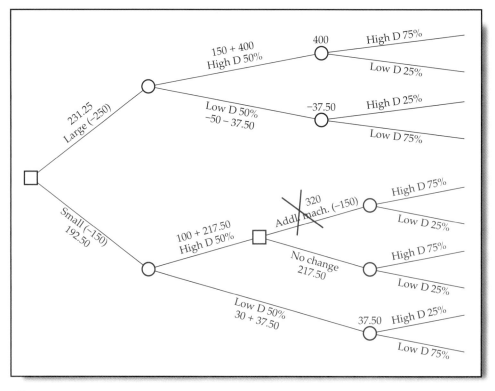

Figure 14.4
Decision Tree Analysis

nify that we will ignore this branch as we continue our evaluation. So, if first-year demand is high with a cash flow of $100, the present value of the upper branch will be $217.50 + $100, or $317.50.

One more branch needs to be addressed. If the small machine is selected and demand is low in the first year, then the second-year expected value of the cash flow will be $37.50 (0.25 × 150 + 0.75 × 0). Adding the first-year cash flow to this branch, we obtain $67.50 ($37.50 + $30). To complete the calculation of the net present value for the small-machine alternative, each of the two present values must be multiplied by 0.5, since this is the probability that the first year's demand will be high/low: 0.5 × 317.50 + 0.5 × 67.50 equals $192.50. Subtracting the cost of the smaller machine, $150, we find that the net present value is $42.50. The final step is to compare the expected net present values of the two alternatives. The expected NPV if the large machine is acquired is $−18.75; if the smaller machine is selected, it is $42.50. Thus, it is obvious that the smaller machine is the better choice. Indeed, the large machine would have been unacceptable in any case, as its net present value is negative.

The preceding solution is not quite complete, as the decision is being made on the basis of expected net present value alone. There has been no calculation of standard deviations, so we have, in effect, ignored the differences in risk between the large- and small-machine alternatives. As mentioned in note 6 of this chapter, risk can also be measured by the use of utility analysis. Each of the outcomes could have been assigned an expected utility, and instead of maximizing net present value, as we did in this example, the objective would have been to maximize utility.

REAL OPTIONS IN CAPITAL BUDGETING

The subject of decision trees, just discussed, points to a possible event we have not discussed previously: a capital budgeting decision does not have to be set in concrete at the beginning of the project.

Up to now, in analyzing capital budgeting decisions, we made estimates of costs, cash flows, life of the project, and probabilities of outcomes, and then proceeded to calculate the net present value or the internal rate of return. But we did not consider that there might be an opportunity for making changes in some aspects of the project while it is in progress or to make adjustments even before the project is started. The ability to make changes is commonly referred to as **real options** that are imbedded in the capital project.[13]

These real options may increase the value of a project above that resulting from a straightforward discounted cash flow calculation. The value of the option is the difference between the project's value with and without the option. We can represent this result with the following simple equation:

Value of the project = NPV + option value

Indeed, if such an option is taken into consideration, it may result in the acceptance of a project that was considered unacceptable without the option. (In other words, it can convert a project with a negative NPV to one with a positive NPV.)[14]

There are various forms of real options:

1. *Option to vary output.* Some projects can be structured to permit operations to expand if demand rises above expectations (this is usually called a *growth option*), or to contract operations if demand falters. It may even allow for a temporary shutdown of production.
2. *Option to vary inputs—flexibility.* A plant may include the possibility of operating with different types of fuel. While the original cost of the plant may be higher, switching from a more expensive fuel to a less expensive one may make the project more favorable. Another potential flexibility is that of taking advantage of different technologies depending on input costs.
3. *Option to abandon.* If, after the project has been started, results turn sour, it is possible that abandoning the project will improve its payoff. If the project can be sold for a price higher than the present value of its expected cash flows, or if

---

[13]Real options have a similarity to financial options, which are an important subject in managerial finance. An option gives the holder the right, but not the obligation, to take an action in the future.
[14]For a more detailed introduction to real options, consult the following articles: A. K. Dixit and R. S. Pindyck, "The Options Approach to Capital Investment," *Harvard Business Review,* May–June 1995, pp. 105–115; and N. Kulatilaka and A. J. Marcus, "Project Valuation Under Uncertainty; When Does DCF Fail?" *Journal of Applied Corporate Finance,* 5, 3 (fall 1992), pp. 92–100. A leading book in this field is Lenos Trigeorgis, *Real Options,* Cambridge, MA: MIT Press, 1997. For a recent article on this subject, see P. Coy, "Exploiting Uncertainty," *Business Week,* June 7, 1999, pp. 118–124.

its facilities can be utilized more favorably in another part of the company, then abandoning the project will enhance its value.

4. *Option to postpone.* An oil company may profit by postponing the extraction of oil from its field, if the current prices are low but are expected to rise in the future. A company may postpone the introduction of a new product pending completion of market research to better evaluate the product's potential.

In both of these cases there is, of course, a cost involved in the postponement, whether it is the cost of delaying cash inflows or of incurring the expense of market research. However, the benefits of the postponement may exceed these costs, and thus create a positive value for the postponement option.

Another reason for postponement may be the expectation of decreases in interest rates. Lower interest rates would decrease the project's required rate of return and thus increase its present value. It must be remembered, however, that by postponing action, the company may lose the "first-mover" advantage.

5. *Option to introduce future products.* A company may be willing to launch a product with a negative NPV, if doing so gives it an option to gain an advantage when later versions of the product are introduced.

An Abandonment Option

We will conclude this brief introduction to real options with a simple example. We will see that by including the option to abandon the project, we will convert a project with a negative NPV to a positive one.

The data for this project are as follows (all dollar amounts are in thousands):

1. The life of the project is 2 years.
2. The original cash outflow is $8,000.
3. The potential cash inflows in year 1 are $3,000 or $6,000, each with a probability of 50 percent.
4. If the first year's cash inflow is $3,000, the second year's cash inflows will be either $2,000 or $4,000, each with a probability of 50 percent.
5. If the first year's cash inflow is $6,000, the second year's cash inflows will be $5,000 or $7,000, each with a probability of 50 percent.
6. The project can be abandoned at the end of year one. The expected abandonment value is $3,500.
7. The project's discount rate is 10 percent.

The calculations are shown in Table 14.9. The upper third of the table shows the NPV calculation if abandonment is not included. The cash flows and their present value at period 0 are shown. Then the probabilities are calculated. Each of the four potential outcomes has a probability of 25 percent. The present value of the cash flows is $7,810, and the expected NPV is a negative $190. Thus, the project would be rejected.

In the second third of the table we show the present value at the end of period 1 of the year 2 cash inflows. We can see that if the first year's cash inflow was $3,000, and the second year's were either $2,000 or $4,000, the PV of these two cash flows at the end of year 1 is $2,727, less than the abandonment value. The expected PV_1 of the two higher cash flows is $5,455, well above the abandonment value.

Table 14.9
An Abandonment Option

EXPECTED NET PRESENT VALUE CALCULATION

PERIOD 1		PERIOD 2		TOTAL				EXPECTED
CF	PV_0	CF	PV_0	PV_0	P_1	P_2	$P_1 \times P_2$	PV_0
		2000	1653	4380		0.25		1095
3000	2727				0.5			
		4000	3306	6033		0.5	0.25	1508
		5000	4132	9587		0.5	0.25	2397
6000	5455				0.5			
		7000	5785	11240		0.5	0.25	2810

Total expected present value	7810
Initial investment	8000
Expected net present value	−190

PRESENT VALUE OF PERIOD 2 CASH FLOWS AT END OF PERIOD 1

PERIOD 2			EXPECTED
CF	PV_1	P_2	PV_1
2000	1818	0.5	909
4000	3636	0.5	1818
			2727
5000	4545	0.5	2273
7000	6364	0.5	3182
			5455

NET PRESENT VALUE WITH ABANDONMENT

PERIOD 1			EXPECTED
CF	PV AT 0	$P_1 \times P_2$	PV_0
3000	5909*	0.5	2955
	9587	0.25	2397
6000			
	11240	0.25	2810

Total expected present value	8161
Initial investment	8000
Expected net present value	161

*$(3000 + 3500)/1.1 = 5909$

In the last section of the table, we substitute the abandonment value of $3,500 into the calculation, and compute the expected PV_0. The expected PV_0 is now $8,161, which gives us a positive NPV of $161. With the abandonment option included, this has now become an acceptable project. The value of the option to abandon is $351.

We did not calculate the standard deviation for this problem. However, had we done so, it would have been lower when the option was considered than when we calculated a straight NPV without the option. Thus, inclusion of the option did not only increase the NPV of the project, but it also decreased its riskiness.

INTERNATIONAL APPLICATION: RISK IN CAPITAL BUDGETING

 In this chapter we have discussed methods to account for risk in the capital budgeting analysis of a corporation. When a corporation operates across national boundaries and is analyzing a long-term investment to be made in, for example, one of its foreign subsidiaries, it must take into consideration at least two additional sources of risk: exchange rate risk and political risk. We will discuss briefly both of these and then cite several real-life recent examples of political risk.

An increase in risk due to multinational operations can be accounted for either through decreasing cash flows (the certainty equivalents discussed previously) or through increasing the discount rate (see discussion of the risk-adjusted discount rate in this chapter). While both methods should ideally give the same final answer, the adjustment of cash flows is sometimes favored.

Exchange Rate Risk

A company is exposed to three types of exchange rate risk:

1. Operating (or economic): This measures the change in the present value of cash flows resulting from *unexpected* changes in exchange rates.
2. Transaction: This exposure occurs due to changes in exchange rates affecting existing outstanding obligations.
3. Accounting (or translation): This occurs due to the necessity of translating a subsidiary's financial statements denominated in a foreign currency into the parent's currency in the preparation of a consolidated statement. Changes in exchange rates can affect the consolidated equity.

In the context of capital budgeting, the first of the three, operating exposure, is by far the most important. It must be noted that exposure results only from unanticipated changes in the exchange rate. Expected changes should have been included in the analysis of the capital budgeting proposal. While a company can try to manage its transaction exposure by using various types of hedges, this cannot be accomplished in the case of operating exposure. A major reason for this is that hedging, which is limited to a few currencies, is usually done for relatively short periods, while capital budgeting projects often tend to extend over a considerable number of years into the future. The firm can best attempt to protect against this exposure by diversifying its operations over many countries, as well as diversifying its fundraising activities over a number of capital markets.

Political Risk

Political risk can be defined as an action by a foreign government that is detrimental to the firm. Four types of such action can be enumerated:

1. *Regulation:* Such an action can include changes in taxes, labor law rules, minimum wages, and price controls. It should be noted that such regulation can affect local companies in the foreign country as well.
2. *Discrimination:* Potential actions include restrictions on the repatriation of dividends, special labor conditions, tariff and nontariff barriers, and also imposition of administrative rules (red tape) that will make operations prohibitively expensive. Such actions are probably the most frequent.
3. *Expropriation:* A government takes over foreign property, usually with the intention of operating the business itself. Expropriation can be done with fair compensation and with inadequate or no compensation. Of course, the question of what is "fair" is an extremely difficult one to answer.
4. *Wars and disorders:* These can lead to destruction of a firm's property.

It is important for a company to attempt to forecast political risk using the best information and advice that it can obtain. There is also the potential of insuring through the U.S. government–owned Overseas Private Investment Corporation (OPIC). This insurance can be obtained in dealing with developing countries and covers inconvertibility, expropriation, war, and political violence. Furthermore, a company can also reduce political risk by negotiating agreements with the government of the foreign country. There are also operating and financial strategies a company can adopt to decrease political risk. This brief discussion of financial risk cannot go into the details of such strategies; thorough descriptions can be obtained from books dealing with multinational corporate finance.[15]

The Political Risk Services Group rates 140 countries for political (as well as economic and financial) risk. In a recent tabulation (November 2001), Somalia, Iraq, Sudan, Nigeria, and Indonesia were judged to be the five most politically risky countries. On the other hand, the Netherlands, Luxembourg, Finland, Denmark, and Switzerland were rated as the least politically risky.[16]

Examples of Political Risk

1. Political, as well as economic, turmoil in Zimbabwe and Zambia have "eroded southern Africa's ability to attract foreign investment over the next two or three years" according to a report by BusinessMap, a South African investor strategy firm. Over the past two years, political violence and economic crises have created a significant deterioration in the prospects for investment in that region. In January 2002, Anglo American, a mining group, decided to withdraw its copper investment in Zambia at a cost of $350 million.
2. Credit Suisse First Boston (CSFB) was supposed to be one of the underwriters for a large share offering by China Unicom, the second largest mobile operator in China. The share issue was estimated by some analysts to be worth more

---

[15]Two of the books on this subject, which have been mentioned before, are David K. Eiteman, Arthur L. Stonehill, and Michael H. Moffett, *Multinational Business Finance,* 9th ed., Boston, MA: Addison-Wesley, 2001, chapters 6, 7, 8, and 13, and Dennis J. O'Connor and Alberto T. Bueso, *International Dimensions of Financial Management,* New York: Macmillan, 1990, chapters 6 and 11. Materials in these two texts have been utilized in this narrative.
[16]Alan Levinsohn, "New Geopolitics Spotlights Political Risk Management," *Strategic Finance,* January 2002, pp. 38–43. The Political Risk Services Group can be accessed on the Internet at www.prsgroup.com.

than $7 billion. However, it was reported that CSFB was excluded from this transaction "after arranging two investment seminars featuring senior Taiwanese government officials." The report said further that "the decision was made by Beijing's top political leaders."

3. Foreign corporations are discouraged from making investments in Norway because of the prevalence of state ownership. This may result in an undervaluation of Norwegian companies "as foreign investors are demanding discounts to offset the risk of what they describe as a 'politicized financial environment.' "

4. Investments amounting to $200 million in Angola by the diamond group, De Beers, are on hold while a dispute is being addressed in London and Hague courts. The argument is over an alleged breach of contract when the Angolan government created the Angola Selling Corporation (Ascorp). This monopoly was awarded marketing rights over diamonds. The potential for business in Angola is great, particularly because the war between the government and Unita rebels appears to be winding down. But seeming corruption and the breaking of contracts by the government have contributed to deterring investment in the country's diamond mining. Among various actions, the government decreased the sizes of some concessions when it created Ascorp, which also appears to be offering below market prices to mining companies.

5. The Occidental Petroleum Company has had to contend with frequent disruptions in its operations in Colombia due to attacks by guerilla groups that are battling for economic and military control of the oil region near Arauca. The pipeline that transports oil from the Caño Limón region to a port on the Caribbean was bombed 170 times in 2001, an increase from 99 times in 2000. The company's workers have also been extorted, and even murdered. The company has had to pay about 50 cents per barrel of oil for security costs.[17]

Containing International Risk

Operating internationally entails some additional risk, but a company can manage these exposures (and possibly benefit) by diversifying its operations and finances.

Suppose that due to a temporary disequilibrium, costs of production among different countries diverge. The company may be able to shift its production and sources of materials and components from one country to another. Or, if product prices and profitability shift among countries, so can a company's marketing efforts. If temporary deviations occur in interest or exchange rates, a company may find it possible to decrease its cost of capital by moving its financing sources. Finally, a diversification strategy may avoid some of the dangers of political risk.[18]

---

[17]James Lamont, "Investors Losing Confidence in Southern Africa, *Financial Times,* January 31, 2002; Eric Ng, "CSFB Dumped from Share Deal over Taiwan Link," *South China Morning Post,* September 1, 2001; "Kowtowing to Beijing," *The Wall Street Journal Europe,* September 3, 2001; Kristin Haug, "Norway's State Ownership Scares Off Corporate Investors," *Dow Jones International News,* June 18, 2001; Nicholas Shaxson, "De Beers Marks Time in Angola," *Financial Times,* January 25, 2002; Alexei Barrionuevo and Thaddeus Herrick, "For Oil Companies, Defense Abroad Is the Order of the Day," *The Wall Street Journal,* February 7, 2002.

[18]A more complete discussion of this subject can be found in Eiteman, Stonehill, and Moffett, *Multinational Business Finance,* pp. 214–216.

The Solution

GLOBAL FOODS

George Kline is now preparing to perform the risk analysis on the expansion project as requested by the treasurer. Although he is quite familiar with the various risk-adjustment techniques, he heeds the treasurer's suggestion to stay away from statistical refinements. He decides to use sensitivity analysis for his presentation. (As we used the expansion project data in explaining sensitivity analysis, we will now continue with the same data.)

George gives some thought to how to simplify Table 14.6 and show a combination of changes. He decides that he will present three summary estimates: worst case, base case, and best case. The base case will, of course, be the original analysis (developed in chapter 13). The worst case will show all variables on the unfavorable side, and the best case will be the opposite. He tries out several combinations. He believes that certain variables are more likely to contain larger errors than others. For instance, he postulates that production and distribution costs, with which the company has experience in other geographic areas, is a fairly good estimate. However, as this new market is not well known, sales price and quantity are more likely to involve significant error, especially on the downside. Because of severe competition, a considerably higher sales price should not be expected. Also, because the company is attempting to penetrate a new market, the chances of falling short of the base estimate appear to be greater than those of surpassing it. He finally settles on the ranges shown in Table 14.10, which also include the resulting net present values and internal rates of return.

The worst case turns out to have a very negative NPV and an internal rate of return close to zero. To prepare for the presentation, George calculates several cases for which NPV is near zero and the internal rate of return is about 15 percent, which, of course, is the required rate. He is thus able to show the magnitude of the errors that would cause the company to be indifferent to this proposal. Three combinations that provide such results are shown in Table 14.11. Many other calculations could have been made, but at this point George feels that he has a good handle on the presentation.

When the time for the presentation to top management arrived, George, accompanied by the treasurer, brought all of his charts to the conference room. George proceeded with his discussion, summarizing the forecasts and estimates and arriving at the recommended solution. He reviewed with management his sensitivity analysis, and the treasurer completed the presentation by recommending that the company go ahead and begin production in the new region.

George felt that his presentation went well, and the treasurer commended him for a good job. But a few days later, the treasurer called George into his office and told him that management had, at least for the time being, decided not to go ahead with expansion. He explained

(*Continued*)

Table 14.10
Three Possible Scenarios

	WORST CASE	BASE CASE	BEST CASE
Percentage differences:			
Sales	−20	0	+20
Sales price	−15	0	+5
Prod. & distr. costs	+10	0	−10
Variable expenses	+10	0	−10
Net present value ($000)	−3,909	3,552	10,161
Internal rate of return	1.6%	24.2%	37.7%

Table 14.11
Additional Scenarios

	CASE 1	CASE 2	CASE 3
Percentage differences:			
Sales	−10	−5	−7
Sales price	−6	−7	−5
Prod. & distr. costs	+5	+7	+7
Variable expenses	0	+5	+4.5
Net present value ($000)	−8	−2	0
Internal rate of return	15.0%	15.0%	15.0%

that management felt that this was not the right time to expand, given the economy's somewhat cloudy future. Also, they considered the strength of their competition and decided that this was not the time to make the investment. Sensing George's disappointment, the treasurer assured him that he did an excellent job with the data he had. Actually, he said, the vice president of finance had told him to commend George for his substantial effort. "But that's the way things go in a large corporation," he continued. "You see, decisions are not always made on the basis of figures, however thoroughly they were developed. You must remember that in business, once the data have been put together, there is still the judgment factor that must be applied by management. After all, that's what top management gets paid for. I am sure that in the future, this or a similar project will be considered again."

SUMMARY

In this chapter the emphasis has been on incorporating risk into the capital budgeting process. The most common measure of risk in economic and financial literature is the standard deviation, which measures the dispersion around the mean of a distribution of possible outcomes. The coefficient of variation, which puts the standard deviation on a relative basis, helps in comparing projects with unequal expected net present values. The z-statistic is used to ascertain probabilities of an outcome being below a certain amount, above a certain amount, or within a range of amounts.

The calculation of the expected net present value and standard deviation for multiperiod projects under conditions of statistical independence was also discussed.

In real business situations, these calculations are often not employed because of their complexity. Instead, the discount rate is frequently adjusted to incorporate risk; the risk-adjusted discount rate (RADR) is a technique that is dominant in business. Another method of accounting for risk, the certainty equivalent, can give results identical to those obtained using the RADR; however, because of its greater theoretical complexity and the difficulty of defining certainty equivalents, this method is not very popular in business.

Additional techniques were discussed. One whose use is quite widespread—sensitivity analysis—was used in solving the situation presented at the beginning of the chapter. Although it doesn't consider the probabilities of occurrence, this method calculates answers to a series of what-if questions. It pinpoints the specific variables (on either the revenue or the cost side) that will have large and small impacts on the results.

Other techniques also were presented. Simulation analysis requires specification of each risky input to arrive at an expected value and standard deviation. Calculations are relatively simple when independence among the variables is assumed, but can become extremely complex when interrelationships among the variables are taken into account. The decision tree method lends itself to sequential decision making. However, specifying sequences and the effects of one decision on another is extremely difficult. A brief and elementary introduction to real options explained how flexibility can be introduced into the capital budgeting process.

Although many techniques of accounting for risk were discussed in this chapter, it is obvious that none of these methods is completely satisfactory. However, the important lesson of this chapter is that risk is everpresent in business, and anyone engaging in business planning must be aware of the dangers of risky outcomes and be able to cope with the uncertainty of future events. Thus, the awareness of a risky situation may be more important than familiarity with any of the specific methods illustrated in this chapter.

IMPORTANT CONCEPTS

Certainty equivalent: A certain (risk-free) cash flow that would be acceptable as opposed to the expected value of a risky cash flow. (p. 621)

Coefficient of variation: A measure of risk relative to expected value that is used to compare standard deviations of projects with unequal expected values. (p. 618)

Decision tree: A method used with sequential decision making in which a diagram points out graphically the order in which decisions must be made and compares the value of the various actions that can be undertaken. (p. 628)

Expected value: An average of all possible outcomes weighted by their respective probabilities. (p. 614)

Probability: An expression of the chance that a particular event will occur. (p. 613)

Probability distribution: A distribution indicating the chances of all possible occurrences. (p. 613)

Real option: An opportunity to make adjustments in a capital budgeting project in response to changing circumstances potentially resulting in improved results. (p. 631)

Risk: Refers to a situation in which possible future events can be defined and probabilities assigned. (p. 614)

Risk-adjusted discount rate (RADR): A value equal to the riskless (risk-free) interest rate plus a risk premium. The risk-free rate ideally is the pure time value of money, and the risk premium represents a judgment as to the additional return necessary to compensate for additional risk. (p. 621)

Sensitivity analysis: A method for estimating project risk that involves identifying the key variables that affect results and then changing each variable to measure the impact. (p. 623)

Simulation analysis: A method that assigns a probability distribution to each of the key variables and uses random numbers to simulate a set of possible outcomes to arrive at an expected value and dispersion. (p. 626)

Standard deviation: The degree of dispersion of possible outcomes around the mean outcome or expected value. It is the square root of the weighted average of the squared deviations of all possible outcomes from the expected value. (p. 615)

Uncertainty: Refers to situations in which there is no viable method of assigning probabilities to future random events. (p. 614)

QUESTIONS

1. Distinguish *risk* and *uncertainty*. Distinguish *a priori* and *statistical* probabilities.

2. Enumerate causes of business risk.

3. The following are the probabilities and outcomes for an event:

PROBABILITY	OUTCOME
0.25	3,000
0.50	4,000
0.25	5,000

Does the table represent a discrete or a continuous distribution? Distinguish the two.

4. You are comparing two potential mutually exclusive investment projects. You have calculated the expected NPV of project A to be $3,758 and that of project B to be $3,114. Can you be certain that you should recommend to your management to implement project A?

5. If two projects have different expected values, can the standard deviations be used to determine differences in risk?

6. Would a risk-averse person prefer a project whose distribution of potential outcomes can be drawn as a continuous normal curve with a very high peak and a steep decline around the peak?

7. Of what use is the table of values of areas under the standard normal distribution in determining the risk level of a project?

8. Define *coefficient of variation.*

9. "All our projects are discounted at the same interest rate," says the treasurer of a large company. Would you dispute the advisability of such a procedure?

10. Why do companies use the RADR method much more frequently than the certainty equivalent method? Can the two methods arrive at the same result?

11. Is a person who regularly goes to horse races (and places bets) and has insured his house against fire acting inconsistently?

12. Describe and give examples of
   a. Sensitivity analysis
   b. Simulation analysis

13. Explain the use of the decision tree in risk analysis. Is this a useful method? Is it the appropriate method for all types of analyses?

14. Why does the use of "real options" improve capital investment analysis? Under which circumstances would you recommend using real options?

PROBLEMS

1. The Quality Office Furniture Company has compiled the year's revenue expectations and their probabilities:

SALES ($000)	PROBABILITIES
240	0.05
280	0.10
320	0.70
360	0.10
400	0.05

Calculate
   a. The expected revenue
   b. The standard deviation
   c. The coefficient of variation

2. If the probabilities in problem 1 had been 0.15, 0.2, 0.3, 0.2, and 0.15, recalculate the expected revenue, standard deviation, and coefficient of variation. Which of the two projections (in problem 1 and this problem) represents a riskier situation? Explain. Draw a bar graph for each situation.

3. The Learned Book Company has a choice of publishing one of two books on the subject of Greek mythology. It expects the sales period for each to be extremely short, and it estimates profit probabilities as follows:

BOOK A		BOOK B	
PROBABILITY	PROFIT	PROBABILITY	PROFIT
0.2	$2,000	0.1	$1,500
0.3	2,300	0.4	1,700
0.3	2,600	0.4	1,900
0.2	2,900	0.1	2,100

Chapter 14   Risk and Uncertainty

Calculate the expected profit, standard deviation, and coefficient of variation for each of the books. If you were asked which of the two to publish, what would be your advice?

4. Suppose you can make an investment with the following possible rates of return:

PROBABILITY	RATE OF RETURN
0.2	−10%
0.6	10%
0.2	30%

On the other hand, you can invest in a U.S. Treasury bill that earns a certain 7 percent. Evaluate the alternatives.

5. The Cactus Corporation is considering a two-year project, project A, involving an initial investment of $600 and the following cash inflows and probabilities:

YEAR 1		YEAR 2	
PROBABILITY	CASH FLOW	PROBABILITY	CASH FLOW
0.1	$700	0.2	$600
0.4	600	0.3	500
0.4	500	0.3	400
0.1	400	0.2	300

a. Calculate the project's expected NPV and standard deviation, assuming the discount rate to be 8 percent.

b. The company is also considering another two-year project, project B, which has an expected NPV of $320 and a standard deviation of $125. Projects A and B are mutually exclusive. Which of the two projects would you prefer? Explain.

6. The Grand Design Corporation uses the certainty equivalent approach in making capital budgeting decisions. You are given the following data¸ for a particular project:

YEAR	CASH FLOW	CERTAINTY EQUIVALENT FACTOR
0	$−20,000	1.00
1	5,000	0.90
2	5,000	0.90
3	5,000	0.90
4	15,000	0.70

The risk-free discount rate is 4 percent, and the risk-adjusted discount rate is 12 percent. Calculate the net present value. Would you accept this project?

7. You have just been employed in the finance department of the Mahler Transportation Corporation. The first task you have been assigned is to recommend a method for evaluating risky projects. You have studied both the risk-adjusted discount rate (RADR) method and the certainty equivalent method, and you have been asked to evaluate the following project using both methods.

Managerial Economics

A four-year project involves an original cash outflow of $30,000; there will be (after-tax) cash inflows of $10,000 in each of the first three years and an inflow of $20,000 in the fourth year. You estimate that the risk-free interest rate is 8 percent and the project's risk premium is 4 percent.

    a. Calculate the net present value using RADR.

    b. Now calculate net present value using the certainty equivalent method, and show that the two methods give identical answers.

8. Project A has an expected net present value of $500 and a standard deviation of $125. Project B has a standard deviation of $100 and an expected net present value of $300. Which of the two projects would you select? Explain why.

9. Global Industries has calculated the return on assets (ROA) for one of its projects using the simulation method. By simulating the operations 1,000 times, they obtained an ROA of 16.7 percent and a standard deviation of 6.2. The results of the simulation conform quite closely to a normal curve.

    a. Draw a probability distribution using the given data.

    b. The company's objective is to achieve an ROA of 12 percent. What is the probability that the project will achieve at least that level?

    c. What is the probability of ROA being nonnegative?

10. The Great Pine Forest Corporation is analyzing an expansion project with the following information:

Initial investment: $120,000
Depreciation life: five years—straight-line
Project life: five years
Additional working capital at $t = 0$ $20,000
Working capital returned at $t = 5$ $20,000
Expected salvage value at $t = 5$ $15,000
Tax rate: 34 percent
Cost of capital: 12 percent

	YEAR 1	YEAR 2	YEAR 3	YEAR 4	YEAR 5
Revenue	$50,000	$80,000	$80,000	$80,000	$40,000
Cash costs	30,000	30,000	25,000	25,000	25,000

    a. Calculate the present value of this project.

    b. Now conduct a sensitivity analysis as follows:

        (1) Assume the best case to have revenue 10 percent higher than just stated, costs 5 percent lower than given, and salvage value twice the amount given.

        (2) Assume the worst case to have revenue 10 percent lower than given, costs 5 percent higher than given, and salvage value to be 0.

    Show the results for the best case, the most likely case, and the worst case.

11. The Prime Time Printing Company is analyzing a two-year project, which would necessitate the purchase of a printing press. The demand for the product will depend on the expected state of the economy. The company's economist forecasts a 30 percent probability that the economy will be expanding strongly, a 50 percent probability that expansion will be normal, and a 20 percent probability of a weak expansion. These probabilities will hold for the next two years. The com-

pany has a choice of purchasing a large press for $50,000 or a smaller one for $40,000. The present value of potential cash flows (in $000) in year 1, given the state of the economy and the size of the equipment, is as follows:

YEAR 1	LARGE	SMALL
0.3	100	60
0.5	40	40
0.2	−20	20

If year 1 has a strong expansion, then the probabilities and PV of cash flows (in $000) in year 2 will be the following:

YEAR 2	LARGE	SMALL
0.3	180	100
0.5	90	60
0.2	60	40

If year 1 has a normal expansion, then the probabilities and PV of cash flows (in $000) in year 2 will be the following:

YEAR 2	LARGE	SMALL
0.3	80	70
0.5	40	40
0.2	20	30

If year 1's expansion is weak, then year 2's PV of cash flows (in $000) will be:

YEAR 2	LARGE	SMALL
0.3	50	50
0.5	30	30
0.2	−30	10

Calculate the expected NPV, the standard deviation, and the coefficient of variation for each alternative, and recommend which alternative should be selected.

12. The Bentley Manufacturing Company has an opportunity to purchase a patent for the manufacture of a new product for $200,000. It has three possible choices:
   a. It does not purchase the patent.
   b. It purchases the patent at the above price.
   c. It spends $50,000 on additional research to learn more about the feasibility and potential of this product, before deciding whether to purchase the patent.

You have the task of making a recommendation. You have expended considerable effort in familiarizing yourself with this product and you have consulted with technical and market experts at your company. You have made the following estimates.
   a. There is a 60 percent probability that the additional research will show this product to have a good market potential.
   b. If the research results are favorable, the chances are 80 percent that the product will net the company $1,000,000; there is a probability of 20 percent that the income from it will be only $150,000.

c. If the research results are not favorable, there is a 90 percent probability that income will be $100,000 and 10 percent that it will be $800,000.

d. If, however, the company purchases the patent without any more research, your estimates are as follows:

30% probability	$1,000,000
40% probability	500,000
30% probability	150,000

Assume that all above numbers are in terms of present values. Using a decision tree, make your recommendation.

13. It has been your secret wish to own and operate an amusement park when you can afford to make the investment. That time has now arrived. There is a large empty lot at the outskirts of Phoenix, Arizona, owned by the city. The city is willing to lease one-half of this lot for 5 years with an option to lease both it and the other half for the next 5 years. In return for charging you a reasonable rent, the city will take ownership of your equipment at the end of the 5 or 10 years.

You have estimated your original investment to be $250,000. You expect your net cash flows (after lease payments, all other expenses and taxes) to be $55,000 for each of the first five years. If you exercise your option to continue with both parts of the property at the end of year 5, you will need to invest another $150,000 (for additional equipment and a miniature golf course). Because your cash flow estimates are now far into the future, you estimate a 50 percent probability that your annual cash flows will remain the same ($55,000) and a 50 percent probability that they will rise to $100,000 per year for the second five years. Your cost of capital is 12 percent.

a. Is the first five-year project acceptable?

b. What is the value of the total project if you exercise your option? What is the value of your option?

Chapter 15

Government and Industry: Challenges and Opportunities for Today's Manager

The Situation

Bill Adams, the chief information officer (CIO) of Global Foods, was faced with a serious problem. Four years ago, his company had decided to outsource its entire voice and data communications operations to AT&T. A 10-year contract had been negotiated, but the terms and conditions of the contract were subject to a review after five years, and Global Foods had the option to discontinue services if it was not satisfied with AT&T's work.

It had been an interesting four years. When he first put out the RFP (request for proposal), he had been surprised at the number and diversity of the responses. He had thought that there would just be the usual cast of characters such as AT&T, Verizon, and Sprint. But in addition, his local telecommunications company along with a consortium of big consulting companies such as EDS and IBM Global Services had also put in bids. It was at that time that Bill realized that the deregulation of the telecommunications industry had provided customers with many more options to choose from. In the end, Global Foods went with AT&T, because it had recently bought IBM's data network and because it was the most experienced company in the telecommunications outsourcing business. After four years of experience he was not so sure he had made the right choice. He asked his staff to prepare a complete assessment of the situation and to recommend whether the company should continue using AT&T's services for the balance of the 10-year contract.

Introduction

The primary objective of this chapter is to discuss the impact of government policies on managerial decision making. When the government is involved in the market economy, it generally controls the behavior of buyers and sellers through a process of "indirect command." That is, rather than ordering buyers and sellers to allocate resources in a particular way, the government uses market incentives or disincentives. This "visible hand" of the government can take such forms as price controls, rules and regulations, taxes, and subsidies. In using the incentive of profit or the disincentive of loss, the government does not change the basic system of rewards and punishments used in the market. Instead, it simply alters the reward structure of a laissez-faire market so that resources are allocated more in accordance with government policy than with the actions of individual buyers and sellers.

In the following section, we will elaborate on the different roles that government plays in the market economy and the justification for such roles. We will then describe what it is like to do business with the U.S. government, which after all is one of the largest buyers of goods and services in the world. This section was written by Sylvia Von Bostel, a member of the staff of Booz-Allen & Hamilton, one of the world's top consulting companies. Its client list includes a number of agencies and departments of the federal government.

The Rationale for Government Involvement in a Market Economy

There are five major functions the government can perform in a market economy such as that of the United States. First, it provides a legal and social framework within which market participants buy and sell the goods and services produced by the economy's scarce resources. For example, the Food and Drug Administration (FDA) seeks to ensure that food and pharmaceutical companies sell products that meet certain standards of safety and quality.

Second, the government strives to maintain competition in markets for goods and services by trying to ensure that no one seller dominates the market in an unfair manner. Third, the government may decide to play a role in the redistribution of income and wealth. It can do so through the tax system (particularly through income taxes), and also through various types of government subsidies and grants for special-interest groups. For example, one of the major subsidies for middle- and upper-income in the United States is the ability to deduct interest payments on residential mortgages.

The fourth market-related function of government is the reallocation of resources. According to economic theory, a misallocation of resources results whenever a market has certain externalities or spillovers. That is, some of the benefits or costs associated with the production or consumption of a particular product accrue to parties other than the buyers or sellers of a product.

The fifth major function of government in a market economy is the stabilization of the aggregate economy. The market economy is prone to periodic upswings and downswings in economic activity. As you have probably already studied in a course in macroeconomics, governments can employ monetary and fiscal policy to deal with the problems of unemployment and inflation, which usually occur at different stages of the cycle.

One government function that does not quite fit into any of the five main categories is the regulation of natural monopolies. The economic definition of a **natural monopoly** is an industry in which a single firm can serve customers more efficiently than many smaller competing firms because of the predominance of economies of scale. Examples of natural monopolies are electricity and gas utilities and telephone services. However, over the past decade or so, there has been a movement by governments throughout the world to reduce the government ownership or regulation of these natural monopolies. Let us elaborate a bit further on three of the five main functions of government: providing a competitive framework for market participants, the reallocation of resources in the presence of market externalities, and the stabilization of the aggregate economy.

Providing a Legal Framework for Competition: The Antitrust Laws

A thorough interpretation of antitrust laws would carry us beyond the scope of this book.[1] We here provide a brief review of the subject. The beginning of antitrust legislation in the United States dates back to the late nineteenth century in response to the formation of large corporations and the so-called "merger-to-monopoly" wave. While under common law various anticompetitive actions (e.g., price fixing) were not enforceable, stronger positive legal action appeared necessary. The first law to be passed was the Sherman Anti-Trust Act, followed by several others.

The Sherman Anti-Trust Act (1890)   The two important sections of this law were the following:

Section 1: . . . every contract, combination in the form of trust or otherwise, or conspiracy, in restraint of trade or commerce among the several states, or with foreign nations, is declared to be illegal . . .
Section 2: . . . every person who shall monopolize or attempt to monopolize any part of the trade or commerce among the several states, or with foreign nations, shall be deemed guilty of a felony . . .

Section 1 outlawed explicit cartels. Section 2, which appeared to outlaw monopoly, was interpreted by the courts as a prohibition of "bad acts" and not monopoly per se.

The Clayton Act (1914)   The Clayton Act was intended to strengthen and widen the application of antitrust enforcement, and specifically enumerated four forbidden practices:

---

[1]A large number of texts on industrial organization treat this topic thoroughly. An example is Dennis W. Carlton and Jeffrey M. Perloff, *Modern Industrial Organization,* 2d ed., New York: HarperCollins, 1994, chapter 20.

Section 2: prohibits price discrimination that would "substantially lessen competition . . ." It exempted price differentiation due to differences in quality, quantity, and costs of selling and transportation.

Section 3: Prohibits the use of tying or exclusive contracts that would lessen competition.

Section 7: Prohibits the acquisition of other companies through purchase of stock if this lessens competition.

Section 8: Restricts interlocking directorates.

The Clayton Act also provided for the recovery of treble damages by the injured party.

The Federal Trade Commission Act (1914) This law set up a new agency, the Federal Trade Commission (FTC), to investigate violations, enforce antitrust laws, and determine what actions constitute "unfair method of competition," which the law declared unlawful. The Wheeler-Lea Act (1938) extended FTC's authority to the protection of consumers.

Subsequent Acts The Robinson-Patman Act (1936) strengthened the price-discrimination provisions of the Clayton Act to include not only the lessening of competition, but also injury to or prevention of competition "with any person who either grants or knowingly receives the benefits of such discrimination, or with customers of either of them." This act was the result of political pressure by small independent grocery stores to make it difficult for large grocery chains to buy and sell at lower prices.

The Celler-Kefauver Act (1950) corrected some omissions of the Clayton Act. Specifically, it applied the law to mergers accomplished through asset acquisition (the Clayton Act applied only to acquisition of stock).

The Hart-Scott-Rodino Act (1976) imposed a premerger notification requirement on large firms (where the acquiring firm has at least $100 million in assets and $10 million in annual sales).

Some Closing Remarks on Antitrust Laws Over time, the interpretation and enforcement of antitrust laws has varied a great deal. Before leaving this subject, we will briefly discuss the two main schools of thought regarding the purpose of the antitrust law and comment on perhaps one of the most publicized antitrust cases in recent years: the United States Government versus the Microsoft Corporation.

One school of thought suggests that the main purpose of antitrust laws is economic efficiency. The laws act against practices that restrict output and raise prices. But not all mergers and agreements will create economic inefficiencies; instead they may lead to greater efficiency and lowering of costs. Thus, courts should interpret such actions case by case. The final goal of policy should be to enhance consumer welfare.

The opposing school of thought argues that the purpose of antitrust laws is actually to limit the power of large firms, and to protect smaller independent firms regardless of the effects on efficiency. This seemed to be particularly evident in the case of the Robinson-Patman Act, which was explicitly aimed at the protection of small grocery businesses. Obviously, this is an extremely complex issue that has not been solved in all these years, and probably will not for many years to come. An excellent contrast between these two schools of thought is illustrated in the case of the failed attempt by GE to take over Honeywell in 2001. This move was approved by American regulators, but rejected by their European counterparts. (See "International Application" at the end of this chapter for details.)

One of the highest profile antitrust cases in recent years is the U.S. government's case against the Microsoft Corporation. In a nutshell, the U.S. government has charged that Microsoft has used its monopolistic powers to compete unfairly against the Netscape Communications Corporation in the Web browser market. (Microsoft also was accused of unfair practices against other companies; however, we will confine ourselves here to the government's case regarding Netscape.) By bundling its own product, Internet Explorer, with its Windows operating system, the government charged that the company gained an illegal competitive advantage against Netscape's Navigator. The thrust of the government's arguments rested on two points: (1) Microsoft indeed has monopolistic powers that violate current antitrust laws, and (2) Microsoft used these powers to unfairly restrict Netscape's ability to compete.

Readers can well expect that top economists were among the cast of expert witnesses called in to testify on behalf of either side. In a dramatic display of "You've got your expert and I've got mine," the government called in prominent economist Franklin M. Fisher of the Massachusetts Institute of Technology, and Microsoft countered with Richard L. Schmalensee, also of M.I.T. By coincidence (or perhaps not), Professor Fisher was Professor Schmalensee's Ph.D. thesis advisor.

Professor Fisher challenged the fairness of Microsoft's decision to imbed its browser into its Windows operating system, which has more than a 90 percent share of the market. Professor Schmalensee countered by saying that this is like saying that "consumers will be made better off if they are deprived, by court order, of Web-browsing functionality that Microsoft wishes to provide at zero marginal cost and that consumers are free to ignore or replace."[2,3] Professor Fisher argued, saying that the threat is not merely that Microsoft will wrest the browser market away from the current leader, Netscape Communications, but worse, that Microsoft might well use browser domination to eliminate competition in operating systems. He further charged that Microsoft's decision to give away its browser constituted an extreme form of "predatory pricing," designed to drive a competitor out of business.

In late 2001, Microsoft settled with the Justice Department. This settlement is very controversial. Antitrust enforcers from nine states are not satisfied and have decided to pursue the case on their own. U.S. District Judge Coleen Kollar-Kotelly suggested in late 2001 that the case could proceed on parallel tracks. Under the requirements of the Tunney Act, the Justice settlement is subject to additional review. Meanwhile the states could continue preparing for a final round in court.[4] The concerns raised by the state antitrust enforcers and many other critics are quite involved.

---

[2]"Trial's War of Economists Pits Student Against Teacher," *New York Times*, January 25, 1999.
[3]Readers should have no trouble finding material in the popular press about this case. However, two good sources that appeared around the time of the preparation of this edition are "As Microsoft Struggles with Antitrust Case, Tactical Errors Emerge," *The Wall Street Journal*, February 18, 1999, and "For Microsoft, Humbled May Not Mean Defeated," *New York Times*, February 28, 1999.
[4]"States Find Flaws in Deal With Microsoft," *The Wall Street Journal*, November 5, 2001.

Essentially, these critics believe that the settlement will not prevent Microsoft from continuing to use the same type of monopolistic tactics that brought the suit upon them in the first place.[5]

Dealing with Market Externalities: Another Key Function of Government in the Market Economy

In the microeconomic theory of the firm, on which much of managerial economics is based, it can be shown that under conditions of perfect competition, an economy's scarce resources will be most efficiently allocated and social welfare will be maximized. This situation prevails when all costs are fully accounted for in the price of the product. However, there are frequent cases when not all costs are included in the price or when not all costs are compensated. Such situations give rise to externalities and result in market failure.

A **benefit externality** is one where not all costs are compensated. In other words, certain benefits accrue to third parties. For instance, a beautiful private garden will benefit people who walk by but this will not compensate the owner. Benefit externalities (sometimes called positive externalities) also arise in the case of information (several people can read the same newspaper) or from innovations that benefit many people. Because producers of these products cannot appropriate all the revenue, too little may be produced.

But **cost externalities** are the ones with which economists are mostly concerned. These are the cases where a producer does not pay all the costs generated by the product. The most popular example of cost externalities (also called negative externalities) in economic literature is pollution. A factory will produce both the product and pollution. But if it does not have to pay for the cost of the pollution it has created, the product will be priced based only on the "private" production costs. Thus, the product's price will be lower than if it had been fully costed, and too much of the product will be produced. This can be shown on a simple graph for a competitive industry, shown in Figure 15.1.

The marginal cost curve of the product is shown as MC_p. The price of the product will be P_1 and the quantity produced will be Q_1. The cost of pollution is not considered in this result. The marginal cost of pollution is shown as MC_{pol}.

The total cost of the product to the economy, the "social cost," is the vertical summation of MC_p and MC_{pol}, or MC_s. If this cost had been included in the pricing of the product, then equilibrium would have been at P_{opt} and Q_{opt}. Obviously, there will always be some pollution. If pollution were to be completely eliminated, then this industry would have to shut down and produce nothing. But this would not be an ideal situation, as there is demand for the product. The **socially optimal price** will occur at P_{opt}, where the price of the product is equal to marginal social cost. Note that at this point less pollution will be produced (and less of the product also) than under strictly competitive conditions where only MC_p was priced into the product.

[5]There are numerous articles about the controversial settlement besides the one cited above. For example, see "Commentary: Settlement or Sellout?" *BusinessWeek*, November 19, 2001.

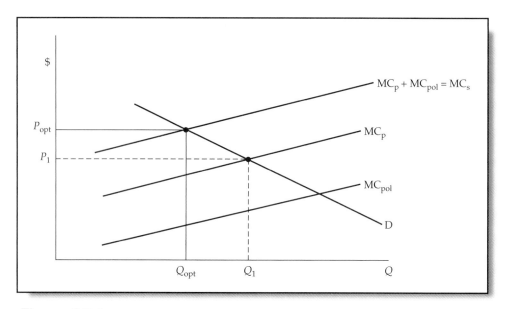

Figure 15.1
Impact of the Marginal Cost of Pollution on Price

How can the optimal equilibrium be attained? The usual prescription is for government to act in one of two ways.[6] The first would be to restrict production to Q_{opt}. The other method is taxation. Ideally this tax would be equal to the MC_{pol} curve. If such a tax were levied, then "externalities would be internalized." A third, rather new way, under the 1990 Clean Air Act, is for the government to set maximum pollution levels, and then sell licenses to companies to give them the right to pollute.

The Coase Theorem: An Alternative Treatment of Externalities In 1960, Ronald Coase advanced the idea that government intervention to eliminate the effect of externalities is not necessary if property rights are correctly and clearly defined.[7] This is often referred to as the **Coase theorem.** Who has the right to pollute and who has the right to keep pollution low? If it were originally decided who owns the property in question, then bargaining between the two parties would result in an optimal solution, without government intervention, at the level that would have been brought about with a correct taxation policy.

Various examples of such a situation can be given. Let us assume a stream, on which we find a chemical plant and a fishing establishment. If the property rights to this stream go to the chemical plant, the fishing company will have to pay the plant to reduce the dumping of its waste into the stream. It will pay just up to the point where the marginal benefit to the fishermen (from harvesting more and healthier fish) will be just equal to the cost incurred by the chemical plant (in dumping its

---

[6]The entire subject of externalities and government intervention was first treated fully by a famous English economist, A. C. Pigou. See *The Economics of Welfare,* 4th ed., London: Macmillan, 1932.
[7]Ronald Coase, "The Problem of Social Cost," *Journal of Law and Economics,* 3 (October 1960), pp. 1–44. This is a very long and complex article. For an excellent brief summary, see George J. Stigler, *The Theory of Price,* 4th ed., New York: Macmillan, 1987.

waste at a less convenient and more expensive location, or actually decreasing its production). On the other hand, if the fishing company has the property rights, the plant will have to pay the fishermen to permit the plant to dump waste. In both cases, the final result will be the same, and will take place at the optimal point that would have been achieved if a correct tax policy (i.e., taxes equal to the marginal cost of polluting) had been imposed.

Other examples of this kind abound. Coase, in his famous article, described the case of farmers growing grain in unfenced fields until a cattle rancher, whose cattle tend to damage the farmers' crops, arrives in the area. In addition, in his article, Coase cited a number of legal cases spanning back to the nineteenth century where the assignment of property rights was crucial in the decision.

While the Coase theorem poses very interesting questions regarding the need for government interference, it is important to look at its limitations. For instance, while optimal production levels are reached whichever party is assigned property rights, income distribution will be affected. In our example, if the chemical plant was awarded property rights, it will gain at the expense of the fishing industry. Thus, normative issues are not addressed by Coase.

But there are additional limitations. First, if transaction costs—i.e., the cost of obtaining an agreement between the two parties—are high, then bargaining may not be an ideal solution. Second, if one company engages in unfair bargaining, no reasonable agreement may be reached. And third, neither side may have complete information regarding the costs and benefits of arriving at the optimal solution.[8]

STABILIZATION OF THE AGGREGATE ECONOMY: MONETARY AND FISCAL POLICY

Monetary and fiscal policy was mentioned previously as government activities designed to stabilize the economy. In light of the 2001 recession in the United States, this function has become a much more important part of the role of government in the market economy. We will discuss each of these briefly.

Monetary Policy

Monetary policy is carried out by the Federal Reserve System (the Fed) through its control of the quantity of money in the economic system and/or interest rates. It is directed at attaining certain goals such as economic activity or price level. Over the years, the specific methods used by the Fed have differed. At one time, its primary concern was the quantity of money. More recently, monetary policy has concentrated on influencing interest rates, specifically the Federal Funds rate.

Banks are required to keep certain cash reserves with the Fed. On any given day, some banks' reserves may exceed requirements. Federal Funds is the name given to

---

[8]A. M. Polinsky, "Controlling Externalities and Protecting Entitlements: Property Right, Liability Rule, and Tax-Subsidy Approaches," *Journal of Legal Studies*, 8, 1979, pp. 1–48.

these excess reserves, which can be borrowed by banks whose reserve balances are deficient. Most of these loans are extremely short term, mostly overnight. It is the rate on these loans that the Federal Reserve targets. Depending on the condition of the economy, the Federal Fund rate target can be lowered, raised, or left alone. This determination is made by the Fed's Open Market Committee, which meets eight times each year. However, the rate also can be changed between meetings; this is what happened several times during 2001.

During the most recent downturn of the U.S. economy in 2001, the Federal Fund rate target was lowered 11 times, by either a quarter or a half of a percentage point each time. This was done to apply the brakes to the economic skid. From a level of 6.5 percent at the end of 2000, the rate declined to 1.75 percent in December 2001. Of course, the announcement of a lower target rate may not always be sustained automatically. In order to bring the rate to its desired level, the Fed may have to engage in open market operations to raise or lower the quantity of money in the economy. Open market operations involve the purchase of government securities in the market in order to increase the money supply as happened in 2001. At other times, when the economy threatens to overheat, resulting in inflation, the Fed may sell securities in the market to decrease the money supply and push interest rates up.

Fiscal Policy

The U.S. government collects taxes to finance expenditures for goods and services as well as transfer payments that have been legislated by the U.S. Congress. Such expenditures are generally based on long-term goals. However, fiscal policy—the changes in the level of taxation and spending—is designed to achieve macroeconomic goals relating to output (gross domestic product) and employment.

By manipulating receipts or expenditures, a surplus or deficit is created. To stimulate the economy, the government—through Congress—will either decrease taxes or increase expenditures (or both), and create a deficit in the federal budget. While both of these actions may stimulate an economy that has descended into a recession, the result of an increase in spending is to enlarge the role of the U.S. government in the economy, which may be considered unfavorable by the part of the population that believes in limited government. However, another part of the population looks at such actions favorably, believing that increased government actions may be beneficial. Again, the actions in the year 2001 present us with good examples of changes in fiscal policy.

One of the new administration's primary goals was to lower the level of taxes in the long run, thus decreasing the government's role in our lives. During 2001, Congress passed a law that decreased income taxes gradually over the next 10 years (other provisions were also included, such as the phasing out of the estate tax). However, since the economy appeared to be turning downward, the Congress included a provision that gave immediate refunds of up to $600 to most taxpayers. This was, of course, intended to give the economy a quick shot in the arm. As the economy appeared to continue its decline toward the end of the year, the administration and Congress embarked on trying to pass an "economic stimulus" package made up of certain tax cut and spending increases. It was passed by Congress and signed by the President in March 2002.

Lags

Although both policies can affect the movement of the economy, it must be recognized that in both cases the effect is not immediate. In fact, there are significant lags in the consequences of both monetary and fiscal actions. First, there is usually a delay in recognizing that a problem exists. While both the Fed and the U.S. government have a large amount of economic data available, they may not be timely or different data may give conflicting signals. (As already mentioned in chapter 6, the onset of the most recent recession was dated March 2001, but this was not announced until December 2001.) Second, after the problem is recognized, there is a delay in implementation. This interval is particularly present in fiscal policy where the action must go through a political process that may be excruciatingly slow. The action can be realized more quickly in the case of monetary policy. Third, even when action is taken, there is a substantial lag for it to work itself into the economy and become effective.

Various economists have tried to estimate these lags. While there is no agreement on the precise size of the lag, we know that it can last more than six months and may at times be as long as a year or more. Thus, it is quite possible that either monetary or fiscal action will actually turn out to be counterproductive. It may become effective when the economy has actually righted itself on its own, and the policy action may either add fuel to an already growing economy or aggravate a decline. The stimulus package passed in 2002 may be just such a case. Even without it, the economy appeared to have bottomed out in early 2002, and any stimulus that it may provide could be too late and could become effective at a time when the economy no longer needs it.

DOING BUSINESS WITH THE U.S. GOVERNMENT

Nowhere else do government policies and procedures have greater impact than on market segments where the government *is* the buyer.[9] Such a market is sometimes described as a **monopsony,** or a market in which the product or service of a number of sellers is sought by only one buyer. In this section, we will focus on the U.S. government because of its size, reach, and impact on the U.S. economy. Conversely, we also will illustrate that a market economy can have a great impact on how the U.S. government acts as a buyer. The challenges of doing business with local and state governments are similar, although there may be specific differences in policies and procedures from those followed by the federal government.

The U.S. government is arguably the single biggest client in the world. In fiscal year 1998, federal receipts totaled $1.722 trillion, or 20.5 percent of gross domestic product. Total outlays were $1.653 trillion or 19.7 percent of gross domestic product.[10] Each year, the federal executive branch purchases about *$200 billion* in goods

---

[9]This section was written by Sylvia Von Bostel, on the staff of Booz-Allen & Hamilton.
[10]"The Budget System and Concepts," *Budget of the United States Government, Fiscal Year 2000,* Washington, DC: U.S. Government Printing Office, 1999.

and services.[11] According to the Federal Procurement Data Center, part of the U.S. General Services Administration, every 20 seconds of each working day the U.S. government awards a contract with an average value of $465,000.[12] In such a market, government policies fundamentally shape the ways in which businesses behave.

The Government Market

Doing business with the federal government is highly complicated. Entire industries have emerged to explain how to be successful in this marketplace. Some companies choose not to do business with the government due to special accounting and reporting requirements, potential liabilities, profit limitations, and other statutory and regulatory controls. On the other hand, many companies have learned how to operate and prosper in this environment.

For the purposes of this discussion, we will approach this subject with three basic questions of *what? when?* and *how?* First, businesses look at *what* they believe the government will buy. This determines the way in which businesses define their product or service offerings. Related to this question is that of *when* the government plans to buy. This is a critically important factor and has an impact on whether short- or long-term investments are required. Third, businesses carefully monitor changes in federal acquisition policies that govern *how* the government will buy. This affects the way in which they develop their bidding strategies. Let us take a closer look.

What the Government Buys *What* the U.S. government buys is influenced by government strategic plans, budget and program input from federal departments and agencies, priorities set by the President, the availability of appropriated funds, congressionally mandated requirements, whether the federal budget is in surplus or deficit, and lots of politics. Businesses monitor this ever-changing environment, their government clients, and the entire federal budget process carefully. While perhaps 80 to 90 percent of the President's budget request is usually enacted, individual programs or projects can be eliminated, cut back, restricted, or limited in other ways. Sometimes Congress adds funding that was not requested. Any of these actions can have a significant impact on a business that has or is seeking a contract with the government.

The federal government's fiscal year begins on October 1, ends on September 30, and is named by the year in which it ends. Fiscal year 1999, for example, began on October 1, 1998, and ended on September 30, 1999. Each January the President announces priority initiatives and proposed funding in the President's State of the Union Address. The formal budget process begins with release of the *Budget of the United States Government* to Congress, which the President is required to submit to Congress by the first Monday in February.[13]

In reality, federal departments and agencies begin building their budgets two years in advance and, in addition to the fiscal year in question, look at "out years," or

---

[11]Retrieved February 3, 1999 from Federal Procurement Data System, General Services Administration World Wide Web site: *fpds.gsa.gov.*
[12]"FPDS . . . the Competitor's Edge," retrieved February 3, 1999 from the World Wide Web: *fpds.gsa.gov/fpds/compete.*
[13]"Citizen's Guide to the Federal Budget," *Budget of the United States Government, Fiscal Year 2000.*

five to six years into the future. The White House, bipartisan commissions, independent panels, interagency councils, inspectors general, the General Accounting Office (the investigative arm of Congress), congressional committees, and federal departments and agencies themselves conduct many reviews that influence budget requests. The Office of Management and Budget (OMB) provides detailed instructions to federal departments and agencies about how to put their budgets together in *OMB Circular A-11,* "Preparation and Submission of Budget Estimates," a document that is updated annually to reflect changes in law. OMB collects the budget requests, "scrubs" the numbers, and puts together the President's budget.

Ultimately, it is the U.S. Congress that authorizes and appropriates the funds that can be obligated and expended for the purchase of goods and services. Once the President's budget is submitted to Congress, the annual appropriations process begins in earnest. There are 13 appropriations bills. In some years they are enacted separately. In others, due to lack of time or breakdowns in negotiations between the White House and Congress on major programs or policy issues, some or all appropriation bills are bundled in a large catchall piece of legislation. Appropriation bills or some stopgap legislation, referred to as "continuing resolutions," must be enacted by October 1 or parts or all of the federal government may be forced to "shut down."

When the Government Buys   *When* the government plans to purchase goods or services is a critical factor in many ways. Learning about a major procurement when the government publishes a request for proposal usually means it is too late to be a player. Competitors who have been tracking the procurement, devising a strategy, and negotiating with teaming partners will have an advantage. For companies that develop and build prototypes and manufacture high-cost items requiring substantial long-term investment, serious delays can threaten their very survival and even lead to merger or acquisition. Unanticipated cancellations due to budget cutbacks or major government shutdowns can result in layoffs, plant closings, and cash flow problems. One need only look at the consolidations that have been occurring in the defense and aerospace industries since the end of the Cold War to see the impact of changes of federal government budgets on private industry. (See the reference on p. 660 to Lockheed's efforts to enter the market for computer services.)

How the Government Buys   *How* the government purchases goods and services has a major impact on bidding strategies. Government acquisition is controlled by two basic laws, the *Armed Services Procurement Act,* applicable to the Army, Navy, Air Force, Coast Guard, and NASA, and the *Federal Property and Administrative Services Act,* applicable to the General Services Administration and all other agencies. The Federal Acquisition Regulation System codifies and publishes uniform policies and procedures for acquisition by all federal agencies. It consists of the Federal Acquisition Regulation (FAR), which is the primary governmentwide document, and agency acquisition regulations that supplement the FAR. The Office of Federal Procurement Policy, part of the Office of Management and Budget, provides overall direction.[14]

---

[14]"Authority·Policy·Laws·Regulations·Selling to the Federal Government," *Government Contracts Reporter,* Commerce Clearing House, Inc., June 14, 1989.

Companies doing business with the government must comply with requirements and controls that do not exist in commercial transactions. These include competition requirements, profit restrictions, audits, bid protest rules, accounting system requirements, prohibitions against gratuities and certain hiring practices, and socioeconomic programs. The Federal Acquisition Regulation is divided into 53 parts. Part 15 deals exclusively with negotiated contracts. Parts 19–26 of the Federal Acquisition Regulation are dedicated to socioeconomic programs, for example, small business programs, the application of labor laws to government acquisitions, environment, conservation, occupational safety, and drug-free workplace, protection of privacy and freedom of information, foreign acquisition, the Indian incentive program, and historically black colleges and universities and minority institutions. Part 30 sets forth cost accounting standards and part 31 deals with contract cost principles and procedures. Part 52 is a long list of solicitation provisions and contract clauses, and includes a matrix listing of FAR provisions and clauses applicable to each principal contract type, for example, fixed-price supply or cost reimbursement research and development. Part 53 provides examples of standard forms, optional forms, and agency-specific forms.[15]

The Government and the Market Economy

As stated, the market economy has a great impact on how the U.S. government acts as a buyer as well. During the 1980s it became apparent that the annual federal deficit and total national debt were reaching unacceptable levels, the Cold War was ending, and the nation was entering a new Information Age. Laws were enacted to enforce budget discipline and the federal government sought ways in which to become more efficient and cost effective. It did this by adapting for its use successful business practices in the private sector such as total quality management, business process reengineering, downsizing, rightsizing, mergers, streamlining acquisitions, and shedding excess infrastructure. From the height of the defense buildup in the mid 1980s until around 1998, the Department of Defense reduced force structure by 35 to 40 percent.[16] Four Base Realignment and Closure (BRAC) Commissions between 1988 and 1995 proposed the closure or realignment of 152 major installations and 235 smaller installations.[17] While not all actions have occurred, approximately $14 to 15 billion in savings were achieved by 1998.[18]

In the 1990s, the federal government accelerated steps to further streamline its acquisition processes, adopt commercial practices, get away from detailed government specifications, buy commercial off-the-shelf items whenever possible, and emphasize performance-based or results-based management. Table 15.1 highlights some of the laws enacted during the 1990s.

One of the major impacts of these acquisition reforms of the 1990s was the increased use of the *Federal Supply Schedules* as a preferred way of doing business. Under the

---

[15]*Federal Acquisition Regulation* as of January 1, 1998, Commerce Clearing House, Inc., 1998.
[16]William S. Cohen, Secretary of Defense, "The Secretary's Message," *Report of the Quadrennial Defense Review,* May 1997.
[17]William S. Cohen, Secretary of Defense, *Annual Report to the President and Congress,* 1998, p. 176.
[18]William S. Cohen, Secretary of Defense, Testimony before the House Armed Services Committee, "Hearing on the President's Fiscal Year 2000 Budget," February 2, 1999.

Table 15.1

Selected Laws Adopting Commercial Practices

Year	Public Law	Key Provisions
1990	Chief Financial Officers Act	• Required the establishment of agency chief financial officers and designated a governmentwide CFO
1993	Government Performance and Results Act	• Established strategic planning and performance measurement requirements for federal agencies.
1994	Government Management Reform Act, which contained the Federal Financial Management Act	• Required agencies and the government as a whole to produce annual audited financial statements • Mandated direct deposit electronic funds transfers for all federal wage, salary, and retirement payments
1994	Federal Acquisition Streamlining Act	• Expanded the types of commercial items and services that the government could purchase using streamlined procedures • Simplified payments for small purchases by increasing the use of governmentwide credit cards
1996	Federal Acquisitions Reform Act	• Expanded the definition of commercial items and services and exempted them from the requirement for certified cost or pricing data and the federal government's cost accounting standards
1996	Information Technology Management Reform Act	• Required capital planning and investment control for information technology • Called for the designation of a chief information officer at each executive agency

Sources: Chief Financial Officers Act of 1990, Public Law 101–576, November 15, 1990; *Government Performance and Reform Act of 1993 (GPRA),* PL 103–62, August 3, 1993; *Government Management Reform Act of 1994 (GMRA),* PL 103–356, October 13, 1994; *Federal Acquisition Streamlining Act of 1994 (FASA),* PL 103–355, October 13, 1994; *Federal Acquisition Reform Act of 1996 (FARA),* PL 104–106, February 10, 1996; *Information Technology Management Reform Act of 1996 (ITMRA),* PL 104–106, February 10, 1996.

Federal Supply Schedules administered by the General Services Administration (GSA), companies apply to provide certain types of commercial items and services and are placed on a list of approved vendors, together with their price lists, which are posted on GSA's Web pages. Qualified vendors are able to market their products and capabilities to federal agencies. Federal agencies are able to find vendors on the list and use streamlined acquisition procedures to meet their requirements. Commercial items and services and off-the-shelf commercial items are also exempt from significant statutory and regulatory requirements, both at the contract and subcontract levels.

Around 1995, under the auspices of the National Performance Review, another phenomenon, sometimes referred to as *entrepreneurial government,* emerged. This brought the adaptation of commercial practices to a new level by actively sanctioning government "franchising," employee stock ownership programs (ESOPs) made up of former government employees, public-public competition, and public-private competition. The *Government Management Reform Act/Federal Financial Management Act of 1994,* cited in Table 15.1, established a franchise fund pilot program in six executive agencies. The fund is used to provide common administrative support services to the designated agency, but can also be used to provide services to other agencies on a competitive basis. As of July 1997, the Environmental Protection Agency, the departments of Commerce, Health and Human Services, Interior, Treasury, and Veterans Affairs were participating in the franchise fund program. Data centers at these six agencies gave up their operating budgets but recover their expenses by charging their own agencies and other government entities for the work they do.[19] US Investigations Services, Inc. (USIS) is an ESOP formed in July 1996 by former federal civil servants in the Office of Federal Investigations, part of the Office of Personnel Management. USIS is the first employee-owned enterprise that involved a former federal agency, and has become the largest private investigations company in North America.[20]

In May 1997, the Federal Aviation Administration (FAA) awarded its Integrated Computing Environment-Mainframe and Networking (ICE-MAN) contract, worth up to $250 million over eight years, to the U.S. Department of Agriculture (USDA) computer center in Kansas City, Missouri. Under that contract, USDA operates the FAA's computer systems for payroll, personnel, and flight safety. Competitors included major corporations such as IBM, Unisys, Computer Sciences, and Lockheed Martin and at least one government agency, the Defense Information Systems Agency.[21]

Federal policy regarding the performance of commercial activities is set forth in *OMB Circular A-76,* first promulgated by the Bureau of the Budget in 1955 and reissued and revised many times since then, most recently in 1996. Circular A-76 states that in the process of governing, the government should not compete with its citizens and shall rely on commercially available sources to provide commercial products and services. When commercial performance of a government commercial activity is appropriate, A-76 requires that the cost of private sector versus government performance be compared to determine who will do the work. It also states that certain functions are so intimately related to the public interest as to mandate performance only by federal employees.[22]

In 1998, the *Federal Activities Inventory Reform Act* (FAIR) required federal agencies to review, inventory, and publicly list those functions that are not inherently

[19]"Battle Lines Drawn on FAA Contract," *Washington Technology,* July 10, 1997, page 1.
[20]"Live Long and Prosper," edited with permission from an article appearing in *Government Executive,* Web site of Foundation for Enterprise Development, *www.fed.org/leading companies/nov97/harper.html.*
[21]"FAA, $150M Iceman Cometh to USDA," *Federal Computer Week,* May 12, 1997, p. 1; "When the Government Hires the Government, FAA Awards Big Systems Contract to USDA, but to Private Contractors, It Doesn't Compute," *The Washington Post,* May 22, 1997; "Battle Lines Drawn on FAA Contract," *Washington Technology,* July 10, 1997, p. 1
[22]*QMB Circular A-76,* March 1996.

governmental and that could therefore be performed by commercial entities. At the same time, FAIR statutorily sanctioned competition between federal agencies and the private sector. To address longstanding concerns in the private sector that government bids in public–private competitions do not fully reflect all costs, FAIR also required the Office of Management and Budget to issue guidance on conducting such competitions. To ensure realistic and fair cost comparisons, FAIR further directed federal agencies to ensure that all costs, including the costs of quality assurance, technical monitoring of the performance of a function, liability insurance, employee retirement and disability benefits, and all other overhead costs, be considered.[23]

These changes over the past 20 years are altering client relationships and redefining what it means to do business with the federal government. Much more business is being conducted using the *Federal Supply Schedules*. More A-76 competitions are being held to determine whether commercial activities should be performed by the government or by commercial entities. There have been major reforms to reduce bid protests and long procurement cycles. The potential value of large federal information technology contracts more frequently reaches or exceeds $100 million. The federal government has created "franchises" and ESOPs. Government agencies are competing against each other to perform administrative services, and companies find themselves bidding against their government clients to provide computer services. In the words of Aldous Huxley, this government market is a "brave new world," one that will certainly bring fascinating challenges in the new millennium.

GOVERNMENT DEREGULATION, MERGERS, AND ACQUISITIONS

For various historic, political, and economic reasons, certain major industries in the United States were subject to considerable government regulation. Telecommunications, electric and gas utilities, airlines, and commercial banks are perhaps the best examples. Beginning in the late 1970s and continuing on through the 1990s, the U.S. government in effect eliminated most if not all regulatory control that it had exercised over firms in these industries. Regardless of the original reasons for their regulation, the Government has assumed that by deregulating these industries, consumers will be better served by lower prices, better service, or more rapid introduction of technology that would ostensibly stem from a more competitive environment.

However, in recent years, the deregulation has apparently resulted in such a fiercely competitive environment that a number of companies in these industries have sought to merge or acquire other companies in order to survive and grow. This is somewhat ironic because one of the great concerns of antitrust policy in the United States has been the level of merger activity. As companies merge, is there a danger that their greater size makes them monopolistic and a threat to free competition? If

---

[23]*Federal Activities Inventory Reform Act (FAIR)*, Public Law 105–270, October 19, 1998.

so, then the very actions of the government to make certain industries more competitive may require it to assert its role as the arbiter of what constitutes "competition."

In commercial banking, the mergers (the combination of two firms or the acquisition of one firm by another) that have grabbed most of the headlines have been among the leading financial institutions. Citicorp merged with Traveler's Insurance to form Citigroup. Chemical Bank and Chase Manhattan merged to become the Chase Bank. Several years later, this commercial bank merged with the investment bank J.P. Morgan to form J.P. Morgan Chase. Bank of America merged with Nations Bank and kept its name after the merger. BankOne merged with First Chicago and did the same thing. Shortly afterward, it acquired one of the nation's largest "monoline banks," First USA.[24] Wells Fargo merged with Norwest. It too kept its name.

In the market for local telecommunications service, the seven Regional Bell Operating Companies that were formed by the breakup of AT&T have been reduced to four. SBC, one of the original seven, merged with Pacific Telesis and Ameritech. The three original "Baby Bells" now operate as one entity: SBC. Verizon is the result of a merger with two original Baby Bells, Nynex and Bell Atlantic, plus GTE, a long distance and local company that had remained independent of the original Bell System of AT&T. U.S. West is now called Qwest when the latter bought out the former. Of the original seven, only Bell South has not been part of any major merger or acquisition. In the long distance market, WorldCom acquired MCI to become MCIWorldCom.

In both the financial and telecommunications sectors, there have also been movements to break up as well as merge different entities. MCIWorldCom broke into two separate entities, MCI (essentially the voice communications business) and WorldCom (essentially the data communications business). AT&T has divested its wireless business and has created a separate entity with Comcast to offer broadband services. Today the entity called AT&T has been left with providing voice communications services to businesses and consumers.

The airline industry in the United States also has experienced some merger and acquisition activity, although not quite as much as in the financial and telecommunications industries. In 2000, United Airlines tried to buy U.S. Air but was prevented from doing so by the government. However, in 2001, the government allowed American Airlines to acquire TWA. After the approval of this acquisition, however, industry analysts have continued to speculate what combinations might form among the other major airlines, Delta, Northwest, Continental, and U.S. Air.

For many decades, the electric utility industry was regulated by state authorities. Rates charged to retail customers had to be approved by these authorities, and were generally based on allowing utilities to earn a particular rate of return on their investment. The electric companies operated in specific regions in which they had a monopoly. Such arrangements assured a rather quiet life for the utility companies, but certainly did not create a need for efficient operations.

This climate began to change in the 1990s when the utility industry moved toward deregulation. California was in the forefront of this trend. In 1996, the state of California passed a law deregulating the electric utility industry, and permitting

---

[24]A monoline bank is one that primarily issues credit cards. Other leading monolines include MBNA and Capital One.

competition and customer choice. The law went into effect in 1998. The situation appeared to be well in hand until the year 2000, when California found itself in the middle of a power crisis. Utility customers suffered through blackouts, and two of the three large California utilities sustained large losses, resulting in one of them declaring bankruptcy. What happened? While the various parties to this debacle tried to assign blame, it became quite clear that there were serious flaws in the deregulation law. The California deregulation law contained a number of provisions, which, when combined, may have led to the difficulties that started in May 2000:

1. Consumers received an immediate 10 percent rate cut. Rates were then frozen at that level.
2. California's public utilities did not have to compete until the year 2002. In the meantime, it was expected that low wholesale prices (compared with the fixed retail prices) would enable the utilities to earn high profits that would enable them to pay off uneconomical investments they had made during the years of regulated rates (these costs are referred to as "stranded costs").
3. Utilities were urged to sell their power-generating plants to independent generators. These companies were expected to be able to generate power more cheaply and efficiently. The California utilities would then purchase their power from these plants as well as others.
4. No long-term contracts for power were to be made. Instead, the law created a new marketplace for power, called the California Power Exchange (CPE). CPE would, on a daily basis, take bids for power for the next day. All utilities were obliged to buy their power through the CPE.

The law went into effect early in 1998, and operated fairly well. In May 2000, the wholesale price of power began rising precipitously, going from $30 per megawatt-hour to $146 in June, and sometime spiking at peak hours to an even much higher level. This resulted in large losses being sustained by the California utilities. As mentioned above retail prices had been fixed, and the higher wholesale prices were considerably above the retail price the utilities were allowed to charge. Ultimately, one of the three large California utilities, PG&E, declared bankruptcy in April 2001.

While the deregulation plan appears to have been flawed, various events and trends contributed to California's problems. During the 1990s, California experienced significant growth. The population rose by 15 percent and the employed labor force rose by 19 percent. Thus, demand for electric power increased substantially. However, during this period, California invested very little to increase its energy production. The reason for this lack is debatable. Some argue that the state's tough environmental laws and a "not in my back yard" (NIMBY) syndrome were the cause, while others contend that low energy prices, excess capacity, and poor profitability are to blame. In addition, the California law discouraged utilities from hedging their price risks. And above that, the freezing of retail prices discouraged Californians from conserving energy.

While consumers in some other states experienced rate increases, the problems created in California did not occur in many states that went ahead with deregulation. Pennsylvania, together with New Jersey and Maryland, is a case in point. In Pennsylvania alone, it appears that consumers have saved $3 billion on their electricity bills over the past three years. Of course, this region of the United States did not experience the phenomenal growth that occurred in California; thus, it was not confronted with California's supply problems. However, some of the success must be ascribed to better decision making on the part of the regulators. Pennsylvania's utilities were permitted to keep their generating plants, and were thus protected from volatile wholesale prices. Furthermore, they could enter into long-term contracts with other generating companies. PPL (formerly Pennsylvania Power & Light) reported profit gains in the year 2000, and expects further profit growth in 2001 and 2002.[25]

We would be remiss in discussing deregulation (and regulation) if we did not at least mention a subject that has been part of the daily headlines throughout the time that we have been completing the final draft of this edition: Enron. Writing about this company and its rise and fall could and will undoubtedly fill volumes. In the context of this chapter, a few brief comments should be made. First, the rise of Enron from a relatively small traditional natural gas utility to a large and complex business that traded in bandwidth as well as energy would not have been possible without the deregulation of the gas and electricity markets. Second, the fall of Enron from the number 1 energy company on *Fortune*'s list of the "World's Most Admired Companies" in 2000 to number 15 in 2001 has resulted in a huge public outcry for greater regulation in many different areas of business activities such as the management of 401k retirement plans, the policy of hiring outside auditors, and the requirements for financial disclosure.[26] Perhaps much more will be learned and can be stated with greater certainty in time for our next edition.

Why Firms Merge

The recent increase in mergers in the deregulated industries is nothing new. The U.S. economy has passed through a number of merger waves since the end of the nineteenth century. During the 1980s and early 1990s, many mergers were motivated by low valuations of the target firms, which had been underperforming. In addition to mergers, this period also saw a large number of leveraged buyouts (LBO's), where public companies were taken private by groups of investors, using large amounts of debt to finance the transaction.[27] In the middle and late 1990s, mergers have been motivated primarily by the necessity to obtain greater efficiencies—economies of

---

[25]A large number of articles and other publications have discussed utility deregulation, and particularly California's problems, over the past several years. Only a few are mentioned here: Brian O'Reilly, "Transforming the Power Business," *Fortune*, September 29, 1997, p. 142; "A State of Gloom: California's Power Crisis," *The Economist*, January 20, 2001; *Manifest on the California Electricity Crisis*, Haas School of Business, University of California Berkeley, January 26, 2001; Mark Gimein, "Who Turned the Lights Out?" *Fortune*, February 5, 2001, p. 110; Jeremy Kahn, "Where Deregulation Isn't a Disaster," *Fortune*, March 19, 2001, p. 40; Howard Gleckman, "Paying the Price in California," *Business Week Online*, April 24, 2001; Laura D. Tyson, "Ignoring California's Energy Crisis Imperils the Economy," *Business Week*, June 4, 2001; Harlan S. Byrne, "Switched on: PPL Got an Early Jump on Deregulation, and It's Paying Dividends Today," *Barron's*, June 18, 2001, p. 20.

[26]"Where Companies Rank in Their Industry," *Fortune*, March 11, 2001. Also see "Bracing for a Backlash: After Enron, Business May Be Subjected to a New Wave of Regulation," *BusinessWeek*, February 4, 2002. Also, in May 2002, the government began investigating Enron for possible manipulation of energy prices in California.

[27]The ultimate goal was, of course, to streamline these companies, make them more efficient (possibly by disposing of some parts of the company), and eventually bring them back as publicly owned companies.

scale or scope—to be able to compete in a global economy. This impetus for merging with or acquiring companies is relevant for any industry where the intensity of competition has increased.

As we have just pointed out, deregulated industries are perhaps the most dramatic example of situations where there is a sharp increase in competition, but certain other industries that have never been regulated also have undergone significant upheaval. In the automobile industry, mergers and acquisitions making the news include the merger of Daimler-Benz with Chrysler, the Ford Motor Company's purchase of Jaguar and of Volvo's motor vehicle division, and BMW's purchase of Rover. After several years of owning Rover, BMW continues to lose money from this operation and its CEO is being severely criticized for this purchase. BMW's current bad experience with Rover shows that not all mergers and acquisitions result in immediate economic gains (later in this section we summarize studies that have tracked the economic consequences of mergers and acquisitions).

At the time this text was being completed, the controversial merger of Hewlett-Packard with Compaq was approved by shareholders. The CEOs of the two companies stressed that a key benefit of the merger was the creation of a new company with sufficient scale to compete on an even basis with IBM and EDS in the market for information technology services.

There are many reasons behind merger activity. The basic motivation for mergers is to increase the value of the combined firms compared to their separate valuations. This simple idea is usually expressed with the following equation:

$$V_{A+B} > (V_A + V_B)$$

where V stands for total market value, and A and B are the two companies involved in the merger.

Among the incentives to merge, some result in increased economic efficiency, but others do not. A partial list of incentives follows:

1. *Synergies in production.* If synergies exist, then the value of the combined companies should exceed the value of the two separately. Among the synergistic results we would find the following:
   a. *Revenue enhancements.* For example, a better distribution system for products when two companies combine may increase sales.
   b. *Operating economies.* These results would include economies of scale and/or scope. Economies could also be achieved through improved research and development (because of complementarities in technical skills resident in the two companies) or "management meshing," where the skills of the management of the companies complement each other. For instance, one company has strong marketing management while the other's managers have technical superiority.
   c. *Financial economies.* The combined company may be able to lower its cost of capital.
2. *Improved management.* In some cases, the acquired firm may lack good management skills, while the acquiring firm has a relative abundance of skilled managers. The merger will create an opportunity for improving the overall management level of the new company by eliminating poor managers.

3. *Tax consequences.* While a merger may not result in increased economic efficiency, it may reduce the tax bill of the two combined companies. If a company has been incurring losses, it will not be paying taxes. It will carry tax losses forward, and may reduce its tax liabilities in the future when it becomes profitable. By merging with a profitable company, it will be able to save taxes immediately, and increase the combined companies' cash flow even in the absence of any synergies.

   Taxes will also be decreased for a company with much cash and no great investment opportunities. If this company were to pay a large dividend, then its stockholders would pay taxes immediately; or if the company were to buy back its stock, stockholders could be liable for capital gains taxes. By using its cash to acquire another company, it will avoid creating tax liabilities.

4. *Managerial power.* Mergers may occur when the acquiring company's managers are seeking to increase their span of authority. While the acquisition of another company may expand the power of managers, it will, in many cases, not result in enhanced efficiency.

5. *Diversification.* During the 1960s, diversification was the ostensible motivation for a large number of mergers. Mergers among companies in unrelated fields of activity predominated. It was said that diversification could decrease the variability of sales and earnings and thus be of benefit to stockholders, even if no synergistic effects were present. This is a flawed argument. There is no reason why stockholders cannot achieve their own diversification by investing in both companies. This would be accomplished much more cheaply, since it would avoid the significant costs that would be incurred in completing the merger.

6. *Market power.* The combination of two or more powerful firms could lead to a decrease of competition in the industry. The result could be lower production, higher prices, and a negative effect on the efficient functioning of the economy. It is with these potential effects that U.S. antitrust laws are concerned.

A large number of studies have investigated the effects of mergers on stockholders and the economy. We summarize their results as follows:

1. There is general agreement that stockholders of the target companies are the big winners, gaining between 20 and 30 percent when their company is acquired. On the other hand, the stockholders of the acquiring firms gain very little, as their stock prices, on average, remain constant. Overall, there appears to be an increase in the value of the combined companies.

2. The evidence regarding increased profitability of merged firms is rather mixed.

3. Merger activity does not appear to have increased the level of industry concentration.

4. There appears to be no decrease in research and development activity of merged firms, contrary to the opinion of some commentators.[28]

---

[28]For an excellent review of recent mergers and acquisitions, including those in industries that we have discussed in this chapter, see "Oligopolies Are on the Rise as the Urge to Merge Grows," *The Wall Street Journal,* February 25, 2002.

International Application: The Failed Attempt to Merge by General Electric and Honeywell

The failed attempt by General Electric to merge with Honeywell in the first half of 2001 provides an excellent example of the international dimension of the role of government in a market economy. What it really illustrates is two opposite philosophies of antitrust held by American and European regulators and government officials. In October 2000, the General Electric Company proposed to merge with Honeywell International, Inc. Prior to this move, Honeywell was in the process of merging with the United Technologies Corporation. After GE topped United's bid, Honeywell and GE prepared for their merger.

The U.S. Department of Justice approved the merger in May 2001. During the past 20 years, the American interpretation of the antitrust laws has been moving in the direction of making decisions on the basis of a merger's effect on consumer welfare. The GE-Honeywell merger appeared to promise production and distribution efficiencies. However, since the merger would affect business in Europe, it had to be approved by the European Commission. After investigation and conferences during the first half of 2001, the European Commission ruled against the merger, despite various concessions made by GE. The basis for the rejection was the merger's potential threat to competitors.

Two major issues appear to influence the Commission's decision:

1. GE and Honeywell, if combined, could "bundle" their products. GE is a major producer of aircraft engines, while Honeywell produces avionics and aerospace products. The merged company would now be able to offer discounts to "customers who bought a package of components and services from GE-Honeywell."[29] Thus, the merged company's competitors would be injured. Several competing companies actively opposed the merger; among them were United Technologies, Rolls-Royce, and Rockwell.
2. GE Capital Aviation Services (GECAS) is one of the world's largest buyers of commercial aircraft which it sells or leases to airlines. The Commission feared that GECAS could require aircraft manufacturers to install GE-Honeywell products on the aircraft ordered by it.[30]

Based on this case, we can say that American government officials appear to favor the demand side of the market (i.e., the buyers of aerospace and related products) while their European counterparts tend to favor the supply side (i.e., the firms that produce these products). We think that the concern about the loss in jobs that inevitably follows such mergers is probably what tilts the Europeans toward the supply side.

---

[29]Andrew Hill and Deborah Hargreaves, "How Monti Turned GE-Honeywell into a Flight of Fancy," *Financial Times*, July 6, 2001.
[30]In addition to the article quoted above, several other articles appeared in the press on this subject. Among these were Mike France, "Europe: a Different Take on Antitrust," *Business Week*, June 25, 2001, p. 40; Gary Becker, "What U.S. Courts Could Teach Europe's Trustbuster," *Business Week*, August 6, 2001, p. 20; Bryan M. Carney, "Blame the EU's Antitrust Rules—Not Monti," *The Wall Street Journal*, July 7, 2001; Philip Shishkin, "Barred Merger Signals U.S.-EU Divergence," *The Wall Street Journal*, July 5, 2001.

The Solution

The staff report that Bill was reviewing was very revealing. Outsourcing is not necessarily the panacea for cost control that everyone seems to imagine. It is true that the vendor's total charge for services is less than the cost that the company believes it would incur by staying "in-house."

However, the company in fact has to have a staff to monitor and work with the vendor to ensure that the various services are carried out according to the service level agreement, or SLA. A large and complex contract such as the one that Global Foods signed with AT&T has multiple SLAs.

After giving the matter considerable thought in consultation with his staff, Bill decided to continue the relationship with AT&T. His reasons were as follows:

1. Both Global Foods and AT&T were relatively new at the outsourcing game and were only just beginning to accumulate the experience and skills to make the relationship pay off.

2. In certain instances where AT&T was not providing satisfactory service, it was because Global Foods was itself not very clear about its requirements. Rather than throwing out the proverbial "baby with the bath water," Bill felt that a reevaluation and possible revision of certain SLAs would be more effective than changing vendors.

3. The competitive environment in the telecommunications industry had been changing over the past few years. Right after the 1996 Telecommunications Act was passed, there were a slew of new telecom companies eager to gain entry into the market who were bidding for contracts at very low prices. This had put downward pressures on pricing in the entire industry and in fact had made outsourcing a lot more attractive strictly from a standpoint of cost (vs. the quality of service). There had ben a drastic shake-out in the market since that time and many of the smaller competitive local exchange carriers (CLECs) had gone bust. This gave the remaining telecom companies, including the incumbent giants such as AT&T, MCI, Verizon, and SBC, slightly more breathing room as far as pricing was concerned. In fact, Bill had read in a recent *Wall Street Journal* article that the telecommunications industry as well as a number of other industries had become more oligopolistic as smaller companies dropped out or companies of all sizes had begun to merge. One statistic cited in the article was that at the end of 2000, there were 330 CLECs challenging the incumbent companies such as Verizon and SBC. A year later, only 150 of them were left.[31] Therefore, the num-

---

[31]"Oligopolies are on the Rise . . ." The situation and solution are completely fictitious, but the consolidation and bankruptcies that have been taking place in the telecommunications industry as a result of deregulation are quite real.

(Continued)

ber of alternative vendors and their cost differential were a lot smaller today than they were four or five years ago.

Shortly after Bill's staff announced to AT&T that the contract would be continued, he got a call from AT&T's Senior Account Relationship Manager for the Global Foods account.

"Hey, Bill, there's a fabulous new Asian-French restaurant that has just opened up downtown. The chef is actually featured on the Food Channel. I'd love to take you and your entire staff there to try out the food, which I understand is fabulous."

"That's really nice of you," Bill responded. "But to be honest, I'm on a diet. Maybe some other time."

SUMMARY

We have illustrated specifically how various business decisions can be influenced by government involvement in the market economy. As we discussed in chapter 1, the primary advantage of the market process over the command and traditional processes is the efficient manner in which market participants allocate a country's scarce resources. Throughout this text, we have tried to show how managers, equipped with an understanding of the major factors of the market process (supply, demand, production, cost, and competition) and various quantitative tools of analysis are able to make optimal decisions to help their firms maximize economic profit.

However, managers often must take government involvement into account in the making of an optimal decision. This is particularly true when managers operate on a global basis and must deal with the laws and regulations of different governments. Coca-Cola's intended purchase of Cadbury Schweppes non-U.S. soft drink business provided a good case in point. To be sure, government laws and regulations can reduce a firm's profits. But at the same time, as we have shown, the government itself is a major customer and so businesses can in fact profit by being suppliers to the government's demand for various goods and services. Today's manager must be equally versed in matters of government as well as private industry.

IMPORTANT CONCEPTS

Benefit externalities: Benefits that accrue to individuals other than those who have paid for a particular good or service, also referred to as *positive benefits, spillover benefits, third-party benefits,* and *social benefits.* The demand for products with external benefits tends to be understated in the market. (p. 651)

Coase Theorem: The idea, developed by Ronald Coase, that government intervention to eliminate the effect of externalities is not necessary if property rights are correctly and clearly defined. (p. 652)

Cost externalities: Costs incurred by individuals other than those who produce a particular good or service, also referred to as *negative costs, spillover costs,* and *social costs.* The supply of goods whose production involves cost externalities tends to be overstated in the market. A good example of cost externalities is environmental pollution. (p. 651)

Monopsony: A market in which there is only one buyer. The government procurement office is often cited as a good example of a monopsony. (p. 655)

Natural monopoly: An industry in which a single large firm can serve customers more efficiently than many smaller ones because of economies of scale. (p. 648)

Socially optimal price: The price of a good or service that is equal to its marginal cost of production. (p. 651)

QUESTIONS

1. What is the rationale for government involvement in the market economy? (Cite the five points presented at the outset of this chapter.)

2. Define *benefit* and *cost externalities.* Explain why situations involving benefit externalities tend to result in an underallocation of society's scarce resources, and why situations involving cost externalities tend to result in an overallocation of society's scarce resources.

3. What is the role of government in dealing with benefit externalities? With cost externalities?

4. Suppose a chemical company was fined for violating certain antipollution laws. As the spokesperson for the Environmental Protection Agency, how would you explain the economic reasons for these actions to angry customers of this company who were forced to pay more for the chemicals as a result of this government action?

5. "The reason the government has to step in and 'internalize' benefit and cost externalities is because people are basically selfish." Do you agree with this statement? Explain.

6. Briefly discuss the Coase theorem. What does this theory imply about the role of government in dealing with market externalities?

7. Based on the information presented in this chapter and on your own reading, do you think Microsoft is operating as an illegal monopoly? Explain.

8. In 1998, American Express announced that it was not going to bid for a renewal of its contract with the federal government to provide its purchasing card for government employees. The government replaced it with Visa and MasterCard purchasing cards. Why do you think American Express decided not to continue this particular business with the federal government? Briefly elaborate.

9. Discuss the economic justification for a merger. In particular, how might these reasons apply to companies now merging in the following industries: oil, automobiles, telecommunications, electric power, commercial banks?

Chapter 16

Managerial Economics in Action: The Case of the Semiconductor Industry

INTRODUCTION

As we stated in the opening chapter of this text, microeconomics is about the study of how scarce resources are allocated among competing uses. And managerial economics is essentially the study of how managers go about making choices regarding the allocation of scarce resources in the best interest of their firm. In making these choices, managers must decide on the answers to the questions listed below in abridged form:

1. What are the economic conditions in a particular market in which we are or could be competing? In particular:
   a. Market structure?
   b. Supply and demand condition?
   c. Technology?
   d. Government regulations?
   e. International dimensions?
   f. Future conditions?
   g. Macroeconomic factors?
2. Should we be in this business?
3. If so, what price and output levels should we set in order to maximize our economic profit or minimize our losses in the short run?
4. How can we organize and invest in our resources (land, labor, capital, managerial skills) in such a way that we maintain a competitive advantage over other firms in this market?
   a. Cost leader?
   b. Product differentiation?
   c. Focus on market niche?

d. Outsourcing, alliances, mergers, acquisitions?

e. International dimension—regional or country focus or expansion.

5. What are the risks involved?

The basic premise of this text is that economic concepts and tools of analysis help managers to find answers to these questions that are in best interest of their firms.

Throughout this text, we have cited numerous examples of companies in a variety of industries (including our hypothetical "Global Foods") that have had to deal with these kinds of questions. We have also tried to show how the concepts and tools of economic analysis can be used in these situations to help the managers of these firms. In this concluding chapter, as was the case in our previous edition, we aim to "put it all together" by selecting and focusing on just one actual industry and one particular firm in this industry to illustrate how economic concepts and tools of analysis can be used to help managers answer the questions above.[1]

We selected the semiconductor industry because it is an excellent example of a market that is continually buffeted by the economic forces of supply and demand. Moreover, new technology is constantly being developed. In this rapidly changing, high-risk environment, the making of decisions is extremely demanding. At the time we were doing our research for this third edition (1998), the entire industry was in the throes of a major global downturn. Key reasons for this were "the global economic slowdown, chronic industry overcapacity, weak pricing and the emergence of the sub-$1000 personal computer (PC)."[2]

It is impossible to select a typical or representative firm in the semiconductor industry. There are thousands of firms with an extremely wide range of market size and focus. In our previous edition, we identified Standard Microsystems Corporation (SMSC) as a company whose recent experiences clearly revealed how challenging it is to compete in the turbulent semiconductor industry. In fact, in the mid- to late 1990s, the firm was fighting for its survival. It was good to learn that SMSC managed to work out its problems and has remained an independent, publicly traded company. Therefore, we have chosen to use this company again to illustrate our points. But in addition, we will talk about a few other companies that have chosen to compete in the volatile semiconductor market with business models that are different from SMSC's. This should give readers an even better appreciation for the challenges of managerial decision making.

As we did in the previous edition, we will present selected sections of the most recent report on the semiconductor industry from Standard & Poor's (S&P) available to us at the time we worked on the current edition. Readers may wish to refer to other more recent S&P reports on this industry or other sources such as Value Line and the research provided by analysts in stock brokerage firms.[3] Information about SMCS and the other semiconductor companies cited in this chapter were found in annual reports, business periodicals, and on their Web sites.

---

[1]Paul Keat and Philip Young, *Managerial Economics: Economic Tools for Today's Decision Makers*, 3d ed., Upper Saddle River, NJ: Prentice Hall, 2000, chapter 16.

[2]*Industry Surveys: Semiconductors,* Standard & Poor's, October 29, 1998, p. 3.

[3]An excellent Web site that provides useful technical background information on the semiconductor industry for the lay person is www.infra.com.

Table 16.1 lists the largest semiconductor companies ranked by revenues in 2000. It shows that the top 10 firms accounted for about 50 percent of total market share, while the revenue generated by thousands of smaller companies made up the other half. The final figures for 2001 are just being produced as we prepare the final draft of this revision. Preliminary figures show some changes such as STMicroelectronics moving up to fourth place.[4] (ST's strategy is presented at the end of this chapter.) Because of its overwhelming domination of the PC microprocessor market, Intel is well above the rest of its competitors. Just to give you an idea of how small the "others" can be, SMSC's fiscal year 2001 (ending 02/01) sales were $163.4 million. This seems like almost a rounding error for Intel, which had total sales of almost $30 billion in calendar year 2000.

The Semiconductor Industry Association (SIA), based in San Jose, California, is probably the most reported source of primary data on the industry. It reported that in 2000 the United States was the world's largest semiconductor end user, consuming 31.3% of the total output. This was followed by Asia/Pacific (25.1%), Japan (22.9%), and Europe (20.7%). There seems to be no doubt that China is emerging as a major country in this industry, from the standpoint of both production and consumption.[5]

Table 16.1

Largest Semiconductor Companies (Ranked by 2000 Revenues, in Millions of Dollars)

Company (Country)	Revenues		% Change 1999–2000	Market Share %
	1999	2000		
1. Intel (U.S.)	26,806	29,750	11.0	13.4
2. Toshiba (Japan)	7,618	11,214	47.2	5.0
3. NEC (Japan)	9,210	11,081	20.3	5.0
4. Samsung (Korea)	7,125	10,800	49.5	4.9
5. Texas Instruments (U.S.)	7,120	9,100	22.0	4.1
6. Motorola (U.S.)	6,394	8,000	25.1	3.6
7. STMicroelectronics (Switz.)	5,077	7,948	56.5	3.6
8. Hitachi (Japan)	5,554	7,282	31.1	3.3
9. Hyundai (Korea)	4,830	6,887	42.6	3.1
10. Infineon (Germany)	5,223	6,715	28.6	3.0
11. Others	84,179	113,305	34.6	51.0
Total market	169,136	222,082	31.3	100.0

Source: Dataquest, Reported in S&P Survey of Semiconductor Industry, May 17, 2001.

[4]*Industry Revenue Share,* Standard & Poor's, December 27, 2001 (industries ranked by 12-month moving average of sales).
[5]*Industry Surveys: Semiconductors,* Standard & Poor's, May 17, 2001, p. 7.

Over the past 40 years, the world's semiconductor industry has grown at an annual compound growth rate of 17 percent. Total global sales for this industry were $204 billion in 2000. Because of the downturn in the industry, the figure for 2001 will be lower. This downturn is just part of a roughly four-year cycle that the industry has been going through in the past four decades. When we were writing the third edition of this text in 1998, the industry was bottoming out of a cycle. Business began to boom from early 1999 and peaked in early 2001. In 2002, as we write this fourth edition, it is in the midst of a downturn again. Forecasts indicate a climb above $225 billion by 2003, although no one agrees on when the next recovery period will begin.

The cyclical nature of the industry is due partly to the macro economy. But the U.S. economy expanded throughout most of the 1990s and the industry still went through its ups and downs. This is because a major source of the cyclicality of the industry is due to its capital intensity, the fairly long lead times involved in production, and the relatively little market power exercised by any one firm or groups of firms. These were the key factors that accounted for the previous industry downturn. Demand was high. Firms then built huge production capacity. When the output from this new capacity hit the market, the resulting increase in industry supply created a glut or "inventory overhang" as industry observers often say. Prices plummeted and the industry went into decline. Eventually, inventories were worked off and the upward part of the cycle began again.

The recovery of the industry in 1998–1999 was helped tremendously by the explosion in new economy investments. Telecommunications, the Internet, and dot-coms were all heavy users of hardware and software that are ultimately dependent on semiconductors. The sharp decline of these businesses and the overall slowdown in the U.S. economy were the major culprits in this most recent downturn. We will go into further detail about this in the ensuing section.

Basically, the making of chips involves three key elements: research and development, design, and manufacturing. Manufacturing also can be divided into two parts: wafer and die manufacturing (called the "front end") and packaging and distribution (called the "back end"). (Perhaps the testing of the finished product could be considered a third part of the manufacturing process.) The front-end process is the most capital intensive. Wafer fabrication facilities, or "fabs," built today can cost up to $3 billion. Back-end processing is more labor intensive and is usually located in lower-wage countries that are also close to the production facilities of the original equipment manufacturers (OEMs). OEMs are the industrial customers of the semiconductor companies; they buy the chips and put them into their products. For example, Dell buys Intel chips for its PCs and Nokia buys STMicroelectronics chips for its mobile phones. Therefore, we can say that the demand for chips is "derived" from the demand for PCs and mobile phones.

Another important feature of the semiconductor industry is the critical role of technology. In 1965, Gordon Moore, a cofounder of Intel, observed that the number of transistors on a chip had doubled every year since 1959, when the integrated circuit was invented. His prediction, that this trend would continue every year, held until 1975, when it began to slow. Moore then said the number of transistors on a chip would double every two years. It actually doubled every 18 months, and this trend became known as Moore's Law.[6]

---

[6]Ibid., p. 20.

This brief background of the semiconductor industry is intended to give readers a better appreciation for the challenges faced by managers of semiconductor companies. In the next section, we will show how the concepts and tools of analysis of managerial economics can be used to illuminate many of these challenges.

INDUSTRY ANALYSIS

Following is the introductory section of an analysis by S&P of the semiconductor industry, reprinted with S&P's permission. Passages pertaining directly to the economic concepts and tools of analysis presented in this text are in boldface type. Each highlighted passage is followed by brief comments and a citation of chapter and pages to which the reader may want to return for additional review.

Downturn Will Hurt—but Only for Awhile

The harshly critical nature of the semiconductor industry was underscored by its rapid transition from boom to bust from mid-2000 to spring 2001.[7] **Unlike most industry downturns, which have their roots in overbuilding of industry plant capacity, this one was instigated mainly by the weakening of the U.S. economy, which caused demand for equipment and products that use chips to slow quite suddenly.**

> *Comment: Some firms seem to be relatively "recession-proof." Among them are those that provide health-care services or sell food and beverages. Other firms are very affected by changes in the macroeconomy. Clearly semiconductor companies fall into the latter category. Stating this in economic terms, we can say that the semiconductor market is very "income elastic."*
>   *Reference: Income elasticity, ch. 4 (pp. 133)*
>   *Additional Comment: Typically, the fall in price originates from the supply side of the market. In this case, the article points out this down cycle was caused more from the downward shift in demand.*
>   *Reference: ch. 3 (pp. 83)*

After a period of exceptional prosperity, end markets for semiconductors began to sputter one by one. Estimates for wireless phone sales were raised in spring 2000, but then reduced in the summer as the sales outlook began to cloud. **By September, personal computer (PC) sales began to sag, and DRAM pricing went soft after a strong summer. By November, inventory congestion in electronic components distribution channels became plainly apparent, indicating widespread weakness in the chip industry.**

---

[7]Ibid., pp. 1–6. Reprinted by permission. As obvious as it is, it is important to keep in mind that this report was written before September 11.

At the turn of the year, it looked as if some of the high-flying specialty chip makers selling into communications and networking equipment market might escape the broader industry's troubles, **but in February 2001, it became clear that all chip segments would be hit hard. During March, semiconductor companies of all stripes reported rapidly weakening order trends that compounded the challenges presented by the inventory overhang. Many company executives said it was the sharpest downturn they'd ever seen.**

Thus the record boom year of 2000 is apt to be followed by a bust in 2001. Global sales in 2000 rose 37 percent to $204 billion, according to the SIA. That stellar performance came on the heels of a recovery year in 1999 when sales rose 19 percent to $149 billion, by SIA figures. From the lofty levels of 2000, global chip sales could show a double-digit decline in 2001, perhaps on the order of 20 percent.

Inventory Overhang Magnifies Downcycle

Over the past 40 years, the semiconductor industry has demonstrated a long-term compound annual growth rate of 17 percent. However, growth has fluctuated dramatically from year to year as the industry has moved through roughly four-year cycles. These cycles are occasionally reshaped by economic shocks from outside the industry, as is the case at present.

Prime suspects for the cause of the current downturn include rising U.S. interest rates in 2000, an abundance of information technology (IT) equipment in place after a five-year period of unusually brisk capital investment by U.S. businesses, and the inability of dot-com companies to continue buying equipment with plentiful venture capital.

In addition, despite improved software tools for managing inventory, the industry has had difficulty in accurately monitoring inventory levels. More con-

tract manufacturers and subcontractors have entered the electronics sector, thereby creating more places on the supply chain where inventory can collect.

Comment: It appears that supply chain management is not yet the panacea for inventory problems.
Reference: See our discussion on supply chain management in ch. 8 (pp. 361).

Before the extent of the inventory overhang became widely known, the SIA forecast in early November 2000 that worldwide chip sales would rise 22 percent in 2001. By early February 2001, the SIA acknowledged that their 2001 forecast was unlikely to be met. By April 2001, private forecasters were predicting double-digit declines for the chip industry in 2001; indeed, California-based consultant VLSI research was projecting an 18 percent drop. Many chipmakers warned that their revenues would be down 20 percent or more in the March 2001 quarter, versus the December 2000 quarter, and might be flat to down on a sequential basis in the June 2001 quarter. Thus, double-digit declines for the industry in full-year 2001 are quite plausible, even if one assumes some improvement in business conditions by late 2001.

Comment: See how quickly forecasts can be proven wrong and how quickly forecasters must readjust their forecasts? In a highly cyclical market such as semiconductors, it is often difficult to apply the forecasting techniques discussed in Chapter 5.
Reference: ch. 6 (pp. 226)

The drop in semiconductor industry activity is reflected in the month-to-month changes in the key statistical series for the industry in early 2001. The SIA data for worldwide chip sales showed March 2001 sales of $14.40 billion, down 4.5 percent year-to-year, and down 7.0 percent sequentially from $15.48 billion in February 2001. The February 2001 figure was down 6.9 percent from the January 2001 level.

A reduction in capital spending on plant and equipment by chip makers is evident in the semiconductor equipment book-to-bill ratio maintained by Semiconductor Equipment and Materials International (SEMI), a trade group based in San Jose, California. In September, October, and November 2000, orders for chip-making gear exceeded shipments, and the monthly book-to-bill ratios were 1.17, 1.16, and 1.12, respectively. (Book-to-bill ratios above 1.0 indicate an industry expansion.) However, the December ratio hit .099, indicating a contraction. The January figure dropped like a rock to 0.89, and the downcycle was confirmed by the February ratio of 0.73 (revised) and the March ratio of 0.64 (preliminary).

Comment: This is an interesting case of "derived, derived demand." The demand for chips is derived from the demand for end-user products such as telecom equipment,

Based on precedents set in prior cycles, S&P expects this series to bottom below 0.60 sometime in mid-2001. The reduced levels of semiconductor equipment bookings confirm that chip makers intend to spend less on their plants in an attempt to cut costs during the downturn. In short, chip makers are reluctant to expand plants because they're pessimistic about chip sales.

All Regions Suffering

Looking at the slowdown by geographic region, the Americas were hit hard as the U.S. economy slipped. The Americas represent about 31 percent of global chip consumption, the largest market by geographic region. The Asia/Pacific region (representing about 25 percent of world sales) has also been hurt badly, and Europe (21 percent) and Japan (23 percent) have not been spared.

The SIA data for March 2001 reveal that chip sales in the Americas dropped 13.4 percent compared with February 2001. Asia/Pacific fell 5.6 percent, while sales in Europe were down 2.0 percent and Japan fell 4.7 percent. On a year-to-year basis in March 2001, sales decreased 10.6 percent for the Americas, 0.7 percent for Europe, and 10.4 percent for Asia/Pacific, but Japan actually showed an increase of 7.0 percent.

Standard & Poor's anticipates that sales will continue to be weak through most of 2001. Sales for certain segments or companies might show a bounce in the third or fourth quarter, whenever inventory congestion clears. That is because, upon achieving normal inventory levels, sales can then move ahead at the pace of underlying demand. Note, however, that the underlying pace of sales is unlikely to be as brisk as it was in 2000.

Another way to assess the slowdown is to check fab utilization rates, especially at the major foundries that serve a wide range of chip makers. In December 2000, the major Taiwan foundries were running near 100 percent; in the spring of 2001, they expect to be running below 50 percent—a very dramatic decline.

PC and Communication Demand Drivers Fade

Historically, the demand side for the semiconductor supply demand equation has been relatively stable, reflecting solid end-market growth of PCs and other electronics applications. Occasionally, however, the chip market has had to contend with unusual forces that alter sales patterns for semiconductors. The present broad economic slowdown, which started in the United States and is rapidly going global, is one such instance. Another recent example is the 1997–1998 Asian financial crisis, which also hindered chip sales.

Yet perhaps the most important recent change in demand trends created an upward lift for sales. The emergence of the Internet spawned many new communications end markets that generate demand for a variety of sophisticated chips. In the present era, both computing and communications markets act as import drives of chip demand.

> **Comment:** *It is much more difficult to forecast changes in demand than changes in supply, particularly when regular changes generally occur on the supply side. When there is no regular pattern of change over time, historical data cannot be used as the basis for future demand. Economists would refer to the kinds of changes in demand that have occurred in the semiconductor industry as "exogenous." In other words, they occur as external shocks to the mathematical forecasting models.*
> *Reference: ch. 6 (pp. 252)*

PC Market Big, but Maturing

Although it may have lost some relative importance in recent years, the PC market is still the principal variable in the chip market, and its health has important implications for semiconductor growth. On the positive side, the PC industry continues to show substantial unit growth and absorb large numbers of chips. Research firm Dataquest estimates worldwide PC unit shipments at 130.5 million in 2000, and looks for 10.7 percent growth to 144.5 million in 2001, and an additional 14.5 percent to 165.5 million in 2002. Dataquest forecasts 212.9 million PC units will ship in 2005, indicating a compound annual growth rate of 10.3 percent over the next five years.

Even modest double-digit unit growth makes PCs look like a relatively strong spot in today's weak global economic environment, although it is lower than the 20 percent plus growth achieved in the boom years of 1995 and 1999. Moreover, following a slump in 2000, new product technology and software introductions may stimulate a return to higher PC unit growth rates. Recently, slower sales trends in this key end market have caused concern about 2001 earnings at PC-centric companies such as Intel Corp., the leader in PC microprocessors, and Micron Technology Inc., one of the handful of top-tier producers of member chips used in PCs.

Communications Customers Sweat It Out

End markets for electronic goods that use communications chips generally decelerated after the PC market slipped in the second half of 2000, but these markets fell from even loftier heights. According to chip maker Atmel Corp. (a maker of a broad range of chips, including logic and flash memory), cell phone sales hit 415 million units in 2000, up from just 275 million in 1999. That may well be terrific growth, but the problem is that the industry was gearing up for as many as 500 million units. For example, based on requests from its customers, Vishay Intertechnology, Inc., a maker of passive components and discrete semiconductors used in wireless phones and many other applications, was preparing for that kind of a number in early 2000. The aggressive ordering of chips in anticipation of a boom led to inventory buildups when growth fell short of projections.

As of early March 2001, Atmel was forecasting that 525 million cell phone units would be shipped worldwide in 2001, heading toward sales of 850 million in 2004. However, on March 15, 2001, Nokia Corp., the leading cell phone manufacturer, toned down its estimate for the 2001 worldwide market to between 450 million and 500 million, from a prior range of 500 million to 550 million. Thus, the wireless handset market remains substantial and is still growing, but might see only single-digit gains in 2001.

Layoffs at customer companies tell the story plainly enough for most communications chip makers. A roster of recent job cuts from the Associated Press dated April 6, 2001, revealed that top communications equipment makers were planning to cut thousands of positions. (The rest of this section, which we will skip over, goes on to cite the major cuts in staff made by companies such as Lucent, Nortel, Ericsson, 3Com, Motorola, and many more.)

Hard Times Lead to Stepped-Up Merger Activity

As companies face a "silent spring" for revenues, many seek to combine forces for a variety of reasons: to realign their product mix, gain size, improve efficiency, or simply to add design engineers, who remain a scarce resource.

For example, Vishay Intertechnology, a maker of discrete semiconductors and passive components, reduced debt and raised cash in 2000 in order to be prepared to make acquisitions at cheaper prices during the downturn. On April 2, 2001, it made an unsolicited bid for General Semiconductor Inc., a maker of discrete semiconductor components, including power rectifiers that would complement Vishay's component lines. Although General Semiconductor declined Vishay's initial offer, perhaps its response will differ if a more generous offer is made.

Also seeking to add compatible lines of product, Microchip Technology Inc. completed its acquisition of TelCom Semiconductor in January 2001 for approximately $260 million in Microchip stock. TelCom's proprietary analog chips can be designed to surround Microchip's microcontrollers on circuit boards that are used in a wide variety of electronic goods.

Although smaller in scale, the Microchip deal was reminiscent of Texas Instrument's purchase of chip maker Burr-Brown in 2000 for stock worth approximately $7.6 billion. Burr-Brown brought in high-end analog design expertise to complement Texas Instrument's digital signal processor (DSP) products. In the modern world of signal processing, which includes temperature, pressure, acceleration, and the like, as well as voice and video signals, the combination of analog chips and digital processors is powerful. The desire to bring analog and DSP capabilities together in-house will likely drive more mergers.

A pairing of high-end analog chip makers, Maxim Integrated Products, Inc. and Dallas Semiconductor Corp., was completed in April 2001. This merger of Dallas into Maxim, valued at roughly $2.5 billion at the time of agreement in February 2001, was sparked mainly by Dallas's quest for top-flight management after the sudden death of its CEO, Vin Prothro. As in many mergers of companies that emphasize proprietary chip design, Dallas's operations will be left intact as it comes under the wing of Maxim.

The downturn has also encouraged at least one spin-off of a chip maker. In late March 2001, Lucent's microelectronics unit was spun off into Agere (pronounced "a-GEAR") Systems, Inc., creating another major independent chipmaker. Pro forma revenue for 2000 was $4.7 billion. About three fourths of Agere's revenue comes from integrated circuits, with the remainder from optoelectronics. Agere will likely experience the same rough going that others in its class have met in the downturn, especially since it carries $2.5 billion in short-term debt.

China Sparkles

Amid the general gloom for the semiconductor industry, China's potential as a major growth market remains a bright spot. Economic growth there is so rapid that market researchers Cahners in-Stat Group projects China's electronics market will be the third largest in the world, after the United States and Japan, by 2003. Many major global chip makers, including Intel, IBM, and Motorola, have offices in China. Part of the attraction is low construction and operating costs, and part is a wide-open mainland market. Many contract manufacturers, which are major consumers of chips, are revving up operations in China. Reports are that the market for cell phones has not slowed in China as it has in the United States and Europe, and is apt to experience a major boom for several decades.[8]

Many chip makers are entering China with relatively small design operations or manufacturing facilities. For instance, in April 2001 networking chip maker Integrated Device Technology Inc. announced it would acquire Newave Semiconductor Corp., a telecommunications chip design shop in Shanghai, with more than 70 engineers. In March 2001, flash memory chip maker Silicon Storage Technology announced an expansion into China with the formation of a local subsidiary in Shanghai and an equity investment in a new wafer foundry, Shanghai Grace Semiconductor Manufacturing Corp. Another joint venture in China is Huaxia Semiconductor Mfg. Co. in Beijing, whose partners include U.S. chip maker Alpha and Omega Semiconductor, Inc. and Shongang Group, a Beijing-based semiconductor maker. Infineon Technologies AG has a back-end packaging plant in China to ser-

---

[8]Sometime in late summer of 2001, industry analysts reported that China had surpassed the United States in total number of cell phone subscribers, with 120.6 million vs. 120 million in the United States.

vice the local market and is reportedly considering a joint venture plant to make transistors and diodes.

These deals are small in the overall picture. Collectively, China is gearing up rapidly for big-time chip production. The Chinese government reportedly aims to have 25 advanced wafer fabrication plants by 2005, including many 8-inch wafer fabs. Lam Research, a U.S. maker of etch equipment for wafer fabrication, forecasts that China will spend $1.2 billion on semiconductor equipment in 2001, up from just $500 million in 2000. The figure may zoom toward $5 billion in 2003. Even so, it is likely to be many years before China is able to produce enough chips for its domestic market, so the country looks like a boom market for worldwide chip makers for many years to come.

Dim Year, Bright Decade

As the semiconductor industry passes through another terrible trough year, it's important to keep in mind that in a year or two a recovery will arrive. Ultimately, the demand for electronics goods will be strong enough to bring the industry back.

Semiconductors are in a remarkable era of rapid technological evolution, which will continue for at least a decade to come. Society is enjoying a golden age of semiconductors. PCs are now commonly available at more affordable prices, and have been downsized to notebook formats, with even better portability to come. Most home computing capabilities will soon be built into cars. And many novel applications are becoming available; for instance, tire pressure can be monitored by chips and displayed on the dashboard.

Broadband Internet access is becoming available in offices and homes, making telecommunications a snap. Wireless phones are not only common, but we may soon see disposable models, calibrated to last for a specified number of minutes. For example, privately held Dieceland Technology Corp conceives of $10 for 60 minutes of talk on its Phone-Card Phone, and a potential global market of 300 million units. **This is an industry where entrepreneurs challenge the goliaths on a regular basis.**

> *Comment: This is a good illustration of the difficulty of saying without question that a market is "monopolistic competition" or "oligopoly." In this example, there are very large, dominant companies that are vulnerable to start-ups that can enter the market fairly easily if they have the right technology.*
> *Reference: ch. 10 (pp. 452)*

All this is occurring with chips made mostly at line widths of 0.18 micron or higher. Now, however, early runs of chips at 0.13 micron are out and, given the industry's track record of incredibly consistent advancements in production techniques, chips at 0.05 micron might be here by 2010. New levels of cost performance will likely alter society's habits as much in the next decade as in the last. The Dick Tracy wristwatch may become a reality—indeed, time electronic gadgets featuring two-way audio/video and other powerful features may not only become available, but also may be cheap.

MANAGERIAL DECISION MAKING IN ACTION

Introduction

We have just given you a view of the semiconductor industry from 30,000 feet in the air. The shifting supply and demand lines and break-even diagrams look just like they do in the textbooks. Now it is time to see the action from the point of view of those on the ground. To be a manager of a firm in this industry generally requires a very different mindset and skill set from a manager in, let us say, our hypothetical "Global Foods." When one is selling food and beverages, the overall growth rate of the industry is relatively low, but at least there are no sharp swings up or down in total industry revenue. Victories are measured by tenth of a percentage point gains in market share. Expenses are measured in the cost of a 30-second commercial aired during the Super Bowl.[9] Critical skills are in advertising and marketing. Executives have MBAs with undergraduate degrees in the liberal arts. When one is producing high-tech chips, technology and competition move so fast that products often have only six to twelve-month development cycles. The entire industry grows three to four times faster than the food and beverage industry, but experiences severe downturns on a regular basis. Victories are measured by the development of complicated new chip designs, breakthroughs in production processes, and the securing of a new relationship with a major OEM. Expenses are measured in research and development (R&D) spending and the depreciation of billion-dollar fabrication facilities. Critical skills are in chip design and manufacturing process management. Executives have MBAs with undergraduate degrees in electrical engineering or Ph.D.s in the sciences or engineering. But managers in both types of industries can use the concepts and tools of analysis of managerial economics to help them make their decisions. So with this in mind, let us review the recent management activities of SMSC. This will be followed by a discussion of the strategies pursued by a sample of other companies, including STMicroelectronics, Taiwan Semiconductor Company, and Virage Logic Inc.

Standard Microsystems Corporation

As described in its 10K report:

> SMSC is a worldwide designer and supplier of leading-edge metal-oxide-semiconductor/very-large-scale-integrated (MOS/VLSI) circuits for the personal computer, peripherals and embedded systems marketplaces. The Company's products provide solutions in Advanced Input/Output (I/O) technology, Systems Logic, USB Connectivity, Local Area Networking and Embedded Control Systems. SMSC is the world's leading supplier of I/O integrated circuits for personal computers.[10]

---

[9]The rate for a 30-second commercial charged by the Fox Television Network for Super Bowl XXXVI was $1.9 million, slightly less than the $2.0 million charged the previous year for advertising during this event. (Based on *New York Times*, February 1, 2001).
[10]SMSC 10K report, filed March 2001.

An excerpt from the CEO's message to the shareholders in its 2001 annual report states that:

> The Company made bold strides in **remaking its business model** [emphasis added] and repositioning itself for accelerated growth. SMSC is now a stronger company with even brighter prospects than it had a year ago.[11]

When we were writing our third edition back in 1998, then CEO Paul Richman reported in his farewell address to shareholders that he had led the implementation of key operating and financial decisions that had put the company in good standing. The firm had solidified relationships with its outsourced wafer foundries, exited from the unprofitable local area network (LAN) systems business, negotiated important agreements with several companies regarding the use of intellectual property licensing agreements, settled some pending major litigation, and substantially increased its R&D spending. But perhaps one of the most important things that the company did was to negotiate certain agreements with Intel that thereby made Intel the Company's largest shareholder. In addition to this added equity funding, Intel provided SMSC with expertise to improve the quality of its output.[12] The new CEO, Steven Bilodeau, then proceeded to develop and implement an offensive rather than a defensive strategy. An important part of this strategy was to remake its business model. This is what it did.

In June 1999, the Company divested its Foundry Business Unit. In the semiconductor world, this made the company officially a "fabless" company. As the company explains in its 10K report, "The Company is a fabless semiconductor solutions provider, which is an increasingly common business model in the semiconductor industry . . . This strategy allows the Company to focus its resources on product design and development, marketing and quality assurance. **It also reduces fixed costs and capital requirements** [emphasis added], and allows the company access to the most advanced manufacturing capabilities."[13] However, the company still conducts its own testing of products near its corporate headquarters in Hauppauge, New York.

But a company's strategy needs to do more than just reduce fixed costs and capital requirements. It also has to increase revenues. In fiscal years 1999 and 2000, almost three fourths of the company's revenues came from sales of input/output (I/O) circuits used in PCs. This product is sold to all the leading manufacturers of PCs, but competition is intense. The real problem is that the PC market has slowed its growth and is approaching maturity. So a key element of the SMSC growth strategy was to reduce its reliance on I/O devices for the PC business and to focus more on the embedded systems products, which are less mature and have more growth potential. It reorganized its company into two main groups: PC products and embedded products. This enabled it to "realize the growth opportunities in each by independently optimizing strategies, tactics, and practices for these two very different businesses."[14] This decision seems to have worked because in fiscal year 2001,

---

[11]CEO Message to Shareholders, SMSC Annual Report, 2001.
[12]Refer to SMSC Annual Report, or Keat and Young, pp. 589–590.
[13]SMSC 10K report, 2001, p. 6.
[14]CEO message to shareholders.

embedded products made up about 33 percent of the Company's revenues, far exceeding the target of 24 percent. Between FY 2000 and 2001, the Company's total revenue increased by 6.6 percent. The company's gross profit margin rose slightly from 30.7 to 30.9 percent. However, it reported an operating loss due mainly to the substantially increased R&D spending from 15.9 to 19.9 percent of revenue. A significant amount of this increase went into its efforts to develop a third major product group for its business: systems logic chipsets.

Based on our review of the semiconductor industry and SMSC strategy and operations, let us imagine how the senior management of SMSC would go about answering the key questions posed at the beginning of this chapter. (To get into the spirit of the exercise, "we" refers to the managers of the company.)[15]

> *What are the economic conditions in a particular market in which we are or could be competing?*
>
> *Market structure?* This market is part oligopoly, part monopolistic competition. Certain segments of the market are dominated by very large firms (e.g., Intel and microprocessors for the PC). Other markets have easier entry and allow for relatively small firms (e.g., Standard Microsystems and the market for I/O devices for the PC).
>
> *Supply and demand conditions?* Regardless of the size of the firms, most firms are affected by supply and demand conditions and therefore do not have very much market power. Prices usually fluctuate because of shifts in supply, but sometimes shifts in demand play an equally if not greater part in this volatility (e.g., the current industry downturn).
>
> *Technology?* It is fast moving, expensive to develop, and very much a critical factor in maintaining our competitive advantage.
>
> *Government regulations?* They are minimal except for certain environmental regulations affecting the manufacturing process.
>
> *International dimensions?* Our industry is truly global, with activities spread fairly evenly throughout North America, Europe, Asia-Pacific, and Japan and to a lesser extent throughout Latin America. In our particular case, most of our customers are located in the Asia-Pacific Rim. Sixty-one percent of our FY 2001 revenue comes from this part of the world. Twenty-four percent comes from North America, 14.8 percent comes from Europe, and less than 1 percent comes from the rest of the world.
>
> *Should we be in this business?* Yes.
>
> *If so, what price and output levels should we set in order to maximize our economic profit or minimize our losses in the short run?* We are primarily price takers for our products. We cannot improve our profit margins by raising price. We can only do so by shifting our resources into those segments where the average selling price is higher relative to our costs of production.
>
> *How can we organize and invest in our resources in such a way that we maintain a competitive advantage over other firms in this market?*

---

[15]Any information contained in these answers that was not discussed above has been taken from the company's 10K and annual reports, 2001.

Cost leader? We strive to be among the low cost producers by outsourcing our manufacturing activities, both front end and back end.

Product differentiation? We continue to spend heavily on R&D and work hard to retain and attract the best design engineers. The best way to differentiate products in this business is to be a technology leader.

Focus on market niche? We have up to now focused primarily on the I/O devices for the PC market. However, we are seeking a greater balance between this product group and the embedded products and also trying to establish ourselves in an entirely new product segment: systems logic chipsets.

Outsourcing, alliances, mergers, acquisitions? We have outsourced our manufacturing completely to outside vendors. We also maintain close relationships with these suppliers as well as with our large OEM customers.

What are the risks involved?[16] The following are the key categories of our risks along with a brief elaboration of such risks. (*Note:* The statements below are direct quotations from the 10K report and are made in the third person. Phrases or words in boldface are indicated by the authors.)

1. *The semiconductor industry.* "The Company competes in the semiconductor industry which has historically been characterized by intense competition, rapid technological change, cyclical market patterns, **price erosion and periods of mismatched supply and demand.** The semiconductor industry has experienced significant economic downturns at various times in the past, characterized by diminished product demand and accelerated erosion of selling prices. In addition, many of the **Company's competitors in the semiconductor industry are larger and have significantly greater financial and other resources than the Company.**"

2. *The personal computer industry.* "Sales of many of the Company's products depend largely on sales of personal computers and peripheral devices. **Reductions in the rate of growth of the PC market could adversely affect the Company's operating results.** In addition, as a component supplier to PC manufacturers, the Company often experiences greater demand fluctuations than its customers themselves experience. **Also, some of the Company's products are used in PCs for the consumer market, which, in recent years, has tended to be more volatile than other segments of the PC marketplace.**"

3. *Product development and technological change.* "The Company's prospects are highly dependent upon the successful development and timely introduction of new products at competitive prices and performance levels, with acceptable margins . . . There **can be no assurance that the Company will be able to identify market trends or new product opportunities,** develop another market,

---

[16]Essential reading for anyone interested in a company, particularly for the purpose of buying its stock, is the statement of risks provided in the 10K report. This statement is much more detailed than the one presented in the annual report. The listing of risks and excerpted descriptions of these risks are taken from SMSC's 2001 10K report.

market new products, achieve design wins or respond effectively to new technological changes or product announcements by others . . ."

EXAMPLES OF OTHER BUSINESS MODELS AND STRATEGIES ADOPTED BY FIRMS IN THE SEMICONDUCTOR INDUSTRY

As noted in SMSC's 10K report, the fabless semiconductor company is an increasingly common business model in the industry. But from a historical perspective, it can really be considered part of an evolution that began four decades ago with a fully integrated company, referred to in the industry as an "integrated device manufacturer," or IDM. These companies did everything "from soup to nuts," to use a quaint expression, or perhaps more appropriately, "from sand to the final end user product." Among the pioneer firms in the semiconductor industry were Fairchild, National Semiconductor, Texas Instruments, and Intel in the United States, and Toshiba and Fujitsu in Japan. Later, Korean companies such as Samsung and Hyundai would adopt the same fully integrated model. Perhaps an even greater degree of vertical integration could be seen with companies such as IBM, Western Electric (now Lucent), Motorola, Toshiba, Siemens, and Samsung. These companies had their own fully integrated semiconductor manufacturing capabilities, which included R&D, wafer fabs, packaging, and testing. They then "sold" their chip output to their hardware manufacturing divisions (e.g., IBM's mainframe computers, Western Electric [AT&T's switch manufacturing division], Motorola and Siemens' telecommunications equipment, and Toshiba and Samsung's computer and consumer electronics products). In this vertically integrated business model, companies are in fact their own OEM customers or their own chip supplier, depending on one's point of view. Some of these companies, such as IBM, Motorola, Toshiba, and Samsung, continue to operate with this business model. However, within the past few years, some have chosen to spin off their chip-making business. In 2000, Siemens's semiconductor division became a separate, publicly traded entity called Infineon Technologies. Shortly after that, Lucent did the same thing with Agere. In 2000, Motorola spun off the lower margin, commodity segment of its semiconductor business. The company formed as a result of this divestment is called ON Semiconductor. In mid 2002, Japan's NEC announced that it was going to spin off its semiconductor division.

Seen in this historical perspective, SMSC and other fabless companies are an extension of the ongoing effort by semiconductor companies to cut costs by reducing their fixed costs (i.e., reducing their operating leverage). Companies that outsource wafer fabrication may still have capital investment in packaging or back-end facilities. But these too can be outsourced to companies that specialize in this activity. SMSC has chosen to outsource both front-end and back-end operations and retains only an in-house testing function.

Readers at this point might be thinking that this appears to be a game of "hot potato." If companies are outsourcing their manufacturing to reduce costs, who would want to take on these activities? The answer at this point is: companies located in the Asia-Pacific region. There are three leading fabrication companies: Taiwan Semiconductor Corporation (TSMC) and United Semiconductor Corporation (USC), also based in Taiwan. The third is a Singapore-based company, Standard Charter. Running fabrication companies requires huge capital investments and a highly skilled and a relatively high-wage work force. These companies believe they have the capital, skilled labor and the management ability to secure the necessary economies of scale and scope and process efficiencies to earn acceptable returns on their owners' investment. Back-end or packaging functions are different. They are relatively less capital intensive, and utilize lower skilled and lower paid labor. Back-end facilities are located in lower wage Asian countries such as China, Malaysia and the Philippines. This is the case whether the facilities are part of a fully integrated company, or a separate entity specializing in this phase of the manufacturing process.

Essentially, those companies who chose to focus on manufacturing, whether front end or back end, are opting for what Michael Porter calls a "cost leadership" strategy. (See chapter 10 for a brief description of this approach.) To maintain a profit using this strategy, costs must continually be reduced. The fabrication companies are constantly making improvements in their production process. The packaging companies also must do this and at the same time search for suitable locations that have people with equal skills or at least the ability to be trained, and who are also willing to work for lower wages. One country offers all of this and more: China. Companies such as Motorola and ON Semiconductor already have established packaging facilities in China. Many others are there or are following suit. Wafer fabrication facilities are also being built. At the time this edition is being prepared, there is great anticipation in the industry for a greatly expanded front-end and back-end manufacturing capacity in China. The two major Taiwanese companies have big plans for shifting much of their manufacturing operations to China.

Leading companies such as Intel and Texas Instruments still maintain a fully integrated business model. But these companies earn a disproportionate amount of their revenue and profit by concentrating on certain segments of the chip market. Intel, of course, still earns most of its money in the manufacturing of microprocessors for the PC. Texas Instruments, a company that produced items such as calculators and watches, decided in the late 1990s to sell off many of its lower end, commodity-type businesses such as memory chips and consumer electronics and concentrate only on certain types of chips. The most important of these are DSP chips.[17] So in this respect, the strategy of Intel and Texas Instruments are what might be called "differentiated and focused."

A major company that has a differentiated and relatively less focused (or broader based) strategy is STMicroelectronics. This company has its headquarters in Switzerland but is really the result of a merger in 1998 between a French and an Italian company. About 10 years ago, STMicroelectronics (then called SGS-THompson) under the leadership of its CEO Pasquale Pistorio, determined that the real growth opportunity for the industry lay not in PCs but in cell phones, TV set-top boxes, and smart cards. The company proved to be right. Moreover, it formed alliances with key OEMs such as Nokia and Hewlett-Packard so that ST could

---

[17]Go to their Web site for a simple technical explanation of what these chips do. Essentially, they are critical in the transformation of analog-to-digital signals.

develop customized chips at the early stage of the product development. For example, ST chips are inside Nokia cell phones and H-P printers. ST is one of the leading companies in the development of new technology in such leading-edge areas as "system-on-a-chip" (SoC).

What is also important to point out about STMicroelectronics relative to our discussion is that this company maintains the traditional, fully integrated business model. It has wafer fabs and packaging facilities all over the world, including such locations as Sicily, Morocco, China, France, and the United States. As noted above, its R&D group has produced one of the best IP "libraries" for SoC and other leading-edge technologies. But interestingly enough, it does outsource some of its packaging functions, and its annual report states that 20 percent of its wafer output will eventually be produced by outsourced fabrication companies.[18]

There is still more in the evolution of the business model in the semiconductor industry. Recently, the ultimate, low-capital company has emerged. This is the so-called "chipless" company. This type of semiconductor firm does not make, test, or sell chips. It only designs them and licenses the IP to companies who then incorporate the designs into the chips that they either make or sell. One of these types of companies recently in the news is Virage Logic Corporation.[19] Virage Logic specializes in developing the IP for SoC, which is the same segment of the industry in which the fully integrated STMicroelectronics has established its leadership. So "in this corner with the red trunks, weighing 7 billion 'pounds' (2001 estimated $ revenue) . . . STMicroelectronics . . . and in the other corner with the blue trunks weighing 34 million 'pounds' (2001 estimated $ revenue) . . . Virage Logic Corporation!"

If there is anything to be learned from many of the dot-coms and their spectacular failure, it is to pay attention to all aspects of a company's business model. Thus far, Virage Logic's "revenue model" is based on license fees. The company has developed joint ventures with such companies as Avanti Technology Inc., Flextronics International Ltd., and none other than Taiwan Semiconductor Company. Virage Logic's relationship with Taiwan Semiconductor indicates to us that just as fully integrated companies are trying to outsource their wafer fabrication, wafer fabrication companies such as Taiwan Semiconductor are trying to expand their capabilities into R&D, the one function that fully integrated and fabless companies continue to keep for themselves. Virage Logic, as a chipless company, offers the opportunity for a fabrication company to jump into this part of the business.

Virage Logic is still in the development phase with all of its partners. When the chips based on its IP are finally produced, the company will begin getting paid royalties. This means some percentage of the revenue for chip sales. Thus far, Virage Logic has been relatively unaffected by the downturn in the chip market because it continues to get a fixed fee for its proprietary design work. But as the CEO of the company admits, "Three years from now, when we will have lots of products in full production, we'd see the effect much more severely of the down cycles . . . [but] our licensing fees should always stay healthy."[20]

---

[18]Information about STMicroelectronics was taken from their 2000 annual report and from "STMicroelectronics: From Niche Player to Goliath," *BusinessWeek,* March 12, 2001.
[19]"A Logical Way to Make Money in the Chip Sector," *Investors' Business Daily,* January 30, 2002.
[20]Ibid.

What is the message from reviewing all of these different business models? In the end, a company still has to make money or "normal profit," to use the terminology of managerial economics. We sincerely hope that this chapter as well as our entire text has given readers a better understanding of the challenges that await managers of firms in the pursuit of this ultimate economic goal.

QUESTION FOR FURTHER STUDY

1. The highly volatile nature of the semiconductor industry means that whatever is written for a textbook will have changed by the time it is published. As we were completing the final draft of this edition, the semiconductor industry had started to show some signs of recovery. Conduct a current analysis of the semiconductor industry. In particular what is the relationship between supply and demand in the industry? What are the main factors affecting demand and supply? How are industry conditions affecting the various types of computer chips (e.g., memory chips and specialty chips that are used in computers, networking equipment, telecommunications devices, consumer electronics, and automobiles)?

Appendix A

Linear Programming[1]

WENDY DESCRIBES THE CASE

WENDY: The Maximus Computer Company (MCC) has four basic computers it sells to students and small businesses. The first, called the "Starter," is a basic, "no-frills" computer. It has most of the amenities that a new user or a buyer on a strict budget could want, including CD-ROM with sound, an entry-level processor, a small hard disk, a modem for Internet access, and a 15-inch monitor. The second model, called the "Midrange," is for more demanding users, offering a faster processor, larger hard disk, more RAM, a DVD player, and a 17-inch monitor. The third model, the "Super," provides just about all the computing power a user could want. It offers even more RAM, a very fast processor, a large hard disk, a DVD player with hardware decoder, and a 19-inch monitor. All but the most demanding users would be very happy with the Super. However, for those who want the very best, the company offers the "Extreme" which offers a state-of-the-art processor, a huge hard disk, the best multimedia package (the latest generation DVD-ROM with a five-piece speaker system), a CD rewritable drive, a 17-inch flat panel display, and so forth.

    Thus, while the company offers only four models, it feels there is enough flexibility to cover most of the target computer audience. It is a small start-up company, and management knows it has to compete against the heavily entrenched products from Dell, IBM, Compaq, Hewlett-Packard, and Gateway. The company philosophy is to ship computers with known-brand components and offer superior service, all at a cost to consumers that is lower than that of the competition.

SILAS: Well, Wendy, I believe I know about the philosophy of the company and its immediate goals. Can you please tell me more about the four models of computers we offer?

---

[1]This appendix was written by Dr. Jack Yurkiewicz, Professor of Management Science, Lubin School of Business, Pace University. The authors are very grateful for Professor Yurkiewicz's contribution.

WENDY: As I said, Maximus makes four models with different levels of features, all with the same customer support. They believe that whatever the sophistication of the machine, customer support should be "top notch" and not deteriorate with the price. In the long run, that will generate customer goodwill and promote our growth in the market.

SILAS: I agree whole-heartedly. Tell me a bit more about the computers themselves.

THE PROBLEM IS DESCRIBED

WENDY: As you know, the computer industry is currently very competitive, and profit margins are low for each model. The net profit on a Starter is $50, for a Midrange it is $120, for a Super it is $250, and for an Extreme it is $300. These figures already take into account material, labor, depreciation, taxes, shipping, and so forth. In other words, these are the net profits to the company for each computer sold.

SILAS: Eventually we can delve into how these values are determined and perhaps how we can increase them, but for now, let's assume that they are sacrosanct. What else can you tell me about the operation?

WENDY: Management has what they call "three operations" that make a computer. They call the first operation **manufacture.** This includes taking the customer's phone call and determining which computer and options he or she wants and getting that information to the management of the production staff. They in turn will get the necessary components and make them available to the workers on the assembly line. The second operation is referred to as **assembly,** where the workers on the assembly line actually put together the computer, according to the specifications of the customer's order. These are skilled workers who take pride in their work, and even though they work on an assembly line, they do not have an "assembly line mentality," for they believe they are making custom products for specific customers. The last operation is called **inspection.** Here we install the software, run various diagnostic tests, and generally check out and pack up the computer before we send it to the customer.

SILAS: I see. Do you have approximate time figures on how long it takes to do these operations?

WENDY: It is a function of the computer. However, they have been doing this for some time now and so the time values do not vary all that much from machine to machine. Thus, for instance, for a Starter, we can assume 0.1 hours for manufacture, 0.2 hours for assembly, and 0.1 hours for inspection. Our units are always in hours.

For a Midrange, we use 0.2 hours to manufacture, 0.5 hours to assemble, and 0.2 hours for inspection. Each Super requires 0.7 hours to manufacture, 0.25 hours to assemble, and 0.3 hours for inspection and testing. Finally, the Extreme requires 0.8 hours to manufacture, 0.2 hours to assemble, and 0.5 hours for inspection. As I said, these numbers really don't vary all that much from machine to machine, but as you can see, they do differ from model to model.

SILAS: Very well. What about your resources? How many people, or should I say, how many people-hours are available to do those three operations?

WENDY: On a daily basis, management informed me that the company has 250 hours available for manufacture, 350 hours available for assembly, and 150 hours to do the inspection and testing.

SILAS: I presume that with all this information, we can proceed to model the problem as a linear program.

WENDY: Indeed, Silas. As I intimated earlier, we can solve linear programs with Excel. Excel comes with an add-on package called Solver that is easy to use and yet powerful enough to solve most mathematical programming problems. All we have to do is make a spreadsheet model of the problem and Solver will do the rest.

SILAS: Well, that certainly is good news. I use Excel and I have made many models. But how do you make a linear program model in Excel?

MODELING THE PROBLEM IN EXCEL

WENDY: Have a look at the Excel spreadsheet model here on my computer, Silas. It is imperative that you first learn how to model a problem in a spreadsheet. Once you master this skill, we can then proceed to discuss how Solver can be used to get the answer for us. Cells B1, C1, D1, and E1 give the labels of our computers, which in linear programming terminology are called *decision variables*. We want the *values* of these variables to appear in cells B2, C2, D2, and E2. Excel's Solver will call these cells the *changing cells*. We put the per-unit profit of each computer into cells B4 through D4. These numbers are traditionally called the *objective function coefficients*. We must enter a formula into cell I2 (which we labeled as the Profit in cell I1) that will give the net profit for all the computers made.

	A	B	C	D	E	F	G	H	I
1		Starter	Midrange	Super	Extreme				Profit
2		0	0	0	0				0
3									
4	max	50	120	250	300				
5						Available	Used	Slack	
6	manufacture	0.1	0.2	0.7	0.8	250	0	250	
7	assembly	0.2	0.5	0.25	0.2	350	0	350	
8	inspection	0.1	0.2	0.3	0.5	150	0	150	

SILAS: I know how to do that. We would type in cell I2 the formula:

$$= B2*B4 + C2*C4 + D2*D4 + E2*E4$$

Algebraically, we are saying, with this formula:

$$50(\text{Starters}) + 120(\text{Midrange}) + 250(\text{Super}) + 300(\text{Extreme})$$

Of course, the value in cell I2 is zero because we have zero values for the number of computers made in cells B2 through E2.

WENDY: That's right. You should know that there is a shortcut to this rather tedious formula. Excel has the built-in function, SUMPRODUCT, which will save us much typing. That is, in cell I2 we can simply type:

$$=\text{SUMPRODUCT}(B2:E2,B4:E4)$$

That says: multiply the values in cells B2 through E2 by the corresponding values in the cells B4 through E4 respectively, and then add up the results. That gives us the same result as your formula. However, it is easier to input, since we need just type in =SUMPRODUCT, highlight the ranges, and type the parentheses. The result is our total profit, which Solver calls the target cell.

SILAS: I suspect that we will be using that SUMPRODUCT function again. Tell me about the other items I see in your spreadsheet.

WENDY: Our model is incomplete. We need to specify the *constraints*. These account for the technological, economic, or other limitations of the system, and restrict the values of the decision variables to some feasible set. We have three constraints in our problem: manufacturing, assembly, and inspection. Our manufacturing constraint is:

$$0.1(\text{Starter}) + 0.2(\text{Midrange}) + 0.7(\text{Super}) + 0.8(\text{Extreme}) <= 250$$

SILAS: That makes sense. The 250 represents the number of people-hours that are available daily. The expression on the left must represent the total number of manufacturing hours used by the four models of computers. In short, the number of manufacturing hours used by the company is less than or equal to the number of manufacturing hours available from the labor.

WENDY: Exactly.

SILAS: Let me see if I can figure out what you entered in the spreadsheet. I see the manufacturing values in the cells B6 through E6. The number of hours of manufacturing available is 250 in cell F6. I'll wager the formula in cell G6 is

$$=SUMPRODUCT(B2:E2,B6:E6)$$

WENDY: That is exactly what I entered.

SILAS: I assume we need similar constraints for assembly and inspection.

WENDY: Precisely. Thus, the assembly constraint says

$$0.2(Starter) + 0.5(Midrange) + 0.25(Super) + 0.2(Extreme) \leq 350$$

and this translates as the number of hours used for assembly is less than or equal to the number of hours available for assembly, or 350.

SILAS: Right, and that is why the formula in cell G7 is:

$$=SUMPRODUCT(B2:E2,B7:E7)$$

This gives us the number of hours used to assemble the computers. Finally, the last constraint should indicate the number of inspection hours used is less than or equal to 150 inspection hours available.

$$0.1(Starter) + 0.2(Midrange) + 0.3(Super) + 0.5(Extreme) \leq 150$$

And the formula in cell G8 is:

$$=SUMPRODUCT(B2:E2,B8:E8)$$

which represents the number of inspection hours that are used for the computers.

WENDY: Right again, Silas. Let's look at the spreadsheet again, only this time with the formulas showing, instead of the values. You'll notice that the formulas in the G column have dollar signs. That is because I copied the formula from cell G6 to cells G7 and G8, and I needed to use the spreadsheet concept of "absolute addressing." This means that the decision variable cells will remain fixed when I copied the formula. The only other thing I have added is a column called "Slack." A *slack variable* for a less-than-or-equal constraint is the difference between the number of units of the resource *available* minus the number of units of the resource actually *used*. It tells us how many units of each resource we have left over in a less-than-or-equal constraint.

	A	B	C	D	E	F	G	H	I
1		Starter	Midrange	Super	Extreme				Profit
2		0	0	0	0				=SUMPRODUCT(B2:E2,B4:E4)
3									
4	max	50	120	250	300				
5						Avail		Used	Slack
6	Man	0.1	0.2	0.7	0.8	250	=SUMPRODUCT($B$2:$E$2,B6:E6)	=F6-G6	
7	Asm	0.2	0.5	0.25	0.2	350	=SUMPRODUCT($B$2:$E$2,B7:E7)	=F7-G7	
8	Insp	0.1	0.2	0.3	0.5	150	=SUMPRODUCT($B$2:$E$2,B8:E8)	=F8-G8	

SILAS: What I would do, at this point, is just try different values for the computer models in cells B2 through E2, all the time monitoring the profit in cell I2. Eventually, I would pick a product mix that would give me the highest profit I obtained. I remember you said that we can get the answer using the technique of linear programming. Please refresh my memory: What does linear programming do?

WENDY: It will find the optimal product mix. That is, it will give me the product mix that yields the highest profit and still not violate any constraints. That is called the *optimal solution.*

USING SOLVER TO GET THE OPTIMAL SOLUTION

SILAS: And you said that Excel had a feature called Solver that can do that? I never even knew about it, and I have been using Excel for years. How does it work?

WENDY: We go to the Tools section on Excel's main menu. There you will see Solver. Just click on it (Figure A.1). If you don't see Solver listed, then you must make it available as an Excel Add-In. Go to Tools and then Add-Ins. You will see a list of possible Add-Ins. Just make sure the Solver box is checked (Figure A.2). Then click on OK. You will only have to do this once; the next time you start Excel, Solver will be available automatically in the Tools menu. If you do not see Solver listed in the Add-Ins section, unfortunately that means it was never installed when Microsoft Office was loaded on your hard drive. You must retrieve the original Office CD and do a "reinstall," which will allow you to pick those features that were not installed the first time. Make sure you find and check Solver and it will be installed. You only need to reinstall those missing features.

SILAS: Well, luckily, I see on my own notebook computer that Solver is available as an Add-In, so the reinstallation isn't necessary. What do I do now?

Figure A.1

WENDY: Let us go through the sequence. You click on Tools on the main menu and then Solver. The Solver dialog box appears after a few seconds. The first thing you need to do is specify the **objective function.** This is the cell that specifies the problem's goal or objective and it *must* contain a formula. Solver calls this the "Target Cell" (Figure A.3). In our case, it is the cell that contains the profit formula and is cell I2. So we just click on cell I2. If the dialog box covers the cell, then just drag it out of the way and then click on I2.

SILAS: The next item is pretty clear. I just choose what kind of problem I have, a maximization one, or a minimization one. I assume the "value of" cell allows me to put in some specified value?

WENDY: Correct. We will almost never use this for we want the *best* target cell value and we want Solver to get it for us. Thus, we can ignore this feature of Solver.

SILAS: The next section is called "changing cells." What does that mean?

WENDY: These are the cells where the optimal solution will appear. That is, these cells show the number of computers that Maximus should make. In our

Figure A.2

Figure A.3

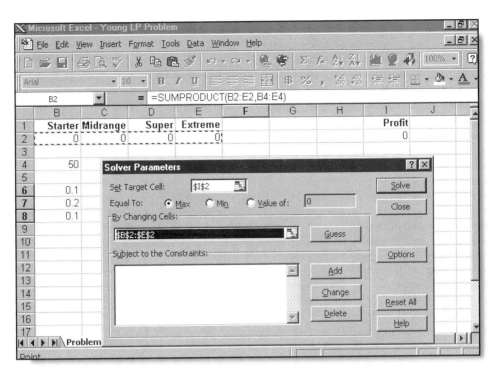

Figure A.4

problem, these are cells in the range B2 through E2. We can just highlight that range or type it in (Figure A.4).

SILAS: OK, that seems easy. Now what about the constraints? I see a section that says "Subject to the Constraints." Do I just type them in?

WENDY: Not quite. You click on Add. After a few seconds another dialog box, called the Add Constraint Dialog Box, appears (Figure A.5). The left field is the *cell reference*. That is a cell or range of cells that tells Solver how much of the resource you actually use. It *must* contain a formula. In our problem, it is the number of hours used for manufacturing, and was the formula in cell G6. We could just click on cell G6. Because the manufacturing constraint was a less-than-or-equal constraint, we need to tell Solver that. That is the default inequality sense. Do you see it, the "<= " inequality sense in the second field? The last field is called "Constraint," and this refers to the cell or range of cells that tell Solver the amount of resources that are available. These are numbers. In our case, it is the number of manufacturing hours available and is the 250 that appears in cell F6. Thus, we just click on cell G6.

Figure A.5

SILAS: I see. I guess we have to do the same for the other constraints. This can get quite tedious if we have many constraints in our problem.

WENDY: True, but there is a shortcut. If all your constraints, or a subset of your constraints, are all of the "<= " form, you can add these all at one time. Make sure the cursor is in the Cell Reference field and just highlight the range of cells that indicate the resources used. In our case, we highlight the range G6 through G8. And then we . . .

SILAS: I get it! They are all "<= " so all we have to do is move the cursor to the Constraints field and highlight the range that has the amount of resources that are available. These are cells F6 through F8. I guess we then click on OK.

WENDY: Right again. If you have additional constraints you click on Add instead of OK. We finally click on OK only after you have entered all the constraints of your problem.

SILAS: I remember that in linear programming we must also specify that the decision variables must all be non-negative. That certainly makes sense for our problem, for we certainly cannot make a negative number of computer models. Do I have to enter those constraints in the same way I did the others?

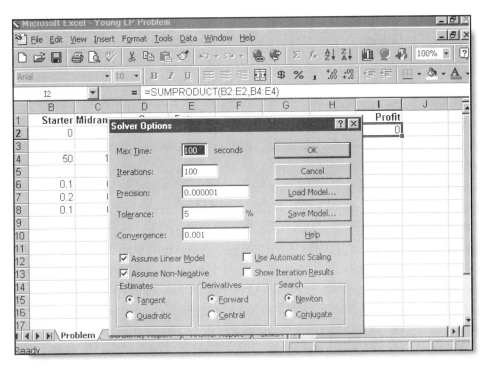

Figure A.6

WENDY: Not if you are using Office 97, Excel 8, or any later version. Do you see in the dialog box the button called Options?

SILAS: Yes.

WENDY: Just click on that, and you can see the two boxes that must be checked (Figure A.6). The first is "Assume Linear Model" and the second is "Assume Non-negative." The first one is important because it will give us important **sensitivity analysis** that we will discuss later, and the second tells Solver to look for solutions in which the variables are all greater than or equal to zero. By the way, if you are using an older version of Excel, this last option is not available, and you have to enter the non-negativity constraints just as you entered all the other constraints. Then you click on OK. The completed Solver dialog box is now in front of you and you are ready to go (Figure A.7).

SILAS: I guess that will do it for entering the model into Solver. I see the "Solve" button and so I will just click on it. Let us see what happens.

WENDY: Fine. Do you see that in a few seconds the computer tells us that Solver found a solution. All constraints and optimality conditions are satisfied. It then asks if you want to "Keep Solver Solution." The obvious answer will be yes, so that box is checked. But Solver also offers three reports, called

Figure A.7

the **Answer, Sensitivity,** and **Limits Reports.** Frankly, we just need the first two, the Answer and Sensitivity one. So when we solve linear programs we always specify that we want these two reports. The Limits Report has limited utility for our needs (no pun intended, Silas, so please do not snicker); therefore, we will not ask for it. Thus, highlight the two reports you want and click on OK. Solver adds two new worksheets to our workbook, each giving a separate report. Also, notice that we got the optimal solution to appear in our specified cells, B2 through E2.

The Original Worksheet

	A	B	C	D	E	F	G	H	I
1		Starter	Midrange	Super	Extreme				Profit
2		0	375	250	0				107500
3									
4	max	50	120	250	300				
5						Available	Used	Slack	
6	manufacture	0.1	0.2	0.7	0.8	250	250	0	
7	assembly	0.2	0.5	0.25	0.2	350	250	100	
8	inspection	0.1	0.2	0.3	0.5	150	150	0	

The Sensitivity Report

CELL	NAME	FINAL VALUE	REDUCED COST	OBJECTIVE COEFFICIENT	ALLOWABLE INCREASE	ALLOWABLE DECREASE
$B$2	Starter	0	−10	50	10	1E+30
$C$2	Midrange	375	0	120	46.67	20
$D$2	Super	250	0	250	170	70.00
$E$2	Extreme	0	−52.50	300	52.50	1E+30

CELL	NAME	FINAL VALUE	SHADOW PRICE	CONSTRAINT R.H. SIDE	ALLOWABLE INCREASE	ALLOWABLE DECREASE
$G$6	manufacture	250	175	250	100	80
$G$7	assembly	250	0	350	1E+30	100
$G$8	inspection	150	425	150	26.67	42.86

The Answer Report

Target Cell (Max)

CELL	NAME	ORIGINAL VALUE	FINAL VALUE
$I$2	Profit	107500	107500

Adjustable Cells

CELL	NAME	ORIGINAL VALUE	FINAL VALUE
$B$2	Starter	0	0
$C$2	Midrange	0	375
$D$2	Super	0	250
$E$2	Extreme	0	0

Constraints

CELL	NAME	CELL VALUE	FORMULA	STATUS	SLACK
$G$6	manufacture	250	$G$6 <= $F$6	Binding	0
$G$7	assembly	250	$G$7 <= $F$7	Not Binding	100
$G$8	inspection	150	$G$8 <= $F$8	Binding	0

THE SOLUTION IS REVEALED

SILAS: Well, I see the optimal solution. Solver tells us to make no Starters, 375 Midranges, 250 Supers, and no Extremes on a daily basis. I must admit that is not what we are currently doing, but Solver says that if we make that daily product mix, our daily profit will be $107,500, which is considerably more than we are currently making. It is interesting that Solver is telling us that we should abandon the "low-end" and "high-end" of the market as compared to offering a "complete product line" for the entire spectrum of customers. We will have to take that up with upper management at our next weekly meeting.

WENDY: I can tell you that I could have predicted something like this. It is a fact of "linear programming life" that the optimal solution would tell us not to make at least one of our computer styles. The reason is that our model had only three constraints, and therefore it is impossible that we will end up making more than three products. *In other words, the number of positive decision variables can never be more than the number of constraints in a linear programming optimal solution.* Thus, I knew, since we had just three constraints, that at least one of our products, the Starter, Midrange, Super, or Extreme, should not be made. However, I did not know which one. The fact that Solver tells us not to make two of these products is a slight surprise, but quite reasonable.

SILAS: Well, as I said, we can take up the solution with upper management. But what does the rest of the output tell us. Is it important?

WENDY: Yes, but before we get into that, I should point out to you that Solver gave us integer optimal values for the number of computer models to make. That will not always happen. In other words, the solution may not be integer-valued. If we want integer solutions, we need to use another technique called **integer programming,** which Solver can also do. However, we will not discuss it now.

SILAS: Very well. I assume that I can ask for your help on that in the future when I need it. Let us get back to all that additional output. Tell me if I need to understand or worry about it.

WENDY: The additional output is what makes linear programming such a rich topic. It is all related to the concept of sensitivity analysis, which tells us how sensitive is our solution to any changes in the data.

WENDY DESCRIBES SLACK VARIABLES

SILAS: Wendy, in the original spreadsheet as well as in the Answer Report, I see a column labeled "Slack" and there are numbers in that column. Since "value" meant the values of the decision variables, what does slack value imply?

WENDY: That has to do with the Simplex Algorithm, the procedure that solves linear programs. This procedure requires that the constraints be equalities, rather than inequalities. Hence, all inequality constraints must first be transformed into equality ones with the aid of new variables called **slack variables.** Non-negative slack variables are added to less-than-or-equal constraints, and similar variables, which are usually called surplus variables, are subtracted from greater-than-or-equal constraints in order to achieve the desired equalities.

SILAS: I think I understand. Because our three constraints were of the form "less than or equal," we needed three slack variables, for each constraint. Is it correct to say that the first constraint, for manufacture, can be written as:

0.1(Starter) + 0.2(Midrange) + 0.7(Super) + 0.8(Extreme) + slack 1 = 250

WENDY: Very good. Since this is the first constraint, the computer adds a new variable, traditionally called slack 1, to the left-hand side of the constraint. The inequality is gone, and the desired equality is achieved. A similar thing is done for the other constraints as well. The program does this automatically. Because there are new variables in the formulation, then their solution must be obtained, in addition to the solution of the original decision variables. The computer gives us the optimal solution to all these variables.

SILAS: The computer output informs us that the value of slack variable 1 is zero. The first constraint had to do with how many person-hours of manufacture we are using. How does one then know the final amount of manufacture person-hours that actually are used?

WENDY: If we substitute the optimal values of the decision variables into the equality form of the manufacture constraint, we shall see. Let me show you.

0.1(Starter) + 0.2(Midrange) + 0.7(Super) + 0.8(Extreme) + slack 1 = 250

or

0.1(0) + 0.2(375) + 0.7(250) + 0.8(0) + 0 = 250

Subject to our rounding, this is exactly the number of person-hours of manufacture that are available, and hence the number of person-hours of manufacture to be used.

SILAS: I see, Wendy. The optimal slack variable 1, corresponding to the manufacture constraint, is zero, which tells us that exactly 250 hours of manufacture are utilized in the optimal solution!

WENDY: Precisely. In technical terms, such a constraint is said to be *tight* or *binding*.

SILAS: I am not sure I understand what you mean.

WENDY: A tight or binding constraint is one in which an optimal slack or surplus variable is zero. That is, such a constraint is satisfied exactly if we substitute the optimal solution in it. No slack or surplus there.

SILAS: I see. That explains the column called "Status" in the Answer Report. Excel is telling us which constraints are satisfied exactly or not, at the optimal solution.

WENDY: Correct, Silas.

Appendix A   Linear Programming

SILAS: Let me see if I have all this information correct in my mind. Since slack variable 3 is zero, then we are using all 150 hours of the inspection time available. The same reasoning for slack variable 2 tells us not all hours of assembly were used. In fact, the 100 slack for assembly indicates that we had 100 assembly hours left over when we implemented our optimal solution. Assembly is thus not a tight constraint. Now I understand, only 250 of the 350 assembly hours are actually utilized.

WENDY: You are right again.

VARIABLE STATUS: BASIC AND NONBASIC

SILAS: Let me return to the solution. Solver tells us that we should produce only Midrange and Super model computers, and not make Starters or Extremes. Since, as you implied, slack variables are new variables that the computer adds to the problem in order to ascertain the optimal solution, then their values are also important and are part of the optimal solution. Thus we have a slack of 100 hours in constraint 2, the assembly time constraint. I shall not ask you how the computer arrived at these answers for I fear the answer involves much mathematics. However, I do notice that some of our variables are positive and some are zero. Obviously those that are positive are important. Do they have a special name?

WENDY: They indeed do. They are frequently called **basic variables.** Basic is a technical term that comes from the simplex algorithm. It refers to the fact that, in the absence of a special case called *degeneracy*, a *basic variable is one whose value is positive.* Also, the number of variables that are positive in the optimal solution equals the number of constraints of the problem if degeneracy is not present.

SILAS: I fear this is getting too intricate for me. Let us forget this notion of degeneracy for now, since you say it is a special case.

WENDY: Quite right, Silas. As I was saying, in the absence of this special case called degeneracy, a basic variable is simply one whose solution is positive. A listing of these variables, and their values, is sometimes called a **basic feasible solution.**

SILAS: I noticed, Wendy, that there are three (if you count slack variable 2) positive or basic variables, and there were three constraints in our problem, ignoring the non-negativity of the variables. Is that a coincidence?

WENDY: No, it is not a coincidence. I alluded to this issue earlier in our discussion. *The number of positive variables is always equal to the number of constraints in the absence of degeneracy.* By the way, those variables that are not positive, that is, that are equal to zero, are called *nonbasic variables.* Once again, we are ignoring degeneracy and we are not counting the non-negativity constraints.

SILAS: I am afraid that sooner or later I must learn the meaning of that ominous term.

WENDY: Yes, if you are to truly understand all the concepts. But we shall defer its discussion to a later time.

SHADOW PRICES ARE DISCUSSED

SILAS: Very well, Wendy. In the interim, I would like to ask you another question. I recall reading an article in *The Times* last week concerning Maximus Computers. The gist of the article was that upper management wanted to achieve a daily profit of $130,000 per day. If we follow the computer's advice and implement the optimal solution, we would achieve a daily profit of $107,500. We are still $22,500 short. I presume that if the company had more resources of manufacture, assembly, and inspection, they could overcome the shortfall?

WENDY: Before I answer your question directly, Silas, I would like to first propose a *hypothetical* example. Now stay with me on this. While it *isn't* the case here, suppose Solver told us that not all 250 available hours of manufacture would be utilized in the optimal product mix. That would imply that there would be some manufacturing time left over; it would be going to waste. Recall we called such a constraint nonbinding. If we were able to get possession of some additional hours of manufacture, all we would achieve is to have even more waste, for that many more hours of manufacture would not be used in our optimal product mix. That is, we would be obtaining the same product mix as before, and the same objective profit, and just additional hours of manufacture not used. Hence obtaining more units of a particular not-fully-utilized resource, as manufacture time is in our hypothetical case, would not get us anywhere as far as increasing our profit. We are "loosening" or "relaxing" a constraint, or getting more resources for that constraint, and achieving nothing.

SILAS: That makes sense, Wendy. What you are implying is that if we want to increase our profit, we must always concern ourselves with loosening a constraint that is tight or binding. As I recall, such a constraint is easily recognized because it has zero slack or surplus. In our present problem, that says all the constraints, except for assembly time, are tight and are thus candidates for relaxing.

WENDY: Precisely.

SILAS: But which ones should I be relaxing? And by how much?

WENDY: Do you notice in the Sensitivity Report there is a column called "Shadow Price"? In linear programming, each constraint has a number associated with it. That number is called a shadow price or dual variable. A shadow price for a particular constraint refers to how much the objective function changes for a unit increase in the right-hand side value of that constraint.

For example, for each additional hour of manufacturing time the firm obtains above the already available 250 hours, its profit will increase by $175. Similarly, for every hour of inspection time the firm gets above the available 150, its profit will increase by $425. The "Constraint RHS" column in the output reminds us how much available resource we have, and the "Shadow Price" column informs us by how much our profit would change if we had more of a particular resource.

SILAS: One more time, Wendy. I see that the shadow price for that constraint is 175, or I assume $175. This tells me that . . .

WENDY: What it tells us is this: for each additional hour of manufacturing the company obtains above the already available 250 daily hours, its profit will increase by $175. The shadow price is sometimes called the constraint's *marginal value,* because it tells us the most the company would be willing to pay, above and beyond what it currently does pay, for an additional unit of the resource. For instance, certainly the firm would not pay $180 beyond what it usually pays for an additional hour of manufacturing time, because its profit increases by only $175 for that extra hour.

RIGHT-HAND SIDE SENSITIVITY ANALYSIS

SILAS: I think I get it. So let me see if I get this correct, we would like to have the company get an additional $22,500 per day. For each hour of extra manufacturing time we hire, the company gets an additional $175 profit. So if the company could hire an additional 22,500/175 or about 128.57 hours of manufacturing time, we would achieve our profit goal.

WENDY: Almost. Your calculations are correct except for one key detail. These shadow prices are valid only over some limited range of the available value. The Sensitivity Report gives that range.

SILAS: I see it. The allowable increase for manufacturing is 100 and the allowable decrease is 80. Please be specific, just what exactly do these numbers tell us?

WENDY: The shadow price for the constraints, as given in the Sensitivity Report, will remain constant as long as the range for the available resources stays between those two values. Thus, if the number of daily manufacturing hours is between 170 (250 − 80) and 350 (250 + 100), then the shadow prices are fixed. Since your calculation called for getting an additional 128.57 hours of manufacturing time, which is above the allowable increase of 100 hours for that constraint, we cannot be certain that the shadow prices are as given. Therefore, your calculation is incorrect.

SILAS: I see. Let me follow your reasoning. I notice that the shadow price for inspection is $425. If we got an additional $22,500/425 or 52.94 hours, we would get to the profit's goal. But because the allowable increase for inspection is only 26.67 hours, this calculation is also incorrect because 52.94 is more than the allowable increase of 26.67. I have answered my own potential question. We can't get the additional $22,500 that way either.

WENDY: Unfortunately, no. Your analysis is correct.

SILAS: Let me try a different tack. Suppose we got some additional hours of manufacture *and* inspection? Let us get enough of *both* resources to achieve the additional $22,500, but still not going outside the allowable range for either one. That should do it.

WENDY: Almost. Unfortunately, our discussion of sensitivity analysis of an available resource infers that we change just *one* resource amount. You are changing *two*. There is something called the **100% Rule** that tells us how to analyze making changes to more than one data item, but we will save that for later.

WENDY DESCRIBES THE 100% RULE FOR RESOURCES

SILAS: I remember that you told me, in our early detective days, that we should not postpone the obvious and to forge ahead to where the evidence leads. Please tell me about the 100% Rule.

WENDY: Very well, Silas. The 100% Rule was developed approximately 30 years after the Simplex Algorithm, and delves into the concept of making more than one change to a resource constraint at a time.

SILAS: Is it complicated to follow?

CELL	NAME	FINAL VALUE	REDUCED COST	OBJECTIVE COEFFICIENT	ALLOWABLE INCREASE	ALLOWABLE DECREASE
$B$2	Starter	0	−10	50	10	1E+30
$C$2	Midrange	375	0	120	46.67	20
$D$2	Super	250	0	250	170	70.00
$E$2	Extreme	0	−52.50	300	52.50	1E+30

CELL	NAME	FINAL VALUE	SHADOW PRICE	CONSTRAINT R.H. SIDE	ALLOWABLE INCREASE	ALLOWABLE DECREASE
$G$6	manufacture	250	175	250	100	80
$G$7	assembly	250	0	350	1E+30	100
$G$8	inspection	150	425	150	26.67	42.86

WENDY: Not really, Silas. The best way to describe the rule is to work out a specific example. Recall that you correctly deduced that we would not be able to achieve the shortfall of $22,500. It may be that we will never be able to overcome that deficiency, but let us try. Look at the Sensitivity Report once again, Silas. Suppose we somehow managed to increase the number of manufacturing hours to 300, or 50 more hours than we currently have. The maximum number of hours we *could* increase manufacture time, and still be assured that the shadow prices do not change, is 100. Our increase of 50 can be thought as an increase of 50/100 = 0.5, or 50 percent of the permissible increase. Let us *also* increase the number of inspection hours from the assumed 150 to 160, an increase of 10 hours. The allowable increase is 26.67, so this increase of 10 represents 10/26.67 = 0.37, or 37 percent of the permissible increase. The 100% Rule states that *if we add the percentage changes (increase or decrease) and if these are less than 100%, then the shadow prices do not change.* Because we had a total change of 50% + 37% = 87% < 100%, then all the shadow prices of our Sensitivity Report do not change.

SILAS: Then I believe I understand. However, these changes still do not help us achieve the $22,500 shortfall. My calculations show that, with 300 manufacture hours (an increase of 50) and 160 inspection hours (an increase of 10), by the 100% Rule, the shadow prices are valid, then our profit will increase by just:

$$175*50 + 425*10 = \$13,000$$

This is well short of the extra $22,500 needed. In fact, I am not sure that, even with the 100% Rule giving us the option of changing more than one resource simultaneously, we can *ever* get the needed $22,500.

WENDY: I am afraid you are correct in the latter analysis, Silas. While the 100% Rule may not perhaps help us in this particular problem, it is useful to know for other problems we may encounter in the future.

MORE RIGHT-HAND SIDE SENSITIVITY ANALYSIS

SILAS: Very well, Wendy. Let me ignore the 100% Rule and the idea of changing more than one resource at a time. Let me return to the concept of a shadow price for a constraint.

WENDY: Very well. What do you want to discuss?

SILAS: The shadow price for assembly is zero. I don't understand that. Can you explain it please?

WENDY: Remember that the shadow price of a constraint tells us how much more we would be willing to pay, above and beyond what we already pay, for an additional unit of that resource. Let me ask you something. Did we use up all of our available 350 hours of assembly?

SILAS: No, because if we make the number of computer models that Solver advises, we would only use up 250 daily hours of assembly. In fact, we would have 100 hours left over, and the slack value of 100 tells me that, correct?

WENDY: Indeed. So if you have 100 such hours not used, why would you want to buy additional assembly hours? Let me rephrase that. What's the most you would pay for an additional hour of assembly?

SILAS: I wouldn't pay anything for it, because I don't need it.

WENDY: Precisely. Assembly time is an example of a *nonbinding constraint.* That means that we do not use all the available resources of that constraint at the optimal solution. *The shadow price of a nonbinding constraint is zero.* On the other hand, if a constraint is binding, or tight, then we are using up all the available resources for that constraint. If you look at Solver's Answer Report, it will tell you which constraints are binding or tight, and which constraints are not binding.

SILAS: I get it. Then we would be willing to pay for some more of that resource, because that resource was all used up at the optimal solution. So *the shadow price for a tight constraint would not be zero.*

WENDY: Again, correct. You just stated a key theorem in the subject of linear programming, called the Complementary Slackness Theorem. Generally stated, if a constraint is tight, then its slack value is zero, and its shadow price will not be zero. If a constraint is not tight, its slack variable is positive and its shadow price is zero. This is true if the problem is not "degenerate."

SILAS: I don't like the tone of that word. What is a degenerate problem?

WENDY: It is not as bad as the term sounds. I will get into its definition later, but I can tell you now that you need not worry about it.

SILAS: Well, that's a relief. Let me just go over this concept of shadow price another time to confirm I got it right.

WENDY: Fine.

SILAS: Suppose a person comes into my office looking for employment. This person says she is skilled in manufacturing. She is willing to work 10 hours a day, and she wants $50 an hour in salary. I normally pay manufacturing workers $30 an hour (which we don't see explicitly in our model, but it is there implicitly, as part of the net profit coefficients of the objective function), so she really wants $20 more than I ordinarily pay my workers. Still, I would hire her. That is because, for each hour she works, the firm gets an additional $175, which is what the shadow price tells me. Therefore, the net profit for the company would be $175 minus the $20 of her extra salary, or $155. We are still ahead and, therefore, I would hire her.

WENDY: Your analysis is sound. Notice that you can hire her to work the 10 hours, because the additional 10 daily hours is less than the allowable increase of 100 hours.

SILAS: I believe I understand. However, another thought just occurred to me. What good is hiring her to do just manufacturing? To build a computer, don't we need manufacturing, assembly, and inspection, all three?

WENDY: A good question, Silas. The computer sees that you have increased just one available resource, manufacturing for instance, and will come up with a new and different product mix based on the available resources. *When you change the amount of available resource to a different value, even if you are in the allowable range, the optimal solution to the problem will change. All that stays the same are the shadow prices.* We generally don't know what the new optimal solution would be, and would have to rerun the problem with Solver to get the new optimal solution. However, I can tell you that the product mix will be different.

SILAS: Very well, let me continue with my example. If I hire this hypothetical person to work an additional 10 hours in manufacturing at $50 per hour, which is $20 more than the $30 per hour I ordinarily pay for manufacturing time, the company would achieve an additional daily profit of $175 − $20, or $155 per hour. Therefore, for the 10 additional hours she works, the company would gain an additional $1,550. However, the product mix—zero Starters, 375 Midranges, 250 Supers, and zero Extremes—would no longer be the optimal solution. Moreover, if I wanted to know what that new solution is, I would have to rerun the problem in Solver to get it. Is that right?

WENDY: Correct. However, I can tell you something about the new solution, even if I don't run the problem again on Solver. If we change the value of an available resource, and we stay within the allowable range, the shadow prices will remain the same. What also remains the same is the "make-up" of the product mix. Those variables that were *basic* before are still basic, and those variables that were *nonbasic* before are still non-basic. What that means is we would still make the same products before we made the change of the resource, although in different amounts. Also, those products we did not make prior to the change, we still would not make. In other words, without rerunning this problem, if you hire this woman to work the additional 10 manufacturing hours, I can tell you for a fact that we should still make Midrange and Super models, but no Starters and Extremes. However, the number of Midrange and Supers will indeed be different from the original optimal values of 375 and 250, respectively, and if we want those amounts, we would have to run the problem again in Solver.

SILAS: That is useful to know. What about the slack for our assembly constraint? Will there still be slack there?

WENDY: Yes. The "optimal solution" means the values of the original variables and any slack variables. Once again, if we make a change in the amount of available resource, and that change is within the allowable range, the optimal solution values will be different. However, those that were positive before will still be positive, and those that were zero before will still be zero. That includes the original variables and the slack variables.

SILAS: I understand. Can you tell me what the rest of the output is all about?

OBJECTIVE FUNCTION SENSITIVITY ANALYSIS

WENDY: Certainly. It is called the **Sensitivity to Objective Function Changes.** Let me propose a hypothetical scenario to you. Consider the Midrange computer. At the moment, the firm assesses a net profit from it of $120. The computer tells us we should produce 375 of them. Now suppose that for whatever reason the per-unit profit of this model Midrange computer were to increase above the given $120 profit. If that profit grew higher, what do you think might happen?

SILAS: It seems to me, Wendy, based on your story, that I would like to make more than the 375 Midrange models that Solver says I should make. Since I presume to have the same limited resources of manufacture, assembly and inspection, if I make more Midrange computers, apparently I would make fewer of some of the other model type, the Super.

WENDY: You are correct. If the profit of model Midrange computers increased, sooner or later we would have a profit in which the optimal solution given would no longer be optimal. Let me reverse the story. Now suppose the per-unit profit of the Midrange decreased below the given $120. What do you think happens then?

SILAS: Clearly, if the profit on this model continued to fall, there must be some value at which I would no longer be happy making the 375 Midrange computers called for in the optimal solution, but would prefer making fewer, or perhaps even none at all. And indeed, if I do make fewer or none, then I would probably make more of some other model to compensate.

WENDY: Correct again, Silas.

SILAS: You seem to be implying, Wendy, that there is some range of values of the profit of Midrange over which we would be content making the 375 called for by the Solver.

WENDY: Not only the 375 Midranges, but the entire product mix will remain the same. You can see the answer in the section involving sensitivity analysis of the variables. There you see, for Midrange, the current profit of $120, an allowable increase of $46.67 (to a maximum allowable profit of

$166.67), and an allowable decrease of $20 (to a minimum allowable profit of $100). This is the range over which the profit of Midrange computers can vary.

SILAS: Without changing the number of Midrange models we will make?

WENDY: More, Silas. Without changing the optimal solution of any of the variables. That is, the entire product mix as called for will still be the same so long as the change in profit of Midranges is within a decrease of $20 and an increase of $46.67. Equivalently, the product mix will not change if our profit of the model Midrange computer is somewhere between $100 and $166.67.

SILAS: How do we know that? I don't understand.

WENDY: It comes from the theory of linear programming and the mathematics behind it.

SILAS: Very well; so be it. However, now let me get a bit hypothetical to see if I understand what you said. If the company discovered that their formulation was in error, and in fact that the per-unit profit of the Super computer was really $200 instead of the assumed $250, an error of minus $50, but less than the allowable increase of $70. Then the answer to the problem is still to produce no Starters, 375 Midranges, 250 Supers, and no Extremes. But what about the total profit of $107,500? Surely that can't remain the same.

WENDY: Clearly not. If we are making the same number of Supers, but are making less money for each one, then the total profit must be lower. In fact, we can easily find it:

$107,500 − 250($250 − $200) = $107,500 − 250($50) = $95,000

SILAS: That seems fairly obvious, Wendy. But I just thought of something. If the profit of an objective function coefficient stays within the allowable interval, then you said all the answers found by the computer stay the same. Does that mean that the slack or surplus variable values stay the same also? And all variables that are zero, or nonbasic, stay that way too?

WENDY: Precisely.

SILAS: That would then imply that the constraints that are tight remain tight, and those that are nonbinding remain nonbinding.

WENDY: Quite correct.

SILAS: Wendy, what happens if the profit on, say, Supers were increased by exactly $170, to $420?

WENDY: At that point, Silas, in the absence of degeneracy, all that happens is that we have alternative optima. That is, there is our current optimal solution set and some other set. Both sets of solutions will have the same objective function value:

$$\$107{,}500 + 250(170) = \$150{,}000.$$

SILAS: There is that ominous word, degeneracy, again.

WENDY: Ignore it for now, Silas. Do you see how really useful the objective function sensitivity analysis is? Once we run the problem on Solver, we can change values on the per-unit profit, and if our new values are within the allowable range, we know that we should make the same number of computer models that Solver found before we made the change. And we didn't have to rerun the problem to get this information.

SILAS: I agree that this is all useful. Let me take the discussion on a different tack. Is my reasoning for the following correct? At the moment the per-unit profit of Starters is $50. The computer says not to produce any, presumably because this profit is too low. If the profit were even lower than the $50, it seems obvious that we would still not produce those Starter computers. In fact, the profit can go as low as we please below the $50, and the optimal product mix would not change. Yet the Solver output shows an allowable decrease of 1.0E+30. What does that mean?

WENDY: The software is using scientific notation. That number is one followed by 30 zeros, an exceedingly large number to be sure. As your common sense surmised, we can have the profit of a Starter go as low as we want, even to "negative infinity," and the product mix would stay the same. That implies that we would still make no Starter computers.

SILAS: Very well. On the other hand, if the per-unit profit of a Starter computer were to increase beyond the given $50, then there must be a point at which the profit is high enough where it would pay to produce the Starters. In other words, the current optimal solution, which says produce no Starters, can no longer be optimal. I am guessing that this per-unit profit for the Starters would have to increase by $10, to $60. What do you say, Wendy?

WENDY: Your analysis is indeed correct. At $60 per-unit profit for a Starter (meaning an increase of $10 from the assumed profit of $50) we have **alternative optima.** That means there is another optimal solution to the problem (another product mix, if you will) with the same profit. Both sets of answers are equally good. That is, we would be indifferent between the two solutions, for the profit would be identical in either case. Once the profit change exceeds this value, we have a new optimal solution in which the Starter model is indeed produced, resulting in perhaps fewer amounts made of some other model computer. What exactly does happen we cannot say. In order to find out we must run the problem again with the new profit of Starter in the objective function. By the way, if the per-unit profit increase of a Starter were exactly $10, because of the nondegeneracy of our problem, we have alternative optima. But what is the objective function value, the total profit of our firm?

SILAS: Since the alternative optima means another solution with the same objective function value, then the profit would be same as that of the current optimal solution in which no Starters are produced. Since we are increasing the per-unit profit of these Starters upward from $50 to the allowable increase of $10, to a limit of $60, and we don't produce any in that range, then the total profit would not change. It remains at $107,500.

WENDY: Yes, your analysis is right on the mark.

SILAS: So if the coefficient of an objective function value is within the allowable interval shown, the optimal solution does not change, but the optimal objective function value or total profit may or may not change. I see. However, you mentioned that word "degeneracy" several times. Just what is a degenerate linear program? It certainly sounds ominous.

DEGENERACY IS REVEALED

WENDY: It is not so threatening as you might imagine. Do you remember that I told you that the number of positive variables in an optimal solution can never exceed the number of constraints? Briefly, the optimal solution to a linear program is called *degenerate if the number of positive variables is less than the number of constraints in the problem.* The problem is not degenerate if the number of positive variables equals the number of constraints. When we count positive variables, we look at the original and slack variables.

SILAS: OK. I understand the definition. That says, for example, that our solution is not degenerate because there are three positive variables in the optimal solution (Midrange, Super, and slack for Assembly time) and there are three constraints in the problem. So what does this imply?

WENDY: Actually, for all practical purposes, nothing. If a problem is degenerate, we glean a little less information from the computer output. For example, if the per unit profit of a Starter were $60, then we have alternative optima. If the problem had been a degenerate one, we would have to rephrase that to read "we might have alternative optima." If the problem was not degenerate (as ours is), we can change that to the more definitive "we have alternative optima." Also, the 100% Rule, which we mentioned earlier, does not work precisely as stated if the problem is degenerate. We shall leave these issues to a more advanced analysis, perhaps in the near future.

SILAS: In other words, I really shouldn't worry too much about it, but I should at least be aware of the concept, is that it?

WENDY: That's right.

THE 100% RULE FOR OBJECTIVE
FUNCTION COEFFICIENTS

SILAS: By the way, Wendy, you mentioned the 100% Rule, which allowed us to change more than one resource value or right-hand side value, at a time. Is there a comparable 100% Rule for changing more than one profit coefficient or objective function coefficient simultaneously?

WENDY: Yes, there is Silas. When we change an objective function coefficient, and we are still in the allowable range as given by Solver, the optimal solution stays the same. The 100% Rule for objective function coefficients says: If we consider the ratios of the changes made (positive or negative) to the maximum possible change in that direction (positive or negative), then the sum of the ratios must be less than or equal to one (or 100 percent if the ratios are in percentages). If these ratios are indeed less than or equal to one, then the optimal solution to the problem will not change.

SILAS: Indeed, the rule is the same as that for the resources or right-hand side, except that now the optimal solution stays the same, while there the shadow prices stayed the same.

WENDY: Indeed, Silas.

SILAS: Let me try a hypothetical example to verify if my understanding is sound. Suppose upper management informs us that the per-unit profit of a Midrange computer dropped from $120 to $110, while at the same time the per-unit profit of a Super computer increased from $250 to $300. The change in Midrange is $10, and the allowable decrease is $20. This represents a ratio of 10/20, or 50 percent. The change in Supers is 50 and the allowable increase for Supers is 170. This represents a ratio of 50/170 or 5/17, or 29 percent. The sum of the ratios is half plus 5/17, which is less than one, or better yet, 50 percent plus 29 percent or 79 percent which is less than 100 percent. That tells me that the optimal solution we had is still optimal. That is, make no Starters, 375 Midrange, 250 Super, and no Extreme computers. The optimal profit can be determined as follows. We still make 375 Midranges, but we are making $10 less on each, for a drop of 375*10 = $3,750. We still make 250 Supers, but are making $50 more on each, for a gain of 250*50 = $12,500. Our net gain is thus 12,500 − 3,750 = $8,750. We add this $8,750 to the original profit of $107,500 to get a total profit of $116,250. Any errors, Wendy?

WENDY: None, Silas.

SILAS: Well, Wendy, I must admit the analysis is not so daunting as I had originally thought. The only item that remains unexplained is the "Reduced Cost" column of the output. You said we would get to it in due time. Is this the time?

WENDY: Yes. If you examine the output you will notice that the reduced cost of a variable is a number other than zero whenever the value of the variable itself is zero, or to put it technically, the reduced cost is not zero when the variable is nonbasic. For our problem, we have nonzero reduced costs for the Starters and Extremes. One interpretation of the reduced cost is this: It tells us how much the per-unit profit of that variable would have to increase before it would pay to produce any. That is, how much the per-unit profit must increase before that nonbasic variable becomes basic. We can see that the current profit of Starters is $50. Not until that per-unit increases by $10 to a total of $60 will we produce Starters. For the Extreme computer, its current profit is $300. Its profit would have to increase by $52.50 to $352.50.

SILAS: Really, Wendy, all that you have just told me could have been obtained from examining the sensitivity analysis of the objective function coefficients of the output. We see those figures you calculated in the "Allowable Increase" column for the two variables in question.

WENDY: Right again, Silas. However, it is our second interpretation of the reduced costs that is even more meaningful. The reduced cost for a nonbasic decision variable tells us how much the objective function value would change per rate of increase of that variable. Hence in our example, if, for whatever reason the firm insisted on making Starters in its product mix, its objective function total profit would *decrease* by $10 for every such computer made. We may think of it as "costing" the company $10 per Starter. That is, this is how much money we are getting less than our optimal $107,500 we could make by producing the optimal product mix. Remember, our optimal mix says to make no Starters. Similarly, if the company wanted to produce Extreme computers, for every Extreme made, the firm would be decreasing its profit $52.50 from the optimal $107,500.

SILAS: So really these reduced costs give us an indication of what the firm's total profit would be if the company produced a nonoptimal or suboptimal product mix.

WENDY: That is one way of stating it, Silas.

SILAS: I think I get it. Are you saying that if I insist on producing an Extreme computer line, for each one I make and sell, the company would be losing $52.50?

WENDY: Right. Of course, the company doesn't "lose" money if it made an Extreme. It would be making $52.50 less than it could if it had not made and sold the Extreme computer.

SILAS: I was wondering about that. Often, companies would not want to drop a product line as it might alienate customers or send a negative message to the marketplace. In particular, I'm not so sure upper management would want to eliminate the Extreme computer line, despite what the optimal solution says.

WENDY: Fine. Then they should know that for every Extreme they sell at the current profit of $300, they are making $52.50 less than the optimal daily profit of $107,500. It is quite common in business for a company to implement a suboptimal solution instead of the optimal solution.

INTRODUCING A NEW DECISION VARIABLE OR PRODUCT

SILAS: Speaking of a nonoptimal solution, Wendy, I read in *The Times* that the marketing people and the R&D people want to produce and sell a new model computer for game players, called the Ultimate. This would be the current state-of-the-art desktop computer. The article said that each Ultimate computer would need 0.9 hours of manufacturing time, 0.4 hours of assembly time, and 0.7 hours of inspection and testing. Could we use what we have learned about linear programming to determine what the minimum per unit profit on such a computer would have to be before it would be beneficial for the company to make any?

WENDY: Yes. Understand that to produce this new computer, we are diverting the valuable resources that we allocated to make the other models. We know what the "loss" of those resources are; they are the shadow prices. Let us calculate, in dollars, how much the resources "eat up" to make just one Ultimate computer:

Manufacturing:	(0.9 hour)*($175/hour)	= $157.50
Assembly:	(0.4 hour)*($0/hour)	= 0
Inspection:	(0.7 hour)*($425/hour)	= 297.50
		$455.00

The concept is called **pricing out a variable.** We see that to make a single Ultimate computer, we need $455 of resources. We want to find the profit minus the cost of an Ultimate, and we want that result to be positive; otherwise, why bother to make an Ultimate? Clearly, for the profit minus the cost to be positive, the profit should be at least $455 for each machine. If the per-unit profit of an Ultimate is over that amount, we should pursue the new product line. If the per-unit profit is below the $455, we should not introduce the Ultimate line. Needless to say, if the profit on an

Ultimate were, say $500, if we ran Solver, we would find that Solver recommends that some Ultimates to be made, and some other computer drop to zero (not be made) to compensate. Recall we have three constraints, so no more than three products can be made in the final product mix.

WENDY GIVES A DOSE OF THEORY

SILAS: Pricing out a variable certainly has its use if we want to introduce a new product to our product line. Does it have any other applications, Wendy?

WENDY: Indeed, Silas, but more from a theoretical point. If you followed the calculations of pricing out, then you should realize what the plan was. We were trying to figure out if it would pay to produce just one new model computer, the Ultimate. Let's ignore the new model for now. We have a model and Solver gave us a solution: in particular, make no Starters, 375 Midranges, 250 Supers, and no Extremes. Suppose I insisted that we make just one Extreme computer in our product mix. To make this one Extreme we need resources, resources that are being used to make the Midrange and Super computers. In particular, to make just one Extreme, we need 0.8 hours of manufacture, 0.2 hours of assembly, and 0.5 hours of inspection. By taking these resources away from the available resources to make Midrange and Super computers, we can think of the situation as Midrange and Super computers had *fewer* amounts of resources than we originally thought. But if you recall, we know the value of these resources, they are called the shadow prices. So to make one Extreme, we need:

Manufacturing:	(0.8 hour)*($175/hour) =	$140.00
Assembly:	(0.2 hour)*($0/hour) =	0
Inspection:	(0.5 hour)*($425/hour) =	212.50
		$352.50

That is, we are using up $352.50 worth of valuable resources (which we used to make the other computers) to make just one Extreme. The profit of an Extreme is $300, and so the profit minus the cost of an Extreme is

$$\text{Profit-Cost} = \$300 - \$352.50 = -\$52.50$$

SILAS: Wait, Wendy. I see the same number as the reduced cost for Extreme computers. Is that a coincidence?

WENDY: Not at all, Silas. In fact, that is how Solver finds the reduced cost of a variable, by pricing it out. Think of Solver now talking to you, saying, "So you insist on making an Extreme computer. Why bother? If you do, you will lose $52.50 for each one you insist on making. Why would you want to do something like that?" That's how Solver knows that it has found an optimal solution. For a maximization problem, the reduced costs of variables are always zero or negative. A negative reduced cost tells Solver not to make that product. If a reduced cost comes up positive, Solver does another iteration, making that product while another product leaves the product mix. Eventually, Solver comes up with a solution in which the reduced costs are all zero or negative, and that implies an optimal solution has been found.

SILAS: Actually, that makes sense. What I don't understand is that those variables we are making, Midrange and Super, have reduced costs of zero. Can you explain that?

WENDY: Certainly, Silas. Remember the concept of pricing out a variable. We want to make just one additional unit of that product. So consider the Super computer. Solver tells us to make 250 units. Suppose, for whatever reason, that you insist on making one more, or 251 all together. That additional Super computer needs 0.7 hours of manufacture, 0.25 hours of assembly, and 0.3 hours of inspection. Let us price out this computer:

Manufacturing:	(0.7 hour)*($175/hour) =	$122.50
Assembly:	(0.25 hour)*($0/hour) =	0
Inspection:	(0.3 hour)*($425/hour) =	127.50
		$250.00

So this extra Super needs $250 worth of resources. However, the profit of a Super is $250, so the profit − cost = $250 − $250 = 0. The reduced cost is zero! Think of it this way. Solver is now talking to you, saying, "Look, I recommend that you make 250 Super computers. You want to make one more. Why? You need $250 worth of resources to make it, and you are bringing in a profit of $250. It is a tie. You are gaining nothing! So why are you going against my recommendation of making 250 such computers? If you want to make one more, you gain nothing, so why bother? In other words, don't do it. Just make the number of Super computers that I recommend, for that is the optimal amount."

SILAS: Solver sounds like a pushy fellow, but I get your point. You are saying that the reduced cost of a variable that we are making will always be zero.

WENDY: Indeed, Silas. That is what is going on "behind the scenes" as Solver tries to find the optimal solution for us.

ON RECOGNIZING ALTERNATIVE OPTIMA

SILAS: Let me ask you another question. You mentioned alternative optima before. That means there is another optimal solution to the linear program with the same profit. If I look at Solver's output, how do I know if the optimal solution that Solver found is unique, or that there are alternative optima?

WENDY: We just have to look at the objective sensitivity analysis in the Sensitivity Report. *In the absence of degeneracy, if we simultaneously see the reduced cost and the value of a variable are zero, we have alternative optima.* Unfortunately, the computer does not tell us what these other solutions are.

SILAS: That says that our problem does have a unique solution. There is no other optimal solution because I don't have any variable whose optimal value is zero and whose reduced cost is zero also. That's pretty easy. What if the problem were degenerate?

WENDY: If you saw that both the optimal value and the reduced cost of a variable were simultaneously zero, then we might have alternative optima. That is the best we could say.

SILAS: Very well, let us forget about degeneracy. I think I even understand *why* your criteria for recognizing alternative optima work. The reduced cost tells us how much our profit would decrease if we made a product that Solver recommends we do not make. But if that value were already zero, and its reduced cost is zero, then we would be indifferent on whether we made it or not. The reason is that the profit would not change. In other words, there is another possible solution to the problem with the same optimal total profit. That is what alternative optima means.

WENDY: That is exactly right.

ADDING NEW CONSTRAINTS

SILAS: I think that is about enough for now. Let me ask you one last question. What would occur in the following case: The firm made its formulation, ran the program, and interpreted the output as we have. Then it discovered that it had omitted an important constraint. Must the entire analysis be performed once again?

WENDY: No, Silas. All we must do, when adding a new constraint to a problem, is substitute the current optimal solution into that constraint and see what happens. If the constraint is not violated, then the original optimal solution is still optimal.

SILAS: What would occur if the constraint is violated?

WENDY: Then I am afraid we would have to run the problem over again to get the new optimal solution.

SILAS: I see. Well, Wendy, I feel that I do understand linear programming much more. If that textbook that I first investigated had treated the subject as you have, from the computer-output point of view, rather than confusing me with tedious calculations involving equations, I might have known the subject much sooner. Thank you for the discussion.

Appendix B

Asymmetric Information[1]

INTRODUCTION

The four types of markets in which firms compete are distinguishable from each other based on size and number of firms, market entry and exit, degree of product differentiation, and existence of mutual interdependence among competitors. But regardless of the market type, economists assume that buyers and sellers have perfect information about market products and prices. The condition of perfect (or at least near-perfect) market information does not always exist. And when this occurs, it poses the problem of what economists call **asymmetric information.** This is a market situation in which one party in a transaction has more information than the other party. For a manager, it is important to understand the potential problems of asymmetric information both because it can directly affect a firm's strategy and because such market failures are often used by governments to regulate industries.

Asymmetric information can lead to poorly functioning markets: too much or too little of a good may be produced. Contracting can be difficult. Fraud is possible. Consumers may fear purchasing goods when they know that the seller knows more about the quality or attributes of a good than they do. In the worst-case scenario, a market may cease to exist or a contractual agreement may never be fulfilled. Many institutions and practices have arisen to mitigate the problems of asymmetric information. Still, for any transaction, when one party has more information than another, the party with more information can use that to its advantage in negotiations. To develop an appropriate strategy for problems of asymmetric information, firms must be aware of any information advantages or disadvantages and what options are available to help it in their position.

The next section describes the two problems that arise with asymmetric information. It is followed by a discussion of various responses that have been devised to address these problems.

---

[1]This appendix was written by Dr. Shannon B. Mudd. The authors are very grateful for Dr. Mudd's contribution.

Markets with Asymmetric Information

Asymmetric information can cause two problems for markets and for those engaging in transactions in a market. The first problem of asymmetric information is called **adverse selection,** and it occurs before a transaction takes place. Prior to a transaction's occurrence, one party may know more about the value of a good being offered than the other. This can complicate the transaction if it is impossible for the information to be credibly conveyed to the other party or if there is a risk of cheating. The negotiated price will be affected, or the transaction may not even take place.

The second type of asymmetric information problem arises after a transaction has occurred. This problem occurs because it is difficult for one party to a transaction to monitor the second party. If the transaction itself changes the incentives of the second party, the problem of **moral hazard** may arise.

For example, suppose "LoudNoises Stereo Systems" enters into a contract to purchase speaker components from "BigBang Audio." BigBang Audio may determine that it is in its interest to reduce the quality of its speaker components in order to increase its profits. If LoudNoises Stereo Systems recognizes that it cannot adequately monitor or enforce a quality level after the contract is signed, it may choose not to undertake the transaction at all in order to avoid the risk of BigBang's cheating.[2]

Example: Adverse Selection—The Market for Lemons

The market for lemons, that is, bad used cars, is a famous example of adverse selection. George Akerlof, who developed this example, was awarded the Nobel Prize in Economics in 2001 for his work in the problem of asymmetric information.[3]

Consider the market for used cars. If I am selling a used car, my experience with it gives me a lot of information about its value, for example, whether it is dependable, whether the air conditioning can handle very hot temperatures on long drives, whether the window shield leaks, whether the battery works consistently, and whether regular maintenance has been performance and recommended repairs made. The buyer does not have this information and is uncertain how to value this car. How much should the buyer pay?

Assume a world in which there are two kinds of used cars: high quality and low quality ("lemons"). If there is perfect information (i.e., both the buyer and the seller could identify whether a used car was a good used car or a lemon), we would simply have two separate markets. There would be a demand for good cars and a supply of good cars. Demand and supply would interact to produce an equilibrium price. The same would work for lemons; supply and demand would interact to produce an equilibrium price and quantity for these cars. We would expect the price for good used cars to be higher than the price for lemons.

---

[2]For more discussions of issues of supply chain management, see chapter 8.
[3]George A. Akerlof, "The Market for 'Lemons': Quality Uncertainty and the Market Mechanism," *Quarterly Journal of Economics,* August 1970, pp. 488–500.

Suppose instead that the owner of the car knows the quality but the buyer does not and the owner cannot credibly convey that information. Suppose also that the number of cars that are of high quality (which are worth $4,000 each) and the number that are of low quality (worth $1,000 each) is the same. How much should the buyer pay? The buyer has a 50 percent chance of a purchased car being high quality and 50 percent chance of the purchased car being of low quality. Suppose the buyer is risk neutral and simply offers the expected value of $2,500 (EV = 50% × $4,000 + 50% × $1,000 = $2,500).[4] But if the seller of a high-quality car can only get $2,500, she may choose not to sell the car. What happens? As some sellers of high quality cars choose not to sell them for $2,500, there will be fewer high-quality cars offered. The probability of purchasing a high-quality car will decrease and the price will drop. In the worst case, no high-quality cars will be offered and the price drops to $1,000. This is inefficient because no buyer is able to buy a high-quality car and no owner of a high-quality car is able to obtain its true value. The market falls apart, because the information cannot be conveyed.

As you may know from personal experience, a market for used cars does exist—and they are not all lemons. What practices have arisen to help this market avoid failure? We discuss this in the next section. But first, let us look at an example of moral hazard.

Example: Moral Hazard—Insurance

The second problem that arises because of information asymmetries is moral hazard; this is a problem of asymmetric information that arises *after* a transaction takes place. It is particularly common in insurance because the firm cannot completely monitor the activities or condition of the insured and the behavior of the insured may affect the probability of a payout.

For instance, consider the decisions faced by an insurance company and an owner of a warehouse that is worth $100,000. The premium charged by the insurance company is based on the expected loss from a fire: the probability of loss times the dollar amount of the loss. However, the probability of a fire can be affected by the institution of a fire prevention program. Suppose that if the fire prevention program were fully implemented it would reduce the probability of fire from 1 percent (.01) to .5 percent (.005), but would cost the firm $50. Furthermore, suppose that if a fire did occur, the warehouse would suffer a complete loss of its value.

Value of warehouse: $100,000

Probability of fire	*Premium = Expected loss*
1% with no fire prevention program	$1000
.5% with $50 fire prevention program	$500

If the fire prevention program were fully implemented, the insurance company would sell the insurance at a premium of $500 (the expected loss of 0.005 × $100,000). However, once the policy is purchased, the insured firm has no incentive to institute

---

[4]*Expected value* is the weighted average of the value of all possible outcomes with the weights equal to the probabilities of those outcomes. For an additional discussion of risk and uncertainty, see chapter 14.

the program. It will be fully covered for a loss due to fire whether or not it institutes the program. Since the program is costly ($50), there is no gain to the firm in implementing it. If the insurance company cannot observe implementation, it cannot make a clause in its contract that it will only pay if the fire prevention program is implemented. It then faces a dilemma of what premium to charge.

How have insurance companies tried to mitigate this problem? One practice is to require co-payments or deductibles in the event of a loss. If the firm must pay out some of its own money in the event of a fire, it may consider the cost of the fire prevention program acceptable. Note that since a loss also becomes costly to the insured, it reduces the problem of moral hazard.

MARKET RESPONSES TO ASYMMETRIC INFORMATION

Let us return to the problem of asymmetric information: How can a buyer learn whether the quality of a product is good? One way is to try to obtain information from other sources. For example, the magazine *Consumer Reports* provides information on the average reliability of various models and years of used cars. This can help the buyer determine the probability that a given car is a good-quality car.

In some markets, it is possible to buy information. For example, bond-rating agencies can provide information on a particular bond about the likelihood that the company will be able to meet its contractual obligations. A limited amount of this information is freely available, but more detailed information is provided at a cost. However, the amount of information is, in general, not as extensive as it could be. This is because information is costly to provide and information suffers from the "free rider" problem. Investors may be able to obtain information without paying for it. Because information providers do not receive compensation from these free riders, the amount of information they produce is less than if all users paid for the information.

REPUTATION

Another way in which a buyer can make educated guesses about the reliability of a good is by relying on the reputation of the seller. Suppose a seller makes a high-quality product. It is able to charge a higher price to reflect its higher costs only if the buyer expects a higher level of quality from the seller. Over time, or with specific advertising, a seller may be able to develop a reputation for producing high-quality goods. However, if it cheats and starts to sell low-quality goods at high-quality prices, the seller will lose its reputation and buyers will no longer be willing to pay for the higher level of quality. It is in the interest of the seller to maintain that reputation and not sell low-quality goods at high-quality prices if it wants to stay in the high-quality market.

Example: Reputation in eBay Auctions

Online auctions suffer from information asymmetries. The buyer cannot directly observe the product and must rely on the seller's description to determine its value. The quality of the information that the seller provides is not directly verifiable. As the auction provider does not usually offer any guarantee, the buyer has difficulty determining the value of the good and the probability that the seller will actually deliver. However, online auctions such as eBay have developed a practice to mitigate this problem of asymmetric information. Sellers may develop reputations in online auctions through feedback from previous buyers. In fact, online auctions report reputational indicators of the seller on the screen for each auction item.

What is the value of a reputation? Melnik and Alm studied this question using eBay auction data on recently issued gold coins.[5] They chose to examine a single homogeneous coin, the 1999 $5 U.S. gold coin. Their results confirm that reputation has a small, but consistent, statistically significant effect on the price received for the good. During the period examined, the coins sold for $32.73 on average. Reputation indicators, constructed by simply subtracting the number of negative feedback comments from the sum of positive feedback comments, ranged from 3 to 3,583, with a mean value of 452. Their results indicate that a doubling of the indicator from 452 to 904 would increase the price received by a seller by $0.18.

STANDARDIZATION

Another institution that has arisen to mitigate adverse selection problems is **standardization of products.**[6] The success of McDonald's restaurants is a good example of the use of standardization. In your neighborhood, you have a good idea about the quality of eating establishments around you, either from your own experience or word of mouth. However, when you travel, you do not know as much. When you see a McDonald's sign, you know exactly what you will get. All McDonald's restaurants are supplied with the same food inputs, and they maintain a level of training for the staff that ensures consistency. There may be a terrific little cafe around the corner, the food of which you would have found to be better. But you did not know what to expect and chose what you knew. With McDonald's, because of the company's strict policy of standardization, you know exactly what to expect.

MARKET SIGNALING

Another important mechanism for combating asymmetries of information is signaling. **Market signaling** can occur if it is less costly for high-quality agents to invest in the signal than low-quality agents. Michael Spence, who shared the 2001 Nobel Prize

---

[5]Mikhail Melnik and James Alm, "Does a Seller's eCommerce Reputation Matter? Evidence from eBay Auctions," *Journal of Industrial Economics*, forthcoming 2002.
[6]This example is based on Robert S. Pindyck and Daniel L. Rubinfeld, *Microeconomics*, 5th ed., Upper Saddle River, NJ: Prentice Hall, 2001, pp. 599–600.

in Economics with George Akerlof and Joseph Stiglitz, was cited for his very interesting work on signaling.[7] The primary example comes from the labor markets.

Example: Education as a Signal in Labor Markets

Envision a simplified world in which there are two kinds of workers: high productivity and low productivity. The characteristics that contribute to these designations are how hard the person works, his or her portfolio of skills, level of responsibility, leadership capabilities, and so forth. At the time of hiring, a firm may not know which type of worker a person is. If the type of worker was immediately identifiable after a person was hired, the firm could immediately discharge low-quality workers. However, many jobs require a large amount of initial training, and it may not be apparent which type a person is for some time. This can be quite costly if the firm is paying wages, payroll taxes and training costs, and other employee benefits. In addition, there are often obstacles that restrict the ability of a firm to fire an employee once that employee has been hired. A firm may have to justify its action and/or pay severance to the fired employee. Can potential employees convey information about themselves, that is, signal to potential employers whether they are high- or low-productivity workers? Donning a suit instead of ragged jeans and a T-shirt is one potential signal. But a low-quality worker can do this as easily as a high-quality worker. To be strong, a signal must be relatively more costly for the low-productivity worker.

Education is considered a strong signal by many employers. To attend school successfully requires a certain amount of perseverance, a level of general skill or intelligence, and so forth, qualities that mark a high-productivity worker as well as a successful student. A firm may be able to judge some of a person's work capabilities by looking at the person's grade point average, the reputation of the school attended, degrees obtained, and length of time in school.

It may be that the school actually contributed to the worker's productivity as well as provided a signal. As a student, you would certainly like to think this. Although investing in education as a signal is certainly valuable, it may not serve as a sufficient motivator to continue to work hard in school, especially if you plan to work for yourself or for a family member.

However, there is scant evidence that education is anything more than a signal. Performing statistical tests to separately identify the value of an education in improving productivity from its value as a signal is very tricky. However, a classic study by Finis Welch examined the performance of family farms to demonstrate the productivity of schooling.[8] If a young person leaves the farm for college and then returns having earned a degree, the value of the college education as a signal is zero, or at least very small, because the person is already known to the family. Are college-educated farmers more productive? According to the study, those with more education do tend to be more successful. They were able to adapt and respond more quickly, especially in an environment of changing technology.

Even if education is not productive, it can serve as a strong signal if it is more costly for low-quality workers to do well than for high-quality workers. A good sig-

---

[7]Michael Spence, *Market Signaling,* Cambridge, MA: Harvard University Press, 1974.
[8]Finis Welch, "Education in Production," *Journal of Political Economy,* Jan/Feb 1970, pp. 35–59.

nal is one in which success at one activity is closely correlated with success at another activity.

Example: Guarantees and Warranties

Guarantees and warranties can serve as a signal because it is more costly to maintain them on low-quality goods than on high-quality goods. A product with a longer warranty is a signal that it is probably of higher quality. Of course you also may need to have information on the reputation of the seller. The warranty is not worth much if it takes two years for something to get fixed or it does not get fixed at all. An interesting example of how a firm can use warranties as a strategy is found in the book *The Reckoning* by David Halberstam.[9] In this history of the motor industry, Halberstam discusses how a warranty was used to change a firm's internal operations. As he tells it, when Lee Iacocca arrived at Chrysler as Chief Executive Officer, the firm had an awful reputation for quality, and for good reason. Iacocca decided to reinstitute the 5-year/50,000 mile warranty that had been used several years before. The other Chrysler managers thought that the policy would be ruinous. They knew the cars were badly constructed and that the program would be very expensive. Iacocca understood that under the current firm systems, the incentives to produce quality cars simply were not there. The indicators by which divisional performance was judged were designed by finance people who had little knowledge of cars. The statistics that they examined had to do with speed of the line, quantity of cars, volume of steel used, and so forth. By instituting the warranty, Iacocca forced the company to pay attention to quality in order to survive. For two years, there was no change in the number of claims and problems reported by dealers. However, in the third year claims began to come down. The quality of cars had begun to improve.

A FINAL EXAMPLE: TWO BANKING SYSTEMS AS RESPONSES TO INFORMATION ASYMMETRIES

Banking systems are classic examples of the problem of asymmetric information. Banks and other lending institutions know less about a borrower's ability and willingness to pay than the borrower. This leads to both problems of asymmetric information: adverse selection and moral hazard. Adverse selection arises because financial institutions charge interest rates that are partially based on their assessment of the ability and willingness of the borrower to pay. Since the assessment is based on an expected number of defaults from low-quality borrowers, the rates may be considered high by high-quality borrowers who may choose to self-finance and not borrow. This produces a tendency for only low-quality borrowers to seek loans, that is, adverse selection.

Moral hazard arises because once a loan is made the borrower may choose to change behavior. For example, a plumber may intend to borrow money in order to buy a machine to help unclog drains. But, once he or she receives the loan, it may seem easier to take the money and bet on a horse based on a "good" tip. If the bank had known

---

[9]David Halberstam, *The Reckoning*, New York: Morrow, 1986.

that this is what the money was going to be used for, it probably would not have made the loan. Moral hazard arises after the loan is made because a borrower may choose not to pay or to engage in activities that the lender would not have agreed to.

There are many ways that banks and other financial institutions, as well as potential borrowers, can try to mitigate these problems. Rajan and Zingales describe two different banking systems that can be seen as alternative responses to the problems of asymmetric information: arm's length banking, as is typically practiced in the United States, and relationship banking, as is typically practiced in Japan and Korea.[10] This description will try to differentiate the two systems, although elements of both systems can be observed in all countries.

Relationship banking systems are characterized by the financier having some control over the borrower. This is typical of the Japanese Keiretsu and Korean Chaebol systems. In these systems, a banking institution is related to a group of other firms through mutual ownership and cross-holding of shares. When the bank lends to one of the members of its Keiretsu or Chaebol, it has inside information about the firm's ability and willingness to pay. This mitigates the problem of adverse selection. In addition, its ownership relationship allows the bank to monitor and exercise some control over its borrower's behavior, avoiding the problem of moral hazard.

In arm's length systems, the banking institution and the lender may not have had any prior knowledge of each other. When the bank considers whether to extend a loan, it asks for information from the borrower about its business history and runs a credit check. In addition, it may require collateral. Practices such as these help to mitigate the problem of adverse selection by making it easier to distinguish high- from low-quality borrowers.

In addition, in arm's length systems, the lender and borrower sign a contract. The contract often includes restrictive covenants, clauses that limit the behavior of the borrower. For example, a borrower may be required to provide periodic financial statements. Or it may be required to maintain its deposits at the bank. The bank can then monitor the firm's activities and performance by examining the reports and the levels of its deposits to determine whether the business is performing as expected. In addition, the firm may be required to put up collateral, for example, purchase a certificate of deposit (CD) which the bank holds until the loan is paid off. The loss of the CD provides the firm with an incentive to make its payments.

The essential characteristics of the two systems are summarized in the following table.

Relationship versus Arm's Length Banking

RELATIONSHIP BANKING	ARM'S LENGTH BANKING
Defining Characteristics	
Financier has power over borrower	Market for funds is competitive
Low transparency in business environment, information not freely available	Well-developed disclosure rules

(Continued)

---

[10]Raghuram G. Rajan and Luigi Zingales, "Which Capitalism? Lessons from the East Asian Crisis," *Journal of Applied Corporate Finance,* Fall 1998, pp. 40–48.

Financier has inside knowledge about borrower	Collateral requirements, borrower must have some capital
	Historical data on firm performance to predict ability to pay
	Credit reports to assess willingness to pay

METHODS FOR LESSENING PROBLEMS OF MORAL HAZARD

Financier has some control of borrower	Enforceable loan contract has covenants that restrict use of funds by borrower
Financier and borrower are linked in the long term. Difficult for borrower to cheat and disappear	Loans have reporting requirements to assist financier in monitoring
Financier control allows direct monitoring of borrower activity	Collateral requirements backed up by rule of law impose cost on borrower from cheating

Is either one of these systems superior? Perhaps it is better to say that the business environment of a country may be more conducive to one or another. In countries in which contract enforcement and information disclosure laws are not well developed, the relationship banking system may be more appropriate. However, even in the United States, relationship banking is important. Firms may prefer to stay with one bank over time because they can develop a reputation as a good borrower. Plus, it is costly to provide information and to convince a lender that a business project will offer the expected return. By building trust and understanding in the relationship, customers are often offered lower interest rates than they would receive if they went to a new bank, unfamiliar with its business and its business practices.

There are advantages and drawbacks to both systems. Relationship banking allows lenders and borrowers to take a longer-term view of the relationship. Financial institutions in a relationship banking system may be more willing to compromise in the short term in order to maintain the relationship and future venues in the long term. However, as relationships and agreements become more complicated and inward looking, interest rates become less and less based on credit risk and other typical market factors. This severely hampers the bank's risk management and can impact its profitability and the prudent construction of its loan portfolio.

Rajan and Zingales point to this as one of the causes of the financial distress currently being experienced in Japan and Korea. They also point to the interaction of the two systems, Western arm's length banking systems lending to Southeast Asian relationship banking systems, as being one contributor to the East Asian financial crisis of the late 1990s. Western arm's length lenders recognized that information disclosure and contract enforcement laws were not as developed as their own systems. In order to reduce the risk in lending to Southeast Asian firms, the Western banks tended to make short-term loans. The fact that short-term lending can quickly be withdrawn made these countries vulnerable to large outflows of capital when the perceived risk associated with such lending increased.

1. It is very difficult for older people to buy private medical insurance at almost any price. While it is true that older people have a much higher probability of illness and therefore claims against insurance, why do insurance companies not offer policies to older individuals at a higher price rise to reflect this?

2. Because credit card companies and banks must charge the same interest rate on credit cards to all borrowers, there is an adverse selection problem with credit cards. How does a credit card company or firm know whether a person will be a high-quality borrower, i.e., one who pays the debts, or a low-quality borrower, i.e., one who does not pay debts? Describe

   a) how the restriction of a single rate leads to an adverse selection problem, and

   b) at least two potential means which credit card companies can use to try to lessen this problem.

Appendix C

Statistical and
Financial Tables

TABLE C.1*a*

Future Value of $1 at the End of *n* Periods

PERIOD	1%	2%	3%	4%	5%	6%	7%	8%	9%	10%
1	1.0100	1.0200	1.0300	1.0400	1.0500	1.0600	1.0700	1.0800	1.0900	1.1000
2	1.0201	1.0404	1.0609	1.0816	1.1025	1.1236	1.1449	1.1664	1.1881	1.2100
3	1.0303	1.0612	1.0927	1.1249	1.1576	1.1910	1.2250	1.2597	1.2950	1.3310
4	1.0406	1.0824	1.1255	1.1699	1.2155	1.2625	1.3108	1.3605	1.4116	1.4641
5	1.0510	1.1041	1.1593	1.2167	1.2763	1.3382	1.4026	1.4693	1.5386	1.6105
6	1.0615	1.1262	1.1941	1.2653	1.3401	1.4185	1.5007	1.5869	1.6771	1.7716
7	1.0721	1.1487	1.2299	1.3159	1.4071	1.5036	1.6058	1.7138	1.8280	1.9487
8	1.0829	1.1717	1.2668	1.3686	1.4775	1.5938	1.7182	1.8509	1.9926	2.1436
9	1.0937	1.1951	1.3048	1.4233	1.5513	1.6895	1.8385	1.9990	2.1719	2.3579
10	1.1046	1.2190	1.3439	1.4802	1.6289	1.7908	1.9672	2.1589	2.3674	2.5937
11	1.1157	1.2434	1.3842	1.5395	1.7103	1.8983	2.1049	2.3316	2.5804	2.8531
12	1.1268	1.2682	1.4258	1.6010	1.7959	2.0122	2.2522	2.5182	2.8127	3.1384
13	1.1381	1.2936	1.4685	1.6651	1.8856	2.1329	2.4098	2.7196	3.0658	3.4523
14	1.1495	1.3195	1.5126	1.7317	1.9799	2.2609	2.5785	2.9372	3.3417	3.7975
15	1.1610	1.3459	1.5580	1.8009	2.0789	2.3966	2.7590	3.1722	3.6425	4.1772
16	1.1726	1.3728	1.6047	1.8730	2.1829	2.5404	2.9522	3.4259	3.9703	4.5950
17	1.1843	1.4002	1.6528	1.9479	2.2920	2.6928	3.1588	3.7000	4.3276	5.0545
18	1.1961	1.4282	1.7024	2.0258	2.4066	2.8543	3.3799	3.9960	4.7171	5.5599
19	1.2081	1.4568	1.7535	2.1068	2.5270	3.0256	3.6165	4.3157	5.1417	6.1159
20	1.2202	1.4859	1.8061	2.1911	2.6533	3.2071	3.8697	4.6610	5.6044	6.7275
21	1.2324	1.5157	1.8603	2.2788	2.7860	3.3996	4.1406	5.0338	6.1088	7.4002
22	1.2477	1.5460	1.9161	2.3699	2.9253	3.6035	4.4304	5.4365	6.6586	8.1403
23	1.2572	1.5769	1.9736	2.4647	3.0715	3.8197	4.7405	5.8715	7.2579	8.9543
24	1.2697	1.6084	2.0328	2.5633	3.2251	4.0489	5.0724	6.3412	7.9111	9.8497
25	1.2824	1.6406	2.0938	2.6658	3.3864	4.2919	5.4274	6.8485	8.6231	10.835
26	1.2953	1.6734	2.1566	2.7725	3.5557	4.5494	5.8074	7.3964	9.3992	11.918
27	1.3082	1.7069	2.2213	2.8834	3.7335	4.8223	6.2139	7.9881	10.245	13.110
28	1.3213	1.7410	2.2879	2.9987	3.9201	5.1117	6.6488	8.6271	11.167	14.421
29	1.3345	1.7758	2.3566	3.1187	4.1161	5.4184	7.1143	9.3173	12.172	15.863
30	1.3478	1.8114	2.4273	3.2434	4.3219	5.7435	7.6123	10.063	13.268	17.449
40	1.4889	2.2080	3.2620	4.8010	7.0400	10.286	14.974	21.725	31.409	45.259
50	1.6446	2.6916	4.3839	7.1067	11.467	18.420	29.457	46.902	74.358	117.39
60	1.8167	3.2810	5.8916	10.520	18.679	32.988	57.946	101.26	176.03	304.48

TABLE C.1a (*continued*)

Period	12%	14%	15%	16%	18%	20%	24%	28%	32%	36%
1	1.1200	1.1400	1.1500	1.1600	1.1800	1.2000	1.2400	1.2800	1.3200	1.3600
2	1.2544	1.2996	1.3225	1.3456	1.3924	1.4400	1.5376	1.6384	1.7424	1.8496
3	1.4049	1.4815	1.5209	1.5609	1.6430	1.7280	1.9066	2.0972	2.3000	2.5155
4	1.5735	1.6890	1.7490	1.8106	1.9388	2.0736	2.3642	2.6844	3.0360	3.4210
5	1.7623	1.9254	2.0114	2.1003	2.2878	2.4883	2.9316	3.4360	4.0075	4.6526
6	1.9738	2.1950	2.3131	2.4364	2.6996	2.9860	3.6352	4.3980	5.2899	6.3275
7	2.2107	2.5023	2.6600	2.8262	3.1855	3.5832	4.5077	5.6295	6.9826	8.6054
8	2.4760	2.8526	3.0590	3.2784	3.7589	4.2998	5.5895	7.2058	9.2170	11.703
9	2.7731	3.2519	3.5179	3.8030	4.4355	5.1598	6.9310	9.2234	12.166	15.917
10	3.1058	3.7072	4.0456	4.4114	5.2338	6.1917	8.5944	11.806	16.060	21.647
11	3.4785	4.2262	4.6524	5.1173	6.1759	7.4301	10.657	15.112	21.199	29.439
12	3.8960	4.8179	5.3502	5.9360	7.2876	8.9161	13.215	19.343	27.982	40.037
13	4.3635	5.4924	6.1528	6.8858	8.5994	10.699	16.386	24.759	36.937	54.451
14	4.8871	6.2613	7.0757	7.9875	10.147	12.839	20.319	31.691	48.756	74.053
15	5.4736	7.1379	8.1371	9.2655	11.974	15.407	25.196	40.565	64.359	100.71
16	6.1304	8.1372	9.3576	10.748	14.129	18.488	31.243	51.923	84.954	136.97
17	6.8660	9.2765	10.761	12.468	16.672	22.186	38.741	66.461	112.14	186.28
18	7.6900	10.575	12.375	14.463	19.673	26.623	48.039	85.071	148.02	253.34
19	8.6128	12.056	14.232	16.777	23.214	31.948	59.568	108.89	195.39	344.54
20	9.6463	13.743	16.367	19.461	27.393	38.338	73.864	139.38	257.92	468.58
21	10.804	15.668	18.822	22.574	32.324	46.005	91.592	178.41	340.45	637.26
22	12.100	17.861	21.645	26.186	38.142	55.206	113.57	228.36	449.39	866.67
23	13.552	20.362	24.891	30.376	45.008	66.247	140.83	292.30	593.20	1178.7
24	15.179	23.212	28.625	35.236	53.109	79.497	174.63	374.14	783.02	1603.0
25	17.000	26.462	32.919	40.874	62.669	95.396	216.54	478.90	1033.6	2180.1
26	19.040	30.167	37.857	47.414	73.949	114.48	268.51	613.00	1364.3	2964.9
27	21.325	34.390	43.535	55.000	87.260	137.37	332.95	784.64	1800.9	4032.3
28	23.884	39.204	50.066	63.800	102.97	164.84	412.86	1004.3	2377.2	5483.9
29	16.750	44.693	57.575	74.009	121.50	197.81	511.95	1285.6	3137.9	7458.1
30	29.960	50.950	66.212	85.850	143.37	237.38	634.82	1645.5	4142.1	10143
40	93.051	188.88	267.86	378.72	750.38	1469.8	5455.9	19427	66521	*
50	289.00	700.23	1083.7	1670.7	3927.4	9100.4	46890	*	*	*
60	897.60	2595.9	4384.0	7370.2	20555	56348	*	*	*	*

* > 99,999

TABLE C.1*b*
Sum of an Annuity of $1 per Period for *n* Periods

NUMBER OF PERIODS	1%	2%	3%	4%	5%	6%	7%	8%	9%	10%
1	1.0000	1.0000	1.0000	1.0000	1.0000	1.0000	1.0000	1.0000	1.0000	1.0000
2	2.0100	2.0200	2.0300	2.0400	2.0500	2.0600	2.0700	2.0800	2.0900	2.1000
3	3.0301	3.0604	3.0909	3.1216	3.1525	3.1836	3.2149	3.2464	3.2781	3.3100
4	4.0604	4.1216	4.1836	4.2465	4.3101	4.3746	4.4399	4.5061	4.5731	4.6410
5	5.1010	5.2040	5.3091	5.4163	5.5256	5.6371	5.7507	5.8666	5.9847	6.1051
6	6.1520	6.3081	6.4684	6.6330	6.8019	6.9753	7.1533	7.3359	7.5233	7.7156
7	7.2135	7.4343	7.6625	7.8983	8.1420	8.3938	8.6540	8.9228	9.2004	9.4872
8	8.2857	8.5830	8.8923	9.2142	9.5491	9.8975	10.260	10.637	11.028	11.436
9	9.3685	9.7546	10.159	10.583	11.027	11.491	11.978	12.488	13.021	13.579
10	10.462	10.950	11.464	12.006	12.578	13.181	13.816	14.487	15.193	15.937
11	11.567	12.169	12.808	13.486	14.207	14.972	15.784	16.645	17.560	18.531
12	12.683	13.412	14.192	15.026	15.917	16.870	17.888	18.977	20.141	21.384
13	13.809	14.680	15.618	16.627	17.713	18.882	20.141	21.495	22.953	24.523
14	14.947	15.974	17.086	18.292	19.599	21.015	22.550	24.215	26.019	27.975
15	16.097	17.293	18.599	20.024	21.579	23.276	25.129	27.152	29.361	31.772
16	17.258	18.639	20.157	21.825	23.657	25.673	27.888	30.324	33.003	35.950
17	18.430	20.012	21.762	23.698	25.840	28.213	30.840	33.750	36.974	40.545
18	19.615	21.412	23.414	25.645	28.132	30.906	33.999	37.450	41.301	45.599
19	20.811	22.841	25.117	27.671	30.539	33.760	37.379	41.446	46.018	51.159
20	22.019	24.297	26.870	29.778	33.066	36.786	40.995	45.762	51.160	57.275
21	23.239	25.783	28.676	31.969	35.719	39.993	44.865	50.423	56.765	64.002
22	24.472	27.299	30.537	34.248	38.505	43.392	49.006	55.457	62.873	71.403
23	25.716	28.845	32.453	36.618	41.430	46.996	53.436	60.893	69.532	79.543
24	26.973	30.422	34.426	39.083	44.502	50.816	58.177	66.765	76.790	88.497
25	28.243	32.030	36.459	41.646	47.727	54.865	63.249	73.106	84.701	98.347
26	29.526	33.671	38.553	44.312	51.113	59.156	68.676	79.954	93.324	109.18
27	30.821	35.344	40.710	47.084	54.669	63.706	74.484	87.351	102.72	121.10
28	32.129	37.051	42.931	49.968	58.403	68.528	80.698	95.339	112.97	134.21
29	33.450	38.792	45.219	52.966	62.323	73.640	87.347	103.97	124.14	148.63
30	34.785	40.568	47.575	56.085	66.439	79.058	94.461	113.28	136.31	164.49
40	48.886	60.402	75.401	95.026	120.80	154.76	199.64	259.06	337.88	442.59
50	64.463	84.579	112.80	152.67	209.35	290.34	406.53	573.77	815.08	1163.9
60	81.670	114.05	163.05	237.99	353.58	533.13	813.52	1253.2	1944.8	3034.8

TABLE C.1b (*continued*)

NUMBER OF PERIODS	12%	14%	15%	16%	18%	20%	24%	28%	32%	36%
1	1.0000	1.0000	1.0000	1.0000	1.0000	1.0000	1.0000	1.0000	1.0000	1.0000
2	2.1200	2.1400	2.1500	2.1600	2.1800	2.2000	2.2400	2.2800	2.3200	2.3600
3	3.3744	3.4396	3.4725	3.5056	3.5724	3.6400	3.7776	3.9184	4.0624	4.2096
4	4.7793	4.9211	4.9934	5.0665	5.2154	5.3680	5.6842	6.0156	6.3624	6.7251
5	6.3528	6.6101	6.7424	6.8771	7.1542	7.4416	8.0484	8.6999	9.3983	10.146
6	8.1152	8.5355	8.7537	8.9775	9.4420	9.9299	10.980	12.136	13.406	14.799
7	10.089	10.730	11.067	11.414	12.142	12.916	14.615	16.534	18.696	21.126
8	12.300	13.233	13.727	14.240	15.327	16.499	19.123	22.163	25.678	29.732
9	14.776	16.085	16.786	17.519	19.086	20.799	24.712	29.369	34.895	41.435
10	17.549	19.337	20.304	21.321	23.521	25.959	31.643	38.593	47.062	57.352
11	20.655	23.045	24.349	25.733	28.755	32.150	40.238	50.398	63.122	78.998
12	24.133	27.271	29.002	30.850	34.931	39.581	50.895	65.510	84.320	108.44
13	28.029	32.089	34.352	36.786	42.429	48.497	64.110	84.853	112.30	148.47
14	32.393	37.581	40.505	43.672	50.818	59.196	80.496	109.61	149.24	202.93
15	37.280	43.842	47.580	51.660	60.965	72.035	100.82	141.30	198.00	276.98
16	42.753	50.980	55.717	60.925	72.939	87.442	126.01	181.87	262.36	377.69
17	48.884	59.118	65.075	71.673	87.068	105.93	157.25	233.79	347.31	514.66
18	55.750	68.394	75.836	84.141	103.74	128.11	195.99	300.25	459.45	700.94
19	63.440	78.969	88.212	98.603	123.41	154.74	244.03	385.32	607.47	954.28
20	72.052	91.025	102.44	115.38	146.63	186.69	303.60	494.21	802.86	1298.8
21	81.699	104.77	118.81	134.84	174.02	225.03	377.46	633.59	1060.8	1767.4
22	92.503	120.44	137.63	157.41	206.34	271.03	469.06	812.00	1401.2	2404.7
23	104.60	138.30	159.28	183.60	244.49	326.24	582.63	1040.4	1850.6	3271.3
24	118.16	158.66	184.17	213.98	289.49	392.48	723.46	1332.7	2443.8	4450.0
25	133.33	181.87	212.79	249.21	342.60	471.98	898.09	1706.8	3226.8	6053.0
26	150.33	208.33	245.71	290.09	405.27	567.38	1114.6	2185.7	4260.4	8233.1
27	169.37	238.50	283.57	337.50	479.22	681.85	1383.1	2798.7	5624.8	11198.0
28	190.70	272.89	327.10	392.50	566.48	819.22	1716.1	3583.3	7425.7	15230.3
29	214.58	312.09	377.17	456.30	669.45	984.07	2129.0	4587.7	9802.9	20714.2
30	241.33	356.79	434.75	530.31	790.95	1181.9	2640.9	5873.2	12941	28172.3
40	767.09	1342.0	1779.1	2360.8	4163.2	7343.9	22729	69377	*	*
50	2400.0	4994.5	7217.7	10436	21813	45497	*	*	*	*
60	7471.6	18535	29220	46058	*	*	*	*	*	*

*> 99,999

TABLE C.1c
Present Value of $1 Received at the End of *n* Periods

PERIOD	1%	2%	3%	4%	5%	6%	7%	8%	9%	10%
1	.9901	.9804	.9709	.9615	.9524	.9434	.9346	.9259	.9174	.9091
2	.9803	.9612	.9426	.9246	.9070	.8900	.8734	.8573	.8417	.8264
3	.9706	.9423	.9151	.8890	.8638	.8396	.8163	.7938	.7722	.7513
4	.9610	.9238	.8885	.8548	.8227	.7921	.7629	.7350	.7084	.6830
5	.9515	.9057	.8626	.8219	.7835	.7473	.7130	.6806	.6499	.6209
6	.9420	.8880	.8375	.7903	.7462	.7050	.6663	.6302	.5963	.5645
7	.9327	.8706	.8131	.7599	.7107	.6651	.6227	.5835	.5470	.5132
8	.9235	.8535	.7894	.7307	.6768	.6274	.5820	.5403	.5019	.4665
9	.9143	.8368	.7664	.7026	.6446	.5919	.5439	.5002	.4604	.4241
10	.9053	.8203	.7441	.6756	.6139	.5584	.5083	.4632	.4224	.3855
11	.8963	.8043	.7224	.6496	.5847	.5268	.4751	.4289	.3875	.3505
12	.8874	.7885	.7014	.6246	.5568	.4970	.4440	.3971	.3555	.3186
13	.8787	.7730	.6810	.6006	.5303	.4688	.4150	.3677	.3262	.2897
14	.8700	.7579	.6611	.5775	.5051	.4423	.3878	.3405	.2992	.2633
15	.8613	.7430	.6419	.5553	.4810	.4173	.3624	.3152	.2745	.2394
16	.8528	.7284	.6232	.5339	.4581	.3936	.3387	.2919	.2519	.2176
17	.8444	.7142	.6050	.5134	.4363	.3714	.3166	.2703	.2311	.1978
18	.8360	.7002	.5874	.4936	.4155	.3503	.2959	.2502	.2120	.1799
19	.8277	.6864	.5703	.4746	.3957	.3305	.2765	.2317	.1945	.1635
20	.8195	.6730	.5537	.4564	.3769	.3118	.2584	.2145	.1784	.1486
25	.7798	.6095	.4776	.3751	.2953	.2330	.1842	.1460	.1160	.0923
30	.7419	.5521	.4120	.3083	.2314	.1741	.1314	.0994	.0754	.0573
40	.6717	.4529	.3066	.2083	.1420	.0972	.0668	.0460	.0318	.0221
50	.6080	.3715	.2281	.1407	.0872	.0543	.0339	.0213	.0134	.0085
60	.5504	.3048	.1697	.0951	.0535	.0303	.0173	.0099	.0057	.0033

TABLE C.1c *(continued)*

Period	12%	14%	15%	16%	18%	20%	24%	28%	32%	36%
1	.8929	.8772	.8696	.8621	.8475	.8333	.8065	.7813	.7576	.7353
2	.7972	.7695	.7561	.7432	.7182	.6944	.6504	.6104	.5739	.5407
3	.7118	.6750	.6575	.6407	.6086	.5787	.5245	.4768	.4348	.3975
4	.6355	.5921	.5718	.5523	.5158	.4823	.4230	.3725	.3294	.2923
5	.5674	.5194	.4972	.4761	.4371	.4019	.3411	.2910	.2495	.2149
6	.5066	.4556	.4323	.4104	.3704	.3349	.2751	.2274	.1890	.1580
7	.4523	.3996	.3759	.3538	.3139	.2791	.2218	.1776	.1432	.1162
8	.4039	.3506	.3269	.3050	.2660	.2326	.1789	.1388	.1085	.0854
9	.3606	.3075	.2843	.2630	.2255	.1938	.1443	.1084	.0822	.0628
10	.3220	.2697	.2472	.2267	.1911	.1615	.1164	.0847	.0623	.0462
11	.2875	.2366	.2149	.1954	.1619	.1346	.0938	.0662	.0472	.0340
12	.2567	.2076	.1869	.1685	.1372	.1122	.0757	.0517	.0357	.0250
13	.2292	.1821	.1625	.1452	.1163	.0935	.0610	.0404	.0271	.0184
14	.2046	.1597	.1413	.1252	.0985	.0779	.0492	.0316	.0205	.0135
15	.1827	.1401	.1229	.1079	.0835	.0649	.0397	0247	.0155	.0099
16	.1631	.1229	.1069	.0930	.0708	.0541	.0320	.0193	.0118	.0073
17	.1456	.1078	.0929	.0802	.0600	.0451	.0258	.0150	.0089	.0054
18	.1300	.0946	.0808	.0691	.0508	.0376	.0208	.0118	.0068	.0039
19	.1161	.0829	.0703	.0596	.0431	.0313	.0168	.0092	.0051	.0029
20	.1037	.0728	.0611	.0514	.0365	.0261	.0135	.0072	.0039	.0021
25	.0588	.0378	.0304	.0245	.0160	.0105	.0046	.0021	.0010	.0005
30	.0334	.0196	.0151	.0116	.0070	.0042	.0016	.0006	.0002	.0001
40	.0107	.0053	.0037	.0026	.0013	.0007	.0002	.0001	*	*
50	.0035	.0014	.0009	.0006	.0003	.0001	*	*	*	*
60	.0011	.0004	.0002	.0001	*	*	*	*	*	*

*The factor is zero to four decimal places.

TABLE C.1d

Present Value of an Annuity of $1 per Period for *n* Periods

NUMBER OF PAYMENTS	1%	2%	3%	4%	5%	6%	7%	8%	9%
1	0.9901	0.9804	0.9709	0.9615	0.9524	0.9434	0.9346	0.9259	0.9174
2	1.9704	1.9416	1.9135	1.8861	1.8594	1.8334	1.8080	1.7833	1.7591
3	2.9410	2.8839	2.8286	2.7751	2.7232	2.6730	2.6243	2.5771	2.5313
4	3.9020	3.8077	3.7171	3.6299	3.5460	3.4651	3.3872	3.3121	3.2397
5	4.8534	4.7135	4.5797	4.4518	4.3295	4.2124	4.1002	3.9927	3.8897
6	5.7955	5.6014	5.4172	5.2421	5.0757	4.9173	4.7665	4.6229	4.4859
7	6.7282	6.4720	6.2303	6.0021	5.7864	5.5824	5.3893	5.2064	5.0330
8	7.6517	7.3255	7.0197	6.7327	6.4632	6.2098	5.9713	5.7466	5.5348
9	8.5660	8.1622	7.7861	7.4353	7.1078	6.8017	6.5152	6.2469	5.9952
10	9.4713	8.9826	8.5302	8.1109	7.7217	7.3601	7.0236	6.7101	6.4177
11	10.3676	9.7868	9.2526	8.7605	8.3064	7.8869	7.4987	7.1390	6.8052
12	11.2551	10.5753	9.9540	9.3851	8.8633	8.3838	7.9427	7.5361	7.1607
13	12.1337	11.3484	10.6350	9.9856	9.3936	8.8527	8.3577	7.9038	7.4869
14	13.0037	12.1062	11.2961	10.5631	9.8986	9.2950	8.7455	8.2442	7.7862
15	13.8651	12.8493	11.9379	11.1184	10.3797	9.7122	9.1079	8.5595	8.0607
16	14.7179	13.5777	12.5611	11.6523	10.8378	10.1059	9.4466	8.8514	8.3126
17	15.5623	14.2919	13.1661	12.1657	11.2741	10.4773	9.7632	9.1216	8.5436
18	16.3983	14.9920	13.7535	12.6593	11.6896	10.8276	10.0591	9.3719	8.7556
19	17.2260	15.6785	14.3238	13.1339	12.0853	11.1581	10.3356	9.6036	8.9501
20	18.0456	16.3514	14.8775	13.5903	12.4622	11.4699	10.5940	9.8181	9.1285
25	22.0232	19.5235	17.4131	15.6221	14.0939	12.7834	11.6536	10.6748	9.8226
30	25.8077	22.3965	19.6004	17.2920	15.3725	13.7648	12.4090	11.2578	10.2737
40	32.8347	27.3555	23.1148	19.7928	17.1591	15.0463	13.3317	11.9246	10.7574
50	39.1961	31.4236	25.7298	21.4822	18.2559	15.7619	13.8007	12.2335	10.9617
60	44.9550	34.7609	27.6756	22.6235	18.9293	16.1614	14.0392	12.3766	11.0480

TABLE C.1*d* (*continued*)

NUMBER OF PAYMENTS	10%	12%	14%	15%	16%	18%	20%	24%	28%	32%	36%
1	0.9091	0.8929	0.8772	0.8696	0.8621	0.8475	0.8333	0.8065	0.7813	0.7576	0.7353
2	1.7355	1.6901	1.6467	1.6257	1.6052	1.5656	1.5278	1.4568	1.3916	1.3315	1.2760
3	2.4869	2.4018	2.3216	2.2832	2.2459	2.1743	2.1065	1.9813	1.8684	1.7663	1.6735
4	3.1699	3.0373	2.9137	2.8550	2.7982	2.6901	2.5887	2.4043	2.2410	2.0957	1.9658
5	3.7908	3.6048	3.4331	3.3522	3.2743	3.1272	2.9906	2.7454	2.5320	2.3452	2.1807
6	4.3553	4.1114	3.8887	3.7845	3.6847	3.4976	3.3255	3.0205	2.7594	2.5342	2.3388
7	4.8684	4.5638	4.2883	4.1604	4.0386	3.8115	3.6046	3.2423	2.9370	2.6775	2.4550
8	5.3349	4.9676	4.6389	4.4873	4.3436	4.0776	3.8372	3.4212	3.0758	2.7860	2.5404
9	5.7590	5.3282	4.9464	4.7716	4.6065	4.3030	4.0310	3.5655	3.1842	2.8681	2.6033
10	6.1446	5.6502	5.2161	5.0188	4.8332	4.4941	4.1925	3.6819	3.2689	2.9304	2.6495
11	6.4951	5.9377	5.4527	5.2337	5.0286	4.6560	4.3271	3.7757	3.3351	2.9776	2.6834
12	6.8137	6.1944	5.6603	5.4206	5.1971	4.7932	4.4392	3.8514	3.3868	3.0133	2.7084
13	7.1034	6.4235	5.8424	5.5831	5.3423	4.9095	4.5327	3.9124	3.4272	3.0404	2.7268
14	7.3667	6.6282	6.0021	5.7245	5.4675	5.0081	4.6106	3.9616	3.4587	3.0609	2.7403
15	7.6061	6.8109	6.1422	5.8474	5.5755	5.0916	4.6755	4.0013	3.4834	3.0764	2.7502
16	7.8237	6.9740	6.2651	5.9542	5.6685	5.1624	4.7296	4.0333	3.5026	3.0882	2.7575
17	8.0216	7.1196	6.3729	6.0472	5.7487	5.2223	4.7746	4.0591	3.5177	3.0971	2.7629
18	8.2014	7.2497	6.4674	6.1280	5.8178	5.2732	4.8122	4.0799	3.5294	3.1039	2.7668
19	8.3649	7.3658	6.5504	6.1982	5.8775	5.3162	4.8435	4.0967	3.5386	3.1090	2.7697
20	8.5136	7.4694	6.6231	6.2593	5.9288	5.3527	4.8696	4.1103	3.5458	3.1129	2.7718
25	9.0770	7.8431	6.8729	6.4641	6.0971	5.4669	4.9476	4.1474	3.5640	3.1220	2.7765
30	9.4269	8.0552	7.0027	6.5660	6.1772	5.5168	4.9789	4.1601	3.5693	3.1242	2.7775
40	9.7791	8.2438	7.1050	6.6418	6.2335	5.5482	4.9966	4.1659	3.5712	3.1250	2.7778
50	9.9148	8.3045	7.1327	6.6605	6.2463	5.5541	4.9995	4.1666	3.5714	3.1250	2.7778
60	9.9672	8.3240	7.1401	6.6651	6.2492	5.5553	4.9999	4.1667	3.5714	3.1250	2.7778

TABLE C.2
Areas Under the Normal Curve

Z	.00	.01	.02	.03	.04	.05	.06	.07	.08	.09
0.0	.0000	.0040	.0080	.0120	.0160	.0199	.0239	.0279	.0319	.0359
0.1	.0398	.0438	.0478	.0517	.0557	.0596	.0636	.0675	.0714	.0753
0.2	.0793	.0832	.0871	.0910	.0948	.0987	.1026	.1064	.1103	.1141
0.3	.1179	.1217	.1255	.1293	.1331	.1368	.1406	.1443	.1480	.1517
0.4	.1554	.1591	.1628	.1664	.1700	.1736	.1772	.1808	.1844	.1879
0.5	.1915	.1950	.1985	.2019	.2054	.2088	.2123	.2157	.2190	.2224
0.6	.2257	.2291	.2324	.2357	.2389	.2422	.2454	.2486	.2517	.2549
0.7	.2580	.2611	.2642	.2673	.2704	.2734	.2764	.2794	.2823	.2852
0.8	.2881	.2910	.2939	.2967	.2995	.3023	.3051	.3078	.3106	.3133
0.9	.3159	.3186	.3212	.3238	.3264	.3289	.3315	.3340	.3365	.3389
1.0	.3413	.3438	.3461	.3485	.3508	.3531	.3554	.3577	.3599	.3621
1.1	.3643	.3665	.3686	.3708	.3729	.3749	.3770	.3790	.3810	.3830
1.2	.3849	.3869	.3888	.3907	.3925	.3944	.3962	.3980	.3997	.4015
1.3	.4032	.4049	.4066	.4082	.4099	.4115	.4131	.4147	.4162	.4177
1.4	.4192	.4207	.4222	.4236	.4251	.4265	.4279	.4292	.4306	.4319
1.5	.4332	.4345	.4357	.4370	.4382	.4394	.4406	.4418	.4429	.4441
1.6	.4452	.4463	.4474	.4484	.4495	.4505	.4515	.4525	.4535	.4545
1.7	.4554	.4564	.4573	.4582	.4591	.4599	.4608	.4616	.4625	.4633
1.8	.4641	.4649	.4656	.4664	.4671	.4678	.4686	.4693	.4699	.4706
1.9	.4713	.4719	.4726	.4732	.4738	.4744	.4750	.4756	.4761	.4767
2.0	.4772	.4778	.4783	.4788	.4793	.4798	.4803	.4808	.4812	.4817
2.1	.4821	.4826	.4830	.4834	.4838	.4842	.4846	.4850	.4854	.4857
2.2	.4861	.4864	.4868	.4871	.4875	.4878	.4881	.4884	.4887	.4890
2.3	.4893	.4896	.4898	.4901	.4904	.4906	.4909	.4911	.4913	.4916
2.4	.4918	.4920	.4922	.4925	.4927	.4929	.4931	.4932	.4934	.4936
2.5	.4938	.4940	.4941	.4943	.4945	.4946	.4948	.4949	.4951	.4952
2.6	.4953	.4955	.4956	.4957	.4959	.4960	.4961	.4962	.4963	.4964
2.7	.4965	.4966	.4967	.4968	.4969	.4970	.4971	.4972	.4973	.4974
2.8	.4974	.4975	.4976	.4977	.4977	.4978	.4979	.4979	.4980	.4981
2.9	.4981	.4982	.4982	.4983	.4984	.4984	.4985	.4985	.4986	.4986
3.0	.4987	.4987	.4987	.4988	.4988	.4989	.4989	.4989	.4990	.4990

TABLE C.3a
Critical Values for the F-Distribution ($\alpha = .05$)

DEGREES OF FREEDOM FOR DENOMINATOR	DEGREES OF FREEDOM FOR NUMERATOR								
	1	2	3	4	5	6	8	10	15
1	161.4	199.5	215.7	224.6	230.2	234.0	238.9	241.9	245.9
2	18.51	19.00	19.16	19.25	19.30	19.33	19.37	19.40	19.43
3	10.13	9.55	9.28	9.12	9.01	8.94	8.85	8.79	8.70
4	7.71	6.94	6.59	6.39	6.26	6.16	6.04	5.96	5.86
5	6.61	5.79	5.41	5.19	5.05	4.95	4.82	4.74	4.62
6	5.99	5.14	4.76	4.53	4.39	4.28	4.15	4.06	3.94
7	5.59	4.74	4.35	4.12	3.97	3.87	3.73	3.64	3.51
8	5.32	4.46	4.07	3.84	3.69	3.58	3.44	3.35	3.22
9	5.12	4.26	3.86	3.63	3.48	3.37	3.23	3.14	3.01
10	4.96	4.10	3.71	3.48	3.33	3.22	3.07	2.98	2.85
11	4.84	3.98	3.59	3.36	3.20	3.09	2.95	2.85	2.72
12	4.75	3.89	3.49	3.26	3.11	3.00	2.85	2.75	2.62
13	4.67	3.81	3.41	3.18	3.03	2.92	2.77	2.67	2.53
14	4.60	3.74	3.34	3.11	2.96	2.85	2.70	2.60	2.46
15	4.54	3.68	3.29	3.06	2.90	2.79	2.64	2.54	2.40
16	4.49	3.63	3.24	3.01	2.85	2.74	2.59	2.49	2.35
17	4.45	3.59	3.20	2.96	2.81	2.70	2.55	2.45	2.31
18	4.41	3.55	3.16	2.93	2.77	2.66	2.51	2.41	2.27
19	4.38	3.52	3.13	2.90	2.74	2.63	2.48	2.38	2.23
20	4.35	3.49	3.10	2.87	2.71	2.60	2.45	2.35	2.20
21	4.32	3.47	3.07	2.84	2.68	2.57	2.42	2.32	2.18
22	4.30	3.44	3.05	2.82	2.66	2.55	2.40	2.30	2.15
23	4.28	3.42	3.03	2.80	2.64	2.53	2.37	2.27	2.13
24	4.26	3.40	3.01	2.78	2.62	2.51	2.36	2.25	2.11
25	4.24	3.39	2.99	2.76	2.60	2.49	2.34	2.24	2.09
26	4.23	3.37	2.98	2.74	2.59	2.47	2.32	2.22	2.07
27	4.21	3.35	2.96	2.73	2.57	2.46	2.31	2.20	2.06
28	4.20	3.34	2.95	2.71	2.56	2.45	2.29	2.19	2.04
29	4.18	3.33	2.93	2.70	2.55	2.43	2.28	2.18	2.03
30	4.17	3.32	2.92	2.69	2.53	2.42	2.27	2.16	2.01
40	4.08	3.23	2.84	2.61	2.45	2.34	2.18	2.08	1.92
50	4.03	3.18	2.79	2.56	2.40	2.29	2.13	2.03	1.87
60	4.00	3.15	2.76	2.53	2.37	2.25	2.10	1.99	1.84
70	3.98	3.13	2.74	2.50	2.35	2.23	2.07	1.97	1.81
80	3.96	3.11	2.72	2.49	2.33	2.21	2.06	1.95	1.79
90	3.95	3.10	2.71	2.47	2.32	2.20	2.04	1.94	1.78
100	3.94	3.09	2.70	2.46	2.31	2.19	2.03	1.93	1.77
125	2.93	3.07	2.68	2.44	2.29	2.17	2.01	1.91	1.75
150	3.90	3.06	2.66	2.43	2.27	2.16	2.00	1.89	1.73
200	3.89	3.04	2.65	2.42	2.26	2.14	1.98	1.88	1.72
∞	3.84	3.00	2.60	2.37	2.21	2.10	1.94	1.83	1.67

TABLE C.3b
Critical Values for the F-Distribution ($\alpha = .01$)

DEGREES OF FREEDOM FOR DENOMINATOR	\multicolumn{9}{c}{DEGREES OF FREEDOM FOR NUMERATOR}
	1	2	3	4	5	6	8	10	15
1	4052	4999	5403	5625	5764	5859	5981	6056	6157
2	98.50	99.00	99.17	99.25	99.30	99.33	99.37	99.40	99.43
3	34.12	30.82	29.46	28.71	28.24	27.91	27.49	27.23	26.87
4	21.20	18.00	16.69	15.98	15.52	15.21	14.80	14.55	14.20
5	16.26	13.27	12.06	11.39	10.97	10.67	10.29	10.05	9.72
6	13.75	10.92	9.78	9.15	8.75	8.47	8.10	7.87	7.56
7	12.25	9.55	8.45	7.85	7.46	7.19	6.84	6.62	6.31
8	11.26	8.65	7.59	7.01	6.63	6.37	6.03	5.81	5.52
9	10.56	8.02	6.99	6.42	6.06	5.80	5.47	5.26	4.96
10	10.04	7.56	6.55	5.99	5.64	5.39	5.06	4.85	4.56
11	9.65	7.21	6.22	5.67	5.32	5.07	4.74	4.54	4.25
12	9.33	6.93	5.95	5.41	5.06	4.82	4.50	4.30	4.01
13	9.07	6.70	5.74	5.21	4.86	4.62	4.30	4.10	3.82
14	8.86	6.51	5.56	5.04	4.69	4.46	4.14	3.94	3.66
15	8.68	6.36	5.42	4.89	4.56	4.32	4.00	3.80	3.52
16	8.53	6.23	5.29	4.77	4.44	4.20	3.89	3.69	3.41
17	8.40	6.11	5.19	4.67	4.34	4.10	3.79	3.59	3.31
18	8.29	6.01	5.09	4.58	4.25	4.01	3.71	3.51	3.23
19	8.18	5.93	5.01	4.50	4.17	3.94	3.63	3.43	3.15
20	8.10	5.85	4.94	4.43	4.10	3.87	3.56	3.37	3.09
21	8.02	5.78	4.87	4.37	4.04	3.81	3.51	3.31	3.03
22	7.95	5.72	4.82	4.31	3.99	3.76	3.45	3.26	2.98
23	7.88	5.66	4.76	4.26	3.94	3.71	3.41	3.21	2.93
24	7.82	5.61	4.72	4.22	3.90	3.67	3.36	3.17	2.89
25	7.77	5.57	4.68	4.18	3.85	3.63	3.32	3.13	2.85
26	7.72	5.53	4.64	4.14	3.82	3.59	3.29	3.09	2.81
27	7.68	5.49	4.60	4.11	3.78	3.56	3.26	3.06	2.78
28	7.64	5.45	4.57	4.07	3.75	3.53	3.23	3.03	2.75
29	7.60	5.42	4.54	4.04	3.73	3.50	3.20	3.00	2.73
30	7.56	5.39	4.51	4.02	3.70	3.47	3.17	2.98	2.70
40	7.31	5.18	4.31	3.83	3.51	3.29	2.99	2.80	2.52
50	7.17	5.06	4.20	3.72	3.41	3.19	2.89	2.70	2.42
60	7.08	4.98	4.13	3.65	3.34	3.12	2.82	2.63	2.35
70	7.01	4.92	4.07	3.60	3.29	3.07	2.78	2.59	2.31
80	6.96	4.88	4.04	3.56	3.26	3.04	2.74	2.55	2.27
90	6.93	4.85	4.01	3.53	3.23	3.01	2.72	2.52	2.24
100	6.90	4.82	3.98	3.51	3.21	2.99	2.69	2.50	2.22
125	6.84	4.78	3.94	3.47	3.17	2.95	2.66	2.47	2.19
150	6.81	4.75	3.91	3.45	3.14	2.92	2.63	2.44	2.16
200	6.76	4.71	3.88	3.41	3.11	2.89	2.60	2.41	2.13
∞	6.63	4.61	3.78	3.32	3.02	2.80	2.51	2.32	2.04

TABLE C.4
Critical Values for the *t*-Distribution

ONE-TAIL α =	.10	.05	.025	.01	.005
TWO-TAIL α =	.20	.10	.05	.02	.01
df =1	3.078	6.314	12.706	31.821	63.657
2	1.886	2.920	4.303	6.965	9.925
3	1.638	2.353	3.182	4.541	5.841
4	1.533	2.132	2.776	3.747	4.604
5	1.476	2.015	2.571	3.365	4.032
6	1.440	1.943	2.447	3.143	3.707
7	1.415	1.895	2.365	2.998	3.499
8	1.397	1.860	2.306	2.896	3.355
9	1.383	1.833	2.262	2.821	3.250
10	1.372	1.812	2.228	2.764	3.169
11	1.363	1.796	2.201	2.718	3.106
12	1.356	1.782	2.179	2.681	3.055
13	1.350	1.771	2.160	2.650	3.012
14	1.345	1.761	2.145	2.624	2.977
15	1.341	1.753	2.131	2.602	2.947
16	1.337	1.746	2.120	2.583	2.921
17	1.333	1.740	2.110	2.567	2.898
18	1.330	1.734	2.101	2.552	2.878
19	1.328	1.729	2.093	2.539	2.861
20	1.325	1.725	2.086	2.528	2.845
21	1.323	1.721	2.080	2.518	2.831
22	1.321	1.717	2.074	2.508	2.819
23	1.319	1.714	2.069	2.500	2.807
24	1.318	1.711	2.064	2.492	2.797
25	1.316	1.708	2.060	2.485	2.787
26	1.315	1.706	2.056	2.479	2.779
27	1.314	1.703	2.052	2.473	2.771
28	1.313	1.701	2.048	2.467	2.763
29	1.311	1.699	2.045	2.462	2.756
30	1.310	1.697	2.042	2.457	2.750
40	1.303	1.684	2.021	2.423	2.704
50	1.299	1.676	2.009	2.402	2.678
60	1.296	1.672	2.000	2.390	2.660
70	1.294	1.667	1.994	2.381	2.648
80	1.292	1.664	1.990	2.374	2.639
90	1.291	1.662	1.987	2.368	2.632
100	1.290	1.660	1.984	2.364	2.626
125	1.288	1.657	1.979	2.357	2.616
150	1.287	1.655	1.976	2.351	2.609
200	1.286	1.653	1.972	2.345	2.601
∝	1.282	1.645	1.960	2.326	2.576

TABLE C.5a
Durbin–Watson Statistic: Significance Points for d_l and d_u (One-Tail Test, $\alpha = .05$)

	k = 1		k = 2		k = 3		k = 4		k = 5	
n	d_l	d_u	d_l	d_u	d_l	d_u	d_l	d_u	d_l	d_u
15	1.08	1.36	0.95	1.54	0.82	1.75	0.69	1.97	0.56	2.21
16	1.10	1.37	0.98	1.54	0.86	1.73	0.74	1.93	0.62	2.15
17	1.13	1.38	1.02	1.54	0.90	1.71	0.78	1.90	0.67	2.10
18	1.16	1.39	1.05	1.53	0.93	1.69	0.82	1.87	0.71	2.06
19	1.18	1.40	1.08	1.53	0.97	1.68	0.86	1.85	0.75	2.02
20	1.20	1.41	1.10	1.54	1.00	1.68	0.90	1.83	0.79	1.99
21	1.22	1.42	1.13	1.54	1.03	1.67	0.93	1.81	0.83	1.96
22	1.24	1.43	1.15	1.54	1.05	1.66	0.96	1.80	0.86	1.94
23	1.26	1.44	1.17	1.54	1.08	1.66	0.99	1.79	0.90	1.92
24	1.27	1.45	1.19	1.55	1.10	1.66	1.01	1.78	0.93	1.90
25	1.29	1.45	1.21	1.55	1.12	1.66	1.04	1.77	0.95	1.89
26	1.30	1.46	1.22	1.55	1.14	1.65	1.06	1.76	0.98	1.88
27	1.32	1.47	1.24	1.56	1.16	1.65	1.08	1.76	1.01	1.86
28	1.33	1.48	1.26	1.56	1.18	1.65	1.10	1.75	1.03	1.85
29	1.34	1.48	1.27	1.56	1.20	1.65	1.12	1.74	1.05	1.84
30	1.35	1.49	1.28	1.57	1.21	1.65	1.14	1.74	1.07	1.83
31	1.36	1.50	1.30	1.57	1.23	1.65	1.16	1.74	1.09	1.83
32	1.37	1.50	1.31	1.57	1.24	1.65	1.18	1.73	1.11	1.82
33	1.38	1.51	1.32	1.58	1.26	1.65	1.19	1.73	1.13	1.81
34	1.39	1.51	1.33	1.58	1.27	1.65	1.21	1.73	1.15	1.81
35	1.40	1.52	1.34	1.58	1.28	1.65	1.22	1.73	1.16	1.80
36	1.41	1.52	1.35	1.59	1.29	1.65	1.24	1.73	1.18	1.80
37	1.42	1.53	1.36	1.59	1.31	1.66	1.25	1.72	1.19	1.80
38	1.43	1.54	1.37	1.59	1.32	1.66	1.26	1.72	1.21	1.79
39	1.43	1.54	1.38	1.60	1.33	1.66	1.27	1.72	1.22	1.79
40	1.44	1.54	1.39	1.60	1.34	1.66	1.29	1.72	1.23	1.79
45	1.48	1.57	1.43	1.62	1.38	1.67	1.34	1.72	1.29	1.78
50	1.50	1.59	1.46	1.63	1.42	1.67	1.38	1.72	1.34	1.77
55	1.53	1.60	1.49	1.64	1.45	1.68	1.41	1.72	1.38	1.77
60	1.55	1.62	1.51	1.65	1.48	1.69	1.44	1.73	1.41	1.77
65	1.57	1.63	1.54	1.66	1.50	1.70	1.47	1.73	1.44	1.77
70	1.58	1.64	1.55	1.67	1.52	1.70	1.49	1.74	1.46	1.77
75	1.60	1.65	1.57	1.68	1.54	1.71	1.51	1.74	1.49	1.77
80	1.61	1.66	1.59	1.69	1.56	1.72	1.53	1.74	1.51	1.77
85	1.62	1.67	1.60	1.70	1.57	1.72	1.55	1.75	1.52	1.77
90	1.63	1.68	1.61	1.70	1.59	1.73	1.57	1.75	1.54	1.78
95	1.64	1.69	1.62	1.71	1.60	1.73	1.58	1.75	1.56	1.78
100	1.65	1.69	1.63	1.72	1.61	1.74	1.59	1.76	1.57	1.78

Note: n = number of observations, k = number of regressors.

TABLE C.5b

Durbin-Watson Statistic: Significance Points for d_l and d_u (Two-Tail Test, $\alpha = .05$)

n	$k = 1$ d_l	d_u	$k = 2$ d_l	d_u	$k = 3$ d_l	d_u	$k = 4$ d_l	d_u	$k = 5$ d_l	d_u
15	0.95	1.23	0.83	1.40	0.71	1.61	0.59	1.84	0.48	2.09
16	0.98	1.24	0.86	1.40	0.75	1.59	0.64	1.80	0.53	2.03
17	1.01	1.25	0.90	1.40	0.79	1.58	0.68	1.77	0.57	1.98
18	1.03	1.26	0.93	1.40	0.82	1.56	0.72	1.74	0.62	1.93
19	1.06	1.28	0.96	1.41	0.86	1.55	0.76	1.72	0.66	1.90
20	1.08	1.28	0.99	1.41	0.89	1.55	0.79	1.70	0.70	1.87
21	1.10	1.30	1.01	1.41	0.92	1.54	0.83	1.69	0.73	1.84
22	1.12	1.31	1.04	1.42	0.95	1.54	0.86	1.68	0.77	1.82
23	1.14	1.32	1.06	1.42	0.97	1.54	0.89	1.67	0.80	1.80
24	1.16	1.33	1.08	1.43	1.00	1.54	0.91	1.66	0.83	1.79
25	1.18	1.34	1.10	1.43	1.02	1.54	0.94	1.65	0.86	1.77
26	1.19	1.35	1.12	1.44	1.04	1.54	0.96	1.65	0.88	1.76
27	1.21	1.36	1.13	1.44	1.06	1.54	0.99	1.64	0.91	1.75
28	1.22	1.37	1.15	1.45	1.08	1.54	1.01	1.64	0.93	1.74
29	1.24	1.38	1.17	1.45	1.10	1.54	1.03	1.63	0.96	1.73
30	1.25	1.38	1.18	1.46	1.12	1.54	1.05	1.63	0.98	1.73
31	1.26	1.39	1.20	1.47	1.13	1.55	1.07	1.63	1.00	1.72
32	1.27	1.40	1.21	1.47	1.15	1.55	1.08	1.63	1.02	1.71
33	1.28	1.41	1.22	1.48	1.16	1.55	1.10	1.63	1.04	1.71
34	1.29	1.41	1.24	1.48	1.17	1.55	1.12	1.63	1.06	1.70
35	1.30	1.42	1.25	1.48	1.19	1.55	1.13	1.63	1.07	1.70
36	1.31	1.43	1.26	1.49	1.20	1.56	1.15	1.63	1.09	1.70
37	1.32	1.43	1.27	1.49	1.21	1.56	1.16	1.62	1.10	1.70
38	1.33	1.44	1.28	1.50	1.23	1.56	1.17	1.62	1.12	1.70
39	1.34	1.44	1.29	1.50	1.24	1.56	1.19	1.63	1.13	1.69
40	1.35	1.45	1.30	1.51	1.25	1.57	1.20	1.63	1.15	1.69
45	1.39	1.48	1.34	1.53	1.30	1.58	1.25	1.63	1.21	1.69
50	1.42	1.50	1.38	1.54	1.34	1.59	1.30	1.64	1.26	1.69
55	1.45	1.52	1.41	1.56	1.37	1.60	1.33	1.64	1.30	1.69
60	1.47	1.54	1.44	1.57	1.40	1.61	1.37	1.65	1.33	1.69
65	.149	1.55	1.46	1.59	1.43	1.62	1.40	1.66	1.36	1.69
70	1.51	1.57	1.48	1.60	1.45	1.63	1.42	1.66	1.39	1.70
75	1.53	1.58	1.50	1.61	1.47	1.64	1.45	1.67	1.42	1.70
80	1.54	1.59	1.52	1.62	1.49	1.65	1.47	1.67	1.44	1.70
85	1.56	1.60	1.53	1.63	1.51	1.65	1.49	1.68	1.46	1.71
90	1.57	1.61	1.55	1.64	1.53	1.66	1.50	1.69	1.48	1.71
95	1.58	1.62	1.56	1.65	1.54	1.67	1.52	1.69	1.50	1.71
100	1.59	1.63	1.57	1.65	1.55	1.67	1.53	1.70	1.51	1.72

Note: n = number of observations, k = number of regressors

Solutions to Odd-Numbered Problems

Chapter 2 Appendix
1. **a.** $Q = 75 - 0.5P$ **b.** $P = 150 - 2Q$
3. **a.** $AVC = 300 - 25Q + 1.5Q^2$
$AC = 1,500/Q + 300 - 25Q + 1.5Q^2$
$MC = 300 - 50Q + 4.5Q^2$
$AVC = 300 + 25Q$
$AC = 1,500/Q + 300 + 25Q^2$
$MC = 300 + 50Q$
$AVC = 300$
$AC = Q + 300$
$MC = 300$

Chapter 3
1. **a.** 800 caps
   b. $10
   c. $20
3. **b.** $P = \$4.00$
5. **a.** $Q_D = 61,000 - 200P$
   b. 0, 26,000, 31,000, 36,000
   c. $80
7. Supply curve shifts to right and demand curve shifts to left. The combined shifts drastically reduced the world market price of sugar.
9. **a.** No, because point elasticity is −.625.
   b. Yes, although the number of units sold would drop from 12,000 to 10,000, the combined impact of an inelastic demand and the increase in advertising would raise total revenue from $36,000 to $40,000. Moreover the incremental revenue is far greater than the $100 increase in advertising expenses.

11. a. $P = 25 - 0.1Q$
   b. $P = 9.29 - 0.007Q$
   c. $P = 90 - 2Q$

Chapter 4

1. $0.2 / -0.1 = -2$
3. b. Point -1.27; arc -1.08
   c. Point 0.45; arc 0.48
   d. Point -1.45; arc -1.25
5. Quantity 5,212; revenue increases.
7. Price $26.73; elasticity -1.73
9. At price = $5.00; arc -2.33, point -2, MR $3.00; at price = $4.00; arc -1.31, point -1.14, MR $1.00; at price = $2.50; arc -0.58, point -0.5; MR $-$2.00
11. a. Elasticity for Brown's shoes may be greater than elasticity for all shoes in general. If elasticity for Brown's shoes is $> /1/$, then price decrease could lead to revenue increase.
   b. Increase 9 percent.
13. a. -1.4
   b. Complementary good; cross elasticity -0.7.
   c. Yes, revenues for ice cream and syrup rise, and probably so does profit.
15. a. 1,800
   b. $0, $100, $25
   c. $TR = 100Q - 0.05Q^2$; $MR = 100 - 0.1Q$
   d. $TR = $42,000$; $MR = 40
   e. $\epsilon = 2.33$
   f. $TR = $48,000$; $MR = 20; $\epsilon = 1.5$
   g. 1,000
17. Elasticity is $-.934$
   Revenue decreases from £159,750 to £155,400.

Chapter 5

1. a. Focus groups, telephone surveys, or historical data on similar products such as VCRs.
   b. Price, advertising expenditures, per capita GDP, price of competing products (e.g., VCRs), or complementary products (e.g., CDs)
3. a. $Q = 91.32 - 0.006P$; (SE 11.4) (SE 0.0009)
   b. Interest rates, advertising promotional rebates.
5. a. $E_p = -1.74$, $E_A = 0.69$, $E_{PC} = 0.10$, $E_M = 0.47$, $E_C = 0.14$
   b. One-tail test could be used for each variable.
   c. Interest rates would be more appropriate for time series analysis.
7. a. Exponents of P_a and P_j indicate a higher degree of substitution between European and Japanese luxury cars than between European and American luxury cars.
   b. Yes, coefficient 1.6 is greater than unity, thereby indicating a luxury product.
   c. Not surprising. Prices of cars could be low relative to the high incomes of those who buy them.

Chapter 6

1. 16 percent; $1,691,277
3. **a.** 16 percent (exact answer is 15.98 percent) **b.** $1,012,680; $1,174,709
   c. 14 percent (exact answer is 14.02 percent) **d.** $995,220; $1,134,551
   e. Growth rate decreases about 1 percentage point each year.
5. **a.** 176.667 + 20.5879t, 176.667 + 20.5879 (11) = $403; Past ten years describe straight line; thus, some confidence that trend will continue.
   b. 382 × 0.7 + 353 × 0.3 = 373. Upward trend makes exponential smoothing an inferior forecasting tool; it underestimates.
7. **a.** $Q = 17,350$
   b. $Q = 17,200$; $Q = 17,400$
   c. $Q = 17,500$
   d. Q decreases by 1,200
9. January $55.4 million; April $104.3 million; July $87.5 million; October $109.6 million.
11. **a.** (1) 848.6 + 959.225 × t
    (2) 2929.367 × (1.124838)^t
    (3) −9351.77 + 2.752893 × GDP
    b. Exponential trend, 19,240.
13. 597.5

Chapter 7

1. **a.** False **b.** True **c.** True **d.** False
3. **a.** 4 units **b.** 1–6, 6–11, 11 and above units of labor.
   c. 9 workers, reduce to 8, no change because still in Stage II.
5. **a.** more to Mexico or possibly Taiwan
   b. either Mexico or Taiwan (Taiwan has lower MP/P but also lower overhead)
7. **a.** and **b.**

VARIABLE FACTOR	QUANTITY	AVERAGE PRODUCT	MARGINAL PRODUCT
0	0.0		
1	7.5	7.5	7.5
2	15.6	7.8	8.1
3	23.7	7.9	8.1
4	31.2	7.8	7.5
5	37.5	7.5	6.3
6	42.0	7.0	4.5
7	44.1	6.3	2.1
8	43.2	5.4	−0.9
9	38.7	4.3	−4.5
10	30.0	3.0	−8.7

9. **a.** $\log Q = 1.889 + .414 \log M$
   b. Fairly satisfactory, could improve if additional independent variables are included.
   c. 2.91, 2.66, 2.51, 2.46, 2.37, 2.22, 2.16

11. **a.** budget line shifts to right
    b. budget line becomes steeper (from X)
    c. budget line becomes flatter (from Y)
    d. budget line rotates and becomes steeper
    e. isoquant shifts to right with bias towards Y
    f. parallel shift of isoquant to the left
13. **a.** CRTS   **b.** CRTS   **c.** IRTS   **d.** DRTS   **e.** IRTS   **f.** IRTS
    g. If exponents sum to unity, CRTS. If they are less than unity, DRTS. If they are greater than unity, IRTS.
15. **a.** 0.75 + 0.3 = 1.05. Increasing
    b.
Labor	Capital	Quantity
100	50	132.9
150	75	203.5
300	150	421.3

    c. 10.9 percent
    d. 7.4 percent; decreasing marginal product   **e.** 2.9 percent   **f.** Constant
    returns to scale

Chapter 8

1.

Q	TC	TFC	TVC	AC	AFC	AVC	MC
0	120	120	0	X	X	X	
1	265	120	145	265	120	145	145
2	384	120	264	192	60	132	119
3	483	120	363	161	40	121	99
4	568	120	448	142	30	112	85
5	645	120	525	129	24	105	77
6	720	120	600	120	20	100	75
7	799	120	679	114.1	17.1	97	79
8	888	120	768	111	15	96	89
9	993	120	873	110.3	13.3	97	105
10	1120	120	1000	112	12	100	127

3. If only relevant costs are included, it would be $188 or $9.40 per fish.
5. **a.** False, decisions are future oriented so managers should use the replacement, not the historical costs of raw materials.
   b. True, this can be explained by the mathematical relationship between marginal and average.
   c. True, declining long run AC means economies of scale and increasing long run AC means diseconomies of scale.
   d. False, marginal cost can also be used in long run analysis because even the "fixed" cost varies in the long run.
   e. False, the rational firm will operate where profit is maximized. This may not coincide with the point of minimum average cost because per unit revenue must also be taken into account.
7. **a.** LRAC = $160 - 20Q + 1.2Q^2$
   LR MC = $160 - 40Q + 3.6Q^2$

b. Because of the particular functional form of the LRAC, we know that this firm experiences economies of scale at about 8 units of output (8.3 to be exact).

9. b & c. Straight line: TC = 94.93 + 0.46

R^2 = 0.91 t = 8.96

Quadratic: TC = 106.68 − 0.13Q + 0.005Q^2

R^2 = 0.99 t_b = −1.41; t_c = 6.70

Cubic: TC = 99.5 + 0.51Q − 0.009Q^2 + 0.00008Q^3

R^2 = 0.999 t_b = 6.30; t_c = −5.07; t_d = 8.36

Cubic function gives best fit.

11. c. (1) Straight-line function; AVC and MC are constant.   (2) TC increases at increasing rate; MC rises.   (3) TC increases at decreasing rate; MC, AVC, and AC decrease.

13. a. & b.

QUANTITY	TOTAL COST	AVERAGE TOTAL COST	AVERAGE VARIABLE COST	MARGINAL COST
1	193.5	193.50	23.50	23.50
4	282.0	70.50	28.00	32.50
7	397.5	56.79	32.50	41.50
10	540.0	54.00	37.00	50.50
13	709.5	54.58	41.50	59.50

c. Marginal cost rises throughout.

Chapter 9

1. The graph indicates the firm is losing money but is earning enough revenue to cover all of its variable cost and contributes the rest to its fixed cost. In the long run, it would have to drop out of the market unless the market price increased or the firm is able to reduce its costs.

3. a. Implies a quadratic total cost function (i.e., law of diminishing returns occurs at outset of production).

b. At Q = 1,500, MC = $157.50; At Q = 2,000, MC = $160.00; At Q = 3,500, MC = $167.50

c. MC = $150 + 0.005, Q = $175, Q^* = 5,000

d. Supply curve is the portion of the firm's marginal cost that lies above the shutdown point.

5. b. Yes   **c.** Produce 14 units because loss would be less than total fixed cost.

7. a. $63   **b.** $50

9. Setting the derivative of the total cost function equal to the derivative of the total revenue function and solving for Q yields the same result as setting the total profit function equal to 0 and solving for Q.

Appendix 9B

1. a. 2,000   **b.** $50,000   **c.** $15,000   **d.** 2,500

e. 2,500 = (37,500 + 15,000) / (P − 10); P = $31

3. AVC = $77; TFC = $120,000

a. $120,000/(100 - 77) = 5,217$ **b.** $521,700

c.

Q	PROFIT
2,000	$-74,000
4,000	$-28,000
6,000	18,000
8,000	64,000
10,000	110,000

5. a. 20,000   **b.** $(60,000 + 15,000) / (9 - 6) = 25,000$ **c.** Undefined (denominator $= 0$); 5   **d.** 3

7. a. 70,000   **b.** (1) 80,000   (2) $70,000 = 1,200,000 / (P - 5)$; $P = \$22.14$
c. (1) $(Q \times 12) - 840,000 = (Q \times 14) - 1,200,000$ $Q = 180,000$ Profit $=$ $\$1,320,000$
(2) 1.64; 1.91   (3) No; equal profit reached at 180,000 units.

9. a. 80,000
b. $100,000
c. 125,000
d. $9.50
e. $3.50
f. 125,000

Chapter 10

1. a. At 50-cent intervals starting from $12.50 and decreasing to $8.00, the arc elasticities are $-1.96, -1.74, -1.55, -1.38, -1.24, -1.11, -1, -0.9, -0.8$.
b. $8.75 would be too low for the students. Optimal price is between $12 and $11.50.
c. Students would suffer a loss if the opportunity cost of their venture were included in the total cost.
d. $8.75 may help to increase the store's revenue. It could even be offered to customers as a loss leader.
3. b. The first firm will have the following MR (starting from $10.00 and decreasing to $3.00 at one dollar intervals): $8.75, $6.75, $4.75, $2.75, $0.75, -1.25, and $-$3.25. The second firms comparable data are $4.33, $2.33, $.033, $-$1.67, $-$3.67, $-$5.67, $-$7.67.
e. Range would be at where the MR line is vertical.
5. a. Although prices are lower, the costs of goods sold are proportionately even lower and so profit margins are often higher for private label goods than for brand name items.
b. Very often the manufacturers of the private products are the very same ones that manufacture the brand names. By selling them as private label products, they save on the marketing expenses.
7. a. $P = \$22$ **b.** Demand would fall, economic profit would approach zero.
c. $P = \$12$.
9. Assume that you have decided $250,000 to be the maximum amount that you could spend for the new product, leaving the rest for the other products. You will probably end up spending this maximum amount (this is the equivalent of a firm charging the lowest possible price).

Chapter 11

1. TC = 6 + 10Q; TR = 15X − 0.5Q²; Profit = −0.5Q² + 5Q −6; Maximum profit = 6.5, at Q = 5 and P = 12.5

3. **a.** (1) Schedule: Q = 7−8, P = $340−360; Equation: Q = 7.5, P = $350 (2) Schedule: Q = 12−13, P = $240−260; Equation: Q = 12.5, P = $250 (3) Schedule: Q = 10, P = $300

   b. (1) Same as above. (2) Same as above. (3) Q = 9, P = $320

   c. In the Baumol model, a change in TFC affects price and quantity.

5. $67.50

7. When TC = $15,000: profit = $21,000, peaches = 400 bushels, apples = 600 bushels. When TC = $25,000: profit = $29,000, peaches = 600 bushels, apples = 900 bushels.

9. **a.** Profit is 34,000
   b. Profit is 38,000
   c. Profit is 36,000
   d. Profit is 38,000

11. **a.** Q = 32
    b. P_x = 68 P_y = 14
    c. Profit = 1998

Chapter 13

1. Buyer must make monthly payments, thus decreasing balance in savings account, and interest earnings will be lower.

3. Sell at the end of year 4. NPV decreases in year 5.

5. Operating cash flows (after taxes)

Year 1	$27,000
Years 2, 3, and 4, each	36,000
Year 5	24,000
PV of operating cash flows	$114,927
PV of salvage (after taxes)	3,404
Additional working capital	−15,000
PV of returned working capital	8,511
Original investment	−150,000
NPV	$−38,158

   Do not make investment.

7. Choice A is preferred, PV cost is $9,924; PV cost of choice B is $11,865.

9. Net present value cost of furnishing car is $13,402. Net present value cost of paying mileage is $11,982. Company should pay mileage.

11. Cost of retained earnings is 14.4%. Cost of new equity is 14.6%.

13.
Bonds	0.28 × 0.066	0.0185
Equity	0.72 × 0.14	0.1008
Weighted cost		0.1193 = 11.9%

15. **a.**
	NPV	IRR
Project C	$10,355	23.0%
Project D	9,237	25.0

   b. Select C; NPV is higher.

Chapter 14

1. a. $320   **b.** $30.98   **c.** 0.097

3.

	Book A	Book B
Expected profit	$2,450	$1,800
Variance	94,500	26,000
Standard deviation	307.4	161.2
Coefficient of variation	0.125	0.090

Depends on attitude toward risk. A has higher profit and higher relative risk.

5. a. NPV = 295; σ = 115; CV = 0.3898

b. Relative risk is about equal, but B's NPV is higher; thus, B could be selected.

7. a. NPV = $6,729   **b.** NPV = $6,729

9. b. Z = (12 − 16.7)/6.2 = −0.76; 77.6%

c. Z = (0 − 16.7)/6.2 = −2.69; 99.6%

11. Large: NPV $58,100; σ $81,270; CV 1.4

Small: NPV $52,300; σ $32,090; CV 0.6

13. a. NPV = −$51,737; not acceptable

b. NPV = $21,671; acceptable

Value of option = $73,408.

INDEX

Note: Page entries in *italics* refer to figures; entries followed by *n* refer to footnotes; entries followed by *t* refer to tables.

omics